In the Days of Billy the Kid

The Lives and Times of José Chávez y Chávez, Juan Patrón, Martín Chávez, and Yginio Salazar

by
James B. Mills

University of North Texas Press
Denton, Texas

© 2025 James B. Mills
All rights reserved.
Printed in the United States of America.

10 9 8 7 6 5 4 3 2 1

Permissions:
University of North Texas Press
1155 Union Circle #311336
Denton, TX 76203-5017

The paper used in this book meets the minimum requirements of the American National Standard for Permanence of Paper for Printed Library Materials, z39.48.1984. Binding materials have been chosen for durability.

Library of Congress Cataloging-in-Publication Data

Names: Mills, James B., 1983- author.
Title: In the days of Billy the Kid : the lives and times of José Chávez y Chávez, Juan Patrón, Martín Chávez, and Yginio Salazar / James B. Mills.
Description: Denton, Texas : University of North Texas [2025] | Includes bibliographical references and index.
Identifiers: LCCN 2025007197 (print) | LCCN 2025007198 (ebook) | ISBN 9781574419627 (cloth) | ISBN 9781574419733 (ebook)
Subjects: LCSH: Billy, the Kid--Contemporaries--Biography | Chávez y Chávez, José, 1850-1923 | Patrón, Juan, 1852-1884 | Chávez, Martín, 1852-1931 | Salazar, Yginio, 1863-1936 | Mexican Americans--New Mexico--Biography | Gunfighters--New Mexico--Biography | Frontier and pioneer life--Southwest, New | New Mexico--History--1848- | LCGFT: Biographies.
Classification: LCC F805.M5 M55 2025 (print) | LCC F805.M5 (ebook) | DDC 364.15/52092 $a B--dc23/eng/20250326
LC record available at https://lccn.loc.gov/2025007197
LC ebook record available at https://lccn.loc.gov/2025007198

The electronic edition of this book was made possible by the support of the Vick Family Foundation.

Typeset by vPrompt eServices.

For Dennis and Bernard

*The corridos tell the tales
of life and death,
of tradition,
legends old and new, of joy
of passion and sorrow
of the people—who I am.*

—Rodolfo Gonzáles

Contents

	Introducción 1
	Prologue 3
Chapter 1	Sons of Nuevo México 7
Chapter 2	The Pretty River 25
Chapter 3	Hombres Malos 45
Chapter 4	The Smell of Blood 65
Chapter 5	Mild Blue Eyes 95
Chapter 6	Lincoln County Warfare 121
Chapter 7	The Burning House 151
Chapter 8	Diablos del Infierno 177
Chapter 9	The Mounted Rifles 199

Photo Gallery 1

Chapter 10	Los Ferrocarriles 217
Chapter 11	El Bilito 241
Chapter 12	The Fallen Prodigy 265
Chapter 13	Cattle, Sheep, and Land 285
Chapter 14	Los Gorras Blancas 311
Chapter 15	Sociedad de Bandidos 351
Chapter 16	Barbarian, He Is! 393

Photo Gallery 2

Chapter 17 The Fading Frontier 419
Chapter 18 Game to the Last 445

Epilogue 475
Endnotes 479
Bibliography 529
Acknowledgments 547
Index 549

Introducción

When I finished writing my biography *Billy the Kid: El Bandido Simpático* several years ago, I realized my work was not finished. Although satisfied that I had given the Hispanos (descendants of Spanish settlers) of New Mexico their rightful voice and place in the personal history of Henry McCarty, alias William H. Bonney, I knew there was still a much broader history that needed to be told. A history centered around the lives and times of four individuals: José Chávez y Chávez, Juan Patrón, Martín Chávez, and Yginio Salazar.

"Someone must one day write this story from the Hispanic point of view," the late Frederick Nolan wrote in the introduction of his *Lincoln County War: A Documentary History*. That was in 1992.

Whether described as Hispanos, Hispanics, Nuevomexicanos, Neomexicanos, Mexican Americans, Chicanos, Latinos, or New Mexicans in our present time, the descendants of Spanish settlers who experienced the Lincoln County War have generally remained little more than an afterthought in most studies of the famous conflict. There have been only a few exceptions, the first being Miguel Antonio Otero Jr.'s *The Real Billy the Kid: With New Light on the Lincoln County War*, published in 1936. The former governor of New Mexico Territory tried to shift some of the focus onto the Hispano perspective, although his efforts were largely unappreciated by Anglo scholars throughout the decades that followed. The late Paul L. Tsompanas picked up the slack seventy-six years later when publishing *Juan Patrón: A Fallen Star in the Days of Billy the Kid* in 2012. The dedicated Daniel Flores independently published his *José Chávez y Chávez: The Outlaw Who Died of Old Age* two years later in 2014.

After spending several years researching and uncovering new information about José Chávez y Chávez, Juan Patrón, Martín Chávez, and Yginio Salazar, I hope to have broadened our knowledge and understanding of their lives and exploits and the Hispano side of New Mexico frontier history. This is a study that extends well beyond the Lincoln County War and into the early twentieth century as we follow the lives and times of a lawman turned outlaw, an intellectual prodigy, a conservative journeyman, and a resilient vaquero. It is also a history of racial conflict, ambition, political rivalry, bravery, greed, vengeance, theft, friendship, romance, good fortune, tragedy, and rebellion in the days of Billy the Kid, the Santa Fe Ring, the White Caps, and the Society of Bandits of New Mexico.

I have never cared for unnecessarily lengthy introductions, so turn the page and take the ride.

James B. Mills

Prologue

Friday, July 22, 1932
Lincoln, New Mexico

The rustic adobe buildings on either side of the dirt road running through Lincoln, New Mexico, were a far cry from the fancy hotels that Douglas Fairbanks Sr. and Johnny Mack Brown usually stayed in. There were no soirees to be found here, only some adobe homes and modest establishments, a humble hotel, a circular stone tower known as the torreón, some dilapidated ruins, and the two-story courthouse at the western end of town. The Hollywood stars arrived in the old frontier town with production manager Charles Lewis around five thirty that Friday evening. As they stepped from their automobile onto a street where many a man had once been weighted down with bullets, their first task was to find some suitable accommodation for the night. Once they had done so, the famous actors began taking in the sights and meeting the locals.

There was one local hombre whom Doug Fairbanks Sr. and Johnny Mack Brown were particularly eager to meet. He could be found with his wife Isabel in a rectangle-shaped house with peeling adobe walls, located three miles to the northwest of Lincoln in Baca Canyon. While it was hardly Fairbanks's close friend Charlie Chaplin's stately mansion in the Hollywood Hills, it was a warm family home built on old-fashioned hard work and kept impeccably clean. Doug and Johnny would meet with several locals, but there was nobody to whom they would listen with more enthusiasm than Yginio Salazar.

When Fairbanks and Brown were greeted by Yginio Salazar's polite handshake, the wiry old-timer with his head of thinning gray hair and bushy moustache probably seemed like a warm-blooded relic. The 72-year-old farmer's dark skin showed the wear and tear of frontier life and having endured many a scorching New Mexico summer. His bowlegged frame moved slowly, as if every rigid step were a struggle—the inevitable result of spending decades riding in the saddle. He had war wounds, too, with the scars from bullets fired into his side, shoulder, and hand fifty-four years earlier.

Yginio Salazar always enjoyed telling the story of how he had played dead in the yard outside the burning McSween home during the summer of 1878. His own acting skills saved his life that night. Had he not successfully fooled his enemies into believing he had already expired, they would have shot him a fourth time and put him in an early grave. Of course, the two Hollywood stars were more interested in hearing about someone else. Someone with whom Salazar had been close friends many years ago. He was the only thing that could bring Fairbanks and Brown to a small, out-of-the-way town in southeastern New Mexico. They wanted to hear about Billy the Kid. Fortunately for the two famous actors, Yginio always enjoyed talking about him too.

Fairbanks and Brown hadn't flown in from Los Angeles for nothing. When their commercial airliner landed in Albuquerque on Thursday, Fairbanks's wife Mary Pickford and the Countess Dentice di Frasso Dorothy Caldwell Taylor had continued flying for New York City while making a brief stopover in Kansas City, Missouri. Doug and Johnny stayed behind and were determined to spend a little time traveling through Billy the Kid country. They had already visited old Fort Sumner in De Baca County, where the famous outlaw was buried decades earlier. The two film stars also stopped for fifteen minutes in Roswell, Chaves County, before their automobile's spinning tires rolled into Lincoln. "It is a very beautiful country," Fairbanks told one reporter. He denied the rumors they were planning to make another movie about Billy the Kid.

Fairbanks's swashbuckling silent film career had declined with the advent of "talkies" in the 1920s. In contrast, Brown had recently shot his way to stardom when playing the lead role in King Vidor's production *Billy the Kid* in 1930. The film was met with derision by some in New Mexico for portraying the outlaw as a heroic figure. Everyone thought they knew who William Bonney was. While many Anglo locals considered the Kid a horrible villain and the worst outlaw to have ever drawn a six-gun, old Yginio Salazar knew better. Those people only knew his famous amigo from the wild stories told about him and what they read in those foolish books and articles. If these two neatly groomed gringos in their expensive clothes wanted to hear some good things about "Beely," they had come to the right hombre.

Yginio looked at the Alabamian actor who had pretended to be his late friend on the silver screen two years earlier. He didn't look much like Billy. He was considerably taller, standing six foot one. A former college football star, Johnny Mack Brown was much more solidly built. He also had dark brown hair and eyes. While the Hollywood star was an impressive looking hombre with a distinct southern drawl, he hardly resembled the short, slender, buck-toothed, blue-eyed desperado whom Yginio knew so well and remembered so fondly. Señor Salazar made sure to inform his guests that Brown was physically "a much bigger man" than his compadre Billy the Kid.

Fairbanks and Brown spent over an hour asking the seasoned vaquero numerous questions through an interpreter. They wanted to know about the men who fought in the Lincoln County War, especially Billy the Kid. Was he a brave fellow? How good of a shot was he? Yginio was used to this kind of thing. An author from Chicago named Walter Noble Burns had interviewed him some years earlier while doing research for a book about the famous bandido. Former governor Miguel Antonio Otero Jr. had arrived in Lincoln during the summer of 1926 to speak with Salazar while writing his own book about the Kid. An enthusiastic historian from Texas named J. Evetts Haley had also interviewed Yginio during the summer of 1927. Almost everyone who came to Lincoln wanted to know about Billy Bonney.

Yginio readily informed Doug and Johnny that Billy the Kid was a very brave man, and a fine shot with both a six-shooter and a rifle. He knew. The elderly farmer had seen it with his own eyes when riding, fighting, and rustling horses alongside the Kid in his younger years. Fairbanks and Brown were also shown around town before their departure, during which time the actors expressed particular interest in the old courthouse where Billy made his famous jailbreak more than half a century earlier. Fairbanks was trying to locate an authentic frontier saloon, but there were none to be found. The film stars departed Lincoln around eight thirty in the morning on Saturday, July 23, 1932. They would stop in Alamogordo on the road to El Paso and were planning to spend some time in Mexico.[1]

As was customary among his people, Don Yginio Salazar had bid farewell to Douglas Fairbanks Sr. and Johnny Mack Brown with a friendly wave and "Adiós." Those two actors were nice men, but they could never truly understand how it felt watching Billy calmly smoke a cigarillo inside the kitchen of the burning McSween home. Nor would they ever feel a searing bullet buried within their flesh. Many young hombres considered themselves cowboys, but none of them knew how it felt riding through the hills knowing that a band of fearsome Apaches could ambush you at any moment. Those actors and young vaqueros may have heard some stories, read a few books, or watched one of those picture shows about the days of Billy the Kid, but Yginio had lived them. He had the scars beneath his shirt, the aching joints, and the sought-after memories to show for it. There weren't too many men like him around anymore either, not even in an old frontier town like Lincoln.

Old Man Salazar's time had passed.

Chapter 1

Sons of Nuevo México

We did not, in fact, come to the United States at all. The United States came to us.
—Luis Valdez

José Chávez y Chávez enjoyed telling people that Native American blood was mixed with his Spanish lineage. While occasionally prone to telling tall tales, he may have spoken truthfully about his ancestry. Centuries of migration and interracial relations in the American Southwest resulted in many Hispanos possessing a bloodline of both Spanish and Native American heritage. An hombre with such a racial mix was commonly described as a mestizo. Although José Chávez y Chávez's parents were both Hispanos, it was possible the blood of Indian ancestors also ran through his veins. José would proudly speak of such a heritage, regardless of its veracity, informing one contemporary that his mother was an Apache, and dubiously claiming to have been kidnapped by Mescaleros as a young boy.[1]

Juan José Chávez and his wife Isadora were living in a place known as Cebolleta when their second child came screaming into the world on March 5, 1850. The small village of Cebolleta (Little Onion), so named for the nearby Cebolleta Mountains, was located in Valencia County in lower northwestern New Mexico Territory. Juan José and Isadora had been married for almost ten years when their son was born, having tied the knot on July 20, 1840. The couple welcomed the birth of a daughter named Juana Chávez in 1842. The 8-year-old Juana now had a younger brother, whom her parents christened José Teodoro Chávez inside the Nuestra Señora de Los Dolores (Our Lady of Sorrows) Church in Cebolleta on March 25, 1850. Juan José and Isadora already shared the common surname Chávez prior to their marriage. Their infant son proudly honored the heritage of both his father and mother by carrying the unique surname of Chávez y Chávez (Chávez and Chávez).[2]

José Teodoro Chávez y Chávez spent his early years in a *placita* (village) encircled by the remnants of a ten-foot wall and two circular guard towers. Cebolleta (modern-day Seboyeta) had started life as a mission for hundreds of Navajo in 1749. The Natives eventually rejected the Spanish colonialists' attempts to convert them to Christianity and dispersed, only to return after the settlement was formally established by the Cebolleta Land Grant in 1800. The Navajo carried out various raids in the early 1800s before an alliance between the Hispano populace and the Laguna tribe proved too much for them. Although much of the landscape appeared barren, there was fertile soil beneath the surrounding mountains where men like José's father could harvest their crops. The Chávez family's village had also become a hotbed for Mexican traders dealing in firearms, liquor, and slaves by the time young José was taking his first steps on the New Mexico terrain.[3]

José Chávez y Chávez was raised in the Roman Catholic faith, which had been practiced in the Americas since the arrival of the Spanish Empire. The young boy would have visited the local Nuestra Señora de Los Dolores Church with his family on a frequent basis. José was undoubtedly present for the christening of his little sister Ana María Chávez shortly after her birth in around 1851. The Chávez family would have also spent time at the Portales shrine roughly one mile north of their village, which had been constructed in a canyon beside a spring in the 1830s. Some of their people traveled from many miles to simply immerse their hands in delightful spring water and offer prayers at the sacred shrine. A party was also thrown for little José and every other child each year on the anniversary of their patron saint. One of the first images to which any Hispano child's eyes became accustomed were the engravings of la Virgen de Guadalupe (the Virgin of Guadalupe) their people kept on the walls inside their homes along with various other saints.

Isadora Chávez kept their small family home in Cebolleta impeccably clean. She was rarely seen by anyone without her rebozo, a long scarf worn over her head. Her husband Juan José wore a wide-brimmed hat while working in the fields and attending to his business in the placita. It was little José Chávez y Chávez's responsibility to help his mother and father with various chores. He was raised with a keen sense of formality, as politeness was highly valued among his people. Elderly males were addressed with "Don" preceding their given name. Females of advanced years received the equally courteous title of "Doña." José was taught to remove his hat and always remain standing whenever speaking to his elders. He was also forbidden to commence eating or drinking before any guests were served their meal and beverage, no matter how hungry or thirsty he may have been at the time. Like any Hispano boy, José spent time playing with his siblings and the other children of their village. In contrast with his two sisters, José was taught how to ride a horse and use a *lazo* (lasso) by his father at an early age. The growing boy could also watch the local horse races and the cockfights held on Sundays in which hombres pitted their most fearsome fowls against each other's amid an excited crowd of onlookers.[4]

José Chávez y Chávez quickly learned to be cautious living on the southwestern frontier. Someone getting shot or stabbed in New Mexico Territory was almost as common as whiskey breath in a cantina (saloon). Native tribes such as the Navajo and Apache were a persistent concern. The military post that became Fort Wingate was located near José's home at the time of his birth. When a band of Navajo stole some livestock from the people of Cebolleta in November 1858, thirty-two of the local Nuevomexicanos went out after them. A bloody fight ensued near the Chuska Mountains, resulting in the deaths of nine Navajo warriors and eight of Cebolleta's Hispano citizens, and another twelve being wounded.[5]

The harsh terrain and unpredictable weather beneath New Mexico's beautiful skies could also be hazardous for a growing young boy. Mountain lions, black bears, and rattlesnakes lurked across the territory's healthy mixture of grassy plains, white desert sands, lava flows, pine forests, mountain ranges, valleys, hills, and flatlands dotted with junipers, sagebrush, Apache plume, and cacti. The Hispanos depended heavily on acequias (irrigation ditches) and a handful of reliable rivers cutting through a landscape with limited rainfall. Nuevo México was no place for the meek or lethargic in frontier times.

The life of the average Nuevomexicano family in the 1800s was one of agrarian routine. Juan José Chávez toiled away in his fields with the same kind of wooden tools his ancestors used with a strong faith that Dios (God) would provide. Life would go on as it always had, or near enough the same. Señor Chávez would have occasionally amused himself by reciting one of the many *dichos* (rhymes) his people enjoyed, such as:

> Las negras son de oro,
> Las trigueñas son de plata,
> Las gueras no mas de cobre,
> Y las blancas de oja de late.
>
> Dark women are good as gold;
> Brunettes like silver win;
> The blondes are only copper,
> And the light ones only tin.[6]

Isadora Chávez spent hours preparing the family meals and crafted homemade clothes and fabrics with a hand-twirled spindle. Whatever vocation Juan José and Isadora Chávez may have had in mind for their *chiquito* (little boy) as the 1850s progressed, they were blissfully unaware their son would live one of most turbulent existences in the history of their homeland.

Farmer. Lawman. Vigilante. Revolutionary. Outlaw. Convict. Their little boy José Chávez y Chávez would do it all.

***

Felipa Martínez Patrón was screaming and soaked with sweat inside her humble farmhouse outside of Santa Fe on November 20, 1852. It would have been little comfort to Isidro Patrón that his rapidly breathing wife was already familiar with the agony of childbirth. As Felipa clenched her fists and gave one final push to bring the couple's third child into the world, the infant's wailing began to echo throughout their adobe home. The exhausted mother was pleased to discover her newborn child was *un hijo* (a son) before the umbilical cord was severed. The precious infant was gently wiped clean and delicately wrapped in a blanket by the local Hispana serving as a midwife.

Winter was rapidly approaching in New Mexico Territory, and the baby needed to be kept warm throughout the coming months. He also needed a name for his christening. As Isidro and Felipa Patrón lovingly gazed at the latest addition to their little family, only one name seemed appropriate. While the couple had been blessed with a daughter named Juana in 1845, they had sadly lost their first son shortly following his birth in 1850. The newborn child was named in honor of his deceased brother, and christened Juan Bautista Patrón. His given name was derived from San Juan Bautista (St. John the Baptist), one of the most celebrated saints in their people's culture.

Juan Bautista Patrón grew up with his family on the outskirts of Santa Fe, meaning *Holy Faith* in Spanish. The Holy City was founded by Spanish colonialists in 1610 and situated in a sandy valley to the south of a large snow-capped mountain in north-central New Mexico Territory. The little Nuevomexicano boy's parents blessed him with the arrival of a younger sister named Encarnación on March 29, 1856. Sadly, Isidro and Juana's fifth child, a boy named Sivoriano, passed away before his first birthday in 1860.[7]

Santa Fe County was founded the year of Juan Patrón's birth in 1852, with the territorial capital naturally serving as the county seat. The entire region had recently suffered through an influenza epidemic that ravaged the health of various Hispanos, Anglos, and Indians, taking the lives of many local Navajo. Mining fever also gripped the countryside. Gold was discovered in the regions to the north and south of the Holy City earlier that year. Silver had also been found in the Taos Mountains to the northeast. "I saw Kit Carson the other day at Taos busy getting his traps ready to go out after beaver," wrote land office receiver and Indian agent John Greiner in Santa Fe.[8]

Juan Patrón probably became familiar with Santa Fe's sandy streets and rows of flat-roofed, single-story adobe houses when accompanying his father Isidro into the Holy City as a young boy. The population were predominantly

Nuevomexicanos, despite the steady flow of Anglos arriving in the territory. The gringos initially saw little promise in the place. "I can hardly imagine how Santa Fe is supported," one Anglo arrival declared. "The country around it is barren. A Mexican will walk about town all day to sell a bundle of grass worth about a dime. They are the poorest looking people I ever saw. They subsist principally on mutton, onions and red pepper." Some of the city's inhabitants were so impoverished, they sold their young daughters into sexual servitude.[9]

Gambling, bailes (dances), drinking, and violence were common in the territorial capital. Some Hispanos still settled their disputes in the streets with old-fashioned duels. Bandidos (bandits) and Indians often waylaid travelers passing through the region or on the famed Santa Fe Trail. The US Army stationed at Fort Union were tasked with protecting travelers on the trail and frequently clashed with the resistant Apache and Navajo. Lawmen were either elected or appointed to keep the peace, although they often differed very little from the offenders they arrested in terms of character. While Pueblos and other Indians lived peacefully on the outskirts of Santa Fe, the majority of young Juan Patrón's fellow Nuevomexicanos in the region were illiterate farmers and *pastores* (sheepherders). That may have been the humble life for which Juan was destined had it not been for the recent arrival of an ambitious French missionary.[10]

Bishop Jean Baptiste Lamy was delivered into New Mexico Territory by the Vatican and received quite the culture shock when arriving in Santa Fe on August 9, 1851. While Nuevo México was home to many exquisite Roman Catholic churches, Father Lamy was horrified by the corruption and practices of numerous padres. Many of them reared illegitimate children in direct violation of their vows. The marriage, baptismal, and burial fees were so exorbitant that unmarked graves were a common occurrence. The bishop and burial fees for the funeral of Gertrude "Madame Tuly" Barcelo in 1852 were an astounding $1,649. "Poor speculation to die in this country," John Greiner publicly balked in reference to the funeral. Some Hispanos were obliged to bequeath one tenth of their yearly increase of their flocks and herds merely to cover the cost of church fees. "The only practical difference between it and Negro slavery is, that the *peones* [peons] are not bought and sold in the market as chattels," recalled one Anglo observer. Bishop Lamy got to work when discovering most of the population were illiterate and began establishing the first of many parish schools.[11]

In contrast with so many Nuevomexicanos of his time, the 7-year-old Juan Bautista Patrón received a strong education after his father admitted him to one of Bishop Lamy's schools in 1859. Juan quickly demonstrated considerable promise in his studies, absorbing knowledge with great enthusiasm and storming through his elementary grades. He learned how to read and write in English with a pleasant cursive scrawl and shocked his family by speaking a foreign language with ease inside their home. He was also taught Latin, Spanish grammar, punctuation, history, geography, orthography, and mythology. The growing boy enjoyed singing, and his hands were soon tinkering with ivory keys while learning how to play the piano.[12]

The American Civil War was raging as Juan Patrón was approaching his teenage years in the early 1860s. Gen. Henry Sibley's forces briefly occupied Santa Fe in March of 1862 while flying a Confederate flag over the city. Sibley also "issued an order for the seizure of all the funds in the Territorial treasury," according to the *Santa Fe Weekly Post.* "The order was executed by his Quartermaster and the money appropriated to either the General's private use or for some other purpose." Hundreds were killed or wounded during the New Mexico Campaign that year, which ended with a Union victory shortly following the famed Battle of Glorieta Pass in the Sangre de Christo (Blood of Christ) Mountains. "The attention bestowed by some of the ladies of Santa Fe upon the sick and wounded Texans in the hospital in this city is worthy of the highest commendation," the *Santa Fe Weekly Post* declared on April 26, 1862. "In health the invalids were regarded as enemies; in sickness and suffering they were administered to with a kindness that might have been shown to friends."[13]

The 13-year-old Juan Patrón was attending classes at St. Michael's College in Santa Fe by 1865. With the conclusion of the American Civil War that year, his adolescent mind was able to focus on his studies without considerations of a gringo conflict. He was now writing essays, learning equations in algebra, studying accounting, identifying chemical elements, and measuring geometric forms in his increasingly crowded small classrooms. Juan's college quickly expanded, and he made a new friend in fellow student Tranquilino Labadie, the son of a highly respected former sheriff and Indian agent.

Juan's new friend Tranquilino Labadie was two years his junior but shared his natural intellect and passion for learning. They also bonded over their shared Roman Catholic faith. The two teenagers sometimes accompanied Bishop Lamy to his small villa in the Tesuque Canyon three miles south of Santa Fe, where they both studied and served as altar boys. Juan and Tranquilino also developed a feverish interest in politics and community affairs as their education progressed. They would remain amigos for the rest of Juan's life.[14]

Although Bishop Lamy recommended Juan Patrón for admission to the University of Notre Dame, the ambitious intellectual had his heart set on entering the world of politics after his final year at St. Michael's College. Juan had grown into a charismatic, articulate young orator, and was determined to make a difference in his community. In 1857 Mexican-American War veteran William Watts Hart Davis had publicly stated that Hispanos lacked "the stability of character and soundness of intelligence that give such vast superiority to the Anglo-Saxon race over every other people." As much as any Hispano in New Mexico Territory, young Juan Bautista Patrón would prove W. W. H. Davis wrong.[15]

Isidro and Felipa Patrón had not brought another illiterate farmer or sheepherder into the world, but rather a man of intellect and enterprise.

* * *

The small Hispano settlement of Manzano was nestled in the eastern foothills of the Manzano Mountains in central New Mexico Territory. The Tigua (Tiwa) people's name for the steep mountain range of deep canyons and piñon-juniper forestation was "closed fist mountains." They seemed impenetrable at first glance, with their highest peak climbing just over ten thousand feet into the sky. Like the picturesque mountains, the village of Manzano had been named for the *manzanas* (apples) growing in two orchards that had been planted there in the early 1800s. It was within reach of those delicious *manzanas* where a boy called Martín Chávez grew up.[16]

José Martín Chávez was born in Manzano, Valencia County, on December 11, 1852. He was baptized eighteen days later inside the

Nuestra Señora de la Inmaculada Concepción (Our Lady of the Immaculate Conception) Church in Tome, Valencia County, on December 29, 1852. His father Juan Chávez was not present that day, so it was left to his mother María Lauriana to oversee her son's baptism alongside the infant's godparents José and Ana María Sisneros. Although he was christened José, the child would always use the name Martín whenever introducing himself.

Martín Chávez's early years were marked with tragedy. Life was hard enough on the southwestern frontier, and it became only harder for little Martín when his father Juan Chávez and mother María Lauriana both died from unknown causes when he was a small boy. Martín needed to be tough to merely survive in the foothills of the Manzano Mountains. Fortunately for the resilient *huérfano* (orphan), his uncle José Chávez and aunt-in-law Apolinaria took him in. Martín also became close with the local Romero family in Manzano, which included a Civil War veteran named Vicente Romero who lived with his young wife María. While growing up with his grandmother Magdalena Chávez and various relatives in Manzano, fate dealt young Martín a kind hand when a padre named José Sambrano Tafoya took him under his wing.[17]

José Sambrano Tafoya had studied theology in Santa Fe and was ordained as a priest at the age of 30 on September 24, 1859. He had been assigned to the Pueblo parish in Picuris before serving as a pastor in Jemez and Cochiti. Padre Tafoya began looking out for Martín and another young boy named Julian Chávez after arriving in Manzano, teaching them both how to read and write. The boys may have accompanied the priest on his occasional trips to a small chapel on the Río Bonito in southeastern New Mexico.[18]

The adolescent Martín Chávez learned more about his people's religious faith and practices than most while being educated by Padre José Sambrano Tafoya. His people held an unwavering belief that la Virgen de Guadalupe, the Virgin of Guadalupe (the Virgin Mary), had appeared on the Hill of Tepeyac in Mexico before a Chichimec peasant named Juan Diego Cuauhtlatoatzin in December 1531. La Virgen de Guadalupe and her apparition believed to have surfaced on the cloak of Juan Diego remained central to the Nuevomexicano system of worship centuries later. The Hispanos relished their many religious and festive events, which were celebrated throughout even the smallest village in their homeland. El día de Santiago (the Feast of Saint James) occurred every year on July 25, during which young señoritas were permitted to ride in the local plaza to signal they were ready for marriage. An annual celebration was also held in honor of Don Diego de Vargas—Diego de Vargas Zapata y Luján Ponce de León y Contreras—the seventeenth-century Spanish governor who had reconquered the region following the Pueblo revolt of 1680.[19]

Martín Chávez would have also heard stories about a secret society called el Fraternidad Piadosa de Nuestro Padre Jesús Nazareno (the Pious Brotherhood of Our Father Jesus the Nazarene), more commonly known as Los Penitentes (the Penitent Ones). The enigmatic Penitentes had established their own moradas (chapels) and sometimes marched in processions led by a priest while dragging large crucifixes or a Carreta de la Muerte (Death Cart) behind them. Members of the brotherhood congregated in white muslin drawers to publicly engage in the art of self-flagellation, whipping themselves and bloodying their backs during Semana Santa (Holy Week) every April. Their hymn of the brotherhood could be heard by observers during their processions:

> Ver a Jesús encarnado
> es cosa muy eminente,
> vá de espinas coronado,
> Nazareno Penitente.
>
> Ay, Jesús de Nazareno,
> que es cosa muy eminente,
> yo te ofrezco este alabado,
> Nazareno Penitente.
>
> Seeing Jesus crimson-gowned
> is a thing so evident,
> going forth nettle-crowned
> as Nazarene and Penitent.
>
> Oh, Jesus as a Nazirite
> so manifestly in my sight,
> I offer you this my lament,
> Oh, Nazarene and Penitent.

Secretive as they were, Los Penitentes still played a role in community affairs. Their moradas sometimes served as a people's court to settle minor disputes among the local Hispano citizens.[20]

In addition to an education, Padre José Sambrano Tafoya bequeathed Martín Chávez with a wooden crucifix. The teenager proudly wore the cross around his neck for the rest of his days, with an instilled sense of toughness, conservatism, and munificence. His life may have gotten off to a shaky start, but young Martín was determined to make something of himself.[21]

* * *

The 27-year-old María Paula (Chávez) Salazar was heavily pregnant with her sixth child in Manzano, Valencia County, during the summer of 1859. Paula was previously married to a deaf farmer named José Ventura Sedillo, the father of her children Lugarda, Francisco, Magencia, and Rómulo. Paula's first husband José passed away following the birth of their fourth child, and the widow subsequently married their longtime family friend Francisco Teofilo Salazar in Tome on September 20, 1857. Lugarda, Francisco, Magencia, and Rómulo Sedillo began using their stepfather Teofilo's surname, and welcomed the birth of their half brother José Salazar in the late 1850s.

The five Salazar children were soon gazing at the latest addition to their family after their mother gave birth to another son in Manzano on September 18, 1859. In keeping with their people's many customs and superstitions, Teofilo and Paula Salazar dared not cut their son's fingernails until he was at least 12 months old. They believed doing so could shorten his lifespan or hinder his eyesight. Teofilo and Paula chose a common baptismal name for their newborn *hijo*. The infant was given the name Higinio, sometimes spelled Eugenio, although the child would later spell his own name as history records it: Yginio. It was a good name, originally of Greek origin and derived from Saint Hyginus, the ninth bishop of Rome.[22]

Teofilo and Paula Salazar had six young mouths to feed and moved their growing family to the Quara and Cienega region of Valencia County by the summer of 1860. Yginio Salazar spent his first few years scampering around the family farm and learning how to handle the chickens and goats. Hens older than seven years were routinely killed from fear they may give birth to a *basilisco* (basilisk), a shapeless, black, deformed chick. His father Teofilo taught him and his slightly older brother José how to harvest crops and ride a horse at an early age. Yginio and his older brothers would have also practiced their lasso skills on the smaller livestock, and occasionally each other, around their homestead.

Paula Salazar taught her musically inclined son Yginio various canciones (songs) in their native Spanish tongue. There were many for Señora Salazar to choose from, such as the children's ballad about an amorous cat named Don Gato:

> Estaba señor don Gato
> En silla de oro sentado
> Con camisita de lino
> Y zapatito bordado.

The Hispano population of New Mexico loved singing their folk songs for enjoyment and as a means of preserving history. An illiterate Nuevomexicano was incapable of writing about his or her experiences and observations with a quill but could contribute to the preservation of history and express their thoughts about love, death, and a variety of topics through song. Popular canciones among the Hispano populace included El Veijo (The Old Man), La Mantira (The Lie), El Borrachito (The Drunken Fellow), Suzanita (Susie), El Covotito (The Little Coyote), and a lovesick ballad of despair called "¡Ay! ¡Ay! ¡Ay!" Sheepherders held a reputation for composing some of the finest folk songs while spending hours in isolation watching over their flocks. "The paisano sings in palatable doubt of his own voice," one Anglo resident of New Mexico recalled. "At all events, his tones are very apt to be husky. He slurs his notes sadly, and is prone to reduplicate them."

In addition to folk songs, Yginio Salazar grew up listening to tales of el Diablo (the Devil), *los dijuntos* (ghosts), and the incarnations of brujas (witches). His people were fearful of the *telecote* (owl), as brujas were believed to take their form and their hooting was considered an evil omen. Almost every abandoned adobe building was believed to be haunted by spirits. Yginio quickly learned to refrain from eating fruit on an empty stomach. The highly superstitious Hispanos also avoided getting married on a Tuesday or gazing at an infant for too lengthy a time from fear of the *mal ojo* (evil eye). Whenever bathing in a river, young señoritas like Yginio's sisters were weary of the *ajolote*—or the *guajolote* in northern New Mexico—the dreaded waterdog. Yginio and his brothers were fearful of *el coco* (the bugaboo), a savage, ugly man or animal that frightened misbehaving young boys.[23]

Teofilo Salazar provided for his family by working as a farm laborer in Valencia County. While the more impoverished Hispanos of Nuevo México lived in stick huts called jacales, the working-class Salazar family were comparatively well-off. Their property was valued at $350, with a personal estate worth $600. The Hispanos had long depended upon a system of peonage in which villagers received varying degrees of financial assistance from their local *patrón* (patron), the wealthiest citizen living in the region. The largest landholders of the wealthier class of Nuevomexicanos in the territory were known as Ricos—a term sometimes used with contempt by the less-fortunate majority.

Although Teofilo Salazar was a capable provider in Valencia County, the laborer eventually decided there was more prosperity to be found in southeastern Nuevo México. The Salazar family packed up their belongings, piled into a wagon, and began making the slow journey toward a little village on the Río Bonito during the American Civil War. "The trip was an adventure," Yginio later reminisced. "I expected to find the trail beset with marauding Apaches, but I found the white man more savage and warlike than the Indians."[24]

The Salazar family did their best to avoid any bloodshed while edging closer to the region where little Yginio lived out the rest of his days.

* * *

Although José Chávez y Chávez, Juan Patrón, Martín Chávez, and Yginio Salazar grew up in different areas of New Mexico Territory, one thing they shared was a childhood immersed with social conflict. The four young Hispanos were born and raised on land only recently annexed by the United States of America. Less than three decades after Mexico had won its independence from the Spanish Empire, the United States seized half of Mexico with the Texas Revolution and the conclusion of the brutal

Mexican-American War in 1848. "I was bitterly opposed to the measure," Ulysses S. Grant later remarked. "And to this day, regard the war which resulted as one of the most unjust ever waged by a stronger against a weaker nation."[25]

The Guerra de Estados Unidos a México (War of the United States against Mexico) began in April 1846, before the United States Congress officially declared war on May 13, 1846. Thousands were killed prior to the signing of the Treaty of Guadalupe Hidalgo almost two years later on February 2, 1848. In signing the treaty, Mexico ceded roughly half of their territory to the United States of America. The surrendered lands of New Mexico, Arizona, California, Texas, Nevada, Utah, and portions of Colorado and Wyoming now belonged to the United States. The finalization of the Gadsden Purchase slightly augmented New Mexico Territory's southwestern border in 1854.

With the United States government calling the shots following the Treaty of Guadalupe Hidalgo in 1848, a steady flow of Anglos began pouring into the newly established territories of the American Southwest. Their arrival was not warmly received by many of the people whom they indiscriminately referred to as "Mexicans." When the Mexican federal government made two hundred thousand pesos available to aid the relocation of families in the lost territories to Mexico in June 1848, roughly one thousand families petitioned to do so the following year in the San Miguel del Vado region alone. "They preferred to lose all [property] rather than belong to a government in which they had fewer guarantees and were treated with more disregard than the African race," recorded Mexico commissioner Ramón Ortiz. While that was an exaggeration, the enmity felt by many Hispanos toward their Anglo conquerors was evident. The California Gold Rush that commenced in 1848 only brought thousands more Americanos west.[26]

In their effort to colonize their territories, the United States installed their own brand of governance and English common law. While the descendants of Spanish settlers throughout the borderlands were not overly nationalistic, they identified more with Mexico's traditional economic structure than the kind of capitalist expansion soon being carried out by the Americanos. Some Hispanos also found the gringos' laws confusing and unjust. "The feeling between the American and Mexican population is worse than ever,"

John Greiner declared in Santa Fe in 1853. "No man thinks of going without his firearms by day, and I presume there is not a single American in the Territory but sleeps with his pistols under his pillow at night. The Mexicans, with a very few exceptions, do not like our government. Should war break out with Mexico, and they be compelled to take sides, they assuredly would take the side of Old Mexico."

Land usage became one of the strongest matters of contention between the Hispano peasantry and the new Anglo establishment in New Mexico Territory. The Louisiana Purchase in 1803 had already brought many Anglo Americans farther southwest, with their numbers increasing following the Gadsden Purchase and the Homestead Act of 1862. While the Treaty of Guadalupe Hidalgo stipulated basic rights for the Hispano populace, such as religious freedom and the right to retain their Mexican citizenship, the US government's refusal to ratify Article 10 of the treaty had failed to recognize the property rights Hispano peasants were afforded during Mexican governance. This not only allowed the Americanos to break up some of larger estates owned by exploitive patróns but also damaged the lives of many modest Hispano farmers. An unfortunate lack of formal education left many illiterate Nuevomexicanos vulnerable to exploitation by Anglo land barons and speculators as the decades progressed. The private-property schemes favored by American and European speculators inevitably conflicted with the Hispano population's legal right to use the waterholes, grazing lands, and timber supplies found on the community grants established by the Mexican government. Some Anglo arrivals also began squatting on Hispano farmlands, sometimes violently driving the "Mexican" inhabitants from their properties, and their actions largely went unpunished.

The Hispano Americans and Anglo Americans of New Mexico Territory also clashed over cultural distinctions. The dark-skinned Nuevomexicanos spoke in a different native Spanish tongue to their Anglo conquerors. They were Roman Catholic rather than Protestant and held less-inclusive community values. The fact that many Hispanos possessed a mixed lineage of Spanish and Native American was also a point of contention with many Anglo arrivals, who considered the "Mexicans" a "mongrel race." Some conservative Americanos were horrified by the affectionate manner with which Hispanos greeted each other in the streets. Whenever a friend visited a Hispano home, they were traditionally greeted with a hug from each member of the family, with the process being repeated before their departure. Hispanas openly smoked cigarillos just like the men, although most refrained from riding horses, as it was considered improper for a female to do so in their community. Many Hispanos preferred burros (small donkeys) rather than horses and used an entirely wooden carreta (ox cart) with loudly creaking wheels to transport their goods or families.

Although hardworking, the Hispano population also possessed a more laid-back outlook on life: *poco tiempo* (in a little while). In contrast with many of their Anglo counterparts, the Hispano community tended to focus on enjoying the present rather than concerning themselves with the future. In the land of *mañana*, there was no need to cease an enjoyable activity today for the sake of something that could just as easily be done the next. Tomorrow would be soon enough, or *pasado mañana* (day after tomorrow). The Americanos always seemed to be in such a hurry. A cigarillo break was a common practice among working-class Hispanos, much to the chagrin of any potential Anglo employers or coworkers. "Es la costumbre de nuestra gente" (It is the custom of our people), the Hispano workers said. While many Americanos mistook them for lazy, most of the Hispano population were content in practicing the same customs and traditions as their ancestors and hardly felt obliged to appease the whims of a foreign people who had seized the Southwest.[27]

To many Anglo arrivals in New Mexico Territory, the Hispanos seemed a backward people with archaic values and strange customs. They were generally viewed with condescension, suspicion, or outright racial prejudice. The Anglo establishment quickly became frustrated in their efforts to "Americanize" Nuevo México to their own liking. Americanos commonly used the racist term "greasers" to describe their "Mexican" counterparts. The Hispanos disdainfully referred to the American and European immigrants in their midst as gringos (foreigners). Although various Anglo males would take Nuevomexicano wives, and cultural barriers were occasionally bridged by specific individuals, the varying degrees of racial tension, distrust, and hostility between Mexican

Americans and Anglo Americans would continue throughout Nuevo México and the American Southwest for decades to come.

In addition to a childhood immersed with social conflict, José Chávez y Chávez, Juan Patrón, Martín Chávez, and Yginio Salazar shared a common destiny. The four of them would all arrive in southeastern New Mexico Territory, where years of racial, political, and commercially related violence awaited them in a place called Condado de Lincoln.

Chapter 2

The Pretty River

Dear native brook! wild streamlet of the West!
How many various-fated years have passed...
—Samuel Taylor Coleridge

The around 3-year-old Yginio Salazar and his family arrived in the small placita on the Río Bonito (Pretty River) in southeastern New Mexico Territory in 1862. Their new home had been settled by Hispanos in a slender valley to the south of the Capitan Mountains around the 1840s. The locals referred to the small village as La Placita. "I was just a boy," Yginio later recalled. "There were about thirty families who lived there." Those families of La Placita had recently suffered through the pillaging and plundering by some Tejanos (Texans) who arrived with the Confederate army eight miles upstream at Fort Stanton the previous year.[1]

The glistening waters of the Río Bonito flowed out of the Sacramento Mountains to the west of La Placita. So did the Río Ruidoso (Rough River) farther south, on which a placita eventually named San Patricio was located. The two rivers conjoined to form the Río Hondo, on which another settlement called Picacho would be established. The Río Hondo continued flowing east until spilling into the Río Pecos, which ran down through all southeastern New Mexico. To the south of the Río Hondo was the Río Feliz

(Happy River), the Río Peñasco, a region known as Seven Rivers, and the daunting Guadalupe Mountains, which remained the domain of the Apache. To the east of the Río Pecos lay the Llano Estacado, a plateau stretching four hundred miles into both Texas and Indian Territory (Oklahoma). It was a tough land for resilient people.

The Salazar family relocated to a small settlement called San José Valle de Missouri, later known as simply Missouri, or Missouri Plaza, in around 1868. Their new home had only recently been established by its predominantly Hispano population roughly twenty-three miles southeast of Picacho. "The Indians never bothered us," Yginio later recalled. "They were afraid of us out there on the plains, but they were very bad in the *cañóns* [canyons] and on the Bonito."[2]

The famous Kit Carson had been ordered to Fort Stanton in 1862 and led violent campaigns to subjugate the Mescalero Apache and Navajo. While small bands of Natives still offered resistance throughout the region, some Mescaleros and Navajos had been transported north to a place called Bosque Redondo by 1868. Hundreds of Navajo died on a forced march from Fort Wingate in what became known as the Long Walk in 1864. Bosque Redondo proved more of a concentration camp than a reservation. Another 1,500 Navajos died there in horrific conditions, with their corpses sometimes being left to float down the Río Pecos. "The soldiers throw the bodies in the river and they float down where we have to drink," recalled a Mescalero Apache named Old Scout Bigmouth. "We see them drift down."[3]

The sufferings of Indians in the Southwest were nothing new in 1868. Many tribes had endured brutal subjugation and slavery at the hands of Spanish colonialists and their descendants for centuries. The Mexican slave trade had long flourished, with young Indian girls fetching a particularly high price to be used as sex slaves. Although the passing of the Thirteenth Amendment to the United States Constitution prohibited slavery on December 6, 1865, some Native Americans continued to be held as slaves in the American Southwest through the use of peonage servitude. Congress successfully passed the Peonage Act of 1867, which enforced the eradication of involuntary servitude in New Mexico Territory. "One of the radical

Senators from Taos County, Juan Benito Valdez, was brought before the U.S. Commissioner for the District of New Mexico on a charge of holding slaves," the *Santa Fe Weekly Post* reported on May 23, 1868. "The evidence showed that he had in his possession *ten Indian slaves* which he held and worked the same as he had done before Congress passed the law abolishing peonage and Indian slavery in this Territory. The Commissioner liberated the slaves and held Senator Valdez over in bail for his appearance at the July term of the U.S. Court in this city."[4]

While many Navajos and Mescaleros endured the horrors of Bosque Redondo, Teofilo Salazar began farming corn, watermelons, oats, wheat, and barley in Missouri Plaza. He often sold his crops to Fort Stanton and cattle drovers from Texas. Any guests who stopped by were cordially invited to smoke a cigarillo made from finely cut tobacco rolled inside a *hoja* (prepared corn husk). Paula Salazar cooked the family meals on a *tinamaiste* over their fireplace or inside an outdoor adobe oven known as an *horno*. Her son Yginio grew up enjoying meals including *carne de rez* (beef), *pollo* (chicken), *gallinas de la tierra* (pheasant and turkey), *carne de borrego* (mutton), frijoles (beans), sopaipillas (fried bread), chile, arroz (rice), *piñones* (pine or piñon nuts), *chaguegue* (Indian corn mush), burritos, tortillas, eggs, dried fruits, and the occasional enchilada or tamale. Red chile ristras could be observed hanging on the arches, doors, porches, windows, and rooftops of every Hispano home in the fall. Like the rest of his people, little Yginio was careful not to drop any salt or a fork whenever dining at a table.

Yginio Salazar frequently helped with the chores, so as not to be like Bartolo the lazy shepherd in Los Pastores, the most famous Nativity play among the Hispanos of Nuevo México. He also continued honing his skills as a young horseman. Vaqueros sometimes demonstrated their dexterity by stooping down to snatch a handkerchief from the ground while riding at full speed. Yginio also observed a game known as *correr el gallo* (running the rooster), which was played by Hispano horsemen on el Día de San Juan (St. John's Day) every year on June 24. An unfortunate rooster was buried in a mound of soil up to its neck while the participants rode at full speed and attempted to pull the bird free by grasping at its greased head. When an hombre successfully pulled the rooster from the soil, the other participants raced after him and tried to rip the bird from his grasp. Another popular sport held on festive occasions was a dangerous game called *el coleo* (ox-tailing), in which vaqueros chased after an ox that had been turned loose on a plain. The speediest rider tried to pull the snorting bullock to the ground with a sudden jerk of the animal's tail.[5]

Missouri Plaza was a bustling place for any boy approaching adolescence to call home. An Anglo settler named Frank Riggins operated a store that sold whiskey to the locals. There was no church in the settlement, although priests sometimes made the hazardous journey in from Tularosa. "The padres used to fight with the Indians, but they usually slipped through," recalled Yginio Salazar. "We had horse races, rooster fights in which we put spurs on the roosters' legs. Had many dances with violin music." The Hispanos prized their frequently held bailes, which featured *cunas*, waltzes, *cutillos*, quadrilles, the fandango, and couples dances like *La Indita* (The Little Indian) and *El Vaquero* (The Cowboy). The musically inclined Yginio became such a proficient fiddle player that he was eventually paid to perform at a baile held in Fort Stanton.[6]

The Salazar family continued farming in Missouri Plaza until they had to move upriver in around 1872 after "all the water was taken out," as Yginio recalled. Things had changed throughout the region by the time they were forced to set up stakes elsewhere. Yginio and his family were now residing in the largest county in America following the establishment of Lincoln County by an act of the territorial legislature on January 16, 1869. While Hispanos still referred to the village on the Río Bonito as La Placita or Bonito, the small adobe town was now officially known as Lincoln, having been named in honor of the assassinated sixteenth president of the United States.[7]

Lincoln County was comprised of twenty million acres stretching 160 miles wide and 180 miles deep across all of southeastern New Mexico Territory. "The Río Bonito is one of the most valuable sections of New Mexico, and is capable of the highest degree of development," the *Santa Fe Weekly Post* had declared on August 21, 1869. The town of Lincoln served as the county seat, with Fort Stanton providing a sense of protection from the Apaches eight miles upstream. The local Hispano farmers relied on the military post for selling produce, and many citizens depended on Santa Fe and the Mesilla Valley for supplies.[8]

A prominent local Hispano named Saturnino Baca had played a hand in the establishment of Condado de Lincoln, having been a Socorro County member of the territorial legislature when the bill to create the new county was introduced. The heavily bearded Saturnino Baca was born in Cebolleta on November 11, 1830. He had served the Union with great success during the Civil War and was promoted to the rank of captain on March 20, 1864. Respectfully known as Capitán Baca to local Hispanos like young Yginio Salazar, the grizzled veteran set up stakes in Lincoln with his much younger wife Juanita and their rapidly growing family.[9]

Like Saturnino Baca, the 20-year-old José Chávez y Chávez had also migrated from Cebolleta into southeastern New Mexico Territory. José arrived in Lincoln County by 1870, having grown into a solid five-foot, ten-inch frame, with thick eyebrows, dark glassy eyes, a moustache, and a firm jawline. He later informed one friend that he was stolen by Mescalero Apaches at the age of 6 and lived with the Indians for more than a decade, although the veracity of this dubious claim can never be determined. He also later claimed to have been a captive of the Navajo for two years. One thing for certain is that José Chávez y Chávez had recently fallen in love with a widow named María Leonora Lucero, formally the wife of a deceased hombre named José Candeleria. The two were married in the Santa Rita Catholic Church in Carrizozo on January 10, 1871. The newlyweds settled on a farm, and their union produced a son named Adecasio Chávez on May 23, 1873.[10]

In addition to farming and providing for his family, José Chávez y Chávez became increasingly proficient in the use of a revolver and rifle. Any hombre who valued his life in Lincoln County needed to be capable of defending himself against ruffians, bandidos, and small bands of Apaches. The *New Mexican* had published a letter from Fort Stanton detailing the deaths of two army teamsters named Hoeffer and McGrath at the hands of some Apaches on September 13, 1870. They had both been killed with arrows and their corpses left naked to rot in the sun. "All that can be done will be done to avenge the murder of the two unfortunate victims of those red fiends," the letter declared. "The night after the murder two citizens en route from Missouri bottom were halloed to by some party of Indians, and informed by them, in no very choice Spanish, that this country belonged to them, and that they purposed to kill every citizen in the vallies."[11]

Courage was strongly valued in a male frontier society often steeped in masculine individualism. No man wished to be thought a coward, lest they leave themselves prone to ridicule, harassment, or aggression. This very much applied in a place like Lincoln County, where violence and theft were extremely common. José Chávez y Chávez would master the use of a six-shooter and a rifle. He also possessed a fiery temper, the kind of steely nerve generally associated with a dangerous pistolero, and a fearsome glare that could unnerve many a man who behaved imprudently. José Chávez y Chávez was not an hombre with whom to take liberties.

***

Juan Bautista Patrón was grieving the loss of his mother when he arrived in Lincoln County in 1870. Felipa Martínez Patrón had recently passed away following a long-standing illness. A short time later Juan's 48-year-old father Isidro had decided to sell the family farm outside of Santa Fe with his son's encouragement. They intended to use the profits to purchase a modest farm just outside Lincoln and open a mercantile store in town. Juan's older sister Juana would remain in Santa Fe County, having married a local farmer named Juan Ramírez and given birth to daughter named Mercedes in May 1870. Isidro, Juan, and Encarnación Patrón headed for southeastern Nuevo México with the success or failure of their venture resting on the 18-year-old college graduate's shoulders. Juan needed to make good use of his education for his family to prosper.[12]

The town of Lincoln appeared vastly different to Juan Patrón's dark eyes when he arrived with his father Isidro and sister Encarnación in 1870. The village looked nothing like Santa Fe, where the people lived in cramped conditions on narrow streets. Lincoln was a pastoral frontier town, with a single dirt road stretching for one mile amid a scattering of adobe houses and several modest tiendas (stores). The circular stone tower known as el torreón on the northern side of the street gave hint of the Apache threat. Picturesque cottonwood and black walnut trees lined the Río Bonito on which everyone depended for subsistence. The river also contained a healthy number of fish to catch. There were roughly four hundred people living in the area, most of whom were Hispanos. Rich soil for farming cabbage, corn, and onions could be found beneath the rolling hills of juniper and piñon running along the north and south of town, where wild turkeys and elk provided additional food sources.[13]

Juan Patrón began confidently strolling through Lincoln in his dapper suits and taking in the sights. The local villagers could often be spotted sitting on blankets in the street while gambling or selling goods such as watermelons and fruits. Cockfights were sometimes held in the plaza. A town minstrel walked from one end of the street to the other while playing the fiddle to announce the holding of a baile on Sunday nights. Juan quickly realized that most of the local Hispanos were illiterate and untouched by the kind of education he had been fortunate to receive in Santa Fe. There was not only an opportunity for Patrón to prosper financially but also the chance to make a positive contribution to the local Hispano community through educational advancements, thereby augmenting the work of his mentor, Bishop Lamy, in southeastern New Mexico Territory.[14]

The 18-year-old Juan Bautista Patrón had grown into a handsome young hombre, with a head of thick black hair, soft brown eyes, pleasant high cheekbones, and a strong nose. He also sported a wispy moustache above a set of full lips and firm chin. Juan looked and sounded like a young man who commanded respect among both his people and the gringos. He began proving himself worthy of deference in Lincoln, with many of the local Hispanos recognizing his education and seeking out his advice on various matters. Many of them would have been shocked that one of their own spoke Inglés (English) so effortlessly when conversing with the handful of Americanos residing on the Río Bonito.

The Patrón family purchased some farming land after their arrival in Lincoln and established their house and store on the south side of the street toward the eastern end of town. The modest twin-peaked building was constructed of adobe, with the inside walls being carefully plastered with yeso (gypsum), also known as *jaspe* around Lincoln. The whitewashed walls were then lined with four feet of brightly colored calico. The usual engravings of saints were hung on the walls just above shoulder height. There were two front doors to the Patrón building on the street: one leading into their private home and the other providing entry to their soon-to-be established store and saloon.

There was no church in Lincoln in the early 1870s. Juan Patrón and his devout Roman Catholic family practiced their faith in several miniscule chapels whenever a padre like José Sambrano Tafoya or a French priest named Francisco Boucart were in town. They were as close-knit as any other Hispano family on the frontier. Juan's duties were to serve as clerk of the family store and assist his father Isidro in farming the family's modest patch of land. Juan's 14-year-old sister Encarnación helped with the chores and was particularly close with her older brother, considering him her *mejor amigo* (best friend).[15]

The Patrón family began making various friends in the generally welcoming and helpful local Hispano community. The Montaño store was barely a stone's throw up the street from the Patrón residence. It was owned and operated by a 36-year-old Civil War veteran from Albuquerque named José Francisco Montaño, who lived with his wife Josefita and their young daughters Vidala and Natividad. As an early Anglo settler in Lincoln named Amelia Bolton later recalled, "The native people of Lincoln, by which I mean the Spanish people, were industrious and immaculately clean, and they made the most of what they had. Their homes, inside and out, and their patios and portals, were regularly scrubbed, swept, and newly plastered with the white native plaster and whitewash. In planting and harvest time they all helped each other—none of them hired help. They were all compadres that is, godfathers, to each other's children and the women were comrades—godmothers."[16]

The Hispano residents of Lincoln also turned up on the Patrón family's doorstep every year on el Día de San Juan (St. John's Day), June 24. After the men, women, and children had bathed in the Río Bonito before sunrise that particular day, they would visit the home of every local family with an hombre named Juan (John) and demand the donation of a live rooster. The cocks were then buried up to their necks one at a time in the middle of the street for the traditional game of *correr el gallo* (running the rooster). "We always locked our door and viewed them from a window," recalled young Amelia Bolton. "It was so wild, it was dangerous to be out."

Miss Bolton was fascinated by Hispano culture, and recalled observing the local funerals with a keen interest:

> When a death occurred, perhaps five or six miles from the cemetery, which was on the edge of town, the body was placed on a board and carried by four or six men, who naturally had to stop from time to time to rest. At each resting place they built a little monument of rocks and placed a wooden cross on top. Whenever relatives passed one of these stations, they always knelt down and offered a prayer. At all adult funerals, two fiddlers played. Flowers were never in evidence at the funeral of a child, particularly of a baby. They considered one so young to be already an angel and all relatives and friends brought bright colored ribbons which they pinned on the angel's dress until it was literally covered with vari-colored bows and streamers.[17]

In addition to the Bolton family, Juan Patrón made the acquaintance of a steadily increasing number of Anglo citizens living in the area. A local Hispano named Mauricio Sánchez had been commissioned as the first sheriff of Lincoln County on May 12, 1869, but an Irish immigrant named William J. Brady had been elected to office four months later on September 6. The 41-year-old Brady had served the Army with considerable success, having assumed command at Fort Stanton for the Union during the Civil War. He now performed his duties as sheriff while residing on a ranch four miles east of Lincoln with his wife María Bonifacia Chávez-Montoya and their children. Major Brady proved a capable frontier lawman, although he also possessed a fierce temper and considerable fondness for draining whiskey bottles.[18]

Juan Patrón also made the acquaintance of Sheriff William Brady's close friend Lawrence G. Murphy, a pale-skinned, red-haired, heavy-drinking Irish businessman. The 36-year-old Murphy had emigrated from Ireland to the United States of America at the age of 16 in early 1851. He subsequently enlisted in the Army and arrived in New Mexico Territory a decade later. Murphy had served the Union steadfastly during the Civil War. He also established the L. G. Murphy & Co. store, a brewery, and a post tradership on the outskirts of Fort Stanton with his German friend and fellow Civil War veteran Emil Fritz in 1866. Murphy and Fritz acquired the contracts to provide fresh beef and corn to the Army at Fort Stanton and the Apaches living on the

Mescalero reservation, sometimes inflating the Indian population numbers to increase the amount of vouchers they could claim. They also established a branch store and hotel at the western end of Lincoln. Murphy had recently been removed from the position of post trader at Fort Stanton, despite serving as the probate judge of Lincoln County by the time young Juan Patrón arrived on the Río Bonito with his family in 1870.

Although Lawrence G. Murphy was a calculating, ruthless businessman with a ferocious temper, he could also be considerably generous and contributed to the advancement of the local community. When the ambitious Juan Patrón discovered there was no school in Lincoln, he opened a classroom for some of the local Hispano and Anglo children in his family's private home. Lawrence Murphy graciously donated his earnings as probate judge to cover Patrón's salary as Lincoln's first schoolteacher. Juan's students began learning mathematics and how to read and write at his educated knee, earning him the appreciation and esteem of various locals.[19]

As Juan Patrón's standing and popularity in the community increased, many of his fellow Hispanos had more grievous concerns than a lack of formal education in the early 1870s. Some of the Americanos arriving in the region were unlawfully squatting on Hispano farmlands and violently driving the families from their homes. When many local "Mexicans" swore declarations against the squatters, Probate Judge Lawrence Murphy issued a proclamation in Spanish published by *The Borderer* on May 19, 1871:

> Many sworn declarations that have been made for us by resident citizens in the disputed boundaries of this county and Doña Ana, and those have taken domicile in conformity with the laws of the lands of the United States in the aforementioned disputed boundaries; and that armed persons in defiance of the law have intruded, in violation of the rights of said citizens... said declarations say that their lives as well as their properties are in imminent danger with said illegal people, and not expecting help from anywhere. Now, however, I L. G. Murphy, probate judge in and for Lincoln County, issue this my proclamation calling in this matter such armed people to desist from their illegal acts while this matter is pending in the District Court and to say such people thusly occupied that they will be held strictly accountable for their actions as disturbers of the public peace and punished accordingly.[20]

The squatting continued despite Murphy's proclamation and further inflamed resentment between the local Hispanos and various Anglo arrivals. To make any real inroads on behalf of his people, the 19-year-old Juan Patrón needed to seek political success in addition to commercial and educational ventures in Lincoln County.

Venturing into the world of politics in New Mexico Territory in the 1870s was like strolling into a rattlesnake den. The governor was appointed by Washington rather than elected by citizens and took residence in the Palace of the Governors in Santa Fe. Although a former Civil War general and minister from Missouri named William A. Pile was in office when the Patrón family arrived in Lincoln County, a Michigan politician named Marsh Giddings was appointed to the position by President Ulysses S. Grant on July 27, 1871. Governor Giddings quickly grew to loathe New Mexico's seemingly lawless and frequently violent atmosphere as much as his predecessor.[21]

For many Hispano farmers and sheepherders in New Mexico Territory, whomever resided in the Palace of the Governors was of little consequence to their everyday lives. The real power in the territory was firmly in the grasp of a confederation of lawyers and robber-barons known as the Santa Fe Ring. Their nonpartisan and increasingly wealthy conglomerate was centered around two University of Missouri graduates named Thomas Benton Catron and Stephen Benton Elkins, who were steadily transforming New Mexico Territory into their own political tributary. Catron and Elkins were doing so with a close-knit circle of friends, including William Breedon—the founder of New Mexico's Republican Party—and an influential seven-foot-tall attorney named William L. Rynerson.

The Santa Fe Ring wielded an unrivaled influence throughout New Mexico Territory, sometimes using bribery, intimidation, voter suppression, and violence to maintain their property, banking, cattle-ranching, and mining interests. The *Santa Fe New Mexican* often served as their mouthpiece in territorial affairs. Thomas B. Catron had studied the land grant system extensively and frequently exploited much of the illiterate Hispano farming community, thereby steadily increasing his personal property holdings until eventually becoming the largest landowner in the country. While the Americano newspapers often portrayed Catron as an enterprising giant, many

Nuevomexicanos viewed him as a silky sow gorging on their homeland who wiped his chin with the territorial legislature and continually belched pesos into his bank account at their expense.[22]

As Juan Patrón was preparing to test the political waters in La Placita, Saturnino Baca was appointed the representative for Lincoln County in the Central Republican Committee of New Mexico in April 1871. A Republican convention was also held in Lincoln County on May 15 that year, during which resolutions were adopted expressing strong dissatisfaction with José Francisco Cháves, their own territorial delegate to Congress. The Republicans of Lincoln County suggested that former secretary of the New Mexico Territory and Indian agent William Frederick Milton Arny was better suited for the position. A fervent Democrat, Lawrence G. Murphy delivered a rousing speech in the summer of 1871 in which he railed against J. Francisco Cháves for New Mexico's exclusion from "the bill passed by congress appropriating the internal revenue collected in the territories to the construction of public buildings." The *Santa Fe New Mexican* publicly derided Murphy's assertions as erroneous, stating that "Col. Chaves did all in his power to have New Mexico included in the bill."[23]

Although still a teenager, Juan Patrón had already achieved political success by the time Lawrence Murphy's close friend William Brady served as the delegate for Lincoln County in the House of Representatives in Santa Fe on December 4, 1871. The young Hispano had thrown his own hat into the political circle by running as a candidate for probate court clerk of Lincoln County in November. When the voters finished casting their ballots, it was a testament to how well regarded young Juan had become throughout the community when he emerged victorious in his first run for public office.[24]

At just age 19, Juan Bautista Patrón was sharing probate court duties alongside Probate Judge Lawrence G. Murphy in Condado de Lincoln.

***

Martín Chávez was 18 years old when residing in Lincoln County with his 60-year-old grandmother Magdalena in 1870. They were not the first residents of Manzano to have migrated into southeastern New Mexico Territory.

A healthy number of Hispanos had ventured from Manzano into the Río Bonito region throughout the previous decade. Martín decided to take up residence in the small placita known as Picacho on the Río Hondo. His new home was said to have been named after the 5,853-foot picacho (peak) three miles to the northwest, or possibly Picacho Hill closer to the east.[25]

Martín established a modest homestead for himself and his grandmother Magdalena on the outskirts of Picacho, where he could farm his crops and begin establishing his place in the local community. There were some familiar faces living in the area. Various members of the Romero family had also arrived from Manzano. The 24-year-old Vicente Romero had recently settled a farm in Picacho with his wife and children after working as a laborer throughout Lincoln County. Martín also spent time around Vicente's nephew-in-law George Kimbrell, an affable gringo from Arkansas who arrived in New Mexico around 1860. Kimbrell worked as a government scout before squatting on a patch of land near Picacho and marrying Vicente Romero's niece Paulita in Tome, Valencia County, on June 29, 1864. Kimbrell had learned Spanish and been warmly welcomed into the Romero family and the local Hispano community.

Vicente Romero also had an 11-year-old niece named Juanita, the younger sister of Paulita Romero-Kimbrell. Juanita "Juana" Romero had been born in Manzano in 1859 and lived with her parents Francisco and Andrea Romero and her younger siblings in Picacho. Juana spent much of her adolescent years around her uncle Vicente Romero, her older sister Paulita, and her brother-in-law George Kimbrell. She also became increasingly familiar with Martín Chávez as the 1870s progressed.[26]

While farming on the Río Hondo, Martín became acquainted with the citizens of Lincoln when traveling up the Río Bonito to buy goods. He would have certainly shaken hands with the young probate clerk named Juan Patrón and acquired items from the Patrón and Montaño stores. Martín may have also done some business with L. G. Murphy & Co., thereby becoming familiar with Probate Judge Lawrence G. Murphy and his heavy-drinking Irish associates James J. Dolan, John H. Riley, and William Brady. The influential Saturnino Baca would have immediately gained Martín's respect. So too would a bilingual farmer named Florencio Gonzáles, who had been educated in France and lived with his young wife Reymunda and their little boy Prospero in Lincoln. Martín also encountered a carpenter from Vermont named George W. Peppin, who had attached himself to Lawrence Murphy and his firm.[27]

Martín Chávez began raising *borregos* (sheep) in Picacho like so many of his fellow Hispanos who had long depended on the wool trade for their livelihood. A Czechoslovakian named Samuel Kohn had established a large wool and hide dealership up in Las Vegas, San Miguel County. Kohn paid ten cents per pound for "unwashed Mexican wool," and twenty-five cents for well-wooled pelts. "Sheep have been raised in this country from time immemorial," declared one observer in 1873. "But a new era has dawned upon New Mexico. Cotswold and Merino bucks have lately been introduced wherewith not only to increase the size of the animals but also the quality and quantity of wool produced. Agencies of eastern merchants have been established in all our principal towns and our wool finds a ready market at our very doors. Having abundancy of cheap labor within our limits, the wages of herders ranging from $5 to $25 and $30 per month, we can truly say that New Mexico is The Country for Stock Raising."[28]

The everyday life of a sheepman like Martín Chávez was one of monotonous routine, broken sleep, and frequent solitude in open pastures. A mayordomo (boss) relied on his hired hands and well-trained sheepdogs to help guide his flock to fresh grazing grounds and protect the animals from predatory wildlife or hostile cowboys. A sheepherder often spent an entire day sat alone in one spot, unless a *corta* (collection of strays) wandered too far from the rest of the flock, before herding the sheep and goats to their *mojada* (sleeping ground) at dusk. Lanterns were placed around the sleeping animals at night to ward off coyotes, bears, and mountain lions. Mayordomos routinely hired extra help throughout lambing season and shearing time each spring. Martín and every other sheepman always kept a watchful eye on the sky above. A *colgada* (hanging) moon indicated weeks of rainfall ahead. A patch of sky known as an *ojo de buey* (ox's eye) that resembled a small portion of a rainbow indicated a period of heavy rainfall was approaching. The relentless howling of coyotes during a winter's night suggested a fierce storm was brewing in the vicinity.[29]

While Martín Chávez had taken a piece of the wool trade, the cattle business was flourishing for a handful of Americanos in Lincoln County. "From the time we stroke the Río Bonito [Fort Stanton] until we reached the settlements on the upper Pecos, all along the valleys and on each side of the different rivers for twenty miles along the tablelands, cattle may be seen partaking of the nutritions grouth [sic] of nature so abundant in these regions," recalled one traveler during the spring of 1873. "The kings of stock raisers and cattle dealers are the Brothers Chisum."[30]

A cattle baron originally from Tennessee named John Simpson Chisum had arrived at Bosque Grande on the Río Pecos with his younger brother Pitzer and one thousand head of longhorns during the summer of 1867. John Chisum had established a partnership with fellow cattleman Charlie Goodnight and since become known as the Cattle King of the Pecos. His distinctly ear lopped jinglebob herds now stretched for many miles along the Río Pecos. The increasingly wealthy and powerful cattle baron held no regard for any small-time ranchers or sheepherders standing in the way of his operation's expansion. He also had a "no questions asked" policy when employing various thieves and killers to protect his interests. Chisum was known for paying a good price for any stolen horses or cattle and his cowboys became notorious for rustling livestock from Indian reservations. "Evidence shows conclusively that in the matter of horse stealing, Mr. Chisum is far ahead of the Indians," an Indian agent eventually reported, describing the cattle baron as "systematically robbing the Indians of their horses through the instrumentality of men whom he hired for the purpose."[31]

John Chisum was hardly unique when it came to appropriating livestock in the American Southwest of the 1870s. Horse and cattle theft were practically a way of life. Anglo rustlers frequently raided stock across Texas, New Mexico, Arizona, and Colorado. Charlie Goodnight was known for sending his cowboys into Mexico to rustle livestock from "greasers," which was barely considered theft in Anglo circles. A small party of Navajos raided some horses, mules, and beeves from Florencio Gonzáles, a rancher from Arkansas named Alexander Hamilton Mills in Agua Azul, the Mescalero reservation, and two other ranchers in Lincoln County on August 9, 1872.

The Hispanos had their own share of rustlers who cut herds from the ranchers and cattlemen throughout the New Mexico Territory. Some of the wealthy Hispano merchants and financiers were willing to purchase stolen stock with no questions asked. A prominent cattleman named John N. "Cattle Jack" Hittson led a posse into New Mexico in 1872 to recover a considerable number of beeves that had been cut from his herds over in Texas. "These God damn greasers have been stealing our horses and cattle for the past fifty years," Hittson remarked. "Two men were recently killed near Fort Stanton for cattle stealing," the *New Mexican* reported on February 18, 1873. When a party of Hispano rustlers from Manzano ran off some cattle from John Chisum's ranch at Bosque Grande the following month, a group of Chisum cowhands recovered the stolen stock after leaving three of the culprits lying dead on the ground.[32]

Martín Chávez quickly learned the wool trade could also be a dangerous one. Anglo cattlemen despised Hispano sheepherders, viewing them as pestilence. Their beeves refused to graze on any terrain previously occupied by sheep until their scent was diluted by rainfall. When Hispano sheepherders continued grazing their flocks on lands that had long been public domain but were now considered private property resulting from land titles, their *borregos* were sometimes killed by an angered cattleman's hired hands. This conflict between Anglo cattlemen and Hispano sheepherders over land and water usage continued for many years and sometimes escalated into violence.[33]

Along with everyone else living in the region, Martín Chávez would have heard the news of two Hispano ranch hands getting shot and killed in February 1873. A 32-year-old rancher from Kentucky named John Copeland had established a homestead seven miles west of Fort Stanton and recently employed two young Hispanos originally from Mesilla. The trouble began when the two ranch hands lit out from Copeland's ranch on a pair of the Kentuckian's horses in the early evening of February 17. Copeland's neighbor John H. Riley also discovered his new saddle had been stolen from his own nearby ranch. The 22-year-old Riley had already undergone an eventful start to the year. One of the L. G. Murphy & Co. associate's cowhands had passed out drunk on the range the previous month and consequently had his frozen feet amputated by the post surgeon at Fort Stanton.[34]

John Copeland and Johnny Riley began tracking the two young Hispanos and soon caught up with one of them. When Copeland discovered his rifle, pistol, blankets, spoons, and other household items had been pilfered, they began interrogating their captive over the whereabouts of his elusive companion.

"¿Quién sabe?" (Who knows?), the Hispano answered.

Copeland and Riley promptly threw a rope around their captive's neck and threatened to lynch him. The Hispano prisoner's resolve rapidly weakened, and he frantically revealed that his fellow thief had split off on a particular route for Tularosa. Copeland set out in pursuit while Riley escorted the "Mexican" back to his ranch, where the thief was "picketed" out for the day.

The vengeful John Copeland took a short cut and rode around twenty miles before he struck the other thieving Hispano's trail and shot him dead. Copeland then returned to his ranch with his stolen stock. Copeland and John Riley eventually agreed to escort their "picketed" Hispano captive to Fort Stanton. They had escorted their prisoner on foot for roughly two miles before the Hispano supposedly tried to make a run for it near a thicket and was fatally shot in the back.[35]

The following day Copeland and Riley arrived at the courthouse in Lincoln and reported their version of events to Probate Judge Lawrence G. Murphy. Juan Patrón was not convinced when overhearing their story. He believed the two young Hispano ranch hands had been coldly murdered, and Copeland and Riley's story was merely an attempt to absolve themselves of liability. Growing increasingly animated, Juan wanted both men arrested immediately and for an investigation to commence. His dormant temper erupted when Copeland and Riley balked at being arrested by a probate clerk without process. Juan started verbally abusing both gringos, and the energized clerk was soon running from house to house to express his outrage to the local Hispanos. Juan solicited enough excitement that Copeland and Riley fled to Fort Stanton in fear of being mobbed by the local "Mexicans."

Juan Patrón raised a posse of eleven heavily armed Hispano ruffians and led them out of Lincoln in pursuit of John Copeland and John H. Riley on the morning of February 19, 1873. They arrived at Copeland's ranch around noon and approached the house with their rifles and revolvers cocked. Copeland was away at the time, but the posse found John H. Riley and post surgeon H. G. Tiedemann on the premises. Juan and his possemen insisted Riley accompany them to his own nearby ranch, cursing him in Spanish during the journey. Tiedemann headed back to Fort Stanton to request assistance.[36]

When the infuriated Hispanos arrived with John H. Riley at the Irishman's ranch, they began feeding their horses with his corn, helped themselves to some food, and smashed up parts of the house. When John Copeland eventually appeared at Riley's ranch, Juan Patrón produced a warrant he had personally signed for both men's arrest. Copeland and Riley refused to be apprehended, and a tense standoff ensued until Lt. A. G. Hennessey arrived from Fort Stanton. Patrón and his posse demanded to be shown the body of the slain Hispano whom Copeland and Riley had been escorting to the fort two days earlier. When Copeland and Riley led them to the Hispano ranch hand's corpse, posse member and notorious pistolero Lucas Gallegos immediately pointed his cocked revolver at John Riley's head.

"You shoot dat man?" Gallegos menacingly asked.

With a pistola in his face, Riley insisted that he was not responsible for the ranch hand's death, while some of the possemen dismounted and began digging a grave for the slain Hispano. As they shoveled the final mound of dirt into the burial site, Riley and Copeland must have felt a supreme sense of relief when Capt. Chambers McKibbin, former Sheriff William Brady, and a detachment of soldiers arrived on the scene. Although a 36-year-old from Ohio named Jacob Lewis "Jackinto" Gylam had succeeded Brady as sheriff of Lincoln County, the Irishman cited his authority as a "U.S. Commissioner" when ordering the soldiers to disarm the Hispano posse and march them to Fort Stanton.[37]

Juan Patrón and his ruffians were put to work at Fort Stanton "earning their bread by the sweat of their brow," as one observer described it. The authorities learned that posse members Juan Gonzáles and Manuel Lucero y Romero were both wanted for murder. "The rest of the gang are equally bad," insisted a letter to the *New Mexican*. "These are the men who the county clerk [Patrón] selected ostensibly to make an arrest without a lawful warrant."

A hasty investigation carried out by Commissioner William Brady quickly led to the acquittal of Copeland and Riley, with the Hispano "rioters being held to bail for appearance in court."[38]

Juan Patrón had learned how things worked in Lincoln County. L. G. Murphy & Co. and their close friend William Brady looked out for each other's interests, having established ties with Thomas B. Catron and the Santa Fe Ring. Corruption also frequently rose through the ranks at Fort Stanton. Juan was eventually indicted by a grand jury in Lincoln for issuing illegal warrants. Although the case against him was never prosecuted, the antipathy he developed for John H. Riley and his Irish associates endured.[39]

The animosity between the Hispanos and Anglos of Lincoln County further escalated with the Tularosa Ditch War in May 1873. "Our mountains are full of good and steady streams, with sufficient waterpower," declared the *Las Vegas Gazette* that month. "But we lack not only the capital, but also the energy and enterprise of our eastern neighbors, and we feel sure that the establishment of manufactories, and the improvement of our herds and flocks would as much add to the welfare of our whole community as to the profit of those capitalists who would invest their money in this way."[40]

The hostilities began after a party of Americanos built dams and irrigation ditches upstream from Tularosa. Many Hispanos were increasingly frustrated with the gringos cutting their irrigation ditches and appropriating their properties, including the farmers of Tularosa in May 1873. When levels of irrigation water began rapidly falling, around twenty-five Hispanos successfully destroyed the waterworks upstream and hindered the efforts to repair them with spurts of gunfire. The Hispano vigilantes rallied around a French priest named Pedro Lassaigne, and the Tularosa ditch conflict raged on for a week with smatterings of violence. Capt. Chambers McKibbin and some cavalrymen were eventually dispatched from Fort Stanton. The troopers exchanged shots with the angry Hispano locals, which brought an end to the open hostilities for the time being, although the conflict over Tularosa water rights persisted.[41]

While Juan Patrón's nemesis John H. Riley accompanied Thomas B. Catron to the district court session in Albuquerque that fall, the Hispanos used their numbers to swing some of the ballots their way in the Lincoln County elections for office in September 1873. Jacinto Gonzáles was elected probate judge ahead of William Brady, Manuel Gutiérrez was elected justice of the peace, Juan Martínez was elected precinct constable, and the 21-year-old Juan Bautista Patrón retained his position as probate clerk. Lincoln County also had a new sheriff in Alexander Hamilton "Ham" Mills, who was married to a Nuevomexicano woman and previously worked for his close friend Lawrence Murphy as a teamster.[42]

The racial tensions in Lincoln County continued to simmer with the steady arrival of various Tejanos, whom the Hispanos generally despised. While numerous Texans were settling small ranches along the Río Pecos, it was the arrival of the Horrell family on the Río Ruidoso during the fall of 1873 that led to an outbreak of unbridled bloodshed.

Even the most peaceable Hispanos of Lincoln County soon had to watch over their shoulders for nothing more than being the descendants of Spanish settlers.

Chapter 3

Hombres Malos

*Our life or yours is the only trade
for soft brown earth and maize.*
—Rodolfo Gonzáles

The hatred that many Nuevomexicanos and Texans felt for each other throughout frontier times can scarcely be overstated. Animosities still lingered from the Texas revolution of the 1830s and the annexation of the Republic of Texas in 1845, which had prompted the Mexican-American War. The Hispano population of New Mexico Territory sided with the Union during the American Civil War primarily out of concern that a Confederate victory would result in Texans lording over their homeland. Nuevomexicanos considered Tejanos the worst kind of gringos. Texans generally viewed Mexicanos as "greasers," "peons," and an inferior race of people.

The *Las Vegas Gazette* reproduced a scathing condemnation of the Mexican race from the *Galveston News* on January 11, 1873. The Texas newspaper had expressed hypocritical outrage and imperialistic antagonism over the banditry occurring on the Río Grande:

> Mexico has had already one sharp lesson at the hand of our government. It would seem that after so plain an exhibition of superior skill, resources and manhood—after so bitter a castigation—she would have had grace

and common sense enough to have confined herself, in all her constitutional vaporings, to the safe side of the law. No sane man can doubt, should there occur a rapture between the Mexican government and our own, that in six months the American flag would be flying over the City of Mexico. . . . Yet the Mexican Government, by permitting the outrages on the frontier of the Rio Grande, has laid itself open to the charge either of a great crime and prospective baseness, or a course of utter folly and presumption. . . . The mongrel population on the West of the Rio Grande is of this character. Doubtless there are enlightened and cultivated men among the Mexicans; but in point of numbers their existence is scarcely appreciable . . . the common people, it is well known, are deplorably ignorant, indolent and vicious. Of a mixed lineage, they display the debasing passions of the aboriginal savage, diverted into the channels of modern brutality, with just enough of the old Spanish blood in their veins to give vim to the sluggish instincts of a nature barely on a level with Hottendot. . . . Let Mexico be made to disgorge the plunder of her thievish borders; let her be made to atone for the insult offered our sovereign territorial rights; let her be made to restrain the lawlessness of her savage yeomanry for all time to come; or else let her be made to know practically again the difference between the American eagle and the Mexican vulture![1]

It was that same degree of prejudice that many Texans brought with them into New Mexico Territory during the 1870s. That included the Horrell brothers and their party of friends, who arrived in Lincoln County during the autumn of 1873.

Merritt, Thomas, Benjamin, Samuel, and James Martin "Mart" Horrell were raised by their parents Samuel and Elizabeth on a ranch outside Lampasas, Texas. The five brothers came from an insular family and developed a reputation for fearlessness and ruffian behavior. "I raised my boys to be fighters," their mother Elizabeth later said. The Horrell boys proved true to form when getting into a scrape with Lampasas County Sheriff Shadrack T. Denson on January 14, 1873. Sheriff Denson had been attempting to arrest the Horrell brothers' friends Wash and Mark Short before receiving a gunshot wound. The townsfolk petitioned for assistance, and Texas State Police Capt. Thomas Williams and six policemen arrived in town to keep things settled.[2]

Mart, Merritt, and Tom Horrell were drinking with some friends in Jerry Scott's saloon when Capt. Thomas Williams attempted to arrest their brother-in-law Bill Bowen for carrying a firearm within the town limits on March 14, 1873. Taking exception to Bowen's impending arrest, the Horrell brothers and their liquored-up buddies opened fire on the policemen. Mart Horrell shot Thomas Williams in the face and the police captain fell dead with two more bullets lodged in his chest. Rookie policemen James M. Daniels and Wesley Cherry were also pitilessly gunned down. Officer Andrew Melville had taken a bullet in the chest and stumbled outside as the Horrell boys and their friends chased after him. The fight then spilled into the street when policeman Henry Eddy opened fired on the culprits as they emerged from the saloon. Mart Horrell received a flesh wound on the back on his head and his one-eyed brother Tom was hit beneath the shoulder blade. Henry Eddy's fellow policeman Andrew Melville survived the day but died the following month in Lampasas on April 10, 1873.

The townsfolk of Lampasas rallied together until Mart Horrell, James Grizzell, and Allen Whitcraft were arrested for their participation in the killing of three Texas state policemen. The incident was dubbed "The Lampasas Horror" by the *Daily State Journal*. On March 20 an inquest jury named Mart Horrell, Tom Horrell, Merritt Horrell, and their friends Bill Bowen, Ben Turner, Joe Bolden, Allen Whitcraft, James Grizzell, Bill Gray, and saloon owner Jerry Scott as the murderers of Captain Williams and his fellow policemen. Adjutant General Frank Britton and a large force were soon combing the countryside for Tom Horrell, Merritt Horrell, and the other guilty parties. Meanwhile, Mart Horrell and Jerry Scott were transferred to the jail in Georgetown in April 1873. The wounded Mart Horrell's incarceration only lasted until his brothers and over thirty of their friends steamed into Georgetown and busted him out of the jail while engaging in a furious shootout with the guards and some of the townsfolk. The Horrell brothers and their cronies ran amok in Lampasas for several months before fleeing into Lincoln County with their families and one thousand head of cattle in the autumn of 1873.[3]

The Horrell brothers were already familiar with New Mexico Territory when arriving on the Río Ruidoso that autumn. The family had traveled through Las Cruces in January 1869, intending to set up stakes in California. Those plans ended after their father Samuel, Tom Horrell, their sister Sarah, and her children were ambushed by Mescalero Apaches in the

San Augustin Pass on January 14. Tom Horrell managed to fight off the Apaches long enough for his sister to escape with her children, but their father Samuel and a man named Theodore Ortega were both killed. The dispirited Horrell family returned to Lampasas rather than continuing their journey to California.[4]

According to a young local girl named Lily Casey, the Horrell brothers and most of their families began setting up stakes in Lincoln County in the fall of 1873 with "a number of associates, who were all more or less desperate fellows." These associates included Ben Turner, Jerry Scott, Tom Bowen, and probably Tom's brother Bill Bowen. The Horrells purchased a ranch on the Río Ruidoso at the mouth of Eagle Creek that had belonged to Frank Reagan and Heiskell Jones, according to Lily Casey and her brother William. "They were scrappers, you bet they were," young Robert A. Casey later said. "They were so tough down there they run them out of Texas."[5]

The atmosphere in Lincoln County was already tense when the Horrell boys and their cavalcade arrived from Lampasas. In addition to ongoing racial conflict, Lawrence G. Murphy had been forced to relocate his entire business operation to Lincoln. His loyal Irish clerk James J. Dolan had tried to shoot Capt. James Randlett when the officer attempted to break up an argument between Dolan and John H. Riley at Fort Stanton on May 16. Although Dolan and Riley made their amends, L. G. Murphy & Co. had been ordered off the post. Murphy's business partner Emil Fritz also began traveling back to Germany in the summer of 1873 after his tuberculosis worsened. Murphy chose a new business partner in the 25-year-old Jimmy Dolan, who compensated for his five-foot, two-inch height with cunning intelligence, ruthlessness, and one of the most volatile dispositions in the territory.[6]

Although L. G. Murphy & Co. remained the leading mercantile enterprise in Lincoln, the 21-year-old Juan Patrón continued succeeding as a businessman himself. The potential for commerce in the Patrón store was broadening, with the *Las Vegas Gazette* announcing the recent discovery of "large veins of coal and specimens of silver ore" in Lincoln County. "Several parties have gone to examine the new discoveries near Stanton and other portions [of] Lincoln County," the newspaper declared. "Lincoln has heretofore been looked upon mostly as a grazing and farming country, but we opine that it will not be six months before a thousand prospectors will be at work in her mountains. When her mineral wealth is once known a rush of new commers [*sic*] will seek her borders. Beside that she has live, wide awake people now."⁷

Juan Patrón may have been salivating over the potential financial gains should prospectors begin arriving on the Río Bonito, but it was the Horrell brothers and their cronies who kept him and many other Hispanos wide awake in the months ahead.

***

The Horrell boys and their friends had barely settled in Lincoln County before hostilities began with the local Hispanos. Although the Horrell family had arrived peacefully and been issued credit notes for thousands of dollars by Lawrence G. Murphy, tensions arose when they claimed some of the locals tried to steal the proceeds they acquired from a cattle sale. The local Hispanos insisted the Horrell party had killed one of their neighbors who had been cutting a ditch, suggesting the conflict over water rights in Tularosa had also surfaced on the Río Ruidoso.⁸

The animosity between the Hispanos and the Horrells began whirling like a dust devil after Ben Horrell and one of his brothers arrived in Lincoln to collect their mail on the night of December 1, 1873. Ben Horrell decided to stick around and began drinking with Jerry Scott and their local friends David C. Warner, Zacharias Crompton, and former sheriff Jacob L. Gylam. It wasn't long before they started making a nuisance of themselves and shooting up the town. Constable Juan Martínez, a "high-strung fellow that thought a good deal of himself" according to one young local, was compelled to intervene. Martínez approached Ben Horrell and his rowdy companions, instructed them to cease their ruffian behavior, and demanded they hand over their firearms. The intoxicated Horrell, Gylam, Scott, Crompton, and Warner begrudgingly complied with Martínez's demand and gave up their guns. The constable left their firearms in the care of Probate Judge Jacinto Gonzáles and returned to the baile being held that night.⁹

Ben Horrell, Jacob Gylam, and their companions continued drinking for roughly an hour before acquiring new firearms and openly threatening the life of Probate Judge Jacinto Gonzáles. Although Postmaster John Bolton dissuaded them from confronting Judge Gonzales, the drunken party soon arrived at a "house of ill-fame," where they threatened the occupants and started randomly firing their guns off in any direction.

Constable Juan Martínez heard gunshots in town for the second time and realized the troublesome gringos had failed to learn their lesson. He would have to not only disarm them but also take them into custody. Martínez recruited some of the locals, which likely included deputies Joe Haskins and notorious pistolero Juan Gonzáles, along with Juan Patrón, Lucas Gallegos, Nico Meras, and other armed Hispanos.[10]

Juan Martínez and his supporters began marching toward the whorehouse with plenty of purpose to confront Gylam, Horrell, Scott, Crompton, and Warner. According to one local, Martínez and David Warner were already bitter adversaries for unspecified reasons. When the constable demanded the liquored-up party surrender their guns for the second time that night and voiced his intentions to arrest them, the inebriated David Warner took exception.

"Don't you surrender to him," Warner told his companions. "You don't have to obey any orders from him."

Jacob Gylam reportedly called Martínez "a damned greaser," and the verbal altercation escalated until the brothel was on the verge of turning into a slaughterhouse. David Warner and Constable Juan Martínez went for their pistols and fired on each other almost simultaneously. They both slumped onto the floor and died from their wounds within minutes. The two parties opened fire, and Jacob Gylam was shot three times. Ben Horrell was also wounded during the exchange. Horrell and Gylam then fled the establishment with the dying Martínez's supporters chasing after them.[11]

Ben Horrell and Jacob Gylam ran toward the Río Bonito and managed to cross its freezing waters before the party of outraged Nuevomexicanos caught up with them. The wounded Gylam and Horrell surrendered and begged for mercy with every visible cloud of whiskey breath they could muster in the chilly night air. The Hispanos were in no mood for clemency after the shooting of Constable Juan Martínez moments earlier. Jacob Gylam was shot ten times at close range, with one bullet from a pistol igniting his clothes and piercing his heart. Ben Horrell was shot multiple times and received several additional slugs in his body after falling dead to the ground. Juan Patrón was later said to have been the hombre responsible for Ben Horrell's death.[12]

The blood-drenched corpses of Jack Gylam and Ben Horrell were still lying outside of town the following morning of December 2, 1873. Someone had sliced off one of Ben Horrell's fingers to obtain a ring he was wearing. Constable Juan Martínez's corpse was now lying in the street with a cross deeply carved into his forehead. With anxieties running high, Justice of the Peace Manuel Gutiérrez wrote a report providing his version of the previous night's events and appealed to Fort Stanton for protection. "The excitement was great," according to one observer in Lincoln, who also "knew that [Gylam] and [Horrell's] friends would gather to avenge them." Maj. John Mason refused Manuel Gutiérrez's request for protection after receiving it in Fort Stanton, stating "there was no necessity for my interference," and "that the troops [are] here for their protection against Indians."[13]

Mart, Merritt, Tom, and Samuel Horrell Jr. were livid when learning of their brother Ben's death. They arrived in Lincoln to collect his corpse and demand an investigation. They wanted the Hispanos responsible tried for murder. Sheriff Alexander "Ham" Mills refused to investigate a shootout involving his own deputies, and the Hispanos asserted that Ben Horrell had been killed while they were carrying out their duty. Threats were levied, and the Horrell brothers warned that "Hell was going to pop." Some of the local Hispanos soon began talking of "cleaning out all the Americans." Like many Texans, the Horrells were no strangers to a feud and returned to the Río Ruidoso with bloodshed on their minds.[14]

The bodies of 38-year-old Severiano Trujillo and another Hispano citizen were soon floating in the Río Ruidoso near the Horrell ranch. Suspicions were immediately raised over their deaths when the corpses were discovered on December 4. The Horrell brothers denied responsibility for the murders, but the locals were not convinced. Deputy Juan Gonzáles and a large party of armed Hispanos gathered on Eagle Creek the following day and threatened to attack "the ranches of Americans." Maj. John Mason soon dispatched Capt. Chambers McKibbin and a small detachment of soldiers to the mouth of Eagle Creek, having instructed them to make their presence known but refrain from any engagement. What began with Constable Juan Martínez reprimanding a handful of liquored-up Americanos in Lincoln was rapidly escalating into a race war.¹⁵

Sheriff Alexander "Ham" Mills decided to support the initiative carried out by Deputy Juan Gonzáles, whom Capt. James Randlett later described as "a noted murderer and horse thief." Juan Patrón later insisted that Lawrence G. Murphy wanted the Horrells out of the country so that he could claim their properties and livestock. On December 5 Sheriff Mills raised a posse of around twenty-five men to accompany him to the Horrell ranch and demand the Texans surrender. The Horrells were willing to surrender to the authorities at Fort Stanton but refused to give themselves up to either Mills or the "scurf of the country." The Horrells and their brethren were all armed with Winchester rifles, and shots were exchanged before the Mills posse backed off and returned to Lincoln.¹⁶

Capt. John Mason reported that "angry feelings still exist and Mexicans still threatening," although things simmered down enough for the Horrells to continue purchasing goods from the Murphy store in Lincoln. This proved to be merely a temporary stalemate after a French priest named Pedro Lassaigne advised Deputy Juan Gonzáles and some Hispanos to set fire to the Horrell ranch and kill the Texans when they tried to flee into the hills. Deputy Gonzáles, described as a "notorious scoundrel, and cutthroat" by Major Mason, quickly began riding for Tularosa to gather reinforcements. When the party of Hispanos failed in their attempt to burn the Horrell ranch in mid-December, the Horrells decided to respond to the threat of being burned alive with swift and deadly action. They also believed Juan Patrón was the Hispano responsible for the death of their brother Ben Horrell weeks earlier.¹⁷

The Horrell brothers rallied more than a dozen of their ruffian friends and began riding toward Lincoln with ruinous intentions on December 20, 1873.

***

Juan Patrón was busy seeing to his own affairs while his 52-year-old father Isidro and younger sister Encarnación attended a baile in Lincoln on the wintry night of December 20, 1873. "A sister of one of our leading Mexican citizens was to be married and it was proposed to honor the happy event by a grand ball in the courthouse," recalled one local. The Patrón family had recently enjoyed their own wedding festivities. The 17-year-old Encarnación had married a sheepherder named Rafael Gutiérrez in the Saint Rita Catholic Church in Carrizozo just two weeks earlier.[18]

The celebrations were in full swing as midnight was approaching. In addition to Isidro Patrón and his youngest daughter, the esteemed Saturnino Baca, his wife Juana, and their children would have been in attendance. José and Josefa Montaño would have also been present. Seated near the Patrón family was a 38-year-old farmer named José Candelario, his wife Pilar Gonzáles, and their two sons Andres and Casimiro. A 30-year-old laborer named Isidro Padilla, his wife Catalina, and their 6-year-old daughter Viviana were also enjoying the festivities. The local minstrels spent the night playing their instruments and singing for all those in attendance, including the unattached señoritas in their brightly colored dresses and shawls. Any hombre wishing to dance with one of the pretty girls was obliged to approach them with the proper etiquette under the watchful eyes of their families.[19]

The Horrell brothers and their supporters could hear the revelries emanating from the dance hall as they approached Lincoln around midnight. The unsuspecting Hispanos were tightly packed inside a confined space, making them an easy target. The Horrell boys and their companions rode to the house of their friend Bill Jones and asked if any of his family were attending the baile. Jones readily informed the heavily armed bunch that no members of his family were inside the dance hall.

"Come on," one of the Horrell party said. "We'll make them dance to *our* music."[20]

The Horrell brothers began trudging through the snow toward the dance hall alongside Zachariah Compton, Jerry Scott, James Wilson, John Walker, and several others. Eyewitnesses later asserted that Capt. James F. Randlett of the US Cavalry was with them and carrying two pistols. The party prepared their lever-action Winchester rifles with a quick snap of the cocking handle as the sound of Spanish lyrics grew louder in their ears. The Horrell boys and their friends then partially surrounded the dance hall. Some of them approached the front doors, while the others positioned themselves outside the windows.

Isidro Patrón and his fellow Hispanos were enjoying themselves when the front doors of the dance hall unexpectedly broke open. A deafening roar of gunfire erupted as the Horrell brothers and their friends began shooting through the doorway and several windows. Many hombres instinctively reached for their wives and children when hearing the thunderous pops and frightened screams of the female attendees. A handful of defenseless Hispanos were cut down by bullets while everyone else scrambled to take cover behind the tables and chairs until the shooting stopped. The satisfied Horrell party then withdrew from the dance hall and quickly rode out of town.[21]

The shaken Hispanos began assessing the carnage inside the dance hall and discovered the fresh corpses of José Candelario, Isidro Padilla, and Dario Valizan lying on the floor. Pilar Candelario, Apolinario García, and Dario Valizan's nephew had been wounded and were soon receiving medical attention. The lifeless frame of 52-year-old Isidro Patrón was also found lying in a puddle of his own blood. "They wanted a Mexican by the name of Juan Patrón," recalled local boy Robert A. Casey. "But he wasn't there, and they got his daddy. He looked a pretty good deal like him, and they killed him."[22]

Having heard the shots along with everyone else in Lincoln, Juan Patrón arrived at the dance hall and learned of his father Isidro's murder. Juan was now the head of his family and did his best to comfort his weeping sister Encarnación. She was fortunate not to have been shot herself. Andres and Casimiro Candelario tried to console their wounded mother Pilar while grieving the loss of their father José. The widowed Catalina Padilla and her young daughter Viviana wailed over the death of Isidro Padilla amid the outpourings of grief, panic, and outrage taking hold of the town. "The court-room walls show many bullet marks, and the floor is bespattered with blood," several newspapers informed the public.[23]

The 21-year-old Juan Patrón became more than the head of his family that night. He also shouldered an increasing responsibility for the Hispano population of Lincoln. The local Nuevomexicanos were looking to him for leadership and reassurance. Many of them predictably wanted retribution against the Horrells and their Tejanos. "The Mexicans swear vengeance, refuse to make peace, and are determined to treat the Texans as they would hostile Apaches," one local observed.[24]

In Tularosa, Padre Pedro Lassaigne began traveling to Lincoln in a buggy when he heard about the baile murders. The French priest held a funeral mass for Isidro Patrón, José Candelario, Isidro Padilla, and Dario Valizan two days after their deaths. Lawrence G. Murphy genially paid out of his own pocket for the four coffins in which the slain Hispanos were buried. A party of vengeful Nuevomexicanos attempted to waylay four Texans spotted in the area later that day. "It's war to the knife," observed one citizen. "As the military declines to interfere, one or the other party must find refuge in the grave-yard." News of the wedding baile ambush reached newspapers as far as the eastern seaboard. "It seems the friends of the Americans previously killed went to Lincoln Plaza last Saturday, where a dance was in progress, and trouble arose between the Americans and the Mexicans, which culminated fatally," the *Newport Daily News* declared in Rhode Island. "Intense excitement prevails, and it is feared more bloodshed will follow."[25]

Juan Patrón realized that a racial powder keg was on the verge of exploding in Lincoln County. He decided to personally appeal to Governor Marsh Giddings in Santa Fe. The governor held a reputation for being somewhat sympathetic toward Hispanos and disapproving of the racial slurs used by Texans and soldiers. Juan left his sister Encarnación in the care of her husband Rafael and Padre Lassaigne, climbed aboard his wagon, and began rolling through the thick snowdrifts to meet with Governor Giddings in the Holy City.[26]

As Juan Patrón was heading for the territorial capital, William Brady would meet with the Horrell brothers on the Río Ruidoso. The Horrells insisted they would not lay siege to Lincoln but would fight to the death if attacked themselves. Lawrence G. Murphy wrote to Governor Giddings and requested the army be used to temper what became known as the Horrell War as the local judicial authorities were "unable to meet the situation."[27]

Maj. John Mason soon asked William Brady to beseech the locals to speak with him at Fort Stanton to "stop the fued [sic] and submit the question to the Civil tribunals." While the Horrell brothers and their friends were reportedly willing to do so, many of the local Hispanos began gathering arms to wage war against the Tejanos. On December 24, Major Mason ordered Capt. Edmund Gustave Fechét and a detachment of soldiers to set up camp on the outskirts of Lincoln to calm the situation. Although La Navidad (Christmas) passed without incident, on December 26 Probate Judge Jacinto González and Justice of the Peace Manuel Gutiérrez wrote a letter to Governor Giddings providing their version of events and declaring "their inability to make arrests." González and Gutiérrez then immediately fled Lincoln and took refuge in the mountains.[28]

Juan Patrón steered his wagon into Santa Fe around December 31, 1873. The journey had been a lousy way for him to spend La Navidad while enduring the unusually cold weather in New Mexico and mourning the death of his father. "The killing was done by Texans in retaliation for the men killed in the beginning of the month at the same place by Mexicans," the *New Mexican* had announced on December 29. "Among the killed was the father of Juan Patron, the county clerk of Lincoln County."[29]

After reaching the territorial capital, Juan sat across from Governor Marsh Giddings in the Palace of the Governors and pleaded his case. The probate clerk provided Giddings with his version of recent events in Lincoln County and identified the Horrell brothers and their friends as the men who had shot up the baile on December 20. The governor proved sympathetic and agreed to intervene. Giddings also expressed his distrust of Maj. John Mason's reports and asserted his belief that the military held a strong prejudice against Hispanos in a letter to Secretary of the Interior Columbus Delano.[30]

Juan made the most of his time in Santa Fe by also taking his case to the *Santa Fe New Mexican* and providing them with details of the baile ambush. "From Juan Patron, clerk of Lincoln County, we have a list of the persons killed and wounded in Placita on the night of 20th ultimo," the newspaper reported on January 2, 1874. News of a shootout occurring in San Patricio on January 4 also reached the Holy City. "It is reported that another fight occurred in Lincoln County, at the village of San Patricio between Texans and Mexicans on last Sunday," the *New Mexican* informed its readers.[31]

Governor Marsh Giddings affirmed his faith in Juan Patrón when issuing a proclamation and offering a $500 reward for the Horrell brothers and their associates in the *New Mexican* on January 9, 1874:

Proclamation by the Governor.

$500 Reward.

Whereas it appears from satisfactory evidence presented to the undersigned, that Zachariah Crompton, E. Scott and three other persons, brothers, by the name of Harrold [sic, Horrell], whose first names are unknown, late of Lincoln, in the Territory of New Mexico, did on the night of the 20th day of December A.D. 1873, at the county of Lincoln aforesaid, aided and assisted by other persons, unlawfully kill and murder Isidro Patron, Isidro Padilla, Dario Balazan and Jose Candelario . . . now therefore, I, Marsh Giddings, Governor of the Territory of New Mexico, by virtue of the power and authority in me vested by the laws of said Territory, do hereby offer and declare a reward of five hundred dollars for the apprehension of the said Zachariah Crompton, E. Scott, and the three persons, brothers, by the name of Harrold, and their delivery to the said sheriff of the county of Lincoln. . . . In testimony whereof I have hereunto set my hand and caused the Great Seal of the Territory to be affixed.

MARSH GIDDINGS.
Governor.[32]

The proclamation from Giddings meant it was now open season for rough hombres like Deputy Juan Gonzáles to pursue the Horrell party. "The Mexican population have nothing to fear from Gonzáles and can commit crime with impunity," Capt. James Randlett had reported earlier that month. The Horrell brothers approached 43-year-old farmer and store owner Robert Casey on the Río Hondo and asked to leave their wives and children with his family. "Although Father disapproved of the actions of the men in their troubles with the Mexicans, he did not think he could refuse to give women and children protection," recalled Lily Casey. "So he permitted them to stay in the mill."[33]

Juan Patrón felt he had served his people well in Santa Fe and began the journey back to Lincoln. He was presumably on his way home when Lawrence G. Murphy headed a mass meeting of Lincoln County citizens to form a vigilance committee at ten o'clock in the morning on January 13, 1874. Juan had no faith left in Murphy by this time. He later suggested the committee was a plot to "dispose and get out of the way obnoxious parties" who were "opposed to their schemes and plots," and the "real object of the committee was to kill me and others." Murphy's initiative was certainly self-serving to some degree. The Irishman clearly had an eye on regaining the office of probate judge when declaring, "Whereas the Probate Judge of the county and justice of the peace of this precinct have abandoned this people, and have went to other counties to reside, in this hour of our need, when their services were so imperatively required in the preservation of peace and of our interests, it therefore behooves [sic] us to consult together as to the best means to supply their places, and restore to this distracted people a sure guarantee of peace, order and protection."[34]

Lawrence G. Murphy was unsurprisingly elected president of the vigilance committee, with José Montaño serving as vice president and John R. Bolton acting as secretary. William Brady motioned for Murphy to appoint a committee comprised of Juan Gonzáles, Rafael Montoya, John B. "Green" Wilson, Mauricio Sánchez, and Brady himself. They were to assign three citizens "in whose hands would be placed the entire charge of the lives, honor, and property of the citizens, until the majesty of the law could be enforced in their behalf by the proper officers." The three men elected to fill those positions were Lawrence Murphy, William Brady, and José Montaño. Murphy's new business partner James J. Dolan was appointed secretary. However power hungry Murphy's intentions may have been, the Irishman's plan unraveled when the vigilance committee was declared illegal before it even came into effect.[35]

Juan Patrón returned to Lincoln after Lawrence Murphy's vigilance committee initiative and resumed his duties as county clerk. Murphy had sent word to the Horrells that he would guarantee their acquittal if they faced trial before the commission, an offer the Texans declined. Everyone was on edge throughout the region. Indian Agent Samuel Bushnell and post trader Paul Dowlin departed Fort Stanton for Santa Fe to meet with Governor Giddings, Judge Warren Bristol, and Maj. William Price on January 17. Bushnell and Dowlin suggested military assistance could restrain the burgeoning guerrilla warfare throughout Lincoln County, insisting "armed parties are moving about over the County—and firing into one another: every person seems to be armed and expecting to be attacked." Judge Bristol provided Paul Dowlin with a letter for Ham Mills, advising the sheriff to turn the warrants for the Horrell brothers over to Major Price when the officer returned to Fort Stanton. Meanwhile, the Horrells made arrangements to sell their cattle to Murphy employee Charles Miller on January 19, 1874.³⁶

Sheriff Mills had already decided to serve the warrants and arrest the Horrell brothers before Maj. William Price and Judge Bristol's letter reached Fort Stanton. Sheriff Mills and Juan Patrón gathered up a posse of around sixty Nuevomexicanos and arrived on the Río Ruidoso on the evening of January 20. Shots were exchanged when they surrounded the Horrell ranch, and Ham Mills was hit in the chest. Fortunately for the sheriff, the bullet struck one of his ribs and passed through his back, and the wound did not prove fatal. Juan Patrón and his fellow Hispanos managed to kill or run off the Texans' horses before escorting the wounded Sheriff Mills back up the Río Bonito. The Horrell boys quickly abandoned their ranch and rode for the Casey ranch on the Río Hondo. "All here is war and rumors of war," one resident of Lincoln wrote the following day. "Every man met is armed to the teeth. Up and down the Río Hondo a number of ranches have been deserted."³⁷

The Horrell brothers and their chums took refuge at the Casey ranch and discussed their next move on the morning of January 21. They decided to escort their families over to Roswell. They also made the determination to "come back and wreak vengeance on the Mexican people," as Lily Casey recalled. "They contemplated nothing short of a complete massacre of the Mexicans at Lincoln." The Horrell boys may have also taken their frustrations out on Frank Reagan, who had sold the Texans a faulty deed to their ranch and recently taken shelter at the Casey ranch. Reagan subsequently disappeared, never to been seen or heard from again in Lincoln County.³⁸

The Horrell boys escorted their families to the Missouri Bottom—formally Missouri Plaza—where their cronies Ben Turner and Edward "Little" Hart decided to ride into Picacho and acquire some corn. The Horrell boys also arranged for Heiskell Jones, Frank McCallum, Jerry Hocradle, and young William Casey to transport their household items over from their abandoned ranch. Jones, McCallum, Hocradle, and Casey successfully drove two wagons to the Horrell ranch and loaded their goods, only to be robbed of everything by a party of militant Hispanos on the return journey. The Horrell brothers declared they would "get lots of the sons of bitches" when learning of the raid.[39]

While the Horrell family's goods were being pilfered, their friends Ben Turner and Edward Hart arrived at a farmhouse over in Picacho. Turner was intending to visit an old Mexican friend and acquire the corn for which he had previously traded. The women of the house denied knowledge of a previous transaction having been made for corn and insisted there were no hombres on the premises. Turner and Hart turned their horses away in frustration. They had barely departed the farmhouse when a shot was suddenly fired through a porthole in an adobe wall. Ben Turner's horse whirled as he fell dead from the saddle, and young Hart began galloping with all possible speed back to the Horrell party on the Missouri Bottom.[40]

The identity of the hombre who killed Ben Turner just outside Picacho was never truly determined, although many believed it was Martín Chávez who squeezed the trigger that day. "It was always said that it was Martín Chávez who did this killing," Lily Casey recalled. "But it was never known positively that this was the case." If Martín was the man who ambushed Turner and Hart, he would have needed little beyond their close association with the Horrell brothers to feel justified in doing so, especially considering their unexpected presence in Picacho during the ongoing feud. The 22-year-old Martín Chávez would have despised the Horrell boys and their fellow Texans as much as any other Nuevomexicano in the region.[41]

Sheriff Ham Mills had received medical treatment for his gunshot wound but remained physically incapable of riding after the Horrells for the time being. Lawrence Murphy had been drunk for a week and became bedridden. It was left to the hotheaded Jimmy Dolan to raise a large posse, although this time Juan Patrón declined to participate. The Dolan posse stormed out of Lincoln and reached the abandoned Horrell ranch on the Río Ruidoso in the early hours of January 25, 1874. They burned the ranch house to the ground and transported the crops back to Lincoln in celebratory fashion.

A drinking splurge in Lincoln that night became so raucous that Sheriff Ham Mills's brother-in-law Steve Stanley ended up pistol whipping several men and getting shot, although his wound was only a minor one.

The following day Stanley shot a 33-year-old blacksmith named William Gill for having refused to join the Dolan posse that raided the Horrell ranch. The wounded Gill survived and managed to reach the safety of Fort Stanton. A young man named Little was also severely beaten and almost lynched before managing to escape to the Casey ranch on the night of January 26. Nobody was arrested for these transgressions.[42]

Juan Patrón and Sheriff Ham Mills were soon rocking back and forth in an ambulance furnished by Maj. David Ramsay Clendenin, having left the chaos of Lincoln behind them. They were heading for Santa Fe to meet with Governor Marsh Giddings and Col. John Gregg to request miliary assistance in what the *New Mexican* soon described as "The Lincoln County War." Maj. William Price reported the sheriff's departure in Fort Stanton on January 28. He also recorded his firm belief that Mills was "perfectly incompetent as sheriff," and "the possibility of getting law or justice before any tribunal except the district judge is and has been simply impossible."[43]

As Juan Patrón and Sheriff Mills were on their way to Santa Fe, the Horrell bunch transported their families to Roswell and prepared to wage war against the Hispanos. They also recruited some Chisum cowboys, who were keen for a fight and more than happy to kill a few "greasers." Major Price believed "the [Horrells] will be able to get a hundred cowboys to aid them, and the end is not yet."

The Horrell brothers were soon riding west along the Río Hondo with around fifty armed supporters. They reportedly shot dead three Hispanos roughly forty miles east of the Casey ranch. "The Texans have the support of the cattlemen on the Pecos River," Price reported in Fort Stanton. "They are perfectly lawless and [intend] visiting their revenge on the Mexicans as a race." Price also gave hint of his own prejudice when declaring, "The town of Placita is composed of some of the worst Mexican element in the Territory." The Horrell gang were in the vicinity of the Casey ranch on January 30 and began riding up the Río Bonito toward Lincoln.[44]

As the Horrell party were edging closer to Lincoln, Juan Patrón and Sheriff Mills arrived in Santa Fe. They met with Governor Marsh Giddings and Col. John Gregg on February 2, 1874. Patrón and Mills requested that soldiers be dispatched to restore order and maintain the peace in Lincoln. Ham

Mills also informed the *New Mexican* that "since he left there, the Texans had killed three men on the way down the Pecos from Bosque Grande, and had also driven all the stock from his [Mills] ranch."[45]

Juan Patrón and Sheriff Ham Mills were unaware the Horrell party had recently set up camp a mile outside Lincoln and were posing an immediate threat to their families. Many of the citizens were in a panic and expecting a slaughter to commence at any moment. The Bolton family abandoned their adobe home and took refuge inside the torreón for the night. Some of the local Hispanos frantically made appeals to Lawrence G. Murphy, who sent a note to the Horrell brothers imploring them "not to attack the town and kill innocent men and women." Murphy also sent them his Mason's ring, knowing one of the Horrell brothers was a fellow Freemason.[46]

Fortunately for the frightened citizens of Lincoln, the large party of Texans began squabbling among themselves after receiving Lawrence Murphy's note and Mason's ring. There were rumors circulating that Governor Giddings was preparing to order military intervention. The Horrell boys demonstrated some measure of restraint and were against the idea of indiscriminately murdering the entire population of Lincoln. Many of their companions were very much in favor of burning the placita to ash. "Morning found us quite safe in the old tower," recalled young Amelia Bolton. "The Horrells had accepted some kind of truce offered by a friend." The Horrell boys and their companions subsequently turned away from Lincoln and began riding back down the Río Bonito.[47]

Although the military assistance requested by Juan Patrón and Ham Mills did not prove necessary in Lincoln, the horde of Texans would not leave the region without drawing some blood from the locals. As Major Price reported, the Horrells made it known that they wanted to kill twelve specific individuals: Lawrence Murphy, Ham Mills, Juan Patrón, Juan Gonzáles, Jimmy Dolan, Stephen Stanley, Joe Haskins, Joe Warnock, and several other Hispanos. When the Texans arrived on the outskirts of San Patricio, they came across a farmer named Severanio Apodaca, whose wife Juanita had only recently been killed by Mescalero Apaches. The 24-year-old Apodaca was hauling a wagonload of grain to Dowlin's Mill when members of the Horrell posse murdered him without hesitation.[48]

After reaching the Río Hondo, the Horrell gang rode into Picacho and stopped at the home of a fellow Texan named James Polk Rainbolt, who headed one of the few Anglo families living in the area. Rainbolt's wife Amanda Drucilla and his sister-in-law Rebecca began preparing some food for their unexpected guests with the help of their daughters. Edward "Little" Hart grew impatient waiting for his breakfast and asked if any "Americans" were living in a small house located across the river. Liberty Rainbolt informed Hart that an American named Joe Haskins lived there but that he was "married to a Mexican."

"Well," Hart casually replied, "we'll just go over there and kill the fellow for that."

Edward Hart, C. W. King, and Thomas Keenan swung into their saddles, rode across the river, and called out "Hello" when reaching the front door of the Haskins home. Deputy Joe Haskins had barely set foot outside his house to greet the visitors when Hart and his two accomplices shot him dead in front of his wife Antonia Gurulé as she watched helplessly through the doorway. "It was as brutal a killing as was ever done in Lincoln County," Lily Casey recalled. "They shot him simply because they had developed a blood lust to kill all Mexicans and as many as possible of Americans who had allied themselves with the Mexicans by marriage or any other way."[49]

The Horrell brothers and their murderous chums continued east along the Río Hondo and spotted six teams of oxen being driven by five Hispanos and George Kimbrell around fifteen miles from Roswell. The five Hispano freighters were immediately shot dead without provocation. The Texans surprisingly spared the life of George Kimbrell, despite him having married a Hispana. The Horrells and their cohorts then arrived in Roswell after stealing four horses from Steve Stanley and relieving 24-year-old rancher Robert Beckwith of his horse, saddle, and revolver. The lanky Zack Crompton, Bill Applegate, Edward Hart, and a man known as Still split off from the group and raided some horses and mules from the Aaron Wilburn–Van C. Smith and Beckwith ranches.[50]

Mart, Merritt, Tom, and Samuel Horrell packed up their families in Roswell and crossed back into Texas. The race war was finally over. Aaron Wilburn and his brother Frank would lead a posse in pursuit of

Zach Crompton, Bill Applegate, Ed Hart, and Still. They caught up with Crompton and Still at Hueco Tanks near El Paso and killed them both around February 18, although Hart and Applegate managed to escape with a large posse of Mexicans chasing after them. "The messrs. Wilburn speak in high terms of the civil and military authorities of old Mexico," a letter to the *New Mexican* declared. "They rendered them all the aid in their power to capture the thieves and recover their stock."[51]

Juan Patrón and Sheriff Ham Mills returned to Lincoln and resumed their duties following the conclusion of the Horrell War. Although warrants were issued for various members of the Horrell bunch, none of them would ever face trial. "Everything seems to be quieted down," Maj. David Clendenin reported in Fort Stanton on February 18, 1874. "The Texans have left the country and the Harrolds [*sic*] are reported back at or near Fort Concho, Texas."[52]

The Horrell boys eventually participated in another conflict, in Lampasas, Texas, which became known as the Horrell–Higgins feud. Of the four remaining brothers, only Sam Horrell lived to experience old age. Merritt Horrell was gunned down by John "Pink" Higgins inside a saloon in Lampasas on January 22, 1877. Mart and Tom Horrell were both killed by a mob of vigilantes while imprisoned in Meridian, Texas, on December 15, 1878. The Hispano population of Lincoln County would have felt they had it coming.[53]

While the Hispano population were enjoying some degree of calm following the departure of the Horrell brothers in early 1874, there was still a considerable degree of racial tension festering throughout Condado de Lincoln. "After the Horrell trouble the Mexicans seemed to have it in for the white people," recalled William Casey. "They never did elect a man to office who had an American wife."

Juan Patrón's leadership during the Horrell War only strengthened his standing as *el guia*: the guiding light of the Nuevomexicanos in Lincoln. This brought the ambitious politíco into greater conflict with Lawrence G. Murphy and his Irish associates. "The people were divided into two parties," Juan later said. "The Mexican element standing behind me, and the Americans, soldiers, and Murphy against me."[54]

The troubles in Lincoln County were only just beginning.

Chapter 4

The Smell of Blood

> *What's happening here, gentlemen,
> is that I'm playing the game of death.*
> —Juan Gelman

San Patricio was the kind of place to which some Anglo travelers would have turned their noses up when passing through Lincoln County. Located ten miles southeast of Lincoln, the modest settlement's small population were almost exclusively Hispanos. The village was originally known as Ruidoso, so named for the nearby river. That changed when an Irish priest oversaw the construction of a church in town in the early 1870s. The placita soon became known as San Patricio, named for the Irish priest's patron Saint Patrick. There were roughly fifteen houses scattered along the town's lone street, each of which had been built with thick adobe walls and rooftop gardens fortified with portholes for fending off Apaches throughout the previous decades.[1]

The 23-year-old José Chávez y Chávez decided to set up stakes in San Patricio in the early 1870s. There were various orchards providing delicious fruits and lush green farming lands along the Río Ruidoso on which to hoe a steady supply of crops. He continued farming, worked as a laborer, and practiced his Roman Catholic faith alongside his wife

Leonora and their son Adecasio inside la Iglesia de San Patricio when the church was constructed.

José Chávez y Chávez was an occasionally boastful young man who took pride in his reputation as a hardcase. He quickly demonstrated the kind of toughness and resolve required for law enforcement on the southwestern frontier. The local citizens subsequently elected José as constable of their precinct for a one-year term in September 1874. His duties as precinct constable included reprimanding or arresting any troublemakers and investigating any robberies, rapes, or murders that occurred in the immediate area. The local farmers and sheepherders also looked to him for protection and guidance if they were attacked by rustlers or hostile Apaches. In a line of work that demanded plenty of sand, the fearless Chávez y Chávez proved highly capable, earning the trust and respect of the local population. That trust and respect was further demonstrated by José's appointment as justice of the peace in what was left of Missouri Plaza in 1875.[2]

Like any lawman on the frontier, José Chávez y Chávez became familiar with most of the locals in his precinct. That included a short, 19-year-old laborer called Sequio Sánchez, who developed a considerable reputation as a pistolero. "He was a bugger," young Robert Casey later said. "Sequio was a little dwarf and a little scoundrel." Constable Chávez y Chávez also became close friends with a teenager named Florencio Cháves, who was 6 years old when his father José was killed at a local baile. "He was killed by Ignacio Gonzáles," Florencio recalled. "Gonzáles ran away." His grandfather had escorted him to San Patricio, where Florencio now cared for his mother and sister above all else.[3]

While José Chávez y Chávez was laying down the law in San Patricio, the ambitious Juan Patrón was contemplating his future upstream in Lincoln. There was no doubt that Lawrence G. Murphy and his new business partner Jimmy Dolan were in control. Murphy had acquired the abandoned Horrell farm and regained the office of probate judge. He also opened the doors of the new L. G. Murphy & Co. store at the western end of town on June 3, 1874. The large two-story building towered over every other one in Lincoln, including the comparatively minuscule Patrón store down the street. The stately structure would soon lend Murphy's firm a new nickname—the House.

It wasn't all good news for the alcoholic Lawrence Murphy that summer. His business operation was still heavily in debt. The *New Mexican* publicly announced that Murphy's close friend and former business partner Emil Fritz had succumbed to tuberculosis in Stuttgart, Germany, on June 26, 1874. The Irishman's clerk William Burns landed himself in hot water for killing Deputy Lyon Phillipowski in a shootout in front of the Murphy store on October 21, although the killing was ruled a justifiable homicide.[4]

Juan Patrón pressed on with his own business ventures in the face of stiff competition from the House while continuing his duties as probate clerk and educating the local children. He also represented Lincoln County alongside Lawrence Murphy, William Dowlin, Charles Fritz, and George Nesmith at a large meeting of territorial Democrats held in Santa Fe on December 15, 1874. Many prominent Democrats traveled from various counties to attend the meeting, which was presided over by Judge José M. Gallegos. Their purpose was to engage in "consultation and organization" and to select an executive committee, central committee, and corresponding secretary. "The time has arrived for a thorough and efficient organization of our forces," they unanimously declared.

Juan Patrón, Lawrence Murphy, William Dowlin, Charles Fritz, and George Nesmith were elected as representatives of Lincoln County for the central committee. The Democrats also took shots at their "political enemies," who had "only succeeded by a system of political chicanery and intimidation," and urged "every legitimate influence in favor of railroad enterprise, the development of our immense mineral and agricultural resources, and particularly in educational facilities for the benefit of the rising generation." As a representative of the Democratic central committee, Juan Patrón was firmly in favor of progress and education for his people, despite becoming a fierce opponent of the corrupt, land-grabbing Santa Fe Ring.[5]

Juan returned to Lincoln County after the meeting in Santa Fe and heard the news of a 27-year-old local farmer named Marcial Rodríguez and his 23-year-old wife María having been brutally killed by Mescalero Apaches on their property around two miles from Fort Stanton in January 1875.

The small band of Mescalero had roamed off the reservation and subsequently engaged in a furious fight with Stephen Stanley, Henry Farmer, and a posse of Hispanos. Stanley was wounded in the leg, and Maj. David Clendenin sent troops to scour the countryside for any Mescalero not confined to their reservation.[6]

Juan Patrón continued dividing his time between Lincoln and Santa Fe despite small bands of Mescalero posing an occasional threat. The Hispano businessman traveled to the Holy City with Sheriff Ham Mills in March 1875. "Juan B. Patron, clerk, and A. H. Mills, sheriff of Lincoln County, are spending a few days in the city," the *New Mexican* announced that month. "They report that peace prevails in that section." As Juan would discover, any peace in Lincoln County was only temporary throughout the 1870s.[7]

Juan also became familiar with a 32-year-old Scottish attorney named Alexander McSween, who had arrived in Lincoln with his 29-year-old wife Susan in an ox-drawn covered wagon on March 5, 1875. "Mr. McSween was quite a handsome man," recalled young Carlota Baca. "Mrs. McSween always looked like a big doll; she was the best dressed woman in Lincoln." Juan Patrón soon befriended the McSweens, who were seeking their fortune in Lincoln County after struggling financially in Kansas. As the only certified attorney on the Río Bonito, the Bible-thumping, red-haired Alexander McSween, or "Mac" as he became known, began taking on various clients, including Lawrence G. Murphy.[8]

Juan Patrón had served two terms as probate clerk by the time his new friend Alexander McSween was setting up stakes in Lincoln County. He felt the time was right to reach for higher office and decided to run as the Democratic candidate for a representative seat in the territorial house. No sooner had Juan's campaign begun when it was revealed that over $20,000 in tax collections had vanished during Lawrence Murphy's tenure as probate judge. Murphy was suspected of lining his own pockets, thereby reflecting poorly on Juan as probate clerk, Ham Mills as sheriff, Pablo Pino y Pino as justice of the peace, and José Montaño as treasurer. Tax assessments had not been made in Lincoln County and returned to the territorial auditor since 1872.

Lawrence Murphy went on the defensive, writing angry letters to *The Borderer* and criticizing the *Santa Fe New Mexican* for suggesting "the banner Democratic county of Lincoln" were responsible for the missing tax funds. The Irishman informed the *New Mexican* that deceased former Sheriff Jacob Gylam, a "Radical Republican," had "robbed the county of over twenty-thousand dollars in public and private funds." Murphy insisted that taxes were not collected for the year 1874 because of the "disturbed state of the country growing out of Radical mal-administration of Indian Affairs." The *New Mexican* was not convinced, describing Murphy as "the big dog of the political tan-yard down in Lincoln," and suggesting the patriarch of the House was "hanging on the ragged edge of irresponsibility." The newspaper further stated that Murphy "seems deficient in knowledge as to his duties," as it was "the duty of the Probate Judge, among other things, to look after the finances of his county."[9]

When the April term of court convened in Lincoln in 1875, Probate Judge Lawrence Murphy tried to charge "the tax delinquency to his brother democrats" as the *New Mexican* described it. Murphy requested the grand jury "summon those officers before you and cause them to render under oath, an account of their official acts as regards the treasury of the county and the territory." The grand jury failed to find any bonds "given by county officers as required by law," considered the officers liable, and lamented their failure to collect county taxes having made it "impossible to take any steps towards the erection of a jail, courthouse, or schoolhouse."[10]

Juan Patrón was subsequently indicted by a grand jury for malfeasance in office. The 42-year-old Justice of the Peace Pablo Pino y Pino was indicted for dereliction of duty. Sheriff Alexander "Ham" Mills and treasurer José Montaño were both indicted for embezzlement. Lawrence G. Murphy escaped indictment by sending a letter of resignation as probate judge to Governor Marsh Giddings. The "big dog of the political tan-yard" in Lincoln County had managed to sidestep any repercussions while shifting the blame away from himself.[11]

Although the indictments against Juan Patrón, Pablo Pino y Pino, Ham Mills, and José Montaño were never prosecuted, their reputations had taken a hit. An anonymous Democrat penned a letter to the *Mesilla News* accusing Juan of "doing the dirty work of the swindling ring [the House] that have been ruling Lincoln County." The letter excoriated Patrón for being "nothing but a Maverick" and someone whom "would be a Radical in a minit [sic] if he think[s] Juan B. Patron would make anything out of it."[12]

Juan refused to let unwarranted slander derail his ambition of winning a seat in the territorial legislature. "The Democrats of Lincoln County have made their local nominations," the *New Mexican* announced on June 9, 1875. "Probate Judge, William Brady; representative, Juan B. Patron; Sheriff, John Newcomb; Probate Clerk, Saturnino Baca." Lawrence Murphy was also praised by the *New Mexican* for quickly offering a $500 reward for the apprehension of a local Hispano ruffian who had recently robbed and murdered a young 8th Cavalry soldier upstream from Lincoln.

Juan Patrón continued campaigning for a representative seat and attended the Fourth of July celebrations held in Santa Fe that year. The territorial capital also hosted the inauguration of a former attorney from Ohio named Samuel Beach Axtell as the new governor on July 30, 1875. The pompous, impressionable Axtell quickly realized where the real power in the territory lay and began cozying up with Thomas B. Catron and the Santa Fe Ring.[13]

There were feverish political hopes in New Mexico as the elections were approaching in the summer of 1875. Juan Patrón had recently found a political ally in Robert Casey Sr., an outspoken critic of the L. G. Murphy & Co. Juan was in attendance when Casey publicly derided Lawrence G. Murphy in a rousing speech at the Democratic convention held in Lincoln on August 1, 1875. The outraged Murphy responded by storming into a meeting, overturning a table, and destroying the stationery in a fit of temper. "You might as well try to stop the waves of the ocean with a fork as to try to oppose me!" Murphy shouted at Patrón and Casey.[14]

Robert Casey decided to eat lunch in the Wortley Hotel after the convention broke up around midday. He was eventually approached by a former employee and ruffian cowboy named William Wilson wishing to discuss eight dollars in back wages. The intoxicated Wilson left town for a couple hours before returning to Lincoln and taking cover behind an adobe wall near the Wortley Hotel. When Robert Casey emerged from the hotel with a satisfied appetite, Wilson took aim with his Henry rifle and fired a shot into Casey's hip from around thirty paces away. The stunned Casey slowly dragged himself around the corner of a nearby house with a bullet lodged near his spine and desperately tried to draw his revolver. Wilson then emerged from hiding and shot Casey below the right eye.[15]

Robert Casey was still clinging to life when he was carried inside the nearby Stanley house. A 35-year-old Chilean post surgeon from Fort Stanton named Carlos Narziso Carvallo tried his best to save him. Casey put up a fight but died from his wounds around four o'clock the following afternoon. William Wilson surrendered to Sheriff Ham Mills after being congratulated by some of his friends, despite one angry citizen calling for him to be lynched. Wilson was then transported to Fort Stanton and locked inside the guardhouse to await his trial. Juan Patrón would have been among those who attended Robert Casey's funeral on August 3, 1875. Lawrence Murphy conducted the funeral service, although members of the Casey family later insisted the Irishman had orchestrated the murder to eliminate a political rival.[16]

Juan Patrón continued his campaign in the wake of Robert Casey's murder, and Nuevo México was buzzing when the elections took place on September 6, 1875. "A prominent Democrat in Lincoln, writing the evening of the 7th, says it is impossible to tell how that county went," the *New Mexican* would report. Juan and his fellow Democrats soon realized they were powerless to stop the Republicans from winning the majority. Florencio Gonzáles, a Republican, was elected probate judge. Eduardo Soto, also a Republican, was elected the new probate clerk. José Montaño, a registered Independent, was reelected as treasurer. A Republican candidate named Eugene Dow had been elected the new sheriff of Lincoln County before being counted out in favor of Saturnino Baca. It was reported that Lawrence Murphy had thrown out enough votes cast for E. A. Dow to ensure Democratic candidate Saturnino Baca was elected sheriff instead. "Murphy controlled everything that there was any money in and dictated who should run for office and who should not," Juan later insisted. "Murphy's power in the county was absolute," Florencio Gonzáles recalled.[17]

Whatever political chicanery in which Lawrence G. Murphy was engaging during the elections in Lincoln County that autumn, Juan Patrón soon had far more grievous concerns than losing to Silver City attorney John P. Risque in his bid to represent the counties of Lincoln, Grant, and Doña Ana in the territorial house.[18]

***

There were some men on the American frontier who could handle their liquor. There were others who became quarrelsome bastards whenever under the influence. Juan Patrón was one of those men. For all his intelligence and erudite manner, the Hispano prodigy was prone to belligerence if he drank too much. While his alcohol consumption was far from excessive, old grievances tended to resurface in his mind and unleash a confrontational disposition whenever he was soused.

If there was anyone in Lincoln County who could elicit hostility from Juan Patrón—especially when the Hispano entrepreneur was immersed in the fog of inebriation—it was John Henry Riley. The two businessmen despised each other. Bitter feelings remained over the shooting deaths of the two Hispano ranch hands in February 1873 and Riley's close association with the House. It would have come as little surprise to both men's closest friends when they ran afoul of each other again in the autumn of 1875.

A buckboard driver later recalled that the trouble started when an intoxicated Juan Patrón began insulting John H. Riley outside the Dowlin store in Fort Stanton on September 15, 1875. They exchanged some heated words until Riley told Patrón to let him alone. In a drunken stupor, Juan refused to let things lie. He began following Riley around the post while repeatedly hurling insults at the Irish businessman and challenging him to a fight. Juan eventually drew his revolver and threatened Riley one last time before carelessly turning his back on his adversary.

Juan was staggering away from Riley when he heard a rapid click behind him. The blast of a Winchester rifle rang in his eardrums a split second later. An excruciating pain jolted through his nervous system as he tumbled to the ground with a horrendous burning sensation in his back and abdomen. Juan had never felt a pain like this before. The bullet fired from John H. Riley's rifle had struck him near his spine and entered his bowels.

The severely wounded Juan Patrón was quickly transported to the post hospital, where surgeon Carlos Narziso Carvallo managed to remove the bullet from his abdomen. Carvallo believed there was little hope for Juan, and the newspapers began all but writing his obituary. "Patron cannot live," the *Mesilla News* announced. "The shot is thought by the Dr. to be fatal," the *New Mexican* reported. "An old feud between John H. Riley and Juan Patron was renewed, and resulted in the fatal shooting of the latter," the *Evansville Journal* informed its readers in Indiana.[19]

While Juan Patrón was supposedly on his deathbed in Fort Stanton, John Riley quickly turned himself over to the authorities. The Irishman pleaded self-defense at a preliminary examination. The case against him was dismissed. "From recent advices from Lincoln, we learn that J. H. Riley, on examination for the shooting of Patron, was discharged," the *New Mexican* reported. "It appears conclusively that he was acting in self-defense." The newspapers were firmly in Riley's corner, despite "the notorious Juan Patron" having been shot in the back. "The whole entire post is in sympathy with R. and feel that he was justifiable," the *New Mexican* declared. "Our informant further states that Riley is sustained by the best portion of the people of Lincoln County."[20]

The "notorious" Hispano businessman would survive the wound inflicted by Johnny Riley, much to the relief of his two sisters and many Hispano supporters in Lincoln County. He would walk with a limp for the rest of his days but was fortunate not to have lost his life or the use of his legs entirely. Juan Patrón had also learned a valuable lesson: never turn your back on the House.

***

Juan Patrón, José Montaño, Charles Vickey, and Sam Wortley were all facing charges of permitting gaming in their establishments when the fall term of court convened in Lincoln on October 4, 1875. Vickey and Wortley both went to trial but were acquitted. José Montaño preferred to plead guilty and pay the fifty-dollar fine. Juan Patrón limped into Judge Warren Bristol's court, and his case was continued to the next term. His new friend Alexander McSween also represented Lawrence Murphy and Jimmy Dolan in nine civil cases to recover various debts.[21]

Like many others in Lincoln at the time, Juan had a vested interest in the pending trial of William Wilson for the murder of Robert Casey. His focus temporarily shifted to Alexander "Ham" Mills when the hot-headed sheriff shot a 43-year-old farmer and married father of two named Gregorio Valenzuela in the left side of his chest with a Winchester rifle for calling him a gringo on October 10, 1875. Valenzuela died the following day. Ham Mills was charged with manslaughter but fled into Texas before standing trial over the latest eruption of racially motivated violence in Lincoln County. Sheriff-elect Saturnino Baca would prematurely take office in his stead.[22]

William Wilson was represented by Santa Fe Ring attorney William L. Rynerson when facing trial for the murder of Robert Casey on October 14, 1875. Juan would have watched the proceedings inside the courtroom and felt justice was served when Wilson was found guilty by an all-Hispano jury. Judge Bristol overruled a motion made by Rynerson for a second trial and sentenced William Wilson to death by hanging on October 18.[23]

While William Wilson's days were numbered, Alexander McSween was making enough money to hire a 41-year-old servant named Tomás Archuleta by the fall of 1875. The Scotsman needed to hire a replacement after Archuleta was stabbed through the heart when visiting the home of a prostitute named Copetona at around one o'clock in the morning of December 8, 1875. The murderer, a "man from Old Mexico" according to one citizen, fled town on a stolen mule before his male accomplice and Copetona were taken into custody. "A soiled dove was the cause of this murder," one citizen declared. "Tragedies such as [these] have ceased to excite the passions of the people of Lincoln County," the *Mesilla News* suggested. "They are accustomed to the smell of blood."[24]

Juan Patrón and Alexander McSween both attended the public execution of William Wilson in Lincoln on December 10, 1875. Juan quickly recognized his mentor Jean Baptiste Lamy's nephew Padre Anthony Lamy standing on the platform and preparing to give Wilson the last rites. The first legal hanging to be carried out in Lincoln County did not transpire as planned. As Sheriff Saturnino Baca was preparing to carry out the sentence, William Wilson looked toward Lawrence Murphy and spoke his final words.

"Major, you know you are the cause of this," Wilson said. "You promised to save me, but—"

Murphy kicked the lever and triggered the trap door before Wilson could finish his sentence. The condemned prisoner danced on air at the business end of a hanging rope for more than nine minutes until being cut down and placed inside a coffin. A curious Hispana opened the coffin lid while the crowd were dispersing and began screaming when she noticed that Wilson wasn't quite dead yet.

"For God's sake!" the woman shouted. "The dead has come alive!"

A noose was fastened around William Wilson's neck for the second time, and he was hanged for another twenty minutes to ensure the execution was carried out. "Wilson was well hung—presumed dead—showed signs of life in the coffin," Alexander McSween later wrote. "Was hung up the second time *con mucho gusto* until really dead."[25]

After witnessing William Wilson's botched hanging, Juan Patrón limped into 1876 without any official political standing in his community for the first time in four years. Lawrence Murphy had recently been appointed to an advisory board representing Lincoln County for the approaching centennial. The Irish Democrat was still very much the "big dog" of the local political tan-yard, despite a wave of Republicanism having swept across the once fervently Democratic Lincoln County. Juan had long grown tired of Murphy's schemes, could sense the political winds shifting, and realized his best chance of winning office in the coming year was to switch parties.[26]

Juan Patrón would stand in further opposition to Lawrence Murphy by becoming a Republican.

***

Martín Chávez was settling into married life as the year 1876 began in Picacho. The 24-year-old farmer and stock raiser had tied the knot with Vicente Romero's 16-year-old niece Juanita "Juana" Romero. The wedding was held in the Our Lady of Sorrows Church in Manzano on August 16, 1875. Padre José Sambrano Tafoya performed the ceremony inside the same church in which Martín and Juana had practiced their Roman Catholic faith as children. Juana's uncle Vicente Romero and wife María served as witnesses. Martín's new brother-in-law George Kimbrell would have also been in attendance with Juana's older sister Paulita.[27]

Martín had returned to Lincoln County after the traditional wedding baile and resumed his farming and wool-trade duties to provide for his young wife on the Río Hondo. He would not let Juanita Romero-Chávez down. Martín was not only succeeding in farming and the wool trade but also emerging as a leader in the local community. The Nuevomexicanos of Picacho respected his intelligence, conservatism, and work ethic. Martín's reputation as the slayer of Ben Turner during the Horrell troubles would have further endeared him to the more hardened hombres throughout the region because he had reportedly demonstrated a willingness to fight and kill in defense of his people.

In addition to becoming the mayordomo (community leader) of Picacho, Martín also befriended Sheriff Saturnino Baca, a fellow Democrat. "From Sheriff Baca, of Lincoln County, we learn that comparative peace and quiet reigns throughout his bailiwick," the *New Mexican* reported on January 4, 1876. "He thinks the execution of the sentence in the case of murderer Wilson will have a most beneficial effect in preventing future outrages." The peace and quiet proved only temporary, and Sheriff Baca recruited a healthy number of deputies throughout 1876. The trustworthy Martín Chávez was one of the hombres Baca handpicked to assist him in carrying out his duties.[28]

When Martín Chávez was commissioned as a deputy sheriff in 1876, a 55-year-old named John B. "Green" Wilson had become the justice of the peace on the Río Bonito after settling in Lincoln with his wife Venedita and their four children. Probate Judge Florencio Gonzáles, post trader Paul Dowlin, and mill operator Joseph H. Blazer were also appointed by the territorial legislature as the first board of commissioners for Lincoln County in February 1876. Martín's duties mirrored those of José Chávez y Chávez during his term as constable in San Patricio. He was also tasked with assisting Sheriff Saturnino Baca in the pursuit of killers, thieves, and hostile Mescaleros; the transportation of prisoners; and attempting to maintain the peace in Picacho whenever necessary.[29]

Any brief semblance of peace in Sheriff Baca's bailiwick was broken up when Stephen Stanley and S. W. Lloyd engaged in an old-fashioned duel just outside Lincoln in early March 1876. The two men had agreed to fire on the count of three before Stanley prematurely shot Lloyd while he was "stepping off his distance," as the *New Mexican* described it. It was unwise to take the word of any man whose life was at risk in Lincoln County. Lloyd survived thanks to the capable hands of a surgeon at Fort Stanton, and Stanley was acquitted at a preliminary examination before Justice Wilson.[30]

Sheriff Baca and his deputies also had to keep an eye on a dangerous hombre named José Domingues in March of 1876. Domingues had recently escaped the guardhouse at Fort Stanton after being sentenced to seven years in the county jail for the murder of Daniel Fisher during a drunken argument in the dining room of the Wortley Hotel in November 1874. "He is an unshackled elephant in the hands of our efficient sheriff, Capt. Baca," a disgruntled local informed the *New Mexican*. "We understand from Capt. Dowlin and Dr. Blazer, county commissioners, that as soon as practicable, steps will be taken to build a jail and courthouse." The locals would still have to wait more than a year for the construction of a jail in Lincoln. "There was no law in those days," local rancher Frank Coe later said. "Public opinion and the six-shooter settled most all cases."[31]

José Chávez y Chávez and the residents of San Patricio would have kept their rifles within reach after a band of Mescaleros stole fifteen horses from the small placita during the final week of March 1876. There was also a sense of uneasiness along the Río Bonito over land titles. A store owner in San Patricio named Elisha Dow and Marcos Estabrook had sought to appropriate almost the entire town of Lincoln at the Mesilla land office the previous autumn. "Things remain in status quo," one local observed. "The parties interested neither advancing or retreating." L. G. Murphy & Co. had recently purchased forty acres of land attached to their establishment. Juan Patrón and Padre Sambrano Tafoya were busy raising funds for the construction of a Roman Catholic church in Lincoln. As three of the town's leading citizens, Lawrence Murphy, Juan Patrón, and Sheriff Saturnino Baca spent the night of Sunday, March 24, 1876, being serenaded by a handful of buffalo soldiers under the charge of Lieutenant Taylor in Fort Stanton. "The Sunday law is not in force here after dark," one citizen remarked.[32]

The residents of Lincoln County were surprised when Governor Samuel Axtell arrived on the Río Bonito as a special guest of Lawrence G. Murphy on April 28. The governor kept residence in the L. G. Murphy & Co. store for the next two weeks. He spent time conversing with some of the locals and spoke with the Mescaleros at the Indian Agency at the behest of district commander Gen. Edward Hatch. Axtell also gave a speech inside Lincoln's small adobe courthouse and encouraged every man to plant a tree for the centennial before returning to Santa Fe with General Hatch on May 13, 1876.[33]

As the United States of America was celebrating its centennial in the summer of 1876, Sheriff Saturnino Baca and his deputies were contending with Juan Gonzáles and his band of rustlers. Once the terror of the Horrell brothers and their fellow Texans, the notorious Gonzáles had since become the terror of stockowners throughout southeastern New Mexico. The former deputy was now stealing horses alongside former Mora County resident Alexander Kelley, Nicodemos Álvares, Manuel Valdéz, Sostenes Archibique, and various other rustlers. The gang made their headquarters at Puerto de Luna in San Miguel County, with their horse-stealing exploits stretching all the way from Pueblo to Socorro. Juan Gonzáles and Alexander Kelley had also recently tried to kill John H. Riley when the Irishman was making a return trip from Santa Fe to Fort Stanton.[34]

"We are having lively times in this county," a resident of Lincoln wrote on July 5, 1876. "There is a party here trying to put down the thieving going on. They have shot the famous Nicodemos Álvarez and also shot and wounded Manuel Valdez and are after the old fox Juan Gonzáles, of worldwide renown as a thief. There will be a meeting here soon to adopt measures calculated to clean out the whole nest of scoundrels." Juan Gonzáles and Manuel Valdéz subsequently fled Lincoln County to avoid capture while their associates Alexander Kelley and Sostenes Archibique herded around fifty stolen horses to Río Abajo in Santa Fe County.[35]

Although Juan Gonzáles escaped him, Sheriff Saturnino Baca managed to arrest a rustler named José Segura in Lincoln on the morning of July 10, 1876. Segura was charged with horse theft at a preliminary examination held by Justice Wilson later that day and unable to raise $1,000 bail. Sheriff Baca and three armed guards were escorting the prisoner to Fort Stanton when they were set upon by seventeen men wearing hoods. The masked vigilantes forcibly took possession of Segura and shot him to death shortly afterward.[36]

José Segura was not the only Hispano rustler whom Sheriff Baca was relieved of that summer. When Baca was escorting a former Chisum vaquero and horse thief named Jesús Largo to Fort Stanton inside a buggy, local farmers Frank Coe, Ab Saunders, Charlie Bowdre, and Josiah "Doc" Scurlock snatched the rustler from the sheriff's custody and lynched him from a nearby tree branch. "The Mexicans were bitter at [Largo], were more bitter than the white men," recalled Frank Coe's cousin George. "He was stealing everybody's horses. He stole Frank's fine stud that he brought in here."[37]

The 20-year-old George Coe had only recently set up stakes on the Río Ruidoso after fleeing the rampant violence sweeping through Colfax County in northeastern New Mexico. The Santa Fe Ring's involvement in the sale of the two-million-acre Maxwell Land Grant in 1870 had eventually led to the eruption of the Colfax County War. When the syndicate that purchased the land grant began violently driving various ranchers from their homes with the Santa Fe Ring's support, a defiant preacher named Franklin J. Tolby reportedly tried to expose the Ring in a letter to the *New York Sun* in July 1875. When Tolby was found dead with two bullets buried in his back two months later, many locals rallied around notorious gunman Clay Allison and waged a war of armed resistance against the land-grabbers. The corpses began piling up and "the pressure was so unbearable, I pulled up stakes and left in the year 1876," as George Coe recalled.[38]

While working-class ranchers were resisting the Santa Fe Ring in Colfax County, Juan Patrón's decision to switch political parties proved a shrewd one. Lawrence Murphy, William Brady, and only six other men attended the Democratic convention held in Lincoln on August 5, 1876. When the local Republicans held their own convention on August 8, an Irish Civil War veteran, "Major" Michael Cronin, was unanimously elected president. José Montaño was elected vice president, and Alexander McSween was elected secretary. The meeting was reportedly harmonious and several rousing speeches were made. Juan Patrón was also chosen as the Republican delegate to the upcoming territorial convention scheduled in Santa Fe. "Our Mexican fellow citizens, chief among them Judge [Florencio] Gonzáles, Juan B. Patron, José Montaño, and F.R. y Lueras, are determined to chase the Democratic cruiser on to corral reef of Salt Creek this year," the staunchly Republican *New Mexican* announced. "Let her strand."[39]

Juan Patrón attended the Republican convention in Santa Fe as the lone delegate from Lincoln County on August 29, 1876. Lawrence Murphy also traveled to the territorial capital in preparation for the upcoming Democratic convention. "Among the strangers in town we notice Hon. M. A. Otero of Bernalillo, Major Murphy and Hon. Juan Patron of Lincoln, Mr. Fred Muller and Vicente Mares of Taos," the *New Mexican* announced. Juan and Murphy would have both observed the advancements being made in the Holy City at the time. Many business houses were being refurnished around the plaza, and a large Catholic chapel adjoining the Academy of Our Lady of Light was being constructed with elaborate Gothic architecture. They also received word of a fatal accident that occurred in Lincoln. Josiah "Doc" Scurlock had accidentally shot and killed his close friend Mike G. Hawkins while examining a self-cocking revolver inside the Murphy store on September 2, 1876.

An educated businessman from San Miguel County named Trinidad Romero was unanimously elected the delegate to the Thirty-Fifth Congress when the Republican Territorial Convention took place in Santa Fe on September 14, 1876. Juan Patrón's fellow Republican John H. Riley was also in attendance, and Probate Judge Florencio Gonzáles was named the representative of Lincoln County on the central committee. "We will encourage immigration to the Territory, the building of railroads, and all enterprises calculated to develop the resources of New Mexico and the condition of her people," the party declared. Santa Fe Ring members Stephen B. Elkins and William Breedon denounced the Democratic party of New Mexico and declared their support for Republican presidential nominee Rutherford B. Hayes, and everyone went home eagerly awaiting the upcoming November elections.[40]

Juan Patrón returned to Lincoln County in preparation for the fall term of court that convened with Judge Warren Bristol presiding on October 3, 1876. Juan was appointed the court interpreter, and Martín Chávez served as a deputy alongside Roberto Bojorquez, Candalario Griego, and Samuel Smith. The gaming charge against Patrón carried over from the previous term was dismissed when acting District Attorney Albert J. Fountain declined to prosecute.

Lawrence Murphy had been appointed foreman of the grand jury and welcomed back his friend Alexander "Ham" Mills with open arms before the court term ended. The former sheriff had returned from Texas to face his manslaughter charge for killing Gregorio Valenzuela the previous year. Mills entered a guilty plea before the court and was given a one-year jail sentence on October 9, 1876. Lawrence Murphy quickly started a petition and Alexander "Ham" Mills was subsequently pardoned by Governor Axtell.[41]

While Lawrence Murphy had won the favor of the governor, Juan Patrón had plans of his own and decided to run for a seat on the recently established three-man Board of Lincoln County Commissioners in the autumn of 1876. He took a break from campaigning in late October when Alexander McSween asked the Hispano businessman to accompany him to Santa Fe. Lawrence Murphy had hired the Scottish attorney to assist with the collection of his late business partner Emil Fritz's $10,000 life insurance policy from the Merchants Life Insurance Company in New York. Fritz's siblings Emilie Scholand and Charles Fritz had since been appointed co-administrators by Probate Judge Florencio González and put up a $10,000 bond. Emilie and Charles granted Alexander McSween power of attorney, requesting the Scotsman travel to New York and handle the case in person.[42]

Juan Patrón, Alexander McSween, and Sheriff Saturnino Baca reached Santa Fe in a buggy on October 27, 1876. They all took rooms in German businessman Paul Herlow's hotel, where they were introduced to an ambitious young Englishman named John Henry Tunstall. The 23-year-old Tunstall had recently arrived in New Mexico Territory with dreams of becoming a highly successful sheep farmer, having previously worked for his wealthy father's mercantile business in Canada and spending time in California. Juan Patrón and Alexander McSween took a liking to the educated Tunstall, and McSween convinced the Englishman to set up stakes in Lincoln County.[43]

Alexander McSween headed for New York to handle the Fritz insurance funds case and John Tunstall decided to accompany Juan Patrón on the journey back to Lincoln. Tunstall departed Santa Fe and spent the night of November 2 in Galisteo. Juan Patrón "called for me about 9 am" as the Englishman recalled. "I should have been on the road about 6 a.m. as the next station was 43 miles off, but consistent with the prudence of the Mexican race, my friend Patron was not ready to start until 10:30." *Poco tiempo*. The tenderfoot Tunstall quickly realized that driving a wagon was not one of Juan Patrón's most judicious talents. As the Englishman later informed his family:

> Our horses were a couple of poor scarecrows that looked as if the harness must gall them all over, our buggy was heavily loaded & had no [brake] & the harness had no breaching, the roads were heavy beyond compass & tolerably supplied with hills. . . . Patron for the first 12 miles (which he told me were the worst of the stage) flogged his horses along up hill & down & fairly exhausted them, he never availed himself of the solid parts of the road, but went right along in the ruts & mud. . . . I ventured to suggest once or twice but it was no use, he was everlastingly gazing at the horizon & flogging away at the horses spasmodically.[44]

Juan Patrón and his frustrated English companion safely arrived in Lincoln around two o'clock in the afternoon of November 6, 1876. Although the pretentious Tunstall considered the voyage to be "torture," and cursed "the entire Mexican race from Patron upwards & downwards" at one point, the tenderfoot was impressed with Juan's character and intelligence. "Patron is a very good sort of fellow & the best educated Mexican I have ever met," the Englishman wrote to his family. "He is quite intelligent & appears to have good principles & certainly kind hearted." Tunstall spent the night in the Patrón residence before taking in the sights around Lincoln the following day and becoming acquainted with the red-haired, large-eyed, and elegantly dressed Susan McSween.[45]

As John Tunstall began familiarizing himself with life along the Río Bonito, Juan Patrón was focused on his political ambitions when the elections took place on November 7, 1876. When the local voters finished casting their ballots, Juan had easily won a seat on the Board of Lincoln County Commissioners alongside 46-year-old farmer Francisco Romero y Lueras and William Dowlin. A local Anglo named James H. Farmer, who had married a Hispana and spoke Spanish, was elected the justice of the peace. The reliable Florencio Gonzáles retained the office of probate judge, Antonio A. Sedillo and Rafael Gutiérres were elected probate clerks, and Murphy-Dolan loyalist William Brady was elected sheriff of Lincoln County for the second time.[46]

Juan Patrón had celebrated his victory and was preparing to take his seat on the Board of Lincoln County Commissioners when the news of Juan Gonzáles's recent demise reached town. The bandido had fled into Valencia County after helping two of his compadres escape the guardhouse at Fort Stanton before he was killed by a sheriff's posse in Bernalillo on the evening of November 18, 1876. "The Territory is well rid of a very bad man and Bernalillo and Lincoln counties are greatly benefited by his summary taking off," the *New Mexican* declared.[47]

Although a posse in Bernalillo saved Saturnino Baca the trouble of dealing with Juan Gonzáles, his final month as sheriff of Lincoln County proved an eventful one. A ruffian named Bill Campbell surrendered to Sheriff Baca after killing Thomas King on the outskirts of Lincoln on December 6, 1876. The disreputable Campbell claimed self-defense and was acquitted by Justice Wilson. Baca also had to contend with a maniacally racist Alabaman named Frank Freeman, who senselessly shot and crippled a Black soldier in the Wortley Hotel later that month. "Efforts were made by Capt. Baca to capture Freeman, but without success," the *New Mexican* announced.[48]

Sheriff Saturnino Baca was in attendance when his friend Lawrence G. Murphy was elected president of a newly formed Lincoln County Farmers Club on December 14, 1876. Sheriff-elect William Brady and Joseph "El Gallo (The Rooster)" Storms were elected vice presidents. Sheriff Baca, Francisco Romero y Lueras, and S. N. Lloyd were appointed to a three-man committee. "The growing agricultural interest of the County would be best promoted by an organization of agriculturalists for the purpose of communicating and recording for mutual benefit," the club resolved. John Newcomb successfully motioned for a copy of proceedings to be sent to the Agricultural Department in Washington. A 26-year-old farmer named Richard M. "Dick" Brewer, who had spent four years working as a cowboy for Lawrence Murphy before purchasing his farm on the Río Ruidoso, motioned for the club to meet again on the first Monday of the following month.[49]

Alexander McSween returned from New York in late December 1876, having acquired the services of Donnell-Lawson and Co. and ensuring the Fritz heirs would receive the $5,800 that Lawrence Murphy's friend Levi Spiegelberg negotiated with Merchants Life Insurance. The Scotsman had signed power of attorney over to Donnell-Lawson before returning to New Mexico. No further litigation was necessary until the Fritz family received half of any potential funds the firm could acquire. Lawrence Murphy had received prior word of McSween's dealings in New York, and the Scottish attorney did not receive a warm reception from Charles and Emilie Fritz-Scholand when returning to Lincoln without the funds. The Fritz family owed their friends at L. G. Murphy & Co. considerable debts. The Scotsman wrote two indignant letters to the Fritz heirs in which he denied any wrongdoing and assured Charles Fritz the funds would be transferred into his account at the First National Bank in Santa Fe. The Scotsman's letters had not been well received, and McSween presented an inflated bill of $3,815 for his services to Probate Judge Florencio Gonzáles on January 4, 1877. The Fritz heirs were convinced they were dealing with a shyster, and the animosities between McSween and L. G. Murphy and Co. grew increasingly bitter.[50]

While Alexander McSween was quarreling with the House, his friend Juan Patrón, Francisco Romero y Lueras, and Will Dowlin took their oaths as county commissioners on January 23, 1877. A board of county school commissioners consisting of Ignacio Gavarro, Martín Sánchez, and John Copeland had also been implemented. The 24-year-old Juan Patrón was elected chairman of the county commission at an organizational meeting, affording him an even stronger degree of influence in Lincoln County affairs.[51]

The need for a jail in Lincoln was demonstrated once again when Lucas Gallegos callously murdered his young nephew Sostero García in San Patricio in January 1877. Gallegos fled north to Las Vegas, San Miguel County, to avoid being arrested by William Brady, who had succeeded Saturnino Baca as county sheriff on January 1. The 26-year-old José Chávez y Chávez had been appointed constable of San Patricio for a second one-year term, and he was also commissioned by William Brady as a deputy sheriff. When Lucas Gallegos was arrested in Las Vegas for horse theft in February, Brady dispatched deputy sheriffs José Chávez y Chávez and 29-year-old Lucio Archulete to bring the fugitive in.

José Chávez y Chávez and Lucio Archulete rode up the Río Pecos for the better part of a week and arrived in Las Vegas on February 24, 1877. San Miguel County Sheriff Benigno Jaramillo delivered Lucas Gallegos into their custody, and the two deputy sheriffs immediately began escorting their prisoner back down to Lincoln on February 26. Lucas Gallegos and his teenage accomplice Catarino Romero were charged with first-degree murder and would remain in custody until facing trial when the fall term of court began in October. Juan Patrón and Sheriff William Brady ensured that a jail had finally been constructed in Lincoln by the time court convened.[52]

Juan Patrón also established a strong friendship with John Tunstall by the spring of 1877. The sandy-haired Englishman had long since forgiven the Hispano prodigy for the unpleasant wagon ride into Lincoln County several months earlier. "I really regret feeling so impatient at him on the road for his bad driving," Tunstall wrote to his family. "For he is a very good fellow & considering [how limited] the chances he has had I think him a wonder."[53]

John Tunstall had developed an affinity for the intellectual Juan Patrón while becoming increasingly chummy with John Chisum and Alexander McSween, who possessed considerable inside information about Lawrence Murphy and Jimmy Dolan's operations. Tunstall abandoned his initial plans of becoming a sheep farmer after realizing the cattle trade provided a greater opportunity to make his fortune. The Englishman had quickly learned of the political and economic structure of New Mexico, as he demonstrated when writing to his family:

> The whole of this country is under the control of a ring composed of two or three lawyers . . . & their practices & power throughout New Mexico are quite astonishing, they are more powerful than priests & that is saying a great deal. . . . Everything in New Mexico, that pays at all, (you may say) is worked by a "ring" . . . now to make things stick "to do any good," it is necessary to either get into a ring or to make one out for yourself. I am at work at present making a ring & have succeeded admirably so far. . . . My ring is forming itself as fast & faster than I had ever hoped & in such a way that I will get the finest plum of the lot.[54]

John Tunstall also bonded with Richard M. "Dick" Brewer while staying at the former Murphy cowhand's farm on the Río Ruidoso. José Chávez y Chávez's young friend Florencio Cháves worked as a ranch hand on Brewer's farm and accompanied Tunstall down to the Río Feliz, where the Englishman found a suitable location to set up stakes after having been dissuaded by Alexander McSween from purchasing Lawrence Murphy's Carrizozo ranch. McSween had informed Tunstall that Murphy had "no good title to the land," causing further enmity with the House. The Irish firm was already feeling threatened by the condescending Englishman's foreign capital.[55]

James J. Dolan and John H. Riley inherited on March 14, 1877, the business operation that Lawrence Murphy had administered for more than a decade. Murphy was growing increasingly weakened with cirrhosis and spending most of his time drinking to dull the pain, not that the Irishman ever needed much incentive to warm his veins with liquor. Dolan had chosen Johnny Riley as his new business partner, and the firm was renamed J. J. Dolan & Co. While the 28-year-old Jimmy Dolan was an astute businessman, their company owed considerable debts and was on the verge of bankruptcy. John Tunstall's ambitions could potentially drive a final nail into the coffin of their enterprise. The Irishman still had his friend Sheriff Brady firmly in his pocket. He had also hired a 22-year-old ruffian named William S. "Buck" Morton to oversee the rustling of Chisum herds on the Río Pecos, and he possessed the all-powerful backing of the Santa Fe Ring.[56]

As Jimmy Dolan was fighting a losing battle against insolvency, Juan Patrón would have realized the long-term effects of the Desert Land Act passed by Congress on March 3, 1877. Any settlers on desert lands of the American Southwest could now legally acquire 640 acres for a twenty-five cent per acre down payment and an additional one dollar per acre after presenting proof of irrigation. The Desert Land Act ensured that land speculation would only increase in Nuevo México as more gringos arrived in the territory. The illiterate Hispanos susceptible to exploitation by crafty Anglo speculators would need an educated leader like Juan Patrón to watch out for them.[57]

***

Like Juan Patrón, the 17-year-old Yginio Salazar had also lost a parent to frontier violence in Lincoln County by the spring of 1877. Yginio later stated that his father Teofilo Salazar was "killed by a shot while arresting a man," suggesting his papá had worked as a lawman, although exactly where or when remains uncertain. His mother Paula eventually remarried a laborer named Francisco Luma, and the family set up stakes in a sawmill camp called Las Tablas in the northern foothills of the Capitan Mountains.[58]

Yginio Salazar had grown into a tall young hombre, with broad shoulders, a head of fine hair, thin eyebrows, and an oval shaped face with a soft, innocent countenance. He began sporting a neatly groomed moustache as soon as he was capable of growing one. For all his timid and slightly effeminate appearance, the Hispano teenager possessed plenty of grit and could handle a horse and a gun with precision.

The plucky Yginio Salazar started working as a cowpuncher for John Chisum, who hired any capable man or teenager for thirty dollars a month. The young vaquero was disinclined to take a backward step when somebody wronged him, and he was determined to settle things with a rustler named Robert "Bob" Beckwith in the spring of 1877. The 26-year-old Beckwith lived on a farm three miles north of Seven Rivers with his parents Hugh Mercer and Refugia Beckwith and many siblings. He had recently ventured north of the Capitan Mountains and stolen several cows from the Salazar family spread.[59]

Yginio seized his chance for retribution when his employer John Chisum decided to go after some of the Seven Rivers rustlers in the spring of 1877. Many of the rustlers had previously worked for the cattle baron and were owed back wages. They were now cutting his herds and selling the appropriated livestock to Jimmy Dolan and John H. Riley. The hostilities began when Chisum foreman James M. Highsaw killed Seven Rivers cowboy and suspected rustler Dick Smith in a shootout on March 28, 1877. Chisum was pleased to hear the news and declared there were six more horse thieves in Seven Rivers who needed to be put in the ground: Robert Beckwith, Louis Paxton, Nathan Underwood, Charles M. Woltz, Thomas "Buck" Powell, and William Johnson.[60]

What became known as the Pecos War escalated when Jimmy Dolan arrived in Seven Rivers to purchase some cattle from Louis Paxton and Nathan Underwood on April 10. Nathan Underwood and his associates were en route to fill the order when they encountered six Chisum cowboys and opened fire on them. When Col. George Purington and Sheriff William Brady both refused John Chisum's requests for assistance, the cattle baron decided to deal with the matter personally. John Chisum, his brother Pitzer, cattleman Robert Wylie, and thirty heavily-armed jinglebob cowhands, including

Yginio Salazar, began approaching the Beckwith ranch on April 20, 1877. "I went with Chisum down after them," Yginio later recalled.[61]

Yginio and his fellow cowhands quickly surrounded the Beckwith home, drove off their horses and mules, and cut off the water supply. Their boss John Chisum sent a note into the house suggesting the women and children vacate the premises before his cowboys laid siege to the formidable ranch house for the next few days. Sheriff Brady had warned Louis Paxton that Chisum was planning to wage war, and the Seven Rivers party inside the fortresslike house were well prepared and provisioned. Many shots were exchanged during the siege, but nobody was hit. Buck Powell and Charlie Woltz managed to escape and rode for La Mesilla, Doña Ana County, to acquire warrants and request assistance from their ruffian friends. Some of Chisum's cowboys eventually lost their nerve, insisting they had been hired to herd cattle rather than wage war. When William Johnson refused to negotiate a truce with Chisum, the frustrated cattle baron withdrew his forces and headed back to his jinglebob herds on April 22, 1877.[62]

A grand jury in Doña Ana County returned indictments against John Chisum, Robert Wylie, Robert Beckwith, Buck Powell, and numerous other participants of the Pecos War. None of them would be prosecuted. Many ranchers in Seven Rivers suspected old John was merely attempting to carpetbag their homesteads, and bitter feelings persisted. "Chisum wanted the little man out of the lower country," rancher and former John Riley cowpuncher William R. "Jake" Owens later insisted. Yginio Salazar also maintained his antipathy for Robert Beckwith and his Seven Rivers partisans.[63]

Although the Pecos War had quickly fizzled out, more blood was spilled in Lincoln when Jimmy Dolan shot and killed his 20-year-old employee Hiraldo Jaramillo in the stables behind the J. J. Dolan & Co. store on May 3, 1877. Dolan claimed that Jaramillo had attacked him with a knife and was shot in self-defense. Juan Patrón and the residents of Lincoln County were even more shocked to learn of the murder of Paul Dowlin, the representative to the legislature of Lincoln, Grant, and Doña Ana Counties, just two days later on May 5. The 47-year-old Civil War veteran was gunned down by a former employee named Jerry Dillon, who subsequently fled into Texas. Representative Dowlin had reportedly made a threat on his former employee's life, and Dillon decided it was a case of first in, best dressed.[64]

The battle lines being drawn in the Lincoln County soil only deepened when John Tunstall decided to establish his own mercantile store in direct competition with the House. "I proposed to confine my operations to Lincoln County," the Englishman wrote to his parents. "I intend to handle it in such a way as to get the half of every dollar that is made in the county by anyone." Tunstall and Alexander McSween were also planning to establish a Lincoln County Bank in town, with their silent partner John Chisum serving as president. The rapacious Englishman, Scottish attorney, and powerful cattle baron were forming a consortium that could usurp the House and eradicate the Irish firm's influence throughout Lincoln County. "Murphy told me that they would have to get rid of McSween and Tunstall," their ally Juan Patrón later recalled.[65]

While another bitter feud in Lincoln County was fermenting, Juan Patrón had made enough money to purchase his own ranch fifteen miles outside of Lincoln and roughly twenty-three miles from the Mescalero reservation line. The commissioner also had an eye on the representative seat in the territorial legislature recently vacated by the late Paul Dowlin. Now a seasoned politician, Juan spent the summer of 1877 rallying the locals and energizing his fellow Republicans in Lincoln, Doña Ana, and Grant Counties to support his candidacy for the position when a special election took place in November. Even some of his Democratic adversaries in Lincoln gave their public endorsement, as the *Las Vegas Gazette* would report:

> Some of the most influential citizens of Lincoln County, among whom we notice F. G. Christie, Jas. J. Dolan, A. H. Mills, B. H. Ellis, Chas [Fritz], Lawrence G. Murphy, A. A. McSween, F. Romero y Valencia, R. H. Ewan, Wm. Brady, sheriff, and others, recommend the election of Mr. Juan B. Patron, an honest, zealous and capable young man of that County, to the territorial legislature, to fill the vacancy caused by the untimely death of the late Paul Dowlin, and ask the cooperation of the good people of Doña Ana and Grant counties for that purpose.[66]

As Juan Patrón was again seeking higher office, he also spent time socializing in Alexander and Susan McSween's new adobe home in Lincoln. Mac hired

Dolan loyalist George W. Peppin to build their hacienda on the northern side of the street under the watchful eye of his wife Susan, who began furnishing both wings of the plush U-shaped house following its completion in June 1877. Juan and Susan McSween shared a passion for playing the piano and probably discussed music on occasion. Susan's sister Elizabeth, her brother-in-law David P. Shield, and their children soon arrived and took residence in the eastern wing of the home. David Shield had recently passed the bar in Missouri and became Alexander McSween's law partner in Lincoln.[67]

Juan Patrón undoubtedly enjoyed chatting and smoking a cigarette with his friend John Tunstall, who frequently stayed with the McSweens that summer while overseeing the construction of his mercantile store adjacent to their home. The Englishman's grand plans were slowly coming to fruition. He had established a ranch on the Río Feliz, bought his way into the cattle business, and hired the reliable Dick Brewer as his foreman. Juan Patrón also made the acquaintance of Rob Widenmann, an overbearing, loud-mouth originally from Michigan. Widenmann had met John Tunstall in Santa Fe that summer and devoted himself to making the wealthy Englishman's life easier.[68]

The Hispano commissioner also became friendly with a 48-year-old Civil War veteran named Isaac "Ike" Ellis, who had recently arrived with his wife and three sons from Colfax County and established his own modest store at the eastern end of Lincoln. The Ellis family were a small part of the steady flow of Americanos arriving in Lincoln County at the time. The mining trade was still booming in the Jicarilla Mountains and attracting various prospectors who spent their days sweating up a storm in pursuit of their fortunes. A prospector named George Ginn had recently invented a machine for dry washing gold ores, and his construction of one in Lincoln with limited materials was causing a considerable stir in the Jicarilla mines. With his keen intellect, Juan Patrón would have found such innovations intriguing.[69]

Juan's friend Alexander McSween was enjoying the comforts of his new home when receiving word on August 1 that Donnell-Lawson in New York had acquired the $10,000 Fritz insurance funds, of which $7,148 would go to the Fritz heirs after the firm deducted their service fees. McSween wrote a letter to the Fritz heirs and declared he was ready to settle the matter, provided

The Smell of Blood

they released him from their $10,000 bond before delivering the funds. The Scotsman then filed a motion with Probate Judge Florencio Gonzáles to be removed from the bond before the Fritz heirs could even reply to his letter, declaring Charles Fritz and Emilie Fritz-Scholand incompetent and intending to misuse the funds should they receive them. The Fritz heirs were unable to draw on the funds without further order from Judge Gonzáles, who instructed Donnell-Lawson to cease taking any further instructions from McSween and transfer the money to the First National Bank in Santa Fe. The insurance funds never arrived, and Jimmy Dolan eventually took matters into his own hands.[70]

Mac had more on his mind than the Fritz insurance funds throughout the summer of 1877. The Scottish attorney, his client Robert D. Hunter, John Chisum, and John Tunstall had established the first Lincoln County Bank inside the Tunstall store. "The safes and necessary paraphernalia are en route," one citizen wrote in a letter to the *Las Vegas Gazette*. Alexander McSween and David P. Shield would keep a law office in one of the back rooms, with the bank serving as an exchange for promissory notes when Tunstall's mercantile store officially opened to the public. John Chisum served as president, McSween acted as vice president, and Tunstall took on the role of cashier. "A check this week drawn on the Lincoln County Bank," the *Mesilla Valley Independent* soon announced. "We had heard that something of the kind was contemplated but this is the first intimation we have received that the Bank was really in existence."[71]

Jimmy Dolan and John H. Riley watched with contempt while the McSween home and Tunstall store were built on land that Alexander McSween had originally purchased from their mentor Lawrence Murphy. They suspected the Scottish attorney had embezzled the Fritz insurance funds and used the money to build his house and stock John Tunstall's store. The two British Protestants and John Chisum were becoming an increasing headache for the Irish Catholic firm, who owed substantial debts to Spiegelberg Bros. and their friend Thomas B. Catron in Santa Fe. John Tunstall also had designs on acquiring the government beef contracts and post tradership at Fort Stanton. "If I could get that position, I could make a great deal of money every year," the Englishman wrote to his family. "As I should so entirely control the county that I could make the prices of everything just to suit myself." Jimmy Dolan sorely needed the money owed by the Fritz family. He became desperate enough to swallow his pride and begrudgingly take out a $1,000 loan with the newly established Lincoln County Bank down the street in what must have been a humiliating experience for the testy Irishman.[72]

Jimmy Dolan's close friend Sheriff William Brady was called upon when an intoxicated Frank Freeman and Charlie Bowdre broke into the McSween home after Freeman maliciously shot a Black soldier in the Wortley Hotel on the night of August 5, 1877. When one of the McSween's Hispano servants shot Freeman in the arm, the two drunken fools fled toward their tethered horses outside the Dolan store. A scuffle ensued when Sheriff Brady tried to arrest them until the troublemakers were restrained by Jimmy Dolan, John Riley, and their associate Jacob B. "Billy" Mathews. Charlie Bowdre returned to his farm after paying a bond of $500. Frank Freeman managed to escape while being escorted to Fort Stanton by some very angry buffalo soldiers. Freeman would hide out at George Coe and Doc Scurlock's ranches on the Río Ruidoso until Sheriff Brady and a detachment of troops eventually caught up with the fugitive and shot him dead in a cornfield.[73]

Juan Patrón and William Brady were both busy overseeing the completion of the first Lincoln jail, built by George W. Peppin in the early autumn of 1877. Juan and his fellow commissioners had doubled the license fees for saloons and merchants and also raised estate taxes in order to pay for it. Located across the street from the Patrón store, the jail consisted of an adobe house built above two underground cells, both ten feet deep and lined with logs brought down from the Capitan Mountains. Access to the cells required the lowering of a ladder through a wooden trapdoor. "No rays of daylight reaches its lower precincts," a reporter from the *Mesilla Valley Independent* would observe upon the jail's completion in early October. "I should judge those who are unfortunate enough to become its inmates will find it a rather difficult undertaking to 'go through' it without the consent of those in charge."[74]

Juan Patrón initially served as the jailer when the Lincoln pit-jail opened. He was also appointed foreman of the grand jury when the fall term of court convened on October 1, 1877. Jerry Dillon was indicted for the murder of

Paul Dowlin during proceedings. Charlie Bowdre pleaded guilty to carrying arms and was fined ten dollars plus court costs. Lucas Gallegos and Catarino Romero were both confined in the new Lincoln pit-jail when their murder cases were continued over to the next term of court. "[Gallegos and Romero] don't mind confinement if they are allowed to live and eat," wrote one citizen in San Patricio. "Gallegos seems the most down hearted of the two: I think he is the oldest scoundrel. Romero is nothing but a boy about 18 or 20 years of age."[75]

When the industrious Juan Patrón wasn't working as chairman of the county commission, a merchant, a jailer, or a grand juror, the Hispano prodigy and Padre Sambrano Tafoya raised enough money to begin the construction of an adobe Roman Catholic church adjacent to the jailhouse, although the structure was never completed. Juan was also enjoying a remarkable amount of nonpartisan support in his ongoing campaign to win a seat in the territorial house. Alexander McSween, Lawrence Murphy, Jimmy Dolan, William Brady, Saturnino Baca, Stephen Stanley, Ham Mills, Charles Fritz, José Montaño, Sequio Sánchez, and even John H. Riley had all signed a letter published by the *Mesilla Valley Independent* in which they collectively endorsed him. "Being assured of the honesty, zeal and capacity of Mr. Juan B. Patrón, we ask for him your generous support, and assure you that the people of Doña Ana and Grant Counties will lose nothing there by," the letter read.[76]

As Juan Patrón was steaming ahead in his campaign to win the vacant representative seat during the autumn of 1877, he could not have imagined that a scrawny, buck-toothed teenager was about to drift into Lincoln County and begin winning the hearts of local Hispanos like no Anglo had ever done before.

Chapter 5

Mild Blue Eyes

Yonder stands your orphan with his gun.
—Bob Dylan

He looked nothing like a desperate horse thief when Yginio Salazar first laid eyes on him. He had the appearance of an innocent schoolboy. The young vagabond was quite a slender little fellow, around 17-years-old, and had yet to undergo his final growth spurt. He stood roughly five foot five at the time, with a head of light brown hair, sharp blue eyes, an aquiline nose, a lantern jaw, and rather girlish hands. His bucked top incisors were immediately noticeable whenever he smiled, which was a frequent occurrence.[1]

The affable teenager who drifted into Lincoln County in the autumn of 1877 was now introducing himself as Billy, having recently taken the alias William H. Bonney. His real name was Henry McCarty, although many knew him as Henry Antrim. Some people simply called him the Kid, or Kid Antrim. When making the youth's acquaintance that autumn, you would never have thought he had recently shot a man over in the Arizona Territory. "There was nothing about him to suggest his steel nerve," Yginio Salazar recalled. "He had the face of an angel; the soft voice of a woman; the mild blue eyes of a poet."[2]

Henry McCarty, alias William H. Bonney, was probably born in New York in 1859. His Irish mother Catherine McCarty had moved him and his younger brother Joseph to Indiana following the death of her husband. "His father died when he was four," George Coe later remarked. Catherine subsequently met a man named William Antrim, with whom they traveled to Wichita, Kansas, in the summer of 1870. From there they had ventured through Colorado and into New Mexico Territory, where Billy watched his mother marry William Antrim in Santa Fe on March 1, 1873. The family soon relocated to Silver City in Grant County, where Billy attended school with his younger brother Joseph. He also began picking up the Spanish language.[3]

Things began falling apart for Billy after his mother Catherine died from tuberculosis in Silver City on September 16, 1874. His stepfather William Antrim was preoccupied with seeking his fortune, and the young teenager learned to mostly take care of himself while living with family friends and in boardinghouses. Billy supported himself by working odd jobs, gambling, and engaging in petty theft. He eventually began hanging around with a 35-year-old thief called George "Sombrero Jack" Schaefer. When Billy was caught in possession of some clothes that Schaefer had stolen from a Chinese laundry in the fall of 1875, the youngster was arrested and locked up in the Silver City jail. He managed to escape two days later by climbing up the chimney and arrived on William Antrim's doorstep in Clifton, Arizona. After being turned away by his indifferent stepfather, the orphaned teenager spent the next two years scraping together a living by gambling and stealing horses with a former soldier called Johnny Mackie in southeastern Arizona.

Billy Bonney also endured two years' worth of verbal and physical abuse at the hands of a hefty blacksmith named Frank "Windy" Cahill in Arizona. Things finally came to a head inside George Atkins's cantina in Camp Grant on the night of August 17, 1877. The boy whom many people called Kid decided enough was enough when Cahill pinned him to the saloon floor and started walloping him in the face. Billy managed to grasp his revolver and fire a bullet into Cahill's belly before scrambling to his feet and quickly fleeing town. Cahill died from his wound the following day. Although the shooting was a case of self-defense by frontier standards, the local authorities ruled Cahill's death "criminal and unjustifiable." The Kid promptly returned to southwestern New Mexico.[4]

Henry McCarty, alias William H. Bonney, continued drifting aimlessly in southwestern New Mexico until he started tagging along with a former Chisum cowboy named Jessie Evans and his ruthless band of killers and thieves known as "the Boys" in late September 1877. The Boys, or "the Banditti" as they were also known, had been stealing horses, robbing stages, murdering citizens, and generally raising all manner of hell for several years. Jessie Evans and his bunch were also closely tied with Jimmy Dolan. They had recently started crossing over into Lincoln County to appropriate livestock, including some horses belonging to John Tunstall, Alexander McSween, and Dick Brewer on September 18, 1877. Dick Brewer, Doc Scurlock, and Charlie Bowdre had tracked Evans and his ruffians into Doña Ana County but returned empty-handed after confronting the gang at Warren H. Shedd's notoriously seedy ranch near the San Augustin Pass.[5]

Billy Bonney presumably accompanied Jessie Evans and the Boys when they lit out from Doña Ana County and arrived in Tularosa on October 9, 1877. The heavy-drinking gang met with their good friends John Riley and James Longwell on the Mescalero Reservation before getting reacquainted with their old chums at the Beckwith ranch in Seven Rivers. When Billy wasn't tagging along with Evans and his band of reprobates, the young drifter spent time meeting some of the locals and looking for work on various ranches. "I first met Billy Bonney in the fall of 1877," recalled Frank Coe. "He looked so young that I did not take him very seriously about work." Billy also tried his luck at the Dolan–Riley cattle camp on Black River. He was quickly turned out when William "Buck" Morton accused the boy of trying to cut in on his lady friend and aggressively banished him from the vicinity.[6]

In contrast with many Anglos who drifted into Lincoln County, young William Bonney spoke fluent Spanish and was able to freely converse with any Nuevomexicanos he encountered. He had also developed into a crack shot with a six-shooter and Winchester rifle. "Was Bilito [Little Billy] a better shot with the Winchester than with the Colt?" Florencio Cháves later said. "Just the same!" Florencio and many Hispanos took an instant liking to the impish Irish teenager, finding him good company and extremely polite. Billy not only spoke their language but also treated Hispano citizens with respect and considerable affection, as if he preferred their company to his own Anglo people.[7]

While young Billy Bonney was snatching horses, looking for work, and meeting some of the locals, the recently completed Lincoln jail became home for Jessie Evans, Frank Baker, Tom Hill, and George Davis in late October 1877. Dick Brewer had been appointed a constable and raised a posse of fifteen men before persuading a reluctant Sheriff William Brady, who despised Brewer's employer John Tunstall as much as his House associates, to help them go after the Boys down in Seven Rivers. The posse had managed to capture Evans, Baker, Hill, and Davis following a shootout at the Beckwith ranch despite Evans's best efforts to shoot Brewer into an early grave on October 17. The posse and their prisoners ran into John Tunstall on the ride back to Lincoln, and upon their arrival the four banditti were locked in one of the underground cells with Lucas Gallegos and Catarino Romero. A local Hispano named Anselmo Pacheco had taken over as jailer and was tasked with providing food and water to four of the most hardened killers in the entire territory.[8]

The prisoners held in the Lincoln jail were afforded one hour of exercise each day while enjoying a little fresh air above ground. "There wasn't any air in that place," Amelia Bolton later said. "I remember some of the men talking about, well, if anybody got in—put in that jail that they want to get rid of, all they had to do was drain the ditch down there by it and drown them—but that was just talk, you know." It was during one of these exercise periods that young Catarino Romero capitalized on a lapse of concentration from jailer Anselmo Pacheco and managed to escape. The 18-year-old Maximiano de Guevara was subsequently hired as the new temporary jailer and handed the keys by Sheriff William Brady.[9]

Maximiano de Guevara would have kept a sharp eye when John Tunstall came into the jailhouse to speak with Jessie Evans, Frank Baker, Tom Hill, and George Davis on November 4, 1877. The Englishman had sent the four ruffians a bottle of whiskey and tried his best to joke with the men who had stolen some of his stock. The conversation inevitably turned sour.

"What you want to know is where your mules are," Jessie Evans sneered. "And you don't get to find out."

"You should go to hell and the mules too before I would ask you for them!" replied Tunstall, who staunchly opposed any possibility of bail for the stock thieves.[10]

Juan Patrón was preparing for the upcoming special election to fill the vacant representative seat when he received a message from escapee Catarino Romero on November 7, 1877. The note informed him that Evans and his chums had filed through their shackles and were digging through the log walls in their cell with tools smuggled to them by sympathizers. Juan immediately informed William Brady and accompanied the sheriff into the jailhouse.

When Juan Patrón examined the jail cells, the information he had received from Catarino Romero proved accurate. Maximiano de Guevara asked for some new shackles to be forged for the prisoners. When Brady merely shrugged his shoulders in response, Juan withdrew any association with the jail in disgust. The sheriff soon arrived half drunk at the Tunstall store and accused the English proprietor of sneaking the tools into the jail for the prisoners. John Tunstall firmly denied having done so and the two men began arguing.

"I won't shoot you now," Brady eventually snarled at Tunstall. "You haven't long to run. I ain't always going to be sheriff."

Juan Patrón and his commission appointed Deputy Lucio Archulete to take over as jailer the following day of November 8, although Sheriff Brady conveniently forgot to hand his deputy the keys. Jessie Evans and his cohorts continued playing cards in their cell, boasting that their chums in Seven Rivers would bust them out sooner or later. The Boys had friends in high places and the fix was in.[11]

***

Juan Bautista Patrón awoke from his slumber in Lincoln with a little more enthusiasm than usual on the morning of November 10, 1877. It was finally election day and time to find out if his months of campaigning in Lincoln, Doña Ana, and Grant Counties to win the vacant seat in the territorial house had paid off. The ambitious Hispano prodigy from Santa Fe had already achieved considerable success in southeastern New Mexico, but this could be his shining moment, until the next one.

Any nervous rumblings Juan Patrón may have felt in his stomach that morning would prove unnecessary when the voters had finished casting their ballots across southern New Mexico Territory. The Hispano commissioner annihilated his opponents Florencio Gonzáles, John Newcomb, Doña Ana County farmer Daniel Frietz, and Silver City miner H. W. Elliott in what became a landslide victory for him.

The *Mesilla Valley Independent* announced on the evening of election day that Juan had already received 337 of the returned Doña Ana County precinct votes ahead of Daniel Frietz's 30, Florencio Gonzáles's 17, and John Newcomb's measly 8. Although Florencio Gonzáles received slightly more of the votes in Grant County, Juan B. Patrón cleaned up on their home turf by winning 202 of the local votes ahead of Gonzáles's 8 in Lincoln County. Juan would ultimately take 529 out of a total 652 votes cast throughout Lincoln, Grant, and Doña Ana Counties.

New Mexico had its newest representative of the territorial house, and he was only 24.[12]

***

For all his recent political success, Juan Patrón was infuriated when learning of the previous night's developments in Lincoln on the morning of November 17, 1877. A former Chisum cowboy and Seven Rivers ruffian named Andrew Boyle had led a heavily armed party of men—including William "Buck" Morton, Jacob B. "Billy" Mathews, and Charlie "Lallacooler" Crawford—into town under cover of darkness and stormed the Lincoln jail. They held off Deputy Lucio Archulete at gunpoint, broke the trapdoor above the cells with heavy sacks filled with rocks, and successfully liberated Jessie Evans, Frank Baker, and their fellow prisoners. Lucas Gallegos naturally seized the moment and lit out of the jail with them.[13]

The outraged Juan Patrón, John Tunstall, and Alexander McSween immediately confronted Sheriff William Brady when hearing the news and demanded something be done. "After the escape, the cells were found to be liberally supplied with files, knives and augers, as also cotton sacks with rocks weighing from ten to twenty pounds," the *Mesilla Valley Independent* reported. "How is that for vigilance?"

Sheriff Brady was as much aligned with the House as the escapees and refused to raise a posse to go after them.

"I arrested them once and I will be damned if I am a-going to do it again!" the sheriff was heard to exclaim.

The Boys and their Seven Rivers cohorts headed south and demanded breakfast at Dick Brewer's ranch on the Río Ruidoso before making off with eight of his horses. They also appropriated San Patricio resident Juan Trujillo's horse, saddle, and guns for Lucas Gallegos on the Río Feliz before returning to the Beckwith ranch in Seven Rivers. Lucas Gallegos acted as their spokesman when informing a newspaper correspondent that "McSween's, Patron's and [Montaño's] death warrants had been signed."[14]

There was no telling what the Boys were capable of, so Juan Patrón needed to watch his back. Jessie Evans and members of his gang had once shot up a dance hall in Las Cruces alongside their friend and notorious badman John Kinney, killing two US Cavalry officers and a Hispano bystander in the process. The brutish Frank Baker had very recently shot and killed an 83-year-old merchant named Chaffre Martíni on the Río Grande for merely asking if Baker had forgotten to pay for some goods when visiting his store. The Boys wouldn't think twice about shooting Juan Patrón to pieces if the opportunity presented itself.[15]

Although Jessie Evans and the Boys were free to issue as many death threats as they pleased, the Lincoln jail did not remain empty for long. Juan Patrón presumably laid eyes on a teenager calling himself Billy Bonney for the first time when the young horse thief was escorted into Lincoln and locked in the pit-jail. The boy they called Kid had been caught in possession of two blue-gray horses he had stolen from the Tunstall ranch on the Río Feliz. "We saw the boy when they'd bring him up, you know, and give him a little air," recalled Amelia Bolton. "He seemed such a young boy."[16]

John Tunstall eventually arrived in Lincoln to speak with young William Bonney. The Englishman needed all the hired guns he could find, so rather than prosecuting the boyish prisoner for horse theft, he offered him a job as a ranch hand. Billy accepted the deal and was soon working on the Río Feliz alongside Dick Brewer, a ruffian named John Middleton, a quiet young cowboy called Henry Brown, an educated part-Chickasaw Indian named Fred

Waite, and young Florencio Cháves. The Kid also spent time bonding with Tunstall supporters Charlie Bowdre, Doc Scurlock, and Frank and George Coe on the Río Ruidoso. Billy Bonney quickly developed an affinity for John Tunstall, possessing a fierce loyalty toward those who showed him kindness. The Englishman was impressed with the teenager's intelligence and pluck, bequeathing him a new horse, saddle, and guns. "My, but the boy was proud," recalled Frank Coe. "Said it was the first time in his life he had ever had anything given to him."[17]

Billy Bonney found a new sense of pride as a Tunstall employee. The teenager dressed neatly whenever possible, sometimes even sporting a flower in his lapel. "He was always a gentleman, no matter where he was," recalled Yginio Salazar. Billy was soon making the rounds in Lincoln and endearing himself to much of the Hispano population, including McSween employee Francisco Gómez. "He was an awfully nice young fellow," Gómez later recalled. "He used to practice target shooting a lot. He would throw up a can and would twirl his six-gun on his finger and he could hit the can six times before it hit the ground."[18]

William Bonney, alias Kid, could ride a horse just like a vaquero, frequently attended the local bailes, and impressed many señoritas with his considerable dancing abilities. He also enjoyed shooting marbles with the local Hispano children behind the Montaño store. "Everybody loved the Keed," remembered Saturnino Baca's 12-year-old-daughter Carlota, who developed a schoolgirl crush on him. "He had an unfailing sense of humor," recalled Yginio Salazar. "He was always ready for some horse-play, to give a joke or to size one. His laughter was as spontaneous as a child's." For all his fun-loving personality, friendliness, and gentlemanly nature, young William Bonney possessed a vengeful streak. He strongly valued bravery and refused to suffer any ill-treatment from anyone. The Kid was a dangerous threat to any potential enemies, and John Tunstall would need the teenager's unflinching nerve and handiness with a gun throughout the stormy months ahead.[19]

***

The slow-burning animosities in Lincoln County intensified when Jimmy Dolan confronted Alexander McSween about the Fritz insurance funds on

December 1, 1877. A hearing was set with Probate Judge Florencio Gonzáles to settle the matter once and for all inside his office on December 7. McSween arrived late and insisted that he had the insurance funds, but he refused to turn them over unless Emilie Fritz-Scholand came over from Las Cruces during proceedings. Judge Gonzáles agreed to his demand and rescheduled the hearing for January 7, 1878. Jimmy Dolan was livid. The Irishman quickly set out for Las Cruces to inform Emilie Fritz-Scholand of the situation and consult with his good friend and Santa Fe Ring member District Attorney William L. Rynerson.[20]

Alexander and Susan McSween departed Lincoln with John Chisum on December 18 to enjoy a vacation in St. Louis. Jimmy Dolan was convinced the Scottish attorney was attempting to flee the territory without handing over the insurance funds. The Irishman promptly escorted Emilie Fritz-Scholand to La Mesilla, where she filed an affidavit for an arrest warrant to Judge Warren Bristol. Alexander McSween was charged with embezzling the insurance funds on December 21. Thomas B. Catron telegraphed the sheriff in San Miguel County and instructed him to detain Alexander McSween and John Chisum in Las Vegas until the arrest warrants arrived, having also levied a trumped-up charge against the cattle baron. The McSweens and John Chisum were unceremoniously hauled back to Las Vegas by a ragtag posse when they tried to continue their journey to St. Louis on December 26. Chisum refused to cooperate with the authorities and remained imprisoned for the time being. Mac advised his wife Susan to continue the journey to St. Louis, and the Scotsman awaited his transportation to La Mesilla to face the embezzlement charge filed against him.[21]

While his friend Alexander McSween was becoming acquainted with the squalid Las Vegas jail, the 25-year-old Juan Bautista Patrón was preparing to climb aboard his buggy and set out on his latest journey to Santa Fe. The Twenty-Third Legislative Assembly was convening in the Holy City on January 7, 1878. Juan would represent the counties of Lincoln, Doña Ana, and Grant throughout proceedings alongside 46-year-old Civil War veteran John K. Houston, a resident of Grant County. Their counterpart in the legislative council was John S. Crouch, an attorney and newspaper editor originally from Tennessee who resided in La Mesilla.[22]

Juan Patrón arrived in Santa Fe and presumably took a room in the Exchange Hotel around January 5, 1878. It was another chance to catch up with his college friend Tranquilino Labadie. The young men had remained *buenos amigos* despite Juan having relocated to Lincoln County seven years earlier. While preparing for the assembly, Juan would have been pleased when discovering most members of the legislature in attendance were Nuevomexicanos. Half the members of the representative house had been unable to reach the capital due to the heavy snowfall across the territory. Juan began socializing with other members of the territorial house at various caucuses and made a highly positive impression on his fellow representatives. The comparatively young Hispano had officially hit the big time in New Mexico politics.

Juan Patrón woke up a little earlier than usual, buttoned his finest white shirt, knotted his string tie into a neat bow, combed his dark hair, and pulled on his Prince Albert coat on the icy-cold morning of January 7, 1878. It was time to get to work. He eagerly headed out onto the snow-coated dirt streets of Santa Fe, limped inside the adobe Palace of the Governors on the main plaza, and entered the legislative chambers of the territorial house and council. This was the most important day of his political career so far.

Juan Patrón took his seat alongside eleven other members inside Representative Hall at noon. The 47-year-old José de Jesús García of Socorro County was elected chairman pro tempore, and proceedings began with a firm slam of his gavel. Juan and the other members-elect submitted their credentials for election to a committee consisting of 36-year-old Perfecto Esquibel of Rio Arriba County, José Baca y Sedillo of Socorro County, and John K. Houston. The credentials were reviewed and approved and the members all duly elected as representatives.[23]

Rep. Perfecto Esquibel motioned for a permanent organization of the Representative House. He also nominated the bilingual Juan B. Patrón to serve as Speaker of the House. When the motions were passed, Juan confidently took his seat and "entertained the members with a few brief remarks, thanking them for the honor conferred upon him," as the *Weekly New Mexican* announced. The newspaper also offered a somewhat tentative endorsement of his election as speaker when detailing his rise to political prominence:

> Hon. Juan B. Patron, the Speaker of the house of the 23d General Assembly of New Mexico, is the youngest man elected to that responsible office since this became a Territory of the United States. He was born in Santa Fe in the year 1852. . . . Emigrating to Lincoln County in 1870, he engaged in merchandizing. In 1871, he was elected County Clerk of that County, an office which he held until 1876, when he was elected one of the County Commissioners. At a called election last fall Mr. Patron was elected to represent the counties of Lincoln, Doña Ana and Grant, to fill the vacancy occasioned by the death of Mr. Paul Dowlin. . . . Mr. Patron is a young man of fine character and business ability, but had little experience in legislative affairs, and none as a presiding officer, especially in as fun-loving a body as all lower Houses have the reputation of being; but with the forbearance of his mates and an aptness to learn, we anticipate that he will fill his new and responsible position very creditably before the close of the present session. The election of Mr. Patron to the Speakership is a compliment to the Southern counties that will be duly appreciated by the people of that section of New Mexico.[24]

Juan confidently settled into his chair as Speaker of the House before some local Hispanos were elected to fill the positions of chief clerk, enrolling clerk, engrossing clerk, doorkeeper, messenger, sergeant at arms, and watchman. Tranquilino Labadie watched with immense pride in the public gallery as his closest confidant oversaw proceedings. He did not remain an observer for long. The 24-year-old Tranquilino was subsequently nominated as interpreter of the House of Representatives by the secretary of the territory on January 10. Rep. Alejandro Branch of Mora County motioned for Labadie's appointment to be approved, and Speaker Patrón called for the votes. He was undoubtedly thrilled when his amigo was appointed after receiving thirteen yeas and eight nays.[25]

Like the *Weekly New Mexican*, the *Mesilla Valley Independent* also expressed its approval of Juan's election as Speaker on January 12, 1878: "Mr. Patron is a young man of great natural talent that has been well cultivated by a liberal education. He is a native of this Territory and is a fine Spanish and English scholar. Mr. Patron is a man of progressive ideas; he fully appreciates the fact that there is ample room for improvement in this Territory, and will lend his aid and influence towards effecting the necessary reforms. We congratulate Mr. Patron upon his election, and the Legislature that it has secured a competent presiding officer."[26]

Governor Axtell had sent a message to the council senate and house of representatives imploring them to keep things simple throughout the Twenty-Third Legislative Assembly. Axtell recommended passing a law "authorizing and directing the county boards of commissioners to call in and fund all their outstanding warrants" with the use of low-interest county bonds. The governor also recommended that county commissioners like Juan Patrón be empowered to serve as a board of health in their respective counties to improve public health, take over the role of school commissioners, establish an office of superintendent of education, and beseech Congress to establish a public education system throughout the territory. Axtell further suggested the creation of a board of prison commissioners to purchase a tract of suitable land for the construction of a territorial prison, the abolishment of any forms of animal cruelty, repealing a statute against carrying arms, and refraining from "establishing any central asylum to the poor" at the expense of New Mexico taxpayers.[27]

The standing committees for both branches of legislature were determined, with Lincoln, Doña Ana, and Grant Counties Rep. John K. Houston serving on the house judiciary. Throughout the next five weeks, the Twenty-Third Legislative Assembly passed thirty-four new general laws, ten acts for local governments, one joint resolution, and eight "memorials" reflecting their stance on various issues. They also passed three pieces of legislation that would have a profound effect on the future of New Mexico by enabling the incorporation of railroad companies, albeit with various bylaws, including the number of directors allowed and American citizenship being required for any members of a railroad corporation. They also established a progressive policy that any shares held by a married woman could be sold or transferred without her husband's signature.

The Twenty-Third Assembly provided further incentive for railroad barons to bring the "iron horse" to New Mexico by exempting all property owned by a corporation from any form of taxation for the first six years after the construction of a railroad line. Not everybody was on board with such a measure. "We are opposed to any such legislation," the *Mesilla Valley*

Independent declared. "If a railroad won't earn enough to pay its just taxes, they had better invest their money in something else that will pay." Despite the Mesilla newspaper's fears that New Mexico would fall "into the maw of one of these mendicant corporations," the iron horse soon began snaking across the territory with the six-year tax exemptions instituted.[28]

Although Juan Patrón's tenure as Speaker of the House during the Twenty-Third Legislative Assembly could largely be considered a personal triumph, he was condemned in various circles for remaining loyal to the Jesuits responsible for his education. His mentor Archbishop Jean Baptiste Lamy's education initiative had spread far beyond Santa Fe with the establishment of Catholic schools in Albuquerque, Taos, Los Alamos, and Socorro. When the question of providing tax relief for the Catholic schools was raised during the Twenty-Third Assembly, the resolute Juan Patrón took a stand on behalf of Archbishop Lamy and the Jesuits, regardless of the political consequences.

A bill from the council senate was placed on Juan Patrón's desk, proposing the chartering of the Association of Jesuit Fathers of New Mexico on January 11, 1878. The corporation would consist of five Jesuit priests tasked with establishment of additional schools and colleges throughout New Mexico and overseeing "the education and development of the youth in all branches of letters, arts, and sciences." Although the association would answer to the courts, they would also be empowered to bestow the diplomas, degrees, and honors usually reserved for the public education system. What's more, all their properties, including real estate, would be exempt from taxes. The provision did not sit well with Governor Axtell—an anti-Catholic Mason—or with other governing officers, non-Catholic legislators, and various members of the territorial press. The 43-year-old Reverend Father Donato Gasparri, the superior of the Jesuits, spent most of the day hovering in the chambers and imploring the Hispano members of the house and council to support the bill. He also made sly appeals to their cultural pride.

"You must be either Mexicans or gringos," Gasparri reportedly told them. "And if you maintain yourselves, you must unite as Mexicans."[29]

The seasoned Rep. Perfecto Esquibel successfully motioned for the Jesuit bill to be removed from Speaker Patrón's desk and filed a motion to refer the bill to a committee. Juan Patrón responded with a short, impassioned speech in which he challenged the motion and called for the vote. When Esquibel's motion was defeated, Rep. José Baca y Sedillo suggested an amendment to the Jesuit bill requiring the association to pay territorial taxes. Juan stood firm in his resolve and promptly called for the vote following an intense debate. Speaker Patrón and Padre Gasparri were satisfied when the amendment was shot down by a vote of fifteen to six. When the call was made for the passage of the Jesuit bill in the late afternoon, the legislation was passed with a vote of fifteen yeas and six nays.[30]

Juan Patrón and the other fourteen representatives who voted in favor of the Jesuit bill may have emerged victorious, but they were soon being hammered by the Anglo press. "The Jesuits control the Legislature!" the outraged *Mesilla Valley Independent* declared. "Such legislation can not be defended," the *Las Vegas Gazette* exclaimed. "It is without excuse." Governor Samuel B. Axtell was appalled and defiantly returned the bill unsigned to both houses of the legislature on January 18. The governor entered the senate chamber at eleven o'clock that morning and delivered a scathing speech in which he admonished the members of the house and council for acquiescing to the Jesuits. Axtell also read aloud a report from attorney general and Santa Fe Ring member William Breedon, declaring the Jesuit bill in violation of the revised statutes of the United States of America.

Juan Patrón remained unmoved in his support for the Jesuits despite his fellow representatives of Lincoln, Grant, and Doña Ana Counties John K. Houston and John S. Crouch voicing their support for Governor Axtell's effort to veto the bill. Axtell's mood would not have improved when the council senate approved the divisive measure following a vote of eleven to two that afternoon. John S. Crouch and J. Francisco Cháves were the only two councilmen who voted to sustain the governor's veto. Speaker Patrón sought a call for all members of the house to be present when the representative votes were recorded, and the Jesuit bill passed with eighteen yeas and four nays. "War between the governor and the majority of the Legislature is fully inaugurated," the *Mesilla Valley Independent* bitterly announced. "The Society of Jesus is the most powerful and insidious secret order in existence."[31]

While Juan Patrón and many of his fellow representatives successfully defied Governor Samuel Axtell in the territorial house that eventful January 18, the Hispano prodigy made some powerful enemies. His growing influence was duly noted by Santa Fe Ring attorney William L. Rynerson in Las Cruces. He was also excoriated by Anglo newspapermen, with the *Grant County Herald* and *Weekly New Mexican* both proclaiming to the public, "It is to the credit of Senator John S. Crouch and Representative John K. Houston that they were among the few who stood by the Governor in this contest. And it is to the lasting disgrace of Juan B. Patrón of Lincoln county that he *mis*-represented his constituency, by siding with and, in his feeble way, even attempting to lead the narrow-minded majority. The people of Grant, Doña Ana and Lincoln will probably bear Mr. Patron well in mind, should he ever again aspire to office."[32]

The *Weekly New Mexican* also ran an excerpt regarding "The Jesuit troubles in New Mexico," published in the *Cincinnati Commercial* the following month, "What may be called the official language of every county in the Territory but two, and all public bodies, from the Legislature down to an alcalde's court, is the bastard Indo-Spanish tongue known as "Mexican," one can see the almost infinite difficulty of fitting such a population for the exercise of the rights and duties of American citizenship."[33]

The headstrong Juan Patrón shrugged off such disparaging remarks from the Americano newspapers and continued his duties as speaker of the house with steadfast conviction. The Twenty-Third Assembly would also override four other measures vetoed by Governor Axtell during proceedings, including a bill that would provide the San Vicente Hospital with one hundred dollars from the territorial funds each month for the care of orphaned children, the sick, and the impoverished. Speaker Patrón guided the legislative assembly through its final proceedings before adjourning sine die on February 15, 1878.[34]

Juan Bautista Patrón climbed aboard his buggy with his representative duties concluded for the time being and began the journey back to Lincoln. Few men had made such an impactful first impression in the territorial house. Although it had been a turbulent five weeks for the Hispano prodigy in Santa Fe, nothing could have prepared him for the rippling effects of the shocking news spreading throughout southeastern New Mexico when he returned to the Río Bonito.

His friend John Tunstall had been brutally murdered, and there would be considerable hell to pay in Lincoln County.

***

While Juan Patrón was seeing to his territorial affairs in Santa Fe, his friend Alexander McSween had been escorted out of the Las Vegas jail by two San Miguel County deputies and returned to Lincoln in their custody on January 8, 1878. McSween remained in the custody of Deputy Sheriff Adolph P. Barrier after Judge Warren Bristol fell ill in La Mesilla and the Scottish attorney's arraignment was postponed until the following month. Deputy Sheriff Barrier sympathized with McSween and sensed the danger posed to his prisoner's well-being by the almost bankrupt J. J. Dolan & Co. and their associates in Lincoln. "I believe that the only thing that saved the life of said McSween was that he was not delivered into the custody of said Sheriff Brady," Probate Judge Florencio Gonzáles later insisted.[35]

Jimmy Dolan and John Riley were increasingly desperate and forced to mortgage their property and cattle holdings to Thomas B. Catron on January 18, 1878. The Santa Fe Ring was deeply immersed in Dolan and Riley's interests in Lincoln County as a result. Alexander McSween and John Tunstall needed to be dealt with in order for J. J. Dolan & Co. to remain in operation and Catron to be suitably reimbursed.[36]

John Tunstall had spent a miserable Christmas suffering with rheumatoid arthritis but decided to accompany Alexander McSween to La Mesilla in late January. With his Scottish friend having been charged with embezzlement of the Fritz insurance funds, Tunstall took a bold public stand against the House before departing for Doña Ana County. The same day the *Mesilla Valley Independent* expressed much of its outrage over the passing of the Jesuit bill on January 26, the newspaper published a letter received from John Henry Tunstall of Lincoln County. The Englishman publicly accused Jimmy Dolan, John Riley, and Sheriff William Brady of embezzling territorial funds:

> Major Brady as the records of this County show, collected over Twenty five hundred dollars, Territorial funds. Of this sum, Alex. A. McSween Esq. of this place paid him over Fifteen hundred dollars by cheque on

the First National Bank of Santa Fe, August 23, 1877. Said cheque was presented for payment by John H. Riley Esq., of the firm of J. J. Dolan & Co., this last amount was paid by the last named gentleman to Underwood and Nash for cattle. Thus passed away over Fifteen hundred dollars belonging to the Territory of New Mexico.... A delinquent tax payer is bad; a delinquent tax collector is worse.[37]

An incensed Jimmy Dolan wrote his own letter to the *New Mexican* refuting Tunstall's claims. The Santa Fe newspaper also announced that "Major Brady has paid into the treasury every cent." What the *New Mexican* failed to inform the public was that the payments had actually been made by Thomas B. Catron on Brady's behalf with the proceeds of Bureau of Indian Affairs vouchers made by John H. Riley. "Brady admitted to me that he had let Riley have the territorial tax money and could not get it back from him," Juan Patrón later recalled. John Tunstall had been on to something. In publicly exposing the latest transgressions of the Irish firm in Lincoln, the Englishman had unknowingly sealed his grim fate.[38]

John Tunstall accompanied Alexander McSween, Deputy Sheriff Adolph P. Barrier, David Shield, and John B. Wilson to La Mesilla, where McSween's hearing was held on February 2 and 4 in Judge Warren Bristol's private home. Bristol ruled that probable cause had existed when the warrant for McSween's arrest was issued and that a grand jury would determine if the Scottish attorney should be indicted for embezzlement when the spring term of court convened in Lincoln on April 8, 1878. Charles and Emilie Fritz's attorney had also filed an affidavit to Judge Bristol for a writ of attachment for $8,000. Bristol addressed the writ to Sheriff William Brady, directing him to seize any property equaling that amount that personally belonged to Alexander McSween or was jointly owned with John Tunstall. Although Tunstall had sworn during proceedings that no official partnership had been established between himself and McSween, the Santa Fe Ring was determined to nail both Brits to the proverbial adobe wall.[39]

John Tunstall, Alexander McSween, Deputy Sheriff Adolph P. Barrier, David Shield, and John B. Wilson were confronted by an enraged Jimmy Dolan and Jessie Evans at Warren H. Shedd's ranch during their return trip to Lincoln on February 5, 1878. Dolan leveled his rifle at Tunstall while the

Englishman was eating his breakfast and challenged him to a fight. Deputy Sheriff Barrier quickly intervened, and the snarling Irishman backed off for the time being.

"When you write to the Independent again, tell them I am with the Boys!" Dolan shouted at Tunstall while storming away.[40]

When the Tunstall–McSween caravan returned to Lincoln on February 9, they quickly learned the writ of attachment sent by Judge Warren Bristol had beaten them back to town and was nestled in Sheriff William Brady's pocket. Brady and his deputies had practically ransacked the McSween home and seized all manner of personal properties to be attached. The sheriff also led House associates George W. Peppin, Jack Long, Follett G. Christie, and James Longwell into the Tunstall store, arrested Rob Widenmann, and ceased all commerce. Although John H. Riley had been gleefully sweeping out the Lincoln jail in anticipation of Alexander McSween's return, Deputy Adolph Barrier believed the Scotsman's life would be in danger if he were turned over to Sheriff Brady. The French deputy decided to keep the grateful attorney under guard in the McSween home instead.[41]

John Tunstall was predictably outraged when learning that Sheriff Brady, "an Irishman, a slave of whiskey," and "a tool" as Tunstall informed his parents, had taken control of his store. The Englishman marched onto the premises with Rob Widenmann, Fred Waite, and Billy "Kid" Bonney to confront Brady and his deputies on the morning of February 11, 1878. Tunstall berated James Longwell over the "damned high-handed business" and declared the Santa Fe Ring the "worst God damn outfit of them all." Fred Waite and Billy Bonney stood behind the Englishman with their Winchester rifles seemingly ready to roar. For all Tunstall's objections, Brady refused to cease the attachment of merchandise but did allow the irate Englishman to take possession of six horses and two mules from the corral.[42]

Alexander McSween was in no position to confront Sheriff Brady while in Deputy Adolph Barrier's custody. Instead, he wrote a letter to the secretary of the interior in Washington. The Scotsman accused House associate Agent Fred Godfroy of appropriating supplies at the Mescalero Agency and distributing spoiled food to the Natives. Although McSween was relying on hearsay from Stephen Stanley, his letter would eventually result in an Indian agent arriving in Lincoln County to investigate the Scotsman's assertions. McSween could do little else with the Santa Fe Ring closing in on him. The Scottish attorney had managed to raise $34,500 in bail bonds, but District Attorney William L. Rynerson refused to accept them.[43]

Sheriff William Brady continued needling John Tunstall by deputizing his close friend Jacob B. "Billy" Mathews and instructing him to lead a posse down to the Englishman's ranch to attach any McSween cattle on February 13, 1878. Dick Brewer, Billy Bonney, and their fellow Tunstall employees had fortified the Englishman's ranch in anticipation of a showdown. The escalating hostilities very nearly erupted in gunfire when Deputies Billy Mathews, George Hindman, and Johnny Hurley arrived on the Río Feliz alongside Manuel "the Indian" Segovia, a deadly gunman named Andrew L. Roberts, Jessie Evans, Frank Baker, Tom Hill, Ponciano Domínquez, and Jack Long. After Dick Brewer tried to calm the situation by inviting the posse to breakfast, Jessie Evans and Frank Baker ended up pointing their guns in Rob Widenmann's face. Deputy Mathews decided to withdraw for the time being, vowing to return with only one man to assist him in rounding up any McSween cattle.[44]

John Tunstall began losing his nerve inside the McSween home on the morning of February 14 when a Black McSween servant called George Washington informed him that John Riley had boasted of raising a large posse to come after the Englishman and his ranch hands. Although Tunstall instructed Billy Bonney, Fred Waite, and Rob Widenmann to return to the Río Feliz, Bonney and Waite had heard enough threats and headed for the Tunstall store. When finding Deputy James Longwell guarding their employer's store on Sheriff Brady's authority and chatting to Stephen Stanley, young Billy Bonney aimed his Winchester rifle in Longwell's direction and told Stanley to get out of the way. Longwell managed to scramble inside and slam the doors shut before the Kid squeezed the trigger.

"Turn loose, you sons of bitches!" Billy shouted. "We'll give you a game!"[45]

Billy Bonney, Fred Waite, and Rob Widenmann subsequently returned to the Tunstall ranch when nobody inside the Englishman's store proved willing to answer the Kid's challenge. John Tunstall spent the next two nights in the McSween home until he rode for the Río Feliz on the evening of February 16, 1878.[46]

While Juan Patrón was riding aboard his buggy on his return trip from Santa Fe and his friend John Tunstall was cautiously returning to his ranch on the Río Feliz, neither of them was aware that Jimmy Dolan and John Riley were about to receive a letter from their friend William Rynerson. The letter—which could aptly be described as a declaration of war—had been penned in Las Cruces on February 14, 1878. District Attorney Rynerson laid out a strategy to deal with John Tunstall, the Englishman's ranch hands, Alexander McSween, Justice of the Peace John B. Wilson, and Juan B. Patrón:

> I believe Tunstall is in with the swindles with the rogue McSween. They have the money belonging to the Fritz estate and they must be made to give it up. It must be made hot for them, all the hotter the better especially is this necessary now that it has been discovered that there is no hell. It may be that the villain Green "Juan Baptista" Wilson will play into their hands as Alcalde. If so he should be moved around a little. Shake that McSween outfit up till it shells out and squares up and then shake it out of Lincoln. I will aid to punish the scoundrels all I can. Get the people with you. Control Juan Patron if possible. You know how to do it. Have good men about to aid Brady and be assured I shall help you all I can for I believe there was never found a more scoundrely set than that outfit.[47]

An exhausted John Tunstall returned to his ranch on the Río Feliz at three o'clock in the morning of February 18, 1878. The Englishman wasn't willing to risk everyone's lives for the sake of some beeves. He instructed his old German cook Gottfried Gauss to stay behind and assist Deputy Billy Mathews in rounding up any cattle when the sun came up. Tunstall also informed a teamster named Bill McCloskey, who had started hanging around several weeks earlier, to ride for the Río Peñasco and fetch "Dutch" Martin Martz to assist old man Gauss in rounding up any attached livestock. The Englishman, Dick Brewer, Billy Bonney, Henry Brown, Fred Waite, and Rob Widenmann would herd their eight horses up to Lincoln at first light.[48]

Jimmy Dolan and John Riley had got the message loud and clear when receiving William Rynerson's letter. Sheriff William Brady subsequently ordered a large posse led by Deputy Billy Mathews to ride for the Tunstall ranch and take care of business. The posse led by Mathews on Brady's authority was comprised of Deputy George Hindman, Deputy Johnny Hurley, William "Buck" Morton, Jessie Evans, Frank Baker, Tom Hill, George Davis, Sam Perry, Manuel "the Indian" Segovia, Andrew L. Roberts, former Sheriff Alexander "Ham" Mills, young Yginio Salazar's adversary Robert Beckwith, various other ruffians, and several local Hispanos.[49]

Deputy Billy Mathews and the posse arrived at the Tunstall ranch on the morning of February 18, 1878. They were disappointed to find only Gottfried Gauss and "Dutch" Martin Martz on the premises. John Tunstall and his ranch hands had set out for Lincoln with their remuda two hours earlier. Jimmy Dolan soon arrived on the scene and began selecting men from their posse to go after the Tunstall party alongside Billy Mathews, who deputized William "Buck" Morton to lead the secondary posse. The rest would stay behind and set up camp. "They would say, 'you go, you go,' and so on, point at each person," recalled Gottfried Gauss. "They were all excited and seemed as though they were going to kill someone." The men chosen to accompany Buck Morton were Deputy George Hindman, Deputy Johnny Hurley, Bob Beckwith, John Wallace Olinger, Sam Perry, Charlie Kruling, Tom Cochrane, Manuel "the Indian" Segovia, Tom Green, Pantaleon Gallegos, Charlie Marshall, George Kitt, and Ramón Montoya. Jessie Evans, Frank Baker, Tom Hill, and George Davis would also accompany them.

"Hurry up, boys!" Buck Morton shouted as he began leading his rough bunch north. "My knife is sharp, and I feel like scalping someone!"[50]

Morton and his heavily armed posse caught up with Tunstall and his companions around five o'clock that evening on a trail passing through a brush-filled canyon near the Parajita Mountains. Bringing up the rear, Billy Bonney and John Middleton heard the posse's horses rumbling behind them and galloped toward Tunstall, Dick Brewer, and Rob Widenmann to warn them of the approaching danger. The outnumbered Brewer, Bonney, Middleton, and Widenmann quickly rode toward a rocky hillside to take cover. Although John Middleton implored his boss to follow him, John Tunstall foolishly turned his horse and approached the posse, presumably intending to parley with them.

When the naive John Tunstall was in range, Jessie Evans fired a shot from his rifle, hitting the Englishman in the chest. Tunstall fell from his saddle and lay prostate on the ground while bleeding profusely. Bill Morton dismounted his horse, approached the helpless Tunstall, and finished the job by firing a bullet from his six-shooter into the back of the Englishman's head. Morton also shot Tunstall's prized horse, and someone decided to crack the already dead Englishman's skull with the butt of his rifle. Deputy George Hindman, Sam Perry, Tom Green, John Olinger, and Charlie Kruling picked up Tunstall's lifeless body and placed it on a blanket next to the dead horse as if they were putting him to bed. It was later said that one of the posse placed the Englishman's hat beneath the head of his fallen steed, considering it an amusing joke.[51]

On their hillside refuge, Dick Brewer, Billy Bonney, John Middleton, and Rob Widenmann all heard the shots in the distance and instinctively knew their employer had been murdered. Taking cover in some nearby trees, they watched as Buck Morton and his posse rode into their line of sight. They immediately recognized Morton and some of the other possemen, including Deputy George Hindman, Deputy Johnny Hurley, Jessie Evans, Frank Baker, Tom Hill, and Pantaleon Gallegos. Rob Widenmann later insisted that he also spotted Jimmy Dolan riding a sorrel horse. Dick Brewer led his three companions to Frank Coe's ranch on the Río Ruidoso before riding into Lincoln later that night to inform Alexander McSween of Tunstall's murder.[52]

When Juan Patrón returned to Lincoln shortly after his English friend's murder, the Hispano representative found the town on the brink of open warfare. Sheriff Brady had already announced his premature judgment that John Tunstall must have been killed while resisting arrest. The slain Englishman's heavily armed supporters were holed up in the McSween home. Many in the community shared their outrage over what transpired. "A good many Mexicans and whites came in," recalled Frank Coe. "Murphy kept his house locked up." A pitifully drunk John Riley showed up at the McSween home professing peaceful intentions and was fortunate not to have been shot dead on the spot. Sheriff Brady quickly appealed to Fort Stanton for assistance, and a detachment of soldiers were soon guarding the J. J. Dolan &

Co. store. Alexander McSween sent word to John Newcomb on the Río Ruidoso to transport John Tunstall's corpse into town.[53]

While offering his moral support to Alexander McSween and the Scotsman's armed associates, Juan Patrón made the acquaintance of a 29-year-old Presbyterian minister and physician named Taylor F. Ealy. The doctor arrived in Lincoln with his wife Mary, their two young daughters, and a schoolteacher named Susan Gates on February 19. They had traveled from Pennsylvania at the behest of Alexander McSween, who had requested the Ealy family oversee the construction of a Presbyterian church and schoolhouse in town. When reaching the McSween home, Dr. Taylor Ealy was shocked to see "about 40 armed men" in "full fighting trim" as he recorded in his diary.[54]

Juan Patrón presumably watched as John Tunstall's cold, battered corpse was hauled out of John Newcomb's wagon and carried inside the McSween house at around six o'clock in the evening of February 19, 1878. When the Englishman's body was laid out on a table in the McSween parlor, William "Kid" Bonney somberly walked up and gazed at his deceased employer's pale, blood-drenched frame.

"I'll get some of them before I die," Billy said and turned away.[55]

The Kid was not the only one in the McSween home determined to reap vengeance upon the House. Dick Brewer headed for San Patricio later that night to recruit his farmhand Florencio Cháves and brought him into Lincoln. Although Alexander McSween and Chisum cowhand Francis "Frank" MacNab offered to pay Florencio *cinco pesos* (five dollars) a day to stick around, young Cháves had commitments back in San Patricio and was reluctant to get involved in a gringo fight.

"No," Florencio insisted. "I got my mother and my sister."[56]

Dick Brewer, William Bonney, John Middleton, and others testified before Justice John B. Wilson during a coroner's inquest held in Lincoln the following morning of February 20. The coroner's jury determined that John Henry Tunstall had been murdered by "bullets shot and sent forth out of and from deadly weapons," which were "held by one or more of the men whose are herewith written: Jesse Evans, Frank Baker, Thomas Hill, George Hindman, J. J. Dolan, William Morton, and others not identified by the witnesses." Justice Wilson then handed the arrest warrants to Constable

Atanacio Martínez. When Martínez expressed his reluctance to serve them, some of Tunstall's former employees threatened to kill him themselves if he didn't brace up and carry out his duty.[57]

Billy Bonney and Fred Waite accompanied Precinct Constable Atanacio Martínez to the Dolan store on the morning of February 21, 1878. Sheriff William Brady quickly leveled his rifle at them and flatly refused to allow the serving of warrants for any of the men on the premises. The sheriff also refused to recognize John B. Wilson's authority as justice of the peace. Brady arrested Constable Martínez, Bonney, and Waite, who were subsequently marched down the street at gunpoint and locked inside one of the pit-jails. The sheriff released Martínez later that evening but decided to keep Bonney and Waite incarcerated for several days.

As a result of their confinement, William Bonney and Fred Waite missed John Tunstall's funeral service, conducted by Rev. Taylor F. Ealy behind the corral of the late Englishman's store on February 22, 1878. Juan Patrón, Alexander McSween, and Probate Judge Florencio Gonzáles—who had helped John Newcomb recover the Englishman's corpse and transport it into town—were all in attendance. Dick Brewer was also present and during the proceedings vowed vengeance against those responsible for Tunstall's murder. The funeral had been carried out as respectfully and quickly as possible. "Soldiers and citizens armed," Taylor Ealy wrote in his diary. "Great danger of being shot."[58]

Juan Patrón would have attended the meeting during which his friends Florencio Gonzáles, José Montaño, Isaac Ellis, and John Newcomb were tasked with confronting Sheriff William Brady at the Dolan store. When discussing matters with Brady, they asked why he was keeping William Bonney and Fred Waite locked in the pit-jail. "Brady replied in substance that he kept them prisoners because he had the power," recalled Florencio Gonzáles. "Brady was a tool for the House." The sheriff also refused to accept any bonds they offered to cover the attached property of Alexander McSween or the late John Tunstall.[59]

Rob Widenmann had recently been appointed a deputy US marshal and arrived in Fort Stanton. He convinced Capt. George Purington to furnish him with a detachment of troops under the command of Lt. Millard Goodwin to assist in the arrest of William "Buck" Morton, Jessie Evans, and their cohorts. Marshal Widenmann, Lieutenant Goodwin, Dick Brewer, John Middleton, Frank Coe, Doc Scurlock, the recently released Billy Bonney and Fred Waite, and a handful of locals arrived at the Dolan store in the early hours of February 23. They failed to find any members of the Morton posse when searching the premises but managed to take back the Tunstall store while arresting Deputies James Longwell, George W. Peppin, Jack Long, Charles Martin, and John Clark in the process. Alexander McSween then charged William Brady with larceny, and the indignant sheriff was forced to pay a $200 bond before Justice Wilson. Brady's loyal deputies George Peppin, Jim Longwell, Jack Long, Charles Martin, and John Clark were bound over to a grand jury and released.[60]

When attending to his own business in Lincoln, Juan Patrón could see heavily armed ruffians with a suspicious glare and an itchy trigger finger everywhere he turned. The battle lines had been firmly drawn, and many of the locals began taking a side. Saturnino Baca and the other citizens who were determined to remain neutral would have been nervously wondering just what was going to happen next. "That insurance business was what started it all, and then they all wanted to kill somebody," Dolan–Riley employee William Wier later said. "Every son of a bitch over there wanted to kill somebody."

Alexander McSween decided to skip town after someone supposedly tried to poison Rob Widenmann on February 24, 1878. The Scottish attorney named John Chisum as executor of his estate when making out a will the following day and headed into the hills under the protection of Deputy Adolph P. Barrier. His friend Rob Widenmann remained in Lincoln and wrote a letter to Sir Edward Thornton, British ambassador to the United States, to inform him that British subject John Henry Tunstall had been murdered by James J. Dolan.[61]

Dick Brewer and a handful of Tunstall partisans realized it was useless to make any appeals to Sheriff William Brady and the corrupt legal system structured to serve House interests in Lincoln County. They would have to take the law into their own hands. "It was said that the Keed swore he would kill every man that was in the posse that killed his friend," little Carlota Baca later recalled. Justice John B. Wilson subsequently appointed Dick Brewer as a special constable and handed him the arrest warrants for eighteen men charged with John Tunstall's murder. Brewer then deputized William "Kid" Bonney, John Middleton, Fred Waite, Henry Brown, Charlie Bowdre, Doc Scurlock, Chisum cowboy Frank MacNab, a cowboy from Texas called Sam Smith, and a part-Cherokee drifter named Jim French. Constable Brewer and his nine deputies swore an "iron clad" oath to never reveal any information that could lead to one of their comrades being either arrested or indicted. They also came up with a name for their posse: the Regulators.

While Juan Patrón's loyalties were firmly with Alexander McSween and the newly formed Regulators, the Hispano prodigy remained in Lincoln when Dick Brewer and his deputies stormed out of town to begin searching for the men responsible for John Tunstall's murder around March 4, 1878. Juan could not afford to risk his political future by participating in what became known as the Lincoln County War.[62]

Chapter 6

Lincoln County Warfare

> *I expect retaliation in a hurry*
> *I see death around the corner.*
> —Tupac Shakur

Martín Chávez was heading toward Roswell on March 9, 1878, presumably to buy some goods and post some mail, when he spotted a fresh trail of horse hooves embedded in the soil. The hoofprints curiously veered off the more commonly used route leading directly to Lincoln. Instead, the tracks left behind by roughly thirteen horses led farther north on a route that passed through Agua Negra and was frequently used by soldiers. Clearly the riders had intended to bypass Lincoln for some reason. When Martín finished surveying the tracks, the former deputy sheriff continued his journey east along the Río Hondo to attend to his business.

Martín arrived in Roswell around four o'clock that afternoon and entered a store owned and operated by a frail 49 year old named Marshall Ashmun "Ash" Upson. The proprietor had worked as a newspaper reporter in New York before eventually heading west. Like Juan Patrón, the heavy-drinking Upson had also worked as a schoolteacher in Lincoln for a time. Martín informed the proprietor of the fresh tracks he had spotted on the trail in from Picacho. When hearing the news, Upson correctly assumed the tracks had been left by the Regulators, their two captives, and William J. McCloskey. They had all stopped in Roswell earlier that day. The curious direction they had taken suggested more blood was about to be spilled in Lincoln County, if it hadn't been already.[1]

Dick Brewer and his Regulators had been searching for the men responsible for John Tunstall's murder when they caught sight of William "Buck" Morton, Frank Baker, Dick Lloyd, and two companions at a lower crossing of the Río Peñasco in the late afternoon of March 6, 1878. The Regulators galloped southward in pursuit of the fleeing culprits for five or six miles until eventually capturing Bill Morton and Frank Baker after the Dolan partisans' horses collapsed on the Río Pecos. Although Dick Brewer had not wanted to take either of them alive, he gave Morton and Baker his word that they would not be harmed should they surrender. This did not sit well with Deputy William Bonney, who supposedly had to be restrained from vengefully shooting Bill Morton on the spot. "I never meant to let them birds reach Lincoln alive," Bonney later told his friend George Coe.[2]

The Regulators had escorted Morton and Baker up the Río Pecos, stayed a night at the plush Chisum ranch on South Spring, and arrived at Ash Upson's post office in Roswell around ten o'clock on the morning of March 9, 1878. John Chisum's blonde-haired niece Sallie had noticed Morton and Baker were both "pale as corpses" when departing her uncle's ranch in the Regulators' custody that morning. Bill Morton knew his chances of survival were slim when handing postmaster Ash Upson a letter he had written back at the Chisum hacienda. The letter was addressed to his cousin H. H. Marshall, an attorney in Virginia. Morton made the risible claim that Tunstall had fired on his posse first and requested Marshall investigate the matter should the Regulators kill him. His friend William McCloskey, who had attached himself to the party on the ride north, tried to alleviate Morton's concerns.

"Billy," McCloskey told him, "if harm comes to you, they will have to kill me first."[3]

It wasn't long before Martín Chávez, Ash Upson, and everyone else began hearing different versions of what happened after the Regulators, McCloskey,

Morton, and Baker rode up the trail leading through Agua Negra that afternoon. Frank MacNab had reportedly shot McCloskey in the head as a suspected traitor. Florencio Cháves later claimed to have accompanied the Regulators on their vendetta ride and insisted Henry Brown was the man who blew McCloskey's brains out. William "Buck" Morton and Frank Baker were shot full of holes by the Regulators when apparently trying to make a run for it. John Middleton later claimed the Regulators decided to bypass Lincoln that afternoon in the belief that J. J. Dolan & Co. would attempt to rescue their two prisoners and that McCloskey was shot by Bill Morton with his own pistol. However things transpired, William J. McCloskey, William "Buck" Morton, and Frank Baker were dead. As far as the Regulators were concerned, a little frontier justice had been dished out for John Tunstall's murder.[4]

The same day the Regulators dusted Morton and Baker in Agua Negra, Governor Axtell arrived in Lincoln after receiving a letter from Sheriff William Brady. The sheriff was doing everything he could to distance himself and his deputies from John Tunstall's murder. "The killing of a man like J. H. Tunstall, by a sheriff's posse so peculiarly constituted as reported, will require much explanation to make it clear and just to an unprejudiced mind," the *Las Vegas Gazette* proclaimed. Thomas B. Catron had also encouraged Governor Axtell to appeal to President Rutherford B. Hayes and request that federal troops be issued to maintain the Santa Fe Ring's idea of peace in Lincoln County.[5]

Governor Axtell predictably spent most of his time in Lincoln with Lawrence Murphy, Jimmy Dolan, and Johnny Riley, although he briefly visited Taylor F. Ealy at the McSween home and exchanged testy words with Rob Widenmann. Threats were soon being made on Taylor F. Ealy's life by House partisans, and a drunk Jimmy Dolan fell off his horse and broke his leg while attempting to shoot an unarmed man the following day in Lincoln on March 10, 1878. "Truly times are so fearfully unsettled here," Ash Upson wrote to his niece in Roswell. Upson had recently observed the bloodied corpse of Frank Baker, whom he described as "the very worse, most beastly murderer this county ever saw."[6]

The Regulators arrived in San Patricio shortly after escorting Bill Morton and Frank Baker to their deaths in Agua Negra. The small placita would often serve as a base of operations throughout their quest for retribution. The Regulators also had an ally in former constable José Chávez y Chávez, who was always up for a fight. "I was talking with my friend, Chávez y Chávez," recalled Florencio Cháves. "I told him it looked like they might fight but I wanted to stay out." Florencio handed his mother thirty dollars and headed for Tularosa in an effort to avoid the escalating warfare. José Chávez y Chávez would not only stick around but also soon joined up with the Regulators.[7]

Although José Chávez y Chávez was eager to join the Regulators and augment his reputation as a pistolero, most of his fellow Hispanos initially refrained from getting involved in a predominantly Anglo conflict. "The Mexicans are very slow," Taylor F. Ealy wrote to his wife Mary. "They tramp out wheat with sheep or goats, fan it by the wind, plow with a stick, keep their guns tied to the plow beam, reap with a sycle. They take pride in doing as the ancients did." Martín Chávez and most of *la gente* (the people) focused on their farming and herding duties throughout lambing season, effectively leaving the gringos to fight things out among themselves. "My husband and I were living on our farm just above Lincoln, New Mexico, all during the Lincoln County War," recalled Lorencita Miranda. "We liked both factions so we never took any part in the war."[8]

While Lorencita Miranda and most other Nuevomexicanos remained neutral for the time being, Governor Samuel Axtell demonstrated his partisanship when issuing a proclamation that removed any semblance of legal standing possessed by the Regulators. Axtell declared John B. Wilson's appointment as justice of the peace by Juan Patrón and the county commissioners "illegal," thereby rendering Wilson's deputization of Dick Brewer null and void. Axtell's proclamation also revoked Rob Widenmann's appointment as a US marshal, ensuring that only Sheriff William Brady and his deputies could carry out any form of law enforcement in Lincoln County. Dick Brewer and his Regulators were now vigilantes.[9]

Although Dick Brewer returned to his ranch on the Río Ruidoso, tensions continued to fester throughout the remainder of March 1878. William Bonney and Charlie Bowdre exchanged fire with Andrew L. Roberts and some House partisans in a running gunfight outside San Patricio later that month. A Cherokee driver killed Tom Hill and shot

Jessie Evans in the elbow when the two banditti attempted to rob the Wagner sheep camp near Alamo Spring on March 14. Evans was eventually captured by Constable David Wood, allowing Rob Widenmann to serve his warrant for the badman and happily see the wounded outlaw confined in the guard house at Fort Stanton.[10]

Sheriff William Brady, Lt. George W. Smith, and a detachment of soldiers scoured the hills in search of Alexander McSween and the Regulators toward the end of March 1878. They eventually rode for the Chisum ranch on South Spring, where old John had recently returned following his release from the Las Vegas jail. Alexander McSween had taken refuge at the hacienda alongside Deputy Adolph P. Barrier and his wife Susan, who had returned from Kansas with an English political activist named Montague Leverson. "This county I am sorry to inform you is under the rule of a gang of thieves and assassins at the head of whom are United States officials," Leverson wrote to President Rutherford B. Hayes.[11]

Alexander McSween was hiding out at the Bottomless Lakes to the east of the Río Pecos when Sheriff Brady and the troops arrived at the Chisum ranch on March 28, 1878. Montague Leverson exchanged barbs with Brady, and Lt. George Smith implored Susan McSween to encourage her husband to come to Fort Stanton until the district court convened in Lincoln the following month. Brady also misinformed Mrs. McSween that the district court would convene on April 1, when proceedings were scheduled to begin on April 8.

Alexander McSween would have known his life would not be worth a silver peso in the House-aligned sheriff's custody, but he decided to accept Lt. George Smith's offer to take refuge in Fort Stanton shortly after Brady and the Cavalry officer led the troops back to the Río Bonito. The Scottish attorney, his wife Susan, John Chisum, Montague Leverson, and a couple of associates set out for Lincoln in two horse-drawn wagons on March 29, 1878.[12]

Mac no longer had to contend with William Brady by the time they arrived.

***

Like many of the Hispanos residing in Lincoln County, the 32-year-old Francisco "Kiko" Trujillo initially tried to steer clear of the escalating warfare between the "Macky Swin (McSween)" and "Marfe (Murphy)" factions in the spring of 1878. It was somewhat difficult for Francisco to continue doing so while living with his wife Margarita, their son Teófilo, and daughter Anna in San Patricio. The Regulators frequently congregated in the placita. Sure enough, Francisco Trujillo, Atanacio Martínez, Sequio Sánchez, and several other local Hispanos followed José Chávez y Chávez's example and began riding with the Regulators shortly after the revenge killings of William "Buck" Morton and Frank Baker were carried out in Agua Negra.[13]

It was also in Agua Negra, recalled Francisco "Kiko" Trujillo, that the determination was made as to who would kill Sheriff William Brady in Lincoln before Alexander McSween arrived in town on April 1, 1878. With their leader, Dick Brewer, having returned to his ranch on the Río Ruidoso, the remaining Regulators were determined to put the House-aligned sheriff in the ground. "Brady was instrumental in having Tunstall killed," Mary Ealy later asserted.[14]

Francisco Trujillo later claimed that Alexander McSween provided the vengeful Regulators with further incentive to take out Brady. According to the San Patricio resident, the Scottish attorney had told them, "As soon as I arrive, Brady is going to try and arrest me and you should not let him get away with it. If I am arrested I shall surely be hung and I don't want to die, while if you kill Brady you shall earn a reward." However accurate Trujillo's recollections concerning the matter, the Regulators decided to take their fight against the House and the Santa Fe Ring directly into Lincoln while Mac was on his way in from the Chisum ranch.

José Chávez y Chávez was disgruntled when the Regulators determined who would ride into Lincoln after eating their lunch in Agua Negra on March 31, 1878. "Bill [Bonney] thought it was best for none of the Mexican boys to go," recalled Francisco Trujillo decades later. An indignant Chávez y Chávez bluntly informed Bonney that none of the gringos in their party were any braver than he was. "Bill explained that Brady was married to a Mexican," Trujillo recalled, "and that it was a matter of policy, all Mexicans being sentimental about their own." When Chávez y Chávez realized the

Kid was not questioning his personal courage, the former deputy sheriff agreed to return to San Patricio and provide any assistance if called upon. Frank MacNab, John Middleton, Fred Waite, Henry Brown, Bill Bonney, and Jim French would ride into Lincoln that evening and spend the night in the Tunstall store. Doc Scurlock and Charlie Bowdre were both married to "Mexican" women and decided to accompany Scurlock's father-in-law Fernando Herrera and several other Hispano allies to the Río Ruidoso.[15]

Sheriff William Brady and his deputies George Hindman, George W. Peppin, Jack Long, and Jacob "Billy" Mathews were heavily armed when emerging from the Dolan store in Lincoln at around nine o'clock on the morning of April 1, 1878. Brady also had some handcuffs attached to his belt and an arrest warrant for Alexander McSween in his pocket. The sheriff and his deputies began strolling down the muddied street toward the eastern end of town, where McSween was expected to arrive that April Fool's morning. Brady briefly stopped to share a laugh with María Mills on the way, blissfully unaware that he and his faithful cronies were walking directly into a guerrilla ambush.

As William Brady and his deputies sauntered past the Tunstall store, the corral gate on the eastern side of the building swung open. Juan Patrón and everyone else's heads snapped in the direction of the Tunstall store as Frank MacNab, Fred Waite, Bill Bonney, John Middleton, Henry Brown, and Jim French unleashed a storm of gunfire on Brady and his four associates. A hundred yards up the street, Amelia Bolton watched in horror as the local sheriff fell into a sitting position with several bullets in him.

"Oh, lord," the sheriff exclaimed.

When Brady attempted to rise back to his feet, the Regulators sent him falling dead into the mud with another round of bullets. George Peppin, Jack Long, and Billy Mathews ran for cover while Deputy George Hindman lay bleeding in the street and shouted for someone to bring him some water. When Ike Stockton helped the wounded deputy to his feet, Fred Waite approached them with his revolver and finished off Hindman by firing shots into his head, back, and side.

Billy Bonney and Jim French emerged from the Tunstall corral when the street had cleared and approached William Brady's fresh corpse. The Kid promptly retrieved his prized Winchester rifle, which the late sheriff had kept for himself after locking Bonney and Fred Waite in the pit-jail six weeks earlier. Billy Mathews had taken cover in the nearby Cisneros house and opened fire on the two Regulators through a window, hitting Jim French in the thigh. The Kid and the wounded French returned to the Tunstall corral before Bonney, Middleton, MacNab, Waite, and Brown emerged on horseback. They galloped east out of town as Brady's remaining deputies fired shots at them. Jim French quickly limped to the McSween home to seek medical assistance from Dr. Taylor F. Ealy. Poor old John B. Wilson had been hit in the ass by a stray bullet outside his home across from the Tunstall store and sought treatment at the Ellis house.[16]

While the Regulators felt wholly justified in their vigilante crusade and considered the killing of Brady and Hindman a case of two more for Tunstall, many of the locals were appalled by their initiative. "The shooting of Brady and Hindman was unfortunate, because it reversed the opinions of many who up to that time had favored the McSween side," Martín Chávez later said. Despite Brady's obvious complicity in John Tunstall's murder, most of the townsfolk could not condone the killing of an elected sheriff under any circumstances. The pregnant and suddenly widowed María Bonifacia Brady was devastated and left to raise her soon-to-be nine children alone. Taylor F. Ealy later summarized the Regulators' outlook on the situation: "Kid, Frenchy, Waite, Little Brown, Middleton, Scurlock. They claim that there is no law here, they can not get law—they claim they are only maintaining the freedom of the county, that it has been ridden to death by a few men—they call it a Ring."[17]

George W. Peppin presumptuously acted as the new sheriff after William Brady was cut down in the street. He immediately appealed to Fort Stanton for military assistance. Capt. George Purington, Lt. George W. Smith, and twenty-five troopers had reached Lincoln by the time the McSween caravan arrived at the eastern end of town. Alexander McSween refused to recognize George Peppin's pseudo-authority but agreed to surrender to Lieutenant Smith as arranged. Peppin merely had to be satisfied with arresting Rob Widenmann, David P. Shield, and McSween servants George Washington and George Robinson. The soldiers were unable to locate the wounded Jim French, who had been hidden beneath the floorboards of the Tunstall store by Sam Corbet after receiving medical assistance from Taylor F. Ealy in the McSween home.

The McSweens, John Chisum, Montague Leverson, David P. Shield, Rob Widenmann, George Washington, and George Robinson were all escorted to Fort Stanton, where the 52-year-old Lt. Col. Nathan Dudley was set to take over command in several days. The heavy-drinking, belligerent Dudley quickly developed an antipathy for the McSweens and the Regulators, although Susan McSween ensured that her husband, David Shield, and Rob Widenmann were confined in the post trader store rather than the guardhouse.[18]

As Alexander McSween prepared for the district court to convene, the Regulators were once again riding under Dick Brewer's command. They had recently bolstered their numbers, with George Coe, Ignacio González, John Scroggins, and the dimwitted "Dirty" Steve Stephens having joined their ranks. "The Murphy faction challenged the McSween faction to meet them at the José Chávez ranch to settle the matter with a pitched battle," Martín Chávez recalled. "The McSween men met the challenge but the Murphys failed to appear."[19]

The Regulators soon met with a correspondent from the *Mesilla Valley Independent*, during which Dick Brewer declared that he "neither advised nor consented" to the killing of William Brady. Some members of the Regulators voiced their intentions to kill Lawrence Murphy, Jimmy Dolan, and John Riley, but indignantly refuted any sympathy for Alexander McSween or connection with his legal affairs. "They say that the only object they have in view is to destroy the original band of thieves and murderers and kill them," the correspondent reported. "They say that if in the prosecution of this design they have violated the laws of the Territory, they are willing to stand the consequences." The Regulators had also heard rumors that Evans gang member Jimmy McDaniels and a party of men from the Río Grande were looking to "take a hand in the quarrel," and vowed to "put an end to their desire to interfere in a quarrel that don't concern them."[20]

After meeting with the newspaper correspondent, Dick Brewer led his Regulators onto the Mescalero reservation in pursuit of Morton posse members George Kitt and Andrew L. Roberts. They were unable to locate Kitt but ran into Roberts at Blazer's Mill with fatal consequences during the early afternoon of April 4, 1878. Dick Brewer and his Regulators were enjoying a meal inside the Godfroy house when John Middleton informed them of the "mighty well-armed" Roberts's presence at the mill. Frank Coe was there on separate business and tried to convince his former neighbor Roberts to surrender peacefully to his Regulator friends.

"No, never alive," Roberts replied. "The Kid is with you, and he will kill me on sight. There is the Kid and Bowdre, and if we had got them last week, we would have killed them."

Charlie Bowdre eventually marched around the corner of the Godfroy house alongside John Middleton, Frank MacNab, Henry Brown, and George Coe, all having volunteered to take the lethal Roberts into custody. Bowdre raised his Winchester rifle as they drew near the doorstep where Roberts and Frank Coe were seated.

"Roberts, throw up your hands!" Bowdre demanded.

"No," Roberts answered, as he raised up with own Winchester.

They both fired their rifles almost simultaneously and Bowdre's shot tore through Roberts's side. The bullet discharged by Roberts ricocheted off of Bowdre's belt buckle and clipped George Coe's right hand, destroying his trigger finger. Roberts then unloaded several more rounds and wounded John Middleton in the chest. Doc Scurlock, Billy Bonney, and some of the other Regulators quickly arrived on the scene, only for Roberts to fire a bullet into Scurlock's holstered revolver and wound Bonney in the arm. "I never saw a man who could handle a Winchester as fast as [Roberts] could," recalled Frank Coe.

When the mortally wounded Roberts took cover inside Henry Blazer's adobe house, Bill Bonney tried to put an end to the standoff with his revolver by sneaking along the side of the house toward the doorway, only to be slammed in the midriff by the nozzle of Roberts's empty Winchester rifle. Dick Brewer lost his temper inside the Godfroy home, threatening to burn Blazer's house down should Henry Blazer or Fred Godfroy not bring Roberts out to him. When both men refused to do so, Brewer slowly headed down the creek bed and positioned himself behind a pile of logs around 125 paces in front of Roberts's adobe refuge. Dick then gave away his position by firing a shot and grazing the doorframe. Roberts took steady aim with the Springfield rifle he had found inside the Blazer home and waited for Brewer to glance over the pile of logs one too many times. When Brewer's blonde locks came into view, Roberts squeezed the trigger and shot the leader of the Regulators through the head, killing him instantly.

With their captain slain, the remaining Regulators decided to withdraw from the standoff and hauled the wounded John Middleton and George Coe into the Ruidoso Valley. Middleton would slowly recover, although Dr. Taylor Ealy eventually had to sever Coe's right index finger. Andrew L. Roberts, alias Bill Williams, died from his wound at Blazer's Mill the following morning of April 5, 1878. Roberts was ironically buried with Dick Brewer inside a large V-shaped coffin on a nearby hill. "Yes, sir," Billy Bonney later conceded. "He licked our crowd to a finish."[21]

***

As guerrilla warfare was raging throughout the countryside, Juan Bautista Patrón and his county commissioners were scrambling to appoint a new sheriff following William Brady's demise. They chose John Copeland. The 37-year-old Kentuckian was appointed to office when the district court convened in Lincoln on April 10, 1878. Proceedings had been scheduled to commence two days earlier but were postponed owing to Judge Warren Bristol's ill health at the time. Precautions were also being taken after Lawrence G. Murphy sent word to Col. Nathan Dudley that the Regulators were planning to ambush Judge Bristol and District Attorney William Rynerson on their way in from La Mesilla.[22]

Juan Patrón's fellow representative John S. Crouch was appointed the court clerk when Judge Bristol and D. A. Rynerson finally arrived in Lincoln on April 10. When the grand jury venire was called, Rynerson immediately challenged the panel on the grounds that the jurors had been selected by John B. Wilson, who was no longer justice of the peace. Judge Bristol set aside the venire and instructed Sheriff John Copeland to select fifteen men to serve as grand jurors and twenty-four men to serve as petit jurors instead.

As Juan would have anticipated, his name was among those brought forward by Sheriff John Copeland when the grand jury was finally organized on

April 13. The Hispano representative was selected along with Joseph H. Blazer, Cresencio Sánches, Jerry Hackcradle, Francisco Pacheco, Wesley Fields, Juan José López, Ignacio de Guevara, R. M. Gilbert, Francisco Romero y Valencia, Andrew Wilson, Camilo Nuñes, Desiderio Zamora, Avery M. Clenny, and Martín Chávez's uncle-in-law Vicente Romero. Three of the jurors were designated as alternates, and Joseph H. Blazer was elected foreman.[23]

Juan Patrón and the other Hispano jurors were not solely focused on the district court proceedings at the time. Their people began celebrating Semana Santa (Holy Week) on Domingo de Ramos (Palm Sunday) on April 14. No amount of shootouts or court proceedings could hinder any Hispanos' devotion to his or her faith during the most important religious traditions of their calendar year. Some of them began an annual pilgrimage to a Roman Catholic church called El Santuario de Chimayó, located north of Santa Fe in Chimayó. The more superstitious Hispanas refused to wash their faces or cut their fingernails throughout the week, believing they would be washing the face and cutting the nails of Jesús Nazareno himself. The Penitentes offered prayers and sang alabados (hymns). They also performed scenes from the play La Pasión (the Passion of Jesus) inside their moradas and during their public processions held on Viernes Santo (Good Friday), although Bishop Jean Baptise Lamy and more conservative Hispanos like Juan Patrón disapproved of the brotherhood's more "savage" acts like self-flagellation.[24]

The district court proceedings finally got rolling in Lincoln on April 18, 1878. The grand jury brought murder indictments against John Middleton, Henry Brown, Fred Waite, and William Bonney for the killing of William Brady. While Judge Warren Bristol made a considerable effort to sway the grand jury in his opening charge, Alexander McSween was acquitted of embezzling the Fritz insurance funds the same day. "We fully exonerate him of the charge and regret that a spirit of persecution has been shown in the matter," the grand jury reported. Judge Bristol, District Attorney Rynerson, and Jimmy Dolan were stunned and outraged. Juan Patrón and his fellow Hispanos would have been far more concerned with offering prayers in a nearby chapel and refraining from eating any red meat throughout Viernes Santo the following day.[25]

Juan Patrón would have been hoping to see justice served when indictments were brought against James J. Dolan and Jacob "Billy" Mathews for accessory to his late friend John Tunstall's murder on April 20. Jessie Evans, George Davis, and Manuel "the Indian" Segovia were also indicted as principals. The grand jury was busy that day, as Charles Bowdre was indicted for the killing of Andrew L. Roberts, and Fred Waite was indicted for the killing of George Hindman. Jimmy Dolan and Billy Mathews each posted their $2,000 bonds, and warrants would be issued for the arrest of the absent Regulators.

All considerations Juan Patrón and the "Mexican" jurors held for the district court were put on the backburner for Domingo de Pascua (Easter Sunday) on April 21, 1878. The Hispanos of Nuevo México were all busy that day attending mass at the local chapel or Roman Catholic church, taking confession, singing hymns, enjoying a feast with their families, decorating hard-boiled eggs, or filling painted eggshells with confetti or perfume with which to gently break over somebody's head when inviting them to dance at a baile that night.

Having enjoyed the Easter Sunday festivities, Juan Patrón was back inside the small Lincoln courthouse when his old adversary John H. Riley was indicted for receiving stolen property on April 23. Constable Atanacio Martínez and a host of McSween partisans were charged with riot and resisting the sheriff. Martínez, Sam Corbet, George Washington, and George Robinson all appeared in court to plead not guilty, and Judge Bristol granted DA Rynerson's request for a change of venue to Doña Ana County. Rob Widenmann was also charged with obstructing a sheriff and resisting a deputy sheriff. He pleaded not guilty and was granted a change of venue with bail set at $500. The murder cases against Jimmy Dolan, Billy Mathews, Jessie Evans, George Davis, Manuel Segovia, Charles Bowdre, and Fred Waite were continued over to the next term of court.[26]

Juan Patrón and Alexander McSween would have felt a sense of jubilation in knowing the House was collapsing when the district court adjourned on April 24, 1878. Jimmy Dolan and John H. Riley had sent a public notice to the *Mesilla Valley Independent* the previous day announcing the suspension of all commerce in the J. J. Dolan & Co. store, declaring "the condition of affairs now existing in this county is such as to make it unsafe for the undersigned to further continue business as they have heretofore done." Their friend Thomas B. Catron would soon foreclose on the properties Dolan and Riley had mortgaged to him three months earlier.[27]

The district court had adjourned when Juan Patrón called for a meeting of citizens to be held inside the small courthouse that afternoon. Many locals gathered inside the adobe building on one hour's notice to "express their sentiments relative to the present troubles." Juan promptly called the meeting to order, nominating Probate Judge Florencio Gonzáles as president of the board, Saturnino Baca and José Montaño as vice presidents, and Alexander McSween and Ben Ellis as secretaries. Florencio Gonzáles then gave a rousing speech that was met with rippling applause from those in attendance. Juan Patrón and José Montaño also gave speeches that were equally well received. Juan Patrón, John Chisum, and Avery M. Clenny were appointed to a committee to "draft and submit resolutions" that were "unanimously adopted" by those present.[28]

The seven resolutions recorded during Juan Patrón's assembly suggested the "present troubles" were only "a continuation of old feuds" and would "now cease as the cause has been removed." The resolutions also offered thanks to Col. Nathan Dudley for his impartiality, and condemnation of Governor Samuel Axtell for his "unworthy" proclamation and his "refusal to investigate our troubles," which "stamp[ed] him as a little, one-sided partisan" and render[ed] him "responsible for the loss of life that has occurred in this county since his visit."

Further resolutions expressed sentiments of racial harmony between the local "Mexicans and Americans" and gratitude for the US officers in Fort Stanton and Sheriff John Copeland. The document was signed by Florencio Gonzáles, Alexander McSween, and Ben Ellis before copies were mailed to President Rutherford B. Hayes, Secretary of War George McCrary, and Governor Axtell, as well as to the *Mesilla Valley Independent* and *Cimarron News and Press* for publication. Juan Patrón, Florencio Gonzáles, and Isaac Ellis would also present the resolutions to Col. Nathan Dudley personally, in "English and Spanish as a token of respect."[29]

For all of Juan Patrón's leadership and initiative, the resolutions drafted that day proved overly optimistic and ineffectual. While Alexander McSween had started a petition for J. J. Dolan & Co. to leave Lincoln County and never return, Jimmy Dolan escorted the dying Lawrence Murphy to Santa Fe. Their allies Governor Axtell and Thomas B. Catron were happy to assist in the war against the Scotsman and the Regulators. John Riley also headed for Las Cruces, where he gave the Regulators "more dirt than any of them" as Frank Coe recalled.

The Regulators were not ready to put their guns away, and Col. Nathan Dudley's impartiality would only last so long. Alexander McSween had drafted a $5,000 reward notice, authorized by John Tunstall's father, for the "apprehension and conviction of the murderers of his son." The notice was published in the *Mesilla Valley Independent* the following month for all to see. The Lincoln County War was far from over.[30]

***

Frank MacNab had taken over leadership of the Regulators following Dick Brewer's death, and he sent word to the ranchers down in Seven Rivers that his vigilantes would clean out those who had played a hand in John Tunstall's murder. Roughly thirty ranchers in Seven Rivers rallied around former Brady deputy William H. Johnson and began preparing for war. "G. W. Peppin told them that this was John Chisum's war," Billy Bonney later recalled. "So they took a hand thinking they would lose their cattle."[31]

The Seven Rivers bunch were comprised of various members of the late Bill Morton's posse, which had carried out the murder of John Tunstall, including Yginio Salazar's nemesis Bob Beckwith, John Wallace Olinger, Sam Perry, and Manuel "the Indian" Segovia. Also in their ranks were local ruffians Marion Turner, "Dutch" Charlie Kruling, Thomas "Buck" Powell, Milo Pierce, Josiah "Joe" Nash, William "Jake" Owens, and a brawny, overbearing psychopath named Ameredith Robert "Bob" Olinger.[32]

The Seven River Warriors began riding northwest toward Lincoln alongside former Brady deputies George Peppin, Jack Long, and Johnny Hurley, soon helping themselves to some of the late John Tunstall's horses on the Río Feliz. They also ambushed Frank MacNab, Frank Coe, and James "Ab" Saunders at the Fritz ranch in the late afternoon of April 29, 1878. Frank MacNab was shot in the chest, fell from his bucking horse, and then was chased into a canyon and finished off by Manuel "the Indian" Segovia with a shotgun blast. Ab Saunders was shot through the hip and ankle while fleeing over a hillock. Saunders's cousin Frank Coe eventually surrendered after his horse was shot in the head and he took cover in a dry arroyo. The Seven Rivers fighters had mistaken Coe for Billy "Kid" Bonney due to their similar height and slender build.[33]

Sheriff John Copeland and the Regulators had received word of the ambush by the time the Seven Rivers bunch escorted Frank Coe, the wounded Ab Saunders, and Frank MacNab's corpse to the outskirts of Lincoln in the early morning of April 30. Sheriff Copeland had demonstrated his partisanship by siding with the vigilante Regulators and appealing to Fort Stanton for assistance. The sheriff and the Regulators had then taken cover on various rooftops and within several homes around town and awaited the arrival of the Seven Rivers bunch with a firm grip on their firearms.

When George Coe spotted "Dutch" Charlie Kruling around four hundred yards distant from the roof of the Ellis store, he took steady aim with his rifle and fired a bullet into Kruling's hip. Juan Patrón, Saturnino Baca, and other citizens remained confined to their homes as the Regulators and Seven Rivers fighters exchanged shots throughout Lincoln for the next few hours. Frank Coe was left unattended by his captors in the Dolan store and quickly took position alongside his comrades. Half a dozen Seven Rivers men were reportedly wounded during the exchanges. None of the Regulators took so much as a scratch.[34]

The latest eruption of gunfire in Lincoln concluded when the overwhelmed Seven Rivers party retreated into the mountains. Capt. George Smith arrived later that afternoon with fifteen soldiers at Sheriff Copeland's behest. He arrested the Seven Rivers men but allowed them to keep their rifles and revolvers. Copeland, the troopers, the Seven Rivers fighters, and the wounded Ab Saunders were then escorted to Fort Stanton. The body of Frank MacNab remained in Lincoln to be buried alongside John Tunstall behind the Tunstall store corral on May 2, 1878. Some of the Regulators accompanied Alexander McSween downriver to San Patricio once Taylor F. Ealy was finished conducting the funeral service.

Alexander McSween appealed to local Justice of the Peace José Gregorio Trujillo in San Patricio, swearing affidavits against eighteen members of the Seven Rivers posse for the killing of Frank MacNab. His friend Juan Patrón was soon observing the chaotic scenes in Lincoln when Sheriff John Copeland returned from Fort Stanton. The sheriff had failed to acquire a military escort from Col. Nathan Dudley to assist him in transporting the loosely confined Seven Rivers prisoners to San Patricio. Dudley had chosen a side in the war and ordered Copeland to ride for Lincoln and San Patricio alongside two of his lieutenants and arrest Alexander McSween, Rob Widenmann, and the Regulators on charges of riot instead.

Sheriff John Copeland did as Col. Nathan Dudley ordered and reluctantly arrested Doc Scurlock, Rob Widenmann, Ignacio González, John Scroggins, Isaac Ellis, Will Ellis, and Sam Corbet when returning to Lincoln. The sickly Sam Corbet was allowed to remain in town, but the rest were escorted to Fort Stanton and locked inside the guardhouse. Copeland then rode for San Patricio and arrested Alexander McSween and George Washington, both of whom joined Doc Scurlock and their allies in confinement at Fort Stanton. Bill Bonney, José Chávez y Chávez, Charlie Bowdre, John Middleton, Frank and George Coe, Francisco Trujillo, and several other Hispano fighters had ridden into the mountains roughly an hour before Copeland arrived.

Col. Nathan Dudley palmed off any responsibility for the many prisoners at Fort Stanton, leaving Sheriff Copeland with little alternative but to reluctantly release the Seven Rivers fighters. They bolted southeast toward the Río Pecos. Copeland also escorted Doc Scurlock and the McSween partisans back to Lincoln several days later. He then swore Scurlock in as a deputy, providing Doc with the legal status with which to assume leadership of the Regulators.[35]

Doc Scurlock and his Regulators regrouped and decided to raid the Dolan–Riley cattle camp near Black River on the Río Pecos on May 14, 1878. They eagerly rustled some livestock from the camp, perhaps unaware the Dolan–Riley herds now legally belonged to the all-powerful Thomas B. Catron. The Regulators also located Miguel "the Indian" Segovia, who had played a hand in John Tunstall's murder and more recently ended Frank MacNab's life near the Fritz ranch. As Francisco Trujillo remembered things,

Segovia was inside an adobe hut with two Texans just across the Río Pecos. Trujillo recalled accompanying Constable Atanacio Martínez, Billy Bonney, and John Scroggins to the adobe building and approaching the front door.

"¿Cómo estás, Kiko?" (How are you, Kiko?), Manuel Segovia called out when spotting Francisco Trujillo outside.

"Ven afuera" (Come on out), Trujillo replied. "Has matado a Macky Nane" (You have killed MacNab).

Segovia emerged from the hut and sheepishly admitted to having shot Frank MacNab, claiming to have done so under the command of Robert Beckwith and from fear of reprisal. The Regulators were in no mood to hear any excuses regarding the recent death of their former captain and took the man known as "the Indian" into custody.

"¡Qué no me maten, Kiko!" (Don't let them kill me, Kiko!), Segovia pleaded to Francisco Trujillo.[36]

The Regulators escorted their prisoner north toward Roswell, presumably intending to sell their stolen livestock to John Chisum at his nearby South Spring ranch. "Old Chisum had promised to pay us $5 for every cow that we would bring in whether his, Murphy's, or anybody else's," José Chávez y Chávez later said. They were roughly two miles south of Roswell when Doc Scurlock, José Chávez y Chávez, and Bill Bonney proposed they put an end to Manuel "the Indian" Segovia.

"Is it not better to take him in and let the law have its course?" Francisco Trujillo naively asked José Chávez y Chávez.

"Come on, Francisco," Charlie Bowdre said, having overheard Trujillo's suggestion. "Let us be running along."

Trujillo and Bowdre rode about fifty yards along the trail before Francisco looked over his shoulder and saw Manuel "the Indian" Segovia trying to escape his captors by galloping away on horseback. José Chávez y Chávez and Bill Bonney quickly spurred their horses and chased after him. They both continued firing shots until Segovia fell dead from his saddle.[37]

Francisco Trujillo, José Chávez y Chávez, Sequio Sánchez, Billy Bonney, and several others gathered around Manuel "The Indian" Segovia's fallen corpse and observed the ramifications of frontier justice. The killing of Frank MacNab had been avenged. Bloodshed was nothing new for the hardened

José Chávez y Chávez, who had already acquired a healthy collection of scars in various fights throughout his years on the Río Ruidoso. His young compadre Bill Bonney broke the silence when casting his blue eyes over the slain Segovia's horse in the distance and glancing at Francisco Trujillo.

"Francisco," the Kid said, "here are the saddle and trappings that I owe you."

Trujillo was not in the mood to go chasing after a dead man's horse and asked Sequio Sánchez to fetch the animal instead. When noticing that Francisco was repulsed by Manuel Segovia's smeared blood on the saddle, the seasoned Doc Scurlock took pity on him. The deputized Regulator offered to exchange saddles with Trujillo for the time being and clean off the blood himself. It had already been a rough day for Kiko.[38]

***

Juan Patrón had a lot on his mind as the summer began on June 1, 1878. A special agent named Frank Warner Angel had arrived in Lincoln County several weeks earlier, having been dispatched by Washington to investigate John Tunstall's murder and the corruption of territorial officials in Nuevo México. The federal investigation was set in motion by the letters Montague Leverson and Rob Widenmann had mailed to government officials throughout the previous months. Angel had publicly announced his arrival in Fort Stanton and began taking sworn statements from some of the locals on May 14.[39]

Juan also had to stomach the recent appointment of another House-affiliated sheriff in Lincoln County. Jimmy Dolan and Lawrence Murphy had arrived in Santa Fe earlier that month to meet with Thomas B. Catron, and he presumably informed Governor Axtell that Sheriff John Copeland failed to post bond as tax collector. Axtell subsequently issued a proclamation on May 28 in which he removed John Copeland from office and appointed George W. Peppin to replace him. Jimmy Dolan had regained control of the legal system in Lincoln County and the Irishman soon returned to the Río Bonito. His dying compatriot Lawrence G. Murphy would remain in Santa Fe for the final months of his life.[40]

Jimmy Dolan had also written a letter that was published by the *New Mexican* on May 25, 1878. The Irishman publicly condemned "the so called regulators" as "assassins" who possessed the balance of "tramps without name or character" and pitifully denied having started "a fight of violence" in Lincoln County. He also accused Juan Patrón of having conspired to assassinate his friend Jessie Evans and the Boys while they were being held in the Lincoln jail the previous year:

> It is now the subject to proof that Juan B. Patron and other villains like him had entered into a conspiracy for the purpose of assassinating men under charge of sheriff Brady and in the county jail, and it is easy of proof that Patron, McSween, and Chism were only deterred there-from by the earnest exertion of Sheriff Brady and a few other citizens who desired the law to be enforced. The night they intended carrying out this brutal act, I was in Mr. Patron's house, the Head Quarters of the would be assassins; and I will here ask Mr. Patron if he remembers asking Sheriff Brady if "the prisoners had any sympathizers present;" and sheriff Brady's answer, "no only in so far as seeing them done justice."[41]

In addition to Jimmy Dolan's hostile letter, Juan Patrón had to deal with other ramifications of the Lincoln County War. The Hispano chairman and his commissioners realized the ongoing warfare was slowing the filing of many tax assessments throughout the countryside. The Patrón commission took a hard-nosed approach in dealing with the matter by levying a 25 percent increase on the assessments of any delinquent taxpayers. The commission also acquiesced to a petition from various taxpayers by increasing the probate judge's salary to $200 per annum. Juan may have viewed William L. Rynerson with contempt, but he dutifully approved payment of $25 to the district attorney for services rendered during the April term of court.[42]

The Patrón store would have been taking a considerable hit financially throughout the spring and early summer of 1878. Lincoln had become a place that many people avoided if at all possible. "Conditions were getting so desperate that everyone had to line up on one side or the other," recalled George Coe. Some citizens were even fleeing their adobe homes and seeking refuge in Doña Ana County for the time being. "The history of Lincoln County has been one of bloodshed from the day of its organization," the *Mesilla Valley Independent* had declared. "A spirit of murder and kindred crimes seems to pervade the very atmosphere."[43]

Juan Patrón inevitably met with Special Agent Frank Warner Angel and provided his sworn statement on June 6, 1878. The 33-year-old, slick-haired Angel listened intently as the most respected and influential Hispano citizen of Lincoln County provided him with details of his various conflicts with Lawrence Murphy, Jimmy Dolan, John Riley, and William Brady throughout the previous seven years. Juan also read the lengthy affidavit that Alexander McSween had submitted to Angel the same day, assuring the special agent that "so far [as] it refers to me, the statements made by me, it is true."[44]

As if Juan didn't have enough on his plate at the time, the commissioner had also been summoned for jury duty when Judge Warren Bristol's court convened in La Mesilla, Doña Ana County, on June 10, 1878. As much as Juan may have wished to see Jessie Evans convicted for the murder of John Tunstall in Bristol's courtroom, traveling to La Mesilla was extremely hazardous for anyone with McSween sympathies at the time. Sheriff George Peppin, John Riley, and William L. Rynerson had acquired the services of the fearsome John Kinney and members of his Río Grande posse to wage war against the McSween faction. Jimmy Dolan reportedly offered further incentive by promising to reward Kinney and his band of ruffians with the late John Tunstall's cattle should they kill Alexander McSween.

With pitiless killers loyal to Jimmy Dolan and Sheriff Peppin scattered along the trails leading into the Mesilla Valley, the apprehensive Juan Patrón sent an urgent message to Col. Nathan Dudley when the Mesilla district court was scheduled to convene on June 10, 1878. He requested a military escort for himself and other local jurors when making their upcoming journey into Doña Ana County, declaring there were "armed men waylaying the roads" with the "purpose of taking our lives." Colonel Dudley complied with Juan's request, providing affidavits that were presented confirming their jury duties. Juan and the other jurors assembled at Fort Stanton three days later and were safely escorted to La Mesilla.[45]

Juan Patrón would have been in attendance when Jessie Evans faced his indictment for the murder of John Tunstall in the Mesilla courthouse. Rob Widenmann also arrived with the military escort to provide testimony, informing John Tunstall's father that Thomas B. Catron immediately "began cathauling me here." Juan presumably shook his head in embarrassment when Tunstall's lickspittle was arrested for the possession of two concealed pistols inside the courthouse. The Hispano representative also may have watched as District Attorney William L. Rynerson laid waste to Widenmann's testimony when he took the stand. Widenmann was forced to admit that he had not actually observed John Tunstall being shot. Jessie Evans naturally denied any involvement in the Englishman's murder, and the notorious badman went free.[46]

Juan Patrón was traveling back to Lincoln when he encountered Indian Agent Erwin Curtis Watkins. The Civil War veteran had recently arrived at the Mescalero agency to investigate the accusations of stock appropriation and poor food distribution that Alexander McSween had levied against Agent Fred Godfroy and J. J. Dolan & Co. back in February. Watkins obtained sworn statements from many locals throughout his investigation, and Juan Patrón provided his own deposition on June 18, 1878. "Statement mostly hearsay, a reliable man although strong McSween partisan," Watkins scribbled in reference to Juan's deposition and character. A backpedaling Alexander McSween admitted that he had been relying on hearsay from Stephen Stanley when providing his own statement. Agent Watkins ultimately concluded that supplies had been borrowed and returned by J. J. Dolan & Co., but he found no evidence of spoiled food having been distributed to the Indians.[47]

Juan scarcely found the time to enjoy a cigarillo after returning to Lincoln before fleeing to San Patricio alongside Alexander McSween and the Regulators on June 19, 1878. Col. Nathan Dudley had granted Sheriff George Peppin's request for military assistance the night before, and John Kinney and his band of marauders had recently reached the Río Bonito to help pursue McSween and the Regulators. Meanwhile, Thomas B. Catron convened a grand jury in Santa Fe on June 21 and filed federal murder charges against Charlie Bowdre, Doc Scurlock, Henry Brown, William "Kid" Bonney, John Middleton, Steve Stephens, John Scroggins, George Coe, and Fred Waite for the killing of Andrew L. Roberts at Blazer's Mill. The leading figure of the Santa Fe Ring insisted the shooting had occurred on federal land in his jurisdiction. Juan Patrón soon grew tired of life on the run and returned to Lincoln. His friend Alexander McSween and the Regulators decided to split into smaller groups and lay low for a few days.[48]

Juan had barely returned to Lincoln before an intoxicated member of Sheriff Peppin's posse threatened to shoot him in the back near the Montaño store. More alarmingly, an uninvited ruffian burst through the back door of Juan's home with a pistol during the night of June 23, 1878. It was Jim Reese, one of Jimmy Dolan and Sheriff Peppin's hired guns. Juan firmly believed Reese would have murdered him that night had "Major" Michael Cronin not also been in his house at the time. The commissioner sent a message to Col. Nathan Dudley the following morning of el Día de San Juan (St. John's Day), asking if he could stay at Fort Stanton for a while. "I have a good deal of business appertaining to the county to attend to," Juan informed the colonel. "Under the present state of affairs in this town, I cannot attend to them." Dudley sent a note in response later that evening recognizing Juan's status as "an honest citizen." He assured the Hispano commissioner that he could find protection at the fort. "I shall try and get up to the post tomorrow, the best way I can," Juan subsequently informed Dudley. "I am exceedingly thankful to you for the kindness you have shown towards me in this matter."[49]

The appreciative Juan Patrón convened his commissioners and ordered payment of a bill from Sheriff George W. Peppin for the construction of a pair of window shutters and a ladder for the Lincoln jail on the morning of June 25, 1878. He then borrowed a horse from a neighbor and accompanied a soldier upriver to Fort Stanton. The Hispano politician was welcome to stay in the post trader's store, for the time being at least.[50]

***

The 18-year-old Yginio Salazar needed only one incentive to begin riding with the Regulators in the late spring or early summer of 1878. Robert Beckwith was on the opposing side. "I got into the Lincoln County War because Bob Beckwith stole some cattle from me," the young vaquero later said. Yginio had already developed sympathies for the McSween partisans while working as a Chisum cowhand. He was determined to get Beckwith one way or another, and he later claimed Alexander McSween threatened to fine him fifty dollars if he didn't join the fight anyway. Like many local Hispanos, Yginio had also befriended Billy "Kid" Bonney, finding him great company. Joining up with little Billy and the Regulators would have been an instinctive move for the young scrapper. "You were either on one side or the other," Yginio later declared. "There was no inbetween."[51]

The Nuevomexicanos of San Patricio were also becoming further immersed in the Lincoln County War during the early summer of 1878. The inhabitants continued providing the Regulators with shelter whenever the vigilantes needed a place to hide out. The sound of gunfire emanating from the outskirts of their placita was becoming an increasingly frequent occurrence. John Kinney and his Río Grande posse were spending a considerable amount of time searching for the Regulators in the Bonito Valley and ambushed Frank and George Coe just outside San Patricio in the final week of June 1878. The Coe boys were fortunate to escape with their lives.[52]

The Regulators also had to contend with Sheriff George W. Peppin and his own posse of ruffians at the time. Jimmy Dolan had recently returned to Lincoln and was able to walk on his damaged leg with the use of a cane. The Irishman was determined to put an end to Alexander McSween and his band of "assassins." His lackey Sheriff Peppin had recently deputized Jack Long, Marion Turner, and William "Buck" Powell in Lincoln. Peppin also deputized Saturnino Baca's brother-in-law José Chávez y Baca, which may have been an attempt to gain the support of local Hispanos and provide the sheriff with a set of eyes and ears among la gente.[53]

Florencio Cháves was still in Tularosa when he received a letter from his beloved mother in San Patricio around this time. A couple of House partisans had recently stolen the thirty dollars that Florencio had left behind for her and his sister when departing back in April. "This bunch got a Mexican and an American to go into our house, broke the trunk," he remembered. Florencio couldn't abide this. He promptly returned to the Río Ruidoso to discuss the matter with his amigo José Chávez y Chávez. "He told me I would have to go over and take chances of getting [the] money back," Florencio recalled. "Mama told me that she knew the man that took that money." Florencio and José Chávez y Chávez managed to capture the hombre responsible soon after. José was determined to kill their Hispano prisoner, but Florencio managed to dissuade him, keeping the Dolan partisan's rifle and six-shooter as compensation instead. Florencio turned the prisoner loose and decided to join up with the Regulators. "That was how I got into the war," he later reminisced.[54]

The Hispanos of San Patricio were going about their business when gunfire erupted in their midst on the morning of June 27, 1878. Deputy Jack Long and five Dolan partisans had decided to try their luck finding the Regulators the night before and positioned themselves just outside of the placita. They were unable to find any of the Regulators but spotted McSween servant George Washington strolling across a wheat field. The Black man threw his hands in the air when bullets started whistling past his head. Deputy Long and his cohorts were escorting their prisoner back to Lincoln when they ran into former sheriff John Copeland, Alexander McSween, Billy Bonney, Charlie Bowdre, Atanacio Martínez, Sequio Sánchez, Jesús Rodríguez, and several others on the outskirts of the village. The two parties exchanged shots, and Jack Long's horse was killed beneath him. The deputy sent a courier to Fort Stanton for assistance, but the Regulators had skinned out by the time the troopers arrived.

Sheriff Peppin and his deputies were no longer able to call for military assistance after Col. Nathan Dudley acknowledged receipt of his new orders from the district headquarters "forbidding the use of the army as a posse comitatus" on June 28. Now having to fight his own battles, Sheriff Peppin used a legal summons to strong-arm fifteen local Nuevomexicanos into service and placed them under the command of Deputy José Chávez y Baca. The sheriff sent them to San Patricio to search for the McSween partisans on July 3, 1878. This time the Regulators were not only there but also well positioned on various rooftops. Deputy Chávez y Baca and his fifteen hombres stormed into San Patricio like conquering heroes at daybreak, only to begin fleeing for their lives when the Regulators opened fire on them. Some of their horses were cut down beneath them, and posseman Julián López was wounded in the arm. "We made it so hot for them they had to back off in a hurry," recalled George Coe.

The besieged Deputy José Chávez y Baca held his position on the outskirts of San Patricio and sent a messenger upriver to Lincoln to acquire some assistance. Jimmy Dolan swung his healing broken leg over his saddle to lead a posse consisting of Sheriff George Peppin, John Kinney, Jack Long, George Davis, former Dolan store clerk Pantaleon Gallegos, Juan José Parada, Lucio Montoya, and various other ruffians to San Patricio.

The McSween partisans had already skinned out and headed east by the time they arrived. Dolan's posse rode after them but were repelled by a burst of gunfire coming from the crest of a ridge four miles east of the placita. Having turned away their pursuers for the time being, Alexander McSween and the Regulators continued riding for the Chisum ranch on South Spring.[55]

The frustrated Dolan party returned to San Patricio and decided to teach the Hispano residents a lesson for harboring Alexander McSween and the Regulators. When Jimmy Dolan ordered every home to be searched, his cohorts began breaking through doors, smashing windows, ransacking houses, robbing the inhabitants, shooting horses, stealing ponies, and terrorizing any "Mexican" in sight. Men, women, and even children were subjected to vulgar insults. The Dolan partisans also physically assaulted a few of the locals and began randomly firing their guns at the farmers working in their nearby fields. The workers dropped their wooden tools and ran for their lives. A local named Juan Lucero was taken prisoner when he proved either incapable or unwilling to provide any information about the McSween party's whereabouts. A 44-year-old laborer named Felipe Silva worked up the nerve to approach Jimmy Dolan and ask him on what authority the roof of the Dow store was being torn down and its inventory pilfered.

"By my orders," Dolan informed him.[56]

The Irishman's posse then headed back up to Lincoln once they were finished their pillaging. Pantaleon Gallegos turned their prisoner Juan Lucero loose during the journey and told him that he could return to his placita. Susan McSween spotted John Kinney leading her mare Pet through town when they returned and assumed the King of the Rustlers had carried out his threat to kill her husband. Susan grabbed a shotgun and confronted the Dolan partisans at the western end of town, threatening to kill someone if her Pet was not returned to her. She then began screaming outside the Baca home, believing Deputy José Chávez y Baca's brother-in-law Saturnino Baca was involved in a conspiracy to kill her husband. The former sheriff was hardly in the mood for false accusations. His wife Juana was due to give birth to another child any day now. Saturnino firmly denied any involvement in a plot to kill Mac. Susan declared in broken Spanish that she had enough money to hire men to kill Capitán Baca and his family before angrily storming away.[57]

While Saturnino Baca was engaging in a war of words with an irate Susan McSween, the residents of San Patricio were rallying around Justice of the Peace José Gregorio Trujillo. Many local farmers were reluctant to resume working in their fields for fear of being attacked by the Dolan party again. A petition requesting military protection was sent to Col. Nathan Dudley in Fort Stanton. Dudley was unable to provide any assistance but offered to provide refuge for any traumatized citizens at the post. He also sent Capt. Thomas Blair downriver to investigate the incident. Juan Patrón was now keeping residence in the post traders store and decided to accompany Captain Blair to San Patricio to serve as an interpreter. His people were suffering.[58]

Capt. Thomas Blair and Juan Patrón arrived in San Patricio with some of the 15th Infantry on July 11, 1878. They visited various houses, with Juan translating the testimony of the Hispano residents for the Americano officer. News of the raid had reached the Regulators and their Hispano allies at South Spring, and some Chisum vaqueros had recently arrived in the placita to protect the locals. José Manuel Gutiérrez informed Blair of the harassment and vulgar insults that he and his female relatives had endured from Deputy José Chávez y Baca, Juan José Parada, and George Davis when they had searched his house. His adobe home was now being guarded by seven armed Hispanos. Captain Blair and Juan Patrón visited the busted-up Dow home, where they spoke to Nepomuceno Carbajal and found panes of broken glass, three broken doors, and the dismantled remains of an upper room. They also took statements from Felipe Silva, María Chávez, Gregorio Jiron, Juan Sedillo, and Francisco García, whose homes had all been broken into by Dolan partisans. Even an adobe house in which some orphaned Hispano children resided had been broken into and busted up. Justice José Gregorio Trujillo informed Blair that "the people had applied to him for protection, which he was unable to afford them," and "much of the wheat in the valley was ready for reaping, but the people were afraid to attend to it."[59]

Although Capt. Thomas Blair had acquired more than enough testimony and observed plenty of physical evidence of the Dolan posse's reprehensible behavior in San Patricio, the officer was unwilling to take the word of the local Hispanos at face value. "None of the statements made to me were under oath, nor were any affidavits presented, only the simply verbal statements of those whose names are given," Blair reported to Col. Nathan Dudley the following day. "I went from house to house and saw the depredations alleged to have been committed by the Sheriff's posse. It is to be understood I do not vouch for the truth of any of the statements made to me, and here presented. What I do know and all I know is that a portion of a house appears to have been recently torn down, and several doors give evidence of having been forcibly entered." A letter signed "Lincoln" was soon mailed to the *Cimarron News and Press*, detailing the assault on San Patricio by "Axtell's sheriff and J. J. Dolan" and "the Rio Grande posse."[60]

While Jimmy Dolan and his partisans would never answer for their actions in San Patricio, if their intentions were to dissuade the local Hispano populace from providing any further support for the Regulators, then it proved a grievous error in judgment. News of their scornful initiative spread rapidly throughout the countryside and only galvanized Hispano support for the McSween partisans. Martín Chávez heard accounts of the Dolan posse's conduct and was suitably appalled. "The Murphy crowd was becoming overbearing, intolerable, and very dangerous," Martín later said. "They helped themselves to whatever they wanted—anywhere. If any one of them found a woman or a girl unprotected or alone, she was treated with insult and horrible usage. Their conduct caused them to be intensely hated."[61]

As the Dolan faction were earning the hatred of many local Hispanos, Alexander McSween and the Regulators arrived at the Chisum ranch on South Spring by July 4, 1878. They spent the next few days at the hacienda fighting off a posse of Seven Rivers men led by Marion Turner, Buck Powell, and Milo Pierce. The Seven Rivers party eventually withdrew from the siege. McSween and the Regulators then headed back toward San Patricio while managing to avoid any pursuers. "We have to look for them like Indians," the frustrated Robert Beckwith wrote to his sister. As Beckwith soon discovered, the Regulators had much bigger plans than merely engaging in another random skirmish out in the open country.[62]

Saturnino Baca emerged from his home in Lincoln and proudly instructed a local boy to fire off several shots in celebration of the birth of his new son on the morning of July 11, 1878. "It is a custom of the Mexican people to fire off their arms when a child is born," Saturnino later recalled. "Especially when a boy is born." When the celebratory shots rang out, the former sheriff quickly spotted some of the Regulators emerging from several buildings and firing off their own guns toward the eastern end of town. They were trying to draw the Dolan partisans out of Lincoln. Saturnino watched as the McSween partisans spent the next hour riding up and down the lower end of the placita. Sheriff George Peppin and his cohorts refused to take the bait, and the Regulators eventually withdrew for the time being.[63]

While Saturnino and Juana Baca had just welcomed another child into the world, María Bonifacia Chávez Brady was fearful of losing one of her own when departing her farmhouse to undertake a twelve-mile journey upriver to Fort Stanton on July 12, 1878. There were tears streaming down the widow's dark cheeks when she finally arrived at Col. Nathan Dudley's quarters. María informed the colonel that Doc Scurlock and two other men had deplorably fired shots at her 14-year-old son William Brady Jr. in a canyon roughly half a mile from their home.

"They have murdered my poor husband," María pleaded. "And not satisfied with this, they now want to kill my boy."

Colonel Dudley sympathized with Señora Brady and suggested the widow bring her son to the fort where he could watch over him. María was unwilling to do so. As dangerous as things were around Lincoln, she desperately needed her eldest son William Jr. to assist with the farming on their homestead. The colonel sent a soldier to guard the Brady home for the next few days instead. "The actions of leading men on both sides, some of whom are holding prominent relations to the government is infamous," Dudley reported to the district headquarters on July 13, 1878. "So alarmed, I am informed, are the laboring classes in some sections of the county, that they do not dare leave their homes to work in the fields."

The same day Col. Nathan Dudley scrawled his latest report in Fort Stanton, the Regulators reinforced their commitment to fight when composing a letter to Thomas B. Catron's brother-in-law Edgar Walz: "We know that your brother-in-law T. B. Catron sustains the Murphy-Kinney party, and take this method of informing you that if any property belonging to the residents of this county is stolen or destroyed, Mr. Catron's property will be dealt with. . . . We know that the Tunstall estate cattle are pledged to Kinney and party. If they are taken, a similar number will be taken from your brother . . . steal from the poorest or richest American or Mexican, and the full measure of the injury you do, shall be visited upon the property of Mr. Catron."[64]

Having issued threats of retaliation against Thomas B. Catron himself, the Regulators once again tried to goad their enemies out of Lincoln on July 14, 1878. Deputy Jack Long and some Dolan partisans initially tried to pursue the McSween men but wisely pulled back and kept position in the torreón. Jack Long knew the Regulators were merely "trying to draw us out" and spotted some of the vigilantes "lying down in ambush in an arroyo waiting for some of us to go after them," as he later recalled. The Regulators eventually gave up and rode off down the Río Bonito.[65]

After failing to lure the Dolan partisans out of Lincoln for the second time, Alexander McSween and the Regulators began riding downriver toward Picacho. They were determined to make a big fight in Lincoln and settle things with the Dolan faction once and for all. To carry out such an initiative, the McSween partisans required a designated leader to come up with an effective strategy. They needed an hombre who was widely respected, sympathetic to their cause, willing to fight, and capable of rallying more "Mexicans" to take up arms against the House and their Santa Fe Ring backers.

They needed Martín Chávez.

Chapter 7

The Burning House

I intend to do battle with them and slay them.
—Miguel de Cervantes, *Don Quixote*

Martín Chávez had already made clear his dissatisfaction with the state of affairs in Lincoln County before stepping outside his adobe home to greet his guests in Picacho on July 14, 1878. Alexander McSween and the Regulators were well aware of Martín's disdain for their enemies when arriving at his doorstep that afternoon. "We knew him to be one of our sympathizers," recalled George Coe. "Although he had never entered actively into an engagement. He was a [former] deputy sheriff, a conservative, and was not satisfied with conditions as they existed." The Regulators also realized how much weight the 25-year-old Martín's word carried with the "Mexicans" residing on the Río Hondo.[1]

Martín greeted Alexander McSween, José Chávez y Chávez, Yginio Salazar, and their compadres before listening to their proposition. There were roughly forty of them. They were all heavily-armed, except for McSween, who never carried a gun. Martín was already familiar with the little buck-toothed fellow known as Kid. Like many of his people, the mayordomo of Picacho had taken a shine to young Billy Bonney, appreciating his gentlemanly manner and warm, fun-loving nature. The McSween partisans had not approached Martín to merely exchange pleasantries, water their horses on the Río Hondo, or dance with some of the local señoritas at a baile that evening. They wanted the former deputy sheriff to lead them into battle.

Martín listened intently as Alexander McSween and the Regulators offered him uncontested leadership over their fighting force. "We took our problem to him and asked him to aid us in solving it," recalled George Coe. "We requested him to take on the leadership of our band, and promised to abide by his decisions and follow his plans." Martín had grown to detest the Dolan faction and readily accepted the offer. This was his chance to set things right, but he needed to come up with an effective strategy for their offensive. Martín determined that their best option was to stealthily make their way into Lincoln after nightfall, corral their horses at the eastern end of town, and position themselves throughout various buildings while hopefully remaining undetected. They needed to "gain a toehold before any resistance could be offered," as George Coe later described Chávez's plan of action.

Alexander McSween and the Regulators agreed with Martín's plan of action, but they needed to bolster their numbers first. Martín utilized his notoriety in Picacho when recruiting more than a dozen of the local "Mexicans" to join their cause. His uncle-in-law Vicente Romero was among those willing to wage war against the House. They decided to ride for Lincoln when the Dolan partisans in town would hopefully be asleep or passed out drunk for the night. Martín and his Hispano recruits gathered as much ammunition and provisions as they could carry before hugging their relatives when it was time to depart. Martín left his worried wife Juanita to take care of their homestead and began leading over fifty men through the darkness upriver toward Lincoln.[2]

Martín Chávez and his horde of McSween partisans successfully reached the eastern end of La Placita without being spotted by any of the locals. They dismounted their horses in the Ellis corral, took hold of their weapons, and began quietly taking their positions. "The townspeople were enjoying the peaceful July night undisturbed as we worked in silence," recalled George Coe. "Chávez placed us in various sections of town." Jimmy Dolan and Sheriff George Peppin were up the street in the Wortley Hotel, having recently sent a large posse led by John Kinney and Buck Powell to search for the Regulators in the vicinity of San Patricio once again. Jack Long, Billy Mathews, Sam Perry, Jimmy McDaniels, George "Roxy" Rose, and a man known as Dummy were sleeping in the torreón.[3]

Martín Chávez ordered Doc Scurlock, Charlie Bowdre, John Middleton, "Dirty" Steve Stephens, and roughly eight more of their men to take position in the Ellis house, much to the surprise of the Ellis family inside. Martín also sent José Chávez y Chávez, Yginio Salazar, Florencio Cháves, José María Chávez, Ignacio González, his uncle-in-law Vicente Romero, and a local sheepherder named Francisco Zamora to accompany Alexander McSween, Billy Bonney, the Kid's new teenage sidekick Tom Folliard, Henry Brown, Jim French, Sam Smith, Tom "Joe Bowers" Cullins, and Joseph J. Smith to the McSween home up the street. Susan McSween, her sister Elizabeth Shield and her five children, and a consumptive law student named Harvey Morris were all surprised by their arrival. "We knew that this would be the center for the battle that was sure to come," George Coe later said.

Martín Chávez headed for the Montaño store alongside Fernando Herrera, Atanacio Martínez, and roughly twenty Hispano recruits. "The night was very dark," he later recalled. José Montaño was away purchasing supplies in Santa Fe at the time. Martín explained the situation to the startled Josefa Montaño, who was on the premises with her children, Scipio and Martena Salazar, the widowed Teresa Philipowski, and Mrs. Ellen Bolton. Martín settled in for the rest of the night alongside his compadres, having also sent a handful of his men into the Patrón store next door. George Coe initially accompanied Martín into the Montaño store but eventually joined his pal Billy Bonney, José Chávez y Chávez, Yginio Salazar, and the others inside the McSween home.[4]

Martín's strategy had proven a master stroke. "He now had all his men in the desired positions without having fired a gun," recalled George Coe. The Dolan partisans and neutral citizens throughout town remained unaware of their presence until morning. "There was not a shot fired," Taylor F. Ealy later wrote. "I nor my family did not know they had entered." Martín and his compañeros remained as quiet as possible inside the Montaño store as the fierce winds blowing through Lincoln rattled the windows and doors. Josefa

Montaño, her children, and the other women on the premises were fully aware that a big fight would commence after sunrise and huddled together in one of the back rooms.⁵

Scipio Salazar emerged from the Montaño store and strolled across the street to the Baca residence after the sun began rising to the east of Lincoln on the morning of July 15, 1878. Scipio alerted Saturnino Baca of the McSween partisans' arrival and advised the *capitán* to keep his guard up. "He told me to be very careful," Baca recalled. "That they wanted to round it up." Martín Chávez and his men were intending to fight it out with the Dolan faction to the last bullet. Many neutral citizens knew something was stirring in Lincoln that morning and were shocked to discover the McSween partisans had effectively taken control of the lower end of town while they were asleep. Jack Long, Billy Mathews, Sam Perry, Jimmy McDaniels, George "Roxy" Rose, and Dummy awoke that morning and realized they would be caught in a turkey shoot should they attempt to vacate the torreón next to the Baca home.⁶

Nobody was more shocked by the McSween partisans' presence in Lincoln than Jimmy Dolan and Sheriff George Peppin. They had merely Lucio Montoya, Pantaleon Gallegos, and a couple of other men at their disposal in the Wortley Hotel that morning. Deputy Jack Long and his cohorts were trapped down the street in the torreón. If the Regulators decided to storm the western end of town, it would be game over. The besieged Sheriff Peppin immediately dispatched an envoy to locate John Kinney and Buck Powell's fearsome posse and bring them back to Lincoln as quickly as possible.⁷

Inside the McSween home, José Chávez y Chávez, Yginio Salazar, Billy Bonney, and their compadres began digging portholes in the walls through which to fire their rifles. They were presumably unaware of the numbers advantage they possessed at the time. George Coe, Henry Brown, and Sam Smith decided to take position in the Tunstall store where the Ellis family were residing. Martín Chávez instructed a handful of his men to climb onto the roof of the Montaño store. The rest of them continued digging their own portholes in the building's adobe walls.⁸

While José Chávez y Chávez, Yginio Salazar, and their compañeros were preparing for war inside the McSween home, the Scotsman discovered that Saturnino Baca's cook was providing food and water to Deputy

Jack Long and the Dolan partisans in the torreón. McSween sent a note to Baca around midday, citing his legal ownership of the land on which they resided and ordering the *capitán* and his family to vacate the premises within three days for allowing "murderers" the "improper use" of his property. Saturnino had not forgotten Susan McSween's recent threat to hire men to wipe out his family. Not only was he offended by the Scotsman's command, but also his wife Juana was in poor health after recently giving birth. The respected former sheriff responded by sending a note to Col. Nathan Dudley, requesting the officer send a few soldiers to provide protection for his frightened family. He also sent a reply to McSween, informing the Scotsman of his wife's illness and suggesting any property claims he made could be settled by law. McSween softened his stance slightly when receiving Saturnino's note, allowing the Baca family to remain on the property for several more days but advising them to vacate their home immediately for their own safety.[9]

In Fort Stanton Col. Nathan Dudley was unable to dispatch any soldiers to the Baca residence, although he did send assistant surgeon Daniel Appel downriver to investigate the matter. Alexander McSween was irritated by Jimmy Dolan's close friend Appel's arrival at his doorstep that afternoon. The Scotsman threatened to burn the Baca family out should they not vacate their house. The increasingly anxious Saturnino Baca promptly sent another note to Colonel Dudley requesting the officer send a wagon in which to transport his sickly wife Juana to Fort Stanton. In the Ellis home, Doc Scurlock insisted the Baca family could leave town peacefully. Scurlock also swore a deposition before Probate Clerk Rafael Gutiérrez in which he denied having recently fired shots at María Bonifacia Chávez Brady's teenage son William Jr.[10]

Dr. Daniel Appel was heading back to Fort Stanton that evening when he spotted a large dust cloud being raised by dozens of ruffians to the west of Lincoln. Jimmy Dolan and Sheriff George Peppin were relieved when John Kinney and Buck Powell's posse stormed into the western end of town. They numbered roughly forty men, including Jessie Evans, Robert Beckwith, Marion Turner, Johnny Hurley, Bob Olinger, Andy Boyle, Milo Pierce, Deputy José Chávez y Baca, and various other Dolan partisans and Seven Rivers men. A sharpshooter named Charlie "Lallacooler" Crawford announced their arrival in town by firing a celebratory shot into the air before they began securing their horses in the Wortley Hotel corral.

In the McSween home, José Chávez y Chávez, Yginio Salazar, and their compadres heard John Kinney and Buck Powell's posse arrive and opened fire on them. The Dolan partisans quickly scattered from the Wortley corral to take cover. Billy Bonney and several McSween men heard the shooting down the street in the Montaño store, where they were presumably discussing strategy with Martín Chávez. The Kid began leading a handful of their men back up the street when Deputy Jack Long and his cohorts spotted them from the torreón. Shots were exchanged as Billy and his compadres dodged their way back to the McSween home. The frustrated Jack Long fired four shots in Bonney's direction and missed with each bullet. The Dolan partisans up the street took position around the Schon and Mills houses and unloaded on the McSween home, shattering the window shutters on the western side of the adobe structure. The two factions continued firing shots back and forth from their respective strongholds until nightfall began impeding their vision, and everyone hunkered down for the night with their ears ringing.[11]

Dr. Taylor F. Ealy and John B. Wilson were almost struck by bullets while making their way down the street to attend to a dying carpenter named Daniel Huff later that night. Deputy Jack Long and his cohorts had spotted them from the torreón and hastily opened fire. Justice Wilson shouted frantically for them to stop shooting and explained the situation. They continued their journey once the firing ceased and were able to attend to Huff, who had been poisoned by an unknown relative. The carpenter died in the company of his distraught Hispano wife and two children soon after.[12]

Although Daniel Huff had proven the only occupant of Lincoln in need of funeral arrangements for the time being, the Dolan and McSween partisans resumed exchanging gunfire shortly after sunrise on July 16, 1878. A handful of neutral citizens remained confined to their homes to avoid the bullets cutting through the air along the Río Bonito the rest of the day. "A good many of the families left town, leaving about twelve families in town," recalled local farmer José María de Aguayo. While many of the Dolan partisans continued firing shots at the McSween home, Sheriff George Peppin sent Charlie Crawford, Lucio Montoya, and a handful of others into the hills

The Burning House

behind the Montaño store. Martín Chávez's hombres positioned on the rooftop suddenly found themselves being fired upon from an elevated position and were forced to climb back down into the store before anyone was hit. "There were no casualties," Martín recalled.[13]

Jimmy Dolan and Sheriff Peppin had grown frustrated with their inability to make any inroads by late afternoon. Their partisans had only managed to chip off pieces of adobe wall and shatter two of the McSween home's windows with their bullets. José Chávez y Chávez, Yginio Salazar, Billy Bonney, and their compadres continued returning fire through their portholes and from the rooftop. Martín Chávez and his Hispano fighters in the Montaño store weren't going anywhere either, nor were Doc Scurlock and the Regulators in the Ellis home. Sheriff Peppin promptly sent a note to Col. Nathan Dudley in Fort Stanton. "If it is within your power to loan me one of your howitzer, I am of the opinion the parties for whom I have said warrants will surrender without firing a shot," the sheriff requested.[14]

Col. Nathan Dudley strongly wished to assist the Dolan partisans when receiving Peppin's request for a howitzer but remained legally incapable of providing any military assistance by order of his superiors. The colonel dispatched Pvt. Berry Robinson to Lincoln with a note lamenting his inability to intervene and freely expressing his moral support for the Dolan faction. "My sympathies and those of all my officers are most earnestly and sincerely with you," Dudley implored. "Were I not so circumscribed by law and orders, I would most gladly give you every man and material at my post to sustain you in your present position."[15]

Pvt. Berry Robinson galloped out of Fort Stanton and was roughly five hundred yards from the western end of Lincoln when several bullets snapped past him. The startled buffalo soldier bolted to the Wortley Hotel, where Jimmy Dolan and his partisans dubiously claimed the shots had come from the roof of the McSween home. Sheriff Peppin was disappointed that Colonel Dudley was incapable of providing a howitzer, but he handed Private Robinson a note in which he informed the cavalry officer that the McSween partisans had fired upon one of his soldiers.[16]

McSween employees Sebrian Bates and George Washington were almost cut down themselves while lowering the corpse of Daniel Huff into a freshly dug grave behind the Tunstall store corral that evening. Deputy Jack Long, Billy Mathews, and their cohorts in the torreón had spotted the two Black men and needlessly opened fire on them. Bates and Washington dumped Daniel Huff's corpse inside the hole and ran for their lives. Martín Chávez waited until nightfall to dispatch McSween employee Joe Dixon to retrieve some water from the Río Bonito for collective use inside the Montaño store. "You could not see any person in town except [N——] Joe and myself," recalled José María de Aguayo. "My children were crying because they were hungry and I had to go about and look for milk and other necessaries."

Hardly anyone in Lincoln was able to get any sleep as the McSween and Dolan partisans continued firing shots at each other throughout the night of July 16. "The situation of the inhabitants was very much compromising and very sorrowful, possessed of terror," remembered José María de Aguayo, who had decided to remain in town with his family throughout the ongoing siege. "None of the inhabitants of Lincoln could attend to their business, nor go after water," Saturnino Baca recalled. The former sheriff and a handful of the locals resorted to sneaking out of their homes after nightfall to "fill up the barrels" from the Río Bonito.[17]

All was surprisingly quiet in Lincoln on the morning of July 17, 1878. It was so quiet that Charlie Crawford, Lucio Montoya, and the handful of Dolan partisans on the hillside to the south of the Montaño store got the idea in their heads that the McSween partisans must have fled town under cover of darkness the previous night. The weary Saturnino Baca curiously watched from his home as Charlie Crawford and Lucio Montoya began strolling down the southern hills toward the Montaño store. Perhaps the siege in La Placita had come to an end following two days of upheaval. "My wife was sick in bed and my children all frightened," Baca later asserted.[18]

As Saturnino Baca quickly learned, the grizzled veteran was not the only hombre who had caught sight of Crawford and Montoya strolling down the hillside that morning. Martín Chávez had also spotted the two Dolan partisans inside the Montaño store. The McSween partisans were still positioned in their various strongholds throughout Lincoln and had no intention of leaving any time soon. Martín Chávez handpicked two hombres to accompany him outside and take the fight directly to the Dolan men slowly approaching the store.

Charlie Crawford and Lucio Montoya were still over four hundred yards from the Montaño store when the hot-tempered Fernando Herrera decided to make Martín Chávez's task a little easier. The red-haired Basque Hispano took steady aim with his 45-120-555 Sharps rifle and fired a shot at one of the Dolan men on the hillside. Saturnino Baca watched from his home as the bullet ripped through Charlie Crawford's hip. The grievously wounded Crawford slumped to the ground, and the startled Lucio Montoya began running for his life down the hillside. He ground to a halt when he spotted Martín Chávez and two hombres thirty yards in front of him. Time seemed to stand still for the briefest of moments before Lucio instinctively fired a shot at Martín. "He miraculously missed me," Chávez recalled. Montoya then began sprinting up toward the Cisneros house.

The relieved Martín Chávez and his two men chased after Lucio Montoya and pursued him into the Cisneros home. Martín could find no trace of the young man who had tried to shoot him when searching the house and correctly assumed that Montoya had taken refuge next door in the Romero home. "We went next door to the Romero house, but he told us that no one had passed by," he remembered. They searched the home anyway but were again unable to find Montoya inside. Martín and his two companions eventually gave up their pursuit and headed back to the Montaño store. Little did they know that Lucio Montoya had been concealed inside a box in the Romero living room and listening the entire time. Montoya then took a desperate initiative. The Hispano sharpshooter disguised himself in women's clothing, wrapped a rebozo over his head, and joined Sheriff Peppin and his associates at the Wortley Hotel. None of them were game enough to retrieve the wounded Charlie Crawford lying helpless in the hills as gunfire erupted once again from the Montaño store and the McSween and Ellis homes.[19]

In Fort Stanton Col. Nathan Dudley was incensed when learning someone had taken a shot at Pvt. Berry Robinson over in Lincoln, describing the incident as an "infamous outrage." The colonel dispatched Capt. George Purington, Capt. Thomas Blair, Dr. Daniel Appel, and five buffalo soldiers downriver to investigate. "Both parties are reported to me as being determined to fight it out to the last round of ammunition," Dudley informed the district headquarters. "The Dolan & Riley faction, I fear, will get the worse of it."

Capt. George Purington and the troops reached Lincoln around midday and listened to Jimmy Dolan and Sheriff George Peppin's version of recent events at the western end of town. When they arrived at Alexander McSween's doorstep soon after, the Scotsman firmly denied that anyone in his home had fired shots at Private Robinson. The cavalry officers didn't believe the Scottish attorney and determined that someone on the roof of the McSween home had tried to shoot one of their buffalo soldiers. Dr. Daniel Appel and the troops then retrieved the wounded Charlie Crawford before heading back to Fort Stanton, where Crawford died from his wound one week later.[20]

Juan Patrón was still residing in the post trader's store at Fort Stanton when Col. Nathan Dudley approached him that evening and accused the businessman of being a McSween spy. The colonel declared his intention to take action in Lincoln and did not want anybody reporting his movements. Juan Patrón refuted Dudley's accusation, insisting he was not spying on McSween's or anyone else's behalf at the post. Dudley caustically offered to furnish Patrón with an ambulance if he wished to travel downriver to the McSween house in Lincoln. Juan informed the colonel that he "did not care about going to the McSween home" but could go wherever he pleased. Dudley's face reddened with anger in having to deal with someone who was not intimidated by his authority. He aggressively ordered Juan to vacate the post within an hour. When Dr. Daniel Appel appealed to Dudley on Juan's behalf, the colonel declared that Patrón could remain in Fort Stanton, provided the Hispano commissioner slept in close quarters so the officer could keep an eye on him.[21]

The McSween and Dolan factions continued firing shots at each other in Lincoln throughout the night of July 17, 1878. The 23-year-old Ben Ellis was eventually caught in the crossfire when he was shot in the neck by one of the Dolan men while feeding his horses. A couple of the Regulators inside the Ellis house sneaked down to the Tunstall store to retrieve Dr. Taylor F. Ealy, who was also fired upon by Dolan partisans when attempting to reach the Ellis home and administer some medical assistance. Ben Ellis would have to wait until morning to receive any care. "Bullets were flying all the time every day through town," recalled José María de Aguayo, who was taking his life in his hands any time he ventured outside his home to acquire necessities for his family.[22]

Andrew Boyle demonstrated plenty of nerve when managing to sneak down the street to speak with Deputy Jack Long, Billy Mathews, and their cohorts in the torreón before sunrise. Jack Long, Billy Mathews, and their companions eagerly accompanied Boyle back to the Wortley Hotel under cover of darkness. Jimmy Dolan had a plan, and with a bit of Irish luck, they would soon be able to surround the McSween home.[23]

***

It was getting rather ripe inside the McSween house by the morning of July 18, 1878. José Chávez y Chávez, Yginio Salazar, Billy Bonney, Florencio Cháves, Vicente Romero, and their compadres all reeked of sweat and gunpowder after spending four nights and three days in close confinement. Martín Chávez and his men inside the Montaño store were also getting rather malodorous. It was impossible to maintain a steady supply of water from the Río Bonito under the circumstances, and sanitation was becoming an issue. It was much safer to relieve oneself in a bucket than to risk getting shot by one of the "Marfe" men when venturing outside to use a privy.

For all the unpleasant aromas wafting into their nasal passages, the McSween partisans still held the advantage in Lincoln. Fernando Herrera had taken out Charlie Crawford, whom Martín Chávez later described as "one of the Murphy's best sharpshooters." They had also managed to wound Seven Rivers fighter William H. Johnson and two other Dolan men. Inside the McSween home, Joseph J. Smith boasted in a letter to his former employer in Roswell that Juan Patrón's would-be assassin Jim Reese had "cried because he was on the wrong side." Their friend Taylor F. Ealy also managed to reach the Ellis home that morning and administer sorely needed medical care to Ben Ellis. "The wound was a bad one," recalled Mary Ealy. "The man had lost much blood."[24]

In Fort Stanton that morning, Juan Patrón decided it was best for him to vacate the post. The Hispano prodigy limped his way to Colonel Dudley's quarters to bid the officer farewell and thank him for his hospitality despite their quarrel the previous day. "I told him I was very sorry that he could suspect me as a spy," Juan later recalled. The businessman informed Dudley that he was leaving, but did not wish to "take a part in the fight." He was heading north to Las Vegas, San Miguel County, where he could "stay sometime until peace was restored." Dudley agreed that Las Vegas was a good place for Juan to seek refuge and suggested his life was probably in danger at Fort Stanton anyway. Juan then set out for the Río Hondo for a few days before traveling to Las Vegas.[25]

As Juan Patrón was doing everything he could to avoid the ongoing warfare, Jimmy Dolan, John Kinney, Sam Perry, George Rose, and several others climbed into their saddles at the western end of La Placita that afternoon. They began riding upriver toward Fort Stanton as the steady pops of gunfire back in Lincoln grew fainter in their ears. Col. Nathan Dudley was in a foul mood when they arrived at the post, and Jimmy Dolan appealed to the officer for assistance. The McSween men were better positioned, and it was their only chance to put an end to the siege down in Lincoln. Dudley readily agreed, instructing the Irishman to "go down and stand them off" until the troops arrived around noon the following day. The temperamental colonel then instructed Dolan and his partisans to vacate the post before nightfall.

Col. Nathan Dudley needed an excuse for defying his orders and convened a meeting with his officers. He announced his official directive was to "take all the available forces at my command to proceed to Lincoln" the following day, for "the sole purpose of giving protection to women and children, and such non-combatants." The colonel and his troops eventually retired to their quarters in preparation to set out for Lincoln the following morning.[26]

After getting as much sleep as he could manage the night before, Martín Chávez was ready to continue the fight inside the Montaño store on the morning of July 19, 1878. Little did the former deputy sheriff know, this particular Friday would result in a series of events that remained firmly etched in his memory for the rest of his days. Alexander McSween was still confident of victory alongside Martín's uncle-in-law Vicente Romero up the street, informing Ash Upson that "right will triumph" in a letter that morning.

The Burning House

José Chávez y Chávez, Yginio Salazar, and Florencio Cháves were prepared for whatever may come. Their young amigo Billy "Kid" Bonney had not demonstrated even the slightest hint of apprehension during the now five-day siege. "He was cool and cheerful as if he were playing a game rather than fighting for his life," recalled Yginio Salazar, who was in awe of the Kid's determination and courage. "The Murphy's told some woman in town that they got a condemned cannon and was going to bombard the town," their comrade Joseph J. Smith had informed his former employer in Roswell. "But we didn't scare worth a dam."[27]

The McSween partisans spent most of the morning trading shots with Jimmy Dolan and Sheriff Peppin's men, until the fighting suddenly came to a halt as noon was approaching. Martín Chávez could sense that something was happening outside and gazed through one of the Montaño store windows. He was shocked to see a procession of blue uniforms slowly coming down the street. Col. Nathan Dudley, Capt. George Purington, two other officers, one company of Black cavalryman, and one company of Black infantry had all arrived from Fort Stanton. They numbered thirty-five men in total. Colonel Dudley had spoken with Jimmy Dolan and Sheriff George Peppin at the Wortley Hotel before leading his officers and companies down the street, having stated for the record that he was in town to offer protection for the women and children, not to provide any assistance to either faction.[28]

Martín Chávez watched as the troops came to a halt for several minutes before continuing down the street and stopping directly in front of the Montaño store. His curiosity surged when Colonel Dudley and his officers dismounted their horses and some of the buffalo soldiers began setting up camp on the opposite side of the street. They had brought a twelve-pound howitzer, a gatling gun with two thousand rounds of ammunition, and three days' worth of rations.

Martín quickly scribbled a note inside the Montaño store and handed it to Joe Dixon, who was to deliver the message to Alexander McSween. As the appointed leader of their partisans, Martín needed to find out exactly what was happening and stepped outside the Montaño store through a side door. He approached the Americano officers standing in the street and was quickly spotted by Capt. George Purington.

"This is one of McSween's men," Purington informed his white-haired superior officer.

"Colonel, you want to kill me and my men in the house?" Martín asked Col. Nathan Dudley in broken English.

The old campaigner ignored Martín's query and gestured toward a handful of buffalo soldiers approaching them. Martín looked in their direction and spotted the turning wheels and heavy barrel of a howitzer. His dark eyes widened as the soldiers positioned the weapon in front of the Montaño store and aimed the brass cannon directly at the front door. The colonel and his troops were clearly in town to assist the "Marfe" faction.

"If a single shot is fired by your men, I will blow your house to pieces," Colonel Dudley warned Martín, also advising that any women or children inside should vacate the premises immediately.

Martín scornfully turned on his heels and headed back to the Montaño store, instructing his men to shoot the buffalo soldier operating the howitzer if there was any sign he intended to use it. Colonel Dudley flew into a rage when overhearing Martín's command and shouted for Justice John B. Wilson to scribble a warrant and arrest the "damned son of a bitch." For all his defiance, Martín knew the fight was as good as over after spending five long days in the Montaño store with his men. The adobe walls of their stronghold could not withstand the force of a cannon blast if the colonel ordered his soldiers to light the fuse.[29]

Joe Dixon delivered Martín's note to Alexander McSween in the Scotsman's home four hundred yards up the street. The pragmatic Chávez had suggested they vacate the premises, as it looked like the army had come to blow them all to pieces. José Chávez y Chávez and Billy Bonney both spotted three cavalrymen passing by the McSween home in the street and heading up toward the Wortley Hotel. The soldiers walked by the front of the house again with Sheriff George W. Peppin moments later. "We all became alarmed seeing Peppin guarded by the soldiers," recalled Susan McSween. Colonel Dudley had also sent Dr. Daniel Appel to fetch Isaac Ellis from his home at the eastern end of town and warned that he would blow the Ellis house to the ground if any of the Regulators inside fired upon his troops.

The Burning House

Dudley then told Sheriff Peppin there were enough Dolan partisans to drive the McSween partisans out of Lincoln.[30]

Inside the Montaño store, Martín Chávez could see the howitzer pointed directly at the front door every time he looked through a window. The handful of men he positioned in the Patrón store five days earlier had already fled down the street to the Ellis home after spotting the brass cannon in the vicinity. Martín swallowed his pride and decided it was time to do the same. He was responsible for everyone's lives, including the women and children inside the Montaño store, and felt it was best to withdraw from Lincoln for the time being rather than try to take on the army and their heavy artillery.

"Sigueme" (Follow me), Martín said to Fernando Herrera, Atanacio Martínez, and the rest of his Hispano fighters.

Some of Martín's men threw blankets over their heads to conceal their identities before following him out the back door of the Montaño store. They quickly headed down the street and safely reached the increasingly crowded Ellis home two hundred yards away, joining Doc Scurlock, Charlie Bowdre, John Middleton, more than a dozen other partisans, and the Ellis family inside. Col. Nathan Dudley had spotted Martín and his men as they were running down the street and ordered his soldiers to turn the howitzer in the direction of the Ellis home. Sheriff George Peppin, Robert Beckwith, John Jones, Johnny Hurley, and several other Dolan partisans then approached the Ellis home and demanded the Regulators surrender.[31]

Sheriff George Peppin and his companions started shooting when they spotted Martín Chávez and his men on horseback after mounting up in the Ellis corral. Martín and his compadres returned fire and wounded John Jones before turning their horses and riding for the northern hills across the river, with bullets cutting through the air around them. Martín and his men managed to cross the Río Bonito without getting cut down and took cover in a gulch. Colonel Dudley was furious with Sheriff Peppin for allowing them to escape. Martín was not about to abandon his wife's uncle Vicente Romero and the others inside the McSween home either. He ordered his men to leave their horses behind in the gulch after everyone caught their breath and take position on a hillside running behind the Río Bonito.

While Martín Chávez and his hombres continued the fight in the northern hills, the arrival of Col. Nathan Dudley and the troops had reinvigorated the Dolan partisans and turned the tide in their favor. Sheriff Peppin had sent Marion Turner to the McSween home with a handful of warrants, only for the Seven Rivers gunman to be turned away when Jim French shouted obscenities through a window. José Chávez y Chávez and his compadres were also dealing with a discouraged Alexander McSween inside their stronghold. The Scotsman's resolve was rapidly weakening after exchanging notes with Colonel Dudley, who had responded to the Scotsman's inquiries with sarcasm. Many of the Dolan partisans began taking cover in various adobe buildings and were closing in on the McSween home. Sheriff Peppin had decided to burn them out, and Yginio Salazar's adversary Robert Beckwith was soon strolling up the street with a bucket of coal oil.

The persistent Martín Chávez and his men tried to provide their compadres in the McSween house some assistance by exchanging long-range shots with the Dolan partisans from the northern hills. Col. Nathan Dudley eventually spotted Martín and his hombres on a hillside and ordered his soldiers to aim the howitzer and gatling gun in their direction. Martín knew they would all be slaughtered if the Army used their heavy weapons and quickly led his men out of range.[32]

Across the river, Col. Nathan Dudley threatened to arrest John B. Wilson, who was again serving as the justice of the peace, for dereliction of duty should he refuse to provide a warrant for Alexander McSween and his partisans for allegedly trying to shoot Pvt. Berry Robinson several days earlier. Sheriff George Peppin was keeping close to the colonel in the Army camp across the street from the Montaño store. The sheriff subsequently deputized Robert Beckwith, who was handed the warrant begrudgingly provided by Justice Wilson. Peppin also instructed Beckwith, John Kinney, Johnny Hurley, Sebrian Bates, and Joe Dixon to gather some wood and carry it up the street to the McSween house.[33]

Susan McSween soon emerged from her adobe home and huffily stormed in the direction of Col. Nathan Dudley's camp. She exchanged some heated words with Sheriff Peppin, who tersely informed her that the men inside her home would be taken dead or alive. Susan then demanded to speak with

Colonel Dudley, who emerged from his tent in no mood to converse with her. When Susan asked the colonel why it appeared the Army were there to assist with the burning of her house, Dudley reiterated that he was in town to provide protection for woman and children. He also declared that Susan had no business harboring the likes of "Billy Kid," Jim French, and "other men of the same character." Dudley and the steely Mrs. McSween began arguing after the officer vowed to blow her house to pieces should anyone fire a shot at his soldiers. When Susan screamed that the Army were consorting with "known thieves and murderers" and planning to murder her husband, the enraged officer ordered some of his soldiers to remove her from his sight.[34]

Susan headed back up the street and was appalled when she spotted three soldiers standing near her home while Deputy Jack Long and Dummy poured coal oil onto the floor of the northeast kitchen. George Coe spotted the two Dolan partisans from the Tunstall store granary and fired a shot at Jack Long, who hastily tossed a light onto the kitchen floor. Long and Dummy then took cover inside the privy behind the McSween home. When the Regulators began taking potshots at the outhouse, Long and Dummy climbed through the privy hole to spend the rest of the evening safely standing in a pool of human waste. Elizabeth Shield quickly managed to douse the fire Jack Long had started in the northeast kitchen with a bucket of water she had fetched from the Río Bonito.[35]

Sheriff George Peppin was still determined to burn the Regulators out and instructed Andrew Boyle and a handful of partisans to sneak into the stables behind the McSween home later that afternoon. Andy Boyle managed to remain undetected while using some timber and a sack of shavings and chips to start a fire next to the northwest kitchen of the McSween house. The Dolan partisans threw coal oil onto the adobe walls before scurrying back to the stables, and the flames began engulfing the northwest end of the U-shaped building. Martín Chávez and everyone else in the valley soon spotted a stream of black smoke rising into the sky above Lincoln. "We could see the flames and smoke from our house," recalled Lorencita Miranda, who remained confined to her home in the hills above town.[36]

José Chávez y Chávez, Yginio Salazar, Billy Bonney, and their compadres tried to put out the fire in the northwest kitchen, only to be driven back when Andrew Boyle and his cohorts unloaded on them from the McSween stables. As the flames began advancing down the west wing of the house, the self-absorbed Susan McSween's immediate concern was her precious piano. Some of the young men inside her home tried to move the heavy instrument at her insistence but quickly gave up. There were more pressing concerns as beads of sweat began rolling off their skin and everyone's clothes dampened as if they were trapped inside a large *horno*. It was probably the closest thing to hell the devout Roman Catholic Hispanos could imagine. They did their best to fight off the encroaching flames while trying to shield their stinging eyes amidst a haze of thick, disorientating smoke. It was little use, and everyone began steadily backtracking through each room to preserve their lives. A keg of gunpowder stored near the northwest kitchen exploded, and the fire continued slowly spreading until the entire west wing of the McSween home was ablaze.

The Dolan partisans had their enemies trapped and continued peppering the windows and doors of the burning McSween house with bullets. The increasingly desperate Regulators returned fire with enough venom for Col. Nathan Dudley to order his buffalo soldiers to take cover behind some unfinished adobe walls down the street. When the flames inevitably started creeping into the east wing of the McSween house, everyone instinctively looked to young Billy Bonney for leadership. "The Kid was the bravest man I ever knew," Yginio Salazar later said. "He did not know what fear meant." When Billy spotted the distraught Alexander McSween cowering in a corner alongside his wife Susan, he grabbed hold of the Scotsman and shook him. The Kid implored Mac to show a little backbone and insisted they would make a break. They weren't dead yet. There was still a chance.[37]

Billy also suggested it was time for the women and children to vacate the burning house, telling Susan McSween that "dresses ain't made for running." Susan initially protested, wishing to remain with her husband. She eventually appealed to Capt. Thomas Blair when spotting the officer and a handful of soldiers outside the Tunstall store with a wagon. The troops were preparing to escort the Ealy family to a safer location. Susan McSween, Elizabeth Shield, and the five Shield children accompanied them down the street to the relative safety of the Patrón store. Josefa Montaño became distressed by the sight

The Burning House

of the burning McSween home up the street and appealed to Col. Nathan Dudley for protection. The cavalry officer refused, insisting that he did not have enough soldiers to provide any assistance to the women and children in the Montaño store.[38]

In the northern hills, Martín Chávez decided to assist his comrades inside the McSween home by leading an attack on the Dolan store. The former deputy sheriff may have been bested by Colonel Dudley and his heavy artillery, but he had not given up on his uncle-in-law Vicente Romero and the hombres trapped inside the burning building across the river. Martín and his compañeros left their horses in a gulch before heading for the Río Bonito with a firm grip on their rifles. They crossed the Bonito's waters, headed up the riverbank, and stealthily approached the Dolan store without being detected. They kept their rifles focused on the front doors, but nobody emerged. "We did get close to the store but none of the crowd came out," Martín recalled. The Dolan partisans were positioned around the McSween home down the street.

Martín and his men withdrew from the western end of Lincoln and headed back toward the Río Bonito as the sun began sinking behind the hills. Martín kept a watchful eye while carefully approaching the rear of the blazing McSween home and observing the fiery carnage. He shouted for everyone inside to come out, but there was no response. "Whether or not we were heard, I've never known," Martín later said. "The fact is that nobody came out." Martín and his parched companions took a drink from the Río Bonito before returning to their horses in the northern hills. "It was impossible for us to be of any assistance," Martín lamented years later. "But we remained in the vicinity to be on hand in case they did escape."[39]

Martín had done what he could. It was all up to little Billy and his compadres inside the burning McSween house now.

***

The crackling flames on the verge of consuming the entire McSween home were providing a shimmering glow along the Río Bonito after nightfall. Billy Bonney noticed that it was almost as light as day outside in the McSween yard. The Kid, José Chávez y Chávez, Yginio Salazar, Florencio Cháves,

Vicente Romero, José María Chávez, Ignacio González, Francisco Zamora, Alexander McSween, Tom Folliard, Jim French, Tom "Joe Bowers" Cullins, Joseph J. Smith, and Harvey Morris were all huddled in the northeast kitchen as nine o'clock was approaching. It was the only room of the house that had yet to burn up entirely. The relentless fire was rapidly closing in on them, and it was almost time to make their break. Billy had tried to hand Alexander McSween a shotgun, but the Scotsman was still refusing to bear arms. "McSween was a God-fearing man who depended upon his Bible," Yginio Salazar remembered. Their comrades George Coe, Henry Brown, and Sam Smith had escaped out the back of the Tunstall store and safely reached the Río Bonito around fifteen minutes earlier.[40]

Yginio Salazar gazed around the sweltering kitchen and noticed that many of his exhausted compadres looked demoralized. Their hangdog expressions told the story. It was doubtful that all of them would reach either the Tunstall store or the Río Bonito alive. Their only means of escape was through the kitchen door leading into the yard outside, where the Dolan partisans would surely spot them. They had removed their boots to soften the sound of their footsteps when crossing the yard and could feel the heat emanating from the rest of the house coming up through their feet as if el Diablo was reaching for their souls. "When it began to look as if we should all be killed, the other men stood about silent, with long faces, hopeless," recalled Yginio Salazar. All except Billy Bonney, who appeared entirely unfazed by their predicament. He was even smiling, as if about to request a dance with some pretty señorita at a baile. José Chávez y Chávez prided himself on being the hardest man in any room, but even he could not believe how calm young Bill appeared under the trying circumstances.[41]

"Te ves muy contento" (You look very at ease), José said to the Kid, with a hint of resentment in his voice.

"¿Bueno, por qué no?" (Well, why not?), Billy answered. "No sirve de nada emocionarse" (No use getting excited).

Yginio Salazar couldn't believe his ears. He also couldn't believe his eyes when Billy took out his tobacco pouch and began casually rolling a cigarillo. "He did not spill a flake," Salazar recalled. "His hand was as steady as steel." The kitchen roof above their heads would soon collapse into a heap

The Burning House

of smoldering adobe and flaming vigas. When a small hunk of burning wood broke loose from the ceiling and landed on the table beside little Billy, he tried to lift everyone's spirits by leaning over and lighting his cigarillo with the flames burning through the piece of debris. He then took a drag on his cigarette and slowly exhaled the smoke from his lungs with noticeable enjoyment. The Kid looked at Yginio and grinned, letting his slightly older amigo in on the joke. "If you had seen Billy the Kid roll that cigarette and smoke it," Salazar later declared, "señor, you would have known at once that he was a brave man."[42]

The Kid's tall, red-haired Texan sidekick Tom Folliard was the first to step through the kitchen door into the McSween yard around nine o'clock. He was closely followed by Harvey Morris, José Chávez y Chávez, Billy Bonney, and Jim French. A shot rang out as they reached the gate, and Harvey Morris slumped dead onto the ground. Tom Folliard, José Chávez y Chávez, the Kid, and Jim French quickly leaped over the law student's corpse and exchanged shots with Robert Beckwith, Johnny Hurley, John Kinney, Andrew Boyle, and several others while approaching the Tunstall store.

Bill Bonney managed to shoot John Kinney in the mouth in the ensuing chaos, clipping off a piece of the badman's sandy moustache. The Kid and Chávez y Chávez also glanced in the direction of the southwest corner of the Tunstall store, where it appeared three white soldiers were firing shots in their direction. José Chávez y Chávez, Bill Bonney, Tom Folliard, and Jim French then began sprinting for the safety of the Río Bonito. "I went slowly until I saw the soldiers fire," recalled Chávez y Chávez. "Then I went with all my might." The four of them were fortunate to reach the riverbank without taking a bullet in the back.[43]

Florencio Cháves, José María Sánchez, Joseph J. Smith, and Tom "Joe Bowers" Cullins also scrambled out of the McSween yard and managed to reach the Río Bonito without getting cut down. "Why we were not all killed, I never could understand," recalled Yginio Salazar, who emerged from the northeast kitchen of the McSween home with Ignacio González. They tried to make a run for it after Ignacio declared his willingness to surrender before he opened fire on the Dolan partisans. González was subsequently shot in the arm but managed to make it through the gate and escape to the river.[44]

Yginio Salazar had barely run twelve paces from the kitchen door when it happened. He suddenly felt as if someone had punched him in his side with an invisible fist. There was a rush of numbness where the blow was struck, rapidly followed by a horrific burning sensation. His initial confusion quickly gave way to the realization that he had been shot through his side. He then felt another powerful thump in his back as a second bullet punctured his flesh and buried itself in his shoulder. The young scrapper was already feeling lightheaded when a third bullet struck his hand and only added to his agony. Yginio instinctively tried to remain on his feet, but the blistering pain was unbearable. He began stumbling on his weakened legs in a daze before everything went dark as he collapsed onto his back in the McSween yard.[45]

As blood trickled from the unconscious Yginio Salazar's wounds, the overwhelmed Alexander McSween had accidentally butted heads with one of his partisans and taken cover behind a pile of wood alongside the northeast kitchen. Vicente Romero and Francisco Zamora took cover inside the nearby chicken house. McSween called out to their enemies and asked if they were willing to accept his surrender. Deputy Robert Beckwith assured the Scotsman he would do so before stepping into the yard with Andrew Boyle, Josiah Nash, John Jones, and Dummy. The unarmed McSween emerged from behind the pile of wood and cautiously approached the Dolan partisans.[46]

Everyone except the senseless Yginio Salazar then heard another burst of gunfire.

***

Yginio Salazar wasn't exactly sure where he was when he first regained consciousness. It suddenly came back to him when the searing pain of his three bullet wounds took hold of his senses once again. He was desperate for a drink of water and could hear laughter amid the glimmering warmth emanating from the blazing McSween home. A handful of Dolan partisans were enjoying a gulp of whiskey and sharing a joke as they strolled among the bloodied corpses lying in the yard. The wounded Salazar and slain Harvey Morris were no longer the only two men with blood seeping into the ground beneath them. Alexander McSween now lay dead just outside the kitchen doorway with five bullets in him. Vicente Romero and Francisco Zamora had also been shot to death by the Dolan partisans and were sprawled out alongside the Scotsman's fresh corpse. Yginio's enemy Robert Beckwith had also been killed when receiving a bullet through his eye from either Romero or Zamora.[47]

As Andrew Boyle, Milo Pierce, John Kinney, and several other Dolan men were sharing a laugh in the vicinity, Yginio realized his only chance of survival was to play dead. He quickly closed his eyes. It was a long shot, but it was the best strategy he could manage under the circumstances. He tried his best to ignore the throbbing pain of his wounds, relaxed all his muscles, and let his body go limp as if having already met his maker. Yginio tried to remain calm when he heard footsteps approaching him. "It was a wonder that the twitch of an eyelid or the tremor of a muscle did not betray me," the wounded Regulator later said.[48]

Andrew Boyle decided to make sure the young "Mexican" lying in the yard was truly dead. It took every possible grain of tenacity that Yginio possessed not to wince or groan as Boyle began kicking him where a bullet had passed through his side. The 18-year-old vaquero believed his number was up when the Seven Rivers gunman continued laying his boot in with considerable force. "If he had kicked me only once more I think I must have groaned or yelled," young Salazar recalled. "The pain was so terrible." His continued silence hardly seemed to matter when Boyle pressed the nozzle of his Winchester rifle into the left side of his chest. It was all over for him now. Adios.

"Don't waste another shot on that damn greaser," the nearby Milo Pierce insisted. "He is already dead, and we may need all our ammunition later on."

Yginio felt a sense of eternal relief when Andrew Boyle withdrew the rifle from his chest and walked away. He might just live to see 19 after all. While his adversary Robert Beckwith's corpse was transported to the Dolan store up the street, the bodies of Alexander McSween, Vicente Romero, Francisco Zamora, and Harvey Morris were left in the yard to be pecked at by the chickens. The Dolan partisans disregard for the bodies of their enemies also proved a stroke of fortune for young Salazar, who would have surely given himself away had the "Marfes" tried to pick him up and carry him off somewhere.[49]

Yginio Salazar spent the next few hours lying motionless in the McSween yard while the Dolan partisans celebrated their victory in Lincoln. The amateur thespian occasionally opened his eyes when curiosity got the better of him, and he observed the dancing and heavy drinking in the street. George Washington and Sebrian Bates were forced to play the violin and guitar while Jimmy Dolan, Sheriff George Peppin, and their partisans kicked up their heels, sang, drank, and laughed the night away. "They had no fear," the wounded Salazar recalled. "Colonel Dudley and his soldiers were there to protect them."

When the Dolan victory party eventually wound down, Yginio began slowly crawling out of the McSween yard, leaving a trail of blood behind him. He managed to reach the Río Bonito without being spotted and eagerly gulped some water like a dehydrated bullock. The young Regulator then collapsed twice while staggering through the darkness toward the eastern end of Lincoln, naturally taking care to avoid Colonel Dudley's camp across the street from the Montaño store. Francisco Romero y Valencia and Ben Ellis both refused to allow the wounded Hispano inside their homes when he desperately pounded on each of their doors.[50]

Yginio firmly believed he was dying when he looked across a field and spotted a light gleaming from within José Otero's house, where his sister-in-law Nicolecita Pacheco was residing at the time. Otero initially slammed the door in young Salazar's face before Nicolecita recognized his voice and let him in. The wounded McSween partisan soon passed out again in front of the fireplace. The concerned Nicolecita had tears streaming down her face while Otero removed the unconscious Salazar's bloodied black shirt with a butcher knife and put her brother-in-law to bed. At least the young vaquero would die comfortably.[51]

Yginio Salazar was as surprised as anyone that he was still breathing inside the Otero home the following morning of July 20, 1878. "I have always thought I must have been under the protection of guardian angels," he later said. The wounded Hispano wasn't out of the proverbial woods just yet. Dr. Daniel Appel was called upon to administer medical care to the McSween partisan that morning. The bullet fired into Salazar's side had passed straight through and the resulting wound was not a serious one. Dr. Appel was more concerned with the bullet that had entered his patient's shoulder. The slug had passed downward and to the left. The army surgeon was unable to remove the ball, which remained lodged in Yginio's back for the rest of his days. If his wounds didn't fester, the young scrapper would survive after plenty of bed rest with one hell of a story to tell.

Dr. Daniel Appel was dressing Yginio's wounds when John Kinney kicked the door in after following the trail of blood young Salazar had left behind him the previous night. Kinney stormed inside with three other Dolan partisans, took one look at the wounded young Hispano, and voiced his intention to finish him off. There was a rumor circulating that Salazar's amigo Billy Bonney had been the man who shot Robert Beckwith the previous night. John Kinney, whom Yginio later described as "one of the worst fellows on the Murphy side," wanted to even the score by killing one of the Kid's friends in return. Dr. Daniel Appel insisted that he would see Kinney and his three companions hanged if they murdered his patient and escorted the ruffians back outside. "He saved my life," Yginio later said.[52]

While Yginio Salazar was having his wounds bandaged in the Otero house that morning, Martín Chávez, José Chávez y Chávez, Billy Bonney, and the rest of their surviving partisans were observing the scenes in Lincoln from across the Río Bonito in the northern hills. Sheriff George Peppin assembled a coroner's jury comprised of Justice John B. Wilson, Octaviano Salas, José García, Felipe Mes, Maximiano Chávez, and José Serno to examine the corpses of Alexander McSween, Vicente Romero, Francisco Zamora, and Harvey Morris that were still lying outside the charred remains of the McSween home. The Dolan partisans also began looting the Tunstall store and appropriating the saddles left behind by the Regulators in the Ellis corral. Susan McSween eventually told some of the local Hispanos to take whatever they wanted from the Tunstall store rather than see its inventory in the hands of "Peppin's gang of murderers." The indignant widow also declined to attend her late husband's funeral. Alexander McSween's unwashed corpse was wrapped inside a blanket and buried behind the Tunstall store corral that afternoon.

Col. Nathan Dudley readied his troops around four o'clock in the afternoon for the journey back to Fort Stanton. Robert Beckwith would be buried at the post with military honors. There were false rumors circulating that the remains of José Chávez y Chávez and Tom "Joe Bowers" Cullins were buried beneath the ruins of the McSween home. Colonel Dudley had also heard false reports that Billy Kid and Jim French had been burned alive, but he could not "vouch for this" in his report to the district headquarters later that night. Francisco Zamora's body had been collected by his relatives for burial. Vicente Romero's corpse was transported back to Picacho by members of the Romero family. "According to information I received later, Vicente Romero was maliciously murdered," recalled Martín Chávez. "I shall never forget the night they took forcible possession of Lincoln and set fire to the McSween home."[53]

For all of Martín Chávez's dismay over the killing of Vicente Romero the previous night, the former deputy sheriff did not feel compelled to avenge his uncle-in-law's death. He already had a young wife to console and a grieving aunt-in-law to contend with back in Picacho. He also felt that any further fighting against the Dolan faction was pointless now that Alexander McSween was dead. Martín led his men north to the Agua Sol ranch in the firm belief that the Lincoln County War was over, although he would need to discuss things with his amigo Billy Bonney and the other leading members of the Regulators before returning to the Río Hondo.[54]

"Mr. McSween, Sheriff Brady, and the others that lost their lives in the war weren't bad men," Carlota Baca later said when trying to put the Lincoln County War into perspective for subsequent generations. "But as at that time the gun was the real law, and they crossed someone they were disposed of by the gun. Jimmie Dolan, Young Riley, Billie the Keed, and other men that lived by the quick draw of the gun weren't really mean men, for they never killed unless their lives were at stake; they weren't murderers, but men of the frontier days." Carlota understood that any man who wielded a gun in frontier society also possessed a certain degree of roughness. Some of those men were just rougher than others.[55]

Carlota Baca and the residents of Lincoln County soon discovered just how appallingly rough some men of frontier times could be.

Chapter 8

Diablos del Infierno

You're nobody 'til somebody kills you.
—The Notorious B.I.G.

"Your decision has been reached simply because you are a coward," Billy Bonney harshly told Martín Chávez. "We have no other recourse than to fight. I have no family, and bit by bit, I intend to get even with them."

Martín probably expected such an intrepid response from his young amigo when informing the Kid of his plans at the Agua Sol ranch in the Capitan Mountains. While Billy surely knew Martín was no coward, the blue-eyed pistolero was displeased the former deputy sheriff and many of their Hispano fighters were intending to return to their families on the Río Hondo. "After learning of McSween's death, we felt that further fighting with the Murphy faction was useless," Chávez recalled. "As spokesman for our group, I told the Kid our decision."[1]

Billy Bonney was determined to continue the fight, and those who shared his feelings rallied around him as their new leader. Martín Chávez was equally resolute in his decision to return home. "I told him I could not join him," Martín later said. "And we parted as good friends." José Chávez y Chávez, Atanacio Martínez, Fernando Herrera, Ignacio González, and

Ramón Barragon decided to keep riding with the Kid for the time being. The remaining Regulators soon returned to the Río Ruidoso and began acquiring new mounts. "Some of our horses were given to us, some we swapped for, and others we swiped off the range," remembered George Coe.[2]

The 26-year-old Martín Chávez returned to Picacho after shaking hands with Billy Bonney and tried to console his wife Juana and widowed aunt-in-law María Romero. "Thus ended my participation in the Lincoln County War," the former deputy sheriff later said. Martín would have watched with a heavy heart as Vicente Romero's corpse was laid to rest in the local cemetery. The former Civil War bugler had left behind his four children Demetria, Pablo, María del Carmon, and 3-year-old Marcus Romero when accompanying Martín into Lincoln. Like the slain Francisco Zamora, the 32-year-old Vicente Romero's name would have been lost to history had he not been killed by the Dolan partisans in the McSween yard that fateful night. "The bloody feud of the people in [Lincoln] County has caused the death of several prominent and good men," the *Las Vegas Gazette* declared. "It seems strange, at this distance, that the war should reach such bloody and disastrous results."[3]

As Martín Chávez resumed his farming duties on the Río Hondo, the wounded Yginio Salazar was quietly loaded into the back of a wagon and transported out of Lincoln around July 21, 1878. Francisco Pacheco escorted Yginio into the northern foothills of the Capitan Mountains, where the young scrapper was briefly reunited with his mother Paula and stepfather Francisco Luma in Las Tablas. While the wounded Hispano was pleased to see his family again, there was a chance the Dolan partisans would come looking for him there. Francisco Pacheco subsequently escorted Yginio farther north to Fort Sumner in San Miguel County. The plucky teenager spent the next six months confined to a bed at the former Army post as his wounds slowly healed.[4]

Hostilities were still prevalent throughout Lincoln County when José Chávez y Chávez, Atanacio Martínez, Fernando Herrera, Ignacio González, and Ramón Barragon accompanied Billy Bonney, Tom Folliard, Doc Scurlock, Charlie Bowdre, Henry Brown, John Middleton, Jim French, George Coe, Frank Coe, and several others onto the Mescalero reservation on August 5, 1878. The remaining Regulators had decided to raise funds by rustling some horseflesh from the Indian Agency. While Billy Bonney and his

Anglo companions stopped for a drink at a spring half a mile from the agency, Atanacio Martínez and the Hispano contingent continued down the trail until they were fired upon by a couple of disgruntled Apaches. Former Dolan clerk Morris J. Bernstein overheard the shots at the agency, quickly emerged on the scene, and was gunned down by Atanacio Martínez during the resulting chaos. Bernstein's killing was strongly condemned by the Mesilla and Santa Fe press, although the *Cimarron News and Press* insisted Martínez had shot the agency clerk in self-defense:

> It is positively asserted that Bernstein was killed by a Mexican who was with a party going from San Patricio to Tularosa to assist in recovering a lot of stolen stock in the possession of Frank Wheeler and others then at San Nicolas . . . [Bernstein] rode up on one Mexican and fired two shots at him: the man took shelter behind a tree. Bernstein still advancing rode close to the tree and fired again at the man, who returned the fire and killed Bernstein. The Mexican says he acted strictly in self-defense and will . . . deliver himself up for trial. His name is Atanacio Martinez.

Billy Bonney and the Regulators still managed to steal the horses and mules from the agency corral despite Agent Fred Godfroy, a handful of soldiers, and three Apaches having fired dozens of bullets in their direction. The Regulators herded the stolen livestock back to Frank Coe's farm on the Río Hondo. Col. Nathan Dudley quickly instructed Lt. Millard Goodwin and a detachment of soldiers to pursue them. "Yes, we were outlaws," George Coe later said. "Had to make a living some way."[5]

José Chávez y Chávez and his fellow Regulators managed to elude Lieutenant Goodwin and arrived at the Chisum ranch at Bosque Grande on August 13. John Chisum was in St. Louis at the time, having recently decided to move his cattle operations onto the Texas Panhandle. Billy and his Regulators accompanied old John's brothers and their families north into San Miguel County and reached Fort Sumner on August 22, 1878. "Two candi hearts given me by Willie Bonney," Sallie Chisum wrote in her diary on the day of their arrival.[6]

When Billy Bonney wasn't pursuing Sallie Chisum's charms in Fort Sumner, he would have also visited his wounded amigo Yginio Salazar, who was always pleased to see the Kid's impish grin. Billy was undoubtedly amused when hearing of how his resourceful compadre had fooled the Dolan partisans by playing dead in the McSween yard. The Kid befriended many of the local Hispanos and quickly felt at home. "[Billy] was a lady's man, the Mex girls were crazy about him," recalled Frank Coe. "He spoke their language well. He was a fine dancer, could go to all their gaits and was one of them."

Fort Sumner was originally an army outpost for the disastrous Bosque Redondo reservation until it was abandoned in 1869. The Navajo had finally been relieved of their suffering after signing the Treaty of Bosque Redondo and resettled on a new reservation along the New Mexico–Arizona border. Fort Sumner now belonged to the wealthy Maxwell family, with whom the Kid would have conversed when organizing a baile at the dance hall near their two-story home. Billy and his Regulators spent the night dancing with the local señoritas and swinging them high in the air.[7]

José Chávez y Chávez almost sullied the Regulators' enjoyable stay in Fort Sumner when getting into a fierce argument with a local farmer named Telesfor Jaramillo behind the Maxwell house one night. José amiably extended his hand to the intoxicated Jaramillo, who refused the handshake and imprudently called the dangerous Regulator a thief. Telesfor had disrespected the wrong hombre. The enraged Chávez y Chávez drew his revolver and threatened to kill the married father of three for daring to insult him. He may well have done so, had Doña Luz Maxwell not overheard the two men and emerged from her home with her 15-year-old daughter Paulita Maxwell. "This Chávez y Chávez was a bad fellow," young Paulita later said. The matriarch of the Maxwell family grabbed Telesfor Jaramillo by the arm and tried to lead the drunken farmer inside her home before José shot him down.

"No matelo. Está borracho" (Don't shoot him, he's drunk), Doña Luz implored. "Espera a que este hombre sobrío y entonces matelo" (Wait until he's sober and settle it).

"No importa si es boracho o no" (I don't care whether he's drunk or sober), José snarled in response. "¡El no puede echar insultos a mi!" (He can't insult me!).[8]

Fortunately for Telesfor Jaramillo, little Billy Bonney overheard the commotion and came rapidly walking toward them. Paulita Maxwell had heard about the Kid's exploits in the Lincoln County War but had never seen him in the flesh. She was surprised the desperado looked so boyish and innocent. The young ladies' man would have also noticed the attractive Paulita's large brown eyes curiously gazing at him.

"Don't let this man kill my friend!" Doña Luz Maxwell pleaded to the Kid.

"Don't be afraid, señora," Billy replied, politely tipping his hat with a confident smile. "I'll straighten this out."

Billy turned to José Chávez y Chávez and calmly spoke to him in his native tongue. Whatever the Kid said, it was enough to convince José to holster his revolver. Billy respectfully took his fellow Regulator by the arm and led him away from the Maxwell home, saving Telesfor Jaramillo's life in the process and having just made the acquaintance of the young señorita destined to win his heart.

José Chávez y Chávez may have been dissuaded from shooting Telesfor Jaramillo into an early grave that night, but he also demonstrated that he was an hombre to be either respected or feared. The 28-year-old Chávez y Chávez valued a fearsome reputation far more than any notions of restraint. His regard for the Kid was the only reason Jaramillo was still breathing.[9]

The Regulators continued riding up the Río Pecos and arrived in Puerto de Luna, where they were welcomed with open arms by the local Hispanos. Billy Bonney then led his men farther north until reaching Anton Chico, where they learned that San Miguel County Sheriff Desiderio Romero had arrived from Las Vegas to arrest them. The Kid and his vigilantes confronted the Romero posse in the Sánchez saloon and scared them out of town without firing a single shot. The Regulators enjoyed some more bailes until eventually holding a "war pow-wow." Frank and George Coe announced they were done fighting and stealing horses for a living, having decided to accept a job herding cattle for Frank's brother-in-law on the Colorado border.[10]

Billy Bonney, José Chávez y Chávez, and the remaining Regulators decided to carry on the fight against the House and returned to Lincoln County.

***

Juan Bautista Patrón was keeping a room in Wagner's Hotel when he attended the ninth annual exhibition inside the Immaculate Conception Parish in Las Vegas, San Miguel County, on August 27, 1878. The Hispano politician had taken his seat in front of a carpeted stage when the festivities commenced at nine o'clock that morning. The parish walls were anointed with cloth and various needleworks crafted by the sisters and pupils of the convent. Speeches were made, songs were sung, premiums were distributed to both boarding and day scholars, several theatrical acts were performed, and a handful of students were crowned with a wreath for good conduct. The exhibition was considered a roaring success, and Juan stood along alongside everyone else to applaud local merchant Charles Blanchard's closing address. "Hon. Juan Patron of Lincoln, Pablo Anaya of Puerto de Luna and John Harrison of Anton Chico were among those in attendance at the exhibition Tuesday," the *Las Vegas Gazette* proudly informed its readers several days later.[11]

Juan Patrón would have been pleased the educational system was slowly progressing in Nuevo México. The Hispano politician would have been further pleased when learning that President Rutherford B. Hayes had removed Governor Samuel B. Axtell from office on September 4, 1878. The "little, one-sided partisan" was given the boot after Agent Frank Warner Angel's submitted his reports to Washington. President Hayes chose Civil War general Lewis Wallace as Axtell's replacement, much to the chagrin of Wallace himself, who was hoping for an ambassadorship. The 51-year-old Wallace was briefed in Washington before reluctantly traveling to New Mexico Territory. Railroad tracks were also edging closer to New Mexico courtesy of the Atchison, Topeka, and Santa Fe Railway Company. The advent of the railroad would provide an astute businessman like Juan B. Patrón with further opportunities for prosperity when Nuevo México finally became linked with the eastern states.[12]

Juan was still reluctant to return to Lincoln County, even if he no longer needed to fear his would-be assassin Jim Reese. The ruffian had been shot and killed by the Sánchez brothers in Tularosa on August 2, 1878. The bitter feelings between the Regulators and Dolan partisans were still prevalent on the Río Bonito. Susan McSween was keeping residence in the Patrón store in Lincoln, fearful that she would be murdered by the Dolan faction or arrested by Col. Nathan Dudley. The Regulators gave Dudley cause for concern when returning to Lincoln in late August and daring the Dolan partisans to do something about it. "Jim French, Kidd, Scroggins, Waite, and three others of the McSween ring hold the town of Lincoln," Dudley reported to the district headquarters.[13]

Jim French, Charlie Bowdre, and Doc Scurlock took turns acting as bodyguards for Susan McSween and sleeping outside the Patrón building. "I guess we owed it to the widow of the old penny pincher Mac," Jim French later wrote. "But she never even thanked us, never even offered us breakfast." John Chisum and Isaac Ellis had also lost their use for the Regulators. "We don't ask no favors of them God dam them," John Middleton wrote to Rob Widenmann. Some of the Regulators also threatened and harassed Saturnino Baca, believing him responsible for Colonel Dudley's presence in Lincoln during the five-day siege. Capitán Baca eventually packed up his large family and sought sanctuary in Fort Stanton. "Papá's life was in danger," recalled Carlota Baca. "We were advised to move to the post."[14]

The Regulators engaged in a little unabashed outlawry when rustling some horses and cattle from the Fritz ranch on September 6, 1878. They began herding the stolen stock northward, also escorting Charlie Bowdre and Doc Scurlock's families and possessions to Fort Sumner, where both men had decided to set up stakes. José Chávez y Chávez and many of his compañeros split off from the vigilante group before Billy Bonney, Tom Folliard, Fred Waite, John Middleton, and Henry Brown herded the stolen horses onto the Texas Panhandle. The Kid and his four Anglo companions spent weeks selling off the stolen nags to local ranchers, gambling, and socializing in and around Tascosa. José Chávez y Chávez had presumably returned to his family in San Patricio with his cut of the appropriated cattle profits.[15]

Juan Patrón was reunited with Susan McSween in Las Vegas after the headstrong widow fled Lincoln on September 17, 1878. Susan took a room in Wagner's Hotel before eventually staying at her sister Elizabeth's home. Their mutual friend John Chisum also checked in at the Wagner Hotel by the end of month. Susan McSween used the $5,000 she had received from John Tunstall's father to hire an asthmatic, one-armed lawyer named Huston L. Chapman to pursue charges against Col. Nathan Dudley for the murder of her husband. Those with a vested interest in politics were anticipating Lew Wallace's arrival in Santa Fe, and Juan decided it was finally time for him to return to Lincoln.[16]

The politico set out for the Río Bonito as an unprecedented reign of terror was about to sweep across Condado de Lincoln.

***

A former Texas lawman named John Selman, alias John Gunter, had recently fled into Lincoln County after his rustling buddy, Shackelford County Sheriff John Larn, was executed by vigilantes in Fort Griffin, Texas, on June 22, 1878. The angry locals had realized who was really responsible for the ongoing appropriation of their livestock and taken matters into their own hands. The 38-year-old John Selman and his brother Tom, alias "Tom Cat," formed their own gang on the Río Bonito shortly after the five-day siege in Lincoln.[17]

John Selman's gang was comprised of former Seven Rivers Warriors and some of the lowest characters to ever set foot in the Bonito Valley. Members included Augustus "Gus" Gildea, William R. "Jake" Owens, Bob Speakes, John Nelson, "Rustling Bob" Bryant, V. R. Whitaker, John "the Prowler" Collins, Jim Irvin, Charles Snow, and a Texan named Reese Gobles, who was once convicted of raping a 10-year-old girl. The gang began stealing horses and making a general nuisance of themselves. They called themselves Selman's Scouts, although they became more widely known as the Rustlers.[18]

Selman's Scouts were in the vicinity of Fort Stanton when they arrived at William H. Hudgens's rented brewery on September 26, 1878. The gang asked Hudgens to purchase some ammunition on their behalf at the post. When Hudgens refused to assist the band of ruffians, several of them rode into Fort Stanton to purchase a large amount of bullets at the fort themselves. Col. Nathan Dudley spotted the horse thieves and temporarily locked them inside the guardhouse. Dudley also made sure all the ammunition was returned with a full refund before releasing the prisoners and ordering them off the post.[19]

The disgruntled Rustlers regrouped on the outskirts of Fort Stanton that evening and headed back to the brewery rented by Will Hudgens. When the gang realized Hudgens wasn't home, they fired shots into the building and began ransacking the place. Selman and his men smashed up the windows

Diablos del Infierno 185

and dragged Hudgens's wife and sister outside, where they "abused and mauled" both women as Col. Nathan Dudley later described it. One of the gang walloped a man named Sheppard over the head with a revolver when the old-timer voiced his objections over the appalling treatment of the ladies. "Three of the party were known by Sheriff Peppin as belonging to the so called Riley & Dolan outfits and one was an escaped convict from Texas," Colonel Dudley would report. "Gunter [John Selman] is still suffering from wounds received a short time ago. He is from Texas and said to be a very bad man."[20]

John Selman and his band of saddle-scum were not finished demonstrating just how bad they were and stormed into Lincoln like a herd of unhinged beasts. The gang broke into several adobe homes, smashed up the furniture, terrorized citizens, and tore the clothing from various women's bodies. They also ransacked Avery Clenny's store at La Junta and burned Frank Coe's vacated ranch on the Río Hondo. "The wives and daughters of good citizens being daily insulted by them, driven into the mountains, hiding to save their lives, almost in sight of the post," an appalled Col. Nathan Dudley informed his superiors.[21]

The Rustlers were not satisfied when they arrived at José Chávez y Sánchez's ranch twelve miles south of Lincoln on September 28, 1878. Chávez y Sánchez's teenage sons Clato and Desiderio were cutting hay with an intellectually disabled boy named Lorenzo Lucero in a field when the ruthless gang approached them. John Selman and his rotten bunch shot all three Hispano boys dead out of pure malice and appropriated any horses they could find on the property. The heartbroken José Chávez y Sánchez and the rest of his family fled their farm and sought refuge at the nearby Fritz ranch.[22]

Selman's Scouts headed for the Río Hondo after committing three motiveless murders and arrived on Martín Sánchez's farm in Picacho. The 14-year-old Gregorio Sánchez genially provided John Selman and his gang with some watermelons to feast on. The bloodthirsty Rustlers expressed their gratitude by shooting the Hispano teenager three times before departing. Martín Sánchez quickly carried his wounded son to Martín Chávez's home. As the mayordomo of Picacho, Martín Chávez sent an urgent request for medical assistance to his recent adversary Col. Nathan Dudley at Fort Stanton.

This was no time for partisanship or old grievances. Everyone needed to pull together regardless of their allegiance during the Lincoln County War.[23]

Martín Chávez's friend August Kline reached Fort Stanton and informed Col. Nathan Dudley of the outrages occurring downriver. Dudley quickly dispatched post surgeon Dr. William B. Lyon to Martín Chávez's home in Picacho. The colonel also assigned an officer and twenty buffalo soldiers to provide protection for mail contractor August Kline and Postmaster Ash Upson. The bereaved José Chávez y Sánchez soon arrived at Dudley's parlor to procure coffins for his two murdered sons Clato and Desiderio. "I respectfully ask, in the name of God and humanity, that I be allowed to use the forces at my command to drive these murderers, horse thieves, and escaped convicts out of the country," the officer pleaded to his superiors on September 29, 1878.[24]

Dr. William B. Lyon was on his way to Picacho when the post surgeon was informed that 14-year-old Gregorio Sánchez had already succumbed to his wounds in Martín Chávez's home. Funeral arrangements were made for the murdered boy in Picacho, and Dr. Lyon visited with José Chávez y Sánchez's family at the invitation of Charles Fritz. "Found the whole family in a most pitiful condition, the father and mother almost crazed with grief, and in a state of constant terror," the army surgeon would report. "The war is no longer the faction war of Dolan and McSween, but seems almost altogether confined to depredations and murder by a band of miscreants."[25]

John Selman and his miscreants were not finished with their depredations just yet and arrived at the Bartlett grist mill eleven miles below Fort Stanton. The Rustlers dragged the wives of two Bartlett employees out of their nearby homes, ripped off their clothes, and gang-raped both defenseless women. One of the naked victims managed to reach Martín Chávez's ranch around two o'clock in the morning to report the sickening crime. Martín Chávez, August Kline, and many locals went searching for the other victim. They found the trembling woman lying in a brush. August Kline headed for Fort Stanton to report the incident to Col. Nathan Dudley but allowed the victims and their families some discretion when refusing to provide their identities. Dudley dispatched Capt. Henry Carroll and twenty buffalo soldiers to provide some manner of protection for the local citizens, one of whom had recently asked the Rustlers who they were.

"We are devils just come from Hell!" one of the deviants replied.[26]

Juan Patrón returned to the Río Bonito and found his community in a complete state of turmoil. Lincoln County had hosted its share of badmen throughout the years, but this was madness. Judge Warren Bristol declared that it was impossible to hold court in Lincoln County that October under the present conditions. Lew Wallace had taken his oath as governor in Santa Fe and pleaded with President Rutherford B. Hayes to place Lincoln County under martial law. Hayes was not in favor of criminals being tried, convicted, and hanged by a military commission, although he did issue a somewhat condescending proclamation on October 7, 1878. The president commanded the citizens of Lincoln County and New Mexico Territory to cease "aiding, countenancing, abetting, or taking part in such unlawful proceedings." He also warned the population to "return peaceably to their respective abodes on or noon of the thirteenth day of October." Probate Judge Florencio Gonzáles, Justice John B. Wilson, Saturnino Baca, Francisco Romero y Luma, Nicholas Torres, J. Gregorio Trujillo, and George Kimbrell signed a petition the following day and sent it to Governor Lew Wallace. They demanded military protection for the citizens of Lincoln County under terms of the Treaty of Guadalupe Hidalgo.[27]

Juan Patrón and various citizens could no longer wait for military protection and decided to deal with Selman's Scouts themselves. Sam Corbet and Isaac Ellis led a posse of citizens armed with buffalo guns in pursuit of the Rustlers. They chased the gang from the Fritz ranch to Martín Chávez's property in Picacho. Juan Patrón also led a large posse of local Hispanos in pursuit of Selman's bunch after the gang fled toward Roswell. "Juan Patrón will be down from [Lincoln] this evening with twenty-six men," Sergeant George Davis reported on October 11, 1878. Racial tensions persisted in Lincoln County, and the impending arrival of Juan Patrón and his armed Hispanos did not sit well with the Anglo landowners and cattlemen in the region. The Hunter & Evans Stock Association quickly sent one of their agents to Col. Nathan Dudley, informing the officer that "a fight would be inevitable between the stockmen and this body of Mexicans if the latter attempted to regulate matters in this section."[28]

Selman's Scouts killed their own member "Rustling Bob" Bryant and left his corpse floating in the Río Pecos before most of the gang fled into Seven Rivers. While John Selman and his brother Tom escaped into Texas, Juan Patrón and his armed Hispanos pursued two members of the Rustlers into San Miguel County and captured them north of Fort Sumner. The thought of four murdered boys and multiple violated women was enough to ignite a vengeful fire in any man's belly. Juan decided to follow the Regulators' example and carried out some vigilante justice by executing both members of the Rustlers, leaving one of them hanging from a tree branch on the outskirts of Puerto de Luna. The político would have felt they had earned it.[29]

***

The 25-year-old Juan Patrón was growing disillusioned with Lincoln County when resuming his duties as chairman of the county commission in the fall of 1878. The continued threats on his life, as well as his time spent in San Miguel County, gave him cause to reconsider his options moving forward. The Hispano politician still carried out his duties efficiently when convening the commission that October. The Patrón commission appointed the boards of registration for Lincoln County's six precincts and duly named the judges for the elections scheduled for November. The commission would fail to register in time for the territorial elections, however. There were soon rumors that an entire Hispano family from Seven Rivers had been slaughtered on the Río Pecos in West Texas. Juan decided not to run for reelection in Lincoln County that November, further illustrating his consideration of setting up stakes elsewhere in Nuevo México.[30]

Juan Patrón would not have shed any tears when learning of Lawrence G. Murphy's death in Santa Fe on October 20, 1878. The infamous Irishman succumbed to cirrhosis and was buried in the Masonic and Odd Fellows Cemetery the following day. "I was very small for my age when I first went to work for the Murphy, Dolan company," Hispano-Anglo teenager Abran Miller later recalled. "I got my clothes and board and Mr. Murphy gave forty dollars to my mother, each month. I soon made them a good cowhand and then I got sixty dollars a month." Although Jimmy Dolan, John Riley, and their House partisans mourned the loss of a friend, Juan Patrón and his fellow McSween partisans felt a sense of elation over Murphy's demise. "Everybody rejoiced over it," remembered Frank Coe.[31]

While Juan Patrón continued his duties in Lincoln, his friend Susan McSween and her attorney Huston L. Chapman were continuing their crusade against Col. Nathan Dudley in Las Vegas. Chapman started writing various letters to Governor Lew Wallace, declaring Dudley "criminally responsible" for Alexander McSween's death. They also traveled to Santa Fe and met with the governor personally to plead their case. Wallace readily agreed that Dudley had demonstrated partisanship during the five-day siege in Lincoln and afforded Susan McSween with a "special safeguard" when she returned to the Río Bonito the following month. Dudley responded to Susan's campaign against him by procuring affidavits from Sheriff George Peppin, Deputy Jack Long, Saturnino Baca, Dr. Daniel Appel, and her former employee Francisco Gómez alleging the widow was a "profane, lewd, and unreliable woman" who engaged in sexual liaisons with various citizens outside of wedlock.[32]

Having taken residence in the Palace of the Governors in Santa Fe, Lew Wallace quickly grew to loathe New Mexico. The proud Hoosier was looking for a quick fix in Lincoln County so he could get the hell out of the territory as soon as possible. He never wanted the position in the first place, and he was far more concerned with trying to write his biblical novel *Ben Hur: A Tale of the Christ*. The governor also realized who was really running things in New Mexico. "I came here and found a 'Ring' with a hand on the throat of the territory," he would inform one old friend. "I refused to join them, and now they are proposing to fight me in the Senate."[33]

Lew Wallace issued a proclamation that he hoped would rapidly settle things in Lincoln County on November 13, 1878. Wallace declared a "general pardon for misdemeanors and offenses" committed by military officers and those not under indictment for unlawful activities during the period from February to November 13, 1878. Those under indictment would still have to answer to the courts. The ink was barely dry on Wallace's proclamation before the reluctant governor appealed to Secretary of State William Evarts for an ambassadorship on November 24. "The progress made in suppressing the insurrectionary troubles in Lincoln county [which was my] special mission here [is] accomplished," Wallace prematurely insisted. "Do you not think me entitled to a promotion?"[34]

Juan Patrón welcomed his friend Susan McSween back to Lincoln when the determined widow arrived with Huston Chapman and took residence in the vacant Baca house on November 23, 1878. Billy Bonney and Tom Folliard also returned from the Texas Panhandle that month after their comrades Fred Waite, Henry Brown, and John Middleton decided not to return to Nuevo México. José Chávez y Chávez, Doc Scurlock, Charlie Bowdre, Jim French, and various local Hispanos continued hanging around town with Bonney and Folliard. "A greater portion of the McSween element was composed of Mexicans," George Kimbrell later recalled. The McSween partisans began congregating at Maximiano de Guevara's home with Huston Chapman, and the one-armed attorney continued mailing letters to Governor Wallace. "The McSween men are willing to stand their trial in the proper county of the territory, or to observe your proclamation, provided, the other side, or 'ring' observe it, but they will never allow themselves to be arrested by murderers like Col. Dudley and Sheriff Peppin," Chapman informed the governor.[35]

The return of Billy Bonney and various Regulators put enough wind up Col. Nathan Dudley for him to pen his own letter to the *New Mexican*. The officer excoriated Governor Wallace for suggesting any military officers had committed offenses during the Lincoln County War in his proclamation. Dudley also laid waste to Wallace's assertions that the hostilities in Lincoln County had ceased when writing to the district headquarters on December 17, 1878. "If His Excellency, the Governor, thinks peace and order prevails in Lincoln county, he is the worse fooled official I ever saw," the colonel insisted. "If he has ever taken any action that could be construed into contributing on establishing serenity to the well disposed and peaceable portion of the community, I am not aware of it." Wallace was not impressed, having already requested that District Commander Gen. Edward Hatch relieve Dudley of his command at Fort Stanton.[36]

The ongoing hostilities in Lincoln broiled over again when Sheriff George Peppin encouraged an allegedly intoxicated 2nd Lt. James French to arrest Doc

Scurlock and several Regulators at Maximiano de Guevara's home on the night of December 13. The Regulators were nowhere to be found when Lieutenant French broke in through the door and began insulting de Guevara and his wife. The officer and three of his buffalo soldiers then arrested a young Hispano for carrying a revolver outside John Copeland's house before getting into a fierce argument with Huston Chapman and Susan McSween at the Baca residence. John Copeland also shot and wounded a 19-year-old Dolan supporter named Juan "Johnny" Mes later that night and quickly turned himself over to the authorities. Huston Chapman, Susan McSween, and Maximiano de Guevara swore warrants against Lt. James French the following day, although the officer would be cleared of any wrongdoing by a military tribunal. Juan Patrón and José Montaño had both sworn affidavits that Lieutenant French had not been intoxicated during his stay in Lincoln. John Copeland was acquitted for shooting young Juan Mes, who was fortunate to survive the bullet wounds he had received in his chest and abdomen.[37]

Animosities persisted along the Río Bonito throughout the remainder of the year. The impetuous Huston Chapman continued his campaign against Col. Nathan Dudley with Susan McSween's full support. Juan Patrón, José Montaño, John Copeland, and A. J. Ballard served as bondsmen when Susan took her oath as administratrix of the McSween, Tunstall, and Brewer estates. Billy Bonney and the remaining Regulators continued to freely roam around Lincoln, and Colonel Dudley eventually prohibited the McSween partisans from visiting Fort Stanton except to collect their mail. George "Dad" Peppin was feeling the heat and officially resigned as sheriff, thereby annulling the appointments of his deputies. Jimmy Dolan, Jack Long, and Billy Mathews subsequently fled to Fort Stanton to seek Colonel Dudley's protection on December 27. In a letter penned at Fort Stanton on New Year's Eve, Dolan informed Governor Wallace that conditions in Lincoln County would improve if Huston Chapman was "silenced."[38]

Lincoln County desperately needed a new sheriff to maintain any semblance of law and order following George Peppin's resignation. Martín Chávez's brother-in-law George Kimbrell was duly appointed to office on January 1, 1879. The 36-year-old Kimbrell was respected by many citizens and held good relations with the local Hispanos. In contrast with his predecessors William Brady, John Copeland, and George Peppin, the new sheriff had remained neutral throughout the Lincoln County War. "The effort to restore peace and order in Lincoln County seems to be a hopeless undertaking," the *Mesilla Valley Independent* suggested on January 11. "A spirit of contention and strife seems to float about in the very air."[39]

Sheriff George Kimbrell's task of restoring peace was made slightly easier when Susan McSween and Jimmy Dolan cemented a truce in early January 1879. Susan also hired a cattle detective named Charley Scase to retrieve the Tunstall cattle which had been stolen by rustlers during the summer. Susan's attorney Huston Chapman swore out a warrant for Col. Nathan Dudley and headed for Las Vegas, intending to appeal to Gen. Edward Hatch in Santa Fe for the orders to have Dudley arrested for complicity in Alexander McSween's murder. Juan Patrón accompanied the belligerent attorney to Las Vegas, although Chapman failed in his quest to have Dudley arrested. Much of the population was buzzing in anticipation of the arrival of the railroad. "Las Vegas will soon be the principal shipping point for all New Mexico," the *Mesilla Valley Independent* declared.[40]

While Juan Patrón was spending more time in San Miguel County, the 20-year-old Yginio Salazar was finally healed up and back on his feet. The young vaquero resumed riding with Billy Bonney, José Chávez y Chávez, and the remaining Regulators in Lincoln by mid-February. "Lincoln County aspires to a newspaper and a land office," the *New Mexican* skeptically announced in Santa Fe. "Homesteads and paper bullets would be decided progress for that section. Give them anything if they will only behave themselves."[41]

Governor Lew Wallace was still reluctant to visit southeastern New Mexico, so it was left to William Bonney to put an end to the Lincoln County War when organizing a peace meeting with Jimmy Dolan, Jessie Evans, and his longtime enemies. The Kid was tired of fighting and even willing to stand trial if necessary. Jimmy Dolan and Jessie Evans received Bonney's message in Fort Stanton and agreed to meet with Kid Antrim and his comrades in Lincoln to discuss peace terms.[42]

Yginio Salazar was waiting alongside Billy Bonney, Tom Folliard, Tom "Joe Bowers" Cullens, and possibly José Chávez y Chávez and Martín

Chávez, as evening approached in Lincoln on February 18, 1879. When Jimmy Dolan, Jessie Evans, Billy Mathews, Edgar Walz, George van Sickle, James Redman, and disreputable Catron cowboy Bill Campbell rode in from Fort Stanton, the two parties cautiously took cover behind some adobe walls. Bad blood rarely washed away easily on the Río Bonito. Jessie Evans suggested it was impossible to negotiate with the Kid and voiced his intention to kill him.

"We have met for the purpose of making peace," Billy Bonney shouted in response. "I don't care to open negotiations with a fight, but if you'll come at me three at a time, I'll whip the whole damned bunch of you!"

Edgar Walz tried to calm everyone down until cooler heads prevailed. William Bonney and Jimmy Dolan eventually emerged from cover and shook hands in the street. They encouraged their companions to do the same. Handshakes were made all around and everyone headed into a saloon to celebrate the suspension of hostilities. They all enjoyed a drink and even sang songs together. The two factions also made a pact in which they agreed to neither kill any member of the opposing party nor provide any evidence against them in future. It was time to "lay aside our arms and go to work," as William Bonney later described it. The Lincoln County War was finally over.[43]

Peace agreement or not, Sheriff George Kimbrell was still compelled to do his duty when he spotted young Bill Bonney and Yginio Salazar in the saloon. He possessed a warrant for Bonney for murder and a warrant for Salazar for resisting the sheriff. The Kid subsequently informed Kimbrell that if the warrant for him was for murder, then he would not be taken alive. The sheriff promptly exited the saloon, saddled his horse, and rode for Fort Stanton to request military assistance. Jimmy Dolan and some of his men continued drinking heavily and insisted Billy Bonney and his compadres accompany them outside so as not to break up the party. The Kid and his friends reluctantly agreed, not wishing to appear unfriendly.[44]

Juan Patrón had returned from Las Vegas with Huston Chapman earlier that evening and may not have been in the best of moods at the time. The Jesuit bill he had steadfastly supported during his time as speaker of the house had just been annulled in Santa Fe. Juan also would have been able to hear the peace celebrations from inside his store. Some of the revelers began singing, firing shots in the air, and ringing cow bells in the street. Juan probably rolled his eyes or something similar, but at least the two factions weren't trying to kill each other anymore.

The exhausted Juan Patrón cordially stepped outside to greet the peace party when they unexpectedly arrived at his doorstep. His pulse began racing when Bill Campbell suddenly pointed a pistol in his direction. Juan quickly took cover behind the other members of the party while the intoxicated cowpuncher loudly threatened to murder him. Billy Bonney, Yginio Salazar, and their compadres shielded their Hispano associate and successfully dissuaded Campbell from doing so. The peace party then headed back up the street, and Juan quickly returned to the relative safety of his store after surviving yet another attempt on his life.[45]

Bill Campbell was leading the peace party back up the street when he bumped into Huston Chapman, with a partially bandaged face, near the torreón. The one-armed lawyer had corralled his horses behind the Baca home after returning from Las Vegas with Juan Patrón. He was battling with neuralgia and was on his way to a neighbors' home to acquire some bread with which to craft a poultice for his face.

"Who are you and where are you going?" Bill Campbell barked.

"My name is Chapman, and I'm attending to my business," the one-armed lawyer replied.

Billy Bonney sensed trouble and tried to leave, only for Jessie Evans to grab him by the collar and ensure he stayed put. When Huston Chapman refused to join the celebrations, Bill Campbell stuck the barrel of his revolver into the lawyer's chest and insisted he dance for them.

"You cannot scare me, boys," Chapman insisted, refusing to entertain the malicious Campbell and his cronies. "I know you and it's no use. You have tried that before. Am I talking to Mr. Dolan?"

"No, but you're talking to a damned good friend of his," Jessie Evans menacingly replied.

The drunk Jimmy Dolan then fired a shot into the ground. Bill Campbell fired a bullet from his own pistol a moment later, shooting Huston Chapman in the chest.

"My God, I am killed!" the lawyer screamed, as flames engulfed his shirt due to the close proximity of Campbell's revolver.

The mortally wounded Chapman tumbled into Edgar Walz's arms before his lifeless body collapsed onto the street. Bill Campbell proudly boasted of his actions while leading the peace party farther up the street toward Frank McCullum's restaurant, located where the McSween home had previously stood.

"I promised my God and General Dudley that I would kill Chapman," Campbell exclaimed. "And I have done it!"

Bill Campbell also vowed to murder Susan McSween's cattle detective Charley Scase before leading his companions inside the McCullum eatin' house. Jimmy Dolan and his men ordered some oysters for supper, intending to continue the celebrations. Bill Campbell encouraged Edgar Walz to place a revolver beside Huston Chapman's corpse so it would appear to have been a case of self-defense. When Walz nervously refused, Campbell handed the pistol to William Bonney after the Kid offered to plant the weapon at the scene. Billy left the restaurant and immediately headed for the Ellis home at the western end of town rather than assisting Campbell. The Kid and his pal Tom Folliard quickly rode for San Patricio, wishing to avoid any association with Huston Chapman's murder. Yginio Salazar decided to do the same. Even a successful peace meeting with Jimmy Dolan's crowd had resulted in bloodshed.[46]

Sheriff George Kimbrell returned to Lincoln with Lt. Byron Dawson, assistant surgeon William B. Lyon, and twenty buffalo soldiers as midnight was approaching. "I have seen thus evening in the town of Lincoln County, N.M., William Bonney, alias Kid, charged with murder, and a Mexican, Salazar by name, charged with resisting the sheriff," Kimbrell had informed Col. Nathan Dudley in Fort Stanton. They searched for Billy and Yginio in several homes but were, naturally, unable to find them. Kimbrell and the troops eventually found Huston Chapman's one-armed corpse still lying in the street. Lieutenant Dawson instructed his buffalo soldiers to assist Justice John B. Wilson in transporting Chapman's body into the nearby courthouse, where Dr. William B. Lyon performed an autopsy.[47]

The murder of Huston Chapman set off a wave of panic in Lincoln. Many citizens feared the lawyer's death would lead to a renewal of guerrilla warfare throughout the county. Juan Patrón was among the those who signed a petition for the stationing of troops in Lincoln to assist Sheriff Kimbrell the following morning of February 19, 1879. The petition also included the signatures of Justice Wilson, José Montaño, Saturnino Baca, Ben Ellis, Sam Corbet, Edgar Walz, John Copeland, Susan McSween, and various others in addition to Kimbrell himself. Col. Nathan Dudley dispatched Lt. Millard Goodwin and twenty-one buffalo soldiers to assist the sheriff in Lincoln later that evening.[48]

Sheriff George Kimbrell also requested six soldiers to accompany him to San Patricio in pursuit of William Bonney and Yginio Salazar on February 20, 1879. Bonney, Salazar, and their amigos proved elusive while hiding out for the next couple of weeks. Sheriff Kimbrell had his work cut out for him, even with a detachment of soldiers remaining in Lincoln for the rest of the month. The outrage expressed over Huston Chapman's murder had a particular vehemence on the heels of the successful armistice organized by Billy Bonney. "Chapman has been killed in cold blood," the *Mesilla Valley Independent* reported. "The old existing feud has doubtless caused the murder. The killing is lamentable in the extreme; the good citizens of Lincoln County have expressed as satisfied that peace had been restored; old citizens that had left returned to their homes satisfied that the laws would be obeyed, and started out fair for an era of peace and progress."[49]

Susan McSween did not give up her crusade against Col. Nathan Dudley in the wake of Huston Chapman's murder. The widow hired a seasoned attorney named Ira Leonard to continue her litigation. The balding New Yorker promptly arrived from Las Vegas and publicly declared charges against Colonel Dudley for abetting Alexander McSween's murder, arson, theft, threats against Justice John B. Wilson, and slander on March 1, 1879. He also filed the charges to Secretary of War George W. McCrary several days later. Ira Leonard was determined to take on the Santa Fe Ring. He also became Lew Wallace's trusted advisor in Lincoln and personally encouraged the governor to make a long-overdue journey to the Río Bonito. Meanwhile, Capt. Henry Carroll informed Wallace that the rumors were true: a family of nine Nuevomexicanos had indeed been slaughtered by the Jones boys and their accomplice John Collins below Pope's Crossing on the Río Pecos in West Texas.[50]

Although the slaughter of a family of "Mexicans" appears to have been little concern to Lew Wallace, somebody needed to answer for the murder of Huston Chapman. The Hoosier had no alternative but to finally set out for Lincoln County and would look to Juan Patrón for assistance when he arrived.

Chapter 9

The Mounted Rifles

You must become a servant of the people.
—César Chávez

Juan Patrón greeted Lew Wallace with a polite handshake shortly after the governor arrived in Lincoln with Gen. Edward Hatch and a military caravan on March 5, 1879. The 51-year-old Wallace took a room in the Montaño store. General Hatch set up quarters in Fort Stanton. The governor soon began strolling along the Río Bonito and discussing the recent troubles with Juan Patrón, Sheriff George Kimbrell, and various other citizens. While Lincoln was probably the last place he wanted to be, the Hoosier quickly developed an immense respect for Juan Patrón, immediately recognizing his intelligence and considerable influence with the locals. The Hispano prodigy was clearly someone capable of assisting him in settling things down in Lincoln County as rapidly as possible.[1]

Governor Lew Wallace may have taken his sweet time in traveling to Lincoln, but he quickly took action when he finally arrived. His first task was to apprehend those responsible for Huston Chapman's murder. Wallace informed Gen. Edward Hatch that Jimmy Dolan, Bill Campbell, Jessie Evans, and Billy Mathews were apparently hiding out in Carrizozo. Lt. Millard Goodwin and a detachment of soldiers subsequently arrested Campbell,

Evans, and Mathews at Lawrence G. Murphy's old ranch and escorted them to Fort Stanton on March 6, 1879. Wallace also relayed information to General Hatch that Billy "Kid" Bonney and Tom Folliard were reportedly hiding out with Yginio Salazar and his family in Las Tablas. Sergeant Israel Murphy and nine buffalo soldiers were sent out after them but failed to locate any of the former Regulators. Bonney and Folliard had been charged as accessories to Huston's Chapman's murder despite not having played any part in the attorney's death.[2]

Governor Wallace presented a scathingly critical assessment of Nathan Dudley to Gen. Edward Hatch in Fort Stanton and requested Dudley be relieved of his command on March 7, 1879. General Hatch merrily obliged and appointed Capt. Henry Carroll as the new post commander. Nathan Dudley was furious and inevitably appealed to Washington for a court of inquiry to be held so he could potentially clear himself of exceeding his orders during the five-day siege the previous summer. Juan Patrón was satisfied with the governor's initiative and organized a public meeting in Lincoln the following day, during which Wallace gloated of having carried out "the best day's work ever done for the citizens of Lincoln County."[3]

On March 11 Governor Lew Wallace wrote a list of former Regulators, Dolan partisans, and members of the Selman gang whom he felt should be arrested "as speedily as possible." The list of names was delivered to Capt. Henry Carroll, whom Wallace encouraged to "rush the 'Black Knights' and their confederates without rest and regardless of boundary lines." Yginio Salazar was the only Nuevomexicano on the list, and the twenty-fourth name the governor jotted down. His slightly younger amigo Billy Bonney was the fourteenth name recorded by Wallace: "John Slaughter, Andrew Boyle, John Selman, Tom Selman, Gus Gildea, J. Irvin, Reese Gables, 'Rustling' Bob, Robert Speaks, The Pilgrim, John Beckwith, Jim French, 'Doc' Scurlock, 'Kid' Wm. Bonney, Tom O'Folliard, Charles Bowdry, Henry Brown, John Middleton, Fred Waite, J. B. Mathews, James J. Dolan, George Davis (Tom Jones), Frank Rivers, Igenio Salazar, John Jones, James Jones, Marion Turner, Caleb Hall (Collins), Haskell Jones, Buck Powell, James Tyson, Jake Owens, Frank Wheeler, Joseph Hill (Olney)."[4]

Although some of the men on Governor Wallace's list avoided capture, Capt. Henry Carroll managed to arrest Jimmy Dolan a short time later. The Irishman was transported to Fort Stanton, and joined his friends Jessie Evans, Bill Campbell, and J. B. "Billy" Mathews inside the guardhouse. The governor also provided Carroll with a list of registered cattle brands in an effort to stamp out rustling in Lincoln County. The post commander was instructed to deliver any unbranded stock to Lincoln and arrest anyone unable to produce a bill of sale for any cattle in their possession.[5]

Having witnessed Huston Chapman's senseless murder shortly after establishing a truce with Jimmy Dolan in Lincoln, William Bonney wrote a letter to Governor Wallace on March 13, 1879. The Kid always believed himself to be on the right side of things during the Lincoln County War, and he offered to provide testimony against Jimmy Dolan and his longtime enemies in exchange for a clean slate. "I have indictments against me for things that happened in the late Lincoln County War," Billy respectfully informed the governor. "I was Present when Mr. Chapman was [murdered], and know who did it and if it were not for those indictments I would have made it clear before now. If it is in your power to [annul] those indictments I hope you will do so, so as to give me a chance to explain." Wallace seized his opportunity to procure a valuable witness and sent Kid Antrim a note two days later. The governor instructed Bonney to secretly meet with him at Justice John B. Wilson's home in Lincoln at nine o'clock on the night of March 17. "I have authority to exempt you from prosecution, if you will testify to what you say you know," Wallace assured the Kid. "The object of the meeting at Squire Wilson's is to arrange the matter in a way to make your life safe."[6]

On March 15, 1879, the same day Lew Wallace scrawled his reply to William Bonney, the governor approached Juan Patrón in Lincoln to discuss the establishment of a county militia. Wallace instructed Juan to gather up a force of between thirty to sixty men whom the Hispano prodigy could trust to assist the local authorities and help restore order in Lincoln County. The governor insisted that all the volunteers possess their own horses and firearms and be ready to ride whenever called upon, and further encouraged Patrón to recruit men from outside the Lincoln precinct. The militia would be dubbed the Lincoln County Rifles. Their general expenses would be covered by notable citizens, although Wallace advised that any "extravagant purchases will not be allowed or recommended for payment."[7]

Juan Patrón agreed to assume the post of militia captain and spent the next few days recruiting more than forty able-bodied men throughout the region. Capitán Patrón acquired the services of Ben Ellis and Martín Sánchez to serve as his first and second lieutenants. Martín Chávez was an obvious choice for recruitment, and the leading citizen of Picacho proved a willing volunteer. Juan also recruited José Chávez y Chávez, Florencio Cháves, and Sequio Sánchez in San Patricio. Yginio Salazar was permitted to sign up, having presumably convinced the authorities of his innocence regarding Huston Chapman's murder and taken a slap on the wrist for resisting the sheriff. His older brother José Salazar and Apolonio Sedillo of Las Tablas signed up as well. Capitán Patrón also recruited sharpshooter Fernando Herrera, José María Sánchez, Camilo Nuñez, Ramón Montoya, Estólano Sánchez, Jesús Rodríguez, and various other local Hispanos. Elias Gray, Alex Rudder, J. C. Wilkons, and George Washington also volunteered.[8]

While Juan Patrón was assembling his Lincoln County Rifles, the cautious William Bonney sneaked into Lincoln to meet with Governor Lew Wallace in John B. Wilson's abode on the night of March 17, 1879. Wallace assured the Kid that he would receive protection while providing testimony against the Dolan partisans the following month after a staged arrest was carried out by Sheriff George Kimbrell. "In return for doing this, I will let you go scot-free with a pardon in your pocket for all your misdeeds," the governor promised the young desperado. Billy placed his trust in Wallace and returned to the San Patricio region later that night to await Sheriff Kimbrell's arrival. The Kid was safe among the local Nuevomexicanos, the vast majority of whom adored him. "Everyone who knew him loved him," Yginio Salazar later said.[9]

Juan Patrón and his Lincoln County Rifles were called into action when Governor Lew Wallace received word that Jessie Evans and Billy Campbell had escaped Fort Stanton with the assistance of their shady guard "Texas Jack," whom the silver-tongued Evans had convinced to flee the post with them. Wallace knew better than to request assistance from Dolan sympathizer

Capt. eorge Purington and quickly sent a note to Juan Patrón in the early hours of March 19, 1879: "Be good enough to send word to all your men to turn out as soon as possible to join in the hunt for Jesse Evans and William Campbell, who escaped from Fort Stanton last night. Say to your men that, as Governor of New Mexico, I offer a reward of $1,000 for Evans and Campbell."[10]

Juan Patrón, Martín Chávez, José Chávez y Chávez, Yginio Salazar, and the rest of the Lincoln County Rifles set out in pursuit of the fugitives. Jessie Evans and Bill Campbell's escape also gave Billy Bonney cause for concern. He knew they would murder him if learning of his arrangement with Governor Wallace. On March 20, 1879, the Kid sent a message to Wallace through John B. Wilson, asking the governor what he should do next. The governor assured Kid Antrim that Evans and Campbell's escape made no difference to their arrangement. Billy then sent Wallace a letter assuring him that he would "keep his appointment," expressing his concerns over being "killed like a dog unarmed" and his distrust of Lt. Millard Goodwin at Fort Stanton. The Kid also offered some advice on how to capture the elusive Evans and Campbell. "You will never catch those fellows on the road," Bonney insisted. "Watch [Fritz's house], Captain Baca's ranch and the brewery[.] They will either go to Seven Rivers or to Jicarillo Mountains[,] they will stay around close until the scouting parties come in . . . it is not my place to advise you, but I am anxious to have them caught, and perhaps know how men hide better than you."[11]

While Juan Patrón and his Rifles returned to Lincoln after spending two days combing the countryside for Jessie Evans and Bill Campbell, the Kid and his loyal pal Tom Folliard were taken into custody by Sheriff George Kimbrell below San Patricio on March 23, 1879. Bonney and Folliard were escorted to Lincoln and stationed inside Juan Patrón's store. Governor Lew Wallace sat down with William Bonney that night and recorded various pieces of incriminating information the Kid provided him about the Dolan partisans, the Boys, and the Rustlers. Billy was renowned for being loyal to his friends and did not reveal any information about his fellow Regulators or many amigos. Kid Antrim and Tom Folliard settled into agreeable confinement in the Patrón store, playing cards with Sheriff George Kimbrell and eating well. Billy was permitted to roam around Lincoln with his guns and visit friends, provided he always returned to the Patrón store. "If he'd just give you his word, you could trust him with it," young Robert Casey later said.[12]

Although trying his best to "settle down," as he later described it, William Bonney was naively unaware that Lew Wallace could not have cared less about him. The governor considered the teenager an expendable ruffian who could provide him with little more than some useful inside information and testimony. Wallace also couldn't understand the local Hispanos' strong affections for Bonney. The old general was shocked when observing the local minstrels playing outside the Kid's window at the Patrón store one night. "A precious specimen nick-named 'The Kid,' whom the sheriff is holding here in the Plaza, as it is called, is an object of tender regard," Wallace wrote to Secretary of Interior Carl Schurz. "I heard singing and music the other night; going to the door, I found the minstrels of the village actually serenading the fellow in his prison."[13]

Despite viewing his prize witness William Bonney with contempt, Governor Wallace was still determined to see Jessie Evans and Bill Campbell back in irons. He implored Juan Patrón to assemble a fresh posse of nine Lincoln County Rifles to go after the fugitives. Juan sent his second lieutenant, Martín Sánchez, to Fort Stanton with a request for five days' worth of rations and ammunition. Dolan loyalist Capt. George Purington staunchly refused. Juan subsequently approached José Montaño, who was willing to distribute the necessary supplies. Martín Sánchez soon led the squad of militiamen out of Lincoln and spent the next six days searching for the two gringos along the Río Pecos. Jessie Evans and Bill Campbell had fled into Texas, and the frustrated Martín Sánchez returned to Lincoln empty-handed on March 29, 1879. Although the Rifles would not be collecting Governor Wallace's $1,000 reward, they did manage to capture various Dolan partisans and escort them to Fort Stanton.[14]

Juan Patrón personally led ten of his Lincoln County Rifles north after Governor Lew Wallace received word that Charles Meriwether Bowdre and Josiah "Doc" Scurlock were hiding out at a ranch ten miles east of Fort Sumner in San Miguel County. The former Regulators were still under federal indictment for the killing of Andrew L. Roberts at Blazer's Mill during the Lincoln County War. Juan Patrón and his hombres wisely refrained from riding the more commonly used trails and traveled only at night. They startled a sleeping Doc Scurlock after crossing the county line and took him into custody during the night of April 11, 1879. Charlie Bowdre was nowhere to be found. Juan began leading his Rifles and their prisoner back toward the Río Bonito the following morning, also sending a message to his first lieutenant, Ben Ellis, down in Lincoln:

> I got Scurlock but Charlie Bowdre was gone. Day before yesterday, while passing through here, I was informed that a party of nine well-armed and mounted men had passed through Taiban and travelling towards Lincoln along the Pecos River. I immediately notified the troops at Roswell of their approach. I conversed with parties just in from the plains, and they say that those chaps are the same "Rustlers," and before they left Texas, they killed two men and robbed them of everything they had. I will await the buckboard from below to learn what direction they went, and if there is a chance for me, I will go down the river.
>
> Be ready up there [in Lincoln] in case the troops let them pass [Roswell]. Those murderers mean mischief, and if they are not captured or killed, they will surely commit murder and rapine. The troops surely have the best chance to have a rub with them since they are notified and posted of their movements. Regards to everybody,
>
> Signed, Juan B. Patrón[15]

Juan Patrón and his Rifles safely escorted Doc Scurlock back to Lincoln despite their concerns over the possible return of Selman's Scouts in the region. Scurlock then joined his old comrades Billy Bonney and Tom Folliard in the Patrón store. The Santa Fe Ring also made their presence known when District Attorney William L. Rynerson and Judge Warren Bristol arrived in Fort Stanton on April 13, 1879, for the approaching district term of court. Bristol quickly used habeas corpus writs filed by Las Vegas attorney Sidney Wilson to ensure that Jimmy Dolan and his captured partisans were released from the guardhouse. Dolan and his allies routinely snickered and laughed at Juan Patrón and his Lincoln County Rifles, derogatorily referring to them as "the Governor's Heel-flies."[16]

The district court convened in Lincoln with Judge Warren Bristol presiding on April 14, 1879. As no term was held the previous autumn, it was left to Judge Bristol, Sheriff George Kimbrell, and court clerk Louis H. Baldy to select names for grand and petit jury duties. The selection process was completed three days later, with Isaac Ellis serving as foreman of the grand jury alongside Martín Sánchez, John Newcomb, Juan Trujillo, and various locals. Justice John B. Wilson was duly appointed as court interpreter. Many members of the grand jury possessed sympathies for the McSween partisans, and Judge Bristol advised them not to display any partisanship throughout what proved to be one of the busiest district court sessions in the brief history of Lincoln County.[17]

Several cases were continued throughout the next two weeks, including the murder indictment against William Bonney, John Middleton, and Henry Brown for the killing of William Brady during the Lincoln County War. Middleton and Brown were long gone, but William Bonney pleaded not guilty and placed himself on county for trial. The Kid had total faith that Governor Wallace would deliver his pardon after providing testimony against Jimmy Dolan, Jessie Evans, and Bill Campbell as agreed. Bonney fulfilled his promise by taking the stand and testifying against his longtime enemies, although the governor was no longer in the vicinity. Wallace had departed Lincoln for Santa Fe when the jury selection process was completed. District Attorney William L. Rynerson soon went after Bonney in the courtroom, determined to see the Kid hanged for the killing of his old friend William Brady. "He is bent on going after the Kid," Ira Leonard wrote to Governor Wallace. "He is a Dolan man." Rynerson successfully filed for a change of venue to Doña Ana County, where he hoped to see William Bonney convicted of murder during the next term of court.[18]

While Billy Bonney continued waiting in Juan Patrón's store for Governor Wallace to deliver his pardon as promised, the grand jury in Lincoln returned over two hundred indictments against fifty men. The majority of those indicted were Dolan partisans, although Jack Long, Marion Turner, Billy Mathews, and various others were granted immunity from prosecution under the guidelines of Governor Wallace's proclamation. William Bonney's loyal sidekick Tom Folliard was also granted immunity when facing indictment for horse theft. George Peppin and a host of Seven Rivers men were indicted for the killing of Frank MacNab the previous year. James Dolan and the absent Bill Campbell were indicted for the murder of Huston Chapman, with Jessie Evans indicted as an accessory. George Peppin, John Kinney, and Col. Nathan Dudley were also indicted for arson in relation to the burning of the McSween home the previous summer. They were all granted a change of venue to Doña Ana County for the next term of court.[19]

Susan McSween's attorney Ira Leonard displayed his nerve by sticking around after two unidentified assailants tried to murder him when firing shots at his room on the night of April 24. Leonard was convinced the Dolan partisans camped on the outskirts of town were responsible. Sheriff George Kimbrell soon received a note containing a brazen threat against his life scribbled around a diagram of a coffin. Lucas Gallegos had since been recaptured and was convicted of murdering his nephew Sostero García over two years earlier in San Patricio. He was sentenced to one year's imprisonment in the county jail on April 26. The grand jury also returned indictments against John Selman and eight members of his Rustlers for various crimes before the district court adjourned on May 1, 1879.[20]

As one court adjourned in Lincoln County, another court quickly convened. Col. Nathan Dudley's request for a court of inquiry regarding his conduct during the five-day siege had been granted, and proceedings began in Fort Stanton with Col. Galusha Pennypacker, Maj. Nathan W. Osborne, and Capt. Henry R. Brinkerhoff presiding on May 9, 1879. Dudley had shrewdly hired the acid-tongued Santa Fe Ring attorney Henry L. Waldo to serve as his counsel. Capt. Henry H. Humphreys and Ira Leonard handled the prosecution. Governor Lew Wallace had returned from Santa Fe and was the first witness to take the stand in Fort Stanton on May 12. The governor provided some lengthy but ineffective testimony before departing Lincoln County for the second time and wishing never to return. A large number of McSween and Dolan partisans, impartial citizens, and soldiers gave frequently conflicting testimony throughout the next six weeks.[21]

Juan Bautista Patrón limped into the courtroom at Fort Stanton and took the stand on May 11, 1879. The Hispano businessman testified in relation to his attempted assassination by Jim Reese, his argument with Colonel Dudley in Fort Stanton during the siege, his being ordered off the post as a suspected McSween spy, and his subsequent departure for Las Vegas. Juan's friends Isaac Ellis, John B. Wilson, and Susan McSween would all testify in relation to Dudley's conduct in Lincoln during the next couple of weeks. William H. Bonney took a break from voluntary confinement in the Patrón store to testify for the prosecution on May 28. Bonney recalled spotting three white soldiers firing in his direction when making his break from the burning McSween home. Colonel Dudley tried to shift the focus onto the Kid's status as a wanted outlaw while the siege was taking place.[22]

José Chávez y Chávez provided the military court with his own recollection of events when taking the stand after his amigo William Bonney was retired as a witness on May 29, 1879. The former San Patricio constable's testimony for the prosecution was translated for the members of the court by interpreter John B. Wilson:

> CAPT. HUMPHREYS: What is your name and place of residence?
> CHÁVEZ Y CHÁVEZ: My name is José Chávez y Chávez, and my residence is San Patricio, New Mexico.
> CAPT. HUMPHREYS: State if you were at the town of Lincoln on the 19th day of July last, if so, state where you were, and what you saw of the movement of the troops, if anything. State all you saw of their actions, if anything that day?
> CHÁVEZ Y CHÁVEZ: I was in the McSween house. I saw the troops come then into the Plaza. I see them only pass to the Plaza. I did not see any other movement in the day. I saw three soldiers pass with Peppin, twice in front of the house of McSween. They did not make any movements.
> CAPT. HUMPHREYS: How long that day were you in the house and where did you come out of the house that day, and if you saw any soldiers about the house, when you come out, if so, state what, if anything, they did?

Col. Nathan Dudley objected via his counsel before Chávez y Chávez answered, and Captain Humphreys modified his question before continuing:

> CAPT. HUMPHREYS: State when you came out of the house, and what you saw, if anything, of the soldiers?

Colonel Dudley objected via his counsel again, on the grounds that it was irrelevant whether any soldiers were in the vicinity or not unless he was present and the troops were there by his order. Captain Humphreys replied that Dudley's conduct was the subject of inquiry as well as the actions of his soldiers while under his command in Lincoln. The court was cleared, closed, and opened following some deliberation. The court then directed Captain Humphreys's question to be answered by the witness:

CHÁVEZ Y CHÁVEZ: When I come out of the house I saw three soldiers in front of the house of Tunstall's next to the house of McSween.
CAPT. HUMPHREYS: State where the soldiers were standing from McSween's house?
CHÁVEZ Y CHÁVEZ: Standing in front of the house of Tunstall going right towards the house of McSween.
CAPT. HUMPHREYS: State what the soldiers did, if anything, after you came out of the McSween house?
CHÁVEZ Y CHÁVEZ: When I was coming out they fired two or three shots.
CAPT. HUMPHREYS: In which direction and at whom were the shots fired, if you know?
CHÁVEZ Y CHÁVEZ: They were fired at [Harvey] Morris and Thomas [Folliard] who were passing there.
CAPT. HUMPHREYS: Had Morris and Thomas come out of the McSween house?
CHÁVEZ Y CHÁVEZ: Yes, sir.
CAPT. HUMPHREYS: What time of the day was it that you came out of the McSween house?
CHÁVEZ Y CHÁVEZ: Directly after dark, I came out.
CAPT. HUMPHREYS: State how far the soldiers were from you when they fired and if it was light enough so you could plainly see?
CHÁVEZ Y CHÁVEZ: It was about 10 yards and I saw the soldiers by the light of the fire.
CAPT. HUMPHREYS: Did you see any soldiers go anywhere that day from the direction of Col. Dudley's camp, if so, where did they go?
CHÁVEZ Y CHÁVEZ: I did not see them, they were in the middle of the town.
CAPT. HUMPHREYS: Was Morris one of the men killed that night?
CHÁVEZ Y CHÁVEZ: Yes, sir.
CAPT. HUMPHREYS: Did you see any other soldiers do anything that day other than what you have stated, if so, state what you saw them do?
CHÁVEZ Y CHÁVEZ: I did not see anything more.

Captain Humphreys stated that he was finished with the witness, and Col. Nathan Dudley began his cross examination:

> COL. DUDLEY: Had you come out of the McSween building when you say you saw the soldiers fire at Morris and Thomas?
> CHÁVEZ Y CHÁVEZ: I was going after them, behind them, and was outside the house.
> COL. DUDLEY: How far were you from the McSween house at the time?
> CHÁVEZ Y CHÁVEZ: About half way between the McSween and Tunstall houses.
> COL. DUDLEY: In which direction were you going, towards the river?
> CHÁVEZ Y CHÁVEZ: Yes, sir.
> COL. DUDLEY: Were you not running at the full height of your speed?
> CHÁVEZ Y CHÁVEZ: I was running when I saw the soldiers fired, and when they did fire, I run my best.
> COL. DUDLEY: Were you not endeavoring to escape from the McSween house to reach the surrounding darkness and did you not exert yourself to the upmost for that purpose, as soon as you emerged from the McSween house?
> CHÁVEZ Y CHÁVEZ: I came out slowly, tolerably slow because they were not firing at the time.
> COL. DUDLEY: Do you swear to say that you went slowly until you got half way to the Tunstall building and that there was no firing whilst you were making that distance?
> CHÁVEZ Y CHÁVEZ: I went slowly until I saw the soldiers fire, then I went with all my might. No Sir, there was no firing when I came out until I got to the point in the middle between the two houses.
> COL. DUDLEY: Do you know Bob Beckwith, if so, had he been killed at the time the soldiers fired, as you say, at Thomas and Morris?

Capt. Henry Humphreys objected, as no reference to Bob Beckwith had been made in the direct examination. Dudley replied he was merely attempting "to fix the time of the killing of Morris" by the witness, and the court directed José Chávez y Chávez to answer the question:

> CHÁVEZ Y CHÁVEZ: I knew him but I had not seen him. I did not know if he had been killed before that, or not.
> COL. DUDLEY: Do you swear and are you certain that Thomas and Morris were ahead of you when the soldiers fired?

CHÁVEZ Y CHÁVEZ: Yes, sir.

COL. DUDLEY: Was there not a fence about the McSween house on the side from which you went out, if so, how did you get over the fence?

CHÁVEZ Y CHÁVEZ: There was no wall, but a board fence. I went out through the gate.

COL. DUDLEY: What kind of building was the McSween house, was it not an ordinary adobe building with a dirt roof?

CHÁVEZ Y CHÁVEZ: Yes, sir, adobe with dirt and boards on top.

COL. DUDLEY: What time, or about what time, was the McSween house set on fire?

CHÁVEZ Y CHÁVEZ: Little after 12 o'clock.

COL. DUDLEY: The house hadn't burned down when you left it?

CHÁVEZ Y CHÁVEZ: Yes, sir, it was burned to the last room.

COL. DUDLEY: Were these soldiers, that you say fired, standing in front of the Tunstall building, if so, how close were they to the front wall of the house?

CHÁVEZ Y CHÁVEZ: They were in front of the house about two yards from the wall.

COL. DUDLEY: About what point along the wall were they standing?

CHÁVEZ Y CHÁVEZ: In front of the corner of the house and the corner that is next to the road.

COL. DUDLEY: Do you mean the road that runs through the town, if not, what road do you mean?

CHÁVEZ Y CHÁVEZ: The road that passes through town.

COL. DUDLEY: Who was with you, if anyone, at the time the soldiers fired at Thomas and Morris?

CHÁVEZ Y CHÁVEZ: Only Bill was just behind me, the man they called the "Kid."

COL. DUDLEY: When did you go into the McSween house, on the 19th day of July last, or prior to that time. If prior, then how many days?

Captain Humphreys objected on the grounds that nothing in the direct examination had led to that point of inquiry. Colonel Dudley insisted the court had the right to know all about José Chávez y Chávez's time in the McSween home. Humphreys's objection was overruled and the court directed the witness to answer the question:

CHÁVEZ Y CHÁVEZ: About three days before.

COL. DUDLEY: Had there not been a conflict going on between the people in the McSween house on the 19th day of July last and Sheriff Peppin and the sheriff's posse, and was not the sheriff and his parry seeking to effect the arrest of persons in the house and were you and the persons with you endeavoring to defeat the sheriff in this attempt?

Captain Humphreys objected, and the court was cleared and closed again after much deliberation regarding the nature of the investigation. The court then opened and directed the witness to answer the question:

CHÁVEZ Y CHÁVEZ: At the time I was in the house. I had not seen the sheriff at no time at the house. Did not see the sheriff then but seen people of his party fighting. I saw them shooting towards the McSween house. There was shooting from the McSween house towards them. I was there but the sheriff did not read any order, don't know if he wanted to arrest anybody or not.
COL. DUDLEY: Who was with you in the house at that time?
CHÁVEZ Y CHÁVEZ: Thomas [Folliard], Harvey [Morris], Bill [Bonney] and [Alexander] McSween, two other Americans, I did not know their names, Francisco Zamora, Yginio Salazar, Vincente Romero, Ignacio Gonzáles, don't recollect any more.
COL. DUDLEY: Do you mean to say that each of those soldiers, you say you saw, fired two or three shots?
CHÁVEZ Y CHÁVEZ: I saw three when they fired once.
COL. DUDLEY: How do you know that those men were soldiers when you escaped from the McSween house?
CHÁVEZ Y CHÁVEZ: Because I saw them.
COL. DUDLEY: By what did you arrive at the conclusion that they were soldiers?
CHÁVEZ Y CHÁVEZ: Because I seen them in soldiers clothes.
COL. DUDLEY: Do you swear that the men had on blue pantaloons?
CHÁVEZ Y CHÁVEZ: Yes, sir.
COL. DUDLEY: Did these pantaloons have stripes down the legs?
CHÁVEZ Y CHÁVEZ: I did not see any.
COL. DUDLEY: Did the men wear caps?
CHÁVEZ Y CHÁVEZ: Yes, sir.
COL. DUDLEY: What kind of coat were they wearing?
CHÁVEZ Y CHÁVEZ: Black blouses.
COL. DUDLEY: Were they white or colored troops?
CHÁVEZ Y CHÁVEZ: White men.

COL. DUDLEY: Did you see them before they fired?
CHÁVEZ Y CHÁVEZ: The fire thinned and at the time, we saw them and they fired.
COL. DUDLEY: Then you did not look at them a great while did you?
CHÁVEZ Y CHÁVEZ: Only while I was passing.
COL. DUDLEY: Were you passing pretty fast?
CHÁVEZ Y CHÁVEZ: When they fired I went in a hurry, yes, when they fired I went pretty fast.
COL. DUDLEY: Did they have belts and cartridges about their person?
CHÁVEZ Y CHÁVEZ: I didn't see any.

Col. Nathan Dudley announced by his counsel that he was finished with the witness, and Capt. Henry Humphreys began a very short redirect:

CAPT. HUMPHREYS: Explain how near the corner of the Tunstall house towards McSween's house the soldiers stood when you saw them first?
CHÁVEZ Y CHÁVEZ: They were close by, about two yards.[23]

José Chávez y Chávez was then retired as a witness. The testimony of William Bonney and José Chávez y Chávez regarding the three soldiers they had spotted while making their break from the burning McSween home was countered when Milo L. Pierce took the stand. The Seven Rivers rancher claimed that he and several other Dolan partisans had been wearing military surplus clothing that evening.[24]

Martín Chávez traveled up the Río Bonito and provided his own testimony in Fort Stanton on May 30, 1879. Like José Chávez y Chávez, the former deputy sheriff only spoke broken English at the time, and his testimony was translated for the court by Justice John B. Wilson:

CAPT. HUMPHREYS: What is your name and place of residence?
MARTÍN CHÁVEZ: My name is Martín Chávez and live at Picacho in Lincoln County, New Mexico.
CAPT. HUMPHREYS: Were you in Lincoln on the 19th day of July last, if so, state where you were, and if you had any conversation with Col. Dudley, that you understood in English, about anything transpiring there that day, if so, state what it was and what you saw, if anything, of the action of the troops or guns that day?

Col. Nathan Dudley objected, citing the ruling previously made by the court regarding any conversation being given of Martín Chávez in the English language. His objection was sustained, and Captain Humphreys modified his question:

> CAPT. HUMPHREYS: Were you in Lincoln on the 19th day of July last, if so, state where you were and what you saw, if anything, of the action of the troops or guns that day?
>
> MARTÍN CHÁVEZ: On the 19th day of July last I was in the house of José Montaño. About 11 o'clock in the day, more or less, I saw from a window troops coming near the house, they halted for a few minutes, afterwards marched forward and stopped in front of the house of Montaño, at this time I went out of the room. When a captain saw me, that was in with Col. Dudley, he said, this is one of the men of McSween. I saw at the time a movement made by Col. Dudley and then I saw a cannon pointed toward the Montaño house. At that time I went out of the house with the men that were there, when I was entering the house of Ellis I saw the same piece turned and directed toward the Ellis house. I went out from there and went down the river and the first time we showed ourselves on a hill, they fired three or more volleys at us. I saw four Americans going ahead of some soldiers that had canteens in their hands towards the house of Ellis. That was before I was far from the house, the Ellis house. Then we went down into a canyon to cover ourselves from the troops. When we was in the highest place I saw smoke at the house of McSween and I knew that the house had commenced burning, and then 8 or 9 of us tried to see if we could liberate those who were in the burning house. The first time we showed ourselves on the hills I heard a holler from one of the men with me. Told me to look at the cannon and I saw a bunch of soldiers walking and they stopped near to the corner of one of the houses that was out of town on the side of the river. I did not see the cannon, and then we retired.
>
> CAPT. HUMPHREYS: Did you see any other movement of the cannon or Gatling that day, if so, state what you saw?
>
> MARTÍN CHÁVEZ: I did not see the gun they call the Gatling gun, which way it was pointed, but I saw it together with the cannon. I did not see any other movement of the cannon that day.

Capt. Henry Humphreys informed the court that he was finished with the witness. Col. Nathan Dudley conducted a brief and uneventful cross examination in which Martín answered various questions regarding the distance between several places in Lincoln, as well as the approximate time that events had occurred on the final day of the siege. Martín was then retired as a witness without a redirect from Humphreys.[25]

Saturnino Baca, José Chávez y Baca, José María de Aguayo, James J. Dolan, Jack Long, George Peppin, and various others would all testify throughout the inquiry. Capt. Henry Humphreys and Ira Leonard were no match for Henry Waldo, who derided the testimony of the McSween partisans during his closing argument with ferocity. "It is a farce on judicial investigation and ought to be called and designated 'The Mutual Admiration Inquiry,'" Ira Leonard had bitterly informed Governor Wallace during proceedings. The military court would ultimately rule that Nathan Dudley had not exceeded his orders during the five-day siege. The colonel was cleared of any charges subject to a court martial on July 18, 1879.[26]

William Bonney had already skinned out of Lincoln before the court of inquiry adjourned upriver in Fort Stanton. The Kid realized Governor Wallace would not deliver his pardon as promised and simply walked out of the Patrón store with Tom Folliard and Doc Scurlock on June 17, 1879. The former Regulators returned to Fort Sumner in San Miguel County. Governor Wallace continued writing his novel, *Ben Hur: A Tale of the Christ*, in Santa Fe. The Hoosier also remained hopeful of receiving an ambassadorship.[27]

Juan Patrón's duties as a militia captain concluded when Governor Wallace dissolved the Lincoln County Mounted Rifles on July 15, 1879. The businessman later submitted an affidavit for the reimbursement of $109.33 for boarding William Bonney, Tom Folliard, Doc Scurlock, and two other prisoners in his store for various amounts of time throughout March, April, May, and June. Martín Chávez continued farming, raising sheep, and providing for his wife Juana in Picacho. José Chávez y Chávez returned to his wife Leonora Lucero de Chávez and their 6-year-old son Adecasio in San Patricio. The spirited Yginio Salazar continued riding with his amigo Billy Bonney, splitting his time between his family's homestead in Las Tablas and Fort Sumner.[28]

For all of Governor Lew Wallace's measures during his time on the Río Bonito, very little had changed in Lincoln County. Juan Patrón found himself at a crossroads in his life. His older sister Juana was living with her husband Juan Ramírez and their daughter Mercedes outside Santa Fe. His younger sister Encarnación was happily married to José "Rafael" Gutiérrez in Tularosa, having given birth to a daughter named María in 1875. Encarnación had more recently bequeathed her older brother with a nephew named Manuel.

Lincoln County had little more to offer Juan Patrón. There was nothing left for him to achieve on the Río Bonito, and Jimmy Dolan would always remain a threat. The Hispano prodigy particularly enjoyed staying with his amigo Tranquilino Labadie and his family in Santa Rosa, San Miguel County. His old college friend Tranquilino also had an attractive, intelligent younger sister named Beatriz.[29]

Juan Patrón had already achieved considerable success in business and politics for a man of 26. He would now make time for romance in his life.

José Chávez y Chávez while incarcerated in the New Mexico penitentiary, ca. 1897. Author's collection.

The Nuestra Señora de Los Dolores (Our Lady of Sorrows) Roman Catholic Church in Cebolleta (modern-day Seboyeta), in which the 20-day-old José Teodoro Chávez y Chávez was baptized on March 25, 1850. Photograph taken by George Wharton James, ca. 1898. Author's collection.

Juan Bautista Patrón as a young man in his early twenties, ca. 1873. Author's collection.

The plaza in Santa Fe, 1866. Courtesy Palace of the Governors Photo Archives (NMHM/DCA), 103021.

Jean Baptiste Lamy, the clergyman who became Juan Patrón's mentor in Santa Fe. Author's collection.

Tranquilino Labadie, who became Juan Patrón's closest friend while attending St. Michael's College in Santa Fe during the 1860s. This photograph was taken in 1912. Author's collection.

Martín Chávez (*left*) with his friend August Kline, ca. 1888. Herman B. Weisner Papers, Rio Grande Historical Collections, New Mexico State University Library, Archives and Special Collections.

The torreón in Manzano, Valencia County, the village in which Martín Chávez and Yginio Salazar were born and where Martín spent his early years. Photograph taken by Charles Loomis in 1885. Author's collection.

Yginio Salazar as a young man in his twenties. Lynda A. Sánchez Collection.

Lincoln, also known as La Placita and Bonito, in Condado de Lincoln (Lincoln County), photographed from the east in the 1870s. *True West* Archives.

Thomas B. Catron, the leading figure of the Santa Fe Ring. The political giant was revered by some and despised by many in New Mexico. Photograph courtesy of Corey Recko.

James J. Dolan and Lawrence G. Murphy (*seated*), ca. 1870s. Chuck Usmar Collection, Albuquerque, New Mexico.

John H. Riley, who became Juan Patrón's nemesis in Lincoln County and almost ended the Hispano businessman's life in Fort Stanton on September 15, 1875. Chuck Usmar Collection.

William J. Brady, ca. 1870s. The Lincoln County sheriff's close association with Lawrence Murphy, Jimmy Dolan, and Johnny Riley brought out the worst in the Civil War veteran. He paid for it with his life in Lincoln on April 1, 1878. *True West* Archives.

The original Patrón house and store in Lincoln during the 1870s. Author's collection.

Hispanas baking bread in an *horno* (adobe oven) outside their home in Taos Pueblo, New Mexico, ca. 1925. Courtesy Palace of the Governors Photo Archives (NMHM/DCA), 004413.

A Nuevomexicano family hanging red chile ristras out to dry in the sun just like their ancestors, ca. 1950. Courtesy Palace of the Governors Photo Archives (NMHM/DCA), 005181.

Saturnino Baca posing for a photograph with his granddaughter, ca. 1888. Considered by some to be "the father of Lincoln County," Saturnino deputized Martín Chávez during his term as county sheriff in 1876. Author's collection.

Florencio Gonzáles, who served various terms as probate judge of Lincoln County and became a good friend to Juan B. Patrón, posing for a photograph in January 1880. Author's collection.

One of the Horrell brothers, although it remains uncertain which one. Author's collection.

Alexander "Mac" McSween. The Scottish attorney's questionable handling of the Fritz insurance funds case ultimately led to the outbreak of the Lincoln County War. Author's collection.

Susan McSween. The vain, headstrong, and resilient "Sue" was always a friend to Juan Patrón. Author's collection.

John Henry Tunstall. The ambitious Englishman's murder ignited the Lincoln County War on February 18, 1878. Author's collection.

John Simpson Chisum, ca. 1880s. Yginio Salazar worked as a vaquero for the cattle baron and participated in Chisum's Pecos War in April 1877. "Uncle John" supported the Regulators during the Lincoln County War before turning his back on them, leading to a bitter dispute with Yginio Salazar's friend Billy "the Kid" Bonney. *True West* Archives.

A group of Mescalero Apaches and a handful of Anglo Americans posing for a photograph outside the Sutler store at the Fort Stanton Mescalero Apache Agency, Lincoln County, ca. 1875. Author's collection.

George W. "Dad" Peppin, ca. 1870s. A faithful lackey of Jimmy Dolan and the House during the Lincoln County War, the former sheriff made peace with Yginio Salazar several years later. George's daughter Emma Peppin eventually married his one-time enemy Martín Chávez's son Benjamin "Bennie" Chávez. Author's collection.

Robert Beckwith, ca. 1870s. Nobody in Lincoln County hated the Seven Rivers rustler more than Yginio Salazar. Author's collection.

Florencio Cháves, a close friend to José Chávez y Chávez, ca. 1927. Author's collection.

Henry McCarty, alias William H. Bonney, more famously known as Billy the Kid, ca. 1880. Although vilified by the Anglo press as a demonic psychopath, El Bilito became a beloved friend and folk hero to the Hispano population of southeastern New Mexico. Author's collection.

Samuel Beach Axtell, the governor of New Mexico Territory and ally of the Santa Fe Ring, in 1876. Author's collection.

José and Josefita Montaño. The respected Nuevomexicano couple's house and store served as Martín Chávez's stronghold throughout the five-day siege in Lincoln during the summer of 1878. Author's collection.

Lieutenant Colonel Nathan Dudley, 1881. The officer accused Juan Patrón of being a McSween spy in Fort Stanton and earned the contempt of José Chávez y Chávez, Martín Chávez, and Yginio Salazar for defying his orders and assisting the Dolan partisans during the five-day siege in Lincoln. Author's collection.

An artist's somewhat fantastical depiction of Billy "the Kid" Bonney making his break from the burning McSween home. This illustration was published with an excerpt from Walter Noble Burns's *The Saga of Billy the Kid* in the *St. Louis Post-Dispatch* on July 4, 1926.

Fort Sumner, New Mexico, ca. 1883. Yginio Salazar spent six months recovering from the bullet wounds he suffered while escaping the burning McSween house at the former military post. The old fort also became his amigo Billy the Kid's adopted home following the Lincoln County War. The Maxwell house is left of center in the background. *True West* Archives.

Paulita Maxwell. The Kid's refusal to leave New Mexico without Pablita ultimately led to his death at the end of Pat Garrett's revolver in Fort Sumner. *True West* Archives.

An Atchison, Topeka, and Santa Fe train steaming north into Mora Canyon, ca. 1887. The arrival of *los ferrocarriles* (the railroads) in New Mexico Territory proved prosperous for some but disastrous for much of the rural Hispano population. Courtesy Palace of the Governors Photo Archives (NMHM/DCA), 038209.

A newborn lamb with its mother in New Mexico, ca. 1915. This was a welcome sight to Martín Chávez and any other sheep farmer in the American Southwest. Courtesy Palace of the Governors Photo Archives (NMHM/DCA), 100489.

Burros being used to transport firewood in Santa Fe, ca. 1886. Courtesy Palace of the Governors Photo Archives (NMHM/DCA), 015243.

George Kimbrell, ca. 1910s. Martín Chávez's brother-in-law and close friend of many decades. Author's collection.

Lew Wallace during his time as governor of New Mexico Territory. The Hoosier never wanted the position and could not wait to leave. Author's collection.

The Palace of the Governors in Santa Fe, 1880. Courtesy Palace of the Governors Photo Archives (NMHM/DCA), 015377.

A political cartoon depicting the Santa Fe Ring as a three-headed snake. This illustration was published in the *Santa Fe Daily Democrat* on October 22, 1880.

Beatriz Labadie-Patrón and her husband Juan Patrón, ca. 1880. Author's collection.

Puerto de Luna, 1880. The Grzelachowski store is on the left. Author's collection.

The captured members of Victorio's band in Chihuahua City, Chihuahua, Mexico, following the death of their leader in 1880. Notice the Apache scalps proudly held aloft by Mexican troops. Lynda A. Sánchez Collection.

Jimmy Dolan (*seated*) and Bob Olinger, ca. 1880. Chuck Usmar Collection.

A handful of cowboys posing outside the Lincoln County Courthouse, formerly the Murphy and Dolan store, at the western end of Lincoln, ca. 1887. The two-story building became the most famous courthouse in the American Southwest after Billy "the Kid" Bonney made his legendary jailbreak on April 28, 1881. *True West* Archives.

An artist's depiction of a shackled Billy "the Kid" Bonney looking through a window inside the Lincoln County Courthouse prior to making his famous jailbreak. This illustration was published with an excerpt from Walter Noble Burns's *The Saga of Billy the Kid* in the *St. Louis Post-Dispatch* on July 11, 1926.

Pat Garrett (*left*), James R. Brent (*center*), and John W. Poe (*right*), ca. 1884. Yginio Salazar held a grudge against Pat Garrett for killing his amigo Billy the Kid but served as a deputy sheriff alongside James R. Brent under Sheriff John W. Poe's authority. Author's collection.

William "Billy the Kid" Bonney's grave in the old military cemetery at Fort Sumner, New Mexico, in 1927. Photograph courtesy of Corey Recko.

Martín Chávez (*standing, center*), delivering a shipment of wool in Las Vegas, ca. 1880s. Author's collection.

Juan Patrón (*left*), Peter "Pedro" Maxwell (*center*), and, reputedly, Pablo Anaya (*right*), 1882. *True West* Archives.

The building in which Michael Maney fatally shot Juan Patrón in Puerto de Luna, photographed in the 1890s. Author's collection.

The Our Lady of Refuge Roman Catholic Church, beneath which Juan Bautista Patrón was buried, in modern-day Puerto de Luna. Author's collection.

Chapter 10

Los Ferrocarriles

What do wheels eat, these wheels
Fixed to their arcs like gods.
—Sylvia Plath

All eyes were on Las Vegas in New Mexico Territory during the summer of 1879. Sometimes referred to as Nuestra Señora de los Delores de Las Vegas (Our Lady of Sorrows of the Meadows) by the Hispano population, the settlement had been established on the western bank of the Río Gallinas in 1835. The square-shaped metropolis was situated in the high country of San Miguel County and home to roughly two thousand predominantly Nuevomexicano residents. The town plaza could be accessed on its four sides via the narrow streets lined with stores, hotels, churches, cantinas, and adobe dwellings. "Here is where the Mexican can be seen in all his genuineness," one Americano observer declared. "He comes with his burro laden down with nearly one-fourth of a cord of wood, sells it to the first purchaser, and leaves town."[1]

A newspaperman from Indianapolis named Anthony M. Conklin and his wife were shocked by the sight of two corpses hanging from the framework of the public well in the plaza when they arrived in Las Vegas that summer. A drunken freighter named Manuel Barela had shot and killed the elderly

Benigno Romero and wounded the old man's companion Jesús Morales without provocation on June 4, 1879. An angry lynch mob dragged Manuel Barela and another prisoner out of the Las Vegas jail around midnight and left their bodies dangling for all to see.[2]

Although still a lively place, the plaza of Las Vegas and its immediate surroundings were considered old news in July of 1879. The Americano newspapers were far more concerned with the large encampment known as New Town, or East Las Vegas, that was under construction one mile away on the eastern bank of the Río Gallinas. The original Las Vegas was now referred to as Old Town by the industrious people raising an increasing number of bathhouses, hotels, stores, and wooden dwellings near the recently established train depot. Nuevo México finally became linked with the eastern states when the railroad tracks leading into East Las Vegas were completed by the Atchison, Topeka, and Santa Fe Railway Company on July 1, 1879.[3]

Los ferrocarriles (the railroads) officially arrived in the territory when the first New Mexico and Southern Pacific train screeched into East Las Vegas on July 4, 1879. "The train-men, the natives, the full-blooded Mexican from his mud hut, and the inhabitants of Las Vegas, all joined in a salute of welcome," one Anglo passenger later recalled. "Alongside of the railroad track, I am told, when the first train halted, and the engine blew its long and shrill whistle, stood many Mexicans who never before had held such a sight." It was the biggest event in the recent history of New Mexico Territory. "The thoughtful minds of the community, as well as the enterprising people who flocking hither from all parts of the country with the view of establishing in trade, have long recognized the importance of the position occupied by Kansas City for the control of the growing trade of the Southwest," the *Mesilla Valley Independent* informed the public.[4]

The iron horse continued transporting Anglo passengers and all manner of freight into East Last Vegas on a regular basis. Laborers were in high demand in New Town, and the freight receipts at the terminal had totaled $78,000 during the month of May alone. Storeowners were now able to order various goods and furniture from the eastern states. Cattlemen could also transport livestock into the territory with unprecedented speed. "Three weeks ago today I came here with the first train, and I saw not a house upon the broad fields hereabouts," railroad engineer Fred Leach Jr. told one correspondent. "Look at it today: the bang of the hammer and the rip of the saw have, as if by magic, done what you see."[5]

The local population rapidly increased as East Las Vegas became a hotspot for ambitious businessmen, gamblers, freighters, stockmen, attorneys, sporting ladies, pistoleros, rustlers, robbers, and ruffians. Justice of the Peace Hyman G. "Hoodoo Brown" Neill and his notoriously crooked police force were soon throwing their weight around. John "Doc" Holliday would arrive there and operate a gin mill. Holliday's friend Wyatt Earp also stopped in Las Vegas before the year was out. It was later suggested that Jesse James spent time there under the alias Mr. Howard, and enjoyed dining at the nearby Hot Springs Hotel. "Every train which arrives brings large numbers of passengers," one correspondent wrote to the *Chicago Tribune*. "One of nature's wonders is the Hot Springs of Las Vegas. They are situated a short five miles from town. These springs are pronounced to far exceed any in America for the curative qualities. I found many visitors and permanent summer-boarders at the hotel. It is contemplated to hasten the already partly completed new hotel and bath-houses: and the Las Vegas Hot Springs are destined to be a most popular and health-giving resort."[6]

Many of the recent Anglo arrivals in Las Vegas also brought a strong degree of racial prejudice against "Mexicans" with them. "*Como la va!* Such is the salutation I offer you—the one with which we, who are well up in Spanish, have learned to greet the lazy and greasy sailors on the ships of the plains," one ignorant Americano announced. "The Mexican peons are not pleasant neighbors." The seeds of an eventual uprising were sewn when some of the gringos saw dollar signs in the "uninhabited lands" upon which many Hispanos resided under the guidelines of community land grants. "Del sonido de las campanas de las iglesias se mueren las ovejas" (The sound of the church bells kills the sheep), was a popular saying among Hispano sheepherders. The arrival of railroad barons and an influx of cattle posed a considerable threat to their migratory lifestyle. What the Americanos called progress, many working-class Hispanos considered land grabbing.[7]

The 26-year-old Juan B. Patrón was fully aware that the arrival of the locomotive in Las Vegas signaled a new era of accessibility and enterprise for Nuevo México in the summer of 1879. The Atchison, Topeka, and Santa Fe Railway Company was also extending the railroad toward Santa Fe. While the arrival of los ferrocarriles in Las Vegas may have played some part in Juan's decision to relocate to San Miguel County before the end of year, the Hispano businessman had recently fallen in love with his longtime friend Tranquilino Labadie's younger sister while staying with the Labadie family in Santa Rosa. Juan's romantic interest in the 21-year-old Beatriz Labadie, as well as his considerations for her family's wishes, were the primary reasons he chose to leave the excessively violent Lincoln County behind him.

Juan Patrón had spent many weeks with the Labadie family before asking Lorenzo and Rallitos Labadie for their daughter's hand. They readily accepted, although Beatriz had been promised to her first cousin Amado Cháves, the eldest son of famous Mexican-American War veteran Lt. Col. Manuel Antonio Cháves, on the day of her baptism. Amado Cháves was 5 years old on the day of Beatriz's baptism, and Lorenzo and Rallitos Labadie were not about to let a formality stand in the way of their daughter's wish to marry the successful young prodigy they already loved like a son. Tranquilino Labadie would have been thrilled by the prospect of becoming Juan's brother-in-law. The St. Michael's College graduates had been close friends for more than a decade. They would now become family.

Juan Bautista Patrón and Beatriz Labadie were married in Anton Chico, San Miguel County, in late 1879. Lorenzo and Rallitos Labadie were understandably apprehensive about their daughter's safety on the Río Bonito and pleaded with their new son-in-law to relocate to San Miguel County. Juan Patrón subsequently packed his possessions into his wagon, readied his horses, and drove his attractive new bride north to Puerto de Luna on the Río Pecos, merely ten miles southeast of Santa Rosa. The newlyweds settled into an old adobe house later described as "primitive living quarters" by one local citizen. Juan and Beatriz's new placita was surrounded by hills within a valley shaped like a crescent moon. A folktale persisted that Spanish conquistador Francisco Vázquez de Coronado had originally named the region Puerto de Luna (Gateway of the Moon) while camping there centuries before, although the name was actually derived from the Luna family who settled there in the 1860s.[8]

While it was hardly the booming Las Vegas, the much smaller Puerto de Luna had potential. Juan Patrón was confident he could succeed there as a businessman and provide for Beatriz, who soon became pregnant with the couple's first child. A 55-year-old Polish immigrant named Alexander Grzelachowski, affectionately known as Pedro Polaco due to his prior associations with the church, was already running a successful mercantile store in town. Juan's friend Pablo Anaya, a successful sheep rancher and respected businessman, also lived in the area with his wife Doloritas and their five children.[9]

Puerto de Luna was known for its orchards and sheep ranches but also held a reputation as a stopover for Hispano and Anglo rustlers. As Juan was settling into married life and preparing for fatherhood, his new hometown was becoming an increasingly popular hangout for those with a penchant for appropriating livestock, including a certain buck-toothed pistolero with whom he was quite familiar.

***

The roughly 19-year-old William Bonney essentially relocated to San Miguel County after Governor Lew Wallace failed to deliver the pardon he had been promised in Lincoln. Aside from occasionally visiting friends in Lincoln County, the Kid began spending most of his time in his adopted home of Fort Sumner. He also spent time gambling and socializing in Las Vegas, Anton Chico, and Puerto de Luna. While it is possible Bonney may have paid Juan and Beatriz Patrón an occasional visit at their new home in Puerto de Luna, there is no record of his ever doing so. The Kid would later write of having aided their mutual friend Pablo Anaya by recovering some stolen livestock on the sheep rancher's behalf.[10]

The 20-year-old Yginio Salazar was still riding with Billy Bonney, Tom Folliard, Charlie Bowdre, Doc Scurlock, and their circle of friends on occasion, although even the hardest gunman was on alert in southern New Mexico at the time. Victorio and Nana had jumped the Mescalero reservation with a band of followers on August 21, 1879. The Apache chiefs had grown tired of the miserable conditions and the broken promises of the White Eye and were determined to fight it out in what became known as Victorio's War.

A master of guerrilla warfare, Victorio consumed many a newspaper editor's time while his band engaged troops and killed dozens of Anglo Americans, Hispano Americans, and Mexicans across the borderlands throughout the next thirteen months.[11]

Lincoln County inevitably hosted more gunplay when former Dolan partisan John Jones shot down John Beckwith during a dispute over stolen cattle in Seven Rivers on August 26, 1879. The late Beckwith's friend Milo Pierce suckered John Jones into a handshake at the Pierce and Paxton cattle camp several days later, just moments before the murderous Bob Olinger fatally shot Jones twice in the back with a Winchester rifle. Billy Bonney was friends with the Jones family and apparently vowed to take care of the widely despised Olinger himself. "Bill [Bonney] was a good man, but Bob Olinger was a damned rascal and deserved killing," Augustus "Gus" Gildea later remarked.[12]

The Kid also returned to rustling cattle and horses that autumn, insisting John Chisum owed him money for services rendered the previous year. "John Chisum hired Billy as a gunman in that Lincoln County War," Fort Sumner resident Jesús Silva later insisted. "When the war was over, Billy went to Chisum for his money, but Chisum wouldn't pay 'im." The Kid and his circle of friends, perhaps including Yginio Salazar, began cutting Chisum herds as a means of compensation. Billy Bonney, Tom Folliard, Charlie Bowdre, Doc Scurlock, and two unidentified Hispano companions allegedly snatched 118 head of Chisum cattle from the pastures of Bosque Grande in October 1879. Billy also continued spending most of his time among the Hispano populace of southeastern New Mexico, most of whom would not have begrudged their friend for stealing cattle from gringos. "Billy liked better to be with Hispanics than with Americans," one of his many amigos Apolicarpio "Paco" Anaya later said.[13]

Billy Bonney and Yginio Salazar probably shook their heads in bemusement when learning that Jimmy Dolan and their longtime enemies were all exonerated of charges in relation to the Lincoln County War during the November term of court in Socorro County. It was a typical Santa Fe Ring affair when District Attorney William L. Rynerson stood before Judge Warren Bristol and succeeded in getting Jimmy Dolan and Billy Mathews acquitted for the murder of John H. Tunstall. "In this county [Dolan] would have without doubt been convicted, but he took a change of venue to Socorro," Tunstall's former cook Gottfried Gauss informed the late Englishman's father. "This is law and justice in New Mexico." The grand jury also cleared Dolan of any liability in the murder of Huston L. Chapman. George Peppin and Nathan Dudley were acquitted of arson, and a host of Dolan partisans who had been indicted for the killing of Frank MacNab all went free. Two court terms had passed and not a single person had been convicted of any charges in relation to the Lincoln County War.[14]

While Jimmy Dolan had recently married Carolina "Lina" Fritz and was looking to regain his status as a successful businessman in Lincoln, Yginio Salazar decided to spend la Navidad (Christmas) with William Bonney in San Miguel County. The local festivities were marred that year when Pablo Anaya's cashier overreacted when a *bastonero* (master of ceremonies) told him to vacate the dance floor at a baile held in Puerto de Luna on Christmas Eve. The offended cashier responded by pulling his revolver and shooting the *bastonero*. The bullet passed through the man's body and struck a 14-year-old girl in the chest, killing her within seconds. The *bastonero* himself died a short time later. The young Hispano cashier was quickly apprehended and transported to Santa Fe on a double-murder charge.[15]

Yginio Salazar and Billy Bonney were driving a horse and buggy through the snow toward Fort Sumner on December 25, 1879. They were eager to enjoy the Christmas Day festivities, and perhaps "chuck some pretty señorita under the chin," as Yginio later described it. The single young hombres were a little too eager, as suddenly became clear when their buggy tipped over when turning off a road in their haste. The sound of their buggy crashing to the ground spooked the large horse they were driving, and the powerful animal proceeded to drag them another fifty feet through the thick snow before finally coming to a halt. Yginio was furious when he finally stood up covered in snow and began cussing in Spanish. Billy rose to his feet laughing, finding the whole thing hilarious. He laughed even more when observing a large clump of snow resting atop his companion's head.

"Just a minute, señor," Billy said to his friend with a toothy smile. "I'll brush you off."

Yginio chuckled for a brief moment before the Kid drew both his revolvers and shot the clump of snow clean off his scalp with rapid precision. *¡Madre de Dios!* Yginio was shocked but could only laugh his ass off in response. "[Billy] made you ashamed of yourself to lose your temper in his presence," the vaquero later said. "*¡Por Dios, caballero!* Billy was a great fellow." The two amigos finished brushing themselves off in less spectacular fashion and continued their journey to Fort Sumner with an amusing tale to tell everyone.[16]

Billy Bonney had to pull a six-shooter with less amicable intentions just two weeks later when encountering a Texan named Joe Grant in Fort Sumner on January 10, 1880. Grant had arrived at the old fort the night before and inquired about the Kid's whereabouts. He curiously tried to make a wager that he would kill a man before Bonney the following day. The Texan became increasingly raucous while the Kid was enjoying a drink with Jim Chisum, several Chisum cowboys, and some of his amigos in a saloon that morning. "We, the Hispanics, were talking, some standing at the bar, and others sitting on chairs," local sheepherder Paco Anaya later recalled. "Grant ordered two drinks, one for him and one for Billy."

Joe Grant took exception when Billy Bonney happily invited a 56-year-old Indian from Puerto de Luna named Francisco Tafolla to join them, declaring that he couldn't "line up with someone who lines up with Indians." Billy took several steps away from the bar after the offended Tafolla stormed out of the saloon to retrieve his gun, intending to kill the loudmouthed Tejano. Joe Grant drew his revolver while the Kid's back was turned.

"Hey, Bill!" Grant shouted.

Billy spun around and lucked out when Grant's pistol misfired. The Kid speedily drew one of his own revolvers and shot Grant three times in the chin area before the Tejano could try it again. Billy then asked Paco Anaya and his amigos to serve as witnesses and accompany him to Justice of the Peace Alejandro Segura's home in nearby Cabra Arenoso. "The judge interrogated us all, and then decided that Billy was free," recalled Paco Anaya. "Many thought that [William Bonney] was a bad man. No, Billy was good, but if someone wanted trouble with him, he was ready and wasn't afraid of anything." Joe Grant was buried in the northeast corner of the old military cemetery in Fort Sumner, having fatally lost what Bonney described as "a game of two."[17]

Yginio Salazar decided to rustle a little horseflesh alongside Billy Bonney the following month, in February 1880. They were accompanied by a local horse thief named Pasqual Chávez, a wannabe pistolero known as Billy Wilson, and Mose Dedrick, a 20-year-old Hoosier who dabbled in counterfeiting and sold appropriated beef. The five ruffians managed to swipe forty-eight horses from the Mescalero reservation and sold off the rustled ponies along the Río Pecos. The Hispano and Anglo citizens of New Mexico despised the Mescalero Apaches and would have hardly been concerned about purchasing stolen Indian ponies. "Some Apache Indians under Chief Victorio captured me, a muchacho, about 14 years of age, while I was herding sheep on the hills in the Rito Lake canyon," Felipe Padilla later recalled. "One of the braves struck me across the face with a quirt; then the Indians, thinking perhaps they had killed me, ran their horses at full speed westward."[18]

While Yginio Salazar was busy stealing horses from the Mescaleros that winter, the 27-year-old Juan Patrón was preparing to depart Nuevo México for the first time in his life.

***

Juan Patrón continued spending time in Santa Fe when he wasn't seeing to his duties in San Miguel County throughout early 1880. The Hispano businessman presumably left his wife Beatriz with her relatives in Santa Rosa when returning to the Holy City for the territorial legislative assembly in January. LeBaron Bradford Prince, a former senator in New York who had traveled west and become chief justice of the New Mexico Territorial Supreme Court, would convene a public meeting in the council chamber to discuss the hot topic of immigration. Governor Lew Wallace was called to the chair as presiding officer before Chief Justice Prince gave a rousing speech, encouraging the formation of an official Immigration Bureau. Henry Waldo and various judges from throughout the territory echoed the chief justice's sentiments. Secretary William G. Ritch was there as a special guest and spoke in favor of Anglo immigration when called upon. George T. Anthony, the former governor of Kansas, was also in attendance as a representative of the Atchison, Topeka, and Santa Fe Railway Company.[19]

Juan Patrón would have applauded when the territorial legislature passed a militia bill as a matter of public necessity, although it was advised to "scan closely all bills and to refuse to pass any appropriations, except when trimmed down to the most economical basis." The legislature recognized the work of Juan Patrón and his Lincoln County Rifles the previous year, and a sum of $2,200 was appropriated to cover their expenses. Juan would receive a total of $441.54 for his service and general expenses as militia captain. José Montaño was reimbursed the sum of $565.73 for his financial support of the militia. Susan McSween received $43.65, and Isaac Ellis received $144.00 for supplying provisions. Additionally, $1,000 would also be dispensed among the militiamen for their varying degrees of service. José Chávez y Chávez received $58.50, whereas Martín Chávez received $6.00 for lesser duties. Yginio Salazar was paid $43.50 for his services, while his older brother José Salazar received $34.00.[20]

Juan Patrón also attended an elaborate reception hosted by Chief Justice L. Bradford Prince and his wife Hattie at their luxurious home in Santa Fe on January 22, 1880. The costly event was described as the "boss social affair of the season" by one attendee. Beatriz Patrón's previously intended spouse Amado Cháves and Lt. Clarence A. Stedman served as ushers, cordially greeting Juan Patrón and the many guests who arrived. J. Francisco Cháves and the other members of the legislative council were there, as were all but two members of the territorial house. Governor Lew Wallace, Secretary of State William G. Ritch, Gen. Edward Hatch, US Attorney Sidney M. Barnes, George T. Anthony, and Frank Springer were in attendance, as were Santa Fe Ring members Thomas B. Catron, Henry Waldo, William Breedon, and Judge Warren Bristol. Numerous other politicians, military officers, judges, attorneys, and prominent businessmen were also in attendance with their wives and families. So were a host of attractive ladies "who lent their charming presence to brighten the whole and bewilder the individual," as one male guest asserted. Juan and the other attendees were able to observe fancy toilets, which had been crafted by Parisian artisans during their taste of high society on the southwestern frontier.[21]

The old Santa Fe Trail was rendered obsolete when the Atchison, Topeka, and Santa Fe Railway officially reached the Holy City to great fanfare on February 9, 1880. Although the railroad company had initially intended to bypass Santa Fe due to its mountainous surroundings, the local voters had funded the construction of an eighteen-mile spur track leading north from Galisteo into the territorial capital. Juan Patrón was probably among the large crowd of officials and citizens who gathered at the Sante Fe train depot at eleven o'clock that morning. A procession of students proudly waved American flags while the St. Michael's College and 9th Cavalry bands alternately played tunes on opposing sides of the railroad track for all those in attendance.

The excitement was palpable at the Santa Fe train depot when Governor Lew Wallace, Gen. Edward Hatch, Chief Justice L. Bradford Prince, and County Commissioner Abram Staab hammered the final spikes into the railroad track to the sound of rabid applause. L. Bradford Prince and Maj. José D. Sena then gave speeches that were met with equal enthusiasm. The citizens and officials of Santa Fe would soon be able to travel to and from Kansas City, Missouri, further opening the door for commerce and immigration. "Monday was a glorious day for Santa Fe," the *Weekly New Mexican* declared. "The completion of this railroad removes the last and only impediment to her rapid advance, and each day hereafter will see an increase of population and of wealth." Nuevo México would never be quite the same again.[22]

The respected Juan B. Patrón was among those invited to participate in an excursion to Kansas City, Missouri, soon after the railroad was completed. George T. Anthony had received a telegram from William B. Strong, the general manager of the Atchison, Topeka, and Santa Fe Railway Company, inviting the officers, legislative council, house of representatives, and prominent citizens of New Mexico to embark on a return excursion to the Missouri River. Governor Lew Wallace decided to remain behind when the arrangements were made. Secretary William G. Ritch, Chief Justice L. Bradford Prince, auditor Trinidad Alarad, and treasurer Juan Delgado would accompany the territorial council, the house of representatives, some invited guests, and more than a dozen ladies on the week-long return journey. Juan Patrón was one of the sixty emissaries who took their seat on a special train comprised of four coaches at the Santa Fe depot on February 15, 1880. A large crowd of citizens cheered and waved them off as the train rolled out at eight o'clock that night.[23]

George T. Anthony ensured Juan Patrón and the other passengers were able to relax and enjoy the journey as the train passed through Lamy, Ribera, Las Vegas, and Raton Pass before entering Colorado. The locomotive railed through Trinidad, La Junta, Las Animas, and old Granada before Juan Patrón observed the vast plains of Kansas when traveling across the Jayhawker State. The excursion train rolled through Dodge City before stopping in Lawrence, Kansas, at around ten thirty in the morning of February 17, 1880. Juan and the delegates visited the University of Kansas, where Speaker of the House Rafael Romero gave a speech in Spanish that was translated for the Anglo listeners by J. Francisco Cháves, the president of the legislative council. Romero expressed his hope that Nuevo México would someday be home to similar universities. The Santa Fe delegation then returned to their coaches and continued their journey east around midday.[24]

Juan Patrón and his fellow emissaries were greeted by Mayor George M. Shelley; the president of the board of trade, C. H. Prescott; the president of the city council, T. B. Bullene; and various prominent businessmen when their train pulled into Kansas City, Missouri, on the afternoon of February 17, 1880. They were all wined and dined at the Union Depot Hotel and then escorted to the enormous Bullene, Moore, Emery and Co. department store on 1016-1018 Grand Avenue. "The vastness of the establishment caused the eyes of the pretty Mexican women to open with astonishment, and they loath to leave," recalled one Anglo observer. Although Juan Patrón spoke English, many of his fellow Hispano delegates needed interpreters while also visiting the stockyards, the Plankinton & Armour packing house, the local Nave & McCord grocery store, the Smith & Keating establishment, and a few public-school buildings. "The businessmen of the city would very much like to have the entire party remain twenty-four hours longer," the *Kansas City Times* reported. "All through New Mexico, a new field is given to the merchants here and they mean to profit by it."[25]

The New Mexico party departed Kansas City, Missouri, early in the morning of February 18, 1880. They also visited Leavenworth, Atchison, and

Topeka in Kansas before beginning the over eight-hundred-mile journey back to Santa Fe. Secretary William G. Ritch called for a meeting during the return trip as the locomotive neared Trinidad, Colorado, on February 20. The secretary of state suggested the drafting of resolutions expressing gratitude to the Atchison, Topeka, and Santa Fe Railway Company, as well as the officers and citizens of the cities they had visited in Kansas and Missouri. Juan Patrón and the other passengers all signed the adopted resolutions, expressing a "hearty thanks" to the railroad company; the governor of Kansas, John St. John; and "the various cities visited with great pleasure." The excursion was deemed a glowing success when the train returned to Santa Fe, and Juan headed home to his wife Beatriz in San Miguel County.[26]

Puerto de Luna probably seemed smaller than usual when Juan Patrón returned home in late February following his eye-opening excursion to the Missouri River. He had barely resumed his duties there before being called upon by his father-in-law Lorenzo Labadie after the latest shooting occurred in Las Vegas. A 23-year-old waiter named James Allen had recently informed traveling liquor salesman James A. Morehead that the hotel cook was unable to fry him some eggs in the St. Nicolas Hotel late one night. Allen's temper flared when Morehead made a sarcastic remark while ordering fried eggs several days later around ten o'clock in the morning of March 2, 1880. The two men began tussling and the robust Morehead got the better of it. The humiliated Allen retrieved a pistol from a nearby room, called Morehead a "son of a bitch," and threatened to kill the St. Louis native if he didn't drop to his knees. Morehead refused and tried to snatch the revolver from the waiter's grasp. A local African American potter unsuccessfully tried to separate the two men before Allen fired a bullet through the unarmed Morehead's side. The waiter was arrested while calmly preparing a table in the dining room a short time later. He waived examination at a preliminary hearing and was locked inside the filthy Las Vegas jail. The popular James Morehead died in agony between the hours of ten and eleven o'clock that night.[27]

Rumors began swirling around Las Vegas that an angry lynch mob would seize James Allen from the local jail and administer their own brand of neck-stretching justice. San Miguel County Sheriff Desiderio Romero stationed extra guards outside the jailhouse each night. The concern for James Allen's safety reached fever pitch after the prisoner's counsel took a change of venue to Santa Fe County on March 11, 1880. Chief Justice L. Bradford Prince ordered for Allen to be transferred immediately into the custody of Santa Fe County Sheriff José D. Sena in the Holy City. The officials in Las Vegas asked the seasoned Lorenzo Labadie, who had been the sheriff of both Santa Fe and San Miguel Counties in his younger years, to ensure James Allen was safely escorted to the territorial capital.[28]

The 54-year-old Lorenzo Labadie needed men he could trust to help him transport James Allen from Las Vegas to Santa Fe without the locals getting wise to it. The former lawman looked to his son-in-law Juan Patrón, their mutual friend Pablo Anaya, and former Santa Ana County Commissioner Amado C. de Baca. They all readily agreed to help Don Lorenzo, and the four hombres were duly authorized as a special posse to transport Allen to the Holy City.[29]

Juan Patrón and Pablo Anaya took rooms in Herlow's Hotel before they arrived at the Las Vegas jail with Lorenzo Labadie and Amado C. de Baca at eleven o'clock on the cold night of March 12, 1880. They successfully escorted James Allen in a carriage to the train depot in East Las Vegas, only to be informed their train was running three hours late. Labadie, Patrón, Anaya, and de Baca quickly led their slender prisoner into a nearby house without being spotted. They remained hidden from view until their train finally arrived at four o'clock in the morning. The special posse shuffled Allen on board and escorted him to Santa Fe before anyone in Las Vegas even realized the prisoner was missing. Lorenzo Labadie, Juan Patrón, Pablo Anaya, and Amado C. de Baca were all commended for their service to the courts and returned to San Miguel County.[30]

James Allen was convicted of murder in the first degree and escorted back to the Las Vegas jail to await execution that August, before managing to escape with five other prisoners that November. The former waiter and his fellow escapee George Davidson were shot to death by Las Vegas deputies Desiderio Apodaca and Francisco Martínez several days later.[31]

***

While the railroad was providing some citizens with unprecedented business opportunities, many gringos were seeking their own kind of fortune in Lincoln County during the summer of 1880. A prospector named George Wilson had uncovered a vein of gold ore in a valley twenty-eight miles northwest of Lincoln the previous year. News of his discovery spread rapidly. A mining camp was established, which transformed into a boomtown after a full-scale gold rush commenced. The new settlement was named White Oaks, after a nearby river, although the region had long been known as Malpais (Badlands), owing to the volcanic fields of lava flow located eight miles to the west of the mining town.

White Oaks became a typically rough boomtown, frequented by prospectors, salesmen, cattlemen, cowboys, gamblers, sporting ladies, pistoleros, and rustlers. The *Las Vegas Daily Gazette* proclaimed the mining town "the new El Dorado" when publishing a letter they received in March 1880. "What we need most, is for some enterprising man," one vainglorious resident of White Oaks had written. "I would say that he need fear no competition from the fossils of Lincoln plaza, who are most heartily and emphatically damned by all who have the misfortune to be compelled to deal with them."[32]

As fortune-seeking Americanos were pouring into White Oaks, the "fossils" of Lincoln were contending with mob violence during the summer of 1880. A young man named Harriman became intoxicated, was arrested for an unknown offense, and locked inside the Lincoln jailhouse on July 3, 1880. Although Harriman was reportedly a quiet, innocuous young man who had merely succumbed to drunken foolishness that day, he was shot dead by "reckless men" who stormed into the jail that night. A deputy sheriff was apparently named as an accessory to Harriman's murder and was killed by a mob of ruffians who stormed the jailhouse on the night of July 4, 1880. Another angry mob reportedly dragged a prisoner out of the adobe jail and hanged him from a nearby tree branch the following night of July 5. A handful of locals would arrive in Santa Fe and inform the *New Mexican* of the "reign of terror" that occurred in Lincoln throughout the Independence Day celebrations along the Río Bonito.[33]

A little Hispano boy residing in Lincoln named Aristotle "Harry" Aguayo later recalled that José Chávez y Chávez was probably the hombre who killed the young prisoner named Harriman inside the jailhouse on the night of July 3, 1880. The 6-year-old Aristotle vividly remembered playing marbles with another young boy named Adolfo Romero near the torreón one evening in Lincoln around that time. The boys soon spotted the solidly built José Chávez y Chávez walking down the street in their direction. Aristotle noticed that José was carrying a brand-new Winchester rifle as he casually strolled past them.

"Hello, boys," José said in Spanish. "Playing marbles are you?"

Aristotle Aguayo and Adolfo Romero responded politely before José Chávez y Chávez approached the nearby jailhouse and disappeared inside. The boys continued shooting marbles until they heard two loud bursts of gunpowder coming from the building.

"Oh, God!" an Americano prisoner screamed inside.

Aristotle and Adolfo listened intently until an angry, familiar voice broke the deathly silence moments later.

"No [expletive] gringo can take my gun away from me and get away with it!" José Chávez y Chávez shouted inside the jailhouse.

Aristotle Aguayo and Adolfo Romero watched in astonishment as the former deputy sheriff emerged from the adobe building with his Winchester rifle and shuffled back up the street after killing one of the shackled prisoners inside the jailhouse. Aristotle's father José Aguayo spotted José Chávez y Chávez calmly riding out of Lincoln with a loaded packhorse the following morning.[34]

The 30-year-old José Chávez y Chávez was still living with his wife Leonora Lucero de Chávez and their 7-year-old son Adecasio in San Patricio that summer. His amigo Florencio Cháves had recently married Teodora, the eldest daughter of the deceased William Brady and widowed María Bonifacia Chávez Brady, and he eventually took work as a jailer up in Lincoln. José Chávez y Chávez sometimes boasted of having killed William Brady himself, despite not having been present when his fellow Regulators gunned down the House-aligned sheriff during the Lincoln County War.[35]

For some, José Chávez y Chávez was a sociable hardcase with an admirable nerve. To others, José Chávez y Chávez was *muy malo*—a true badman.

***

The wool trade was becoming an increasingly promising enterprise for Martín Chávez during the summer and autumn of 1880. The arrival of the railroads in New Mexico Territory had increased the demand for shipments of wool in Pennsylvania and New York. "No industry among us, probably, has made more steady advance in the quality of its work than wool manufacturing," the *Las Vegas Gazette* declared. "Sheep husbandry, when backed by intelligence, skill, and large capital, is probably as certain a road to competency and even fortune as this road affords." Martín Chávez had yet to accumulate large capital from his backbreaking labor but possessed the intelligence and skill to further succeed in sheep husbandry in Picacho.[36]

When Martín Chávez wasn't transporting shipments of wool to Las Vegas, the 27-year-old farmer enjoyed visits from his 14-year-old cousin Ambrosio Chávez, who had moved from Manzano to Lincoln with his parents in 1879. Martín and his 21-year-old wife Juana would have watched on when the widowed María Romero married an hombre called José Trinidad Vigil the previous year. María continued raising the four children her late husband Vicente Romero had left behind, and she would also have five additional children with Señor Vigil. Juana's older sister Paulita and her husband Sheriff George Kimbrell would have their fifth child, a son named Guillermo (William), in August 1880. Martín and Juana had been married for five years but had yet to conceive a child of their own.[37]

Martín and Juana also enjoyed visits from their helpful friend William Bonney in Picacho. "Kid stayed with me many nights," Martín later recalled. Bonney was always welcome in the homes of many Hispanos whenever riding through Lincoln County. The Kid also spent time dealing monte in White Oaks and even played cards with Sheriff George Kimbrell without fear of arrest. "He had worlds of friends," young Aristotle Aguayo later said. "Billy was an outlaw, but he never was bad."[38]

Martín Chávez would always remember the time Billy Bonney and his sidekick Tom Folliard arrived at his farm in Picacho shortly after his property had been raided by local rustlers. Sweat was dripping from Martín's brow as he struggled to plow his fields with the only horse in his possession when Bonney and Folliard arrived leading a pack horse fitted with their camp materials.

"I'm glad you boys came along with three horses," Martín said when greeting them. "Somebody has stolen mine and I can't get along with one horse."

Billy Bonney immediately dismounted his bay mare and began removing his materials from the pack horse. He instructed his pal Tom Folliard to do the same. The Kid and his stout sidekick fitted their camp outfit onto their saddle horses, leaving the pack horse to assist Martín with his farming duties. Martín offered to return the pack horse when Bonney and Folliard stopped in a few days later, having since purchased a new horse of his own.

"Never mind about that, Martín," the Kid said. "You can keep him."

The former deputy sheriff insisted and eventually persuaded Bonney and Folliard to take the animal back. "Billy was one of the kindest and best boys I ever knew, and far superior in many respects to his pursuers," Martín later said. "The Kid knew Martín well and often stayed at his house," his cousin Ambrosio Chávez recalled. Martín and Billy both lost parents at an early age, which would have made for a natural rapport. Bonney often talked about his mother Catherine when conversing with friends. Martín undoubtedly spoke of his deceased parents Juan and María Lauriana.[39]

Martín Chávez enjoyed horse racing as much as the next hombre and accepted a challenge from some Texans who hitched their covered wagons near Picacho on one occasion. "They had a fast horse that they wanted to race against a mare that my cousin Martín had," recalled Ambrosio Chávez. "The Texas people bet three fat beeves that their horse could outrun Martín's mare." The overconfident Tejanos were furious when Martín's mare won the race by a considerable margin, and they refused to honor the wager. The disgruntled Chávez returned to his ranch without the three plump beeves he had won fair and square.

When Billy Bonney paid Martín a visit a short time later, the former deputy sheriff told his amigo about the horse race with the Tejanos and their refusal to honor their bet. "Billy asked Martín if he wanted those beeves, and of course Martín said that he did," remembered Ambrosio Chávez. "He wore two guns and had on two belts of cartridges." The Kid informed Martín that he would collect the wager on his friend's behalf and laughed when Juanita Romero-Chávez and her female relatives tried to dissuade him from fear that he might get killed. Billy calmly rode out to the Texan's camp and shot dead three of their finest cows. He then returned to Martín's ranch and told his amigo to send for his beef. The Tejanos were so unnerved by the Kid's actions, they immediately broke camp and left the vicinity. Their fellow Anglos rarely took up for "Mexicans" in such a manner, and the Kid had a reputation as a desperate young man. "Billy was a perfect gentleman and a man with a noble heart," Martín Chávez later insisted.[40]

For most of the Hispanos throughout the region, Billy "the Kid" Bonney had become the social bandit of Nuevo México—a bandido they could cheer for. An audacious desperado who spoke their language, preferred their company to his own Anglo race, wore sugarloaf sombreros like them, dressed like them, sang with them, danced with them, understood their culture, and treated them with generosity and affection. "He was kind and good to poor people," his compadre Yginio Salazar recalled. The Hispanos of southeastern New Mexico embraced the youthful bandido as a local hero, sometimes referring to him as Bilito (Little Billy) or El Chivato (the Little Goat). "He never had a Mexican for an enemy, they all loved him, and would do anything for him," recalled Carlota Baca. "He was a nice fellow and well-liked by the natives," remembered local boy José Montoya. "He was awful good to the Mexican people and stayed with them most of the time."[41]

While William Bonney enjoyed the unwavering support of most Hispanos in southeastern Nuevo México, his outlawry was growing more brazen after he failed to receive his pardon from Governor Lew Wallace. "He was warm-hearted to a degree, absolutely loyal to a friend," recalled Frank Coe. "But unfortunately with little scruples as to either the lives or property of those who opposed him." The Kid had a chip on his shoulder and continued rustling horses and cattle from local Anglo ranchers and the wealthy cattlemen on the Texas Panhandle.[42]

Billy Bonney was particularly aggrieved with John Chisum over the money he insisted the cattleman owed him and continued cutting jingle-bob herds with a circle of friends and associates. Tom Folliard and Charlie Bowdre were still riding with the Kid, although Doc Scurlock had relocated to Texas with his family in early 1880. Yginio Salazar had returned to Las Tablas after briefly dabbling in horse thievery. The Kid, Folliard, and

Bowdre were often accompanied by fellow rustlers Billy Wilson, Tom Pickett, and an unsavory former Las Vegas policeman called Dave Rudabaugh. They sometimes grazed their stolen livestock in a secluded region seventy miles southeast of Fort Sumner known as Los Portales. A crooked army veteran named Pat Coghlan and his middleman Tom Cooper paid twelve dollars a head for appropriated cattle in Tularosa. Bonney's friends Daniel, Samuel, and Mose Dedrick were also willing to purchase stolen beeves in White Oaks.[43]

The Hispanos may have loved "Beely" like one of their own, but the Anglo citizens of White Oaks considered Bonney and his circle of rustlers a menace. The Kid's one-time friend Deputy Will Hudgens had relocated to the mining town and quickly grew tired of them. New Mexico Territory needed to change as the railroads expanded, and rustlers like William Bonney had to become as much a thing of the past as possible. Charlie Goodnight and the influential cattlemen on the Texas Panhandle were equally determined to put an end to stock thievery. Jimmy Dolan, John Chisum, and the Santa Fe Ring also wanted the Kid gone.[44]

Sheriff George Kimbrell would face stiff competition for his office after John Chisum and Roswell rancher "Captain" Joseph Lea decided Lincoln County needed a sheriff who would pursue William Bonney rather than play cards with him. The man they had in mind was a lanky former buffalo hunter originally from Alabama who had previously dabbled in cattle theft himself while living in Fort Sumner. He was familiar with William Bonney and his hideouts but also willing to go after him. His name was Patrick Floyd Jarvis Garrett.[45]

***

Juan Patrón's life changed when he took on a whole new form of responsibility in September 1880. That was the month his wife Beatriz gave birth to their first child, a daughter whom they christened María Theresa Consuelo Rayitos Patrón. The proud parents referred to their little bundle as Rayitos and doted on her with the typical enthusiasm of first-time parents. Juan had been given another reason to smile during the summer. His younger sister Encarnación and brother-in-law Rafael Gutiérrez had brought their third child into the world, a daughter named Juana Saturnina Gutiérrez, in June 1880. *La familia lo es todo*.⁴⁶

While splitting his time between Puerto de Luna and Santa Rosa, Juan Patrón befriended the local padre Auguste "Antonio" Francois Joseph Redon, who could sometimes be observed merrily chatting with William "Kid" Bonney outside a church in Anton Chico. Juan had noticed that Puerto de Luna had only a small chapel in which Roman Catholics could practice their faith. While his ambition of establishing a church in Lincoln had never come to fruition, the Hispano businessman and the French priest organized a campaign to raise funds for the erection of a church in Puerto de Luna. Juan encouraged the local businessmen to donate money to the cause, while Padre Redon solicited funds from his flock. They eventually raised $1,200 in their hopes of establishing a parish seat. Melquiades Ramírez donated a portion of land and the construction of a local Roman Catholic church began.⁴⁷

Juan Patrón had married into a family of Democrats and switched parties for the second time after settling in San Miguel County. Having successfully ridden the Republican ticket during his final years in Lincoln, the Hispano businessman attended the Democratic convention in Las Vegas on October 13, 1880. The convention was called to order by county sheriff and member of the county central committee Desiderio Romero at ten o'clock that morning. Juan Patrón was elected temporary secretary until the delegates finished arriving in the afternoon and a permanent organization was effected with the election of Pedro Vasquez as president of the convention. Juan's father-in-law Lorenzo Labadie was elected as one of the vice presidents, while his brother-in-law Tranquilino Labadie and Judge Arthur Morrison were elected permanent secretaries.

The Democratic convention was eventually convened in Baca Hall owing to the large attendance and continued long into the night. Speeches were made and the ticket nominations were determined. Tranquilino Labadie had earned the nomination for county clerk. In addition to the speeches made at the convention, the sound of gunfire was also heard in Las Vegas that night when 20-year-old Dionicio García shot the middle-aged Augustine Montoya with a small caliber pistol outside a dance hall on the south side of the city.

García was quickly locked inside the jailhouse. Montoya managed to pull through the following morning after receiving the last rites from a padre.[48]

As Juan Patrón and his wife Beatriz were setting down roots in San Miguel County, the Hispanos and Anglos of New Mexico Territory breathed a collective sigh of relief when learning of Victorio's demise. The Apache war chief and a band of followers were surrounded by Mexican soldiers under the command of Col. Joaquin Terrazas in Tres Castillos, Chihuahua, Mexico, on October 14, 1880. Victorio and some of his warriors tried to fight off the Mexican soldiers with what little ammunition they possessed but were eventually slain the following morning. "Caught like rats in a trap, and unable to retreat, the Indians fought desperately," the *Las Vegas Gazette* declared. Several of Victorio's band managed to escape. The rest were taken prisoner.[49]

It was later said that the enigmatic Victorio stabbed himself in the heart after running out of bullets rather than allowing himself to be captured by the Mexicans. "That their deeds have retarded the advancement of New Mexico and especially of its southern counties cannot be denied," the *New Mexican* declared. "They were shot down by the Mexican troops like vermin which should be exterminated in any manner." Although reviled by the White-Eye and Mexicans of the borderlands, the defiant Victorio had cemented his place in Apache folklore as a legendary symbol of resistance.[50]

***

George Kimbrell knew he had a fight on his hands to retain the office of sheriff as the elections approached in October 1880. Lawrence G. Murphy's old financial backer Joseph A. Larue took control of the Democratic convention in Lincoln that month, voicing his strong support for Pat Garrett and disdain for the incumbent sheriff. Larue now owned the former Tunstall store, and his clerk Jimmy Dolan also spoke in favor of Garrett's election. Santa Fe Ring member David Easton even shoved Kimbrell supporters aside to reach the speaker's stand and deride the sheriff for having friendly relations with outlaws. Kimbrell's opponent also enjoyed the unwavering support of John Chisum, post trader Will Dowlin, and influential rancher "Captain" Joseph Lea.[51]

The 30-year-old Patrick Floyd Jarvis Garrett was pushed as the man to end outlawry in southeastern New Mexico and won a close vote as the

Democratic party's nomination for sheriff of Lincoln County. While Pat Garrett's reserved nature was ill-suited for campaigning, the long-legged Alabaman was hard to miss. He stood six feet, four inches tall, with dark hair, hazel eyes, and a thick moustache. The candidate certainly looked the part, despite having no previous experience hunting outlaws. He was also a good storyteller, possessed a dry sense of humor, spoke fluent Spanish, and, most importantly, knew how to handle a gun with precision. Garrett had spent years working as a buffalo hunter in Texas and once killed a skinner named Joe Briscoe during an argument at their campsite near Fort Griffin.[52]

George Kimbrell decided to run for reelection despite Pat Garrett's narrow victory at the Democratic convention in Lincoln. The sheriff still possessed the support of many Hispano farmers, including his brother-in-law Martín Chávez. Kimbrell also had a supporter in William "Kid" Bonney, who campaigned in Las Tablas for the incumbent sheriff's reelection. William Bonney was already familiar with Pat Garrett, having spent time around him in Fort Sumner. The tall Alabaman had settled in Bonney's adopted home in early 1878. The Kid even attended Pat Garrett's first wedding at the old fort in November 1879, although the marriage proved short-lived when the bride Juanita Martínez died from a medical condition the following day. Garrett then spent time stealing and butchering some of the local Hispano's cattle with his friend Barney Mason. He had since moved to Roswell after marrying Fort Sumner resident Apolinaria Gutiérrez in Anton Chico on January 14, 1880.[53]

While Pat Garrett was looking to make a better life for himself as a frontier lawman, William Bonney was involved in an increasingly serious romance with Paulita Maxwell in Fort Sumner. The Kid also sent word to Ira Leonard looking for a way out of the outlaw life, still hoping to receive his pardon. The 16-year-old Paulita Maxwell later insisted that Billy and Pat Garrett were friends in Fort Sumner, often gambling and engaging in shooting contests together. "As far as anybody knew at the time, [Pat Garrett's] only qualification for the office was his intimate friendship with the Kid and his men," Paulita later said. "He was familiar with all their old trails, their favorite haunts, their secret places of rendezvous and refuge." Whatever the true nature of their relationship, Garrett had sand and knew Bonney well enough to pursue him like nobody ever had before. "Pat Garrett, who took up pursuit of the Kid for them, was a cow thief himself, as everybody in Fort Sumner knew," Yginio Salazar later insisted. "He went back on [the Kid] for money and for the promise of office."⁵⁴

William Bonney had no intention of leaving Nuevo México at the time and was as dangerous as a diamondback when threatened. "Billy didn't bother anybody unless they were out to get him," recalled Yginio Salazar. "If he was your friend, he was your friend, but he was hard on anybody who talked about getting him if he knew it."⁵⁵

Pat Garrett was sometimes a man of few words, but his actions said plenty.

Chapter 11

El Bilito

In a nation of frightened dullards there is a sorry shortage of outlaws, and those few who make the grade are always welcome.
—Hunter S. Thompson

William H. Bonney knew Pat Garrett would pursue him if the Alabaman was elected the sheriff of Lincoln County on November 2, 1880. What the Kid didn't know was that a secret service agent named Azariah Wild had recently arrived in Nuevo México to pursue his rustling associates Billy Wilson and Tom Cooper. They were both suspected of running a counterfeiting operation. The real culprits were William H. West and the Dedrick brothers, who had handed Billy Wilson four counterfeit $100 bills when purchasing a livery from him in White Oaks. Wilson had put the counterfeit notes into circulation when purchasing goods from the Larue and Montaño stores in Lincoln.

Agent Azariah Wild had arrived in Santa Fe from New Orleans and subsequently reached Lincoln with Edgar Walz on October 4, 1880. Agent Wild had never even heard of William Bonney when first arriving in the territory but quickly learned of the Kid's existence when meeting with Ira Leonard, Joseph A. Larue, Jimmy Dolan, and José Montaño on the Río

Bonito. It was presumably Jimmy Dolan who suggested his old adversary William Bonney was responsible for the counterfeiting operation, although Agent Wild reported having "found no evidence thus far to support their suspicions."[1]

Miserable in the freezing conditions and missing his family, Azariah Wild was taken for a ride by various locals with their own agendas. The agent's list of suspects quickly ballooned to eighteen individuals. Among those suspected of involvement in the counterfeiting operation were Sheriff George Kimbrell and Susan McSween's second husband George B. Barber. Agent Wild's investigation became farcical when Edgar Walz tried to convince the government agent that his employee James DeVours could prove there was a gang of thieves numbering a preposterous 161 men responsible for all the cattle theft and counterfeiting in Lincoln County. DeVours was only willing to give up the goods for $1,000. He failed to show up when Wild arranged to meet with him.

Ira Leonard had also shown Agent Azariah Wild a letter he had received from William Bonney in which the Kid had professed being "tired of dodging the officers." Wild wasn't willing to promise anything, but he was open to the idea of using Bonney as a witness in exchange for the pardon he was promised by Governor Lew Wallace. The agent was far more concerned with capturing Billy Wilson and Tom Cooper, having appointed Johnny Hurley and Bob Olinger to serve as deputy US marshals and make the arrests when the warrants arrived from Santa Fe.[2]

Charlie Bowdre was also looking for a way out and had been exchanging letters with Pat Garrett's close friend "Captain" Joseph Lea. The former Regulator was reportedly willing "to give the whole thing away for a consideration." Dave Rudabaugh, Tom Pickett, and Billy Wilson only made things hotter for their rustling associates when they robbed a mail carriage on October 16, 1880. William Bonney was named as a suspect in Agent Wild's reports, despite not having been present when the stage robbery occurred.

Agent Azariah Wild had also spent time in Fort Stanton, where he was informed that "Wilson and his gang" had recently stolen sixty-eight head of cattle from "a man named Ellis," four-hundred head of cattle from "another party," and eight horses from John Chisum. Wild also reported having heard that "a force of desperados" operated out of Fort Sumner, a place the agent described as "the headquarters of all bad men for nearly the whole country." Any ruffian who engaged in banditry in southeastern Nuevo México was being lumped in with "Billy Kid" and his circle of rustlers in San Miguel County. Sheriff George Kimbrell managed to arrest a mail robber named Benjamin Franklin Hill in late October and was undoubtedly embarrassed when his prisoner escaped a few nights later.[3]

Billy Bonney needed the support of the Hispano populace more than ever when Pat Garrett defeated George Kimbrell in the election for sheriff of Lincoln County on November 2, 1880. The tall Alabaman had received 320 votes ahead of Kimbrell's 179 in a county with a population of roughly 2,500 people at the time. "Nothing ever gave Fort Sumner such a shock of surprise as Garrett's selection by the cattle interests to be sheriff of Lincoln County," Bonney's love interest Paulita Maxwell later said. Sheriff George Kimbrell was pressured into appointing Garrett as one of his deputies. The Anglo cattlemen and ranchers wanted something done immediately about Bonney and his circle of rustlers, and their man Garrett would not take office until January 1, 1881.[4]

Agent Azariah Wild received the warrants for the arrest of Billy Wilson, Tom Cooper, and a rustler called James Finley on November 8, 1880. When Sheriff-elect Pat Garrett and "Captain" Joseph Lea arrived in Lincoln the following day, Wild simply crossed out Johnny Hurley's name on one of his deputy marshal commissions and scribbled in Garrett's name instead. Plans were then made to raise a posse comitatus to "make a raid on Fort Sumner." Deputy US Marshals Pat Garrett and Bob Olinger tried to locate Tom Cooper and James Finley over in White Oaks but returned to Lincoln empty-handed. Garrett was also keeping a close eye on Bob Olinger, whom the sheriff-elect was cautious to even sleep around and later described as "born a murderer at heart."[5]

Azariah Wild also received a visit from a White Oaks miner and former Texas Ranger named James W. Bell. The 27-year-old Jimmy Bell had fled Texas two years earlier after being released on bonds for his involvement in the murder of a farmer named Ratliff Morrow. The tall miner had recently befriended Pat Garrett and was looking to make a deal with Agent Wild on behalf of two counterfeiters operating in White Oaks. The federal agent was desperate to return to his wife and four children in New Orleans and was willing to make a deal with anyone who could make his job easier.[6]

Sheriff-elect Pat Garrett and "Captain" Joseph Lea returned to Roswell intending to raise a posse on November 14, 1880. A snowstorm kept them stationed there for the time being, although Garrett managed to send word to his friend Barney Mason up in Fort Sumner. Mason possessed inside information about William H. West and the Dedrick brothers' counterfeiting operation in White Oaks. He was also familiar with William Bonney and had allowed Billy Wilson to board in his home at Fort Sumner. Pat Garrett convinced Agent Azariah Wild to hire his chum Mason as an informant. Wild also heard that a cattle detective called Frank Stewart was leading a posse and two wagons over from the Texas Panhandle at the behest of the recently established Canadian River Cattleman's Association. Stewart and a dozen cowhands had been tasked with either apprehending or killing Billy Bonney and the rustlers who were cutting herds.[7]

Pat Garrett and Bob Olinger continued raising a posse in Roswell while informant Barney Mason headed over to White Oaks to spy on William H. West, Tom Cooper, and the Dedrick brothers. Nobody seemed to know exactly where William Bonney was at the time. Barney Mason informed Agent Wild that the Kid and Billy Wilson departed Fort Sumner to begin herding sixty stolen horses north to the Canadian River on November 15, 1880. Pat Garrett later claimed the Kid, Tom Folliard, Tom Pickett, and a rustler named Robert "Buck" Edwards had stolen eight horses from the Grzelachowski ranch and were selling them off near White Oaks around the same time, on November 16, 1880.[8]

Wherever William Bonney was throughout the previous week, his rustling activities began catching up with him when he ran into a posse led by Deputy Sheriff Will Hudgens six miles north of White Oaks on November 22, 1880. The Hudgens posse had already arrested Moses Dedrick and W. J. Lamper on the trail before Bonney, Dave Rudabaugh, Billy Wilson, "Buck" Edwards, and a Texan named Joe Cook exchanged shots with them at Coyote Springs. The Kid, Rudabaugh, and Wilson managed to escape and headed north to their friend Jim Greathouse's ranch. Moses Dedrick was released on bonds in

White Oaks and soon fled the territory with his brothers Daniel and Samuel. Their counterfeiting associate William H. West did the same.[9]

William Bonney, Dave Rudabaugh, and Billy Wilson found themselves besieged by another White Oaks posse at the Greathouse ranch on the morning of November 27, 1880. Constable Tom Longworth had raised a posse consisting of Will Hudgens, James W. Bell, a blacksmith named James Carlyle, and various heavily armed locals. They had followed Bonney, Rudabaugh, and Wilson's trail from Coyote Springs and taken position behind various barricades around the Greathouse ranch during the night. Tom Longworth had returned to White Oaks to gather reinforcements and left gunman James Carlyle in charge when the posse took Greathouse employee Joe Steck hostage that morning. The posse dispatched Steck to deliver a message to the Kid and his cohorts, demanding their surrender. Billy Bonney laughed at the notion of surrendering and assured Steck that he wouldn't be harmed. The Kid sent Steck back outside with a message of his own. He demanded to know who was in charge of the posse and invited their leader inside to talk things over.

James Carlyle headed into the ranch house and demanded Bonney, Rudabaugh, and Wilson surrender. The Kid decided the posse was merely a lynch mob when Carlyle was unable to produce any official papers. Billy informed Carlyle that he would have to remain inside the ranch house and lead the way out after sunset. The White Oaks posse eventually grew tired of waiting and dispatched Jim Greathouse's partner Fred Kuch inside with another message. They were intending to "storm the fort," as Joe Steck later described it. As Steck and Fred Kuch emerged from the ranch house to take cover, James Carlyle tried to escape by crashing through a window. Carlyle was quickly struck by three bullets and fell dead. Steck and Kuch ran for their lives when the White Oaks posse fired more than fifty shots at them from all directions. Joe Steck dived onto the ground and was nearly shot in the head several times before the firing stopped.

The White Oaks posse strangely withdrew, leaving James Carlyle's bloodied corpse lying in the snow. William Bonney, Dave Rudabaugh, and Billy Wilson simply strolled out of the ranch house, headed to the nearby Spencer ranch to enjoy a meal, and began making the eighty-mile journey to

Anton Chico on foot. The White Oaks posse insisted Carlyle had been shot by the Kid and his associates. William Bonney claimed that Carlyle was accidentally "killed by his own party, they thinking it was me trying to make my escape." Joe Steck and Fred Kuch buried James Carlyle's corpse to the northeast of the Greathouse ranch before the White Oaks posse returned with Johnny Hurley and some reinforcements. They burned the Greathouse and Spencer ranches to the ground after failing to locate the elusive outlaws.[10]

As Billy Bonney, Dave Rudabaugh, and Billy Wilson were heading back to San Miguel County, the determined Pat Garrett, Bob Olinger, Barney Mason, and a heavily armed posse arrived in Fort Sumner around December 2, 1880. They had already captured two fugitives named John Joshua Webb and George Davis, both of whom had recently escaped from the Las Vegas jail. Garrett was informed by an Anglo local that Tom Folliard, Charlie Bowdre, and Tom Pickett could be found at their friend Tom Yerby's ranch twenty miles to the northeast of Fort Sumner. Garrett and several possemen rode out and were soon chasing after Tom Folliard in a running shootout on the trail. The Kid's pal easily outran them on a superior mount and had fled the Yerby ranch with Bowdre and Pickett by the time Garrett and his companions arrived.[11]

The frustrated Pat Garrett returned to Fort Sumner before leading a handful of men on the seventy-mile ride southeast to Los Portales. Garrett managed to find the Kid's hideout very easily, later describing it as "impassable except to the initiated," which may suggest the sheriff-elect had been there before. The posse found only two cows grazing in the vicinity and some salt and musty flour inside the small cave in which Billy Bonney and his associates had set up camp. Pat Garrett and his men butchered a yearling for supper and headed back to San Miguel County the following morning.[12]

Pat Garrett was informed that Charlie Bowdre wanted to talk with him when he stopped at the Brazil-Wilcox ranch on the journey back to Fort Sumner. The sheriff-elect arranged to meet with the former Regulator at a crossing two miles outside the old fort the following afternoon. Garrett showed Bowdre a letter from "Captain" Joseph Lea assuring him of a chance to start over should he sever ties with the Kid's circle of rustlers. "I told him if he did not quit them or surrender, he would be pretty sure to get captured or killed," Pat Garrett recalled. The sheriff-elect then returned to Fort Sumner and dismissed all the members of his posse except Barney Mason.[13]

Pat Garrett and Barney Mason escorted J. J. Webb and George Davis to Puerto de Luna and turned the prisoners over to San Miguel County Sheriff Desiderio Romero and his posse of drunken hooligans they had encountered on the trail. A notorious bandido named Mariano Leiva tried to pick a fight with Garrett at the Grzelachowski store, declaring that he would "like to see any damned gringo arrest him." Pat eventually slapped Leiva off the porch, and the intoxicated ruffian pulled his pistol. Garrett drew his own revolver and blew a hole in Leiva's shoulder, sending the wounded bandido running off in the opposite direction with his tail between his legs. Garrett then tried to ignore the Romero posse's buffoonery while helping them escort George Davis and J. J. Webb to Las Vegas. He also dispatched Barney Mason to find cattle detective Frank Stewart over in Anton Chico and arrange for them to meet up in Las Vegas.[14]

Billy Bonney, Dave Rudabaugh, and Billy Wilson finally arrived in Anton Chico and then returned to Fort Sumner shortly after Pat Garrett had departed. The Kid wasn't pleased when reading the December 3, 1880, edition of the *Las Vegas Gazette*. The editor, J. H. Koogler, had published a provocative article declaring "Billy the Kid" the captain of a gang of desperados numbering between forty and fifty men, and therefore responsible for practically every act of banditry committed in southeastern Nuevo México. "The gang is under the leadership of 'Billy the Kid,' a desperate cuss, who is eligible for the post of captain of any crowd, no matter how mean or lawless," the *Gazette* declared. "Shall we suffer this horde of outcasts and the scum of society, who are outlawed by a multitude of crimes, to continue their sway on the very border of our country?"[15]

While Billy Bonney was responsible for some of the rustling occurring in the region, he was riled by J. H. Koogler's exaggerations. The local Hispanos' favorite bandido wrote a defensive letter to Governor Lew Wallace on December 12, 1880. The Kid insisted that James Carlyle had been killed by his own posse and denied leadership of a large gang. "There is no doubt but what there is a great deal of stealing going on in the territory, and a great deal of property is taken across the plains as it is a good outlet," Billy informed Governor Wallace. "But so far as my being at the head of a band there is nothing of it." Bonney had a tendency to stretch the truth sometimes, and Wallace issued a public notice drawn up by Secretary William Ritch on December 14, 1880:

BILLY THE KID

$500 REWARD

I will pay $500 reward to any persons
who will capture William Bonny, alias The Kid, and
deliver him to any sheriff of New Mexico.
Satisfactory proofs of identity will be required.
LEW WALLACE
Governor of New Mexico[16]

The name "Billy the Kid" and embellished tales of his outlawry began spreading far and wide across the borderlands. The newspapers would continue exaggerating Bonney's activities, portraying the young rustler as a heartless psychopath who would kill any man on a whim. His reputation quickly became as fearsome as the late Victorio's. While many bandidos would have immediately fled the territory, the stubborn Bilito still possessed the loyal support of many Hispanos willing to provide him with shelter and information about his pursuers. The Kid was not about to abandon his querida Paulita Maxwell either.[17]

While the territorial press was making Billy the Kid the most famous outlaw in the American Southwest, Pat Garrett needed reinforcements. He offered Frank Stewart a share of the reward money in Las Vegas. Stewart agreed but had already sent his Panhandle posse ahead to White Oaks before departing Anton Chico to meet with the sheriff-elect. Garrett, Stewart, and Barney Mason rode after the Panhandle boys and caught up with them the day after their departure from Anton Chico. Cowpunchers Jim East, Lou Bousman, Tom Emory, Lee Hall, Lon Chambers, and Bob Williams agreed to continue the hunt for Bonney's circle of rustlers. The other half of the Panhandle posse decided to continue their journey to White

Oaks instead. "The Mexicans were not dependable, and the Americans did not all like Garrett, so he had to ask help from us cowboys in Texas," Jim East later said.[18]

Pat Garrett, Frank Stewart, and their posse rode for Puerto de Luna and arrived in the placita on the evening of December 16, 1880. They bedded down for the night and recruited the assistance of Grzelachowski ranch hands Juan and José Roival. Their numbers were further bolstered by Charles Rudulph and English cattleman George Wilson. Pat Garrett sent José Roival down the Río Pecos to Fort Sumner to act as a spy before leading the posse through a fierce snowstorm toward the Kid's adopted home that night. The posse initially concealed themselves within Pete Maxwell's orchard and tried to keep a low profile after arriving in Fort Sumner during the early hours of December 18. Billy Bonney and his associates were nowhere to be found, having ridden for the Wilcox-Brazil ranch on the Taiban the previous night. Pat Garrett detained a local Hispano who spotted them snooping around before the posse eventually bunked down in the old Indian Hospital to the northeast of the plaza.[19]

Pat Garrett and Barney Mason tried to acquire any information about William Bonney's whereabouts during the morning of December 18, 1880. The Hispanos of Fort Sumner resented the posse's presence and gave them nothing. The gringos were after their friend Bilito. "Nearly all the Mexicans were friendly to the Kid," recalled Jim East. "Garrett told everybody to stay in Fort Sumner and for no one to leave on pain of death. He was afraid someone would slip out and tell the Kid." Garrett's fears were well-founded. A local farmer named Higinio García rode east for the Wilcox-Brazil ranch to inform Bilito of the posse's presence after convincing the tall Alabaman to allow him to leave the grounds and fetch a little milk for his infant son Hilario.[20]

Pat Garrett noticed 16-year-old Juan J. Gallegos suspiciously watching his every move in Fort Sumner on the morning of December 19, 1880. Garrett interrogated the teenager long and hard enough for him to reveal that he was spying on Billy Bonney's behalf. The shaken Gallegos eventually agreed to act as double agent. The sheriff-elect also detained Bonney's friend José Valdéz and forced him to scribble a note informing the Kid that Garrett and his Tejanos were on their way back down to Roswell. Garrett wrote another note to Manuel Brazil and Thomas Wilcox, neither of whom were overly fond of the Kid and his ruffians, assuring them the posse were staying put. The sheriff-elect handed Juan Gallegos both notes and sternly instructed him to return to his stepfather Thomas Wilcox's ranch and deliver each message to the intended recipients.[21]

Pat Garrett, Frank Stewart, and their possemen detained the Kid's amigos Jesús Silva, Higinio García, and Jesús Verelles in addition to the already-captive José Valdéz. They kept their Hispano hostages under guard in the old Indian Hospital while expecting Billy Bonney and his associates to ride in from the Brazil-Wilcox ranch on the night of December 19, 1880. "[Garrett] was smart and cunning and above all, careful," Yginio Salazar later said. Lon Chambers was standing guard outside around eight o'clock when he spotted some shadowy figures riding through the thick fog toward the Indian Hospital. The deputy ducked inside to inform his companions, and Pat Garrett took cover with his Winchester rifle behind a post and dangling harness on the porch. Billy Bonney, Tom Folliard, Charlie Bowdre, Dave Rudabaugh, Billy Wilson, and Tom Pickett had taken the bait.[22]

Tom Folliard was the first to reach the old Indian Hospital and about to dismount when he heard a familiar voice shout, "Halt!" Tom instinctively went for his pistol and Pat Garrett shot him in the left side of his chest. Folliard screamed in pain as the rest of the posse began randomly shooting at the outlaws. The Kid and his companions quickly turned their horses and headed back toward the Taiban. The fatally wounded Tom Folliard soon returned to the Indian Hospital slumped over his saddle horn and groaning in pain. Pat Garrett and the posse carried the tall Texan inside, laid him onto a blanket, and resumed their card game in front of a warm fire. The Kid's 19-year-old sidekick cursed Garrett for a "long-legged son of a bitch," took a small drink of water, and died a short time later. Thomas O. Folliard was buried in an unmarked grave next to Joe Grant in the northeast corner of the old military cemetery the following day.[23]

Pat Garrett, Frank Stewart, and their posse caught up with Kid's bunch again in the early hours of December 23, 1880. Manuel Brazil had shown Garrett the tracks in the thick snow leading toward a small rectangular rock house at Stinking Spring—a place the Hispanos referred to as Ojo Hediendo and El Ojo del Taiba—four miles east of the Wilcox-Brazil ranch. The posse had taken their hostages José Valdéz, Jesús Silva, Higinio García, and Jesús Verelles with them. They stealthily approached the rock house while Billy Bonney and his four companions were sleeping inside. Pat Garrett, a handful of possemen, and their Hispano captives laid on their blankets in a small hollow thirty feet in front of the rock house door. Frank Stewart and the rest of the posse, with an anxious grip on their Winchester rifles, took position on one side of the stone structure and waited for the sun to rise.[24]

Pat Garrett was taking no chances. He had described William Bonney's sugarloaf sombrero to the posse and instructed them to shoot the Kid on sight. Charlie Bowdre was wearing a similar-looking sombrero when he emerged from the rock house to feed their horses at dawn. Garrett and his companions opened fire, having mistaken Bowdre for the Kid and shooting the unsuspecting former Regulator in the chest and leg. "[Garrett] would never give the man he was looking for the slightest possible chance to defend himself," Yginio Salazar bitterly said years later. Bowdre stumbled back inside the rock house only to emerge moments later with his pistol holstered and his hands raised. The 31-year-old Charles Meriwether Bowdre collapsed into Lee Hall's arms and died on Lou Bousman's blanket several minutes later.[25]

Billy Bonney's bay mare had spent the night inside the rock house, but the Kid's plan to make a break on horseback was foiled when Garrett shot down one of his companion's horses in the doorway. Bonney and Garrett exchanged sarcastic pleasantries, and the posse took turns firing shots at the rock house throughout the rest of the day. When the posse began cooking supper that evening, the aroma of the food was enough to entice the hungry William Bonney, Dave Rudabaugh, Billy Wilson, and Tom Pickett to finally surrender. Higinio García later told his brother-in-law Paco Anaya that Bonney had emptied his bladder onto the pile of rifles, revolvers, and gun belts inside the rock house before emerging with his hands raised.[26]

Barney Mason immediately raised his rifle to shoot the Kid when he emerged from the rock house but was dissuaded from doing so when his fellow possemen Lou Bousman, Lee Hall, and Jim East threw down on him. Lou Bousman had spent a little time around Bonney on the Texas Panhandle and threatened to kill both Mason and Pat Garrett if a single shot was fired in the Kid's direction. Pat Garrett ordered for Billy's wrists and ankles to be tied with rope before the young bandido happily shook hands with his amigos Higinio García, Jesús Silva, José Valdéz, and Jesús Verelles.

"I won't shake these damned Texans' hands," the Kid informed them in Spanish.[27]

Billy Bonney and his fellow captives were permitted to enjoy a feed before they were escorted back to the Wilcox-Brazil ranch for the night. Pat Garrett had initially regretted Charlie Bowdre's death that morning until Manuel Brazil informed him of the former Regulator's intention to kill the sheriff-elect the next time they met. The Kid and his companions were kept under close guard during the night and loaded into a wagon alongside Charles Bowdre's corpse the following morning.[28]

Manuela Bowdre had to be restrained from punching and kicking Pat Garrett when the posse and their captives arrived in Fort Sumner around eleven o'clock on the morning of December 24, 1880. The distraught widow walloped Jim East over the head with a branding iron when he and Lou Bousman carried her husband Charlie's corpse into her home. "Poor girl, it broke her heart when Charlie Bowdre was killed by Pat Garrett and his man-hunters," Paulita Maxwell recalled. Garrett commendably offered to pay for her slain husband's funeral clothes and burial. Charles Meriwether Bowdre was planted next to Tom Folliard and Joe Grant in the northeast corner of the old cemetery. The sheriff-elect also paid the local blacksmith to forge some irons with which Billy Bonney and Dave Rudabaugh were shackled together.[29]

Pat Garrett, Frank Stewart, and their prisoners were eating some chuck when they were approached by a former Navajo slave named Deluvina Maxwell. The 32-year-old Deluvina had been purchased by the late Lucien B. Maxwell as a child and worked as the family housekeeper. She had also become William Bonney's surrogate mother in Fort Sumner, happily washing and ironing his clothes, cooking his meals, and affectionately referring to him as *mí chiquito* (my little boy). "She worshipped him," recalled Paulita Maxwell. "To her mind, there was never such a wonderful boy in all the world."[30]

Doña Luz Maxwell had sent Deluvina to ask the posse if "Beely" could be permitted to visit with her daughter Paulita in their home. Pat Garrett consented, although the Kid was kept chained to Dave Rudabaugh while visiting with his *querida* (beloved). "The lovers embraced, and [Paulita] gave Billy one of those soul kisses the novelists tell us about," recalled Jim East. "We had to pull them apart, much against our wishes." Deluvina Maxwell also gave her little Billy a knitted scarf to help keep him warm. The Kid returned the favor by handing Deluvina one of the four copies of his tintype photograph, much to the Navajo woman's delight.[31]

Billy Bonney, Dave Rudabaugh, Tom Pickett, and Billy Wilson were soon loaded into a wagon and escorted thirty-seven miles up the Río Pecos to Puerto de Luna, where the Kid enjoyed his last Christmas dinner in the Grzelachowski store on December 25, 1880. Pat Garrett, Frank Stewart, and the remaining members of their posse then continued escorting the prisoners northeast until arriving in Las Vegas to considerable fanfare on December 26. Pat Garrett was the toast of the town, having proven himself a highly capable frontier lawman in a remarkably short period of time. The Kid and his associates were locked inside the rancid jailhouse on Valencia Street, where a reporter from the *Las Vegas Gazette* slipped inside and interviewed Bonney the following morning.

"There was a big crowd gazing at me wasn't there," the Kid remarked. "Well, perhaps some of them will think me half man now; everyone seems to think I was some kind of animal."[32]

In the few weeks since the *Las Vegas Gazette* had bequeathed him the nickname "Billy the Kid," the around 20- or 21-year-old Henry McCarty, alias William H. Bonney, had become a national celebrity. Even newspapers in New York began publishing reports of the youthful desperado and his frequently exaggerated exploits. Bonney wasn't particularly impressed by his newfound fame.

"I don't see any money in it," the Kid would inform another reporter from the *Las Vegas Gazette*. "Everything that has been done in that country is laid to me."[33]

While Tom Pickett would remain in Las Vegas to face charges for rustling, Pat Garrett, Frank Stewart, and their posse had some trouble when trying to escort William Bonney, Dave Rudabaugh, and Billy Wilson to Santa Fe on the morning of December 27, 1880. Sheriff Desiderio Romero and a large mob of predominantly Hispano citizens gathered at the train depot in East Las Vegas intending to seize former city policeman Dave Rudabaugh. The locals believed Rudabaugh had murdered jailer Antonio Lino Valdéz when trying to bust his friend J. J. Webb out of the Las Vegas jailhouse eight months earlier. Pat Garrett and Frank Stewart held their nerve, eventually threatening to arm their captives if the hostile locals didn't disperse. The Kid casually leaned out the window and jawed with a reporter during the chaos. He then waved his sugarloaf sombrero in the air as the train finally began rolling toward the territorial capital.[34]

Pat Garrett, Frank Stewart, and their possemen escorted Billy Bonney, Dave Rudabaugh, and Billy Wilson into Santa Fe during the evening of December 27, 1880. The Kid and his associates were turned over to Deputy US Marshal Charles Conklin and locked up in the city jail on Water Street. "The arrival here of the prisoners created a good deal of excitement and Sheriff Garrett is the hero of the hour," the *New Mexican* declared the following day. Pat Garrett wasn't the sheriff of Lincoln County just yet, and William G. Ritch was serving as governor after Lew Wallace had taken a leave of absence to attend to some business in New York and Washington. Governor Ritch refused to hand the reward money over to Garrett, as the tall Alabaman presently held no legal authority as sheriff. John Chisum's friend Marcus Brunswick and Santa Fe Ring attorney William Thornton advanced the $500 reward to Pat Garrett and Frank Stewart instead. The national banks of Santa Fe and Las Vegas, as well as a handful of prominent Anglo citizens, also raised an additional $900. Frank Stewart and his cowboys soon headed back to the Texas Panhandle with their share of the reward money. Pat Garrett returned home to his pregnant wife Apolinaria and officially became the sheriff of Lincoln County on January 1, 1881.[35]

William Bonney spent the next three months in the Santa Fe jail while newspapers across the United States continued playing up his exploits and transforming "Billy the Kid" into a national sensation.

"I'm getting up a terrible reputation," Bonney told one journalist from the *Las Vegas Gazette*.

In his desperation the Kid wrote four letters to Governor Lew Wallace, requesting the governor come and speak with him in the jailhouse. Wallace ignored him. The Hoosier was looking forward to finally leaving the territory. His proposal for resignation was accepted by President James A. Garfield, and Lionel A. Sheldon was set to take over as governor of New Mexico in the spring.[36]

Billy Bonney, Dave Rudabaugh, Billy Wilson, and fellow inmate Edward "Choctaw" Kelly had almost dug their way out beneath their cell wall in late February when another prisoner snitched on them. "These men are desperados and should be caged like beasts," the *New Mexican* declared when news of the escape attempt reached them. The heavily-shackled Billy Bonney had to be satisfied with receiving the occasional visit from amigos, including the 20-year-old Miguel "Gilley" Antonio Otero Jr., whom the Kid had befriended during the train ride in from Las Vegas. "I liked the Kid very much," Otero Jr. later said. "He had a reputation for being considerate of the old, the young, and the poor."[37]

While Miguel Antonio Otero Jr. would eventually leave his own considerable mark on New Mexico history, his young friend Billy the Kid was soon transported to La Mesilla in Doña Ana County. William Bonney was arraigned before Judge Warren Bristol for the murder of Andrew L. Roberts inside the Mesilla courtroom on March 28, 1881. His attorney Ira Leonard did enough to ensure the federal indictment against him was rescinded on April 6. Judge Warren Bristol then pushed for Ira Leonard to step down as Bonney's attorney. The court subsequently appointed Albert J. Fountain and John D. Bail to represent the famous outlaw during proceedings.

William L. Rynerson's close friend Simon B. Newcomb was now the US district attorney and equally determined to see Bonney hanged when the Kid stood trial for his participation in the killing of William Brady. "If he was present, encouraging, inciting, aiding in, abetting, advising, or commanding this killing of Brady, then he is as much guilty as though he fired the fatal shot," Judge Bristol informed the local Hispano jurors during proceedings. The jury found Henry McCarty, alias William H. Bonney, guilty of murder in the first degree on April 9. The Kid was back in the courtroom several days later when Judge Warren Bristol sentenced him to be hanged by Sheriff Pat Garrett in Lincoln. His execution was scheduled for May 13, 1881. "I expect to be lynched going to Lincoln," the Kid subsequently told a reporter from the *Mesilla News*. "Advise persons never to engage in killing."[38]

William Bonney's longtime enemies Bob Olinger, John Kinney, and Jacob "Billy" Mathews knew plenty about killing while they were helping to escort the Kid into Sheriff Pat Garrett's custody at Fort Stanton on April 21, 1881. Garrett and Bob Olinger then escorted the Kid downriver to Lincoln. Billy was confined in Lawrence G. Murphy's old bedroom in the upstairs northeast corner of the former J. J. Dolan & Co. store, which now served as the county courthouse after being purchased by the board of commissioners. Pat Garrett assigned his deputies Bob Olinger and James W. Bell to guard their famous prisoner every hour of the day. Billy remained handcuffed at all times. A sturdy pair of leg irons also kept him chained to the hardwood floor. He was only permitted to leave his makeshift cell when being escorted out back to use the privy. "A line had been drawn down the center of the Kid's room and he had been ordered to stay on one side of it," Martín Chávez recalled. The late John Tunstall's former cook Gottfried Gauss was now living behind the courthouse and prepared Bonney's meals. A local Hispano boy named Severo Gallegos affectionately picked wild berries and cherries for the famous bandido to enjoy.[39]

Martín Chávez traveled up the Río Bonito intending to visit his amigo William Bonney in the Lincoln courthouse. The muscular Bob Olinger allowed Saturnino Baca, Juana Baca, and Sam Corbet to visit his prisoner but wouldn't let Martín anywhere near the Kid. "He declared that I had been too friendly with him," Chávez recalled. While James W. Bell guarded the Kid without malice, "Pecos Bob" relished in taunting Bonney with his double-barreled Whitney shotgun and kicking his shins. "Olinger thought he could control the Kid by scaring him," Martín Chávez later said. Billy wasn't scared but merely irritated. The Kid despised the brutish Olinger and waited for a chance to square things up with him.[40]

Pat Garrett liked William Bonney personally and treated him in a firm but cordial manner. "There were many good traits about Billy," the sheriff later said. "He wasn't what you'd call a killer. He never made a gunplay he didn't mean, and he never shot up a town or committed any such foolishness.

I've met worse men than Billy." Sheriff Garrett also knew Bonney would do anything required to preserve his own life by escaping. He frequently warned his deputies Bob Olinger and James W. Bell to never let their guard down. Olinger merely laughed and suggested he could turn the Kid loose and easily round him up like a helpless, little goat. "I cautioned those fools not to take an eye off him," Garrett recalled.[41]

What Sheriff Pat Garrett didn't know was that a rescue plan was being put together by some of the Hispanos over in San Patricio and Picacho. They were not about to sit back and let their Bilito dance on air. Sequio Sánchez and his wife Isabella were helping to raise a party of local hombres to storm into Lincoln and bust the Kid out.

"They'll never hang him," Isabella Sánchez was overheard assuring the distraught Josefa Anaya in Picacho. "We've got fourteen men now to take him out and that's plenty. But we'll get more, and they'll not hang him."

While many Hispanos were praying for their "Beely" to be delivered from the hangman's noose, the rescue plan proved an unnecessary initiative. The resourceful and desperate Bilito took matters into his own famously capable hands.[42]

***

Yginio Salazar had not seen William Bonney for months when his amigo surprisingly arrived at his family's home in Las Tablas during the night of April 28, 1881. Billy was supposed to be locked up over in Lincoln and awaiting his execution the following month. Instead, the Kid was looking for a friendly place to bed down for the night with the red blankets tied behind the saddle on his pony. Yginio and his family welcomed Billy with open arms as they always did, although his compadre wanted to avoid confined spaces and decided to spend the rest of the night in the hills near their house. It wouldn't take long for word to spread of what had transpired back in Lincoln just hours earlier.[43]

The 21-year-old Yginio Salazar had been less pleased to see Sheriff Pat Garrett strolling around Las Tablas the previous day. The sheriff had reluctantly left Billy Bonney in the custody of his deputies Bob Olinger and James W. Bell in Lincoln before stopping in Las Tablas to collect taxes and licence fees. Pat spent the night over in White Oaks while visiting his friend John W. Poe, who had succeeded Frank Stewart as cattle detective for the Canadian River Cattleman's Association. Garrett was still in White Oaks when Billy Bonney showed up at the Salazar home after escaping jail in Lincoln.[44]

William Bonney made his move around six o'clock in the evening of April 28, 1881. Bob Olinger had escorted five prisoners from Tularosa down the street to the Wortley Hotel for supper, leaving Bonney to dine with James W. Bell in the courthouse. Bell foolishly let his guard down while following Bonney back upstairs after escorting him outside to the privy. Billy spun around at the top of the stairs and walloped James Bell twice over the head with his handcuffs. Bell's revolver spilled out of his holster while tussling with the prisoner, and the Kid dived onto the floor to retrieve it. Bonney grabbed the pistol and told Bell to throw up his hands but squeezed the trigger when his guard tired to make a run for it down the stairs. A bullet struck James Bell in his right side before the deputy ran out the back of the courthouse and died in the arms of a stunned Gottfried Gauss.

Billy hadn't wanted to kill James W. Bell but was looking forward to greeting Bob Olinger with the deputy's own Whitney shotgun. Olinger leaped up from his table in the Wortley Hotel when he heard gunfire coming from the courthouse and ran up the street to investigate. Bonney watched as the psychopathic deputy strolled directly into the line of fire beneath the eastern window of his makeshift cell. Olinger stopped in his tracks when old Gottfried Gauss informed him that Bonney had just killed Bell.

"Hello, Bob," the Kid called out from the window above.

Billy emptied both barrels of the heavy shotgun into the large deputy's face, shoulder, and side. Olinger was already dead when his muscular frame hit the ground. Smoke was pouring from both barrels of the Whitney when the Kid smashed it over the windowsill and angrily tossed the broken weapon at Olinger's fresh corpse.

"You damned son of a bitch," Billy snarled. "You won't corral me with that again."

The Kid quickly called out to Gottfried Gauss, assuring his old German friend that he wouldn't hurt him. Gauss tossed Billy a mining pick before heading off to fetch a horse from courthouse stables. The Kid also instructed

12-year-old Severo Gallegos to lend Gauss a hand and fetch him a bridle. "A man that is sentenced to be hanged just has to get away some way," Gallegos later said. Billy stepped onto the upstairs porch of the courthouse to justify his actions to the townsfolk, declaring that he was left with no choice but to shoot James W. Bell when the deputy tried to run. The Kid described himself as "standing pat against the world," and announced that he had no desire to kill anyone else but would do so if someone tried to prevent his escape.

The Kid spent over an hour trying to remove his leg irons with the mining pick Gottfried Gauss had thrown him. "He came to the conclusion to await a better chance, tie one shackle to his waist-belt, and start out," recalled the old German, who had fetched a pony belonging to clerk Billy Burt and tied two red blankets behind the saddle. William Bonney shook hands with everyone in the vicinity and swung into the saddle for the second time after initially having a little trouble with the skittish pony. The Kid promised to send the animal back to its rightful owner and informed the townsfolk that they "need not look for him this side of Ireland." He then calmly rode west out of Lincoln while singing a tune.[45]

Billy Bonney stopped at several Hispano homes before arriving at the Salazar homestead later that night. José Córdova and Scipio Salazar were able to remove the Kid's leg irons before he rode through the Capitan Mountains and greeted Yginio Salazar with a handshake. Bonney spent the next couple of days with Yginio and his family after arranging for Billy Burt's pony and saddle to be returned to Lincoln as promised. It was just like old times at the Salazar home, except their friend Bonney was now the most wanted hombre in the American Southwest.[46]

The Salazar family made Billy a gift of a good sorrel horse and new saddle when it was time for him to ride on. "I told him to leave this place and go to old Mexico," recalled Yginio Salazar. "Kid said he was going to Bosque Redondo." Billy was planning to ride for old Mexico, but he wasn't going without Paulita Maxwell. The Salazar family each gave Billy a farewell hug before he rode south toward the Río Peñasco, presumably intending to confuse his trail before heading north for San Miguel County. It was the last visit Yginio Salazar ever recieved from his blue-eyed compadre. He would never forget him.[47]

Pat Garrett would not forget about Billy Bonney either. The sheriff returned to Lincoln in a foul mood after receiving word of the Kid's jailbreak. He led more than one posse in search of Bonney's trail, but they found nothing. John W. Poe quickly arrived from White Oaks with his wife Sophie after hearing word of Bonney's escape. "Soon we took up residence in the courthouse," recalled Sophie Poe. "Each time I went down to the mess, I had to walk over the stains of Bell's blood whom the Kid killed."

Pat Garrett knew William Bonney would never be taken alive again. The sheriff would have to kill him if he stuck around. The problem was la gente. Pat knew there was little use in trying to chase after Bonney while the bandido was hiding out among the Hispanos. "[Billy] had many friends who were true to him," the sheriff later said. "Harbored him, kept him supplied with territorial newspapers, and with valuable information concerning his safety." Pat Garrett was not about to go chasing after the Kid like a foolhardy cavalier, no matter how much pressure he was under. Instead, he sent out some feelers and patiently bided his time.[48]

Much of the pressure on Pat Garrett's shoulders was coming from the press. The territorial newspapers were in hysterics over Billy the Kid's escape. The *Las Vegas Daily Optic* sensationally described Billy as a "young demon," the "terror and disgrace of New Mexico," and someone with a name "synonymous of all that is malignant and cruel." Governor Lew Wallace issued another $500 reward notice for William Bonney, alias Kid, while preparing to leave New Mexico behind him. Bonney's spectacular jailbreak in Lincoln only broadened his fame, and even newspapers across England, Scotland, and Ireland began publishing stories about the young fugitive. The *St. Louis Daily Globe-Democrat* went so far as to proclaim that Billy had "ravished women" and "killed some forty men." "This is terrible," the *Santa Fe New Mexican* declared. "Lincoln County will be remanded of the worst reign of terror it has had yet." Most of the Hispano population of southeastern Nuevo México felt the exact opposite about the situation. "Everyone was glad to see the Kid escape," Martín Chávez later recalled.[49]

The relieved Martín Chávez was probably surprised when his amigo William Bonney stopped at his ranch in Picacho to stay a night before riding north up the Río Pecos to Fort Sumner. The Kid was always welcome in

Martín's home, so what was one more night between amigos. The former deputy sheriff also gave Billy the same advice as their old comrade Yginio Salazar. Martín implored his young friend to ride for old Mexico or "any place a long way from here." Billy wasn't leaving without marrying Paulita Maxwell and convincing her to ride for the border with him.

"No," the Kid insisted. "I go with my wife. If I die, I am satisfied, for I die for her."[50]

Billy Bonney swung his slender frame into his creaking leather saddle and grasped the reins in his small hands when it was time for him to depart the following morning. Martín Chávez and his wife Juana had accompanied their young guest outside to see him off with a traditional hug and affectionate wave. Billy then began riding for old Fort Sumner with a sharp tap of his heel into his horse's side. Martín watched as his amigo began slowly shrinking into the distance for the final time. He might just marry Pablita Maxwell and make it to old Mexico after all. *Vaya con Dios*, Bilito.

***

"Billy, the Kid is killed," the *Las Vegas Daily Optic* informed the public on July 18, 1881. The news spread rapidly throughout New Mexico Territory, North America, and across the Atlantic Ocean to Great Britain. William Bonney had returned to Fort Sumner and spent a couple of months trying to convince the 17-year-old Paulita Maxwell to marry him and accompany him to old Mexico. The young lovers were apparently planning to elope when the Kid made the fatal mistake of entering Pete Maxwell's bedroom around twelve thirty on the morning of July 15, 1881. "They had to sneak up on him in the dead of night to murder him," Martín Chávez later said.[51]

Sheriff Pat Garrett had been sitting inside the darkened bedroom with Pete Maxwell, who was firmly against the notion of his younger sister Paulita marrying the famous bandido. Maxwell had successfully back-channeled news of Bonney's whereabouts to Garrett's deputy John W. Poe, whom Billy had encountered in the shadows of the Maxwell porch outside just moments earlier. The last words on the Kid's lips after entering Maxwell's bedroom were "¿Quién es?" (Who is it?). Two shots roared from a nervous Pat Garrett's revolver, one of them striking the unsuspecting bandido near the heart and quickly rendering him "tan muerto como una Piedra" (as dead as a stone), as Hispano newspaper *La Voz Del Pueblo* later described it. He was around 20 or 21 years old.[52]

The Hispanos of Fort Sumner were outraged when discovering their friend and local hero "Beely" had been killed. Deluvina Maxwell pounded Pat Garrett's chest and cursed him for a "pisspot" and a "son of a bitch" after the Navajo housekeeper and Jesús Silva confirmed Billy's death inside Pedro Maxwell's bedroom. "[Garrett] was afraid to go back in the room to make sure of whom he had shot!" Deluvina later said. "I went in and was the first to discover that they had killed my little boy." Sheriff Pat Garrett and his deputies John W. Poe and Thomas "Kip" McKinney retreated into the Maxwell home for the night when the local Hispanos began hurling insults at them and behaving in a threatening manner. "If a leader had been present, Garrett and his two officers would have recieved the same fate they dealt Billy," recalled the Kid's amigo Francisco Lovato.[53]

Deluvina Maxwell and various señoritas spent the night crying and praying over William Bonney's corpse while conducting a wake inside an old carpentry shop. "The Keed was gone but many Spanish girls mourned for him," Carlota Baca later said. Henry McCarty, alias William H. Bonney, more famously known as Billy the Kid, was buried to the southwest of the northern entrance in the old military cemetery at Fort Sumner on the afternoon of July 15, 1881. Almost the entire population of Fort Sumner accompanied his coffin to the cemetery and paid their respects. "My friend Bilito is dead," Florencio Cháves later said. "He was in many ways a good boy. Not half so bad as many others of his time here, anyway, not half so black so some stories make him."[54]

Sheriff Pat Garrett soon arrived in Santa Fe with a coroner's jury report written in Spanish to collect the $500 reward offered by Lew Wallace for killing William Bonney, alias Kid. The sheriff was again met with resistance from acting Governor William Ritch, but eventually recieved the reward money to which he was entitled. Jimmy Dolan also raised more than $560 from the citizens of Santa Fe and delivered Garrett the sum of $1,150 for getting rid of "the worst man the territory has known." Sheriff Pat Garrett quickly became the most famous lawman in America. He was roundly praised by Anglo newspapers across the country for striking a blow against outlawry. "The hero of the hour in New Mexico, the king lion of the territorial menagerie, is Patsey Garrett," the *St. Louis Globe-Democrat* declared on August 3, 1881. A fable was circulated that Billy Bonney had killed twenty-one men— one for each year of his life. It was a myth so poetic that even some of the Kid's amigos grew to believe it over time. The Hispano reaction to William Bonney's death, however, was generally in glaring contrast with that of many Americanos in the summer of 1881. "I knew Garrett," Martín Chávez later said. "Coward."[55]

The Hispano population of southeastern Nuevo México had seen plenty of bandidos come and go in their time, but "Beely" was different. He was their outlaw. "He was a bad man to some of his own race, but always a friend of the Spanish people," recalled Fort Sumner resident Seledon Trujillo. While the Anglo press and sensationalist writers continued portraying William H. Bonney as a bloodthirsty cutthroat responsible for an exaggerated number of killings, the Nuevomexicanos cherished the Kid's legacy as that of a kindly, generous friend, and a folk hero who had waged war against the crooked gringos running things in their homeland. "All the wrongs have been charged to Billy, yet we who really knew him know that he was good and had fine qualities," Martín Chávez later said. Even Hispanos who hadn't known El Bilito personally would smile at the mention of his name and delight in reciting *cuentos* (folktales) of his daring exploits.[56]

For many Nuevomexicanos like Martín Chávez and Yginio Salazar, their amigo Billy the Kid was an outlaw who stood for something.

Chapter 12

The Fallen Prodigy

I have touched with hand so bold
a once-bright star that fell dead . . .
—José Martí

Juan Patrón, his wife Beatriz, and their young daughter Rayitos were spending much of their time with their Labadie relatives in Santa Rosa when Billy the Kid was killed in July 1881. While Juan Patrón's reaction to William Bonney's death remains lost to history, we do know the Hispano prodigy was focused on his business interests that summer. He had already opened a mercantile store and saloon in Puerto de Luna. He also obtained a sizeable land grant and established a ranch in a region known as Agua Negra several miles outside the placita. Juan dedicated himself to the cultivation of a large orchard on his family's 160-acre homestead rather than raising sheep like most of the locals. The industrious entrepreneur took on additional work as a subcontractor for the mail routes.[1]

The 28-year-old Juan Patrón and his father-in-law Lorenzo Labadie both served as grand jurors during the district court session in Las Vegas in August 1881. One of the murder cases they deliberated over was that of Anacleto Chávez, who had fatally stabbed an hombre named Román Gallegos in Santa Fe on February 26, 1881. Although Chávez's wife had provided damning testimony against her husband during the coroner's inquest held in Santa Fe, the residents of Las Vegas were shocked when the petit jury delivered their verdict. Anacleto Chávez was found guilty of murder in the fifth degree on August 16, 1881. The prisoner was sentenced to pay a fine of $100 and then released. "It thus seems that killing a man is worth no more than running a gaming table," the exasperated *Las Vegas Gazette* declared the following day.[2]

Juan Patrón undoubtedly visited his older sister Juana, brother-in-law Juan Ramírez, and 12-year-old niece Mercedes when returning to Santa Fe and attending the territorial legislative assembly in February 1882. "Juan B. Patrón of Santa Rosa, is one of last Sunday's arrivals," the *New Mexican* announced on February 7, 1882. Tensions ran high in the council chambers that month when a bill proposing the reimbursement of Bernalillo County Sheriff Perfecto Armijo's expenditures was referred to the finance committee rather than immediately passed. Sheriff Armijo had been widely praised for his bravery and dedication after capturing the notorious Mariano Leiva, Escolastico Perea, Miguel Barrera, "California Joe," and Faustino Gutiérres—the gang responsible for the murder of "Colonel" Charles Potter in October 1880. An incensed Hispano representative suggested racial prejudice was behind the bill's referral to the finance committee, arguing that if Lincoln County Sheriff Pat Garrett had received $500 for capturing Billy the Kid, then Perfecto Armijo should receive the sum of $2,500 for having captured five dangerous fugitives.[3]

After satisfying his political appetite in the territorial capital, the 29-year-old Juan Patrón presumably returned to San Miguel County by the time his wife Beatriz gave birth to their second child in March 1882. The couple's 18-month-old daughter Rayitos was blessed with a little brother, whom the proud parents christened Juan Secundino Ramón Jesús Patrón. Now a father of two young children, Juan was looking to get back into the political game after spending the previous four years on the sidelines.[4]

Juan Patrón won a minor victory when attending the registration board meeting held in Las Vegas on October 3, 1882. The widely respected businessman was elected a member of the three-man board of registration for San Miguel County Precinct No. 21 for the upcoming elections. Juan had far greater aspirations than merely winning a place on the local board of registration when attending the Democratic "People's convention" in the Las Vegas courthouse on October 18, 1882. The convention was called to order that morning by prominent Anton Chico businessman Eduardo Martínez. Gross, Blackwell & Co. proprietor Jacob Gross and 51-year-old farmer Tomás C. de Baca served as vice presidents. Two members of each precinct were appointed for the purpose of forming a ticket, and the nominations were determined later that night.[5]

The ticket ratified at the Democratic convention was declared "The People's Ticket" when published by the *Las Vegas Gazette* on October 19, 1882. Francisco "Frank" Antonio Manzanares was nominated for delegate, Tomás C. de Baca for probate judge, Richard Dunn for county sheriff, Jesús M. Tafoya for county clerk, and Félix Martínez for county treasurer. Juan Bautista Patrón was undoubtedly thrilled when learning that he and St. Nicolas Hotel manager William H. Keller had won the Democratic nominations for the territorial council. The Hispano prodigy was back in the game.[6]

Juan spent most of the next three weeks campaigning in San Miguel County for a seat on the territorial council. It was a natural progression for him after successfully campaigning for a representative seat in the territorial house five years earlier. His name appeared alongside William H. Keller's on "The People's Ticket" in the November 5 edition of the *Las Vegas Gazette*. The ticket was published again when the voters cast their ballots on November 7, 1882. The local Democrats had gained ground when the votes were returned, although the Republicans still held the majority in San Miguel County. In the race for the two county seats in the territorial senate, Republican candidate Andres Sena emerged supreme with 2,564 votes. William H. Keller won a seat when finishing second with 2,115 votes. Juan B. Patrón had to settle for third place with an impressive 1,950 votes. It was enough votes for Juan to finish ahead of Republican candidates George W. Prichard and Celso Baca, but not enough for him to win a seat on the territorial council. Although the businessman came up tantalizingly short of winning a seat by merely 165 votes, the narrow margin gave him cause for optimism moving forward.[7]

The 30-year-old Juan Patrón moved on from his political setback and focused on expanding his business interests in Puerto de Luna.

The entrepreneur had developed a friendship with a 29-year-old local businessman named William Baxton Giddings, who was born and raised in Agua Negra, San Miguel County. The two men spent a little time together in Las Vegas, with their presence in town being noted by the *Las Vegas Gazette* on December 8, 1882. Patrón and Giddings decided to partner up and opened a hotel in Puerto de Luna the following year. Although Juan's political aspirations had yet to come to fruition, his business ventures and two young children would keep him occupied in San Miguel County throughout 1883.[8]

Juan Patrón appeared before Justice of the Peace Tomás Gallegos in a small settlement called Los Colonias, located fourteen miles northwest of Santa Rosa, on February 16, 1883. A brakeman for the Atchison, Topeka, and Santa Fe Railway Company named George W. Mitchell owed the Patrón store an unpaid debt of $99.99. Justice Tomás Gallegos issued a writ of attachment and assigned Constable Santiago Alborado to deliver the writ to Mitchell and oversee its return on February 23. George Mitchell's attorney James F. Steck subsequently filed a motion for the dismissal of the writ due to insufficient evidence. Justice Tomás Gallegos overruled the motion in his judgment, declaring that a total sum of $150 covering the attachment and any additional costs was to be paid by George W. Mitchell on March 3, 1883. The aggrieved Mitchell ensured that his attorney submitted an affidavit for Justice Gallegos's judgment to be set aside during the district court session in Las Vegas that summer.[9]

While Juan Patrón's business interests were paying off in San Miguel County, his temper landed him in hot water again during the St. John's Day festivities in Puerto de Luna on June 24, 1883. Juan probably had too much to drink that day when quarrelling with Andres Sena, the hombre who had won the local majority vote for a seat on the territorial council the previous November. While the nature of their dispute remains lost to history, things became so heated that Juan reportedly pulled his revolver and threatened to shoot the councilman on the spot. The 42-year-old Sena was not only a council member but also a widely respected merchant, stockman, freighter, and postmaster in Los Alamos. Although Juan didn't carry out his threat to shoot Andres Sena on el día de San Juan, he was indicted for assault in a menacing manner, carrying a deadly weapon, and opening his establishment on a Sunday by a grand jury in Las Vegas in August 1883.[10]

Juan would face all three charges against him in the district court the following year. In the meantime, the businessman celebrated his thirty-first birthday with his pregnant wife Beatriz, daughter Rayitos, and son Juan Jr. on November 20, 1883.

***

The 29-year-old Martín Chávez and his wife Juanita were living on their sheep ranch in Picacho, Lincoln County, when something unusual occurred in October 1882. Juana gave birth to a son named David Billescas that month. David was not Martín's child, although the sheep farmer would adopt the infant and refer to him as his "step-son." It is doubtful Martín would have done so had his wife been unfaithful, which may suggest the 22-year-old Juanita Romero-Chávez was raped earlier that year. The name of the newborn child's genetic father remained absent from future Chávez family records. Martín Chávez would raise the boy as if he were his own and teach him the art of sheep husbandry.[11]

Martín Chávez also maintained his close friendships with his brother-in-law George Kimbrell and August Kline in Picacho. Kline had recently established his own ranch on the Río Hondo, and the German farmer received praise for the high-quality shipments of corn and wheat he transported to Las Vegas. "Specimens of the corn and cane are on exhibition the Gazette office, and is as fine as if raised on the rich prairies of Iowa and Illinois," the *Las Vegas Gazette* informed its readers in 1882. "Vegetables grow in profusion and require but little cultivation."[12]

Picacho had a population of roughly one hundred residents when August Kline's ranch served as the polling place for those in the precinct to cast their ballots on election day in November 1882. Martín Chávez and Señor Kline eventually posed for a photograph with their arms linked in a testament to their friendship. Martín's old mentor Padre José Sambrano Tafoya had also settled in Picacho. The priest continued his work as a missionary on the Mescalero reservation, having dedicated himself to converting as many of the Natives to Catholicism as possible.[13]

Martín Chávez may not have cared for Pat Garrett, but the long-legged Alabaman had proven an effective frontier lawman, even if William Bonney's famous jailbreak necessitated the construction of a new jail behind the courthouse in Lincoln. Pat Garrett and his ghost-writer Ash Upson also published a book titled *An Authentic Life of Billy the Kid the Noted Desperado of the Southwest* in 1882. The sheriff provided valuable insight about his pursuit of William Bonney, although the rest of the poorly selling book was largely a work of mythology from Ash Upson. Martín Chávez's significant role in the five-day siege in Lincoln was not acknowledged in the postmaster's frequently inaccurate depiction of events.[14]

Pat Garrett decided not to run for reelection as sheriff by the autumn of 1882. Instead, the famous lawman campaigned for a seat in the territorial council. Like Juan Patrón, the 32-year-old Pat Garrett narrowly came up short in his bid to win a seat on November 7, 1882. The Alabaman's former deputy John W. Poe easily won the vote for sheriff of Lincoln County the same day. John William Poe succeeded Garrett as sheriff and began proving himself a capable frontier lawman on January 1, 1883.[15]

While Martín Chávez continued raising sheep in Picacho and transporting shipments of wool to Las Vegas, his former comrade José Chávez y Chávez was working as a laborer over in San Patricio during the early 1880s. The notorious pistolero and his wife Leonora bequeathed their 8-year-old son Adecasio with a baby sister named Beatriz Chávez in around 1881. The 33-year-old Chávez y Chávez eventually took work as a sheepherder up in San Miguel County to provide for his growing family. He may have traded war stories with Juan Patrón while working for a sheep rancher near Santa Rosa.[16]

Shortly after arriving in San Miguel County, José Chávez y Chávez made the acquaintance of a one-legged hombre named Regino Gutiérrez. Gutiérrez was a former buffalo hunter, and his leg had been amputated in Anton Chico after he accidentally shot himself while fleeing hostile Indians in his younger years. One thing José and Regino had in common was a tendency to brag about their marksmanship. The two hombres occasionally engaged in "friendly boasts," until Gutiérrez's pride could stand no more. The former buffalo hunter flew into a rage and challenged José to prove how much of a marksman he was by trying to hit one of his index fingers from a distance of twenty-five yards. Never one to back down, José accepted the challenge and took aim. Regino Gutiérrez spent the rest of his days with only nine fingers.[17]

José Chávez y Chávez also made the acquaintance of a fellow *pastor* named José García y Trujillo, who worked on a nearby sheep ranch in San Miguel County. On one occasion the former Regulator and his amigo were smoking cigarillos under a tree on the western bank of the Río Pecos when a pack train on its way to the Arizona Territory pulled up on the other side of the river. The two sheepherders watched while the freighters tried to ford the stream. The water was moving too rapidly at the time, and the horses driving the pack train began flailing. José Chávez y Chávez and José García y Trujillo quickly tore off their clothes, jumped into the water, and helped guide the floundering animals across the Río Pecos before disaster struck the freighters and their pack train.

The 35-year-old José García y Trujillo was both shocked and impressed when José Chávez y Chávez showed him the various scars on his body after helping the freighters continue their journey to the Arizona Territory. The former Regulator had been wounded multiple times throughout the years. "He had an innocent face," García y Trujillo recalled decades later. "Didn't look as though he could break a dish, but he was bad with a gun. ¡*Qué hombre!*"

José García y Trujillo had also spent a little time around José Chávez y Chávez's old compadre William Bonney in San Miguel County. He held the famous bandido in high regard. "*Muy generoso hombre* [A very generous man], Billy the Keed," the sheepherder recalled. "All the Mexican people, they like him. He give money, horses, drinks, what he have. *Siempre muy caballero, muy senor* [Always very polite, very much of a gentleman]. Everybody like the Keed. *Su vista penetrava al corazon de toda le gente* [His face went to everybody's heart]." José García y Trujillo refused to believe that someone as savvy as William Bonney had been killed at the end of Pat Garrett's revolver that night in Fort Sumner, insisting the legendary bandido must have somehow miraculously escaped across the border. Billy the Kid became larger than life.[18]

While El Bilito remained a beloved folk hero to la gente in southeastern Nuevo México, the late William Bonney's former rustling associates Billy

Wilson and Tom Pickett were being cursed by the Hispanos of San Miguel County during the early months of 1884. Reports had reached Las Vegas that four Hispano laborers named Teodoro Ulivari, Cisto Gutiérres, Melquiades Flores, and Juan Lerma were senselessly murdered by Billy Wilson, Tom Pickett, and two rustlers known as Yank Beale and Pony Williams in Seven Rivers on January 8, 1884.[19]

Teodoro Ulivari, Cisto Gutiérres, Melquiades Flores, Juan Lerma, and five other unarmed Hispano laborers were reportedly approaching Bill Griffith's saloon in Seven Rivers after running out of supplies while digging an acequia in the lower Pecos Valley on January 8, 1884. "There's a gang of greasers coming up the road," Pony Williams had supposedly informed his companions inside the saloon. "Let's have some fun with them." Billy Wilson, Tom Pickett, Yank Beale, and Pony Williams had reportedly stampeded toward the nine Hispanos and opened fire, murdering Cisto Gutiérres, Teodoro Ulivari, Melquiades Flores, and Juan Lerma in the process. The five surviving Hispanos had apparently fled north, and the bodies of the four victims were supposedly buried in an unmarked grave in Teodoro Ulivari's hometown of La Cuesta.[20]

"Mexicans Massacred," the *Las Vegas Gazette* announced on January 10, 1884. "Details of the bloody affair reaching this city yesterday, furnishing one of the most revolting chapters in the history of New Mexico bloodshed." A posse of citizens had reportedly chased Billy Wilson, Tom Pickett, Yank Beale, and Pony Williams across the Mexican border. Governor Lionel Sheldon was appalled by the news and quickly issued a public proclamation on January 11, 1884: "Now, therefore, I do hereby offer a reward of $300 for the capture and conviction of the murderer or murderers of each said murdered parties, to be paid out of the territorial funds, on proof of capture and conviction of such murderer or murderers."[21]

Word of the "pure cowboy deviltry" and "cold-blooded fun" reached newspaper editors as far east as Pennsylvania and Connecticut. The *Las Vegas Gazette* suggested former sheriff Pat Garrett was the man to pursue the fugitives. "Sheriff Poe is a good officer and we believe will also do his duty in the premises," the *New Mexican* insisted on January 11, 1884. "The good name of the territory and the peace of Lincoln County demands the capture and punishment of these murderers."[22]

According to Ash Upson, some shooting had recently occurred in Seven Rivers, but not in the sensational manner reported by the newspapers. The former journalist sat down in Roswell and wrote a letter to the *White Oaks Golden Era* under his usual pseudonym Pecos on January 28, 1884. Upson insisted that only the 26-year-old Cisto Gutiérres had been killed in Seven Rivers, and the laborer had been shot by a lone Americano near Bill Griffith's saloon on December 11, 1883. Thomas Fennessey, James McBee, W. R. Cummings, and A. H. Barrett were arrested a short time later on a complaint filed before Judge Edmund Thomas Stone. "There was no Billy Wilson, no Tom Pickett, no rustlers there—no four men killed, no flight of rustlers nor pursuit by citizens," Upson firmly declared.[23]

Sheriff John W. Poe reiterated Ash Upson's assertions when mailing his own letter to Governor Lionel Sheldon: "One Mexican was killed at Seven Rivers on December 11 in a drunken row, and four or five arrests followed, but the evidence was wanting and they were discharged. I think the guilty man has escaped into Texas. Billy Wilson nor Tom Pickett have not been in this county for nearly three years. There has not been four men killed in this county in the last eighteen months. I am at a loss to know the motives of parties circulating reports of crime in Lincoln unless they envy the county's prosperity and peace."[24]

While Lincoln County was enjoying a less violent atmosphere than in previous years, things were never quite as tranquil as Sheriff John W. Poe professed. Saturnino Baca reportedly lynched former McSween servant George Washington in Lincoln after the Black man had eloped with his daughter Josefina in June 1882. Pat Garrett had viciously pistol-whipped a 27-year-old lawyer named William M. Roberts in Lincoln for allegedly disrespecting him on September 19, 1882. A Kentuckian named William S. Pearl was lynched by a party of soldiers in Lincoln several days after drunkenly shooting Pvt. John Downey during an auction in Fort Stanton on January 2, 1883. A shoe salesman named Peter Mackel had fatally shot Frank Kiser in the chest for having "destroyed his daughter's virtue" in White Oaks on March 15, 1883. Seventeen-year-old John S. Neal shot and killed J. N. New in self-defense on the Río Peñasco on June 19, 1883. Simeon E. Welding exchanged bullets with Judge Samuel S. Terrell and his brother Frank Terrell during a land dispute near Lincoln on February 4, 1884. José Gonzáles killed another Hispano named Torres in Tularosa on February 9, 1884, and Milton V. Nixon shot ranch hand Tomás Valentine between the eyes on the Río Peñasco on February 20, 1884.[25]

"Lincoln County is more orderly and peaceable now than it has ever been," Sheriff John W. Poe insisted in February 1884. Ironically, for all the violence still occurring throughout the region, the sheriff wasn't altogether wrong in his assessment.[26]

***

Juan B. Patrón was probably among the two hundred Hispanos who attended a mass meeting held inside Baca Hall in Las Vegas on the night of March 7, 1884. There were also twenty Anglo citizens in attendance that night. For once there wasn't a hint of racial tension or political partisanship as the crowd gathered inside the hall. This was a different kind of meeting. The two hundred "Mexicans" and twenty Americanos were united against a common enemy: Thomas B. Catron and the Santa Fe Ring. An increasing sense of anti-bossism was taking hold among various citizens in San Miguel County as the 1880s progressed. The arrival of the railroads and rising competition for land and resources was only further inflaming resentment among working-class Hispanos throughout the region.[27]

Tranquilino Labadie served as interpreter when the meeting was called to order by Deputy Constable José de la Cruz Pino. Former mayor and local Republican jefe Eugenio Romero was duly appointed chairman and handed Tranquilino a message he had received. Those in attendance were disappointed when Labadie read aloud the message from territorial councilman J. Francisco Cháves, an eloquent public speaker and opponent of the Santa Fe Ring. "Colonel" Cháves was held up in Lamy and would not reach Las Vegas in time for the meeting. "The disappointment was indeed great," a *Las Vegas Gazette* reporter in attendance recalled. "For it had been hawked about that the corruption which has existed at Santa Fe since the day that Tom Catron set foot on New Mexican soil would be ventilated and the tyrant king arraigned before the common people."[28]

Former territorial treasurer Juan Delgado, the respected Eduardo Martínez, a prominent local Democrat named Tomás Tafoya, and Don Eugenio Romero all gave speeches intended to "agitate the public pulse." Chairman Romero took particularly fierce aim at Thomas B. Catron, describing the leading figure of the Santa Fe Ring as a "hydra-headed interloper," a "self-constituted king," and "an evil conniver that has created more misery in New Mexico than any other individual that ever had legal standing." Romero's speech was met with rabid applause, and resolutions were drawn up by a committee expressing opposition to Catron and his land-grabbers. A reporter from the *Las Vegas Daily Optic* had recently queried Thomas B. Catron himself about the existence of the Santa Fe Ring and his association with it. Catron had suggested that "if there was such an organization as the Santa Fe Ring, he certainly belonged to it and was proud of it."[29]

While the seeds of an uprising were beginning to germinate in San Miguel County, the 31-year-old Juan Patrón was preparing to welcome his third child into the world. The Patrón family had moved in with their Labadie relatives in Santa Rosa for the final stages of his wife Beatriz's pregnancy. Lorenzo and Rallitos Labadie doted on their grandchildren Rayitos and Juan Jr. and kept a close eye on their heavily pregnant daughter whenever their son-in-law attended to his business interests over in Puerto de Luna. They were thrilled when Beatriz Patrón gave birth to a baby girl on March 19, 1884. The newborn child was named after Beatriz's older sister Delores and christened María Delores Felipa Patrón.[30]

Juan Patrón had missed the birth of his daughter Delores in Santa Rosa. He was busy preparing to stand before an old adversary inside the Las Vegas courthouse at the time. The once-disgraced former governor Samuel Beach Axtell had been appointed chief justice of the New Mexico Supreme Court by President Rutherford B. Hayes two years earlier. Judge Axtell was presiding over the district court session in Las Vegas on March 20, 1884, when Juan faced his indictments for assault, carrying a deadly weapon, and failing to adhere to Sunday law. Juan's attorney Miguel Salazar proved worthy of his legal fees inside the Las Vegas courthouse that day. "The only important criminal case tried yesterday was that of Juan Patron, for threatening to shoot Andres [Sena] at Puerto de Luna last St. John's Day," the *Las Vegas*

Gazette announced. "He was tried by jury and acquitted." Juan entered a guilty plea for keeping his establishment open on a Sunday and paid a fine of two dollars. The final indictment against him for carrying a deadly weapon was dismissed.[31]

Juan was back inside the Las Vegas courthouse with US District Attorney "Colonel" George W. Prichard the following morning of March 21, 1884. George Mitchell had hired Columbus Moise to represent him after his previous attorney James F. Steck had filed an appeal to set aside the judgment made by Justice of the Peace Tomás Gallegos in Patrón's favor the previous year. Mitchell insisted Steck had inadequately represented him when filing the motion for an appeal during the previous term of court. Justice Tomás Gallegos had submitted an affidavit explaining his judgment, and the civil case was dismissed by the district court.[32]

Juan Patrón returned to Santa Rosa and proudly cradled his newborn daughter Delores after fulfilling his legal commitments in Las Vegas. Beatriz and their little ones remained in Santa Rosa while her husband and her father Lorenzo Labadie traveled north and arrived in Las Vegas on April 1, 1884. They both registered at the Plaza Hotel before riding the rails to Santa Fe the following day. Juan and Lorenzo attended to some unspecified business in the territorial capital before making another stopover in Las Vegas on their way back to Santa Rosa.[33]

The 31-year-old Juan Patrón needed to take care of his own business in Puerto de Luna when preparing his surrey (small carriage) outside the Labadie home in Santa Rosa in the early hours of Monday, April 7, 1884. The 3½-year-old Rayitos Patrón did not want her father going anywhere without her that morning. "He had just returned from Santa Fe," she recalled decades later. Rayitos wrapped her little arms around her papá's leg and begged him to take her with him. Rallitos Labadie eventually had to pull her granddaughter away when it was time for her son-in-law to depart. Señora Labadie comforted Rayitos as the teary-eyed toddler watched her father set out for Puerto de Luna.[34]

Juan Patrón soon ran into his brothers-in-law Román Labadie and Cresenciano Gallegos while attending to his business in Puerto de Luna on April 7, 1884. They all agreed to meet up in 69-year-old Irish businessman

"Governor" Charles Hayes Moore's saloon for a drink before heading back to Santa Rosa together. The construction of the Our Lady Of Refuge Church for which Juan and his friend Padre Auguste Redon had campaigned was almost complete. The Roman Catholic church still needed a roof but was ready to open its doors to the public.

Juan also exchanged a respectful glance with a 26-year-old cowboy named Michael Erskine Maney outside the Moore establishment around four o'clock that afternoon. The slender Texan was leading his horse into the Moore corral shortly after riding into town. Maney had enjoyed several meals in the Patrón saloon while staying in Puerto de Luna the previous December. The affable cowpuncher had arrived that day to cash a money order on behalf of his childhood friend and employer George C. Peacock, the foreman at the J. J. Cox ranch located sixty miles to the southeast.[35]

Juan Patrón entered the Moore saloon after concluding his business affairs in Puerto de Luna at around seven o'clock in the evening of April 7, 1884. He limped through the establishment and joined his brothers-in-law Román Labadie and Cresenciano Gallegos at a gaming table run by saloon operator William Ruth. The cards didn't fall his way that evening. Juan lost every dime in his possession while playing monte. The disgruntled businessman headed over to the bar after going bust at the table and approached Michael Maney. The cowboy was enjoying a drink after dining with William Ruth earlier that evening. Juan asked Maney if he would buy him a whiskey. The Texan thought a lot of the educated Nuevomexicano and cordially agreed.

Michael Maney continued buying drinks for Juan whenever the local merchant requested another one. Maney eventually asked his drinking companion how he had fared playing monte that evening. Juan admitted that he had gone bust but insisted he could win his money back if his new friend loaned him a dollar. The Texan generously provided him with a silver dollar and accompanied the businessman over to the monte table. Juan quickly lost the dollar trying to "pick the lady." He then stumbled back toward to the bar with Maney and saloon operator William Owens.[36]

Juan was already soused when he threw back another shot of whiskey with Michael Maney and William Owens at the bar. Owens suggested the intoxicated businessman accompany him over to L. P. Tracy's saloon in the nearby Grzelachowski store.

"Do you want me to go with you and Juan?" Michael Maney asked.

"Yes, come on," Owens replied.

William Owens tried to keep the stumbling Juan Patrón upright as the three men sauntered down the street toward the Grzelachowski store. They quickly discovered the Tracy saloon was closed when they arrived. The proprietor had closed his establishment and gone to bed earlier than usual that night. When they woke L. P. Tracy from his slumber, the Missourian staunchly refused to open his saloon for them. Michael Maney then began leading his companions back up the street to the Moore saloon.

As William Owens maintained a firm grip on the staggering Juan Patrón, the intoxicated businessman noticed through his foggy vision that Michael Maney was carrying a .44 Colt revolver on his hip.[37]

"Hey, damn you, what are you doing with that six-shooter?" Juan suddenly barked. "Why do you want to be carrying it?"

Maney looked in the direction of his two companions with a puzzled expression before answering Juan's bizarre question.

"My carrying a six-shooter is nothing more than a habit," the cowboy assured him.

"Are you carrying it for me?" Juan slurred in a haze of whiskey-fueled paranoia.

"I am not carrying a six-shooter for anyone," the perplexed Maney replied.

"Nobody but a damn coward would carry a six-shooter!" Juan shouted. "Damn you, I'll get my six-shooter and kill you!"

Michael Maney couldn't believe what he was hearing after treating Juan in such an amiable and generous manner that night. The cowpuncher and William Owens quickly entered the Moore saloon, leaving Juan to limp off in the direction of his store in a drunken stupor. Owens informed his companion of Patrón's reputation for becoming "abusive and dangerous when drinking" as they returned to the bar inside "Governor" Moore's saloon. Hopefully, the inebriated businessman would collapse in a cot somewhere and sleep it off.[38]

Juan Patrón's limp appeared more pronounced than usual as he unsteadily ambled through the night air toward his store. The businessman had always been an aggressive drunk. His mind was further clouded with an increasing sense of paranoia. Ruffians from Lincoln County had occasionally shown up looking for him throughout his previous four years in Puerto de Luna. "They tried to lure him from his home," Rayitos Patrón recalled hearing from her grandmother Rallitos Labadie in later years. "But they were not successful in trapping him, although he would have met them in the open had not my uncles and grandfather prevented the encounter." Juan was convinced Michael Maney was intending to kill him when retrieving his army Remington .44 revolver inside his store. He stuffed the pistol firmly behind his waist belt and headed back to the Moore saloon.[39]

Juan entered the Moore establishment around ten thirty and immediately spotted Michael Maney standing at the bar. Neither of them said a word. They didn't have to. The two men kept their eyes locked on each other as the Hispano businessman with a belly full of whiskey limped across the room toward the gaming table. Juan's brother-in-law Cresenciano Gallegos was trying to win a little money. Juan continued glaring at Maney while keeping one hand firmly on the handle of his Remington revolver and placing the other on his brother-in-law's shoulder.

"Let's go, buddy," Juan said to Gallegos, his eyes remaining locked on the Texas cowboy standing ten feet away. "It's time we go home. I am sleepy."

"Take your hand off your six-shooter," Michael Maney insisted, understandably feeling threatened.

Juan merely tightened his grip on his Remington when Maney finally spoke to him as if he were readying himself to throw down on the Texan. Maney was ready to reach for his own revolver when instructing the drunk businessman to remove his hand from the Remington a second time. Juan then made his decision in a whirlwind moment of liquored-up bravado. He tried to pull his Remington pistol from out of his waist belt, only for the barrel to get momentarily caught in his trousers. It was enough time for Maney to smoothly draw his .44 Colt revolver from his holster and fire the first shot.

The bullet slammed into Juan Patrón's chest a split second before he squeezed the trigger of his Remington and fired a shot in the cowboy's direction. He fired wide and the bullet stuck the adobe wall to the right of his intended target. Juan was fading quickly as he stumbled in the direction of a laborer named Gregorio Baros. The dying businessman unintentionally fired a second shot from his revolver, wounding the 41-year-old bystander in the arm. Juan Bautista Patrón then collapsed onto the saloon floor as his heart stopped beating. A shining light for the Hispano population of Nuevo México had been extinguished.[40]

Michael Maney wildly fired two more shots from his revolver as Juan Patrón fell dead in front of the wounded Gregorio Baros. One of the bullets struck the coal oil lamp providing a dim glow throughout the saloon that night. A rush of panic took hold of Michael Maney in the sudden darkness of Charles Moore's establishment. He was a Texan, and he had just shot one of the local Hispano community's favorite sons. The 26-year-old cowboy scrambled out of the saloon and sprinted four hundred yards to the Río Pecos from fear of being shot or lynched by the locals. Maney anxiously positioned himself behind several large boulders along the riverbed and prepared to make a stand if necessary.[41]

A crowd of anxious citizens were gathering outside the Moore saloon as Justice of the Peace Pablo Anaya, William Owens, William Ruth, and bartender Thomas Jones entered the establishment. William Ruth could barely see his hand in front of his face before reigniting the coal oil lamp and casting a gleam of light over Juan Patrón's corpse lying facedown on the saloon floor. The late businessman's Remington pistol lay beside him merely six inches from his right hand. The saddened Pablo Anaya refused to wait for a formal inquest to be held and knelt beside his friend's warm body. He failed to find a pulse and pronounced Juan Bautista Patrón dead shortly after eleven o'clock. Anaya then picked up his slain friend's Remington and handed the pistol to a local farmer without examining the weapon. It was sloppy work from the local justice of the peace.[42]

Cresenciano Gallegos found the bullet hole that Juan Patrón's pistol had left in the adobe wall of the saloon during the shootout. He removed the small silver crucifix he was wearing around his neck and jammed it inside the hole to serve as a modest memorial for his slain brother-in-law. Justice Pablo Anaya then turned Juan Patrón's bloodied corpse over to Cresenciano and Román

Labadie. They wrapped the body inside a saddle blanket, loaded the fresh corpse into the late prodigy's surrey, and began driving the small carriage back to the Labadie home in Santa Rosa. There was no easy way to tell the sleeping Beatriz Patrón when they arrived. The Labadie family tried to console the heartbroken widow when she observed her husband's body lying in the surrey. "The scene of sorrow can never be forgotten by those present," the *Las Vegas Daily Optic* reported. Beatriz's three children Rayitos, Juan Jr., and Delores would have to grow up without their beloved papá.[43]

A posse comprised of fifty locals stormed out of Puerto de Luna in various directions on horseback to locate Michael Maney at first light on April 8, 1884. The Texan surrendered peacefully when George V. Davidson and Nicolas Griego got the drop on him in the Cañón de Dios five miles outside of town around eight o'clock that morning. Maney was escorted back to Puerto de Luna and underwent a preliminary hearing before Justice Pablo Anaya. Many of the devastated local Hispanos wanted to stretch the Texan's neck beneath a tree branch as soon as possible. "Everybody was crazy with excitement," recalled George V. Davidson. There were also unfounded rumors that Maney had been hired to carry out an assassination. Fourteen local ranchers rode into Puerto de Luna that evening, purchased guns and ammunition in the Grzelachowski store, and menacingly positioned themselves in a corral seventy yards from where the preliminary hearing was held. Michael Maney asserted that he had plugged the widely respected Patrón in self-defense. "I was scared because he threatened to kill me," the Tejano informed Justice Pablo Anaya. "When he took his pistol out, I shot him."[44]

Michael Erskine Maney was charged with murder and locked inside the local jailhouse when the preliminary hearing finally ended around two o'clock in the morning of April 9, 1884. As the sun rose over the hills at dawn, Justice Pablo Anaya assigned Nicolas Griego, George V. Davidson, and George Giddings—the older brother of the late Juan Patrón's business partner William Baxton Giddings—to escort the despised prisoner eighty miles north to Las Vegas. "Those intending violence had not the nerve to begin any operations," recalled George V. Davidson. "We left Puerto de Luna for Las Vegas with a guard of eight men." The heavily armed posse escorted Michael Maney into Las Vegas on the afternoon of April 11, 1884. Some of the locals expressed feelings of hostility toward Maney when they arrived, although many citizens had left town earlier that day in their carriages to watch members of Los Penitentes engage in self-flagellation throughout the countryside in morbid fascination.[45]

Michael Maney was safely delivered into the custody of Sheriff José Santos Esquibel and locked inside the Las Vegas jailhouse. The Texan faced a preliminary charge of murder before Chief Justice Samuel B. Axtell and was scheduled to stand trial during the next district court session in August 1884. Reports of Juan Patrón's demise were published by newspapers in California, Kansas, Missouri, West Virginia, Tennessee, Wisconsin, Maryland, Ohio, Indiana, Nebraska, Illinois, Montana, New York, and even Canada. "Juan B. Patron, a wealthy citizen and ex-Speaker of the Territorial Legislature, was assassinated," the *Montreal Star* informed its readers on April 12, 1884.[46]

The bereaved Lorenzo Labadie and several others sent letters to the *Las Vegas Gazette* insisting that Juan Patrón's death had been an unprovoked murder carried out with icy deliberation. "Information reached the city yesterday that Juan B. Patron, one of the best known Mexican citizens of the territory, had been murdered in cold blood at Puerto de Luna," the *Gazette* announced on April 11, 1884. The *Santa Fe New Mexican* described the killing as "one of the most cowardly and cold-blooded deeds on record" the following day. "It is believed that [Michael Maney] was hired to kill Patrón, because he knew of the evil doings of some of the men in that section of country," the *Albuquerque Evening Democrat* proclaimed. "Justice should be sure and speedy, as it was an unprovoked, deliberate, well-planned murder."[47]

George Giddings went so far as to suggest that Juan Patrón's killer had been hired "to pick a quarrel and kill him by parties who opposed Patron's father, and finally secured his assassination during the Lincoln County War." Michael Erskine Maney was no assassin, and four of the five Horrell brothers were dead. The 26-year-old cowboy also had no connection with Jimmy Dolan, John H. Riley, the Santa Fe Ring, or anyone else bearing a grudge against the late Hispano entrepreneur. "Maney has a good education and has never drank liquor to excess," the Texan's employer George C. Peacock informed the *Las Vegas Daily Optic*. "He never was quarrelsome and he always enjoyed a good reputation."[48]

The death of Juan Patrón was a bitter loss for many in the community, but the intoxicated businessman was the aggressor when the shooting occurred. Michael Maney had drawn and fired his .44 Colt revolver in self-defense. One resident of Puerto de Luna wrote a letter to the Las Vegas *Stock Grower* calling for a calmer response from citizens:

> The killing of a well known, public, spirited, and useful citizen, by an obscure cowboy is likely to generate in the public mind undue and ungovernable prejudice against the accused.
>
> To put the affair at Puerto de Luna, between Juan B. Patron and Michael Maney before the public in its proper form, we have but to say that it was simply a matter of time, as to which should get the first shot. Evidence before the coroner's jury shows that Patron's pistol caught in his clothes as he attempted to draw it. Otherwise he would in all probability been first to fire. Again the reputation of the deceased for quarrelling and madness (while drinking) is second to none; while that of Maney, during the six months that he has been among us, is remarkable for peace and quietness. While the circumstances do not render Maney free of crime, they most certainly clear him of the charge of being an assassin. He told a plain, straight story at the examination, which corresponded with the evidence; offered no excuses, but expressed sorrow, when told of the result of his shooting; and an honest listener was impressed with the belief that his sorrow was not on account of being caught.
>
> Then let not the relatives and friends of the deceased, clamor for the blood of the homicide, who only lives because he was quicker than his antagonist.
>
> J. M. J.[49]

Having assisted in the capture of Michael Maney and his transportation to Las Vegas, stockman and former cattle detective George V. Davidson also defended Juan Patrón's killer when speaking with a reporter from the *Las Vegas Gazette*. "A great wrong has been done [Maney], of that I am certain," Davidson professed. "The case is apparently not understood at all, as it will be when it comes up in district court. It is true that one of the best citizens of the county has lost his life, and as a natural consequence the feeling runs very high against the man who killed him. However, it is well known liquor made Juan Patrón a very different man than what he was when sober, a courteous and affable gentleman."[50]

Juan Bautista Patrón was laid to rest beneath the almost completed Our Lady Of Refuge Catholic Church in Puerto de Luna on Thursday afternoon, April 10, 1884. It was an honor usually reserved for saints, and a testament to how much the late businessman meant to the local Hispano populace. Padre Auguste "Antonio" Francois Joseph Redon performed the service, and a large multitude of citizens paid their respects at the funeral. The outpouring of grief from Juan's immediate family, Labadie in-laws, and devoted Hispano supporters was considerable. "The sorrowing wife and relatives have the sympathies of the good people in every part of the territory," the *Las Vegas Gazette* announced two days later.[51]

"He was a man of extraordinary ability, was a shrewd businessman, and had filled various positions of public trust," the *Las Vegas Gazette* declared on April 11, 1884. "Juan B. Patron was one of the brightest and best informed young men of native descent in New Mexico, and a man of unusual promise," the *New Mexican* announced the following day. "A bright future was before him and had he lived he would doubtless have made an enviable record in public affairs in New Mexico. The shock and grief over his untimely death are universal."[52]

While some Americanos mourned him, the Hispano population of Nuevo México were particularly crestfallen over Juan Patrón's demise. La gente had lost a charismatic, articulate leader, and an incisive voice for their community in the face of Anglo expansion throughout their homeland. Although his political influence had waned during his final years, there is no telling what the Hispano prodigy may have achieved had his life not been cut short at the age of 31. "My father had many friends," Rayitos Patrón later wrote. "He was always spoken of as a king and a just man who befriended many and prevented the impoverishment of a great number of native people." If only her esteemed father had laid off the whiskey that night in Puerto de Luna.[53]

Juan Bautista Patrón's legacy remains a testament to what the descendants of Spanish settlers born into the humblest of conditions could achieve in frontier times if merely afforded the education and occasion to do so.

Chapter 13

Cattle, Sheep, and Land

Nothing grows in this earth
without diligence and cut knuckles.
—Valerie Martínez

Martín Chávez was in Las Cruces when he learned of Juan Patrón's death in April 1884. The 31-year-old sheep farmer had been summoned to serve on the grand jury for the district court session in Doña Ana County that spring. The local population was still in shock over the murder-suicide that had recently occurred in the small village of Doña Ana just six miles north of Las Cruces. A 35-year-old store and saloon owner named Domingo Montoya had recently accused his wife Josefa Melendes-Montoya of infidelity. Domingo studiously settled all of his business affairs before shooting the 25-year-old Josefa in the abdomen, chest, and head inside their home at around six o'clock in the evening of March 31, 1884. The once-respected businessman then blew his own brains out. The deceased couple's six orphaned children were subsequently taken in by their late mother's Melendes relatives.[1]

Martín Chávez and the other Hispano grand jurors in Las Cruces had to juggle their Semana Santa celebrations with a demanding workload in

April 1884. The grand jury returned fifty-five federal indictments and sixty-nine territorial indictments throughout proceedings. The famous Pat Garrett was also in town on petit jury duty that month. There was considerable excitement when former Kinney gang member Charles "Pony Diehl" Ray was convicted of cattle theft. "A man who steals a cow is, in the eyes of Las Cruces people, the worst man in America," Grant County Commissioner James Lewis Vaughn snidely remarked after attending court. "While a man who commits a cold-blooded murder gets a bouquet and a certificate of good character."[2]

Martín had cause for celebration after returning to Picacho once the district court session closed in Las Cruces in April 1884. His wife Juanita realized she was pregnant with his first child. Martín continued transporting shipments of wool to Las Vegas, although sheep farmers like himself were having to contend with an influx of *ganado* (cattle) following the formation of the Lincoln County Stock Association in March 1883. The venture proved highly successful for the association's president William E. Anderson, vice president John W. Poe, secretary "Major" Michael Cronin, Pat Garrett, Joseph A. Larue, "Captain" Joseph Lea, Jacob "Billy" Mathews, James J. Dolan, José Montaño, Florencio Gonzáles, and various others throughout the region. Stock numbers rapidly increased as the cattle trade became the leading enterprise in Lincoln County. Martín Chávez realized things were changing in his homeland and began taking an increasing interest in local politics and public affairs.[3]

Although Martín Chávez was accustomed to the fragility of life in Nuevo México, the former deputy sheriff was no less devastated when death reached for his mentor José Sambrano Tafoya in late June 1884. The padre was thrown from his buggy when the neck-yoke broke while driving his team down a rocky hillside above Lincoln. The 54-year-old priest landed on his head and suffered a fractured skull. Martín was presumably at José Sambrano Tafoya's bedside when his mentor died several days later. Deputy Sheriff James R. Brent informed the *Lincoln County Leader* of the tragic accident, and local citizens mourned the loss of the missionary responsible for the baptism of more than a hundred Natives on the nearby Mescalero reservation. The late reverend had even converted and baptized the infamous Mescalero war-chief San Juan. The place where Padre José Sambrano Tafoya's accident had occurred outside Lincoln soon became known as Priest Canyon.[4]

While Martín Chávez mourned the Catholic priest responsible for his education, his former partisan Yginio Salazar had to contend with the law during the summer of 1884. The 24-year-old vaquero believed a man should always stand his ground and fight. The young scrapper wasn't fooling around when he got into an unspecified dispute with James M. Bennett, a formidable ranch hand living on the Cienega del Macho to the northeast of Las Tablas. Whatever the source of their differences, the former McSween partisan fired a shot at Bennett with his revolver around July 1, 1884. It wasn't a warning shot. Yginio was trying to kill him.[5]

The 46-year-old William F. Blanchard was justice of the peace for Precinct No. 8 in Lincoln County when Yginio Salazar took a shot at James Bennett that summer. The Civil War veteran issued a warrant for Salazar's arrest in White Oaks on July 1, 1884:

> To the sheriff or any constable of Lincoln County, greeting:
>
> You are hereby commanded to arrest and take the body of Yginio Salazar . . . so that you have his body before undersigned, Justice of the Peace, within and for Precinct No 8 County of Lincoln, at my office in White Oaks, said county, then and there to answer unto a charge of shooting at one James M Bennett with a revolver shooting with intent to kill him, the said James M Bennett. This in the vicinity and territory aforesaid on or about the 1st day of July 1884.
> And this do you forthwith under the penalty of law.
> Given under my hand this 1st day of July A.D. 1884
>   W. F. Blanchard, Justice of the peace.[6]

Deputy George L. Ulrick subsequently arrested Yginio Salazar and delivered him to Sheriff John W. Poe on July 19, 1884. Yginio was charged with assault with intent to commit murder at a preliminary hearing and bound over to the grand jury for the next district court session in Lincoln County. His intended target James Bennett would also have to answer to the district court after discharging his Winchester rifle in more newsworthy fashion the following month.[7]

The 25-year-old James Bennett, his 27-year-old brother Thomas Bennett, and their friend George Dickey had been quarreling with a prominent cattleman from Texas named Ephraim Wilson Richards for several months. The animosity only escalated when the 32-year-old Richards drove his former employee George Dickey off his ranch at gunpoint and told him never to return during the spring of 1884. Some of the locals were expecting trouble when Dickey and the Bennett brothers established a ranch of their own just above the Richards estate near the Cienega del Macho. E. W. Richards suspected that Dickey and the Bennett boys were doing the bidding of his bitter rival Melvin "Mel" Emyor Richardson, another prominent cattleman in the area.

Ephraim Richards and his ranch hand Henry Lackey headed north when realizing the water supply had been partially cut off while constructing a cabin at a spring on the morning of August 15, 1884. Richards's ranch hands Frank Collins, George Pringle, William Green, George Paxton, Josh Cummins, and M. F. McBride soon heard gunshots in the distance and galloped north after their employer's wounded horse returned to their camp alone. They found the fatally wounded Henry Lackey sprawled out on a blanket. Lackey informed his coworkers that Ephraim Richards was lying dead on the ground about fifty yards away. He insisted they had been ambushed by George Dickey and the Bennett brothers. The ranch hand died roughly half an hour later. James Bennett had shot the 20-year-old Henry Lackey in the left side of his abdomen with his Winchester rifle. George Dickey had killed Ephraim Richards with a shotgun blast. Richards's corpse was retrieved by his employees later that afternoon.

James Bennett, Thomas Bennett, and George Dickey quickly turned themselves over to the authorities in Lincoln, claiming Ephraim Richards and Henry Lackey were intending to jump their ranch and tried to waylay them. Sheriff John W. Poe and Justice of the Peace José M. de Aguayo escorted the three prisoners back to the scene of the crime and conducted an examination. Poe found footprints in the soil behind a three-foot high brush seventeen steps from where Richards fell dead. "Thirty-two steps southerly from Richards was found another ambush, with foot-marks behind of two persons, as reported by Sheriff Poe," the *Lincoln County Leader* informed the public.

The evidence suggested Ephraim Richards and Henry Lackey had ridden directly into an orchestrated ambush. Justice Aguayo held a coroner's inquest and placed James Bennett, Thomas Bennett, and George Dickey under bonds of $1,000 each to appear before a grand jury during the next court session. Mel Richardson and Johnny Hurley provided the bonds and the three prisoners were released. Ephraim Richards and Henry Lackey were buried in the cemetery outside White Oaks on the afternoon of August 17, 1884.[8]

Although Yginio Salazar had yet to settle down himself, his family had grown in Las Tablas by the summer of 1884. His stepfather Francisco Luma had recently passed away, and his 59-year-old mother Paula now lived in the adobe house next door with his older brother José Salazar, his wife Ginovera, and their 2-year-old son Teofilo. The 18-year-old Ginovera Lucero Salazar was heavily pregnant with the couple's second child and would give birth to a daughter named Amalia in the coming winter. Yginio's older brother Rómulo (Román) Salazar also lived a stone's throw away with his wife Victoriana and their 5-year-old daughter Emeteria.[9]

Yginio Salazar also made peace with his old adversary George W. Peppin by the summer of 1884. The former McSween partisan had served as a witness when Peppin filed a preemption declaratory statement to the land office in Las Cruces on April 14 that year. He did the same for a local woman named Ignacia Gómez on August 22, 1884. While Yginio Salazar and George Peppin were now on amicable terms, other animosities still lingered in the aftermath of the Lincoln County War. Yginio occasionally quarreled with the late William Brady's second eldest son Robert "Roberto" Brady. "I used to fight with Higinio Salazar every time we met because he was one of Billy the Kid's gang," young Robert Brady later recalled. "I always had a hatred of them because they killed my father."[10]

Yginio Salazar and Martín Chávez both served their community in the run-up to the elections during the autumn of 1884. The county commissioners Edmund Thomas Stone, Andrew Wilson, José Montaño, and probate clerk Sam Corbet convened in Lincoln to resolve various matters on October 7, 1884. Martín Chávez was appointed the road supervisor for Precinct No. 4. He would commence work after filing a bond of $100 payable to the territory. Martín's friends George Kimbrell, August Kline, and Frank McCullum were appointed judges of election for Precinct No. 4 when the locals cast their ballots the following month. The 25-year-old Yginio Salazar and Scipio Salazar were appointed to the board of registration for Precinct No. 6. The board of county commissioners also approved a bill of $10.53 from Deputy George Ulrick for carrying out the arrest of Yginio Salazar back in July.[11]

As Yginio Salazar was preparing to face indictment when the district court convened, Martín Chávez attended the People's Convention held inside the Lincoln courthouse at two o'clock on the afternoon of October 15, 1884. Martín Chávez, Florencio Gonzáles, José Montaño, Florencio Cháves, Saturnino Baca, George W. Peppin, Michael Cronin, Sam Corbet, Scipio Salazar, Deputy George Ulrick, Francisco "Kiko" Trujillo, and other locals had signed a public declaration inviting any citizens "in favor of economy and reform in the conduct of local affairs." Nominations were declared for the upcoming elections, and resolutions adopted expressing support for all candidates "irrespective of their political adherence to any party."[12]

While Martín Chávez was dabbling with third-party politics, Sheriff John W. Poe's political considerations were briefly set aside when the news reached Lincoln that Deputy Sheriff Jasper N. Corn had been shot and killed by Nicolas Aragón twenty-seven miles south of Las Vegas. Aragón had been arrested for horse theft earlier that year by Deputy James Brent and George Kimbrell but had managed to escape the Lincoln jailhouse on May 28, 1884. Sheriff Poe had recently learned the escapee was hiding out near Puerto de Luna and dispatched the reliable Jasper Corn to bring him in. Nicolas Aragón outran Deputy Corn and fatally shot the 24-year-old Tennessean with his Winchester rifle near Gallinas Springs shortly after sunrise on October 19, 1884. "Aragon will undoubtedly be captured, either dead or alive," the *Las Vegas Gazette* insisted. Governor Lionel Sheldon issued a $500 reward for the capture and delivery of the dangerous bandido.[13]

As Nicolas Aragón became the outlaw of the moment, Yginio Salazar would have noticed Pat Garrett's familiar lanky frame among the grand jurors when the district court opened with Judge Warren Bristol presiding on October 24, 1884. The former Regulator would always resent Garrett for having killed his amigo Billy the Kid. Yginio was preparing to stand trial for taking a shot at James Bennett only for the grand jury to announce there was no indictment to be found against the plucky vaquero. Judge Bristol ruled that the case against Yginio Salazar was "hereby dismissed and that said defendant as to the charge herein go hence without delay." While the charge of assault with intent to commit murder against Yginio Salazar was dismissed by the court, James Bennett, Thomas Bennett, and George Dickey were indicted for the murders of Ephraim W. Richards and Henry Lackey. The three men entered a plea of not guilty, and their cases were carried over to the next term of court.[14]

Yginio Salazar had returned to Las Tablas by the time John W. Poe defeated independent candidate Frank Lesnett to retain the office of sheriff when the elections were held on November 4, 1884. Poe's friend Jimmy Dolan had reestablished himself as a merchant in the former Tunstall store in Lincoln and won the confidence of enough voters to secure the office of county treasurer. Although Martín Chávez had yet to taste political success, the sheep farmer was given a reason to celebrate that month. His wife Juana gave birth to his first biological child in Picacho on November 29. Martín's 2-year-old adopted son David Billescas would soon have a little brother following him everywhere. Martín and Juana christened their infant son José "Modesto" Francisco Chávez.

While Martín and Juana Chávez had brought new life into the world, word soon reached the Bonito Valley that Yginio Salazar's former employer John Simpson Chisum had breathed his last in Eureka Springs, Arkansas. The 60-year-old cattle baron died from medical complications after undergoing surgery to remove a growth from his neck on December 23, 1884.[15]

***

Lincoln was steadily progressing with the construction of various new buildings and the booming cattle trade bringing in considerable revenue by January 1, 1885. The local population had increased as Lincoln County became an attractive place for various businessmen, cattlemen, and ranchers to set up stakes. Pat Garrett, John W. Poe, and the Lincoln County Stock Association had ensured a decrease in rustling activity, having offered various rewards for the apprehension of any man who violated stock laws throughout the region. The Lincoln County Stock Association claimed ownership of a staggering 286,800 cattle, horses, and mules by the end of the year.

The late Juan Patrón's ambition of establishing a church in Lincoln was finally realized when John B. Wilson's saloon was purchased by the county commission and transformed into a house of worship. There were also plans for the construction of a local schoolhouse directly east of the two-story courthouse at the western end of town.[16]

Having won a second term as sheriff, John W. Poe was not about to let Nicolas Aragón slip away after killing his deputy Jasper Corn the previous autumn. Sheriff Poe; his deputies James Brent, Johnny Hurley, Barney Mason, William Duford; and Las Vegas resident James Lane caught up with Aragón at the outlaw's home three miles below Chaperito, San Miguel County, in the early hours of January 25, 1885. The 28-year-old Nicolas Aragón remained hidden in the shadows of his adobe house while his wife Ruperta and several other women surrendered when Sheriff Poe kicked in the door around three o'clock in the morning. Aragón waited until the women were escorted into the building next door before taking aim with his Winchester rifle and shooting Johnny Hurley through the bowels.

"I am killed!" the former Dolan partisan shouted when the bullet struck.

Sheriff Poe and his companions surrounded Nicolas Aragón's home and exchanged shots with the fugitive as a standoff ensued. The fatally wounded John Hurley died in the care of Señora Aragón in the house next door around twenty hours later. "This broke Mr. Poe's heart, and he swore he would fight to the death to get his man," Sophie Poe later said. That was no easy task, as Nicolas Aragón continued fighting off the posse like a wounded mountain lion, almost shooting both Sheriff Poe and Deputy James Brent in the head. The bandido staunchly refused to surrender to an Americano.

Sheriff John Poe dispatched James Brent to retrieve Pat Garrett in Las Vegas the following morning. Garrett was in Texas at the time, and Deputy Brent returned with San Miguel County Sheriff Hilario Romero instead. Nicolas Aragón had been wounded in the head and left knee before finally surrendering to Sheriff Romero on the morning of January 27, 1885. John W. Poe and his remaining deputies then escorted him to Santa Fe. "Thus ends the wild career of a very desperate character," the *Las Vegas Gazette* declared. John Hurley was buried next to Jasper Corn in James Whitmore's private graveyard twenty-five miles south of Las Vegas.[17]

Sheriff John W. Poe had lost two reliable men at the end of Nicolas Aragón's rifle in the space of four months. He needed some new deputies. The sheriff ironically procured the services of an hombre who had proudly called Billy the Kid his compadre. The 25-year-old Yginio Salazar was sworn in as a deputy sheriff by John W. Poe in early 1885. The former vigilante was a proficient horseman and experienced gunman and had served in the Lincoln County Rifles under the esteemed Juan Patrón's command. Few men had taken three bullets in a single evening and lived to tell about it. Yginio also knew how rustlers operated, having spent time stealing horses alongside New Mexico's most famous desperado.[18]

While Yginio Salazar became an officer of the law, Michael Erskine Maney was soon running from the authorities. The affable Texan stood trial before Judge Samuel Axtell for the killing of Juan B. Patrón inside the Las Vegas courthouse on December 5, 1884. His father Henry Maney, an esteemed lawyer in Seguin, Texas, hired Sydney M. Barnes and the firm of Lee & Fort to represent his son in court. Attorney General William Breedon and US Attorney Thomas B. Catron handled the prosecution. The jury was evenly split after much deliberation and unable to render a verdict. Maney's lawyers motioned for a change of venue to Santa Fe County, and another trial was scheduled for July 1885. Michael Maney was transported to the territorial capital but managed to escape the jailhouse with another prisoner named Richard Elliot on the morning of May 10, 1885. Sheriff Hilario Romero was unable to locate the two fugitives, and Governor Lionel Sheldon issued a $500 reward for Maney's capture.

Michael Erskine Maney presumably fled back to Texas, but eventually he returned to Nuevo México after the authorities lost interest in pursuing him. By 1910 the Texan was living with his wife Barbara Mae (Caldwell) Maney in Doña Ana County, where the couple raised their son Henry and daughters Alice, Agnes, Allie, and Virginia. The man who shot Juan Patrón in self-defense lived a quiet, peaceful existence until his death in Las Cruces on February 11, 1942.[19]

***

Deputy Sheriff Yginio Salazar and Martín Chávez had either witnessed or heard of just about every form of frontier violence in their time, but nothing quite like what occurred in the mining settlement called Bonito during the early hours of May 5, 1885. Martin Nelson had been born in New Hampshire in 1861. Like so many young men of his time, he had ventured west and eventually traveled from Nebraska into Lincoln County around 1881. Nelson set up stakes in "Bonito City," located twenty-five miles north of Lincoln. The residents of Bonito considered the 24-year-old miner a sociable and good-natured citizen. They had even once elected him as the local constable. Little did they know their friend Martin had a malignance lurking inside him that even a hardened bandido like Nicolas Aragón would have struggled to comprehend.

Martin Nelson was sharing a room with 40-year-old Dr. William H. Flynn, 16-year-old John William Mayberry, and 5-year-old Edward F. Mayberry in the two-story Mayberry boarding house in Bonito at around three o'clock in the morning of May 5, 1885. For reasons known only to himself, Nelson decided to steal Dr. William Flynn's watch while his companions were sleeping. When Dr. Flynn was awoken by the sound of his watch being pilfered, Nelson quickly walloped the pharmacist over the head with his six-shooter. The 43-year-old William F. Mayberry overheard the commotion and headed upstairs to investigate. Nelson shot Dr. William Flynn through the heart as Mr. Mayberry reached the landing. He quickly shot the owner of the log house in the same fashion. Nelson then turned his attention to William Mayberry's two sons, shooting teenager John Mayberry in the face and neck, and blowing 5-year-old Eddie Mayberry's head off while the frightened boy still lay in the cot he had been sharing with his killer.

Having already murdered four citizens, Martin Nelson headed downstairs and procured his Winchester rifle. A 36-year-old miner named Peter Nelson, originally from Austin, Texas, entered the back door of the Mayberry house after hearing the gunshots across the street. Martin Nelson added another victim to his tally when fatally shooting the concerned neighbor in the chest and side. The 39-year-old Mrs. Amanda Mayberry grabbed her 10-year-old daughter Nellie Maude Mayberry and frantically ran out the front door. Nelson followed them into the street and shot the pregnant

Mrs. Mayberry in the back. He also shot little Nellie Mayberry through her side. The wounded girl scrambled into the cellar of a nearby residence while Martin Nelson kicked her mother's warm corpse into a ditch and covered the body with a plank of wood. Nelson then calmly entered the cellar and leveled his Winchester rifle at the trembling Nellie.

"I might as well send you to hell with the balance of 'em," the murderer said.

Nellie pleaded for her life until Nelson finally agreed to let her live, so long as she promised to attend his hanging. Nelson then returned to the Mayberry home and fired a wayward shot at a local businessman named Consbrook when he emerged from George Huber's store. Consbrook quickly alerted his neighbors, and a number of citizens began arming themselves. Townsfolk surrounded the Mayberry house, unaware that Nelson had already fled the mining camp under cover of darkness. Justice of the Peace DeWitt Clinton Taylor and nine armed citizens were still guarding the Mayberry home to prevent Nelson's escape when the murderer showed up at a local woman's house around eight o'clock that morning as if nothing had happened. Nelson headed down the street after eating breakfast and aimed his Winchester rifle at one of the men standing outside the Mayberry house. He squeezed the trigger and fatally shot 42-year-old German miner Herman Beck in the back.

"Take to the brush, you sons of bitches!" Nelson shouted as he ran toward the nine remaining guards outside the Mayberry home.

Justice DeWitt C. Taylor gave the order to open fire, and the guards sent the deranged Martin Nelson tumbling to the ground with three bullets in his chest. Nelson climbed back to his feet with a rush of adrenaline before a fourth bullet cut him down permanently. Justice Taylor and his men then rushed inside the Mayberry home in search of any survivors. They found only pools of blood, which had dripped through the cracks between the wooden floorboards above their heads. Taylor solemnly led his men upstairs to where the shooting began. "The sight there made many an old miner's eye drip like moss on a dewy morning," recalled one eyewitness.

News of the "Bonito Horror" quickly spread from coast to coast. The mass shooting was even reported by the *New York Times* two days later. "Seven deaths, and probably eight, caused by one man!" the *White Oaks*

Golden Era exclaimed in disbelief. Sheriff John W. Poe dispatched Deputy James Brent to deliver his condolences to the townsfolk and express admiration for Justice D. C. Taylor and the men who had taken down the murderer. Dr. William H. Flynn's body was embalmed and shipped to his relatives in Boston, Massachusetts. William F. Mayberry, Amanda Mayberry, John Mayberry, Eddie Mayberry, Henry Nelson, and Herman Beck were buried high upon a hillside outside Bonito on May 6, 1885. Martin Nelson's "miserable carcass" was thrown into a crudely constructed box and buried in a flat beneath the same hill. Nellie Maude Mayberry survived the gunshot wound inflicted by Nelson. She eventually married a businessman named Charles F. McGee in Iowa and died a grandmother in California decades later.[20]

The mass shooting in Bonito was still on a lot of people's minds when the district court convened in Lincoln on May 11, 1885. Martín Chávez sat on the grand jury while Deputy Sheriff Yginio Salazar served on the petit jury throughout proceedings. Local attorney George T. Beall Jr. and "Colonel" Albert Jennings Fountain secured a verdict of not guilty for James Bennett, Thomas Bennett, and George Dickey after the three men stood trial for the murder of Henry Lackey on May 16. The grand jury was unwilling to pursue the indictment against the Bennett brothers and Dickey for the murder of Ephraim W. Richards on the grounds that the cattleman had reportedly threatened the perpetrators. A 47-year-old butcher named Lyman Sprague Allen was convicted of criminal carelessness for the accidental shooting death of Sam Anderson. Allen was sentenced to five years in the almost completed New Mexico Territorial Penitentiary located fifteen miles south of Santa Fe. John C. Joy was convicted of cattle theft and sentenced to five years in the penitentiary. An Irishman named James McCarthy received seven years for murder.[21]

Catarino Romero had recently been recaptured following his escape from the old Lincoln pit-jail in the autumn of 1877. "While a free man, the natives feared him," the *White Oaks Golden Era* insisted. "For when drunk he would do anything, no matter how fiendish or cold-blooded, to satisfy his brutish temper." Romero was found guilty of murder in the second degree during the district court session in May 1885. Judge Stephen S. Wilson sentenced him to life imprisonment in the territorial penitentiary. Warden

James E. Gregg was already housing forty prisoners in the penitentiary when Romero was sentenced, although construction of the multileveled facility was not completed until the following month. The authorities soon closed a contract for the installation of 150 incandescent lights by the US Electric Light Company of New York, the same company that supplied lighting for the Brooklyn Bridge. Catarino Romero would not live to see them. The jailer Joseph Smith Lea shot Romero four times when the prisoner attacked him with a stove hearth and tried to flee the Lincoln jailhouse on the evening of June 4, 1885. Lea was discharged following an inquiry. "While the killing of a human being is to be deplored, it is not worthwhile to shed tears over [Romero's] death," the *Golden Era* remarked.[22]

Deputy Sheriff Yginio Salazar and Deputy Sheriff James R. Brent procured their Winchester rifles in preparation to assist Sheriff John W. Poe with the transportation of prisoners Lyman S. Allen, John C. Joy, and James McCarthy to Santa Fe in the early hours of July 1, 1885. George T. Beall accompanied them on the journey to represent the prosecution when Nicolas Aragón stood trial for murder later that month. They reached the Holy City without any trouble and delivered the three prisoners to the penitentiary authorities. Yginio Salazar presumably headed back to Lincoln before John W. Poe, James Brent, and George Beall checked in to Herlow's Hotel on July 6, 1885. The district court convened that day, and Sheriff Poe and Deputy Brent both provided testimony during the upcoming trial of Nicolas Aragón for the murder of John Hurley. "Nicolas Aragon, the latest criminal celebrity, is a little wheezen-faced Mexican, 28 years old, with a keen 'snakey' black-eye," the *New Mexican* declared. "His hard face indicates abundant brute force."[23]

Nicolas Aragón became the subject of wild speculation prior to his trial. The Las Vegas press sensationally reported that he once rode with Billy the Kid and was a participant in the murder of "Colonel" Charles Potter. Aragón firmly denied both baseless allegations. The prosecution team of Attorney General William Breedon, Assistant Attorney General Marshall A. Breedon, and George T. Beall had secured a change of venue from Las Vegas. They believed it would be difficult to convict Aragón in San Miguel County owing to the support of his friends and relatives. A petit jury comprised of local

Hispanos may have been reluctant to condemn one of their own to death for shooting a couple of gringos from Lincoln County. Aragón's wife Ruperta had also raised funds to secure the legal services of Victory & Read and former Santa Fe County Sheriff José D. Sena.[24]

Nicolas Aragón was arraigned in the district court and placed on trial for the murders of John Hurley and Jasper Corn on July 15, 1885. José D. Sena argued for the defense that the shot that killed John Hurley was "fired in the dark, with no one to swear that they actually saw the accused fire it." Aragón was acquitted of murdering Johnny Hurley by the Hispano petit jury on the morning of July 17, 1885. "He owes his escape from just punishment to the wily scheming of Sena, who worked upon the feelings of his countrymen so as to blind their sense of justice," the *Lincoln County Leader* bitterly remarked. Attorney General William Breedon motioned for Aragón to be remanded to jail and stand trial for the murder of Jasper Corn in Colfax County following another change of venue. Nicolas Aragón was convicted of murder in the second degree by a jury in Springer, Colfax County, and sentenced to life imprisonment in the territorial penitentiary on September 25, 1885.[25]

***

Lincoln County was continuing to evolve in a variety of ways when Yginio Salazar filed bills totaling $14.35 to the board of county commissioners for his services as a deputy sheriff in October 1885. Public schools had been established in almost every precinct. Hundreds of illiterate Hispano and Anglo children were now learning to read and write throughout Lincoln County. Superintendent Alexander G. Lane had worked tirelessly that year to expand the public school system. The 50-year-old Dr. Lane had also received assurances from County Treasurer James J. Dolan that the Irishman would provide the funds necessary to furnish every school with the textbooks adopted for the next five years. "That the watchword of progress now, from the Atlantic to Pacific, is, 'grade the county schools,' is true," the *Lincoln County Leader* declared. The public school system may have been progressing, but there was contention over whether the children of New Mexico Territory should be educated in English or Spanish. "This is an American people and government," one local

Anglo insisted. "Mexicans should learn English rather than that Americans should acquire the Spanish language."[26]

Although more children were learning how to read and write in Lincoln County than ever before, numerous Hispano sheepherders were more concerned with hostile cowboys throughout the summer and autumn of 1885. A *pastor* named Dionicio Cháves reported that five hundred of his sheep had been slaughtered in one night on the ranges of Carrizozo in early June 1885. Cháves had recently sold his sheep ranch to an Irish cattleman named James A. Alcock and made the mistake of herding his flock in the vicinity. "We don't believe in cattlemen killing sheep, nor do we believe in sheepmen killing cattle," the *White Oaks Golden Era* insisted. "Each industry needs the protection of our meagre laws: property is too expensive to be slaughtered and left to rot on the range."[27]

A land agent from Texas called M. J. Denman and his cowboys were making life miserable for the Hispanos residing in Seven Rivers throughout 1885. "For several years past, but few Mexicans have been allowed to live within these limits, peaceably and without molestation," Ash Upson revealed on December 3, 1885. "Many Mexicans have been killed outright, without provocation, several have been wounded, and many more driven away from their homes by intimidation and threats of shooting, assassination and mob-violence." The majority of claims made under the Desert Land Act in the Pecos Valley were fraudulent. When M. J. Denman accused Lincoln County Stock Association President Charles Bishop Eddy of having acquired much of his acreage illegally, cattleman Charles H. Slaughter and various Anglos exposed Denman's harassment and murder of local Hispanos in a sworn deposition on December 10, 1885. "The Mexican settlers in this part of the county have always been objects of hatred to the class of border ruffians to which said Denman belongs," declared Charles Slaughter. What Slaughter failed to mention was that numerous illiterate Hispano farmers had been duped by his friend Charles Eddy into selling their lands for less than one dollar per acre.[28]

While some Nuevomexicanos were suffering at the hands of land agents and cattlemen, the wheel of technological advancement had continued turning in Lincoln County with the connection of a telephone line between Fort

Stanton and the Mescalero Apache Agency by the autumn of 1885. A large adobe brewery had recently been constructed just above the fort by Civil War veteran Charles R. Biederman, Swiss blacksmith John Ruffley, and German brewer H. L. Muller. "These gentlemen are making an excellent quality of beer," the *Golden Era* announced.

There was plenty of cerveza (beer) on offer when a grand Christmas Ball was hosted by Scipio Salazar and Atanacio Martínez inside Sais's Hall in Lincoln on the night of December 25, 1885. Musicians had been brought in from Albuquerque for the occasion, and many of the attendees wore their fanciest clothes. James Brent wore a blue outfit with golden brass buttons. Atanacio Martínez wore a noticeable red necktie, Joseph Smith Lea wore a cashmere suit trimmed with leather, and the famous Pat Garrett showed up in a fashionable woolen suit and tight leather boots. Deputy Sheriff Yginio Salazar was probably in attendance and dressed as sharply as possible that night. "Lincoln is becoming famous for these entertainments," the *Golden Era* remarked. "A commodious hall will soon be needed to accommodate all who wish to attend."[29]

The placita that had long been the most dangerous municipality in New Mexico Territory now held a reputation for grandiose functions rather than continuous bloodshed.

***

José Chávez y Chávez had relocated to Las Vegas at some point during the early 1880s. He left his wife Leonora Lucero de Chávez and their children in San Patricio to allow himself the freedom to come and go as he pleased. Having spent time working as a laborer and sheepherder, the literate Chávez y Chávez resumed his career as a temperamental frontier lawman in San Miguel County. He later recalled temporarily working as a policeman under José Santos Esquibel in 1882. A subpoena related to the Michael Maney case filed in the district court of Las Vegas in December 1884 bears the name "José Chavez, Deputy," suggesting the former Regulator had been deputized by Sheriff Esquibel at a later date.[30]

José Chávez y Chávez was working as a policeman under Sheriff Hilario Romero in Las Vegas by 1885. Although records of his activities are difficult to trace, José demonstrated his occasional propensity for brutishness in the line of duty when assaulting a 12-year-old Italian boy named Vicenzo Lorenzo on June 29, 1885. José paid a fine of fifteen dollars for assaulting the youngster, and the *Las Vegas Gazette* would report that "Officer Chávez" was arrested the following day for having used "threatening language towards one of the witnesses in the trial." José was temporarily locked in the city jail after failing to raise the $500 bond set by Justice of the Peace William J. Steele.[31]

José Chávez y Chávez also became familiar with the boyish Robert "Bob" Ford while working as a city policeman in Las Vegas. The 23-year-old Missourian had achieved worldwide fame by fatally shooting Jesse James in the back of the head while the outlaw was dusting a picture inside the living room of his home in St. Joseph, Missouri, on April 3, 1882. Ford considered himself a brave and noble hero for having betrayed his gang leader, although most of the population viewed him as a sniveling coward. His brother Charley Ford was already dying of tuberculosis when he committed suicide in Missouri on May 6, 1884. Robert Ford arrived in New Mexico Territory and opened the Bank Saloon with former James Gang member Dick Liddel on Bridge Street in Las Vegas by January 1885.[32]

Robert Ford joined the frequently corrupt Las Vegas police force after his saloon on Bridge Street failed to turn a profit. "If any citizen of the meadow town hereafter disobeys the law, Bob will bring him to a sense of his duty to good government when said citizen may be hanging a picture," the *Albuquerque Democrat* caustically remarked on March 27, 1885. Although San Miguel National Bank cashier Miguel Antonio Otero Jr. considered Ford "pleasant to meet" and "good natured," the Missourian was shunned by most citizens like "a mad dog." Bob didn't help matters by continually boasting of his shooting Jesse James and supposed marksmanship with a revolver.[33]

Sheriff Hilario Romero eventually grew tired of Robert Ford's crowing and decided to call the officer's bluff. Romero suggested the little gringo engage in a shooting contest with his fellow policeman José Chávez y Chávez on the outskirts of Las Vegas. A crowd of citizens followed them out of town and gathered around to watch as Sheriff Romero placed a coin on a fence post to serve as the target. Robert Ford took a shot at the coin and missed by a considerable margin. José Chávez y Chávez then stepped forward, drew his revolver in a flash, and sent a bullet through the center of the coin with ease. As the citizens applauded Chávez y Chávez's deadly marksmanship, Ford began whining that the shooting contest was somehow unfair.

José Chávez y Chávez was in no mood for Robert Ford's protests and challenged the wannabe pistolero to an old-fashioned duel. José suggested they stand back to back, take twenty paces when given a signal, and then shoot to kill. When staring into the dark, glassy eyes of a real badman, Ford suddenly lost his nerve and backed down. The Missourian soon packed his belongings and departed Las Vegas, much to the relief of those who had grown tired of his macho posturing. Robert Ford lived up to his reputation for cowardice but had saved himself from a trip to the coroner's office that day.[34]

José Chávez y Chávez would have killed him without the slightest hesitation.

***

Yginio Salazar's duties as a deputy sheriff in Lincoln County concluded when James R. Brent succeeded John W. Poe as sheriff in January 1886. Yginio filed a bill totaling $6.50 for his services as a deputy sheriff to the board of county commissioners on January 4. He also attended a grand baile to celebrate James R. Brent's new role as sheriff in Lincoln on January 30. Jimmy Dolan and Josh Church ensured it was a night to remember when mixing the drinks, and almost everyone in attendance quickly became soused.

"All promenade to your seats!" Yginio cried during the festivities to signal when a dance had concluded.

Six months later Yginio was probably in attendance for the wedding of Sheriff James Brent and Carlota Baca inside the Lincoln Church on July 3, 1886. Carlota wore a white satin dress on her big day, complete with a wreath and "a flowing veil that enveloped her entire form" as one eyewitness recalled.[35]

The 26-year-old Yginio Salazar began taking a more serious interest in politics following his stint as a deputy sheriff. He quickly achieved success when attending the Republican Convention held in Lincoln on August 31, 1886. Salazar, William Caffrey, Wallace Holt, and George B. Barber were nominated and unanimously elected as delegates to the Republican Territorial

Convention scheduled to be held in San Miguel County the following month. Yginio and his fellow delegates were in attendance when the esteemed J. Francisco Cháves verbally eviscerated Governor Edmund G. Ross—a Democrat from Ohio who had been appointed to office by President Grover Cleveland the previous year—during the territorial convention in Las Vegas on September 6, 1886. "Colonel Chaves flayed the old governor alive and the old man was in the gallery listening to it all," the *Albuquerque Journal* informed the public.[36]

Although partisan politics remained as hostile as ever, Yginio Salazar continued living a relatively quiet life in Lincoln County, aside from one violent incident during the summer of 1888. For whatever reason, former McSween partisan Atanacio Martínez struck and pummeled his old comrade Señor Salazar in Lincoln on July 23, 1888. Rather than seek revenge like he may have done five years earlier, the 28-year-old Salazar swore an affidavit before the *jues de paz* (justice of the peace) José Córdova two days later. Córdova issued a warrant for Atanacio Martínez's arrest so the former constable could be "dealt with according to law." Yginio Salazar's time as a deputy sheriff appears to have tempered the combative inclinations of his youth.[37]

While Yginio was still enjoying the single life in Lincoln, Martín Chávez and his pregnant wife Juana were busy raising their boys David and Modesto downriver in Picacho. Martín also attended a mass meeting of citizens in Lincoln in January 1887. The purpose of the congregation was to express staunch opposition to a proposal by the territorial legislature that a new county be carved out of a significant portion of land centered around Roswell in eastern Lincoln County. The 34-year-old Martín Chávez, Sheriff James Brent, Saturnino Baca, George Peppin, Emil Fritz, August Kline, Michael Cronin, and roughly two hundred other citizens were present when José Montaño and James J. Dolan were appointed to "represent the feelings of the majority of the people of Lincoln County" during the mass assembly. "We demand of our representatives in the legislature that they do not act in the matter until they have heard the voice of the people of this county," José Montaño recorded in an adopted resolution during proceedings.[38]

Having voiced his objection to the carving up of Lincoln County, Martín Chávez and his wife Juanita welcomed the birth of their daughter Josefa

"Josefita" Chávez in Picacho on March 20, 1887. As a former pupil of Padre José Sambrano Tafoya, the conservative Martín Chávez would have mourned the loss of Jean Baptiste Lamy the following winter. The late Juan Patrón's mentor had resigned as archbishop of Santa Fe several years earlier and succumbed to pneumonia in the territorial capital at the age of 73 on February 13, 1888. "He passed away as he lived, calmly and beautifully, a smile of Christian contentment encircling his noble face like a halo of glory," the *New Mexican* declared.

With three young mouths to feed, Martín Chávez represented his precinct as a member of the Democratic County Central Committee at the Democratic Convention held in Lincoln on April 20, 1888. The sheep farmer made a somewhat radical political move several months later. Martín decided not to attend the next Democratic Convention held in Lincoln on August 31, 1888. Instead, the former deputy sheriff attended the People's Convention, comprised of Republicans and a handful of Democrats, on September 1, 1888. Martín Chávez, John A. Brothers of White Oaks, and William H. H. Miller of Roswell subsequently emerged as the nominees for the board of county commissioners on the People's ticket. "[Martín Chávez] is a robust type of native born citizen, whose ability or honor will not be questioned by anybody," the *Lincoln County Leader* declared on October 20, 1888. "He will see that such of our roads as are under county surveillance are passable and will not make a [sieve] out of the county treasure for the benefit of the favored few." Martín secured a respectable number of votes but ultimately fell short of winning a seat on the commission in the November elections. Meanwhile, the staunch Democrats of Lincoln County were shocked when 32-year-old Texan and School Superintendent Daniel C. Nowlin won the vote for sheriff ahead of the incumbent Democratic candidate James R. Brent.[39]

For all the vehement objections of Martín Chávez and numerous citizens of the Bonito Valley in early 1887, the territorial legislature passed a bill for two new counties to be carved from land comprising eastern Lincoln County in February 1889. Chaves County, reportedly named after highly successful businessman Felipe Cháves of Belen, would comprise the northeastern portion of Lincoln County, with Roswell serving as the county seat. Eddy County, named after stockman Charles Bishop Eddy, would be carved out of the lands to the south of Chaves County, with the town of Eddy initially serving as the county seat. "The new counties are attached to the county of Lincoln for legislative representation and the three shall jointly elect one councilman and one representative," the *New Mexican* announced on February 25, 1889.

While Martín Chávez and every other farmer in southeastern New Mexico relied on their acequias for sustenance, former sheriff Pat Garrett and Charles B. Eddy were looking to make a fortune by drastically expanding irrigation after a severe drought put a dent in the local cattle trade in 1886. Garrett and Eddy had formed the Pecos Irrigation and Investment Company, acquired the promotional efforts of newspaperman Charles W. Greene, secured some wealthy investors, and launched a profitable irrigation scheme throughout the Pecos Valley. Their enterprise grew until Garrett was forced out when he was no longer able to match the financial contributions of their supremely wealthy investors. As Charles B. Eddy's pockets grew deeper, the irrigation scheme proved costly for numerous illiterate Hispano farmers—many of whom could not even spell their own names—when they were tricked into selling their land and water rights to irrigation company officials for a few measly dollars. The gringos took with one hand while providing employment opportunities with the other, as Anglo contractors relied heavily on Hispano American and Mexican laborers to "water" the land.[40]

As Condado de Lincoln began shrinking around him, Martín Chávez continued carving out a future for himself and his family in Picacho. He also made peace with Lucio Montoya, the one-time Dolan partisan who had taken a shot at him during the Lincoln County War. Lucio had since married María Inez Miranda, who had given birth to their daughter Floripa Montoya on January 11, 1885. "Years later when we were at peace, I had many hearty laughs with Lucio Montoya," recalled Martín Chávez. The two hombres often chuckled about Lucio having hidden inside a box in the Romero house and disguised himself in women's clothing to escape Martín's wrath during the five-day siege in Lincoln.[41]

Martín and Juana Chávez's three children David Billescas, Modesto Chávez, and little Josefita Chávez all attended the public school in Picacho when they were old enough. David Billescas and Modesto Chávez were probably receiving an early education from local schoolteacher Thomas Kayse by 1890. While Judge Alexander L. Morrison—the president of the Republican League of New Mexico in Santa Fe—had recently established Republican League clubs in White Oaks, Lincoln, and Picacho, the 37-year-old Martín Chávez attended the Democratic Convention held in Lincoln on August 14, 1890. He was among the fourteen delegates elected to attend the Democratic Convention scheduled to take place in Roswell, Chaves County, on August 21, 1890.[42]

Around the time Martín Chávez was preparing to represent the Democrats of Lincoln County over in Roswell, a Picacho resident named Casimiro Billescas vanished while searching for some of his sheep on a nearby hill. Billescas suffered from heart disease, and the high altitude proved too much for the *pastor*. A local Hispana spotted his corpse lying on the hilltop four days later.[43]

***

While Martín Chávez and Yginio Salazar were now residing in a much smaller Lincoln County, their old compadre José Chávez y Chávez continued making a living for himself in what became the largest county of New Mexico Territory in 1889. San Miguel County was now home to roughly 24,204 inhabitants. The county seat of Las Vegas had even surpassed Santa Fe and Albuquerque as the most populated metropolis in all of Nuevo México. "Grazing land in unlimited quantities can be had for the money or good paper," one Anglo resident of Las Vegas declared in February 1889. "And with a sufficient quantity of water, what more can be asked by an intelligent stockman or farmer?" José Chávez y Chávez worked as a city policeman under Sheriff Lorenzo López in the increasingly crowded Las Vegas. He also worked for a businessman and seasoned mining agent from Omaha named James H. Hunter, who opened a livery stable on Bridge Street.[44]

San Miguel County was enjoying an unprecedented degree of political and commercial influence in New Mexico Territory, but many of the poorer Hispanos were fiercely disgruntled in early 1889. The development of the railroads and resulting wave of industrial capitalism had inevitably favored the interests of a commercial elite in New Mexico Territory throughout the previous decade. Many local Hispanos had grown tired of Anglo speculators and a handful of upper-class Nuevomexicanos disregarding the 496,446-acre Town of Las Vegas Land Grant established by the Mexican government in 1835. The Santa Fe Ring, various wealthy cattle ranchers, and Anglo squatters frequently stretched the boundaries of their land claims by fraudulent means, thereby denying the rural Hispanos of their legal right to the water, grass, and timber supplies on community lands as guaranteed by the Treaty of Guadalupe Hidalgo and the United States Congress. The use of barbed wire fences by various ranchers and merchants to enclose thousands of acres cut off numerous Hispanos from their local schools, churches, waterholes, and sheep trails.[45]

With the benefit of hindsight, it was only a matter of time until the resentment felt by many impoverished Hispanos boiled over into some form of militant resistance against what the Americanos called progress. In the spring of 1885, the General Land Office concluded an exhaustive four-year investigation and submitted reports implicating government officials, various cattle ranchers, territorial politicians, and railroad companies of committing land fraud throughout much of New Mexico Territory. Governor Edmund G. Ross had also given hint of the potential for rural discontent in Nuevo México when submitting his annual report to the secretary of the interior in 1885. The former senatorial representative of Kansas had expressed his dissatisfaction with the United States government's failure to safeguard the community land titles being "absorbed into great cattle ranches, merely for the purpose of getting control of water courses and springs, and thus keep out settlers and small herds." The systematic land fraud in New Mexico Territory and nonfeasance of the US government continued despite these reports. The situation became unbearable for many working-class Hispanos of San Miguel County by 1889. ¡Es todo![46]

The resentment that many poorer Nuevomexicanos held for the wealthy Anglo and Hispano landholders of San Miguel County was exemplified by the class-struggle ideology and revolutionary aspirations of three brothers. Juan José, Pablo, and Nicanor Herrera were born into a large family sired by their late father Manuel Herrera and their deceased mother María Paula Archibeque-Herrera. The well-educated Juan José Herrera, the eldest of the three brothers, was born in El Pueblo, San Miguel, on November 22, 1837. He served as a captain for the Union during the Civil War, thereby earning himself the nickname El Capitán. Juan José also worked as an Indian Agent before temporarily vacating New Mexico after some form of scandal resulted in him abandoning his French wife Elisa Pinard in 1866. In addition to English and French, El Capitán had learned several native dialects while traveling through various states and territories before returning to San Miguel County. Juan José was indicted for the "assault with intent to commit murder" of an hombre named Dionicio García during the summer of 1886 before entering the world of politics in Las Vegas the following year.

The robust Pablo Herrera had been born on March 2, 1844. Pablo was also well-traveled, having worked as a freighter in Wyoming Territory alongside his younger brother Nicanor in the late 1860s. He later hauled freight alongside older brother Juan José in Ojitos Fríos, San Miguel County, during the early 1870s. Pablo had drawn wages as a laborer in Routt, Colorado, and Rio Arriba County, New Mexico, following the death of his wife during the early 1880s. The spirited Pablo also got into a scrape with a saloon owner named Wallace Gould in Los Ojos (Park View), Rio Arriba County, on the night of November 24, 1887. Gould struck Pablo twice with a loaded billy when the laborer refused to vacate the establishment. Herrera responded by grabbing the proprietor and cutting him three times with a small pocketknife. He was taken into custody by Sheriff Louis M. Ortiz and sentenced to one year and three days in the territorial penitentiary for assault with intent to commit murder in April 1888. The *New Mexican* later claimed Herrera was sentenced for stabbing former deputy sheriff Dan Sullivan, describing him as "a very bad man." The feisty laborer served six months in the penitentiary before he was pardoned by Governor Ross in October 1888. Pablo Herrera was ready to take on the world when joining his brothers Juan José and Nicanor in San Miguel County following his release from prison.

Nicanor Herrera was born on November 28, 1846. The long-haired, bearded Nicanor worked alongside his older brother Pablo in Wyoming Territory in the 1860s, established a farm outside Las Vegas by 1870, and drew wages as a laborer in La Cebolla Valley, Mora County, during the early 1880s.

It was later suggested that Nicanor was the meanest of the three Herrera brothers, although others insisted he was merely the most animated.[47]

Juan José, Pablo, and Nicanor Herrera had remained close throughout the years and were determined to challenge the political and economic system in their homeland. The Herrera brothers joined an American workers federation called the Knights of Labor, a national union which had accumulated over one hundred thousand members by the mid-1880s. The neatly groomed Juan José Herrera had spent time helping to organize some of the coal and lumber camps in the Rocky Mountains of Colorado on behalf of the union during his travels. Juan José subsequently established the first three Caballeros del Trabajo (Knights of Labor) chapters in San Miguel County.

Juan José Herrera was also aware that an independent political faction comprised of left-wing agrarian populists and workers known as the People's Party were gaining traction in the Midwest and eastern states on the back of a wave of American populism throughout the late 1880s. Herrera's next move was to assist Civil War veteran and East Las Vegas resident Francis A. Blake and some Anglo members of the Knights of Labor with the establishment of the People's Party of New Mexico. Juan José made an even bolder statement when learning that an Anglo neighbor operating the Black Tree Trunk Ranch near San Gerónimo was denying la gente their right to graze stock on the community land with a lengthy barbed wire fence. Herrera angrily shoved the unrepentant gringo into a rain barrel when confronting him. He then cut down the despised fence to the delight of the local Hispanos.

Although the People's Party of New Mexico failed to accumulate many votes during the 1888 elections, the support for the Herrera brothers and their radical ambitions increased among the Hispano farmers, laborers, sheepherders, ranch hands, and railroad workers of San Miguel County. Juan José Herrera and his brothers had rallied enough support from the impoverished Hispanos living in the region of El Salitre, El Burro, Ojitos Fríos, and San Gerónimo to oversee the formation of a more secretive organization by early 1889. They soon made their existence known to the predatory capitalists and corrupt officials they despised.[48]

A militant working-class uprising was about to commence in San Miguel County, and José Chávez y Chávez would be in the very thick of it.

Chapter 14

Los Gorras Blancas

Be fair and just and we are with you,
do otherwise and take the consequences.
—Los Gorras Blancas

They seemed to have come from nowhere. The band of dark-skinned riders wearing white hoods suddenly galloping across the terrain near San Gerónimo, San Miguel County, during the night of April 26, 1889. While they would have made for an intimidating sight to any observer, the party of masked individuals were not intending to shoot or lynch anyone that night. Nor were they about to carry out an arbitrary raid. Their intention was to liberate some of the land upon which their people had freely roamed for decades. The band of mysterious Nuevomexicanos riding through the darkness of San Miguel County that night were devoted members of a newly established and highly secretive organization called Los Gorras Blancas (the White Caps).

The masked hombres moved quickly when reaching the lengthy barbed wire fence that two Englishmen named W. D. Quarrell and William Rawlins had recently erected around their ranch on Tecolote Creek. The stealthy vigilantes began cutting the entire four miles of barbed wire—the devil's hat-band—into pieces. They also set fire to every fence post before rapidly dispersing in the moonlight. Los Gorras Blancas had successfully carried out their first raid, leaving W. D. Quarrell and William Rawlins with merely $800 worth of useless barbed wire fragments and charred kindling.[1]

If Juan José, Pablo, and Nicanor Herrera were not participants in the raid themselves, they would have been satisfied when hearing the reports of their comrades who destroyed Quarrell and Rawlins's fence during the night of April 26, 1889. It was a good start, but plenty more late-night raids would need to be carried out before the land-grabbers got the message. Their white hoods—made from flour sacks with two punctures serving as eyeholes—provided a measure of anonymity for themselves and a healthy dose of intimidation for anyone they encountered. The Herrera brothers may have gotten the idea when reading about the White Caps of Arcola, Illinois, in a news item published by the *Las Vegas Daily Optic* several weeks earlier. A band of hooded Anglo vigilantes had recently destroyed a commissioner's barn in Tuscola, Illinois, after their letters opposing the intended construction of a drainage canal in their community were ignored by officials. It was later suggested that Juan José Herrera had drawn inspiration from the Ku Klux Klan, although El Capitán was not motivated by racial hatred.[2]

Stealthy members of Los Gorras Blancas continued leveling fences in Agua Sarca, Bernal, and San Gerónimo under cover of darkness throughout the spring of 1889. One party of night riders carried out a more aggressive raid when burning territorial surveyor Edward F. Hobart's newly built house to the ground near the Las Vegas Hot Springs. The White Caps were not dissuaded when the late Juan Patrón's former attorney Miguel Salazar tried to procure indictments against Juan José Herrera, Pablo Herrera, and nineteen other local Hispanos for fence cutting in Las Vegas on May 3, 1889. Whatever happened, they would all remain silent. Every member of Los Gorras Blancas had been sworn to secrecy on pain of death and answered to seven appointed tenientes (lieutenants) within their organization.[3]

When W. D. Quarrell and William Rawlins rebuilt their barbed wire fence on Tecolote Creek, a band of White Caps cut it down for the second time in June 1889. Rawlins and Quarrell stubbornly rebuilt the fence again, only for members of Los Gorras Blancas to pay them another destructive late-night visit. The hostilities escalated when a handful of unidentified "Mexicans" fired shots at Quarrell and his ranch hand Tom Williams while the two men were driving some stock from their corral around eight thirty on the morning of June 27, 1889. Tom Williams took a bullet in his thigh and W. D. Quarrell's horse was shot dead beneath him. The *Las Vegas Daily Optic* obliviously suggested the "Mexicans" responsible for the shooting were either bandidos or members of Los Penitentes "in order to get rid of the men who do not believe in their worship."[4]

Although their raids were initially carried out against Anglo ranchers, Los Gorras Blancas were motivated by a sense of class conflict rather than ethnic hostility. The White Caps did not racially discriminate in their vigilante crusade, as demonstrated when they destroyed wealthy Hispano merchant José Y. Luhan's barbed wire fences, crops, haystacks, farm machinery, lumber, and sawmill in the mountainous village of San Ignacio during the summer of 1889. They also tore down a barbed wire fence belonging to a former Republican delegate named Gregorio Varela eight miles west of Las Vegas around July 10, 1889. No hombre in San Miguel County, regardless of his ethnicity, was safe from Los Gorras Blancas if disregarding the Las Vegas Land Grant. The masked vigilantes were as much against Ricos as they were against Americano land-grabbers.[5]

The White Caps' numbers rapidly increased as they continued recruiting dissatisfied young workers, and even an elderly Civil War veteran and pensioner named Teodoso Salas in El Salitre. The organization also needed hardcases who were willing to get their hands dirty. This included Porfirio Trujillo, a local bandido who had spent a one-year stretch in the territorial penitentiary for horse theft. The 39-year-old José Chávez y Chávez also fit the bill. The former Regulator was a proud Nuevomexicano and seized his opportunity to resume hostilities against the same kind of bossism he had opposed during the Lincoln County War. Chávez y Chávez began moonlighting as a member of Los Gorras Blancas while still drawing wages as a policeman under Sheriff Lorenzo López in Las Vegas.[6]

When José Chávez y Chávez wasn't burning the candle at both ends in San Miguel County, the notorious hard-ass made a considerable impression on the Padilla family of Galisteo that eventful summer. José Delores Padilla and his wife Marcellina had welcomed their ninth child into the world on June 24, 1889. The couple were escorting their infant son up the Río Pecos to Anton

Chico for the child's baptism several weeks later when they encountered José Chávez y Chávez and a band of ruffians on horseback. When informed of the Padilla family's intentions, José offered to serve as the infant's *padrino* (godfather). He further insisted on personally transporting the baby upriver to Anton Chico and overseeing the baptism himself. The Padillas fearfully agreed, not wishing to offend the temperamental policeman. José Chávez y Chávez and his compadres headed north with their little *hijo* in what all but amounted to a case of kidnapping.

José and Marcellina Padilla anxiously prayed for their baby's welfare inside their adobe home for several days until José Chávez y Chávez turned up on their doorstep cradling his new godson as promised. The policeman had chosen the name Adecasio Juan Padilla for the infant, Adecasio also being the name of his own son. José and Marcellina Padilla later told their *hijo* about his tumultuous christening, which quickly became a family legend. Adecasio Juan Padilla took pride in being the godson of the infamous José Chávez y Chávez, and he entertained his own children and grandchildren with the story of his baptism decades later.[7]

***

The officials of San Miguel County and the territorial press were slow to comprehend exactly what was happening as Los Gorras Blancas continued their late-night raids throughout the summer of 1889. Twenty more Caballeros del Trabajo (Knights of Labor) chapters suddenly emerged throughout the region, and usually in the vicinity of where the bands of hooded night riders carried out their raids. The local Hispanos remained silent about the situation, and Governor L. Bradford Prince was preoccupied with his trip to Lincoln County that July. The governor gave a rousing speech in White Oaks on Independence Day before spending time in Lincoln and Fort Stanton. "Gov. Prince returns from his visit to Lincoln County thoroughly delighted with the condition and prospects of that section," the *New Mexican* announced on July 20, 1889.[8]

While Lincoln County had finally settled down, San Miguel County was rapidly becoming its successor as the most anarchistic county in Nuevo México. Having already issued warnings to Sheriff Lorenzo López, who was a leading member of Los Penitentes and distant relative of Juan José Herrera, a band of Gorras Blancas cut down several miles of the former judge's barbed wire fence and destroyed his crops in Romeroville during a late-night raid in August 1889. The White Caps carried out further raids that month against a 39-year-old Virginian rancher named James Wilson Lynch outside Romeroville and a prominent farmer named J. Placido Romero in Peralta, Valencia County.[9]

After trying to ignore the organization's activities for months, the *Las Vegas Daily Optic* interviewed Chief Justice Elisha Van Buren Long and formally acknowledged the existence of Los Gorras Blancas on October 23, 1889. The leading newspaper of San Miguel County echoed the sentiments of Justice Long when implying the vigilantes were justified in their disaffection over land usage but condemned the cutting of fences by "lawless mobs." The *Optic* suggested there were legal means to deal with those putting up barbed wire fences on community land, insisting the local population were "not ready to turn their government over to a self-constituted mob, who propose to take the administration of the law in their own hands."[10]

While many local Nuevomexicanos sympathized with the hooded night riders, the 37-year-old District Attorney Miguel Salazar's loyalties were firmly with the land speculators of San Miguel County. Although Chief Justice Elisha V. B. Long privately recognized that the Las Vegas Grant was indeed a community grant, the 53-year-old Hoosier could not condone any form of violent resistance from "Mexicans." District Attorney Salazar and Chief Justice Long would ensure that a grand jury returned further indictments against various alleged fence cutters during the upcoming district court session in Las Vegas.[11]

The district court had convened in Las Vegas when sixty-three members of Los Gorras Blancas rode into town and startled various citizens around midnight of November 1, 1889. They were all wearing their traditional white hoods, lengthy black coats, and slickers, and were armed with rifles and revolvers. When the White Caps failed to locate Sheriff Lorenzo López at the jailhouse, the party of insurgents gathered outside the courthouse in an act of open defiance. They also shouted threats and insults through the windows of District Attorney Miguel Salazar's home before galloping out of town.

"There is a secret organization of fence cutters in the country to the southwest of Las Vegas," the *Las Vegas Daily Optic* informed its readers. "A number of murders have been committed in that community during the past six months, and a large amount of fencing cut, and the grand jury has been investigating those lawless acts and trying to bring the perpetrators to justice, and it is likely for this reason that the White Caps attempted to terrorize the community and thus put a stop to the investigations of the grand jury."[12]

The grand jury continued their investigations in Las Vegas despite the brazen attempt to dissuade them. Chief Justice Elisha V. B. Long ordered the arrest of a local Black man known as Romualdo Fernandez for refusing to answer the grand jury's questions about Los Gorras Blancas on November 9, 1889. "It is thought he knows much more about the fence cutting than he desires to tell," the *Las Vegas Daily Optic* insisted. Fernandez spent several days in jail before admitting to having passed by White Cap meetings held in El Salitre and El Burro but insisted that he was unable to identify any of the participants. Chief Justice Long ordered for Fernandez to be escorted back to the jailhouse. "If anyone happens to see [Los Gorras Blancas] or know about their crimes, he will not testify for fear of being killed," District Attorney Miguel Salazar later remarked.[13]

Miguel Salazar would also report that Los Gorras Blancas carried out a raid twenty-seven miles southeast of Las Vegas while the grand jury were struggling to accumulate testimony against them in November 1889. "The fence of an American, whose name I do not remember, and who was the agent of the R. R. Co. at Rowe, was also destroyed," Salazar recalled. The railroad agent, one Daniel B. Hampe, overheard the destruction of his fence that night and approached the hooded perpetrators with a loaded shotgun. He quickly retreated when the White Caps fired several shots in his direction. Los Gorras Blancas also continued expanding their operations across county lines that month when burning fifteen tons worth of haystacks belonging to Severino Trujillo in Guadalupita, Mora County. "White Caps will do well enough for the effete East, but they are entirely out of place in the progressive West," the *Las Cruces Sun-News* amusingly declared on November 9, 1889. "San Miguel County has disgraced the whole territory of New Mexico."[14]

It was not until the final day of the district court session in Las Vegas that indictments were returned against members of Los Gorras Blancas for riot and fence cutting on November 25, 1889. District Attorney Miguel Salazar had procured confessions from three prisoners being held in the county jail for unrelated misdemeanors. The three hombres supposedly confessed to being members of the White Caps and having participated in the destruction of W. D. Quarrell and Sheriff Lorenzo López's barbed wire fences. It wasn't much, but it was enough for the grand jury to issue twenty-six indictments against forty-seven suspects, including Juan José Herrera, Pablo Herrera, Nicanor Herrera, 34-year-old Dario Atencio, Civil War veteran Rafael Lujan, José Lucero, Antonio Lucero, Juan Ortiz, Apolonio Trujillo, Manuel Montaño, and pensioner Teodoso Salas. While none of them could face trial until the district court session convened the following April, Sheriff Lorenzo López was instructed to carry out the arrests as soon as possible.[15]

Although indictments were returned against the Herrera brothers and some of their comrades, the working-class Hispanos were given cause for celebration on the final day of the district court session. Three brothers named José, Francisco, and Pablo Padilla had each fenced in 160 acres of community pastures in 1887 for the express purpose of ensuring their people could utilize the land while also preventing any form of privatization by the Americanos. A representative of the Las Vegas Land and Cattle Company named Philip Milhiser had inevitably sought legal action against them. The monumental district case of *Milhiser vs. Padilla* had stretched for two years until Chief Justice Elisha V. B. Long ruled in favor of the Padilla brothers on November 25, 1889. It was a victory for some of la gente, although the Las Vegas Land Grant issue remained unresolved.[16]

Sheriff Lorenzo López and his deputies were able to arrest Juan José Herrera, Pablo Herrera, Nicanor Herrera, Teodoso Salas, and fifteen other suspected members of the White Caps without any trouble in early December 1889. "[Salas] is quite an old man to be engaged in such work," the *Las Vegas Daily Optic* remarked. It quickly became clear the level of support Los Gorras Blancas enjoyed when three hundred Hispano citizens followed the law officials and their prisoners into Las Vegas. Sheriff López promptly sent a telegram to Governor L. Bradford Prince requesting fifty rifles and additional ammunition on December 11, 1889. "I fear jail will be attacked by a mob," the sheriff pleaded. Territorial Adjutant General Edward W. Wynkoop quickly arrived from Santa Fe with the rifles and ammunition as requested. "For a while it looked like war, but better counsel prevailed," the *New Mexican* would report. "Col. Wynkoop says Sheriff Lopez is handling the affair bravely."[17]

A crowd of Hispano men, women, and children continued gathering outside the jailhouse in support of the Herrera brothers and their fellow prisoners on a daily basis. "Large parties of their friends coming into town," Col. Edward Wynkoop informed Governor L. Bradford Prince, who soon arrived in Las Vegas to investigate the situation himself. "One Santos Gallegos, of Anton Chico, was murdered at 3 o'clock yesterday morning while in camp near Kearney's Gap, another crime laid at the door of the White Cap marauders," the *New Mexican* announced on December 12, 1889. Governor Prince later reported that White Cap and willful outlaw Porfirio Trujillo had indeed shot a man at Kearney's Gap, although the recipient of Trujillo's bullet was merely wounded rather than killed.

The tensions in Las Vegas only increased when more suspected White Caps were arrested, and the defiant Pablo Herrera reportedly assaulted at least one of his jailers. Chief Justice Elisha V. B. Long realized the prisoners in the overcrowded Las Vegas jail could not stand trial for several months and lowered their bonds from $500 to $250 for each offense. The Herrera brothers and their compatriots raised the money with the assistance of their supporters and were released on bonds on December 16, 1889. They received a hero's welcome from over three hundred of their relatives, supporters, and members of the Knights of Labor when emerging from the jailhouse doors. Their female supporters waved American flags while others sang the abolitionist ballad "John Brown's Body" as the large crowd marched through the streets of Las Vegas in celebratory fashion. "These people, in some way, consider themselves martyrs," the *Las Vegas Daily Optic* disdainfully remarked. The newspaper also compared Los Gorras Blancas to the radicals of the French Revolution when accusing the organization of lacking deference for the church or the priesthood.[18]

The Herrera brothers and their compadres had barely left town before a large party of White Caps rode into Las Vegas late one night in December 1889. Their objective was neither intimidation nor destruction of property but rather the posting and distribution of a manifesto titled Nuestra Plataforma (Our Platform). The manifesto—almost certainly written by the educated hand of Juan José Herrera—sharply explained their principles to anyone who could read Spanish:

Our Platform

Not wishing to be misunderstood, we hereby make this our declaration.

Our purpose is to protect the rights and interests of the people in general; especially those of the helpless classes.

We want the Las Vegas Grant settled to the benefit of all concerned, and this we hold is the entire community within the grant. We want no "land grabbers" or obstructionists of any sort to interfere. We will watch them.

We are not down on lawyers as a class, but the usual knavery and unfair treatment of the people must be stopped.

Our judiciary hereafter must understand that we will sustain it only when "Justice" is its watchword.

The practice of "double-dealing" must cease.

There is a wide difference between New Mexico's "law" and "justice." And justice is God's law, and that we must have at all hazards.

We are down on race issues, and will watch race agitators. We are all human brethren, under the same glorious flag.

We favor irrigation enterprises, but will fight any scheme that tends to monopolize the supply of water courses to the detriment of residents living on lands watered by the same streams.

We favor all enterprises, but object to corrupt methods to further the same.

We do not care how much you get so long as you do it fairly and honestly.

The People are suffering from the effects of partisan "bossism" and these bosses had better quietly hold their peace. The people have been persecuted and hacked about in every which way to satisfy their caprice. If they persist in their usual methods retribution will be their reward.

We are watching "political informers."

We have no grudge against any person in particular, but we are the enemies of bulldozers and tyrants.

> We must have a free ballot and a fair count. And the will of the majority shall be respected.
>
> Intimidation and the "indictment" plan have no further fears for us. If the old system should continue, death would be a relief to our sufferings. And for our rights our lives are the least we can pledge.
>
> If the fact that we are law abiding citizens is questioned, come out to our homes and see the hunger and desolation we are suffering; and "this" is the result of the deceitful and corrupt methods of "bossism."
>
> Be fair and just and we are with you, do otherwise and take the consequences.
>
> The White Caps, 1,500 Strong and Growing Daily[19]

District Attorney Miguel Salazar later described the White Caps' *plataforma* as "anarchical, revolutionary, and communistic." While there was an element of truth in all three of Salazar's assertions, the manifesto also professed sentiments of patriotism, antiracism, and above all else, anticorruption. Although Nuestra Plataforma failed to outline a specific long-term solution to the "deceitful and corrupt methods of bossism," the message from the vigilante organization was clear: those who had grown fat at the expense of the common people were the enemy.[20]

Los Gorras Blancas refrained from carrying out any more organized raids until the winter passed, although several of their hard-headed members continued engaging the authorities in anarchical fashion. Having spent the previous two months dodging Sheriff Lorenzo López and his deputies, little Porfirio Trujillo and his gang of bandidos burned an eighty-ton stack of hay on the sheriff's spread in Romeroville that December. Several members of the White Caps reportedly fired shots at a passing train near the San Miguel station during the night of December 23, 1889. The following month cattlemen Stan, Joel, and William Goodley of El Cuervo received a written notice from "the commission of death and fence-cutters" warning them to vacate the countryside.[21]

There was probably nobody more relieved by the decrease in Gorras Blancas operations than Governor L. Bradford Prince in early 1890. The 49-year-old New Yorker was under considerable pressure while preparing to lead a delegation to Washington, DC, to propose statehood for New

Mexico Territory. Factionalism, political infighting, and much of the East and Midwest viewing the Hispano population of Nuevo México as "grossly illiterate, superstitious, and morally decadent," ultimately crushed the delegation's proposal. Governor Prince, Thomas B. Catron, J. Francisco Cháves, and other advocates for statehood had to continue waiting for New Mexico Territory to be admitted to the Union.[22]

***

It became clear that Los Gorras Blancas had merely been waiting for the winter to pass when they launched a stunning offensive against the Atchison, Topeka, and Santa Fe Railway Company on March 6, 1890. An estimated three hundred members of the White Caps cut nine hundred railroad ties in half near San Miguel after subcontractor Eugenio Romero reportedly refused to pay his workers a royalty of one cent per tie. While the *Las Vegas Daily Optic* declared the railroad company "a constant drain against us," the newspaper insisted that "lawlessness is never a good regulator of evil."[23]

After striking against los ferrocarriles near San Miguel Station, more than two hundred members of Los Gorras Blancas rode into Las Vegas to distribute more copies of Nuestra Plataforma during the night of March 10, 1890. "Once I saw more than a hundred pass my home at night, two abreast," recalled county clerk Miguel Antonio Otero Jr. *Las Vegas Daily Optic* editor Russel A. Kistler tried reasoning with the White Caps in a lengthy editorial two days later:

> Citizen "White Caps," come let us reason together. Your interests as citizens of San Miguel county are the same as those of all other law-abiding people in this community.... Some of these laws are bad, but we must never repeal them by the same methods by which they were enacted. It will not do to trample even a bad law underfoot, simply because it is bad. That would be revolutionary and tend to disorganization of society and the consequent unsafety of life and the destruction of all property rights.... We must all obey the law so long as it remains in force upon our statute books, and if it is not a good law in its practical effects, if it works an injury to the people in general, elect men to the legislature who will get it repealed and a good law enacted in its place.... But when you allow your organization to be used to commit a

wrong or do an injury to your neighbor you weaken its power for good, drive away from your support good men who sympathize with your general purposes so far as known, harden and strengthen public opinion against you, and to the extent of your wrongdoing cast yourselves outside of the pale of the law. . . . In all that you do that is in accord with the law, you will find THE OPTIC your friend. In the doing of wrong and the committing of overt acts and acts outside the law and injuries to private individuals or the public, it cannot accompany you. . . . Now we are free to say that we subscribe to much of what you set forth in your "platform." But we don't approve, but on the most heartedly condemn the adoption by you of the name "White Caps." You are good citizens, joined together for lawful and laudable purposes, purposes for which you need not be ashamed to be seen and known of all men. . . . Now then, citizens, we ask you to consider these suggestions. Let us have no more cutting of ties by anyone. No more cutting fences even if they are unlawful.[24]

Los Gorras Blancas were not swayed by Russel Kistler's public appeal and continued their militant campaign. They also appeared to enjoy some semblance of moral support from Spanish-language newspaper *La Voz Del Pueblo* (The Voice of the People) in Las Vegas. "People get tired of waiting forever and sometimes they arouse themselves to action," the newspaper declared on March 15, 1890. Although the Nuevomexicano periodical's educated founder Nestor Montoya and publisher Félix Martínez refrained from openly condoning the cutting of fences, *La Voz Del Pueblo* voiced its support for the Knights of Labor while publicly condemning "capitalists, monopolists and land grabbers."[25]

Los Gorras Blancas expanded their operations by stopping freighters on various roads in San Miguel County in March 1890. If the driver of any team hauling railroad ties wasn't charging their contractors five dollars for every shipment, the White Caps unloaded the ties from the freight wagons and destroyed them. "Lumber teams have also been molested for the same reason," the *New Mexican* would report. Russel A. Kistler quickly changed his tune when realizing his public plea had fallen on deaf ears, demanding "something effective be done by the strong arm of the law to check and punish the White Caps in their mad, determined career." Los Gorras Blancas soon posted another notice around Las Vegas instructing the local

Hispano populace to refrain from cutting railroad ties and lumber unless for a price approved by the organization. They also asked la gente not to work for any employer unless their salary and the work itself received their approval. The notice was ominously signed, "White Caps, Fence Cutters and Death."[26]

The self-indulgent Porfirio Trujillo provoked further hostility from the *Las Vegas Daily Optic* after arriving in the village of Pecos, located six miles above Rowe, on March 23, 1890. Trujillo and his pistol-packing wife left another member of the White Caps named Espirio watching their horses outside of town while the notorious bandido forced two store owners to hand over a fancy suit, some cash, and a large supply of alcohol at gunpoint. "The liquor was made to be passed freely and everyone was compelled to drink," recalled one resident of Howe. "[Trujillo] made several different men and women dance, firing an occasional shot when they did not dance to suit him. In this way he passed most of the night, terrorizing the people."[27]

Francisco "Frank" Antonio Manzanares, the former delegate to Congress, mailed letters to his successor Anthony Joseph and United States Secretary of the Interior John Willcock Noble stating that "the unsettled condition of land grants was responsible for all these White Cap outrages" on March 29, 1890. As if to reinforce the assertions of Manzanares, a party of Gorras Blancas reportedly torched Mora County resident M. G. Gordon's old planing mill below the Las Vegas Hot Springs later that night. French tailor Frank Le Duc's adjacent house had also gone up in flames, although Le Duc later asserted that "tracks showed that two men were engaged in those burnings, and he believed that they lived in the adjoining village." A short time later, six members of Los Gorras Blancas confronted Miguel Salazar outside the district attorney's office in Las Vegas. They wanted to know what Salazar intended to do with the indictments against them for fence cutting and riot.

"Push 'em to the full extent of the law," the determined Salazar informed them.[28]

While Miguel Salazar was investigating the origins of Los Gorras Blancas and preparing for the district court to convene, editor Russel A. Kistler went on the offensive when publicly accusing Juan José Herrera of being the leader of the fence-cutting organization. Kistler demanded Herrera prove his innocence to the people of San Miguel County and explain the reason for his sudden departure from New Mexico Territory in 1866. "There is no denying the fact that [Herrera] is generally charged with being the instigator and leader, and the state of outlawry which now exists is charged directly to him," the *Las Vegas Daily Optic* announced on April 5, 1890. The 52-year-old Juan José Herrera sat down in Las Vegas two days later and wrote a letter to Russel Kistler in response:

> I have noticed an article in your editorial column branding me as a dangerous man in the community. This does me an unfair and uncalled for injustice, and although the same is assumed to some from the editor, I am satisfied it is but the outgrowth of a continuous scheme of persecution carried on by certain designing politicians, who, for no other purpose than political aggrandizement, are willing to sacrifice the interests and peace of the entire community. The unnecessary scare in your city about what the so-called "white-cap element" is about to do, is agitated by their willing tools and emissaries to poison the minds of your people, in order to get your support to prevent the rapid downfall of these designing politicians, who through their corruption and mis-doings, are the sole cause of the present discontent.
>
> As a citizen of this county, I defy any man, be he who he may, to say that I have in any manner, or at any time, advised destruction of property of any individual. . . . I, as a member of the Knights of Labor of New Mexico, stand pledged and ready to settle all differences that may arise regarding wages, by arbitration between communities representing the business men and the working men and the working men of San Miguel county in a friendly, conventional and lawful manner. At the same time, I also stand pledged to assist in supressing any unlawful movement carried on by the "white caps," or any other organization, against the private interests of any individual. . . . I have never heard the least mention in the councils of the Knights of Labor, or in any other place, that such a brutal act as destroying the property of innocent citizens should be even listened to by them . . .
>
> I wish to say that there are facts connected with my leaving the Territory at the time, in 1866, that I do not now wish to bring to public notice, on account of reasons that might affect others more than myself. And I do not care to pursue an innocent woman into the grave . . .
>
> I will continue to fight these designing politicians in a political way to the bitter end, so far from my assisting in any manner, or even suggesting, to disturb the peace and quietude of our community,

I stand ready to render my life in its defense. While I was born in New Mexico, I rejoice in feeling that I am an American, that proud title which embraces all nationalities and races of people that live under our flag and constitution; and I am ready to work and fight to sustain every principle and institution that belongs to our common country.

Yours,
Juan J. Herrera[29]

Juan José Herrera's letter was an eloquently written denial of any association with Los Gorras Blancas and their raids, but District Attorney Miguel Salazar and others were not convinced. El Capitán did not expressly deny his ordering the destruction of property but merely challenged any man to say that he had. Herrera's obvious attempt to distance the Knights of Labor from the White Caps was the result of a growing divide between the two organizations. Although sharing an enmity for land-grabbers and mutual support for worker's rights, the prominent Anglo members of the Knights of Labor were firmly opposed to the cutting of fences by the "Mexican people," whom they described as "of the poorer class" and "ignorant." That was an opinion shared by District Attorney Miguel Salazar, who dismissed Los Gorras Blancas as "ignorant people, easily deceived, and swayed by such wicked and evil designing persons, as this leader and his lieutenants are."[30]

The inherent class snobbery of Anglo members of the Knights of Labor and District Attorney Miguel Salazar diluted their understanding of the impoverished insurgents they were maligning. While most of Los Gorras Blancas had received little—if any—formal education, for a supposedly "ignorant people," their modus operandi demonstrated considerable acumen. The vast majority of their members maintained their anonymity, avoided detection and indictment, and shrewdly carried out their raids with a minimum of civilian bloodshed. Los Gorras Blancas were also careful not to burn anyone alive, as every building they torched was unoccupied at the time. These were not the operations of a mindless rabble who had been manipulated into wicked servitude, but rather a meticulous band of socially conscious revolutionaries, admittedly interwoven with some crafty ruffians. District Attorney Miguel Salazar was underestimating his adversaries.

As the district court session was rapidly approaching, the 37-year-old Manuel Cabeza de Baca wrote a letter to Governor L. Bradford Prince on April 15, 1890. The probate judge of San Miguel County informed Prince that his expensive barbed wire fence had recently been cut and suggested the formation of a militia to deal with Los Gorras Blancas. A railroad bridge had also recently gone up in flames near the Las Vegas Hot Springs. "Numerous complaints had been filed with the county commissioners, asking them to hire detectives and 'secret officers' to bring to the courts the perpetrators," county clerk Miguel Antonio Otero Jr. later recalled. The White Caps also continued their push for increased hauling rates that month. "It is reported from an authentic source that the so-called 'white caps' have ordered Mexican freighters and forwarders to raise the freight tariff from seventy-five cents a hundred pounds to $1.50., threatening to demolish the wagons, kill the teams and ruin the harness of those who do not comply with the order," the *Las Vegas Daily Optic* announced on April 19. There were additional reports that bands of White Caps had burned several houses near Red River and on the Vermajo up in Taos County.[31]

District Attorney Miguel Salazar had high hopes when the fourth district court session opened on the morning of April 21, 1890. Presiding over the court was 53-year-old Judge James O'Brien, an Irish-born Civil War veteran and former state senator from Minnesota who had only recently arrived in the territory following his appointment as chief justice of the New Mexico Supreme Court by President Benjamin Harrison. It was a lengthy district court session that spring, with Thomas B. Catron, "Colonel" George W. Prichard, Frank Springer, Elisha V. B. Long, and various other attorneys handling the over four hundred cases on the docket. A special commission was appointed to fill several vacancies on the grand jury, and an almost entirely Hispano petit jury including Lincoln County luminary Florencio Gonzáles were sworn in. County Clerk Miguel Antonio Otero Jr. had recovered from a recent illness and was in attendance throughout proceedings.[32]

News soon reached Las Vegas that Los Gorras Blancas had struck again while the district court was in session. A party of White Caps had burned Italian foreman Albert Alberti's intended new house on the old Jacobi ranch on Mora Road three miles outside of Las Vegas during the night of May 3, 1890.

"I am satisfied that a secret organization is responsible for some acts, still I believe that others entirely out of the White Cap league are the authors of outrages to satisfy private animosities," Albert Alberti later remarked. It was a good time for any ruffian to settle personal grievances under the guise of Gorras Blancas insurgency in San Miguel County. "This is the fourth building burned in that vicinity without any apparent cause in the last six weeks, not to say anything about the railroad bridge," the *Las Vegas Daily Optic* declared. "A Pinkerton would seem necessary in that immediate locality."[33]

When the time came for Miguel Salazar to push his twenty-six indictments against Juan José Herrera, Pablo Herrera, Nicanor Herrera, José Lucero, Antonio Lucero, Dario Atencio, Rafael Lujan, Teodoso Salas, Juan Ortiz, Apolonio Trujillo, Manuel Montaño, and thirty-five other suspected members of Los Gorras Blancas for fence cutting and riot, the district attorney was left wanting. The three witnesses from whom Salazar had procured confessions during the previous term of court were nowhere to be found. Sheriff Lorenzo López had spent thirty days trying to locate them throughout the countryside, but to no avail. "The court then, under the pressure of counsel for the defendants for an immediate trial, and seeing no chance of procuring the witnesses for the Territory, dismissed all those cases from the docket," Salazar bitterly recalled. The district attorney suspected his three witnesses had been silenced by Los Gorras Blancas in bloody fashion. "The general belief is, that those witnesses have been killed and disposed of by the white caps, and in that way prevent prosecution against them," Salazar informed Governor L. Bradford Prince.[34]

The Herrera brothers and their compadres defiantly gathered in the plaza outside the Las Vegas courthouse with hundreds of their Hispano relatives and supporters shortly after Judge James O'Brien dismissed all charges against them on May 19, 1890. "For three hours were harangued by members of their crowd, some shooting pistols in the air, and all in the most excited way, denouncing the public officers and the laws," Governor Prince later wrote. Prince would have been further dismayed when learning that Chief Justice James O'Brien sympathized with the Hispano insurgents like an old Irish rebel. "To a casual and impartial observer, ignorant of antecedent causes, the so-called outrages are the protests of a simple, pastoral people against the establishment of large landed estates, or baronial feudalism, in their native territory," Judge O'Brien informed the governor. "The term White Cap, when used in any other sense, is, in my opinion, a misnomer."[35]

While the Herrera brothers and hundreds of Hispanos were causing a stir outside the courthouse in Las Vegas, Porfirio Trujillo surprisingly surrendered to Eugenio Romero at the respected county assessor's ranch the same day. The dangerous fugitive was transported to the district court and arraigned on indictments for carrying deadly weapons, discharging firearms, and resisting an officer on May 19, 1890. "Trujillo has been 'in the woods,' a fugitive from justice for the past year," the *New Mexican* declared. The bandido entered a plea of not guilty to all three charges. Trujillo was then released on $200 worth of bonds despite remaining under indictment for his alleged participation in the killing of three Rock Creek sheepherders named Joseph Leckie, Julian Tessiere, and Jesús Trujillo several years earlier in Santa Fe County.[36]

Exactly where the 40-year-old José Chávez y Chávez was throughout the chaotic district court session in the spring of 1890 remains uncertain. While José continued performing his duties as a city policeman in Las Vegas, it is impossible to determine the extent of his covert activities as a member of Los Gorras Blancas. Whatever late-night raids in which he may have participated, the former Lincoln County Regulator successfully concealed his identity beneath his *gorra*. He kept his mouth shut like a good soldier. José had plenty of experience at dodging pursuers and was good at keeping secrets. The devout Roman-Catholic policeman had also joined the supremely tight-lipped Penitentes and left various scars upon his back while engaging in self-flagellation.

If José Chávez y Chávez was inclined to participate in raids carried out by Los Gorras Blancas, the muscular Penitente received ample opportunity to do so throughout the summer of 1890. White Cap operations only increased after Judge James O'Brien dismissed all charges against the Herrera brothers and their compadres.[37]

***

Twenty-four miles southeast of Las Vegas, a 37-year-old farmer from Maryland named John Boon Snouffer found a note attached to one of his fence posts near the railroad settlement called Fulton in late May 1890. The note warned Snouffer and his neighbor W. C. Wright, a station master for the Atchison, Topeka, and Santa Fe Railway Company, to vacate their farms within fifteen days. A short time later, six masked hombres with Winchester rifles and drawn revolvers confronted Snouffer and "informed him not to remove the electric light poles which he was getting out under contract for Las Vegas under penalty of death." A band of Gorras Blancas subsequently burned down the farmer's recently furnished house during the night of June 4, 1890. The White Caps soon returned to cut both Snouffer and W. C. Wright's barbed wire fences, also shooting Wright in his thigh and the back of his neck during another late-night raid. "The next act was the burning of my store after which I deemed it unsafe to stay there any longer," Snouffer recalled. The frightened farmer moved to Las Vegas with his wife Elizabeth and their four young children. "The fence cutters are alienating all sympathy from them by their lawless acts," the *Las Vegas Daily Optic* declared. "These barbarians must be brought to justice."[38]

Civil War veteran and attorney "Captain" Lewis C. Fort's barbed wire fence had already been leveled on his Tie Camp ranch twelve miles northwest of Las Vegas when his house was razed to the ground during another late-night raid on the evening of June 15, 1890. "Mr. Fort thinks that it is possible for a building to be burned down in New Mexico, that was not fired by the White Caps or other miscreants," the *Las Vegas Daily Optic* skeptically announced two days later. A barbed wire fence belonging to Ozra Amander Hadley, the former acting governor of Arkansas and president of the Northern New Mexico Stockgrowers Association, was also cut down farther northeast in Watrous, Mora County. One of Hadley's employees was wounded when confronting the hooded night riders and protesting the destruction of his employer's fence.[39]

Los Gorras Blancas continued their raids on an unprecedented scale throughout the remainder of June 1890. G. O. Scott, who had arrived from Denver several months earlier after purchasing the old Lynch milk ranch near Tecolote from Las Vegas liveryman Robert Oakley, reported that five miles of his barbed wire fence had been cut and his house ransacked. French-Canadian merchants Frédéric-Alexis Desmarais and Octave Geoffrion's fences were cut to pieces near Tecolote Creek around the same time. By the end of the month, three railroad bridges had been burned, sixty telegraph poles cut down, and barbed wire fences leveled on Mary Ann Hommel's ranch in Conchas, the recently widowed Louisa Desmarais Bernard's ranch in Trementina, and former ladies' hat manufacturer George G. Heckle's ranch on Red River in Taos County.[40]

As White Cap insurgency swelled throughout the countryside, the Herrera brothers and roughly seven hundred members of Los Caballeros del Trabajo lit beacon fires on the hilltop above the old fairgrounds of Las Vegas and marched through the metropolis with pitch blue torches on the night of July 3, 1890. Juan José, Pablo, and Nicanor Herrera then hosted a grand baile that lasted until the early hours of the morning. Governor L. Bradford Prince was in town when the Herrera brothers and roughly two thousand members of Los Caballeros del Trabajo held their own parade amid the usual Independence Day festivities in Las Vegas on the afternoon of July 4, 1890. Some Americano spectators were undoubtedly shocked when they spotted Sheriff Lorenzo López, who had recently left the Republican party after a falling out with his brother-in-law Eugenio Romero, happily leading the large procession on horseback. The demands for "Free schools for our children" and "War against the public officials who don't account for their administration," as well as exclamations such as "We seek protection for the worker against the monopolist," were displayed on various banners as the local Knights marched through the streets of Las Vegas in broad daylight. "El pueblo es rey, y los oficiales públicos son Sus sirvientes humildes que deben obedecer Sus mandatos" (The people are king, and public officials are her humble servants who must obey her mandates), they collectively shouted.[41]

Los Caballeros del Trabajo gathered in the old town plaza to host a grand barbeque after their eye-opening demonstration in Las Vegas. *La Voz Del Pueblo* editor and Knights of Labor member Nestor Montoya proudly introduced the organization to the locals before Juan José, Pablo, and Nicanor Herrera gave rousing speeches. East Las Vegas Mayor Edward Henry and former Republican legislator Theodore B. Mills attended the barbeque and publicly praised their efforts. Governor L. Bradford Prince gave a short address to the public following the customary fireworks display, thanking everyone for the patriotic celebration and wishing them Godspeed. "Yesterday's parade of the Knights of Labor was quiet, orderly, and gentlemanly," the *Las Vegas Daily Optic* announced the following day. "There was no display of power, except as franchised citizens; no drunkenness; no trouble of any kind."[42]

Having recently recovered from a nervous breakdown, Governor L. Bradford Prince finally began his crusade to stamp out the White Caps in the summer of 1890. Prince believed the secretive organization enjoyed the unspoken support of at least half the population of San Miguel County. He also suspected Los Gorras Blancas and Los Caballeros del Trabajo were one and the same. Prince had long been accused of aligning with the Santa Fe Ring, had recently been controversially quoted describing the Hispano population of New Mexico as "greasers," and had his own considerable financial investments to safeguard from a potential revolution. "The villain who dares occupy a public position without being elected by the people shall be hanged," proclaimed one of the banners displayed by Los Caballeros del Trabajo during their Independence Day parade in Las Vegas. Charles Bent, the first American governor of Nuevo México, had been assassinated inside his home by Pueblo natives at the behest of Mexican insurgents just four decades earlier during the Taos Revolt of January 1847. LeBaron Bradford Prince was no fool. While the Independence Day demonstration held by the local Knights of Labor was an orderly affair in Las Vegas, the White Caps continued their militant operations throughout the month of July 1890.[43]

As parties of Gorras Blancas patrolled the outskirts of Las Vegas on a nightly basis, other bands of White Caps carried out multiple raids against prominent businessman Eduardo Martínez, stockman José Sánchez, and farmer Candelario Rael in Anton Chico. "Fence cutters are after Eduardo Martinez in Anton Chico," the *New Mexican* announced on July 12, 1890. Los Gorras Blancas struck again when cutting barbed wire fences belonging to Sheriff Lorenzo López, Francisco "Frank" Antonio Manzanares, Eugenio Romero, and Canadian merchant Charles Blanchard during the night of July 17, 1890. Some local businessmen and Anglo ranchers were appalled when the 54-year-old Sheriff López capitulated with the White Caps by tearing down the rest of his fence himself. The *Las Vegas Daily Optic* initially reported that *La Voz Del Pueblo* publisher Félix Martínez's fence was also cut, until the proud Nuevomexicano informed a correspondent that he had recently coiled his own barbed wire voluntarily.[44]

W. J. Mills, who worked as the foreman of Wilson Waddingham's ranch in Romeroville, was surprised to find a note written in Spanish attached to a gatepost less than one hundred yards from his quarters on the morning of July 19, 1890. The Americano could only scratch his head in confusion until someone translated the politely written warning for him:

> Sir
> This notice is with the object of requesting you coil up your wire as soon as possible from the North and South sides. They are fences which are damaging the unhappy people and we request you further to coil up your wire as soon as you can to the agricultural land, and if you do not do it, you will suffer the consequences from us.
>
> Your Servants,
> The White Caps.[45]

W. J. Mills enclosed a copy of the notice with a letter detailing recent events to Governor Prince, who was corresponding with various citizens whom the White Caps had raided. Prince also received a letter courtesy of Secretary of the Interior John W. Noble signed by Civil War general and former governor of Massachusetts Benjamin F. Butler on July 21, 1890. The letter included a list of twenty-five "outrages" allegedly committed by Los Gorras Blancas during the previous fourteen months. The governor issued a public notice later that day, offering a $100 reward "to the person or persons furnishing information leading to the conviction" of anyone responsible for the destruction of fences, railroad ties, or any property in San Miguel County. "I am afraid that unless an effective and strong remedy is used against the said leader and its lieutenants, the organization will increase throughout the territory to monster proportions," District Attorney Miguel Salazar informed Prince in a letter of his own. The White Caps of Nuevo México were now the subject of newspaper reports in Missouri, Kansas, Indiana, Minnesota, Pennsylvania, Connecticut, New Jersey, and various other states across the country. This wouldn't do at all.[46]

Los Gorras Blancas were not discouraged by Governor Prince's $100 reward notice. That quickly became evident when a band of White Caps raided Louisa Desmarais Bernard's ranch for the second time and destroyed her rebuilt barbed wire fence in Trementina during the night of July 25, 1890. The fact that Louisa was the sole provider for her six children following the recent death of her husband Joseph Bernard left an especially bitter taste in the mouths of those opposed to the White Caps and their raids. What's more, the widow's ranch had been constructed on government land rather than the communal pastures of the Las Vegas Land Grant. The White Caps struck again when cutting down forty rods of fencing along a rancher named Clark's cornfield to the west of the Las Vegas Land Grant the following night. "There remains no doubt now but that the fence-cutting is done by a handful of agitators who can restrain or turn loose the dogs of destruction at will," the *Las Vegas Daily Optic* remarked.

The "dogs of destruction" were at it again when fourteen miles of barbed wire fence belonging to Col. Roswell G. Wheeler was cut to pieces on his Pagosa pastures east of Las Vegas while the former Indian agent was away on business in Alameda, California, on July 28, 1890. "The fence-cutter is getting more numerous and more decidedly ubiquitous than ever," the *Las Vegas Daily Optic* declared. "It has been suggested by a thinking citizen, for many years a resident in Las Vegas, that Maj. Miguel Salazar, the prosecuting attorney, request the court at its next session to reinstate those indictments against the fence-cutters, which were dismissed in May by Judge James O'Brien."[47]

Governor L. Bradford Prince meant business when issuing a proclamation in both Spanish and English on August 1, 1890. The officials of the Atchison, Topeka, and Santa Fe Railway Company had informed him they would no longer purchase crossties in New Mexico Territory on account of White Cap insurgency, thus depriving San Miguel County of $100,000 in annual revenue. Prince openly condemned the "companies of masked men" who had been "organized for the purpose of performing such evil deeds," and called upon "all good citizens to aid the civil authorities in the discovery of the perpetrators of these crimes." The governor insisted that "two wrongs cannot make a right," and that "order must and will be restored."

He also publicly threatened Los Gorras Blancas with the potential establishment of a territorial militia or calling upon the United States army to wipe out their insurrection. "The White Caps must go and at that speedily," the *New Mexican* declared. "If the ordinary methods of the law are not sufficient, why extraordinary methods must be taken."[48]

Having read Governor Prince's proclamation, Juan José and Pablo Herrera stormed into the *Las Vegas Daily Optic* headquarters in East Las Vegas to confront Russel A. Kistler and his staff on the morning of August 4, 1890. The animated Pablo Herrera insisted the "political bosses in San Miguel County" were "directly blameable for all this fence-cutting business," and held "a silent hand in all the depredations being perpetrated by the so-called White Cap element." Pablo further insisted that he could produce the necessary evidence to support his claim. "Out with it, Don Pablo—out with it," the *Daily Optic* implored later that evening. The same day, Los Gorras Blancas instructed the Hispano railroad workers in Rowe and Fulton to quit their positions if they failed to receive an increase on their current wage of $1.40 per day's work or "suffer the consequences." Thirty railroad workers employed by John Lawrence Laub at Rowe Station promptly went on strike, refusing to cut any more ties until their demands were met. J. L. Laub's store was eventually burned to the ground during a late-night raid.[49]

True to his word, Governor L. Bradford Prince had requested assistance from Washington in the form of federal troops and suggested hiring detectives to infiltrate the White Caps in a letter to Secretary of the Interior John W. Noble on August 11, 1890. "There can be no doubt that there is a secret oath-bound organization in San Miguel County, and extending now into the adjoining counties," Prince informed Noble. "It is believed to be confined entirely to natives of New Mexico, and almost entirely to the most ignorant class. As nearly as can be ascertained, a few active and educated men have arranged this organization." Although his request for military assistance was denied, Prince tried using the Nuevomexicano insurgents' religious faith against them. The governor approached Archbishop Jean-Baptiste Salpointe in Santa Fe and urged him to "exert an active influence against the formation of such secret societies for illegal purposes."[50]

In his quest to divide and conquer the Hispano insurgents, Governor Prince found an ally in Terence Vincent Powderly, the grand master of the national Knights of Labor. Prince wrote to the 41-year-old Pennsylvanian asking him to impose his authority and weed out members of the union engaging in the destruction of property in New Mexico Territory. Powderly also received a letter from New Mexico signed by Frank C. Ogden and several other Anglo Knights whining about the infiltration of their organization by "ignorant" Hispanos and "the self-called White Caps." A passive utopian, Terence V. Powderly had long been opposed to the use of force, and even peaceful strikes, within his union. This conflicted with Juan José Herrera's hard-nosed militant convictions on the southwestern frontier. After all, it was through armed revolution that the United States of America had been founded and Mexico had won its independence from the Spanish Empire decades earlier.[51]

Juan José Herrera and Governor L. Bradford Prince were both in attendance for a public meeting called by Chairman Stephen E. Booth and his board of commissioners to address the White Cap rebellion inside the Las Vegas courthouse on August 16, 1890. Nestor Montoya served as interpreter while his fellow Caballeros del Trabajo member Félix Martínez delivered a stirring speech in which he called for the eradication of both land-grabbers and fence cutters. His address was very well received by the large crowd, including Russel A. Kistler. "While fence-cutting is wrong, in the eyes of the law a heinous crime, still the crime of grabbing land, fencing up pasturage, water, wood and road-ways from the people to whom the privilege of access belongs, is a still greater crime," Kistler soon wrote in the *Las Vegas Daily Optic*. Governor Prince could read the room and tried to keep the focus on fence cutting when addressing the crowd. The New Yorker estimated that four-fifths of those in attendance held sympathies for the White Cap organization. Juan José Herrera gave a speech of his own and naturally denied leadership of Los Gorras Blancas. Nobody knew what nobody knew. The very next night, a band of White Caps destroyed five and a half miles of barbed wire fence on the Phoenix Farm and Ranching Company's pastures one mile west of Watrous in Mora County.[52]

A sense of common ground between those opposed to land grabbing and those opposed to both land grabbing and fence cutting was solidified during the mass meeting in Las Vegas. Juan José Herrera realized many local citizens, even some of those firmly against White Cap insurgency, were now ready for a political revolution in San Miguel County. While routinely condemned by the territorial press, Los Gorras Blancas undeniably played a leading role in awakening much of the local populace to the corruption plaguing their homeland and the realization that social and political change could be possible. "Land-grabbers and boodlers have long lived off the poor people in this fair land," Russel A. Kistler proclaimed in the *Las Vegas Daily Optic* on August 18, 1890. "For years and years, it has been made the speculation ground for cast-off politicians, the has-beens of the effete east." While the leading newspaper in San Miguel County was espousing remarkably similar sentiments to the declarations made by the White Caps in Nuestra Plataforma, Juan José Herrera and his brothers decided that politics was the way forward. Los Gorras Blancas remained active for the time being, although on a much smaller scale.[53]

As public sentiment was shifting in favor of political and economic reform in San Miguel County, a pronunciamento was distributed and posted throughout Las Vegas announcing the establishment of an independent political party called el Partido del Pueblo Unido (the United People's Party) on August 25, 1890. The declaration had been signed by Theodore B. Mills, Juan José Herrera, Nicanor Herrera, Nestor Montoya, Probate Judge Manuel Cabeza de Baca, Francis A. Blake, and twenty-seven other prominent Hispano and Anglo citizens. *La Voz Del Pueblo* naturally served as the new party's mouthpiece, and the pronunciamento was published by Russel A. Kistler and the *Las Vegas Daily Optic* later that evening.

"A cry of discontent has become general among the people of San Miguel County on account of party abuses committed against the sovereignty, and public and private interests of the same, especially the interests of the working people," the pronunciamento read. "Now, therefore, in compliance with the wishes of a great many of the citizens of this county, it is requested by these presents, that a meeting of the people of the whole county, by means of a representation of one delegate from each precinct, which delegate shall represent the will of the people of his respective precinct as a member to act as a Central committee man in the organization of a party to be called The United People's Party." The objective of the meeting was described as "obtaining a determined and absolute reform of the administration of public affairs in our county, which change we hope shall inure to the benefit and welfare of the community," and scheduled to take place inside the Las Vegas courthouse the following Monday. In the meantime, Nicanor Herrera begrudgingly paid a fine of fifty-two dollars, pending an appeal, following his arrest for carrying a concealed weapon in Las Vegas on September 2, 1890.[54]

For anyone paying attention, it was surely no coincidence that when Juan José Herrera decided to take on the system through political means that White Cap raids suddenly decreased throughout the autumn of 1890. El Capitán was now more focused on trying to change the system from the inside.

***

El Partido del Pueblo Unido held their first meeting inside the Las Vegas courthouse as scheduled on September 8, 1890. Theodore B. Mills was elected president and Nestor Montoya elected secretary. Félix Martínez, *La Voz Del Pueblo* staff members Juan Gallegos and Enrique H. Salazar, and merchant Manuel Silva were elected to the executive committee. The new committee called for local citizens to attend the United People's Party's first convention, scheduled to commence in the Las Vegas courthouse on September 15. In the meantime, *La Voz Del Pueblo* continued promoting the United People's Party as a viable alternative for disillusioned Republicans and Democrats: an anti-monopolist party to represent the interests of working-class farmers, laborers, mechanics, and ranchers rather than a political and commercial elite.[55]

Having abandoned the Republican Party and joined el Partido del Pueblo Unido, Sheriff Lorenzo López had recently opened a threatening letter inside the Las Vegas post office. The typed message was an attempt at blackmail regarding the city policemen like José Chávez y Chávez and José Valdéz serving under Sheriff López's authority in Las Vegas:

MR. SHERIFF: It is a notorious fact that the men you have as policemen are prominent members of the "white cap" or "nights of labor" organization and, under such circumstances, are not fit persons to protect the lives and property of the community. You being the high officer of this county and who, by virtue of your office, is supposed to guard the law and order of this district, ought to, in justice to yourself and the good people of this county, discharge those men at once and put in their places honest and honorable men, not belonging to any lawless organization; and, if you do not discharge those officers, the good people will believe such a charge. We give you a fair warning, for, if you do not heed this, our protest, it will be our duty to report you to the judge of this district, to the prosecutor, to the governor and the county commissioners.

TAXPAYERS OF SAN MIGUEL COUNTY

Lorenzo López disregarded the warning, having already decided not to run for reelection as sheriff that year. Theodore B. Mills mentioned the letter López had received during his speech at the United People's Party committee meeting on September 8, describing it as "an earnest of what extreme measures would be resorted to by the opposition to the people's movement" and dismissing its anonymous author as a "debaucher," a "thief," and a "coward."[56]

The establishment of el Partido del Pueblo Unido became a hot topic throughout the countryside, and roughly two thousand residents of San Miguel County arrived in Las Vegas for the commencement of the new party's convention on September 15, 1890. Some citizens had traveled over three hundred miles to be there. Theodore B. Mills and Nestor Montoya gave speeches for the 1,500 people squeezed inside the judicial hall as hundreds of other arrivals listened intently outside the courthouse walls. The convention lasted for three days, with the party's platform reinforced for all in attendance. El Partido del Pueblo Unido wanted the Las Vegas Land Grant issue resolved by the legislature in accordance with the Treaty of Guadalupe Hidalgo as soon as possible. They also demanded considerable improvements to the public school system, among various other issues.[57]

It quickly became apparent that Thomas B. Catron and the Republicans of Santa Fe were feeling a little threatened by the emergence of el Partido del Pueblo Unido when their *New Mexican* mouthpiece began devoting considerable space in their daily newspaper to attacking "the White Cap-United People's party." The *New Mexican* declared the Republicans the "party of law and order" and suggested, "The White Cap party is drooping" as early as September 8, 1890. "The leaders of the White Cap-United People's party in San Miguel County are showing the cloven hoofs," the newspaper declared the following day. "All they want is offices and the spoils of power and office. They care not a continental red cent for the well being or welfare of the poor dupes who have done their bidding heretofore and have committed illegal acts, deeds of lawlessness and outrages under the cover of darkness and mask."[58]

Following a relatively quiet August, the White Caps made up for lost time during one carefully orchestrated raid in Mora County in September 1890. A large band of Gorras Blancas destroyed nine miles of R. G. Head's barbed wire fence on the Phoenix Farm and Ranch Company's pastures one mile west of Watrous, fourteen miles of "the devil's hat-band" on Mahlon Harrold's nearby property, an additional five miles of Ozra Amander Hadley's barbed wire enclosure, and four miles of fence belonging to Civil War veteran "Captain" William B. Brunton, all during the night of September 18. "The enormity of the work required to destroy the fences shows that no small number of men were at work, as they must have been no less than three hundred engaged in the crime," the *Las Vegas Daily Optic* declared. "The White Caps do their work very effectually, cutting of the posts about half way from the ground, and cutting the wires between every post so that it is impossible to use the material again," the *New Mexican* bitterly announced.[59]

While the White Caps put away their *gorras* for the remainder of the month, Juan José, Pablo, and Nicanor Herrera assisted Félix Martínez with the organization of a county ticket at the United People's Party convention held in Las Vegas on September 30, 1890. Proceedings lasted through the night until a ticket was finalized the following morning. Pablo Herrera, Nestor Montoya, Pablo Aragón, and Chaperito resident Félix García emerged as the nominees for the house of representatives. Theodore B. Mills, Las Vegas policeman José Valdéz, and Hermerejildo Vigil won the nominations for the territorial council. Lorenzo López's 27-year-old son José L. López was nominated for county sheriff, Dionicio Martínez was nominated for probate judge, Las Vegas *Stock Grower* editor R. F. Hardy was nominated for probate clerk, Jesús María Tafoya was nominated for treasurer, and Charles F. Rudulph was nominated for superintendent of public schools. José Montoya, laborer Antonio Solano, and Las Vegas Street Railway Company Superintendent John Shank were nominated for the board of county commissioners.[60]

Antonio Joseph, a self-serving Freemason and suspected member of the Santa Fe Ring, also attended the United People's Party convention in Las Vegas. The opportunistic Democrat reportedly donated $1,400 to the independent party's campaign funds in exchange for their support in his ultimately successful bid for reelection as New Mexico's delegate to Congress. When the Democrats of San Miguel County declined to organize a ticket of their own for the upcoming elections, instead preferring to ride the coattails of the people's movement, the Republicans of Santa Fe naturally derided el Partido del Pueblo Unido as mere puppets of the Democratic Party. "A good many decent and patriotic Democrats in San Miguel County will vote for the Republican ticket," the *New Mexican* insisted. "A vote for Joseph means a vote for the White Cap element and lawlessness in New Mexico." While Antonio Joseph represented the kind of political and commercial elite the hardliners of el Partido del Pueblo Unido opposed, the party needed all the campaign funds they could acquire. They would also need Democratic voters like the late Juan Patrón's father-in-law Lorenzo Labadie when election day arrived.[61]

As Republicans were scrambling to discredit an unnervingly popular independent party that could upset the political order of things, the United People's Party pressed on with their campaign in San Miguel County. Russel A. Kistler quickly turned away from them when learning "fence cutters" were on their "mongrel ticket" and resumed his feverish support for the Republican Party. "The election of the white cap element to control the county affairs, would be the direst calamity which ever befell any community," the *Las Vegas Daily Optic* melodramatically declared. "War, pestilence, famine, earthquake and tornado might combine to devastate San Miguel County, and the result would be less hurtful to its future prosperity than would be the putting of this lawless element into control of the county." The United People's Party still enjoyed the support of *La Voz Del Pueblo* and its political allies the *Albuquerque Democrat* and *Albuquerque Journal*. The *Albuquerque Journal* suggested that a newspaper should "procure its information as regards the character of those who compose the people's movement in San Miguel County" from sources other than Thomas B. Catron and Max Frost, the secretary of the New Mexico Bureau of Immigration and editor of the *Santa Fe New Mexican*.[62]

Although the White Caps did not carry out any raids during the month of October, some of their remaining members made their existence known in Santa Fe County as the elections drew closer. One hundred Gorras Blancas paraded through Lamy with a strip of white cloth concealing their horses' loins and distributed notices to the public during the night of October 25, 1890. The same band of White Caps eventually rode to José Leon Madrid's home around midnight. They fired their pistols into the air and left a note warning the Republican to keep his mouth shut about them or "suffer the consequences." They also posted a notice at Colorado businessman H. D. McAllister's nearby charcoal ovens operated by the Sayle brothers:

> All who have work for the ovens are required to receive the sum of $3 per cord for cutting and hauling wood, to haul and deliver in the yard, and all choppers to receive $1 per cord, and all persons hiring men at less than this are required to raise these rates at once or accept the consequences from an indignant public.
>
> THE PEOPLE[63]

The *New Mexican* reported that forty citizens of Santa Fe County who were "known to be working for the success of the Republican county ticket" had received threatening anonymous letters from the local White Caps several days later. Forty-five-year-old Lamy resident Lucien N. "John" Fewell, who had recently been dubiously acquitted for the murder of Edward Norman

Bacheldor in Española four years earlier, delivered the letter he had received to *New Mexican* editor Max Frost for publication:

> John Fewell alias Pistol Johny (murder) Yow Think Yow are smart by Looking out and working agints Friends. Friends of the People, the People (on the Democratic Ticket). Yow Had Better Stop this at once, and keep away on Election day from Lamy; for Your Wifes and Childrens Sake.
>
> THE PEOPLE[64]

The *New Mexican* soon announced the installment of an "Election Law" forbidding anyone other than election officials, two partisan challengers, and every individual voter from stepping within ten yards of any polling place on election day. Anyone convicted of violating the provision would either receive a heavy fine or be jailed for at least three months.[65]

"The chief trouble with the people's party is that it lacks people," a Republican campaigner snidely declared in San Miguel County on October 29, 1890. Later that evening, Juan José Herrera, Pablo Herrera, Félix Martínez, R. F. Hardy, Antonio Solano, janitor Albino Baca, Delegate to Congress Antonio Joseph, and the esteemed Lorenzo Labadie all boarded a train in Las Vegas with a four-piece band to give speeches at a grand rally organized by the United People's Party in the town of San Miguel. "The attendance of voters from all the surrounding settlements was quite large," the *Las Vegas Daily Optic* begrudgingly admitted. "If desertions from the people's party, so called, continue as they have during the last five days, our majority will approximate 2000," an anonymous Republican wrote in Las Vegas on November 1, 1890. "It is said that even the White Caps have morning sickness and meditate suicide when they think about that unhallowed, chumpy, illiterate, so-called people's ticket."[66]

The overconfident Republicans were horrified to find out just how many voters el Partido del Pueblo Unido had at their disposal when election day finally arrived on November 4, 1890. The United People's Party had cleaned house once all the ballots were counted across the sixty-three precincts of San Miguel County. Nestor Montoya, Pablo Aragón, Félix García, and ex-convict Pablo Herrera were elected to the house of representatives. Theodore B. Mills and Hermerejildo Vigil both won a seat in the territorial council. Dionicio Martínez annihilated his Republican opponent Ramón Ulibarrí to win the office of probate judge, R. F. Hardy won the election for probate clerk, Jesús María Tafoya was elected county treasurer, and Charles Rudulph slaughtered Republican incumbent Dr. John Barney Pettyjohn to become the new superintendent of public schools. People's candidates José Montoya, Antonio Solano, and John Shank were elected to the board of county commissioners, Nepomuceno Segura was elected county assessor, and policeman José Valdéz was elected coroner. In the biggest shocker of them all, Partido del Pueblo Unido candidate José L. López easily defeated Republican jefe Eugenio Romero to win the office of county sheriff.[67]

The people had spoken and shifted the political landscape of San Miguel County with one trip to the ballot box on November 4, 1890. The *Santa Fe New Mexican* and *Las Vegas Daily Optic* suddenly had very little to say about "the White Cap element," beyond publishing the election results and howling that "illegal voting under the supervision of the White Cap bosses" must have occurred. "Out of all the surprises that were in store for the Republican Party, the County of San Miguel was the paralyzer," the *Albuquerque Democrat* declared. "For many years that County has been controlled by the political parasites who make their headquarters of operation in the capital of the Territory."

In addition to the usual campaign victory celebrations taking place throughout the countryside, Juan José Herrera proudly led six marshals and five hundred supporters carrying torches and flags through the streets of Las Vegas one night like a conquering hero. "¡Qué viva el Partido de Pueblo Unido en el Condado de San Miguel! (Long live the United People's Party in San Miguel County!), they shouted for all within earshot. Even Russel A. Kistler objected when Juan José and Pablo Herrera were indicted for "resisting officers in the lawful discharge of their duties" and their younger brother Nicanor was indicted for discharging his revolver in the plaza. "Why not others, if they?" the *Las Vegas Daily Optic* asked. "It's alright and proper to prosecute, but will not do to persecute."[68]

With the rousing success of el Partido del Pueblo Unido in the county elections, White Cap raids largely ceased throughout the countryside.

The organization had served its purpose and dissolved into small splinter groups of hooded agitators. "Occasionally one would hear of small groups of White Caps cutting fences and burning barns, but nothing more on a large scale," recalled Miguel Antonio Otero Jr. "Gradually the roughnecks disappeared, and quiet was restored throughout San Miguel County."[69]

***

Pablo Herrera was uncharacteristically wearing a seventy-dollar suit of clothes donated by businessman Marcus Brunswick when arriving in Santa Fe with his fellow delegates Nestor Montoya, Pablo Aragón, Félix García, Theodore B. Mills, and Hermerejildo Vigil in late December 1890. While his younger brother Nicanor would also arrive in the Holy City with his family, their older brother Juan José spent most of his time that month trying to broaden their radical influence in Albuquerque. A former convict himself, Pablo visited the territorial penitentiary and discussed various matters with the inmates before entering the legislative chambers of the territorial house and council on the morning of December 29, 1890.[70]

As crowds of people continued flocking to the territorial capital, Pablo Herrera, Nestor Montoya, Pablo Aragón, and Félix García swore their oaths and took their seats in the house of representatives after the Twenty-Ninth Legislative Assembly of New Mexico Territory convened on the morning of December 29, 1890. Their Partido del Pueblo Unido compatriots Theodore B. Mills and Hermerejildo Vigil took their respective seats in the territorial council alongside Thomas B. Catron, J. Francisco Cháves, and eight other delegates. "Never was so much interest manifested in any public assemblage," the *New Mexican* declared. "Prominent citizens were present from every quarter of the territory." J. Francisco Cháves was elected president of the assembly ahead of Theodore B. Mills following the arrival of territorial secretary Dr. Benjamin Morris Thomas that afternoon.[71]

The 45-year-old Pablo Herrera mostly remained silent for the first fifteen days of the Twenty-Ninth Legislative Assembly as various bills were presented and passed. Pablo was unimpressed with what he observed. He was also aware that his mere presence in the chamber was a major point of contention with the Republican reactionaries in attendance. The *New Mexican* had barely waited for the assembly to open before excoriating the representatives of San Miguel County in the Spanish-language edition of their newspaper. *El Nuevo Mexicano* described Pablo Herrera, Nestor Montoya, Pablo Aragón, and Félix García as "obedient submissive slaves" and "pawns" of Juan José Herrera, the "preacher of justice," the "instigator of outrages," and "the soul of the White Caps of San Miguel County." The Republican newspaper further accused *La Voz Del Pueblo* publisher Félix Montoya of acting as an intermediary agent between Los Gorras Blancas and the Democratic Party in a conspiracy "to rob the ticket box of the Galisteo precinct." In a fit of sour grapes, the *Nuevo Mexicano* suggested life imprisonment for fraudulently elected representatives, insisting "the blindfold with which these impostors covered their faces has been torn."[72]

Pablo Herrera finally stood up and addressed the assembly after Nestor Montoya produced a petition signed by seven hundred residents of Santa Fe County calling for the inmates of the territorial penitentiary to manufacture more bricks on January 15, 1891. Herrera announced that everyone may have thought him a fool for remaining silent but that he had been waiting patiently until something that mattered to him was aired. He then surprised many in attendance when stating that he had "a better time when he was in the New Mexico penitentiary" than during the previous fifteen days in the council chambers. Declaring himself a "representative of the people," Herrera suggested that making shoes or other materials would be more productive for the inmates and provide more revenue for New Mexico than the construction of bricks. He then returned to his seat with "no more to say" for the time being. "The Hon. Pablo Herrera, whom the most conservative members have wanted to abuse so much, and in truth, he is not one of the most perceptive of the chamber; it is notable because he does not use his words unnecessarily," the *Voz Del Pueblo* remarked two days later. "But at the critical moment, of all questions, he is first in the line of formality for justice and duty."[73]

Pablo Herrera made his voice heard again when J. Francisco Cháves presented a legislative act that would establish common schools in New Mexico Territory and create the position of superintendent of public instruction on January 26, 1890. Pablo declared it "a very important law" and wanted the act "approved in three or four days" to allow him time to read and consider it. The other Hispano representatives requested at least two days to examine the details of the act. This led to an intense debate between Pablo Herrera and representatives William Burns and Albert Bacon Fall, both of whom wanted the act approved immediately. The school law was eventually passed by the legislature, with the superintendent of public instruction being appointed with the council's approval. Public schooling became compulsory for every child not attending private school between the ages of 8 and 16 for a minimum of three months each year. Every teacher required knowledge of the English language so the "Mexican" students would learn how to speak like Americanos.[74]

Any considerations of public schooling were briefly set aside when two hombres tried to assassinate Thomas B. Catron during a committee meeting held inside his office on the night of February 5, 1891. The councilmen were discussing a bill recently proposed by Theodore B. Mills when two shots were fired through a glass window in the direction of Catron's chair around 7:45 that evening. The two assailants, later described as of medium build and each wearing black slouch hats, quickly spurred their horses and galloped out of the Holy City. The would-be assassins had been unaware that Republican councilman and Grant County attorney José Arturo Ancheta was sitting in Catron's chair when they fired one blast from a shotgun and one bullet from a Winchester rifle through the window. Ancheta was struck in the shoulder, head, and left side of his neck by five buckshot, although his wounds did not prove fatal.

Thomas B. Catron immediately tried to implicate Los Gorras Blancas when interviewed by the *New Mexican*, insisting the attempt on his life "undoubtedly had its origin in the condition of affairs that has existed in this county for the past two years." The legislative assembly placed $20,000 at Governor Prince's disposal the following day. A $5,000 reward for anyone who could provide information leading to the arrest and conviction of those involved in the shooting was posted. Governor Prince also requested assistance from James McFarland, who worked in the Denver office of the Pinkerton National Detective Agency. Detectives Charles A. Siringo and Charles T. Leon were subsequently dispatched to infiltrate Los Caballeros del Trabajo and the remaining White Caps in San Miguel County. Meanwhile, the *Las Vegas Daily*

Optic published a notice recently posted by the remaining members of *Los Gorras Blancas* on the property of an anonymous citizen:

> Mr.——: You are hereby notified to take away all wire along the —— as soon as possible. If you fail to do it, we are going to kill every man that we may find guarding the fences. This we will do! You were notified about the fact, some time ago and failed to do so; and now, we will see if, at this warning you fail again. If you don't do it, we will tell you that the first man we will meet has to die, and this we will do very soon; and, also, the fence will be destroyed. Whereas you are subject under this notice, and under the Spangled Banner, that the first man we find in that fence shall lose his life, and his family shall perish; and, also, you will suffer the consequences imposed upon you by 1,000 men.
> WHITE CAPS[75]

While Pablo Herrera and many working-class Hispanos were disappointed the would-be assassins had missed their intended target in Santa Fe, the Twenty-Ninth Legislative Assembly proved a harsh lesson in the brutal reality of New Mexico politics for those representing el Partido del Pueblo Unido. The party possessed the numbers in San Miguel County but remained a small minority in the legislature. Their fellow representatives and councilmen were red-blooded capitalists with no interest in agrarian or economic reform. Although Pablo Herrera won praise for voting in favor of Santa Fe remaining the territorial capital, when he presented House Bill No. 182 related to the protection of laborers, miners, and employees, Rep. Albert Bacon Fall successfully motioned for the bill to be tabled indefinitely. Several other bills presented by representatives of el Partido del Pueblo Unido in the interest of safeguarding the impoverished were vetoed by Thomas B. Catron and his Republican delegates. For a man of action like Pablo Herrera, it was all too much to stomach. Although Theodore Mills expressed his thanks to all those present throughout the session, Herrera stood up and delivered a scathing farewell address before the assembly closed on the night of February 26, 1891.[76]

"Gentlemen, I have served several years time in the penitentiary but only sixty days in the legislature, the present house of representatives," Pablo informed the assembly. "I have watched the proceedings here carefully.

I would like to say that the time I spent in the penitentiary was more enjoyable than the time I spent here. There is more honesty in the halls of the territorial prison than in the halls of the legislature. I would prefer another term in prison than another election in the house."[77]

Pablo Herrera returned to what would become a significantly smaller San Miguel County after expressing his disgust with the political process in New Mexico. The legislature had approved an act to create the County of Guadalupe out of the land comprising southern San Miguel County, with Puerto de Luna serving as the county seat. "The population of San Miguel County by the late census is 24,167," declared Governor Prince when returning the bill to the council chamber. "The inhabitants included in the new county by the same census are about 4,697. This would still leave San Miguel County in a condition requiring another division in a short time, and the new county would not have population enough to entitle it to even one representative." Despite the governor's objections, the bill to establish Guadalupe County was passed with two-thirds of the votes on February 26, 1891. Pablo Herrera's mood would not have improved when he was suspended from the Order of the Knights of Labor for unspecified reasons at an assembly in Tiptonville, Mora County, shortly after his return to Las Vegas.[78]

El Partido del Pueblo Unido may have won the elections in San Miguel County, but the people's movement had slammed into a political adobe wall in Santa Fe. The key positions of influence such as governor, treasurer, and district attorney were still filled by appointment rather than election and therefore remained beyond the reach of those with revolutionary aspirations in Nuevo México. Although Nestor Montoya's fence law had been passed by the legislature, thereby making it illegal to destroy fences on any property with legitimate title or erect a fence on any pastures without legal ownership, the Las Vegas Land Grant issue remained unresolved.[79]

Juan José Herrera continued trying to evoke resistance against the system as much as possible under the circumstances. El Capitán spent time garnering additional support in Chaperito, assisted former sheriff Lorenzo López with the examination of local delinquency records during a county commission meeting in Las Vegas, and organized Caballeros del Trabajo assemblies throughout the spring of 1891. He also received praise from

La Voz Del Pueblo for his "heroic and patriotic efforts" for the "protection of the poor against despotism."

Nicanor Herrera continued working alongside his older brother Juan José as an organizer for the Knights of Labor and wishing death upon Thomas B. Catron. Although James McFarland of the Denver Pinkerton Agency initially believed former Santa Fe County sheriff, anti-Ring Democrat, and grand master workman for the Knights of Labor Francisco "Frank" Chávez was behind the attempt on Thomas Catron's life in Santa Fe, undercover operative Charlie Siringo insisted Nicanor Herrera was a prime suspect when writing a letter to Governor L. Bradford Prince in April 1891. Siringo described Nicanor as the "worst of the White Cap leaders" and claimed the "fine looking specimen of the Mexican race" had declared that Catron must "die before the next election."[80]

For the antagonistic Pablo Herrera, his trailblazing journey from the territorial penitentiary to the house of representatives would transition into a downward spiral that began inside a saloon owned by a disreputable hombre named Vicente Silva, a close associate of José Chávez y Chávez.

Chapter 15

Sociedad de Bandidos

I've got clouds in my eyes, blood on my hands.
—Tito & Tarantula

The 41-year-old José Chávez y Chávez dressed in a dapper suit with a baton hanging from his belt during the day and a pistol resting on his hip at night when patrolling the streets of Las Vegas in early 1891. He looked like the quintessential frontier lawman, with his solid build and neatly groomed hair and moustache. Nobody doubted the policeman's nerve or willingness to fulfill his duty in the face of danger. Officer Chávez y Chávez occasionally worked various other jobs around San Miguel County, frequently laughed and chatted with citizens, and served the local community by sitting on the petit jury during the district court session in the spring of 1891. He was also politically active, having joined the United People's Party following his covert stint as a member of Los Gorras Blancas.[1]

José Chávez y Chávez was making a respectable living as a city policeman and had purchased a house on the outskirts of Las Vegas. It wasn't enough for the seasoned lawman. Rather than run for sheriff or political office on the People's ticket, Officer Chávez y Chávez chose to pursue a path of organized crime to supplement his income. He did so by joining an organization that proudly referred to itself as la Sociedad de Bandidos de Nuevo México (the Society of Bandits of New Mexico). Although the Society of Bandits were supporters or members of el Partido del Pueblo Unido, their activities were driven by self-interest rather than resistance against land barons. They wanted to get rich by any unlawful means available to them.[2]

Vicente Silva was the third child brought into the world by his father Antonio and mother Dolores Perea-Silva in Bernalillo County in 1845. Like so many Hispanos of his time, Vicente grew up in a poor but respectable family and remained illiterate for the rest of his days. The Silva family eventually relocated to San Miguel County, where Vicente became the head of his family following the death of his father Antonio during the 1870s. While his younger brother Jesús María Silva became a ranch hand for the Maxwell family and a close friend of the famous Billy the Kid in Fort Sumner, the 35-year-old Vicente was working as a laborer to provide for his mother Delores, his paralyzed brother Teodocis, and his niece Higinia Mares in an adobe house on Pacific Street, East Las Vegas, in 1880. It was around that time when Vicente married the 26-year-old Telésfora Sandoval, later described as "not a beautiful woman" but one who "did not lack charm." Her most noticeable features were her stunning dark eyes and thick lashes. Vicente and Telésfora adopted an abandoned baby girl whom liveryman John A. C. Minner found in his stable in March,1885. They named their adopted daughter Emma Silva and doted on her with considerable affection.[3]

The 46-year-old Vicente Silva was operating a two-story saloon and brothel known as the Cantina Imperial (Imperial Saloon) on Moreno Street in West Las Vegas by 1891. The proprietor lived on the second floor with his wife Telésfora, their adopted daughter Emma, and his brother-in-law Gabriel Sandoval, who helped run the noisy saloon, gambling rooms, and dance hall downstairs. The establishment was notorious for selling cheap liquor and offering an array of prostitutes, including one woman known as La Golondrina (the Swallow) and two heavyset females known as Las Elefantas (the Elephants). "At all hours of the night his place was busy with a motley crowd of ruffians," recalled Miguel Antonio Otero Jr. "Not alone men but many women frequented the place, all of them drinking bad whiskey, singing, and using insulting language."[4]

In public the auburn-haired, light-skinned Vicente Silva always dressed neatly in a white shirt and vest. He resembled an Irishman more than a Nuevomexicano. The saloon owner knew how to turn on the charm and make anyone feel at ease in his presence. "He was pleasant, sweet-tempered, and agreeable with everyone he met," recalled Miguel Antonio Otero Jr. The *Las Vegas Daily Optic* had even recommended Silva for the nomination for probate judge on the United People's Party ticket in September 1890.[5]

Behind closed doors Vicente Silva was a perverted, ruthless gangster, with a hair-trigger temper and an insatiable hunger for money. He was also an abusive husband, frequently hitting his wife Telésfora Sandoval de Silva if she displeased him or failed to keep her mouth shut about his business. Although his popular saloon was turning a profit, Vicente wished to solicit a lot more dinero from the local community. The "singing room" on the first floor of his Cantina Imperial also served as a conference room for la Sociedad de Bandidos de Nuevo México; the proprietor's criminal organization comprised over two dozen Hispano ruffians and shady policemen.[6]

José Chávez y Chávez not only joined the Sociedad de Bandidos de Nuevo México but also become a leading member. He answered only to Vicente Silva, who ran his Society of Bandits much like a Mafia family. José's fellow policemen Julian Trujillo and 36-year-old Eugenio Alarid also claimed membership, along with rough hombres like Guadalupe "El Lechuza" Caballero, Manuel "El Mellado" Gonzáles y Baca, Procopio Rael, Nestor Herrera, Patricio Maes, Remigio "El Galivan" Sandoval, Zenon Maes, Germán Maestas, Pablo Lucero, Pedro Baca, Jesús Vialpando, and the fearsome Dionicio "El Candelas" Sisneros. "They were as tough a bunch of bad men as ever gathered together outside a penal institution," recalled Miguel Antonio Otero Jr. "It was a closed corporation, each bandit pledging his life, not only to secrecy but to stand together, even unto death." Vicente Silva also purchased a ranch known as Monte Largo near the San Pedro mines in southern Santa Fe County to serve as a headquarters for the exclusively Hispano organization's rustling activities. "Cattle and horse stealings were soon on the increase," remembered Miguel Antonio Otero Jr.[7]

It was inside Vicente Silva's raucous saloon that Pablo Herrera quarreled with his 29-year-old nephew Meliton Ulibarri—one of the sons of Pablo's older sister Juanita Paula Herrera-Ulibarri—in early May 1891. Meliton was angry that his uncle had recently insulted his older brother Gumecindo Ulibarri's wife Romanita during a family dispute in the married couple's home. Meliton demanded an explanation, and a heated argument ensued. Pablo decided to teach his nephew a lesson by having him arraigned before Justice of the Peace Clemente Angel for threatening him.[8]

Juan José, Pablo, and Nicanor Herrera were among the large crowd gathered outside the Don Rumaldo Baca Building in the old plaza of Las Vegas when their nephew Meliton Ulibarri's preliminary hearing took place at three o'clock in the afternoon of May 11, 1891. Juan José Herrera was dismayed when Vicente Silva denied having heard Meliton Ulibarri threaten Pablo Herrera inside his Imperial Saloon when the proprietor took the stand. The tension between the local Republicans and members of the United People's Party was already palatable in the crowded plaza when El Capitán confronted Silva in the doorway of the courthouse around four o'clock. The two hombres began arguing until all hell broke loose when the Herrera brothers' political rival Doroteo Sandoval tried to intervene and expressed his satisfaction with Vicente Silva's testimony. Threats and insults were levied, pistols were drawn, and sticks, stones, and punches were thrown as a riot erupted in the plaza.[9]

Deputy Sheriff William "Billy" Green, who had once served an eighteen-month sentence in the territorial penitentiary for horse theft, tried to break up the riot by firing several shots from his revolver into the crowd, one of which was allegedly aimed at Constable José L. Galindre. The 24-year-old Green was beaten over the head and robbed by members of the crowd before fleeing inside the district courtroom. Juan José Herrera grabbed Doroteo Sandoval's 33-year-old son Florencio around the throat when the younger Sandoval approached him with a raised fist in the ensuing chaos. In response, the ornery Pablo Herrera drew his knife and thrust the blade six inches deep into Florencio Sandoval's chest on the corner of the courthouse porch. The 52-year-old Doroteo Sandoval was also stabbed several times in his face and left side by either Pablo or Nicanor Herrera, both of whom were struck in the head with sticks and rocks during the melee.[10]

Pablo and Nicanor Herrera accompanied their older brother Juan José to his adobe home while the wounded Doroteo Sandoval was carried inside his own nearby dwelling once the riot had subsided in the plaza. Although Doroteo would pull through, his son Florencio Sandoval succumbed to his own stab wound shortly after providing his dying testimony to notary Patricio Gonzáles on the porch of the courthouse:

> *Knowing that I am about to die, I make this statement*:
> Do you know who cut you?
> *Yes, I do. Pablo Herrera did it, with a knife.*
> Are you sure of this?
> *Yes, I am.*
> Where did you receive the wound from Pablo Herrera?
> *At the side of my heart.*
> Do you make this declaration, because you expect to die?
> *I think I am going to die.*
> Which Pablo Herrera cut you?
> *The brother of Juan and Nicanor.*
> Where did this happen?
> *At the corner of the porch of the old Baca building, May 11th, 1891.*
> Sworn and subscribed to, in the presence of Antonio Cajul and Leonardo Duran, before me, Patricio Gonzales, notary public.[11]

Sheriff José L. López, Deputy Billy Green, and a posse arrived on Juan José Herrera's doorstep that evening and escorted all three Herrera brothers to the jailhouse. Juan José, Pablo, and Nicanor were locked behind bars pending a preliminary examination by Judge Henry Stiles Wooster. "Great excitement prevails on the streets among the native people, and it is feared that the end is not yet," the *Las Vegas Daily Optic* announced that evening. Sheriff José L. López needed extra help that month, and policeman José Chávez y Chávez later submitted a bill of twelve dollars to the county commissioners for having spent six nights guarding the jailhouse.[12]

Once the Republicans of Santa Fe received news of the stabbings, they predictably jumped at the chance to condemn the Herrera brothers and their radical brand of politics. "From all accounts the killing of Sandoval by Pablo Herrera on yesterday at Las Vegas was a cold-blooded murder," the *New Mexican* declared on May 12, 1891. "The murders committed at Las Vegas on yesterday are but the very natural outcome of the lawless and dangerous teachings of the White Cap bosses." *La Voz Del Pueblo* took a more cautious approach by calling for a full investigation before condemning any of the parties involved. "On the one hand, there is an affidavit from the late Florencio Sandoval, declaring that he received his wound from the hand of Pablo Herrera," the Hispano newspaper announced. "Doroteo Sandoval's wounds are said to have been received by Pablo Herrera on the one hand, and by Nicanor Herrera on the other. On the other hand, it is said that it was not Pablo Herrera who injured the deceased Florencio, while others say that he did it in defense of his life, seeing himself attacked and threatened by several of those who participated in the tumult."[13]

Juan José Herrera was charged with assault with intent to commit murder and released on $2,000 bail, after some difficulty securing bonds, on May 16, 1891. Pablo and Nicanor Herrera initially waved examination to await the determination of a grand jury, although Nicanor had a change of heart when learning that Doroteo Sandoval would survive the stab wounds he had suffered in the plaza. Nicanor was granted bail for the sum of $3,000 after securing bonds and released from the jailhouse a short time later. Pablo Herrera was charged with murder in the first degree and remained behind bars. Sheriff José L. López escorted Herrera and another prisoner named William Bryant Tipton to the Mora County jail "for safe keeping" in early June 1891.[14]

While Pablo Herrera bided his time in Mora County Sheriff Agapito Abeyta's custody, his older brother Juan José and publisher Pedro García established their own Spanish-language newspaper in Albuquerque in June 1891. Those opposed to the Knights of Labor and Los Gorras Blancas in San Miguel County had recently formed their own organization called el Sociedad de los Caballeros de Ley y Orden y Protección Mutua (the Society of Knights of Law and Order and Mutual Protection). With an estimated 1,500 members, the United Protection Association started publishing a newspaper called *El Sol de Mayo* to contend with *La Voz Del Pueblo* and attack anyone associated with the people's movement in San Miguel County. White Cap insurgency had also come under fire from the local Jesuits' newspaper the *Revista Catolica*, which excoriated Los Gorras Blancas and the formation of secret societies in the community.[15]

Juan José Herrera used his own newspaper, *El Defensor del Pueblo*, to fire back at *El Sol de Mayo* and the *Revista Catolica*. He even publicly criticized the late Archbishop Jean Baptiste Lamy, his successor Archbishop Jean-Baptiste Salpointe, Vicar General Peter Eguillon, and the clergy of New Mexico Territory itself. This caused considerable outrage in both conservative and liberal circles. An Indignation Meeting was eventually called to order inside the Santa Fe courthouse on the night of August 10, 1891. Thomas B. Catron served as chairman while an appointed committee drafted resolutions "denouncing this outrage upon civil and religious liberty" for publication in the *New Mexican*, *El Sol de Mayo*, and the *Revista Catolica*. "We condemn the said [*El Defensor del Pueblo*] and declare it to be a scandalous, vicious and immoral publication, representing nihilistic tendencies unworthy of a civilised community," one of the resolutions professed.[16]

When the 52-year-old Juan José Herrera wasn't attacking the clergy of Nuevo México with Marxist fervor, there was still the Las Vegas Land Grant issue for him to contend with that summer. The territorial legislature had passed an act during the Twenty-Ninth Legislative Assembly in Santa Fe for the establishment of a board of trustees to determine which inhabitants held legitimate title on the communal pastures of the Las Vegas Land Grant. While el Partido del Pueblo Unido regulated a convention held in Las Vegas to determine the process for establishing a board of trustees in July 1891, the five resolutions proposed by Félix Martínez reflected a more conciliatory form of antimonopolism than Juan José Herrera had in mind. The resolutions allowed for any individual who had lived on the Las Vegas Land Grant for a minimum of five years to establish legitimate title within the next five years. Although a maximum ownership of 160 acres per individual was enforced, and no communal pastures could be allocated without approval from the board of trustees, Martínez's resolutions still provided an opportunity for future settlement. That was not what the Herrera brothers and Los Gorras Blancas had been seeking with their militant campaign.[17]

When Juan José Herrera was indicted for assault with intent to commit murder by a grand jury in Las Vegas in November 1891, his seasoned attorney and United People's Party member John D. W. Veeder ensured that El Capitán did not serve any prison time. Nicanor Herrera also avoided a prison sentence but spent most of the next twelve months suffering from a blood-related illness in Albuquerque. Their brother Pablo Herrera was transported back to Las Vegas from Mora County and indicted for murder in the first degree for the fatal stabbing of Florencio Sandoval during the district court session. His case was continued over to the next term of court, despite prosecuting attorney "Captain" Lewis C. Fort's strong push for an immediate trial.[18]

While Pablo Herrera was denied bail and remained in the Las Vegas jailhouse, Sheriff José L. López and Deputy José Valdéz arrived in Santa Fe with a handful of prisoners recently sentenced to time in the territorial penitentiary on November 15, 1891. Among their prisoners was the notorious Porfirio Trujillo. Judge James O'Brien had sentenced the one-time member of Los Gorras Blancas to twelve months of imprisonment for assault with intent to commit robbery. It was Porfirio Trujillo's second term in the territorial penitentiary, but it would not be his last.[19]

***

The Republicans of Santa Fe demanded an explanation when Pablo Herrera was released from the Las Vegas jailhouse after District Attorney Lewis C. Fort, Félix Martínez, Enrique Houghton Salazar, and Dr. Miguel F. Desmarais provided $6,000 worth of sureties on May 25, 1892. District Attorney Fort quickly wrote a letter to the *Las Vegas Daily Optic* explaining his actions during the court session in Las Vegas that month:

> The man whom [Pablo Herrera] is charged with killing was killed at a time of great excitement, when a large crowd of persons were closely assembled together, and much excitement prevailed, and there is likely to be much conflict in the evidence as to the material facts, under these circumstances . . . upon information furnished me, by those most interested in the prosecution, a very large proportion of the jury were friendly to Herrera, and it seemed, not only to me, but to those directly interested in the prosecution, that I would be more likely to secure a conviction under more favorable circumstances and that it was best not to allow the case to go to trial at the last term, as to go to trial under the circumstances existing meant an acquittal for Herrera. . . . It is less expense to the county that he should be on bail, as an examination

of the records of the board of county commissioners will show that it has already cost the county a large sum for his maintenance. Everyone knows he will stand trial. I have not the slightest doubt but he will be present, and if I remain in office as district attorney, he will certainly be prosecuted with all the vigor and power I can command.[20]

Although Pablo Herrera was free on bonds to spend time preaching his radical politics to the impoverished Hispanos of Rio Arriba County, the people's movement suffered a grievous blow when former Santa Fe County sheriff Francisco "Frank" Chávez was gunned down in the territorial capital. The influential Democrat and grand master workman of the New Mexican Knights of Labor had stirred up considerable opposition to the Santa Fe Ring before he was shot four times from behind a telegraph pole near the Guadalupe Bridge just after ten o'clock on the night of May 29, 1892.

The murder of Francisco Chávez sent shockwaves throughout Nuevo México, and a lengthy investigation began. Some suspected Frank Chávez's old adversary Francisco Gonzáles y Borrego, a member of a Republican Button Gang, was responsible. Félix Martínez and others firmly believed Thomas B. Catron and the Santa Fe Ring were behind the assassination. *La Voz Del Pueblo* subsequently published a sonnet in Spanish honoring the fallen caballero:

> Rebrame el huracán, callen las aves
> El cielo enluten negros nubarrones
> Vistan las calles fúnebres crespones
> Que ha muerto el popular Francisco Chávez
>
> Murió tu amigo; Pueblo! ¿No lo sabes?
> Le asesinaron vándalos felones,
> Murió por defender tus conviceiones,
> Justo es su nombre en tu memoria grabos
>
> Desde el cielo, su sombra protectora
> Vela de su país por los destinos
> Y por su anciana madre que le llora
>
> Ciñe del mártir la inmortal corona,
> Y al ver á sus cobardes asesinos,
> Le inspirán compasión y les perdona.[21]

As political violence remained the order of the day in New Mexico Territory, the 42-year-old José Chávez y Chávez continued working as a lawman in Las Vegas in 1892. José submitted a bill of thirty dollars for his services as a city policeman during the month of February, but he may have needed to purchase a new home after failing to pay the property tax on his house and lot in Precinct No. 26 the previous year. His homestead and various other properties were sold cash-in-hand to the highest bidder by Sheriff José L. López to satisfy delinquent taxes for the year 1891 during the month of May 1892. Chávez y Chávez either handed López the cash that month or eventually purchased another home on the outskirts of Las Vegas after the auction. The policeman supplemented his income by working as a vaquero for the sheriff during the summer. "José Chávez y Chávez drove a herd of López's steers in from El Cuervo today," the *Las Vegas Free Press* announced on August 3, 1892.[22]

When José Chávez y Chávez wasn't patrolling the streets of Las Vegas for Police Chief José Mares or driving herds of cattle for Sheriff López, the policeman demonstrated his propensity for political violence after "Colonel" George W. Prichard denounced the United People's Party during a speech at a Republican–Union League convention in Las Vegas on October 6, 1892. José and several Hispano ruffians were gathered outside a saloon in the plaza the following morning when they spotted the staunch Republican strolling in their direction. Chávez y Chávez took a vicious swing at Prichard when he came within reach but missed his target. The attorney then exchanged words with the angry Hispanos in an incident the *New Mexican* naturally described as a case of "White Cap lawlessness."[23]

The *Las Vegas Free Press* would report that Juan José Herrera—now working as a deputy for Sheriff José L. López—had started a fight at the same Republican–Union League convention and been forcibly removed from the premises. "When a party has to resort to getting up fights in a hall to try to injure its opponents, it is pretty nearly gone up," the *Las Vegas Free Press* remarked. *La Voz Del Pueblo* described such reports as "malicious and false," insisting Deputy Herrera had escorted one of their journalists to the convention and was beaten by members of the crowd when trying to arrest two Republicans for repeatedly insulting him. "Our reporter was an eyewitness to the whole thing, and he knows the truth of the case," the Hispano newspaper insisted.[24]

Political animosities continued while the United People's Party held their own convention inside the Las Vegas courthouse in early October 1892. El Partido del Pueblo Unido was drawing inspiration from the national People's Party, which had been founded earlier that year by leading members of the Farmers' Alliance, the Greenback Party, and various independent labor organizations. While former Union Gen. James B. Weaver of Ohio had emerged as the national People's Party nomination for president of the United States during the summer, el Partido del Pueblo Unido was hoping to repeat their previous success at the ballot boxes during the upcoming November elections in San Miguel County. Juan José Herrera was appointed to a committee for permanent organization during the people's convention on October 10, 1892. His younger brother Nicanor Herrera had recovered from his lengthy illness and was appointed to a credentials committee during the same session.[25]

The same day Juan José and Nicanor Herrera received their appointments, their Republican political opponent Manuel Cabeza de Baca sat down in Las Vegas and wrote a letter to Governor L. Bradford Prince regarding Porfirio Trujillo's impending release from the territorial penitentiary: "I understand that efforts have been made to have Porfirio Trujillo out of the Penitentiary, before his time is up, we have discovered that he is a member of a secret organisation or committee, appointed by the bosses of the white caps to murder several of our best citizens, and prominent republicans, of this county and we ask and request from you that such a thing will never happen and that you will keep him in the pen until his time is up." Manuel Cabeza de Baca's plea to Governor Prince proved futile when Porfirio Trujillo was released from the territorial penitentiary one month early for good time on October 12, 1892.[26]

The same day Porfirio Trujillo was released from the penitentiary, the irrepressible Pablo Herrera made a considerable impression on those attending the People's Party convention in Las Vegas on October 12, 1892. Pablo had grown disillusioned with the direction of the party and was ruled out of order when taking the floor after John D. W. Veeder was nominated for the territorial council. He refused to be silenced. "[Pablo Herrera] made a speech denouncing the chairman [Theodore B. Mills] and the action of the convention all through and stating he would withdraw from such a corrupt crowd," recalled one journalist in attendance. "He then withdrew from the room, followed by one-half of the convention." While Pablo Herrera was finished with politics, his older brother Juan José emerged as the nominee for probate judge of San Miguel County on the People's ticket several days later. El Capitán immediately introduced a resolution declaring *La Voz Del Pueblo* the "official organ of the County of San Miguel."[27]

Pablo Herrera was not the only hombre who had grown disillusioned with the United People's Party by the autumn of 1892. Sociedad de Bandidos member Patricio Maes was supposedly planning to leave el Partido del Pueblo Unido and become a Republican. His jefe Vicente Silva considered this an act of treason. Silva already suspected Maes had become an informant for the authorities and organized a Sociedad de Bandidos meeting in his saloon on Moreno Street during the early hours of October 22, 1892. José Chávez y Chávez was in attendance when Patricio Maes stood trial before "prosecutor" Vicente Silva and a "war council" for the "crime of high treason." A letter Patricio Maes allegedly wrote to the editor of *El Sol del Mayo* announcing his resignation from the United People's Party and declaring his intention to join the Republican Party was produced as evidence to support the charge of treason. The accused hombre professed his innocence but was eventually sentenced to death. A noose was fastened around Patricio's neck before José Chávez y Chávez, Eugenio Alarid, Julian Trujillo, and various other members of their society quietly escorted the condemned "traitor" to the Río Gallinas bridge.[28]

The local authorities found the corpse of Patricio Maes hanging from the Río Gallinas bridge after sunrise on October 22, 1892. His death quickly became a political tool when a Republican club was named in his honor several days later. The editors of *La Voz Del Pueblo* questioned the Republicans' sincerity in doing so, insisting the "Mafia party" was merely trying to gain political advantages. The Hispano newspaper also published an affidavit in which the victim's brother Felipe Maes professed that he had always known his sibling Patricio "as a Republican" and declared the letter his brother had supposedly sent to *El Sol de Mayo* announcing his defection from el Partido del Pueblo to the Republican Party an "impossible mystery to solve." Felipe Maes insisted that "my brother Patricio Maes was not murdered for political reasons by the Partido del Pueblo" in an affidavit signed by witnesses Juan José Herrera and Juan Quintana. The truth of the matter was that nobody knew exactly why Patricio Maes had been murdered. The *Las Vegas Free Press* quickly grew tired of waiting for answers. "We should like to ask why the authorities have not done something to find the [murderer] or murderers and also why no reward is offered for their detection?" the newspaper asked on October 29, 1892.[29]

While the murder of Patricio Maes remained a mystery to the local authorities, the Republicans of Santa Fe could only whine that "lawlessness and intimidation to an unparalleled degree was the order of the day in the county of San Miguel" after the United People's Party cleaned house at the ballot boxes on November 8, 1892. Antonio Joseph winning a strong majority of the vote against Thomas B. Catron to remain New Mexico's delegate to Congress was a particularly bitter pill for them to swallow. Although the United People's Party lost one seat in the territorial house to the recently established Guadalupe County, they defeated the Republicans to win every other political office available to them in San Miguel County. Félix Martínez and John D. W. Veeder were elected to the territorial council, Enrique H. Salazar was elected superintendent of public schools, Charles "Carlos" Rudulph was elected probate clerk, and Lorenzo López defeated Eugenio Romero to win another term as county sheriff. Juan José Herrera also won a close vote against Republican candidate Plácido Sandoval to win the office of probate judge. His first official act was the appointment of George W. Prichard as the new administrator for the Republican party of San Miguel County to secure any lingering debts. This backfired when "Colonel" Prichard approached the *New Mexican* claiming that Republican tickets were pilfered from ballot boxes in Los Alamos and Arroyo de los Yutas on election day, and further insisted that numerous residents of Tecolote had voted for the United People's Party more than once.[30]

Politics was probably the last thing on Pablo Herrera's mind when facing a lengthy term in the territorial penitentiary in November 1892. The former representative's penchant for stabbing his adversaries had caught up with him when he was indicted for the murder of Florencio Sandoval by a grand jury in Las Vegas that month. "The jurors have been secured and impanelled who are to decide the case of the territory vs Pablo Herrera," the *New Mexican* eagerly announced on November 18. Judge James O'Brien was not satisfied when the petit jury found Pablo Herrera guilty of murder in the third degree and recommended a sentence of ten years imprisonment at four o'clock the following afternoon. O'Brien instructed the jurors to return to their room and deliberate further until agreeing on the severity of the crime. The judgment of the court was further delayed when Herrera's attorneys motioned for a new trial.[31]

The 47-year-old Pablo Herrera had yet to receive his sentence from the district court when he casually pulled on his overcoat, walked out of the Las Vegas jailhouse, and fled into the mountains on the afternoon of December 9, 1892. "Mr. Herrera was not an ordinary prisoner, nor was he treated as such," the *Nuevo Mexicano* reported. "He enjoyed privileges that other prisoners do not ordinarily enjoy, but despite that he was royally bored in jail and longed to enjoy the delights of freedom to his heart's content." A posse consisting of Sheriff José L. López and deputies Juan José Herrera, José Chávez y Chávez, Serafin Baca, and Billy Green quickly set out in pursuit but failed to locate the fugitive. "No one has any expectations of his being recaptured," the *Las Vegas Daily Optic* despondently remarked. Pablo Herrera had more than enough support from local Hispanos willing to aid him in avoiding capture by the authorities, some of whom were not overly keen to catch him in the first place. "If it weren't that we don't want to hurt sensitivities, we would congratulate Don Pablo Herrera for his lucky evasion; but we consider that it would be in very bad taste to do so," the *Nuevo Mexicano* sympathetically announced. "What we will say is that the main duty of a prisoner when he no longer has hope of freedom is to try to get it in the best way he can."[32]

According to the *New Mexican*, three hombres believed to be Pablo Herrera and Sociedad de Bandidos members Germán Maestas and Procopio Rael fired four shots at city policemen on the western outskirts of Las Vegas on January 16, 1893. The law officials reportedly fired seven shots in retaliation. "It is supposed from the traces of blood [the policemen] either hit a horse or a man in the attacking party," the leading newspaper of Santa

Fe informed its readers. However accurate the *New Mexican*'s depiction of events, it is understandable why such reports convinced a liberal traditionalist like Miguel Antonio Otero Jr. that Los Gorras Blancas, la Sociedad de Bandidos, and el Partido del Pueblo Unido were "one and the same," as he wrote in his later years. Pablo Herrera spent most of the next twenty-three months hiding out in the mountains.[33]

El Partido del Pueblo Unido continued governing San Miguel County with moderate success, although the Herrera brothers' dream of forging a united Hispano-American populace in defiance of Anglo encroachment and bossism was steadily dismantled by political infighting. Persistent attacks by reactionary officials and the United Protection Association didn't help their cause either. As the debate continued over exactly what constituted a "community grant," Juan José Herrera and Félix Martínez differed in their outlook on the matter. Councilman Martínez was willing to appease the commercial class of San Miguel County so long as the rights of Nuevomexicanos were not dismissed. Probate Judge Herrera believed the pastures of the Las Vegas Land Grant belonged to its inhabitants and should therefore remain off-limits to any self-serving businessmen. Although renowned for his generosity, the wealthy Sheriff Lorenzo López's social and political outlook was more in line with traditional patronage rather than antimonopolism. His son-in-law Enrique H. Salazar disliked Félix Martínez and left *La Voz Del Pueblo* to establish his own newspaper called *El Independiente*. Probate Clerk Charles Rudulph also ended up feuding with prominent Knights of Labor Secretary Ezequiel C. de Baca and being publicly scorned by the organization.[34]

As for the rapacious José Chávez y Chávez, the policeman continued engaging in banditry with Vicente Silva and la Sociedad de Bandidos de Nuevo México. Officer Chávez y Chávez and his fellow policemen Julian Trujillo and Eugenio Alarid were tasked with keeping their jefe informed of any potential moves made by the authorities, thereby providing the organization with a degree of impunity while carrying out their various crimes. Society member Germán Maestas later confessed to having been involved in more robberies and rustling activities than he could remember during his time in Vicente Silva's orbit, including the robbery of four priests at gunpoint on the San Juan River. "The cattlemen of San Miguel, Mora, and Guadalupe counties were suffering crippling losses of livestock and horses that mysteriously disappeared," recalled prominent Las Vegas attorney Manuel Cabeza de Baca. "No one knew who had stolen them or where they had been taken."[35]

According to Julian Trujillo and Germán Maestas, later described as "one of the most despicable scoundrels of the entire gang," their associate José Chávez y Chávez was involved in the premeditated robbery and brutal murder of a 50-year-old school director named Carpio Sais on the night of December 28, 1892. Maestas rode into Las Vegas that day to meet with José Chávez y Chávez, Julian Trujillo, and Pablo Lucero to discuss their next score. When José informed Germán of the plan to rob old Carpio Sais, it was made abundantly clear they would have to kill the school director to ensure that he remained silent. Germán readily agreed to participate and was tasked with keeping an eye out for any potential witnesses while the crime was committed.

Germán Maestas was delayed when purchasing a bottle of whiskey in a saloon, and his three associates waiting outside decided to carry out the plan without him. José Chávez y Chávez, Julian Trujillo, and Pablo Lucero lured the unsuspecting Carpio Sais to a secluded location where they robbed the school director of $130 before stabbing and stoning him to death as quietly as possible. The three murderers then buried Carpio's bloodied corpse in an undisclosed location. José Chávez y Chávez, Julian Trujillo, and Pablo Lucero cursed Germán Maestas for a coward when finding him in the saloon. They handed their associate $9 and warned him to keep his mouth shut or suffer the same fate as their victim. The body of Carpio Sais was never officially recovered.[36]

While nobody at the time suspected José Chávez y Chávez was a stone-cold killer, every newspaperman in the territory soon had a horrifying tale of organized crime to piece together that would propel the policeman's notoriety to greater heights for all the wrong reasons.

***

Vicente Silva was increasingly paranoid after wealthy rancher "Captain" Refugio Esquibel filed charges against him for stealing four of his prized horses in October 1892. The leader of la Sociedad de Bandidos abandoned his family in Las Vegas before he was indicted by a grand jury for horse theft on November 7, 1892. Silva spent most of the next two months in Mora County or at his hideout in the mountains near Los Alamos thirteen miles northeast of Las Vegas. The bandido shaved his head and began growing a lengthy gray beard to avoid detection. He also became obsessed with the notion that his wife Telésfora and brother-in-law Gabriel Sandoval would enlighten the authorities about the full extent of his criminal activities during his absence.[37]

Vicente began missing his adopted daughter while hiding out and ordered his faithful henchman Guadalupe "El Lechuza" Caballero to kidnap the 8-year-old Emma Silva down in Las Vegas. The young girl subsequently disappeared without a trace outside the girls' academy at around ten o'clock in the morning on January 22, 1893. Telésfora Sandoval de Silva was distraught, and *La Voz Del Pueblo* announced a "liberal reward" for anyone who could find the missing student. Guadalupe Caballero had lured Emma into a covered wagon that morning and transported the schoolgirl to his jefe in Mora County as instructed. Sociedad de Bandidos member Manuel Gonzáles y Baca later insinuated that Silva raped his 8-year-old adopted daughter while she was in his depraved company.[38]

The 48-year-old Vicente Silva allegedly paid a late-night visit to his wife Telésfora in Las Vegas after orchestrating their adopted daughter's kidnapping and assured his better half that little Emma was safe with him in Los Alamos. He then resumed hiding from the authorities and frequently stayed at the home of his 38-year-old mistress Rosario Lucero de Baca on the edge of Las Vegas. Silva was fixated on the notion that Telésfora and her brother Gabriel Sandoval would report his criminal activities to Sheriff Lorenzo López. He soon began plotting their murders with various members of his Sociedad de Bandidos, falsely informing his associates that Telésfora and Gabriel were having incestuous relations.[39]

The 14-year-old Gabriel Sandoval was incensed over the kidnapping of little Emma Silva, whom he adored as much as his older sister Telésfora. The teenager kept a close watch on Rosario Lucero de Baca's house and naively approached policeman and Sociedad de Bandidos member Julian Trujillo about the matter in front of the Imperial Saloon in Las Vegas on the evening of

February 7, 1893. He wanted his brother-in-law Vicente arrested and Emma brought home as quickly as possible. Guadalupe "El Lechuza" Caballero overheard their conversation and quickly informed his jefe at Rosario Lucero de Baca's home on the edge of town. Vicente Silva told Caballero to keep an eye on young Sandoval and instructed his friend José Chávez y Chávez to locate Julian Trujillo and Eugenio Alarid.

The 42-year-old José Chávez y Chávez was strolling along National Street to the west of the old town plaza when he spotted Julian Trujillo and Eugenio Alarid approaching him outside the First National Bank a short time later. José instructed his fellow officers to accompany him down Gonzales Street until they reached Demetrio Perez's house. Vicente Silva was waiting for them behind a nearby adobe wall. Julian Trujillo had already agreed to meet Gabriel Sandoval in the Imperial Saloon that night and Silva laid out their plan. Vicente would head over to the ruins of a deserted house on Moreno Street in a secluded area roughly two hundred and fifty yards from the San Miguel County courthouse. José Chávez y Chávez, Julian Trujillo, and Eugenio Alarid would meet with young Gabriel in the Cantina Imperial at eight o'clock as scheduled. When Silva fired a bullet from his pistol a short time later, the officers would invite his brother-in-law to accompany them down Moreno Street to investigate.

José Chávez y Chávez, Julian Trujillo, and Eugenio Alarid arrived at the Imperial Saloon around eight o'clock as planned. José and Eugenio headed inside while Julian stood just outside the doorway. Chávez y Chávez soon spotted Gabriel Sandoval leaning against a counter. The plucky youngster had just finished quarrelling with Guadalupe Caballero inside the establishment, calling El Lechuza a "pimp" and a "tool" of his thieving brother-in-law. Some of the hombres in the saloon were stunned by Sandoval's outburst and asked Caballero why he had let the boy get away with speaking to him in such a manner.

"His fire will soon be lowered," Caballero calmly told them.

José Chávez y Chávez called out to Gabriel Sandoval, and the two of them enjoyed a couple of drinks before a shot was fired down the street. Sandoval readily agreed to accompany Chávez y Chávez, Trujillo, and Alarid to investigate the shooting and followed the three policemen out of the saloon.

Sandoval was thrilled when Officer Chávez y Chávez told him that his brother-in-law Vicente was at his mistress Rosario's house and they were going to arrest him as they headed down Moreno Street in the wintry night air. José Chávez y Chávez and Eugenio Alarid suddenly grabbed Gabriel Sandoval and disarmed him when they reached the ruins of an abandoned old house. The two policemen kept a firm grip on the teenager's arms as Vicente Silva emerged from behind an adobe wall with a knife in his hand.

"You are here, you scoundrel," Silva said to his terrified brother-in-law. "You have been rogering your own sister."

Vicente stepped forward and thrust the knife into the left side of Gabriel's chest while José Chávez y Chávez and Eugenio Alarid simultaneously walloped the teenager over the head with their revolvers. They continued doing so until Sandoval's body went limp before they dragged his battered corpse inside the adobe ruins. Vicente ordered Alarid to keep watch on the corner of Moreno and Pacific Streets and instructed Chávez y Chávez and Trujillo to wait for him at Rosario Lucero de Baca's house. Silva then sauntered off to inform Guadalupe Caballero that "the business was fixed up" and ask his faithful henchman to saddle a horse and bring the animal to Rosario's house.

Vicente Silva asked for some water when joining José Chávez y Chávez and Julian Trujillo at Rosario Lucero de Baca's house and washed Gabriel Sandoval's blood from his hands. When Guadalupe Caballero arrived with his saddled mare, Vicente gave him a dollar and told him to go buy them some whiskey. They all took a drink before Silva removed some money from his belt and handed five dollars to José Chávez y Chávez, Julian Trujillo, Guadalupe Caballero, and his mistress Rosario.

"Let us go," the bandit chief told his male companions.

Vicente Silva stealthily led José Chávez y Chávez, Julian Trujillo, and Guadalupe Caballero over to the abandoned ruins on Moreno Street to dispose of his brother-in-law's corpse. Silva and Trujillo each grabbed one of their young victim's arms while Caballero lifted the lifeless teenager's legs. José Chávez y Chávez led the way while holding the reins of Caballero's mare and keeping a sharp eye out for any witnesses until his companions carried the fresh corpse into a corral behind the Imperial Saloon. The murderers tossed

Gabriel Sandoval's body into a deep privy vault, concealed the corpse with clumps of dirt and woodchips, and quickly dispersed. Silva and Caballero rode northeast to their hideout in Los Alamos. Officers Chávez y Chávez, Trujillo, and Alarid continued patrolling the streets of Las Vegas as if nothing had happened.[40]

The following morning a young boy approached José Chávez y Chávez on the street and told him that Telésfora Sandoval de Silva had requested his presence at her home. When José arrived on Telésfora's doorstep, the concerned woman informed him that her brother Gabriel had not come home and asked if the policeman had seen him the night before. Chávez y Chávez told her that he had seen Gabriel standing in the doorway of the Cantina Imperial and accompanied her brother, Julian Trujillo, and Eugenio Alarid to the police office around nine o'clock. As far as he knew, his three companions then headed over to the Buffalo Saloon to get some sleep. Telésfora immediately sent for Julian Trujillo, who denied having seen Gabriel Sandoval at all the night before. Trujillo suggested the boy may have left town for San Marcial. Telésfora was puzzled by this, stating that her brother only possessed the fifty cents she had given him.[41]

José Chávez y Chávez and Julian Trujillo didn't have any answers for the concerned Señora Silva and resumed patrolling the streets with their batons.

***

It was business as usual for la Sociedad de Bandidos when Vicente Silva, Manuel Gonzáles y Baca, Antonio José Valdéz, Martín Gonzáles y Blea, Dionicio Sisneros, and Florentino Médran robbed German merchant William Frank's store in Los Alamos during the night of April 6, 1893. The hooded bandidos rolled up in a stolen wagon before breaking into the store and loading up several barrels of whiskey, some inventory, and the safe. They broke the safe open at a nearby river and happily took possession of the $4,000 in notes, $125 in school warrants, and $35 cash they found inside. Silva and his associates also paid homage to famous Spanish social bandit Diego Corrientes Mateos by setting fire to William Frank's account books to ensure the German merchant was incapable of collecting thousands of dollars in debts from the locals. "This is the boldest robbery of recent years in San Miguel County," the *New Mexican* announced.[42]

Although the existence of la Sociedad de Bandidos remained a well-kept secret, rumors were circulating that Vicente Silva was somehow responsible for the lynching of Patricio Maes the previous autumn. Shortly after the robbery of William Frank's store, the Society of Bandits suffered their first real setback when valued member Procopio Rael was convicted of carrying arms by a petit jury in Las Vegas in early May 1893. The 37-year-old Rael was also indicted for three other offences and believed to have participated in the recent assault and robbery of Isaac Jacobson in Tecolote.

"Procopio, you seem to be in rather bad luck," Judge James O'Brien remarked after the defendant pleaded not guilty.

"Yes, your honor," the bandido replied. "They can throw stones, but they can't hit me."

Procopio was stunned when Judge O'Brien sentenced him to twelve months in the territorial penitentiary merely for carrying arms. Sheriff Lorenzo López and Special Deputy Enrique H. Salazar subsequently delivered the outlaw to the penitentiary authorities in Santa Fe on May 8, 1893.[43]

Vicente Silva had a problem of his own in Las Vegas at the time. Telésfora Sandoval de Silva was deeply troubled by the mysterious disappearance of her brother Gabriel two months earlier. The bandit chief had pleaded ignorance. He even pretended to search for the missing teenager with his distressed wife. Telésfora had approached prominent attorney Manuel Cabeza de Baca about her brother's disappearance, although a search conducted by some Las Vegas policemen proved ineffective. Having already contemplated Telésfora's murder for months, Vicente decided it was time to silence his wife. He dispatched Guadalupe Caballero to Las Vegas with a phony letter from the deceased Gabriel Sandoval inviting Telésfora to Los Alamos.[44]

While Vicente Silva was trying to lure Telésfora Sandoval de Silva to his hideout in Los Alamos, his associate José Chávez y Chávez would have to answer to Judge Henry Stiles Wooster after assaulting Albino Baca in Las Vegas in early May 1893. "Jose Chaves Y Chaves did unlawfully and in a gross and insulting manner, did assault said affiant (Albino Baca)—and then strike, beat, and kick and slap said affiant's body and face," the court determined. Judge Wooster ordered the policeman to pay a fine of $15.36 plus court costs and released him under a bond of $50.00 on May 15. José Chávez y Chávez decided to leave town for a while and spent the next three months working up in Maxwell City, Colfax County.[45]

It was a good time for José Chávez y Chávez and anyone else engaging in banditry to lay low in New Mexico Territory. The 50-year-old William Taylor Thornton, a seasoned attorney and former mayor of Santa Fe, was clamping down on outlawry following his appointment as governor by President Grover Cleveland the previous month. "Gov. Thornton said this morning that he was determined to leave no stone unturned that would in the least tend to check crime in New Mexico and that he proposed to put a stop to all classes of outlawry," the *New Mexican* had announced in the territorial capital. Thornton offered a reward of $200 for the capture of Vicente Silva and a reward of $100 for the apprehension of those responsible for the robbery of William Frank's store in Los Alamos. A sum of $200 was also offered for information leading to the arrest of those responsible for various murders throughout the territory during the previous four years.[46]

"But the most notorious and damaging case is that of Pablo Herrera," the *New Mexican* declared in May 1893. The Republican newspaper expressed considerable dismay that the elusive Herrera had recently been spotted attending Roman Catholic assemblages despite his fugitive status. "On the evening of March 23 or 24, or of someday about that time, Pablo Herrera was seen on the streets of the town of East Las Vegas, seated in a buggy, and conversing with more parties than one, while he was accompanied by his brother, Nicanor Herrera, the latter being on horseback and armed with a Winchester," declared a grand jury in Santa Fe. Governor William Thornton offered a reward of $200 for the apprehension of Pablo Herrera on May 12, 1893.[47]

One week later, the 39-year-old Telésfora Sandoval de Silva finally set out for Los Alamos after Sociedad de Bandidos member Florentino Médran arrived outside her home in a buggy and delivered a letter from her husband on the morning of May 19, 1893. Vicente Silva's letter informed Telésfora that Médran was there to transport her to Los Alamos and suggested she keep her departure from Las Vegas a secret. Señora Silva believed she was about to be reunited with her adopted daughter Emma and younger brother Gabriel when climbing into the buggy with her escort to begin the thirteen-mile journey to Los Alamos that evening. Her nefarious husband and his right-hand man Guadalupe Caballero were waiting for them at Cañada Patosa halfway along the lesser-known route. Vicente Silva greeted Telésfora affectionately, sent Caballero down to Las Vegas to keep an eye on things, and escorted his unsuspecting better half the rest of the way.[48]

Like many a narcissistic crime boss, Vicente Silva had become blinded by his own hubris. The 48-year-old leader of la Sociedad de Bandidos was blissfully unaware that the handful of ruffians waiting for him and Telésfora to reach their hideout in Los Alamos were convinced their jefe had lost his mind—*estaba loco*. If Silva was willing to kill his own wife, then any one of them could be next. Manuel Gonzáles y Baca, Dionicio Sisneros, Remigio Sandoval, Florentino Médran, Martín Gonzáles y Blea, and several others present had also grown tired of their rapacious leader hoarding most of the profits from their various criminal exploits. A few of them were even feeling a little troubled by their conscience in knowing that an innocent woman was about to be murdered.[49]

Vicente Silva led his wife Telésfora into an arroyo two hundred yards from his hideout and stabbed her to death with his Bowie knife shortly after they reached Los Alamos around midnight. He then returned to his bandidos, instructed them to bury his wife's corpse, and boasted there would be no more "squealing down in Las Vegas." Silva's own men shot him to death the moment he turned his back on them. The bandidos carried their slain leader's corpse to the same arroyo in which Señora Silva had been stabbed approximately a dozen times in the chest. The lacerations on the murdered woman's hands indicated that she had put up a fight in her dying moments. The bandits started digging the hole in which they buried the bodies of Vicente and Telésfora Silva side by side beneath the sand. Everyone present agreed to keep their mouths shut about what had just transpired and hoped the corpses were never found.[50]

Orphaned for the second time in her young life, the robust Emma Silva was reportedly sent to Taos by Rosario Lucero de Baca. The little girl was eventually adopted by Frank and Jesse James's maternal uncle Jesse Richard

Cole and his wife Emily Catherine Cole. The Cole family took the 8-year-old Emma back to Clay County, Missouri, where Emily Cole continued raising the girl like one of her own children after her husband Jesse euthanized himself with a pistol shot to the head following a lengthy illness in 1895. The resilient Emma Silva graduated from Kearney High School, attended William Woods University, and married a salesman named Jesse William Waers in Liberty, Missouri, on December 31, 1902. She briefly returned to New Mexico Territory to search for her biological parents and collect a payment from her curator during the summer of 1903. Emma Silva-Waers became a member of the First Christian Church of North Kansas City and the Order of the Eastern Star in Clay County, Missouri, where she lived out the rest of her days and died a great-grandmother in Kansas City on December 6, 1957.[51]

***

Over three hundred residents of Las Vegas sent a message to anyone engaging in banditry on the night of May 29, 1893. Sociedad de Bandidos member Cecilio Lucero had been apprehended and charged with the brutal murder of his cousin Benigno Martínez and his cousin's employee Juan Gallegos three days earlier. The brutality of the double murder six miles east of Las Vegas stirred up considerable public animosity toward the perpetrator. Cecilio Lucero not only fatally shot the sheepherders for unspecified reasons, but he also crushed their skulls with a rock and tied the corpses behind a burro to be dragged around by the animal the rest of the day. Some of the outraged locals decided to take the law into their hands following Lucero's preliminary hearing and stormed the city jail around 9:15 p.m. City Marshal Thomas F. Clay tried to hold them off before the vengeful mob retrieved Lucero from his cell and escorted the prisoner down Sixth Street to the Board of Trade corner.

"A rope!" members of the crowd exclaimed. "A rope!"

The predominantly Hispano crowd dragged Cecilio Lucero west along Douglas Avenue after someone retrieved a five-eighths-inch hemp rope. The mob eventually reached the G. B. & Co. Warehouse, which had previously served as a skating rink. They decided that was the right place to carry out their brand of justice. A noose was fastened around Lucero's neck while the other end of the rope was thrown over the crosspiece of a nearby telegraph pole.

"I did not do it!" Lucero screamed in Spanish. "I did not kill them! The damned cowards that killed my cousin! I would like to kill them all!"

"Up with him!" various members of the crowd shouted in unison.

The raging mob of citizens hoisted Cecilio Lucero into the air around 9:43 p.m. and left him dangling from the telegraph pole. "No attempt at rescue was made at any time," the *New Mexican* would announce. A coroner's jury cut down Lucero's corpse around 10:10 p.m. "Such was the retribution of Silva's confederate bandit," attorney Manuel Cabeza de Baca later remarked without a hint of sympathy.[52]

The lynching of Cecilio Lucero was probably fresh in the mind of 55-year-old Juan José Herrera when arriving in Santa Fe to meet with Governor William Thornton in June 1893. Although described as the "shining light of the People's party" by the *New Mexican*, the probate judge of San Miguel County proved unsuccessful in his bid to secure a pardon for his younger brother Pablo Herrera. The $200 reward remained open to anyone capable of catching the popular fugitive. "The Optic calls on Pablo Herrera to come in and give himself up to the authorities," the *New Mexican* declared the following month.[53]

While Pablo Herrera continued hiding out in the mountains, a petition was passed around East Las Vegas calling for Procopio Rael to be pardoned by Governor William Thornton in August 1893. Thornton acquiesced after receiving a visit from the Procopio's 57-year-old father Martín and pardoned the prisoner on the afternoon of December 4, 1893. The general consensus was that "the ends of justice had been fully subserved by his incarceration in the penitentiary for seven months." Many residents of Las Vegas may have felt otherwise had they been aware of Procopio Rael's complicity in the lynching of Patricio Maes in October 1892.[54]

Shortly after Procopio Rael was released from the penitentiary, *La Voz Del Pueblo* published a lengthy letter from Juan José Herrera. The probate judge of San Miguel County expressed his frustration with the ongoing debate over the Las Vegas Land Grant and voiced his concern for the working-class population should the matter not be resolved in their favor.

El Capitán also took several less-than-subtle shots at wealthy Las Vegas banker Jefferson Raynolds, an associate of Thomas B. Catron and fierce opponent of the people's movement:

> The question of title settlement to the Las Vegas Grant has been the subject of discussion for many years. It had been silent for some time, for the reason that the former Secretary Noble, a member of Mr. Harrison's cabinet, had decided that it was not in any way legal or legitimate, that the claimants claimed more than what would have been segregated from them, and that the rest would be returned to the public domain. The majority of the residents were evidently satisfied with this decision of the Secretary of the Interior, and nothing more had been said until recently, when some philanthropic (the kind that is always in the communities, who say we want everything for the town) have appeared and are determined to get some arrangement whatever it may be. I admit that getting a fix, as suggested by some people, would produce a big enough "potato" for some, and it may be that I even touched a slice, but despite that, I strongly deny that the masses can be benefited by some of the fixes that have been pointed out.
>
> The only one that could perhaps benefit the masses is the one that has as its object the arrangement in favor of the community. But now I ask, who is the community? The majority of those who make up the community are small-scale farmers and working men of limited resources, who either now or later will be forced to mortgage their farms to buy the necessities of life; so that after some time the philanthropic that I have mentioned above, having the *con, perhaps*, will soon keep all the land, and will have satisfied his inordinate greed. So if the initiators of this movement are sincere, and really work for the public good, then the interpretation that should be given to the so-called grant of Las Vegas, is that it would be left, seconded by the Mexican government, "for common rights," which means public domain.
>
> Now Mr. Editor, in support of my assertion that "common rights" means public domain, I wish to cite the colonization laws of Mexico and Spain. It was the custom, and it was legally established by those governments, that whenever there were ten new lands, at once they were recognized by these governments as a municipality, with rights to a mayor, and sometimes, he and the three members of the council had full right to distribute land to the colonists, and these distributions were made to each individual, in accordance with his means for cultivating, and the same was done with all the nine that came after. This was done

in this so-called Las Vegas community grant, until the year 1846. The boundaries established for the so-called Las Vegas Grant were intended for the municipality, to indicate the limits of power of the municipal government, in the same way that the boundaries of the city of Denver, or of the city of Las Vegas, were drawn, but they were never intended as the boundaries of the grant, because if such had been the understanding, none of the lands could have been apportioned by the mayor up to the year 1846, without an unsecured document from the owners thereof, and a mayor would then have had as much right to distribute the land as I have to dispose of Mr. Raynolds's property.

Juan J. Herrera[55]

As the Las Vegas Land Grant issue remained unresolved to Juan José Herrera's considerable irritation, a dispatch sent from Albuquerque to the *Daily Globe-Democrat* in St. Louis, Missouri, insisted the notorious Porfirio Trujillo was raising hell in eastern Bernalillo and Valencia Counties in December 1893. "In the Manzano mountains, east of [Albuquerque], a desperate character named Porfirio Trujillo, who is a murderer, is the leader of a gang of rustlers, and the peaceful settlers are much alarmed," the dispatch read. "This is supposed to be the worst gang in the territory." The *Albuquerque Times* set the record straight a short time later. "Whoever sent that dispatch is trying to earn a dollar at the expense of the good name of this territory and Valencia County," the newspaper declared. "The truth of the Valencia County outlawry is that the leader of the gang of cattle killers operating east of Chilili and south through the Berendo plains is an American and resident of Bernalillo County. It is bad enough to send such unnecessary intelligence broadcast over the country, but it is far worse to saddle the blame on to a Mexican."[56]

For anyone hoping to profit from headlines about Hispano banditry, their wish was granted when the curtain finally fell on la Sociedad de Bandidos de Nuevo México during the spring of 1894.

***

Manuel Gonzáles y Baca was missing his family while locked in the San Miguel County jail in early April 1894. The 30-year-old member of la Sociedad de Bandidos and former city policeman had been arrested for cattle theft in Los Alamos four months earlier. Manuel was looking for a way out when sending a message to esteemed Mora County resident Rafael Romero, a graduate of Notre Dame and Princeton Universities and a prominent Democrat. Romero had recently arrived in Las Vegas to serve as interpreter during the district court session, and Gonzáles y Baca wanted to make a deal with the authorities in exchange for some startling information about a secret society of bandits and the mysterious disappearance of young Gabriel Sandoval fourteen months earlier.[57]

Manuel Gonzáles y Baca spilled his guts when Rafael Romero paid him a visit on the morning of April 11, 1894. The prisoner confessed that he belonged to a secret organization called la Sociedad de Bandidos de Nuevo México and revealed the names of various other members. Manuel further revealed that Gabriel Sandoval was stabbed to death by Vicente Silva in the presence of Julian Trujillo—now the justice of the peace for San Miguel County Precinct No. 10—and some other crooked policemen. Gonzáles y Baca insisted the teenager's corpse had been buried in a privy vault behind the Farmers Hotel, previously known as the Imperial Saloon.

Any degree of skepticism Rafael Romero and the local authorities may have initially felt evaporated when the body of Gabriel Sandoval was uncovered in the exact location provided by Manuel Gonzáles y Baca on the afternoon of April 11, 1894. The corpse had decomposed beyond physical recognition after fourteen months and was identified by the pocket watch and several other items on his person. A coroner's inquest carried out by Justice of the Peace Pablo Ulibarri later that night determined that Gabriel Sandoval's death was caused by "a mortal wound in his breast, between the second and third ribs, on the left side, and inflicted with a two-edged instrument."[58]

The revelations of Manuel Gonzáles y Baca and discovery of Gabriel Sandoval's corpse shocked the local population and quickly became a leading news item throughout New Mexico Territory. "The Bandit Society of San Miguel County, so called, must go!" the *Las Vegas Daily Optic* announced. "Manuel Gonzales y Baca, who 'peached' on his fellows, has been released from jail, on bonds." Although Manuel remained tight-lipped about the deaths of Vicente and Telésfora Silva, warrants were issued for various members of la Sociedad de Bandidos either directly involved or complicit in the murder of Gabriel Sandoval. Sheriff Lorenzo López promptly arrested Procopio Rael,

Martín Gonzáles y Blea, Guadalupe Caballero, and Rosario Lucero de Baca for complicity in Sandoval's murder and escorted them to the county jail.[59]

Governor William Thornton arrived in town and attended a meeting convened by former Sheriff José Santos Esquibel in St. Joseph's Hall, West Las Vegas, on the night of April 12, 1894. Probate Judge Juan José Herrera, Félix Martínez, Rafael Romero, Manuel Gonzáles, and Manuel Cabeza de Baca were appointed to a committee to confer with Governor Thornton "as to what action is best to be taken in the present alarming condition of affairs in San Miguel County." Thornton met with the committee and promised to support District Attorney Lewis C. Fort in his "efforts to see that the laws of the land are faithfully executed" the following morning. Chief Justice Thomas Smith was equally determined to eradicate the Society of Bandits and a thorough investigation began. "Several parties implicated have fled from Las Vegas," the *New Mexican* announced.[60]

While Dionicio Sisneros and several other members of la Sociedad de Bandidos had skipped town like rats fleeing a burning stable, the 44-year-old José Chávez y Chávez stuck around long enough to observe Gabriel Sandoval's decomposed body lying on a piece of tin. The teenager's corpse was later respectfully interred in Las Vegas. Although Manuel Gonzáles y Baca does not appear to have initially named Chávez y Chávez as a participant in Sandoval's murder, the policeman was subpoenaed by Justice of the Peace Pablo Ulibarri and the coroner's jury. They wanted to know if Officer Chávez y Chávez saw Gabriel Sandoval on the night he was murdered and inquired about a mysterious gunshot on Moreno Street shortly before the teenager's disappearance. José testified that Sandoval was in the company of Julian Trujillo when he last saw the boy on the night in question.[61]

Things became much hotter for José Chávez y Chávez after Sheriff Lorenzo López and several deputies captured Germán Maestas five miles north of Lamy on April 14, 1894. Maestas had been charged with the murder of a sheepherder named Pedro Romero the previous month. Romero had married Germán's unofficial wife Rosita "Rosa" Durán while the bandido was serving a two-month sentence in the territorial penitentiary for carrying arms earlier that year. The vengeful outlaw inevitably shot and killed the sheepherder near Los Alamos shortly after his release. Germán initially refused to surrender when cornered by the López posse, wrongly assuming José Chávez y Chávez was among their ranks and believing that he would be killed. He eventually gave up his arms when Sheriff López talked him down and was transported to Las Vegas later that day. Maestas was locked inside the county jail and indicted by a grand jury for the murder of Pedro Romero shortly after his arrival.[62]

The roughly 30-year-old Germán Maestas realized he was probably destined for the gallows. He turned to his religious faith and decided to seek redemption in the eyes of his God by disclosing details about the murders of school director Carpio Sais, Patricio Maes, Gabriel Sandoval, and Telésfora Sandoval de Silva to the authorities. The prisoner revealed José Chávez y Chávez's status as a leading member of la Sociedad de Bandidos and his involvement in several murders in the process. Germán's revelations were corroborated by Manuel Gonzáles y Baca, who had been promised a pardon in exchange for his testimony.[63]

As a result of the information provided by Manuel Gonzáles y Baca and Germán Maestas, warrants were issued for the arrest of Vicente Silva, Dionicio Sisneros, José Tiburcio Montoya, Zenon Maes, Pedro Baca, Marcos Varela, Nestor Herrera, and various other members of la Sociedad de Bandidos for complicity in the murder of Patricio Maes. Further warrants were issued for the apprehension of José Chávez y Chávez, Julian Trujillo, and Eugenio Alarid for their complicity in the murder of Gabriel Sandoval. While Dionicio Sisneros fled in the direction of Arizona, most of the bandidos were quickly apprehended, including José Tiburcio Montoya on the night of April 15, 1894.

Julian Trujillo agreed to testify for the prosecution against his associates shortly after he and Eugenio Alarid were taken into custody. District Attorney Lewis C. Fort needed more witnesses and offered immunity to Ricardo Romero, Lisandro Montoya, Manuel Maldonado, and Hilario Mares—all charged with complicity in the murder of Patricio Maes—in exchange for their testimony. "A public meeting was held at the Opera House tonight for the purpose of expressing the approbation of the community for the energetic action of the governor, chief justice, and other officials in prosecuting crime and enforcing the laws," one resident of Las Vegas wrote on April 20, 1894.[64]

José Chávez y Chávez was unaware the *gato* was out of the bag while attending to some personal business four miles southwest of Las Vegas in Agua Zarca around April 20, 1894. He was surprised to find many of the locals in a state of excitement when he returned to the county seat that evening. "Then it was that I heard a great deal of noise in the plaza here in town, and heard it said that they were looking for me and that they were after me," José later recalled. A local woman informed the policeman that she understood Manuel Gonzáles y Baca and Ricardo Romero had implicated him in the murders of Gabriel Sandoval and Patricio Maes, as well as the robbery of William Frank's store in Los Alamos. José wasn't taking any chances when he learned deputies Billy Green, Arthur Jilson, and Joe Blakely were looking for him, and he quickly fled town.[65]

José Chávez y Chávez put a little distance between himself and Las Vegas until reaching a crest "about a mile and a half west of town," as he later recalled. He kept an eye out for any deputies while hiding out in the timbers for several days with his Winchester rifle. "Then I went to a place called Encinosa, west of town," José later said. "Some days I would go without anything to eat, at others I would get something to eat from the wood haulers." The fugitive eventually sent a message to his friend Serafin Baca, asking the deputy to ride out from Las Vegas and meet with him. Baca arrived alone a short time later and accompanied his amigo to the nearby home of an old woman named Tamosa. Deputy Baca promised to return with some tobacco for his friend before heading back to Las Vegas.[66]

José Chávez y Chávez was awaiting Serafin Baca's return on a nearby ridge a short time later when he spotted a group of men approaching on horseback in the distance. He quickly realized Deputy Baca was returning with a posse rather than some tobacco and began sprinting southwest with all possible speed. José continued running all through the night until reaching Bado de Juan Pais, a small settlement twenty-two miles southwest of Las Vegas in Guadalupe County. Chávez y Chávez had amigos in Bado de Juan Pais but dared not show his face under the circumstances. The exhausted fugitive found a secluded place on the outskirts of the placita to catch a nap around sunrise. He then set off on a seventy-mile journey southwest toward Albuquerque later that morning.[67]

José's legs frequently hurt from rheumatoid arthritis, but he had to keep moving. The fugitive spent some of the next five or six days slowly walking toward Albuquerque until hitching a ride on a passing stranger's wagon. "The man driving the wagon said he was coming from Tascosa and was on his way to Albuquerque," he later recalled. "It was a wagon with a team of burros hitched to it." José bypassed Albuquerque by heading south along the Río Grande toward Sevilleta (La Joya), Socorro County. He then crossed the river, spent several days traveling west in the direction of Acoma Pueblo in the company of some young Pueblo Indians, and arrived on a Navajo reservation in eastern New Mexico. "I worked for the Indians for fifteen days," he remembered.[68]

While José Chávez y Chávez was traveling over two hundred miles from Las Vegas to Navajo country, Chief Justice Thomas Smith brought the hammer down on various members of la Sociedad de Bandidos inside the San Miguel County courthouse on May 2, 1894. For their complicity in the murder of Patricio Maes, Procopio Rael was sentenced to ten years in the penitentiary, Nestor Herrera and Marcos Barela were sentenced to seven years, Pedro Baca and Nicacio Rael received five years, and Zenon Maes was sentenced to four years. They were all transported to Santa Fe at four o'clock that afternoon to begin their prison terms. "The conviction of six of the men breaks up the infamous secret society," the *New Mexican* announced. "These are the men who, at the 'trial' of Maes in Silva's house voted against hanging Maes as advocated by Silva, hence the comparatively light sentences imposed by the court." Germán Maestas received no such clemency when convicted of the murder of sheepherder Pedro Romero the same day. Maestas was sentenced to death by hanging and would remain confined to his cell in the county jail until his execution was carried out later that month.[69]

"Joe Blakely and Billy Green brought Julian Trujillo up from Fort Sumner, yesterday afternoon, and placed him in jail," the *Las Vegas Daily Optic* announced on May 3, 1894. "It is said that he has more startling disclosures at his tongue's end and may yet prove to be a valuable witness for the prosecution in some of the approaching murder trials." Julian Trujillo and Eugenio Alarid were arraigned for their complicity in the murder of Gabriel Sandoval and pleaded not guilty. The following morning Sheriff Lorenzo

López and six deputies escorted Dionicio Sisneros over from Santa Fe and locked him inside the county jail. Sisneros had disguised himself as a traveling musician and crossed the border into Arizona. Santa Fe County Sheriff William P. Cunningham and Deputy Sheriff Page Otero had trailed the fugitive for six days and finally captured him in Tucson.[70]

Chief Justice Thomas Smith and District Attorney Lewis C. Fort continued breaking up the Society of Bandits throughout the remainder of the district court session in May 1894. Dionicio Sisneros was sentenced to life in the penitentiary for his complicity in the murder of Patricio Maes. Manuel Gonzáles y Blea, Librado Polanco, and Remigio Sandoval also received life sentences when convicted of murder in the second degree, although Guadalupe Caballero received only three years after divulging some information to the authorities. Nicanor Gallegos received ten years' imprisonment for his complicity in the murder of Patricio Maes, while José Tiburcio Montoya was sentenced to three years. Former policemen Julian Trujillo and Eugenio Alarid were both sentenced to life in the penitentiary for their complicity in the murder of Gabriel Sandoval.[71]

La Sociedad de Bandidos de Nuevo México was finished, but the question "Where is Vicente Silva?" remained on many people's lips. For all the testimony provided by members of the criminal organization, none of them dared speak a word of their leader's death. A report that Silva and his wife had been captured by a deputy US marshal in Flagstaff, Arizona, was inevitably proven false. An executive proclamation was issued offering a reward of $500 for the capture of the deceased bandido slowly rotting beneath the soil in an arroyo outside Los Alamos. Germán Maestas informed the authorities that Telésfora Sandoval de Silva had supposedly been murdered by her husband. The prisoner was either unaware of Vicente Silva's own death or chose to remain silent about the matter while awaiting his execution. "The hunt for Silva continued, but to no avail," recalled attorney Manuel Cabeza de Baca. "People were convinced that the earth had swallowed him."[72]

As the citizens of Las Vegas pondered the whereabouts of Vicente Silva, the local officials were fully aware that José Chávez y Chávez had successfully fled San Miguel County. The *New Mexican* publicized the territorial government's commitment to apprehending the disgraced policeman on May 11, 1894: "An executive proclamation has been issued offering a reward of $500 for the arrest and conviction of Jose Chavez y Chavez, late of San Miguel County, charged with murder, who is now a fugitive from justice."[73]

With a $500 reward providing ample motivation for any lawman bold enough to pursue him, José Chávez y Chávez was now among the most wanted outlaws in the annals of New Mexican banditry. "Feliciano Chavez, another member of the secret society, accused of complicity in the Maes hanging, was arrested a few days ago," wrote one resident of Las Vegas on May 11, 1894. "This leaves two of the gang at large, but unfortunately they are the principal members of the murderous crowd, they being Vicente Silva and Jose Chavez y Chavez. The latter will, in all probability, be captured soon, but there are doubts as to the capture of Silva."[74]

While José Chávez y Chávez would prove more difficult to apprehend than anticipated, his one-time confederate Germán Maestas was staring death in the face on the afternoon of May 25, 1894. A scaffold had been constructed directly east of the San Miguel County jail within a twelve-foot-high enclosure, inside which some two hundred residents of Las Vegas were eagerly awaiting his execution. A further fifteen hundred people were gathered outside the enclosure and desperate to catch a glimpse of the outlaw's final moments. It was steadily approaching 1:20 that afternoon when Santa Fe County Sheriff William P. Cunningham arrived outside Germán's cell.

"Are you ready?" the lawman asked.

"Ready for what?" the prisoner replied.

"To go down," the sheriff answered.

Germán Maestas assured Sheriff Cunningham that he was ready and appeared entirely unfazed when consulting with the Roman Catholic priest who would accompany him to the gallows. The convicted murderer firmly believed his sins had been forgiven by Dios and said farewell to the other prisoners while being escorted out of the building.

"Where are you going?" the clergyman asked him between prayers.

"To meet God," Maestas confidently replied.

The large crowd of citizens gathered inside the enclosure noticed the peaceful smile on Germán's face when Sheriff Cunningham and the priest escorted him into the yard. The prisoner appeared tranquil when ascending the steps of the wooden scaffold and didn't flinch when his feet and hands were bound with rope. Maestas exhibited no sign of apprehension when the noose was placed over his head, even voluntarily lifting his chin to allow for the rope to be properly adjusted around his short neck and the knot positioned behind his left ear. "There is one mean trait that Maestas could not be accused of, and that was cowardice," one observer recalled. The condemned man declined the opportunity to voice any final thoughts to the crowd, but answered the priest's prayers before a dark hood was pulled over his scalp. The lever was pushed at 1:20 p.m. and Germán Maestas descended through the trapdoor as scheduled. His neck snapped at the end of a short drop, and he was officially pronounced dead five minutes later.[75]

The body of Germán Maestas was turned over to his 59-year-old father Macedonio for burial following a coroner's examination. The executed man's unofficial bride Rosita Durán and their 5-year-old-son Lauteres Maestas presumably attended the funeral. "The hanging of Maestas has taught the rest of the gang a salutary lesson," the *New Mexican* declared on May 25, 1894. "The only thing that now remains to be done to break up the gang entirely is the capture of Vicente Silva and Jose Chavez y Chavez." The following day, *La Voz Del Pueblo* exhibited its disdain for the elusive José Chávez y Chávez when castigating the former policeman in Spanish: "A singular thing that almost always shows that the most cowardly murderers and the most brazen thieves are always laughing their heads off. They all show their teeth: when they are told something, even if it does not deserve laughter, they let out a resounding laugh. As an example of this we cite José Chávez y Chávez, the most cowardly murderer there has ever been: he was always laughing and ingratiating himself with everyone, as if he had been the most meek little lamb in the community."[76]

José Chávez y Chávez later claimed that his decision to flee Las Vegas was partially from fear that Deputy Billy Green would shoot him on sight. "When I got the information that Billy Green was out looking for me, I thought to myself he would shoot me from a corner, and say that I made some resistance, because I knew what kind of a fellow he was," he recalled. While no more of a ruffian than José Chávez y Chávez himself, the 27-year-old William Green would serve as the catalyst of a violent incident that only broadened the racial divide in San Miguel County during the summer of 1894.[77]

Deputy Billy Green, his brother Elias, and their Mexican companion Jesús Villezea were eager to collect some of the reward money for the apprehension of anyone charged with complicity in the murder of Patricio Maes as they transported fatally wounded clergyman Nestor Gallegos into Las Vegas on the morning of July 26, 1894. Deputy Green insisted the fugitive had been shot while resisting arrest. Gallegos informed Justice of the Peace Pablo Ulibarri that the deputy shot him without justifiable cause before dying of his wounds the following day. "When [Green] yelled at me to surrender, I didn't say anything, but just because I moved to climb on a rock he shot me," Gallegos insisted. Justice Ulibarri believed Gallegos was telling the truth, and a warrant was issued for Deputy Green's arrest for the crime of murder.

Billy and Elias Green and Jesús Villezea were in the kitchen of Green's restaurant in West Las Vegas when they spotted Constable José Martínez and deputies Donaciano Sandoval and Simón Aragón approaching them on the night of July 26. "We had barely seen them when they came upon us threatening us with the weapons they brought," José Martínez recalled. Green refused to be taken into custody when Martínez produced a warrant for him. He then opened fire alongside his two companions, shooting Deputy Donaciano Sandoval in the chest and stomach. Sandoval died moments after tumbling to the floor. Constable Martínez and Deputy Aragón quickly exited the restaurant and sought out Sheriff Lorenzo López.[78]

When the sheriff and a posse arrived outside Billy Green's restaurant, City Marshal Thomas F. Clay of East Las Vegas insisted that he was the only one authorized to carry out the arrest. This did not sit well with Sheriff López and his Hispano deputies as decades of ethnic hostility took hold of everyone's senses. A standoff ensued between the two factions while many Hispano and Anglo citizens inevitably began taking sides. "There was a race war brewing, when District Attorney Fort called on the U.S. troops for assistance," the *New Mexican* declared. Things only got worse when a lieutenant and detachment of 10th Infantry soldiers arrived on the scene and tried to disperse the crowd with the bayonets fixed to their rifles. The commanding officer was punched in the face by one of Sheriff López's supporters, and López was struck by a soldier's bayonet in the confusion.

When the deputy finally emerged from his restaurant, Sheriff López and City Marshal Clay each grabbed one of Billy Green's arms and began an impromptu game of tug of war. "It looked like Green would be torn in two by the contending officials," the *New Mexican* remarked. City Marshal Clay was eventually able to take sole custody of Deputy Green with military assistance and escorted the prisoner across the Gallinas River Bridge to East Las Vegas. While permitted to take custody of Jesús Villezea in West Las Vegas, Sheriff López's repeated demands that William and Elias Green be turned over to him were denied. City Marshal Clay and the soldiers feared the two Americanos would be lynched by a mob of Hispano citizens, and District Attorney Lewis C. Fort sent a telegram to Governor Thornton later that night. "People are greatly excited and need your presence here to quiet matters, as great danger of a riot prevails," the attorney pleaded. Sheriff Lorenzo López sent his own telegram to Governor Thornton the following morning. "Can deputy marshals with soldiers interfere with and oppose my arrest of criminal prisoners when I hold warrants for the arrest of same for murder?" López asked. "Is martial law enforced to that extent?"[79]

Racial tensions continued to broil throughout Las Vegas following the incident described by *La Voz Del Pueblo* as an "Encuentro Fatal" (Fatal Encounter), and the subsequent conflict "entre el Americano y el Mexicano" (between the American and the Mexican). The *Las Vegas Daily Optic* bemoaned the unauthorized use of military force as murmurs of a race war began spreading throughout the countryside. Governor William Thornton arrived in Las Vegas and tried to calm the situation on July 28, 1894. His job became more difficult when Chief Justice Thomas Smith ruled that Billy Green was justified when shooting the deceased Nestor Gallegos. Billy Green, Elias Green, and Jesús Villezea were then bound over to a grand jury for the shooting of Deputy Donaciano Sandoval and released on bonds.[80]

The fatal shooting of Deputy Donaciano Sandoval temporarily united the Hispano population of San Miguel County like never before. Political persuasions were cast aside when representatives of el Partido del Pueblo Unido and the Republican Party attended a mass meeting held in a schoolhouse on July 30, 1894. Juan José Herrera, Sheriff Lorenzo López, Félix Martínez, Eugenio Romero, Manuel Cabeza de Baca, Charles Rudulph, Antonio Lucero, Patricio Gonzáles, and various other officials and citizens were all in attendance when the formation of a people's union was announced. "The people of San Miguel County unite under the guild of one party," *La Voz Del Pueblo* declared. Resolutions were passed stressing unity for the common good of the people and condemning the murderers of Deputy Donaciano Sandoval. "Del pueblo, por el pueblo y para el pueblo" (Of the people, by the people and for the people), was the cry heard inside the schoolhouse. News of the mass meeting spread across the countryside and various Hispano residents of Guadalupe and Rio Arriba Counties declared their support for el Partido de Union.[81]

As quickly as the Hispanos of San Miguel County rallied together after the shooting of Deputy Donaciano Sandoval, dissension over their union's leadership and platform destroyed any sense of solidarity by the end of September 1894. Sheriff Lorenzo López and Enrique H. Salazar soon decided to split off from the Unionistas to form their own party, called el Partido Independiente. While flying the banner of el Partido de Union, Eugenio Romero continued supporting Thomas B. Catron, who greatly benefited from the political turmoil in San Miguel County and finally defeated Antonio Joseph in the race for delegate to Congress that November. Although a spirit of resistance against Anglo encroachment and predatory capitalism endured in smaller sects of the Hispano community, the people's movement steadily crumbled under the weight of persistent infighting and factionalism. Like famous Spanish American leader Simón Bolívar in South America decades earlier, Juan José Herrera and his faction of faithful revolutionaries ultimately discovered they had "plowed the sea" after almost touching heaven in Condado de San Miguel.[82]

José Chávez y Chávez could not have cared less about San Miguel County politics when crossing the border into eastern Arizona Territory during the summer of 1894. "I don't remember whether it was in June or the latter part of July," he later said. José eventually reached the Gila River and spent almost three weeks working in various Hispano sheep camps. The fugitive had been hired to keep a tally of the sheep being sheared, but the rheumatoid arthritis in his legs was giving him considerable grief at the time. He soon took refuge in the mountains of Socorro County, just east of the Arizona border. The desperate fugitive boarded in the home of an elderly local hombre and worked as a sheepherder in the area for the remainder of 1894. "At that time, I was working to get enough money to buy a horse, because at that time I had seen a newspaper account and ascertained the amount of the reward offered for my arrest," he later recalled.[83]

While José Chávez y Chávez was hiding out in the mountains of Socorro County, the tenacious Pablo Herrera returned to his farm nine miles outside of Las Vegas by December 1894. The charter member of Los Gorras Blancas kept a low profile when occasionally venturing into the city to visit his amigos and relatives. He was reputedly attempting to raise support for a resurgence of large-scale White Cap resistance. It was also rumored that he was intending to surrender to Sheriff Lorenzo López and submit himself once more to the courts.

Whatever his exact motivations, the 50-year-old Pablo Herrera arrived in West Las Vegas and visited a padre's private home to confess his sins and take communion on the morning of December 24, 1894. He also visited several mercantile stores to formally request that any bonus items be distributed to the local Hispano children for La Navidad. The wanted fugitive then stopped by Edward G. Murphey's apothecary before making his way to the home of 48-year-old laborer Don Catarino Romero.

Pablo Herrera sat down with the Romero family to enjoy a meal unaware that someone had spotted him soliciting presents for the local Hispano children in the plaza. The citizen ran toward the courthouse to inform Chief Justice Thomas Smith of Herrera's presence in the city. "There is no shortage of individuals who are frightened even by their own shadow, and who are always ready to know the faults of others but not their own," *La Voz Del Pueblo* would bitterly report. Chief Justice Smith declared Pablo's presence an "insult to the community." He called on Sheriff Lorenzo López to bring Herrera in dead or alive and issued bench warrants to City Marshal Thomas F. Clay and Constable Billy Green for the fugitive's arrest. Sheriff Lorenzo López was compelled to do his duty as always and raised a heavily armed posse of thirteen men, including his brother Felipe López. The posse approached Catarino Romero's home with their Winchester rifles and split into four groups to cut off any chance of escape.

As nine o'clock was approaching that Christmas Eve morning, Catarino Romero's 17-year-old son Sabino came running into the dining room to inform his father and Pablo Herrera that some armed men were outside their home. Catarino headed for the front door, intending to hold the posse off until convincing Herrera to surrender peacefully. Pablo took this opportunity to make his escape through a door leading into a corral and headed for Nicolás T. Córdova's home. Members of the posse opened fire when they spotted him heading north up the street. Pablo sprinted through Domingo Moore's house, unaware that deputies Felipe López and Porfirio Casaus had taken cover near the door of Jesús Hernández's adjacent home.

When Deputy Sheriff Felipe López spotted Pablo Herrera scrambling into his line of sight, he took aim with his Winchester rifle and fired three times, hitting the fugitive twice in the back. Pablo tumbled into a sitting position and loudly gasped for air as the posse cautiously approached him. Constable Billy Green needlessly fired a shot into the fatally wounded Hispano's left cheek. Pablo Herrera's fresh corpse was quickly carried inside Róuiulo Ulibarri's nearby home while several Nuevomexicano bystanders were arrested after forcibly disarming Billy Green and beating him over the head in retaliation.

Although members of the posse claimed Pablo Herrera had opened fire on them first, other eyewitnesses insisted the fugitive's revolver was still nestled in his holster when he was cut down. News of Pablo Herrera's death spread rapidly, and many local Nuevomexicanos were furious. Chief Justice Thomas Smith promptly sent a telegram to Santa Fe requesting Governor Thornton order "fire-arms in the possession of the Las Vegas militia company turned over to the sheriff that he might be prepared to preserve order." Justice of the Peace José L. Galindre held a coroner's inquest, with Nicolas T. Córdova, Catarino Romero, José Delores Gallegos, Felipe Montoya, Gregorio Varela, and Juan Silva serving as jurors.

While Anglo newspapers happily announced "the dead outlaw" had been taken down, Félix Martínez and his staff at *La Voz Del Pueblo* were shocked and disheartened. "Herrera was the offspring of one of the best families in our county," the Hispano newspaper professed. "Like his brothers he was generous, and he had all the characteristics of a patriotic man. He was a man of courage, for he was never seen to show fear in any difficulty no matter how serious it was. At last, he had to succumb to the fatal decree of destiny and there is nothing left but to pray that God have mercy on his soul." Juan José and Nicanor Herrera soon arrived in Las Vegas to quietly prepare their brother's corpse for burial.[84]

Pablo Herrera was laid to rest in a Roman Catholic cemetery on December 26, 1894. Any sense of renewed large-scale Gorras Blancas resistance had died with him.

Chapter 16

Barbarian, He Is!

Oh, sinnerman, where you gonna run to?
—Nina Simone

The mystery of Vicente Silva's whereabouts was finally solved when Rafael Romero and Manuel Cabeza de Baca paid Florentino Médran a visit in the territorial penitentiary in late February, 1895. Médran had previously hinted that his former jefe was dead but refused to divulge any further information. This time the prisoner informed Rafael Romero and Manuel Cabeza de Baca that Silva and his wife Telésfora were both killed and buried together in an arroyo outside Los Alamos during the spring of 1893. A party of officials from Las Vegas spent several days searching for the burial site until finally exhuming the bodies on March 17, 1895. The rotting corpses were transported to Las Vegas in the back of a wagon around 5:30 that afternoon.[1]

The bodies of Vicente Silva and Telésfora Sandoval de Silva were officially identified during an inquest held in the San Miguel County courthouse on March 18, 1895. "The former had a set of false teeth, a very bald head and long gray beard," the *New Mexican* announced. The body of Vicente Silva was buried "in an unobstructed plain" as Manuel Cabeza de Baca recalled. Telésfora Sandoval de Silva's corpse was respectfully interred in a Roman Catholic cemetery. "Thereby hangs a tale of blood curdling crime that has few equals in western history," the *New Mexican* declared. "For nearly two years officers of the law have been in search of Silva." Meanwhile, Society of Bandits member Jesús Vialpando and his accomplice Feliciano Chávez had been arrested the previous month for the murder of rancher Tomás Martínez and were sentenced to death by hanging in Santa Fe. With confirmation of Vicente's Silva's demise, and most of la Sociedad de Bandidos either behind bars or destined for the gallows, all that remained was the apprehension of Silva's "lieutenant" José Chávez y Chávez.[2]

Governor William Thornton and the territorial authorities would strike another blow against banditry when Deputy Sheriff Thomas H. Tucker arrested Porfirio Trujillo in Las Vegas and escorted him to the Santa Fe County jail on April 20, 1895. "Porfirio Trujillo, whose long criminal record is as black as the interior of a tar barrel, who has repeatedly been in durance vile for deeds of blood and plunder, who has hitherto contrived to escape from the hands of justice, was arrested," the New Mexican proudly announced. The one-time member of Los Gorras Blancas was set to finally stand trial for his complicity in the murders of sheepherders Joseph Leckie, Julian Tessiere, and Jesús Trujillo in Rock Creek, Santa Fe County, on March 5, 1887. "This triple tragedy was a most cowardly and brutal affair," the *New Mexican* declared. "After the men were murdered, the bodies were burned."[3]

La Sociedad de Bandidos had been extinguished, but the apprehension of the elusive José Chávez y Chávez remained a high priority for the territorial authorities. Socorro County Sheriff Holm Olaf Bursum was undoubtedly aware of the $500 reward on the fugitive's head when hearing whispers that Chávez y Chávez was working as a sheepherder under an assumed name near the Arizona border during the spring of 1895. The Norwegian lawman assigned 28-year-old Joseph "José" Wiggins to investigate the matter. Special Deputy Sheriff Joe Wiggins may have been familiar with José Chávez y Chávez, having spent some of his childhood residing in Fort Stanton, Lincoln County, with his Anglo father William and Hispano mother María during the early 1870s.[4]

The 45-year-old José Chávez y Chávez was working as a sheepherder around forty-five miles north of Quemado, Socorro County, when a "half-breed" young man showed up looking for a job in May 1895. Special Deputy

Sheriff Joe Wiggins had found his man and spent several days working undercover alongside the fugitive known as José González. The unsuspecting Chávez y Chávez was rolling himself a cigarillo and enjoying the warmth of a campfire when Wiggins finally made his move on Tuesday, May 21, 1895. The special deputy pointed his gun at the wanted bandido and told him to throw up his hands. José knew the game was up when he spotted the firearm aimed in his direction. He could only smile while slowly rising to his feet and reaching for the clouds above.

"It is no use," Chávez y Chávez conceded. "You have me."[5]

Special Deputy Sheriff Joe Wiggins quickly escorted his captive southeast toward Socorro. José went along quietly, and they arrived in town without incident two days later. Sheriff Holm O. Bursum then began transporting José Chávez y Chávez northeast to Las Vegas. They reached the metropolis by the end of the month. "Sheriff Bursum, of Socorro County, arrived at noon, having in charge Jose Chavez y Chavez, the notorious member of the Silva gang, wanted for participation in four murders," the *Las Vegas Daily Optic* informed its readers. "Chavez was found in Socorro County, on the very border line of Arizona, herding sheep."

Sheriff Holm O. Bursum took credit for the arrest when delivering José Chávez y Chávez to San Miguel County Sheriff Hilario Romero. *La Voz Del Pueblo* declared an *epoca de retribución* when announcing the long-awaited capture of Chávez y Chávez on June 1, 1895:

> Just as the seed produces the plants, so crime produces its expiation; The echo of the news of the verdict of the jury in the case of the Borregos and others had not just calmed down, when another inmate who is charged for one of the most horrible crimes committed in New Mexico arrived at the Las Vegas depot. The subject we are talking about is José Chavez y Chavez, who suddenly disappeared a few days after the discovery of the late Gabriel Sandoval. Chavez was arrested in Socorro County at a sheep ranch by the Socorro County Sheriff. He is now in safe hands, under the guardianship of Sheriff Romero. The time of crime has passed and now the time of retribution is in force.[6]

While the apprehension of José Chávez y Chávez was acknowledged by the territorial press, the local reporters were more concerned with the headline-grabbing trial of Francisco Gonzáles y Borrego, Antonio Gonzáles y Borrego, Laureano "Chino" Alarid, and Patricio Valencia—all charged with the murder of Francisco "Frank" Chávez—over in Santa Fe. Their former associate Juan Gallegos caused a sensation when testifying that Thomas B. Catron had promised the four accused hombres a sum of $700 to carry out the assassination. "No one believed such a statement, not even Catron's enemies," Miguel Antonio Otero Jr. later insisted.[7]

The late Francisco Chávez's mother, Juliana V. Chávez, certainly had her suspicions, having mailed a letter to Thomas Catron accusing him of complicity in her son's murder. "Mr. Catron, you are not above suspicion of knowing more about the assassination of my son than you have ever found it convenient to reveal," Señora Chávez's letter read. "The murderers as far as discovered are political partisans of yours, they frequented your office, were of the same society, sworn with you to mutually protect each other, and you have always defended them in their commissions of crimes." Catron would have to defend himself against accusations of influencing various witnesses after the jury found the Borrego brothers, Alarid, and Valencia guilty of murder in the first degree in Santa Fe on May 29, 1895. The four Hispanos were sentenced to be hanged on July 10, although a review by the New Mexico Supreme Court delayed their execution.[8]

While many were seeking justice for the assassination of Frank Chávez in the territorial capital, José Chávez y Chávez spent the summer of 1895 biding his time in the San Miguel County jail and waiting for the fourth district court to open that November. "The people of the upper Pecos valley are highly pleased that Chavez y Chavez has been landed behind bars," the *New Mexican* declared on June 10, 1895. "He has been a terror to the country, and they now feel easier since he has at last been captured." José sought comfort in his Roman Catholic faith by building a shrine inside his cell and offering prayers before his religious artifacts.[9]

Chief Justice of the New Mexico Supreme Court Thomas Smith was seeking appointment as the chief justice of the court of private land claims in Washington, DC, when Judge Humphrey Bennett Hamilton opened the district court session in Las Vegas on November 4, 1895. José Chávez y Chávez was indicted by the grand jury for complicity in the murder of

Gabriel Sandoval and entered a plea of not guilty. His former Sociedad de Bandidos associate Antonio José Valdéz pleaded not guilty to complicity in the murder of Patricio Maes during the session. Their cases were continued over to the next term of court.

The *Las Vegas Daily Optic* expressed its astonishment when José Chávez y Chávez received a check for twenty dollars "with which to do as he pleases" from an old friend named "Pino" in Belen, Valencia County. "The money would seem rightly to belong to the attorney who will defend Chavez in court," the newspaper remarked. Chávez y Chávez hired Elmer Ellsworth Veeder and John De Witt Veeder of the firm Veeder & Veeder to represent him when his trial commenced the following spring. District Attorney Elisha Van Buren Long and Missouri-born attorney William Gill Haydon would handle the prosecution.[10]

José Chávez y Chávez and Antonio José Valdéz were given something to think about when their former Sociedad de Bandidos associate Jesús Vialpando and his accomplice Feliciano Chávez were hanged for the murder of Tomás Martínez in Santa Fe on the morning of November 19, 1895. The 30-year-old Jesús Vialpando wrote a lengthy statement prior to his execution, providing details about his upbringing, his friendship with Germán Maestas, and the murder of Pedro Romero for which Maestas was hanged the previous year. "My sorrow at this moment is the fate of my poor innocent wife and children," Vialpando wrote. "May heaven protect them! May kind-hearted friends help them in their desolate condition. I beg of my friends to protect my poor children. For them and for my mother I pray to the last."[11]

The year 1896 had barely commenced when another shocking incident occurred in New Mexico Territory. The legendary Billy the Kid's one-time attorney "Colonel" Albert Jennings Fountain and his 8-year-old son Henry both vanished near White Sands while returning to Mesilla from Lincoln on February 1, 1896. The authorities found two pools of blood near their abandoned wagon, but there was no sign of their bodies. "Colonel" Fountain was prosecuting suspected rustlers at the time, including a landowner named Oliver M. Lee, whom many suspected was responsible for the attorney's disappearance. Some pointed the finger at Fountain's adversary and rival landowner Albert Bacon Fall. Despite the efforts of famous lawman Pat

Garrett and various officials, the bodies of Albert and Henry Fountain were never recovered, and the case remains unsolved.[12]

There was much speculation over the disappearance of Albert and Henry Fountain when José Chávez y Chávez and Antonio José Valdéz received a visit from Manuel Cabeza de Baca in the San Miguel County jail in early March 1896. The attorney had almost completed a manuscript about Vicente Silva and la Sociedad de Bandidos de Nuevo México. He wanted his pamphlet to feature photographs of the two prisoners when published in Spanish by Félix Martínez and *La Voz Del Pueblo* later that year. Chávez y Chávez and Valdéz readily agreed and separately posed for a photograph with Chief Justice Thomas Smith's permission. Manuel Cabeza de Baca's occasionally embellished and preachy manuscript, *Vicente Silva y Sus Cuarenta Bandidos* (*Vicente Silva and His Forty Bandits*), was published several months later. "The moral effect that reading it will have on its readers, especially the youth, it will be of infinitely much more value than the minimum price of $1.50 per copy," *La Voz Del Pueblo* announced.[13]

While Manuel Cabeza de Baca would intrigue much of the Spanish-speaking populace with gruesome tales of Vicente Silva and la Sociedad de Bandidos, the notorious Porfirio Trujillo soon paid the price for his own outlawry when receiving a third term in the penitentiary. The former member of Los Gorras Blancas pleaded guilty to murder in the third degree for the killing of sheepherder Joseph Leckie nine years earlier. He was sentenced to three years imprisonment by Judge Napoleon Bonaparte Laughlin in Santa Fe on May 15, 1896.[14]

***

The 46-year-old José Chávez y Chávez was originally set to stand trial for complicity in the murder of Gabriel Sandoval in the San Miguel County courthouse on April 29, 1896. His trial was delayed for several weeks to allow for the conclusion of the lengthy *J. B. Dawson vs. Maxwell Land Grant Company* case. "Jose Chavez y Chavez, one of the chief lieutenants of the Vicente Silva gang, will be tried for his life in the District Court as soon as the present trial of Dawson vs. the Maxwell Land grant is finished," the *Las Vegas Examiner* announced. "Some startling testimony is expected in this trial." J. B. Dawson eventually emerged victorious and the *Territory vs. José Chávez y Chávez* finally commenced on the afternoon of May 27, 1895. "The trial will be watched with a great deal of interest," the *Las Vegas Daily Optic* declared later that evening. "Jose Chavez y Chavez, who will now soon have justice meted out to him, is said to be one of the most desperate of the [Silva Gang], who for a while kept this country in a state of terror."[15]

José Chávez y Chávez was back inside the courthouse with Judge Thomas Smith presiding on the morning of May 28, 1896. A petit jury had been carefully selected and was comprised of Hispano citizens. J. Ramón Maestas, Donaciano Gonzáles, Diego Herrera, J. Gabriel Martínez, Pedro Ribera, Rumaldo Montoya, Jesús María Roibal, Monico Anaya, J. Benavides, Doroteo Vigil, and Lucrecio Lucaro were eleven of the hombres tasked with rendering the verdict. District Attorney Elisha Van Buren Long had prepared a host of witnesses, some of whom were former members of la Sociedad de Bandidos themselves. Manuel Gonzáles y Baca, Guadalupe Caballero, Antonio José Valdéz, José M. Baca, Catarino Romero, Rosario Lucero de Baca, Carlos Rubio, Tiburcio Tenorio, Joe Blakely, Manuel Cabeza de Baca, Serafin Baca, and several others testified for the prosecution throughout proceedings.[16]

Julian Trujillo also testified for the prosecution after receiving his ticket out of the territorial penitentiary on May 15, 1896. Chief Justice Thomas Smith and District Attorney Elisha Van Buren Long had secured a pardon for Trujillo from Governor William Thornton in exchange for the convicted murderer's damning testimony against his former brother in crime. "An execution of this man Chavez will have tendency to hold in check the lawless classes, and something is due to Trujillo," Long had informed Governor Thornton. "Trujillo's evidence has contributed to the conviction of one of the subordinate accomplices and is essential to the establishment beyond doubt of the guilt of the associate principle," Smith insisted. José Chávez y Chávez probably wished he could drive a knife through Trujillo's heart while his former coworker testified against him.

"I'm going to do you up," Trujillo quietly remarked in Spanish when strolling past the seated Chávez y Chávez during the trial.[17]

With his back to the wall, José Chávez y Chávez denied any connection with Vicente Silva or involvement in the murder of Gabriel Sandoval when taking the stand. When examined by his attorney Elmer E. Veeder, the former policeman maintained that Sandoval was in the company of officers Julian Trujillo and Eugenio Alarid before the teenager's disappearance. In his version of events, Chávez y Chávez had accompanied Sandoval, Trujillo, and Alarid from the Imperial Saloon to the police headquarters before his companions retired to the Buffalo Saloon. Elisha V. B. Long then unsuccessfully tried to rattle the defendant while carrying out his cross examination:

> LONG: You and Vicente Silva were intimate friends?
> CHÁVEZ Y CHÁVEZ: No, sir. I know him in his saloon like everyone else.
> LONG: Didn't you work for him on his ranch?
> CHÁVEZ Y CHÁVEZ: No, sir.
> LONG: Were you ever in his employ?
> CHÁVEZ Y CHÁVEZ: Never.
> LONG: Hadn't you been out with him on a good many expeditions?
> CHÁVEZ Y CHÁVEZ: No, sir, never.

José Chávez y Chávez also denied having ever been in the company of Manuel Gonzáles y Baca during Elisha Long's cross examination. José admitted to having drinks with Gabriel Sandoval, Julian Trujillo, and Eugenio Alarid inside the Imperial Saloon on the night of the teenager's disappearance, but denied having heard a gunshot being fired up the street and subsequently escorting young Sandoval to his death:

> LONG: Didn't you lead Gabriel Sandoval right up towards that house?
> CHÁVEZ Y CHÁVEZ: No, sir.
> LONG: Didn't Vicente Silva jump out and seize him by the coat?
> CHÁVEZ Y CHÁVEZ: No, sir.
> LONG: Didn't you draw your gun and knock [Sandoval] over the head with it, sir?
> CHÁVEZ Y CHÁVEZ: No, sir, I didn't see it.
> LONG: And didn't you and Silva take hold of his body, when prostrate and drag it into the house? And in your presence didn't Silva take his dagger and stab the boy in the heart?
> CHÁVEZ Y CHÁVEZ: No, sir, I didn't see anything of that.

LONG: And didn't you drink some whiskey with the murderers right there?
CHÁVEZ Y CHÁVEZ: No, sir.
LONG: And didn't you go from there to the house of Rosario [Lucero de Baca]?
CHÁVEZ Y CHÁVEZ: I have already told you I did not.
LONG: Didn't Guadalupe Caballero come up there after the body was killed?
CHÁVEZ Y CHÁVEZ: I only saw Guadalupe Caballero when he was going up the street.
LONG: Didn't you go to an old unfinished house and wait there for Silva to come back after the murder?
CHÁVEZ Y CHÁVEZ: I had already told you I was not there.
LONG: Didn't you go to Rosario's house?
CHÁVEZ Y CHÁVEZ: No, sir.
LONG: Didn't Silva unbuckle his belt and give you money?
CHÁVEZ Y CHÁVEZ: No, sir.
LONG: Didn't he on that same occasion give Julian Trujillo money?
CHÁVEZ Y CHÁVEZ: No, sir.

José Chávez y Chávez continued providing sometimes vague and unconvincing answers throughout the remainder of District Attorney Long's cross examination. He recalled observing the corpse of Gabriel Sandoval lying on a piece of tin shortly after it was exhumed in West Las Vegas, but absurdly denied having heard anything about the arrest of Manuel Gonzáles y Baca at the time. José acknowledged his friendship with Serafin Baca when detailing his departure from San Miguel County, although he sarcastically denied any connection with his imprisoned Sociedad de Bandidos associate Nestor Herrera.[18]

The Hispano jurors were unconvinced by José Chávez y Chávez's answers, considering the overwhelming testimony against him. They found the defendant guilty of murder in the first degree on June 2, 1896. "It is said that Jose Chavez y Chavez, who was, yesterday, found guilty of murder in the first degree, never turned color or gave the least sign of emotion when the verdict of guilty was read," the *Las Vegas Daily Optic* announced the following day. Elmer and John Veeder knew they had grounds for an appeal and filed a motion for a new trial, but the sentence was a forgone conclusion.

Judge Thomas Smith sentenced José Chávez y Chávez to death by hanging on the afternoon of Saturday, June 13, 1896.[19]

José Chávez y Chávez may have displayed little emotion throughout his trial, but the prisoner was feeling considerably anxious when the New Mexico Supreme Court began reviewing his case in Santa Fe on August 14, 1896. His attorneys Elmer and John Veeder had astutely questioned the credibility of several witnesses for the prosecution based on their own previous discretions and involvement in the murder of Gabriel Sandoval when filing their appeal. Judge Thomas Smith had also sustained the prosecution's objections when Elmer Veeder questioned Julian Trujillo, Guadalupe Caballero, and Manuel Gonzáles y Baca about their own crimes throughout his cross-examinations. The Veeder brothers received another chance to represent their client when the supreme court reversed the fourth district court's decision and granted José Chávez y Chávez a second trial on September 1, 1896. A copy of the higher court's ruling soon reached the San Miguel County courthouse in Las Vegas:

> Where accomplices, previously convicted of crimes, who had been restored to competency as witnesses by pardon, appeared for the prosecution, the court erred in refusing to permit them to state, on cross-examination, the nature of and facts in connection with such crimes of which they had been convicted, in order to impeach their credibility; and in ruling as to one of such witnesses that, if it should appear that the witness had been useful in discovering the crime, it would be no reason for the court to depart from "fundamental principles of law, as it appreciates them," as implying in the opinion of the judge it was truthful testimony.
>
> The court also erred in excluding evidence as to the liberty and favor granted such witnesses by the prosecution notwithstanding their conviction for such crimes, and in confining the inquiries to whether the inducements had been offered by persons having authority. The jury should have been instructed that they must consider the inducements under which such testimony was offered.[20]

José Chávez y Chávez was undoubtedly relieved when learning of the supreme court's decision, although he had missed his son's wedding. Adecasio Chávez married Marines "María" Billescas in Lincoln County on

July 19, 1896. The *Las Vegas Daily Optic* was unimpressed with the ruling of the supreme court and resented the prisoner's suddenly brighter disposition. "Jose Chavez y Chavez, who was under sentence of death, is said to have become very despondent and discouraged for a few weeks before the verdict of the supreme court granting him a new trial," the *Optic* declared on September 7, 1896. "But he now is beginning to regain his courage."[21]

***

The second trial of José Chávez y Chávez for the murder of Gabriel Sandoval commenced inside the San Miguel County courthouse, with Judge William J. Mills presiding, on the morning of November 25, 1896. Once again the petit jury was comprised entirely of Hispano citizens after fifty-nine men were examined for the positions. There would be no racial bias in their ruling. The trial lasted five days until Juan Ortega, the foreman of the jury, read the verdict for the court on the evening of November 30, 1896:

TERRITORY OF NEW MEXICO,
vs. } No. 8755.
JOSE CHAVEZ Y CHAVEZ

We, the jury, find the defendant, Jose Chavez y Chavez, guilty of murder in the first degree, as he stands charged in the indictment.
JUAN ORTEGA,
Foreman.[22]

Judge Thomas Smith had instructed the jury to render a verdict of guilty of murder in the first degree if finding the defendant José Chávez y Chávez guilty of the murder of Gabriel Sandoval. "This is criticized by some, though if Chavez is guilty, it is certainly in the first degree," the *Las Vegas Daily Optic* remarked. "And there seems to be no reason why a jury should be allowed to return a verdict not in accord with the evidence." José Chávez y Chávez was sentenced to death by hanging for the second time, with his execution scheduled to occur in Las Vegas on January 1, 1897. His attorneys Elmer and John Veeder quickly filed another appeal with the New Mexico Supreme Court in the hope of saving their client from the gallows. "Jose Chavez y Chavez will probably be presented with a necktie, as a New Year's present," the *Las Vegas Daily Optic* announced. "It will, however, have six feet of rope attached to it."[23]

José Chávez y Chávez seemingly had three weeks to live when a local citizen named Juan Saiz informed the authorities that he spotted a human foot protruding from what appeared to be a shallow grave three miles east of Las Vegas on the evening of December 10, 1896. Judge Henry Wooster, H. P. Brown, W. W. Prigmore, W. W. Jones, and John Rogers set out to investigate the following morning. They were shocked to find both a foot and the back of a human skull protruding from a shallow grave in an arroyo located roughly one hundred feet from the main road leading into the city. They quickly realized the naked corpse had been cut in half just above the hips when the remains were exhumed. "The legs placed in the grave first, the head and trunk being placed on top of this, face down, and the arms folded up under the trunk," the horrified *Las Vegas Daily Optic* informed the public.[24]

Judge Henry Wooster and his companions transported the severed corpse back to Las Vegas and held an inquest that afternoon. They determined that the unidentified victim died from violent means several years earlier. "Nothing but the skeleton, muscles and skin remain," the *Las Vegas Daily Optic* announced. "The skeleton is that of a man of under size, the hair is of a light colour but may have been bleached having been buried for several years." Some people suspected it was the body of Carpio Sais, who was robbed and murdered by José Chávez y Chávez and his associates in December 1892. Others believed it was the body of an express messenger named Eugene Rossell, who had also vanished and supposedly been murdered by members of the Silva gang several years prior. The *Las Vegas Daily Optic* hoped that José Chávez y Chávez would shed some light on the matter before his execution was carried out on New Year's Day: "Jose Chavez y Chavez, who is now in the county jail in this city, under sentence to hang on the 1st day of January, was one of the leaders of the Silva gang. Perhaps, when he sees the end nearing and that all hope of saving his own neck is lost, he will consent to divulge many a dark mystery that now exists, in consequence of this gang's doings, and among them, that of the man whose bones were exhumed today." José Chávez y Chávez was given cause to remain silent when his attorneys Elmer and John Veeder secured their client another hearing before the New Mexico Supreme Court, thereby postponing his scheduled execution. "His case will not likely be reviewed by that body till next July," the *Las Vegas Daily Optic* begrudgingly announced on December 14, 1896.[25]

At the very least, José Chávez y Chávez would live to experience another New Mexico summer. Francisco Gonzáles y Borrego, Antonio Gonzáles y Borrego, Laureano "Chino" Alarid, and Patricio Valencia were not so fortunate. Although Thomas B. Catron had tried his best to delay their execution—even appealing to President William McKinley—the four hombres were hanged for the murder of Francisco "Frank" Chávez in Santa Fe on April 2, 1897. As far as *La Voz Del Pueblo* was concerned, the executed hombres had merely been pawns in a conspiracy that ran much higher in the capital. "If it is true that the guilty were used, it is indeed a tragedy," the Hispano newspaper professed. "It is sad for New Mexico that her sons should be used. Neo-Mexicanos must be more independent. Do not be misled by *bárbaros* who will ever force you to sacrifice your life."[26]

***

The 47-year-old José Chávez y Chávez had been confined to his cell in the San Miguel County jail for almost two years when he received a visit from Pueblo resident Don Demetrio Rivera and an hombre named Joaquin Vigil on May 17, 1897. The exact nature of their visit remains lost to history, although they were presumably on friendly terms with the prisoner. Demetrio Rivera soon opened a barber shop next to the post office in West Las Vegas. He may well have given José Chávez y Chávez a trim during his visit. José took pride in his appearance regardless of his surroundings and continued awaiting the supreme court's ruling on his conviction for the murder of Gabriel Sandoval.[27]

Sixteen days after José Chávez y Chávez received a visit from Demetrio Rivera and Joaquin Vigil, history was made when President William McKinley appointed the 37-year-old Miguel Antonio Otero Jr. as the first "Mexican" governor of New Mexico Territory on June 2, 1897. Many were shocked by President McKinley's decision, including the relatively young Otero Jr.

himself. Gilley had merely been hoping to win the office of United States marshal when accompanying a delegation to Washington, DC, during the spring. "There were probably thirty to forty New Mexicans in Washington at the time, each pulling wires for his particular candidate," Otero later recalled. Thomas B. Catron, Stephen B. Elkins, and his associates had supported Bernalillo County resident Pedro Perea for appointment, whereas others had thrown their support behind various candidates such as Judge Alexander L. Morrison, former Governor L. Bradford Prince, George H. Wallace, former Wisconsin Congressman Hugh H. Price, Gen. Eugene A. Carr, and Civil War veteran "Captain" Thomas Willis Collier Jr.[28]

Miguel Antonio Otero Jr. voiced his support for "Captain" T. W. Collier at a meeting in the Ebbitt House hotel in Washington, DC. Jefferson Raynolds suggested everyone throw their support behind the educated but inexperienced Gilley for the office of governor. His suggestion was met with deathly silence. While rooming with Hugh H. Price in the Ebbitt Hotel, Miguel Antonio was stunned when President William McKinley endorsed him as a candidate for governor and appointed him to office on June 2, 1897. McKinley clearly felt New Mexico Territory needed some fresh blood and youthful enthusiasm in the Palace of the Governors in Santa Fe. "Mr. Otero has been chosen," the *New Mexican* announced in the territorial capital. "He is quite a young man for the position, being just 37 years of age and the youngest governor New Mexico has ever had."

Miguel Antonio Otero Jr. was inaugurated outside the Palace of the Governors in Santa Fe to considerable fanfare at 11:30 on the morning of June 14, 1897. Although the son of an Anglo mother, Miguel Antonio considered himself as much a "Mexican" as the next hombre, as he made clear during his inauguration speech to the sound of rabid applause.

"It is not the least of my joys to remember on this occasion that I stand before you the first native-born governor of this fair territory," Miguel Antonio informed the large crowd gathered outside the Palace of the Governors. "I am proud of the fact that I am a Mexican! I am proud that at last it has been recognized that in one of us may be embodied the principles of true American citizenship!"[29]

José Chávez y Chávez's life was in Governor Miguel Antonio Otero's hands when the New Mexico Supreme Court affirmed the prisoner's conviction and death sentence in Santa Fe on October 2, 1897. Although the higher court judges found sixty-nine errors in the second trial of Chávez y Chávez, his attorneys Elmer and John Veeder made a grievous error when failing to file a motion for a third trial when stating their objections to Judge Thomas Smith's ruling. José Chávez y Chávez was scheduled to be hanged in Las Vegas between the hours of five o'clock in the morning and five o'clock in the evening of October 29, 1897.[30]

According to one report, José Chávez y Chávez declared that he "didn't care a damn" when informed of the supreme court's ruling. He began spending most of his time in meditation or prayer, having seemingly accepted his fate. His "penitent mood" was noted by a reporter for the *Las Vegas Daily Optic* when briefly visiting with the prisoner on October 11, 1897. "An Optic reporter had a few moments' chat with Jose Chavez y Chavez, the condemned man in the county jail," the newspaper announced. "He says he is ready to meet his God, that he was born to die, and that he does not entertain any fears whatever, of that which is to come, either on earth, or in heaven."[31]

José Chávez y Chávez may have been prepared to die, but his attorneys Elmer and John Veeder had not given up hope of saving their client's life. The dedicated lawyers would appeal directly to Governor Miguel Antonio Otero in Santa Fe. "The general belief, however, is that the penalty of the law will not be carried out in this instance," the *Las Vegas Daily Optic* had announced shortly after the supreme court's ruling. "As others as deeply implicated in the murder have escaped with their lives, only life imprisonment being given them."[32]

Elmer and John Veeder were surely encouraged when Governor Otero demonstrated a proclivity for mercy when commuting the death sentence of a Black man named Henry Daniels to life imprisonment on October 12, 1897. Daniels had been convicted of murder for the shooting death of a young African American named Lafayette Fox in Silver City the previous November and sentenced to death by hanging. Otero stood firm in his convictions after his decision to spare the life of Henry Daniels was met with uproar by many citizens of Grant County. "That Daniels was a 'bad [n———]' there seems to be little doubt," one former resident of Grant County complained to the *Las Vegas Daily Optic*. "Had the verdict of the courts been unmolested, the chances are the Daniels' execution would have had a most salutary effect upon suppressing crime in southwestern New Mexico."[33]

The debate began raging throughout New Mexico Territory over whether José Chávez y Chávez should be hanged for his involvement in the murder of Gabriel Sandoval. Some believed justice would be served in his public execution. Others felt the death sentence was excessive in light of his accomplices Julian Trujillo and Eugenio Alarid both receiving life imprisonment rather than a trip to the gallows. While many Hispanos could not condone the crimes committed by José Chávez y Chávez, the notorious badman was still one of their own. Enough of their people had been hanged in recent years.

Governor Miguel Antonio Otero started receiving letters from various citizens expressing their thoughts on the matter, including Juan Ortega and the Hispano jurors who had returned a second guilty verdict against the condemned prisoner. "We believe that under all the circumstances of the case your Excellency, the Governor of the Territory, should commute the said sentence to imprisonment for life, and we so recommend," Ortega and the Hispano jurors informed the governor. Otero also received a sealed envelope from Lincoln County. Martín Chávez, Yginio Salazar, José Montaño, Saturnino Baca, Florencio Gonzáles, Sequio Sánchez, Florencio Cháves, George W. Coe, members of the Brady family, County Clerk Demetrio Perea, and over two hundred other residents of Lincoln County had signed their names on a petition calling for José Chávez y Chávez's life to be spared. "Residents of the County of Lincoln, New Mexico, believing that the ends of justice would be fully met by the commutation of the death penalty of one Jose Chavez y Chavez," the petition read. "Do respectfully beg your Excellency to commute said death sentence of said Chavez to life imprisonment."[34]

Judge Gideon D. Bantz, Judge Needham C. Collier, and Judge Humphrey B. Hamilton each wrote a letter to Governor Otero expressing their support for commutation after presiding over the Chávez y Chávez case for the New Mexico Supreme Court. In contrast, East Las Vegas attorney Andrieus A. Jones was firmly against the notion. "In my judgment, if you should do this, you will make a grave mistake," Jones wrote to Governor Otero on October 13, 1897. Insurance agent Adin H. Whitmore also expressed his disapproval of commutation when penning a letter to the governor in East Las Vegas three days later:

> I hear it very seriously intimated that you have in contemplation the commuting of the sentence of Jose Chaves y Chaves. I can not believe that you are really considering this matter with such end in view.
>
> If, however, you are so considering it, let me ask you in God's name and your personal interest, to banish even the idea from your thoughts. I honestly feel that politically you can no more afford to commute the sentence of the human monster than you can financially afford to wipe out of existence every vestige of your material possessions.[35]

Respected attorney Frank Springer added his two cents when writing a letter to Governor Otero on October 16, 1897. "Imprisonment for life is no punishment to these people," the lawyer insisted. "Your life and mine were in danger from [José Chávez y Chávez] and his associates a few years ago whenever we walked the streets of West Las Vegas at night." J. M. Cunningham, the president of the San Miguel National Bank, wrote his own short message to Governor Otero the same day. "I have heard that the attorney of Jose Chavez y Chavez has said that his client will never hang," Cunningham declared. "I hope that you will let the law take its course in the case of this tried convicted murderer."[36]

John D. W. Veeder rode the rails from Las Vegas to Santa Fe on the night of October 18, 1897. The attorney met with Miguel Antonio Otero the following morning, during which the 37-year-old Hispano governor scheduled a meeting with Veeder to discuss the Chávez y Chávez case on October 26. "Mr. Veeder appears to be hopeful—as most lawyers always are," remarked one observer. Veeder then returned to Las Vegas, where some Hispano citizens were circulating a petition calling for Chávez y Chávez's life to be spared.[37]

While John Veeder remained hopeful of saving his client from the gallows, Governor Otero received a lengthy letter written by District Attorney Elisha Van Buren Long in East Las Vegas on October 20. Long encouraged Otero to put his faith in the prosecution's evidence and the verdict of the two petit juries and to disregard any notions of clemency for José Chávez y Chávez. "When the evidence in this case is considered, and the duty of

Chavez y Chavez as a police officer is born in mind, and the cold blooded, calculation of the man in aiding to carry out this foul deed, it would seem that hanging was entirely too mild a punishment in such a case," the district attorney insisted. The headstrong Otero responded several days later, informing Long that "I think yourself as well as other citizens of Las Vegas ought to know that I am not in the habit of deciding cases before I hear them."[38]

Governor Otero also received a letter from Raton attorney Charles Springer calling for the execution of José Chávez y Chávez to take place as scheduled. "I wish to enter my earnest protest against the commutation of the sentence of Jose Chavez y Chavez," Springer declared on October 20, 1897. "The greatest curse to New Mexico has been the weak-kneed policy of our courts and former governors, whereby criminals have gone unpunished and have been pardoned for political reasons, which actually encourages people to commit crime." Time appeared to be running out for José Chávez y Chávez when Governor Otero signed a proclamation commanding the sheriff of San Miguel County to carry out the condemned prisoner's execution as scheduled. "Jose Chaves Must Hang," the *New Mexican* announced when publishing the Hispano governor's proclamation for its readers on the evening of October 23, 1897.[39]

Although various attorneys and prominent citizens were firmly against commutation, José Chávez y Chávez's former employer James H. Hunter—now working for the Fremont, Elkhorn, and Missouri Valley Railroad Company in Omaha, Nebraska—pleaded for clemency when typing a letter to his old friend Gilley on October 25, 1897:

HIS EXCELLENCY GOVERNOR, M. A. OTERO.
SANTA FE' N.M.
DEAR GILLEY;-

I WISH TO ALSO TO [*PETITION*] YOU FOR CLEMENCY FOR JOSE CHAVES, WHO IS TO SUFFER THE DEATH PENALTY VERY SOON, IF YOU DO NOT INTERFERE IN HIS BEHALF.
  IN THIS CONNECTION I WISH TO STATE JOSE USED TO WORK FOR ME AND I THOUGHT I KNEW HIM WELL AND I LEARNED SOME OF HIS HISTORY FROM HIS OWN LIPS LONG BEFORE HE WAS EVER ENTICED INTO THE "SILVA GANG." HE TOLD ME HE WAS STOLEN BY THE MESCALERO

APACHES, WHEN HE WAS ONLY SIX YEARS OLD AND LIVED WITH THEM UNTIL ABOUT THE AGE OF 21 AND HAD NO EDUCATION, AND IT WAS AN EASY MATTER FOR ONE WITH SILVAS CUNNING TO ENTICE HIM INTO WRONG DOING.

I HOPE YOU MAY BE ABLE TO SEE YOUR WAY CLEAR TO AT LEAST REDUCE IT TO A LIFE SENTENCE.

[HOPING] FOR YOU LONG LIFE AND PROSPERITY, I AM AS EVER

YOUR FRIEND
J.H. Hunter[40]

To say records of José Chávez y Chávez's childhood and teenage years are scarce would be an understatement. While it is possible José may have been stolen by Mescalero Apaches for a brief period as a young boy, it is equally possible that this was merely a wild story he espoused to garner sympathy or augment his fearsome reputation. Hispanos and Anglos struggled to assimilate when returning to their respective communities after being held captive by Indians for an extended period of time. José Chávez y Chávez demonstrated no sign of any such struggle throughout his time in Lincoln County. James H. Hunter's suggestion that a former precinct constable, justice of the peace, deputy sheriff, and city policeman could have been naively vulnerable to manipulation by Vicente Silva was preposterous. José Chávez y Chávez knew what he was doing.

The execution of José Chávez y Chávez was just three days away when Governor Miguel Antonio Otero met with John D. W. Veeder to review the condemned prisoner's case on October 26, 1897. District Attorney Elisha Long had failed to make the journey over from Las Vegas as requested. Governor Otero decided that he needed more time to examine the evidence before making his determination. John Veeder was relieved when Otero granted his client a reprieve of twenty-eight days at five o'clock that afternoon:

Whereas, the evidence in this case is very voluminous, and time is required to go over it carefully,

Now, therefore, I, Miguel A. Otero, Governor of the Territory of New Mexico, do this day grant to the said Chaves y Chaves, a reprieve of twenty-eight (28) days from the 29th, day of October (the date heretofore set for his execution) until the 26th, day of November, A.D. 1897, in order as above stated that the evidence in the said [case] may be examined.

The Death Warrant heretofore issued from the Executive Office on the 23rd, inst., for the execution of the said Chaves y Chaves on Friday the 29th, of October, is this day declared void.

Done at the Executive Office, this the 26th, day of October, A.D. 1897 Witness my hand and the GREAT SEAL of the Territory of New Mexico. Miguel A. Otero Governor of Territory of New Mexico[41]

Governor Miguel Antonio Otero spent time carefully examining the Chávez y Chávez murder case throughout the next twenty-eight days. Russel A. Kistler was not impressed with the Hispano governor's decision. The *Las Vegas Daily Optic* quickly published details about the murder of Gabriel Sandoval and a photograph of the deceased teenager on October 27, 1897. "J. D. W. Veeder returned, this morning, from Santa Fe, where he had been working to save the neck of Jose Chavez y Chavez, who will in all probability never feel the hangman's noose tighten around his neck," the newspaper announced.[42]

Governor Otero continued receiving letters from prominent citizens while examining the case, including one written by Harry Whigham, the manager of the Raton Coal and Coke Company in Raton on November 1, 1897. "It is generally held that there is a certain class of people in our Territory who respect nothing but a firm hand and that should you change the sentence of the court in the case of Chaves, it would be a step of retrogression," Whigham insisted. "The life of a murderer appears to me to weigh but lightly in the balance against the good of the whole people." Elisha V. B. Long wrote another letter to Governor Otero on November 6 in which the district attorney insisted José Chávez y Chávez "was clearly guilty of an inexcusable and cold-blooded murder," and suggested the "Executive branch" only set aside the rulings of the court in "cases where there has been newly discovered evidence, not considered at the trial." Conversely, Judge Manuel Cabeza de Baca informed the *Las Vegas Daily Optic* that he remained neutral on the matter of commutation and refused to "sign petitions presented to him by both sides."[43]

The territorial press continued applying pressure to Governor Otero during the next couple of weeks. "In Las Vegas, the atmosphere around the condemned man, Jose Chaves y Chaves, is said to be very lurid," the *New Mexican* announced on November 17. "In the meantime, Governor Otero has the case under advisement and is keeping his own counsel." Russel A. Kistler responded to the Santa Fe newspaper's declaration with condescending scorn the following day. "Keeping his own counsel is good!" the *Las Vegas Daily Optic* snidely declared. "Why, every schoolboy in the city knows that Gillie is under sacred promise to commute the sentence of the red-handed murderer to imprisonment for life. By the way, our boy governor ought to read the organic act again and see what his powers and privileges are in the premises."[44]

The "boy governor" was also feeling the heat from Félix Martínez and *La Voz Del Pueblo* in San Miguel County. The Hispano newspaper had received praise from the *Las Vegas Daily Optic* for publishing a scathing condemnation of José Chávez y Chávez's criminal activities and professed religious faith that November. Nobody seemed to mind that *La Voz Del Pueblo* wrongly accused the prisoner of murdering a citizen named Inocencio Borrego, a crime for which Serafin Baca had been charged the previous year:

> Chavez y Chavez is not at the present time enabled to take the life of human beings, but is able to perjure himself, slandering right and left.
>
> The poor, lamented Gabriel Sandoval was assassinated in the most cowardly manner imaginable. His body was thrown into a privy vault. The dirtiest of the dirty, the most horrid of the horrid, but it is said by those that pretend to know, that Chavez, his assassin, will live so he may swear in vain if he can do no worse harm.
>
> Inocencio Borrego, the lamented and honest citizen, faithful husband and fond father, lives no more. His widowed wife sobs daily for his loss. His sad, orphaned children cry for the want of their father. They suffer all sorts of privation, but their recognized assassin, Chavez y Chavez, still lives. Probably that he may in the future repeat more horrors and barbarities and leave more widows and orphans to suffer.
>
> Carpio Sais, the school director's life was taken away whence his Creator had placed it in this world, by the bloody hand of Vicente Silva's first lieutenant, Chavez y Chavez. The schools lost a faithful public servant, and their fund was robbed of its money, but the thief,

assassin and perjurer, it is rumored, shall live so he may remain as a relic of what constitutes a chief of crime.

"Billy the Kid," the bandit, because he committed his murders at the risk of his own life in doing so, had to forfeit his own, but Chavez y Chavez, his first lieutenant, on account of his being such a coward, of such a cold soul and dastardly heart, having always stained his hands with human blood in the dark, when his victims did not see him, it is said, he shall live, so when another chance presents itself, he may use his ready poniard through the back.

It is told us that Chavez y Chavez has an altar in his cell. Barbarian, he is! After knowing in his own conscience that he is the most cowardly of all criminals, he so vilely profanes the religion he proclaims. On the one hand he acts as though he prays, and upon the other, he slanders, right and left.[45]

It seemed everyone had an opinion on what should be done with the "barbarian" José Chávez y Chávez when John D. W. Veeder registered at the Claire Hotel in Santa Fe on the night of November 18, 1897. Veeder appeared before Governor Otero on behalf of his client the following day. William H. Pope represented the territory as District Attorney Elisha Long was unable to attend the hearing. With his client scheduled to be hanged in Las Vegas on November 26, John Veeder suggested there was still time to prepare a new bill of exception and take the Chávez y Chávez case to the supreme court for the third time the following summer. Governor Otero adjourned the inconclusive hearing until the next day, instructing Veeder and Pope to confer with District Attorney Elisha Long over in Las Vegas that night. "If no satisfactory arrangement as above suggested can be agreed upon, the governor as the ultimate arbiter will speedily determine it," the *New Mexican* announced.[46]

Governor Miguel Antonio Otero made his executive decision after receiving telegrams from Elisha V. B. Long, William H. Pope, and John D. W. Veeder the following day. "Judge Long does not ask further postponement of executive decision and territorys [*sic*] case is submitted upon the facts now before your excellency," Long and Pope's telegram from Las Vegas read. "Have read telegram of Long and Pope as you will see from it, no arrangement as discussed can be made," Veeder further informed the governor. Gilley held no personal sympathy for José Chávez y Chávez, but he could not ignore the dozens of errors which had occurred during the prisoner's trials in San Miguel County. With the support of Judge Gideon D. Bantz, Judge Needham C. Collier, and Judge Humphrey B. Hamilton, the Hispano governor decided that life imprisonment was punishment enough for José Chávez y Chávez's crimes and officially commuted his sentence that afternoon:

--- EXECUTIVE OFFICE ---
Santa Fe, N.M. November 20, 1897.

Whereas, Jose Chaves y Chaves, was charged by indictment in the District Court sitting within and for the county of San Miguel and the Territory of New Mexico with the crime of murder in the first degree, and sentenced by said court to be hanged, and

Whereas, said cause and judgement was by an appeal of the said Chaves, taken and removed to the Supreme Court of the Territory of New Mexico, and upon the hearing of said cause in and by the said Supreme Court, the said sentence and judgement of the court below was sustained and affirmed, and

Whereas, this case came up for final hearing before me at the Executive Office on the 19th, day of November, A.D. 1897, and a full and thorough investigation into this case was had, and the hearing of counsel on both sides, and

Whereas, recommendations for executive clemency in the shape of letters from three of the Associate Justices of the said Supreme Court, before whom this case was tried, and such Associate Justices being as follows; N. C. Collier, H. B. Hamilton, and Gideon Bantz; their recommendations being on file in this office, and which for a commutation of the death sentence of the said Chaves, to life imprisonment, and

Whereas, a number of the jurymen in each of the trials of the said cause, and the foreman of each jury in each trial of the said cause, have filed a petition in this, the Executive Office, setting forth reasons why a verdict was given for murder in the First degree in this case in the respective trials of the said Jose Chaves y Chaves, and both the jurymen and the foremen of the said juries recommend that a commutation be extended in this cause.

Now, therefore, I, Miguel A. Otero, Governor of the Territory of New Mexico, by virtue of the authority in me vested, and as above, after a careful and thorough investigation, do this day commute the said death sentence imposed by the said District and Supreme Courts of this territory upon the said Jose Chaves y Chaves to imprisonment in the Territorial Penitentiary at hard labor for the term of his natural life; and do direct that he, the said Jose Chaves y Chaves, be taken from his present place of confinement, by the Sheriff of the County of San Miguel, N.M. to the Territorial Penitentiary at Santa Fe, and therein confined at hard labor for the period of his natural life.

Done at the Executive Office, this the 20th, day of November, 1897. Witness my hand and the Great Seal of the Territory of New Mexico.

Miguel A. Otero
Governor of the Territory of New Mexico[47]

News of Governor Otero's decision reached newspaper editors as far as Los Angeles, California, and Buffalo, New York. José Chávez y Chávez briefly enjoyed nationwide fame as "the last of the Silva gang" to be brought to justice. "Chavez's neck saved," the *Los Angeles Times* informed its readers on the West Coast. "Gov. Otero commutes the sentence of the notorious murderer and outlaw," the *Buffalo Inquirer* announced in the east. "A member of Billy the Kid's band years ago, he is charged with the most brutal crimes, and he was the principal in the murder of young [Sandoval] at Las Vegas five years ago, acting under direction from the Silva gang of outlaws."[48]

While those in favor of commutation had been vindicated, Governor Otero's decision was an unpopular one among other citizens. Las Vegas attorney Andrieus Aristieus Jones organized an indignation meeting and publicly accused Otero of being *"particeps criminis* [a partaker of crime]." Jones subsequently became a fierce enemy of the Hispano governor, until cooler heads eventually prevailed. "Some years later [A. A. Jones] openly apologized and stated that my action in commuting the sentence of Jose Chavez y Chavez was one of the best acts I ever performed during my term of office," Otero recalled.[49]

San Miguel County Sheriff Hilario Romero escorted José Chávez y Chávez to Santa Fe and delivered the prisoner to Warden Edward Henry Bergman on the evening of November 22, 1897. The penitentiary authorities had their hands full that night. Rio Arriba County Sheriff Perfecto Esquibel also delivered six Hispano prisoners of his own. The 64-year old Warden Edward H. Bergman had served the Union during the Civil War and ran a tight ship. The hard labor performed by inmates of the territorial penitentiary furnished Santa Fe with thousands of bricks and pounds of lime on an annual basis. A new cell block had recently been constructed, and Governor Otero had authorized Warden Bergman to allow nine of his best stonecutting prisoners to work in the Holy City under strict supervision. "New Mexico is to be congratulated upon having had as worthy and capable a man as Col. Bergman at the head of so important an institution," the *Albuquerque Journal* declared.[50]

The penitentiary authorities noticed the "Penitente lash marks" on the right side of José Chávez y Chávez's back while the convicted murderer was processed on the night of November 22, 1897. They also spotted two "bullet scars" on the former Lincoln County Regulator's left calf. The 47-year-old prisoner's details were recorded, including his five-feet, ten-inches height, place of birth, and marital status. He was also issued a striped prison uniform. The guards then escorted him to his cell, where he began adjusting to a life of strict routine and hard labor as inmate no. 1089.[51]

José Chávez y Chávez was now a statistic.

Juan José Herrera (*left*), Pablo Herrera (*center*), and Nicanor Herrera (*right*). The heart, soul, and dagger of Los Gorras Blancas and the people's movement in San Miguel County. Author's collection.

Looking down Bridge Street in Las Vegas, New Mexico Territory, ca. 1891. Author's collection.

The only known contemporary depiction of Los Gorras Blancas carrying out a raid. This illustration was published in Las Vegas newspaper *El Sol de Mayo* in 1892. Author's collection.

Members of Los Penitentes engaging in self-flagellation in Abiquiu, New Mexico Territory, in 1893. José Chávez y Chávez was a member of the brotherhood in San Miguel County and participated in self-flagellation, leaving scars on the right side of his back. Author's collection.

LeBaron Bradford Prince, who served as governor of New Mexico Territory during the White Cap uprising and people's movement in San Miguel County. Author's collection.

Lorenzo López, during his time as sheriff of San Miguel County. This illustration was drawn from a photograph and published in La Voz Del Pueblo on October 29, 1892.

Félix Martínez, the well-educated publisher of La Voz Del Pueblo and member of el Partido del Pueblo Unido in San Miguel County. This illustration was drawn from a photograph and published in La Voz Del Pueblo on October 29, 1892.

A political cartoon titled "La Mafia Bolseando a Catron" depicting the Republican "Mafia party" riding the coattails of Thomas B. Catron, circulated by *La Voz Del Pueblo* in November 1892.

Porfirio Trujillo, photographed in the New Mexico penitentiary on May 15, 1896. A member of Los Gorras Blancas and notorious bandido, the perennial jailbird served four terms in the correctional facility. An unidentified person sank an ax into the back of the ruffian's skull in Lower Rociada, San Miguel County, during the night of April 7, 1902. Inmate No. 953: Porfirio Trujillo, 1896, May 15, box 6499, Collection 1970-006: New Mexico Corrections Department Records, State Archives of New Mexico.

Juanita "María" Paula Herrera-Ulibarri, the older sister of Juan José, Pablo, and Nicanor Herrera, seated next to her husband José Ulibarri. A family dispute between Juanita's younger brother Pablo and her son Meliton Ulibarri set off a chain of events that resulted in bloodshed in May 1891. Photograph courtesy of Rock Ulibarri.

Vicente Silva, the infamous leader of la Sociedad de Bandidos de Nuevo México. This illustration was drawn from a photograph and published in the *San Francisco Call and Post* on July 3, 1898.

Telésfora Sandoval de Silva, the ill-fated wife of Vicente Silva. This illustration was drawn from a photograph and published in the *San Francisco Call and Post* on July 3, 1898.

José Chávez y Chávez during his time as a Las Vegas policeman and member of la Sociedad de Bandidos de Nuevo México. This illustration was drawn from a photograph and published in the *San Francisco Call and Post* on July 3, 1898.

An artist's depiction of José Chávez y Chávez's adobe house on the outskirts of Las Vegas. This illustration was published in the *San Francisco Call and Post* on July 15, 1900.

Gabriel Sandoval, the ill-fated younger brother of Telésfora Sandoval de Silva. José Chávez y Chávez was initially sentenced to death by hanging for his involvement in the teenager's brutal murder. This photograph was published in the *Las Vegas Daily Optic* on October 27, 1897.

An artist's depiction of the murder of Gabriel Sandoval in Las Vegas on the night of February 7, 1893. This illustration was published in the *San Francisco Call and Post* on July 15, 1900.

An artist's depiction of a murder carried out by members of la Sociedad de Bandidos. This illustration was published in the *San Francisco Call and Post* on July 3, 1898.

Sociedad de Bandidos member Germán Maestas standing on the scaffold in a dark hood with a noose around his neck just moments before he was hanged for the crime of murder in Las Vegas on May 25, 1894. Author's collection.

Holm Olaf Bursum. The respected lawman escorted José Chávez y Chávez to Las Vegas and took credit for the arrest of the fugitive carried out by Special Deputy Joseph "José" Wiggins in Socorro County during the spring of 1895. Bursum later became the warden of the New Mexico penitentiary in Santa Fe County while Chávez y Chávez was incarcerated in the correctional facility. This photograph was published in the *Carrizozo Outlook* on August 25, 1916.

José Chávez y Chávez posing for a photograph while imprisoned in the Las Vegas jail at the request of Manuel Cabeza de Baca, the author of *Vicente Silva y Sus Cuarenta Bandidos* (*Vicente Silva and His Forty Bandits*), in March 1896. Author's collection.

The San Miguel County courthouse and jail in Las Vegas, ca. 1893. José Chávez y Chávez was very familiar with both buildings. Courtesy Palace of the Governors Photo Archives (NMHM/DCA), 014721.

Miguel "Gilley" Antonio Otero Jr., who befriended Billy the Kid in his younger years and became the first Nuevomexicano governor of New Mexico Territory on June 14, 1897. Otero commuted José Chávez y Chávez's death sentence for the murder of Gabriel Sandoval to life imprisonment on November 20, 1897. The highly successful politician published three memoirs and *The Real Billy the Kid: With New Light on the Lincoln County War* prior to his death in Santa Fe on August 7, 1944. Author's collection.

John De Witt Veeder. The Las Vegas attorney worked tirelessly to save his client José Chávez y Chávez from the hangman's rope in 1897. Author's collection.

Humphrey Bennett Hamilton, ca. 1916. Hamilton was one of the three New Mexico Supreme Court judges who examined the guilty verdicts returned by the San Miguel County district court against José Chávez y Chávez for the murder of Gabriel Sandoval. This photograph was published in the *Carrizozo Outlook* on August 25, 1916.

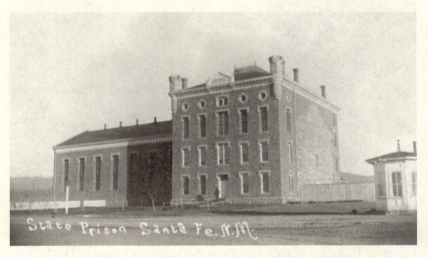

The New Mexico penitentiary in Santa Fe County, ca. 1900. Courtesy of State Archives of New Mexico.

José Chávez y Chávez, also known as inmate no. 1089, while incarcerated in the New Mexico penitentiary. Author's collection.

Martín Chávez and members of his family posing for a photograph with a padre (*far left*). Juanita Romero-Chávez and Martín are both seated, with their granddaughter Anita Santana standing between them. Standing in a row behind them are (*left to right*) their son Benjamin Chávez, their daughter-in-law Trinidad Montoya-Chávez holding a baby, their son José "Modesto" Chávez, their daughter Josefita Chávez-Santana, and their son-in-law Francisco Santana. Courtesy of Ed Romero.

José Chávez y Chávez—clean-shaven with very short hair—while incarcerated in the New Mexico penitentiary. Author's collection.

Scipio Salazar, ca. 1902. Scipio was inside the Montaño store alongside Martín Chávez and his Hispano fighters during the five-day siege in Lincoln in July 1878. He survived the war and became a prominent Democratic political figure, county commissioner, and highly successful sheep farmer in Lincoln County. Scipio also led an unsuccessful campaign for the early release of his friend José Chávez y Chávez from the New Mexico penitentiary during the autumn of 1908. This photograph was published in the *White Oaks Eagle* on January 1, 1903.

The Picacho post office and Martin Chavez & Sons store in Lincoln County, ca. 1910s. That could be Martín Chávez himself standing on the porch in a white shirt. Photograph courtesy of the Historical Society for Southeast New Mexico.

Dionicio Chávez, the son of José Chávez y Chávez and Leonora Lucero de Chávez, ca. 1920s. Dionicio was conceived and born while his father was incarcerated in the New Mexico penitentiary. Photograph courtesy of Margaret Chávez Slayton.

Martín Chávez (*left*) posing for a photograph with George Curry (*right*), ca. 1910s. During his time as governor of New Mexico, Curry believed Martín's old comrade José Chávez y Chávez was a reformed prisoner and granted the notorious badman conditional parole on January 11, 1909. Courtesy of Ed Romero.

The remnants of the Roman Catholic chapel in which José Chávez y Chávez's funeral service took place in Milagro, New Mexico. Photograph courtesy of Josh Slatten.

Berkley Haswell (*left*), playing the lead role in James Hoadley's play *Billy the Kid in Mexico* inside the Stone Opera House in Binghamton, New York, in January 1921. This photograph was published in the *Press and Sun-Bulletin* (Binghamton, NY) on January 4, 1921.

Margarita Salazar, the niece and adopted daughter of Yginio Salazar, on her wedding day in the early 1920s. Herman B. Weisner Papers, Rio Grande Historical Collections, New Mexico State University Library, Archives and Special Collections.

How the entrance to the Palace of the Governors in Santa Fe looked to the elderly Martín Chávez's eyes in the late 1920s. Courtesy Palace of the Governors Photo Archives (NMHM/DCA), 010598.

Walter Noble Burns, ca. 1926. Burns interviewed Yginio Salazar, Martín Chávez, and other friends and contemporaries of the famous William Bonney while working on the manuscript that became *The Saga of Billy the Kid*. The talented writer died in Chicago, Illinois, on April 15, 1932. This photograph was published in the *Chicago Tribune* on May 8, 1926.

Benjamin Chávez with his wife Emma Peppin-Chávez, the daughter of his father Martín's one-time adversary George W. Peppin. Courtesy of Ed Romero.

Yginio Salazar with his wife Isabel, their adopted daughter Margarita, and young members of the Salazar family on the porch of the Salazar home in Baca Canyon on July 9, 1926. Herman B. Weisner papers, Rio Grande Historical Collections, New Mexico State University Library, Archives and Special Collections.

Yginio Salazar (*left*), Isabel Salazar with two young members of the Salazar family (*center*), and former governor Miguel Antonio Otero Jr. (*right*) outside the Salazar family home in Baca Canyon on July 9, 1926. Herman B. Weisner papers, Rio Grande Historical Collections, New Mexico State University Library, Archives and Special Collections.

Yginio Salazar (*left*) and Miguel Luna (*right*), who was playing marbles in front of the Lincoln County Courthouse when Billy the Kid made his famous jailbreak, posing for a photograph outside the Salazar home in Baca Canyon on July 9, 1926. Notice the Salazar family dog relaxing on the porch behind them. Author's collection.

The 66-year-old Yginio Salazar looking like the loneliest man on earth in the face of progress, standing alongside the two automobiles parked outside his adobe home during former governor Miguel Antonio Otero Jr.'s visit on July 9, 1926. Author's collection.

George Coe (*left*) on his fruit farm in Lincoln County on May 12, 1927. Photograph courtesy of Corey Recko.

An advertisement for King Vidor's film *Billy the Kid* playing at the Princess Theatre in Roswell, New Mexico. Published in the *Roswell Daily Record* on December 29, 1930.

Johnny Mack Brown, who played the lead role in King Vidor's motion picture *Billy the Kid*. This photograph was published by the *Los Angeles Evening Post-Record* on December 24, 1930.

Douglas Fairbanks Sr. as he appeared in *Around the World In 80 Minutes*, a documentary film released in December 1931. This image was published by *The Daily Illini* when advertising the film's final showing at the Orpheum Theatre in Urbana, Illinois, on February 11, 1932. Five months later Douglas Fairbanks Sr., Johnny Mack Brown, and production manager Charles Lewis travelled to Lincoln, New Mexico, to speak with Yginio Salazar about Billy the Kid and the Lincoln County War.

José Chávez y Chávez's headstone, which was admirably erected on the correct place of his burial in Milagro by Billy the Kid's Historical Coalition, although the birth year is incorrect. Photograph courtesy of Josh Slatten.

Martín Chávez and Juanita Romero-Chávez's marker in the Rosario Cemetery, Santa Fe. The birth date for Martín Chávez is incorrect. Author's collection.

Yginio and Isabel Salazar's headstone in the community cemetery east of modern-day Lincoln, New Mexico. The birth date and death date for Yginio Salazar are incorrect, as is the death date for Isabel Salazar. There is no question that Yginio would have appreciated the "Pal of Billy the Kid" inscription. Lynda A. Sánchez Collection.

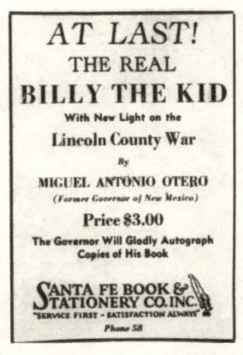

An advertisement for Miguel Antonio Otero's *The Real Billy the Kid: With New Light on the Lincoln County War*. Published in the *Santa Fe New Mexican* on March 3, 1936.

The collection of religious artifacts, paintings, *gorras*, and a photograph of the Herrera brothers on display at the White Caps exhibition in the City of Las Vegas Museum during the spring of 2022. Author's collection.

The "Blind St. Joseph" statue (the saint's eyes are closed) on display during the White Caps exhibition at the City of Las Vegas Museum in the spring of 2022. As Los Gorras Blancas did not carry torches during their late-night raids, it is said that some of their members prayed to this statue to provide them with "eyes" in the darkness. Author's collection.

The Herrera brothers and White Caps mural on the corner of Douglas Avenue and Seventh Street in modern-day Las Vegas, New Mexico. The vigilante group's proclamation, Nuestra Plataforma (Our Platform), is reproduced in its entirety for those who can read Spanish. Author's collection.

Casa de Patron, a former bed and breakfast on the site of the original Patrón house and store in modern-day Lincoln, New Mexico, in 2022. Photograph courtesy of Gordon Fikes.

Chapter 17

The Fading Frontier

It's the end of the world as we know it.
—R.E.M.

Martín Chávez was moving up in the world by early 1898. The mayordomo of Picacho now held a seat on the Lincoln County board of commissioners alongside White Oaks optician Joseph B. Collier and merchant Ira Everett Sanger. When Martín wasn't serving the local populace as a county commissioner, the former deputy sheriff was also prospering as a sheep farmer. He was making enough money to hire a 58-year-old servant named José Sedillo, who resided with the Chávez family on the Río Hondo. The 39-year-old Juanita Romero-Chávez had given birth to her husband's third child, a son they christened Benjamin Chávez, in June of 1893. Five-year-old Benjamin helped his father with various labors and attended the local school with his 13-year-old brother Modesto and 11-year-old sister Josefita. Juanita's 15-year-old son David Billescas also attended school and worked as a sheepman on the family ranch.[1]

Martín had remained politically active and become one of the leading Democrats in Lincoln County. The Hispano sheep rancher had been elected to represent the local Democrats along with fellow delegates George Curry, James F. Hinkle, George Ulrick, and J. Y. Hewitt at the Democratic Territorial

Convention during the summer of 1894. Martín had also won the nomination for probate judge of Lincoln County that year, only to be narrowly defeated by Republican candidate Thomas C. Tillotson on election day. Tillotson finished with 589 of the votes, just ahead of Chávez's 536. Martín had shaken off the loss and represented the local Democrats at the party's territorial convention held in Las Vegas in June of 1896. He then achieved political success when garnering an impressive 617 votes to win his seat on the board of county commissioners that November.[2]

For all of Martín's recent success, things got off to a rough start for the commissioner in 1898. Years earlier George W. Peppin had transferred an account with a balance of $716 to his close friend James J. Dolan. The county commissioners still owed Peppin an additional sum of $984 for the construction of the old Lincoln jail at the time. Dolan unsuccessfully tried to acquire duplicates of the warrants he received from payment of the Peppin account, claiming the originals were destroyed in a fire. The Irishman had gone to the courts, where the case remained until his friend Sheriff Emil Fritz appeared before the board of commissioners and requested that a bond be issued on the Peppin account in August 1897. In their eagerness to settle the claim, Martín Chávez and Ira Sanger issued a bond for the agreed-upon amount of $700.

Joseph B. Collier had been absent from the board meeting and was furious when learning of what transpired. Collier claimed that his fellow commissioners fraudulently issued the bond and insisted the warrants had already been paid for the Peppin account. News of the Dolan Claim subsequently reached various local newspapers by January 1898. It is doubtful that Martín Chávez mourned his former adversary's passing when James J. Dolan suddenly died from a hemorrhage of the bowels at his ranch on the Río Feliz on February 26, 1898. Martín and Ira Sanger were indicted by a grand jury for fraudulently issuing the bond in the settlement of the Dolan claim two months later, although neither man lost his seat on the board of county commissioners.[3]

The widely respected Martín and Juanita Chávez served as witnesses at the wedding of their longtime friend August Kline and the widowed Delores Herrera inside the Santa Rita Catholic Church in Carrizozo on September 13, 1898. Martín and his wife would have also attended the wedding of his cousin

Ambrosio Chávez and Raimonda Sánchez in the same church the following month, on October 24. A short time later Martín resolved a personal matter when appearing before Probate Judge Alf Hunter in Lincoln on November 7, 1898. That was the day Martín filed a petition with the probate court for the official guardianship of David Billescas. The Hispano commissioner loved the teenager like his own biological sons and was delighted when the probate court granted him legal guardianship of his "stepson."[4]

Although Martín's influence in Condado de Lincoln was increasing, the county itself grew smaller when its southwestern pastures officially became Otero County on January 22, 1899. Miguel Antonio Otero Jr. proved a highly effective governor, and the new county was named in his honor. The governor had also overseen the renaming of Guadalupe County as Leonard Wood County in honor of the famous presidential physician and major general of the Rough Riders following the conclusion of the Spanish-American War in the Caribbean and Asia-Pacific the previous year. Otero continued the push for statehood and strongly valued educational advancements. Gilley would personally establish the first secondary school in Santa Fe in 1899.[5]

As Governor Miguel Antonio Otero was guiding New Mexico Territory into a new century, the 46-year-old Martín Chávez's term as a county commissioner had concluded by the time he returned to Picacho after fulfilling some jury duties with former county treasurer R. Michaelis in Socorro during the spring of 1899. Martín, his African American ranch hand George Williams, and George Kimbrell were soon transporting a shipment of wool over to Roswell. They decided to set up camp alongside a lake thirteen miles west of their destination on the night of May 19, 1899.

Martín and his companions were enjoying some supper around their campfire after a hard day's hauling when two shots were fired from behind their wagon just a few yards away. George Williams was struck by both bullets and died almost immediately. Martín and George Kimbrell quickly scrambled toward their wagon, but they could only hear the sound of someone sprinting off into the darkness. "Williams recently married a young Mexican woman at Picacho," the *White Oaks Eagle* announced. "It is thought that his murder is the finale of the bad blood caused by the marriage." The shooter was never identified.[6]

Martín had lost a valuable employee in George Williams and focused on farming his crops on the Río Hondo that summer. The local population quickly turned to him for leadership when the Picacho post office was discontinued without explanation by order of the postmaster general on October 31, 1899. The local Hispanos, most of whom could not speak English, felt their placita had been disrespected and had to pay a contractor fifty cents each month to have their mail delivered from Lincoln. Don Martín and the locals started a petition for the reestablishment of their post office.[7]

As the twentieth century was rapidly approaching, Martín was provided with a hint of future communication when telephone companies discussed establishing a line connecting Roswell, Picacho, Lincoln, Fort Stanton Hospital, Capitan, Nagal, and White Oaks. "It would be a great convenience to stockmen and everybody else, along the line, as a means of quick communication," the *White Oaks Eagle* excitedly declared. "Send your telephone man over the proposed route and see if he doesn't find the different towns ready to take hold of the enterprise."[8]

***

The 39-year-old Yginio Salazar had finally tied the knot in Lincoln County by the autumn of 1899. The former deputy sheriff married a 35-year-old widow named Isabel Paniague, formerly the wife of an hombre named Cenobio Chávez, inside the Saint Rita Catholic Church in Carrizozo on November 29, 1898. Isabel Paniague de Salazar's father Luis Paniague was deceased, but her mother María de los Angeles Chávez was residing in Lincoln and would have attended the wedding. Former McSween employee Francisco Gómez and Ascención Salas served as witnesses during the ceremony. Isabel had a 17-year-old daughter named Pilar from her previous marriage, who worked as a call grader and decided to take her stepfather Yginio's surname. Whatever became of the educated Pilar Salazar beyond the turn of the century remains a mystery.[9]

Yginio and Isabel Salazar established a modest homestead three miles northwest of Lincoln in Baca Canyon. The former Regulator was described as illiterate when census taker William F. Blanchard came knocking on the Salazar family door on June 7, 1900. Yginio remedied that by learning how to read and write before the end of the decade. His mother Paula Salazar de Luma had passed away, and the farmer sometimes honored her maiden name by referring to himself as Yginio Salazar de Chávez. His brother José Salazar worked as a laborer while residing with his wife Ginovera and their children Valentine, Teofilo, Amalia, Renanda, William, Rafaela, and Bartola Salazar near Lincoln. Yginio's half-brother Rómulo (Román) also lived nearby with his wife Victoriana and their children Emeteria, Romelio, and Guadalupe "Lupita" Salazar.[10]

Like the majority of male citizens in Lincoln County, the 40-year-old Yginio Salazar was living the quiet life of a farmer during the summer of 1900. He still had his trusty Winchester rifle to deal with any stock thieves, although that had become less of a concern in recent years. While theft and murder would continue on some level, the wild days of Yginio Salazar's youth were steadily fading into history. Many old ruffians like Hugh Beckwith had passed away, the Apache threat was a thing of the past, and the United States Army had abandoned Fort Stanton in 1896. The old fort now served as a tuberculosis hospital eight miles upstream from Lincoln. Railroad tracks had reached Carrizozo and the El Paso and Northeastern Railway Company began running trains into Capitan. "The ploughshare of a pine-stub, the phaeton with half-ton wheels of wood, and their frontier associates have yielded to steel and iron," New Mexico author Charles Lummis had recently declared. "The *carreta* is no longer a familiar institution. To find it one must go to the utter hamlets, where the shriek of its ungreased wheels—hewn cross-sections of a giant sycamore—still affrights the drowsy land."

While Lincoln remained the same old frontier town it had always been, a younger generation of ambitious merchants, businessmen, and lawyers were now residing in its adobe buildings. The esteemed Florencio Gonzáles had passed away on December 8, 1897. Yginio Salazar and the local Hispano population still celebrated el día de San Juan every year by running the rooster, much to the fascination of many recent Anglo arrivals. The Americanos had their own games, and the Salazar family could now cheer for their local baseball team, the Lincoln Tigers. Bicycle races were held in White Oaks and considered quite the spectacle during Independence Day celebrations on July 4, 1900.[11]

The Salazar family were given cause for celebration when Yginio's brother José and his wife Ginovera welcomed the birth of their daughter Margarita Salazar in Lincoln County on February 22, 1901. For unspecified reasons—perhaps Yginio and Isabel Salazar were incapable of conceiving a child—José and Ginovera Salazar allowed Yginio and Isabel to adopt their newborn daughter and raise the little girl as if she were their own.

The infant Margarita inevitably became the manzana of her adopted father's eye.[12]

***

The 46-year-old Martín Chávez had survived the wrath of the late Jimmy Dolan when leading the McSween partisans into battle during the Lincoln County War, but he could not save his livestock from the unpredictable New Mexico weather in the spring of 1900. A ferocious snowstorm raging across the countryside cost Martín the lives of 147 goats and 180 head of sheep in Picacho on the night of May 15, 1900. Lincoln resident Leslie Ellis and various other sheep farmers throughout the county also recorded significant losses after the storm had passed. "Such losses have never been here before at this time through storm," the *White Oaks Eagle* announced on May 24. "The cause is attributed to early shearing as only recently shorn animals have died."[13]

Although Martín had to replenish some of his stock, the sheep farmer was given a reason to smile when he was appointed the local postmaster following the reestablishment of the Picacho Post Office in late May 1900. Although Martín and residents of Picacho still used horses and goats to tramp out their grain instead of thrashers, farming became a highly profitable enterprise on the Río Hondo that summer. "Crops on the Hondo are better this year than for some years past," one Hispano citizen declared in July 1900. "Martin Chaves has several thousand pounds of wheat and barley sacked and ready for market." Martín, his friend August Kline, George Kimbrell, and several other ranchers had also cultivated impressive fruit orchards on their homesteads. "There is a tremendous yield of apples on these ranches, and the fruit crop generally is very good; peaches, plums, pears, and cherries galore," one local Hispano informed the *White Oaks Eagle*. "In two or three years more, Picacho will be the center of the fruit industry of Lincoln County."[14]

The ambitious Martín Chávez was soon on the campaign trail after securing the nomination for probate judge of Lincoln County on the Democratic ticket for the second time in the fall of 1900. Disappointment followed when he lost the race to Republican candidate Luciano Trujillo when the elections took place in November. Luciano received 764 votes ahead of Martín's 546. Although unsuccessful in his second bid for the office of probate judge, the mayordomo of Picacho entered 1901 having succeeded his brother-in-law George Kimbrell as the justice of the peace for Precinct No. 4 in Lincoln County.[15]

Martín's responsibilities as justice of the peace almost cost him his life in January 1901. The 48-year-old sheep farmer was brutally beaten when trying to calm down a rowdy hombre causing a disturbance and waving a gun around in Picacho that month. "The disturber assaulted Chavez, beating him over the head with a gun," the *Las Vegas Weekly Optic and Stock Grower* announced on January 19, 1901. "Chavez is in a critical condition and will probably die." The San Miguel County newspaper was underestimating the Lincoln County War veteran's resolve. Don Martín recovered from his injuries and continued serving the local community whenever called upon.[16]

Don Martín Chávez's reputation as a leading citizen of Lincoln County only broadened throughout the next couple of years. Everyone knew his name and greeted him with respect. When Martín spoke, others listened. The dependable, educated *huérfano* was readily available for all manner of service to the community, taking a seat on a petit jury in Lincoln and sitting on a grand jury in Socorro in November 1901. Martín then served on the Lincoln County Board of Registration for Precinct No. 4 and acted as a councilman at the Democratic County Convention held in Lincoln during the summer of 1902.

Things were also good at home on Martín's Sunset Ranch in Picacho. Juanita Romero-Chávez was pregnant with Martín's fourth biological child when her husband sold one thousand lambs at $1.25 per head to Roswell citizen William Blackwood in September 1902. Although wolves were giving sheep farmers cause for concern on the Río Hondo that autumn, Martín and various local ranchers were now prospering in the fruit industry. Fruit trees were "breaking beneath the weight of their own production" in Picacho according to one correspondent at the time.

Martín capped off a successful couple of years in Lincoln County by celebrating the birth of his second daughter, Marillita "María" Chávez, in Picacho on November 3, 1902.[17]

***

For all his deserved reputation as a badman, José Chávez y Chávez became a model prisoner behind the walls of the territorial penitentiary southwest of Santa Fe. The convicted murderer spent most of his days making bricks and never caused a disturbance for the guards. Holm Olaf Bursum, the former sheriff of Socorro County who escorted Chávez y Chávez to Las Vegas in the spring of 1895, had taken over as superintendent of the penal institution following "Colonel" Edward Henry Bergman's retirement on May 1, 1899. "Idleness and darkness have been banished from the penitentiary since [Bursum] took charge," the *Albuquerque Citizen* declared in the spring of 1902. The institution was now home to modern machinery and had become an ideal "brick making plant," turning out thirty thousand of "the best brick made in the west every day."[18]

The penitentiary was kept studiously clean and provided good ventilation and lighting for its inhabitants. Many prisoners adorned their neat cells with materials crafted by their own hands. They also made their own clothes and shoes and were free to borrow books from the prison library. José Chávez y Chávez and his fellow inmates could enjoy meals consisting of chicken, turkey, and pork courtesy of the prison barnyard when dining in the mess hall. Superintendent Bursum had recently acquired thirteen acres of surrounding land for the establishment of a "model truck farm" and a large orchard outside the prison walls. "There is almost a score of substantial buildings, including shops, boiler and engine house, hospital, hot-house, livery barn, lime house, brick kilns and other structures," one reporter observed when visiting the institution in the spring of 1902. "At present many men are employed in rearing a much needed massive second wing to the main building."[19]

The 52-year-old José Chávez y Chávez was familiar with some of his fellow inmates, including his former Sociedad de Bandidos associates

Eugenio Alarid, Dionicio Sisneros, and Manuel Gonzáles y Blea. He also served time with the notorious Porfirio Trujillo. The onetime member of Los Gorras Blancas was sentenced to his fourth term in the territorial penitentiary—this time for discharging a deadly weapon—in December 1899. Porfirio served sixteen months before receiving an early release for good time on April 23, 1901. The perennial jailbird returned to his stomping grounds over in San Miguel County.[20]

José Chávez y Chávez and his fellow inmates undoubtedly heard the news of Porfirio Trujillo's fate in the spring of 1902. The four-time convict spent several days drinking liquor after quarreling with his common-law wife Emimia Ortiz in Rociada, a small village located twenty-seven miles northwest of Las Vegas, in early April. The frightened Emimia fled to her father's home in Lower Rociada. When Porfirio eventually learned of his lady's whereabouts, the notorious pistolero arrived outside her father's house to make peace on the evening of April 7, 1902.

A local laborer spotted Porfirio Trujillo lying with his right arm beneath his head in the plaza the following morning of April 8. The laborer assumed the bandido had passed out in an intoxicated stupor and informed his relatives. A member of the Trujillo family soon discovered that Porfirio was neither drunk nor hungover. He was dead. An unidentified party had sunk an ax into the base of the 35-year-old ruffian's skull the previous night.

Sheriff Cleofes Romero set out from Las Vegas to investigate Porfirio Trujillo's death after receiving a telephone call from Rociada on the morning of April 8. The sheriff returned the following night and delivered Porfirio's corpse to his parents Vicente and Julianna Trujillo for burial. "Thus has passed away one or the worst characters and one of the most all round criminals San Miguel County ever knew," the *Albuquerque Citizen* remarked. "The coroner's jury refused to hold anyone responsible for the murder and probably there will be no arrests made until the grand jury brings in an indictment, if it does, next month, when it meets."[21]

José Chávez y Chávez would have also heard news of Juan José Herrera's passing six months later. The 64-year-old founding father of Los Gorras Blancas and driving force of the people's movement in San Miguel County succumbed to typhoid fever inside his modest home in Las Vegas at 7:15 on the morning of October 10, 1902. Thousands of Hispanos throughout the region were devastated. "We say that his death has made a deep impression in the circles of society and not without good reason if we take into account that from the year 1890 to date there has not been a more conspicuous figure in the county or in politics than Captain Herrera," *La Voz Del Pueblo* announced in Spanish the following day. "Captain Herrera was one of the best friends that the working people in New Mexico have ever had and the workers' organizations that he created in this county and in various parts of the territory obeyed his desires that he always harbored to improve the condition of the worker and obtain its elevation in social life."[22]

While much of the Hispano populace mourned the passing of their working-class hero El Capitán, a new board of trustees of the Las Vegas Land Grant appointed by District Judge William J. Mills held their first meeting on December 22, 1902. The late Juan José Herrera would have been horrified that banker Jefferson Raynolds served as president of the board alongside Elisha Van Buren Long, El Agua Para Water Company Manager Frederick Harrison Pierce, wealthy merchant Charles Ilfeld, land speculator Isidoro Gallegos, rancher Félix Esquibel, and former Sheriff Eugenio Romero. Senator Charles Spies, the Veeder brothers, and prominent Republicans of East Las Vegas had successfully pushed for the board of trustees to be appointed by Judge Mills rather than chosen by the people.

The slow disintegration of the Las Vegas Land Grant began as communal pastures were sold to wealthy businessmen, and "wasted lands" were used for irrigation schemes and other ventures. The farmers, herders, and modest ranchers whom Juan José Herrera had represented were largely overlooked in the pursuit of commerce. Albert W. Thompson of Clayton, Union County, purchased fifty thousand acres of the Las Vegas Land Grant with the intention of selling lots to eastern Americanos in 1906. Although small pockets of Hispanos continued sporadically leveling fences throughout the territory, organized resistance against land-grabbers never again reached the heights spearheaded by the Herrera brothers in San Miguel County.[23]

As the Las Vegas Land Grant began shrinking, José Chávez y Chávez's family was growing despite the patriarch serving a life sentence in the territorial penitentiary. It appears José was allowed conjugal visits with his wife Leonora

Lucero de Chávez when she traveled up from San Patricio to see him. Leonora gave birth to a daughter named Bessie Chávez on February 2, 1901. The couple brought another child into the world when Leonora gave birth to a son named Dionicio Chávez on October 9, 1904. José and Leonora's eldest son Adecasio owned his own house in San Patricio by the turn of the century, and provided for his wife Marines "María" Billescas-Chávez by working as a laborer. José and Leonora's daughter Beatriz Chávez eventually married a man named Adolfo López in Carrizozo on April 8, 1905.[24]

In contrast with devoted family men like Martín Chávez, Yginio Salazar, and Juan Patrón, infamous badman José Chávez y Chávez chose to leave his family behind in San Patricio when relocating to Las Vegas in the early 1880s, suggesting he was not the most attentive husband and father in Nuevo México.

***

While the Wright brothers were inventing and flying the first airplane in North Carolina, Martín Chávez was serving his community as the deputy sheriff of Picacho in 1903. Lincoln County Sheriff John W. Owen, a respected Democrat originally from Missouri, had appointed Martín to the position less than two months after taking office on New Year's Day. It was a testament to Martín's ascending reputation that his appointment was announced by the *Las Vegas Daily Optic* on March 7, 1903. Martín would have worked closely with Picacho resident Manuel B. Romero, who was appointed constable of Precinct No. 4 by Chairman Scipio Salazar and his county commissioners later that spring.[25]

Deputy Sheriff Martín Chávez and Constable Manuel B. Romero probably investigated the shootout between 41-year-old former deputy Jasper L. "Jap" Clark and 26-year-old Roswell farmer Bud Hobbs near Picacho on August 4, 1903. A disagreement had led to both men drawing their guns and Clark fired a wayward shot in Hobbs's direction. Hobbs proved more accurate when shooting Clark in his abdomen and side and under his arm during the exchange. Hobbs was quickly taken into custody and released on a $2,000 bond. Jasper "Jap" Clark recovered from his wounds but was convicted of horse theft over in Roswell that November. He was released on a $3,000 bond pending an appeal to the Supreme Court but eventually served time with José Chávez y Chávez and the other inmates of the territorial penitentiary.[26]

After celebrating La Navidad with his family, the esteemed Martín Chávez was mentioned in a poem titled "Amigos de por Jugando." The poem was written by an anonymous resident of Leonard Wood County, and published by *La Voz Del Pueblo* in East Las Vegas on December 26, 1903:

> Al amigo Martin Chavez.
> Yo le debo gran favor
> Que sin llegar á su honor
> Repito ahora y cuando;
> No tengan mucha confianza
> De amigos de por jugando.

> To my friend Martin Chavez.
> I owe him great favor
> That without coming to his honor
> I repeat now and when;
> Don't have much confidence
> From friends by playing.[27]

Martín Chávez presumably knew the reason for his inclusion in the poem and the identity of its mysterious author.

The recent emergence of the automobile proved far more intriguing to many citizens of New Mexico Territory than poetry throughout 1904. The appearance of a "Devil Wagon" on the streets of Albuquerque caused quite a sensation in January that year. "The auto is about ten feet long and has three seats single file for the three operators of the machine," the *Albuquerque Morning Journal* declared. "The machine is a freak, but it is a most ingenious and creditable piece of work." Many citizens of northwestern New Mexico were enthralled when Denver resident J. C. Carlson drove the first "Red Devil" they had ever seen on a return trip from Durango, Colorado, to Farmington, San Juan County, on June 4, 1904. "For 20 miles about [Aztec and Farmington], the farmers came with their families to see the wonderful automobile which went without visible traction power," the *New Mexican* announced. There was soon talk of establishing an automobile line from Roswell to Torrance. "Devil Wagons will make trip in one day," the *Albuquerque Journal* excitedly predicted that autumn.[28]

As an exciting new mode of transportation was providing many in New Mexico with a glimpse of the future, Martín Chávez's old adversary George W. Peppin croaked inside his home in Lincoln on September 12, 1904. The 64-year-old Civil War veteran and former county sheriff was buried in the local cemetery to little fanfare. In contrast, the entire territory was rocked by the assassination of J. Francisco Cháves three months later. The 71-year-old New Mexico historian and political giant was shot through a window while dining in his friend Juan D. Salas's home in Pinos Wells, Torrance County, at around seven o'clock in the evening of November 26, 1904. Governor Miguel A. Otero's older brother Page Blackwood Otero was working as a conservation officer and managed to capture the prime suspect—a mestizo named Domingo Valles—shortly before the body of José Francisco Cháves was interred in Santa Fe on November 30. Domingo Valles allegedly confessed to the assassination while in custody but pleaded not guilty before standing trial in Santa Fe in August 1907. A jury found the defendant not guilty after twelve hours of deliberation, and the murder of J. Francisco Cháves remains officially unsolved.[29]

***

Yginio Salazar switched political parties and became a Democrat by the early 1900s. The 45-year-old farmer had already been selected as a delegate to the local Democratic Convention during the summer of 1902 before attending the convention held in Lincoln on September 20, 1904. Martín Chávez was undoubtedly in attendance that day when Yginio Salazar, Fred Pfingston, and Bernardo Salazar emerged as the nominees for the board of county commissioners on the Democratic ticket. Of the three Democratic nominees, only Yginio emerged victorious when the votes were counted that November. The former deputy sheriff would take his oath as a county commissioner alongside Republicans Paul L. Crause and White Oaks merchant Solomon C. Wiener. "Lincoln County is blessed with an energetic and progressive board of county commissioners," the *New Mexican* reported in Santa Fe on February 17, 1906. "Its chairman, Solomon [Wiener], of

White Oaks, with his colleagues, Captain [Crause], of the Bonito, and Eugenio Salazar, of Lincoln, are watchful of the citizen's interests in the general advancement of the county."[30]

Don Yginio Salazar spent the next two years serving on the Lincoln County Board of Commissioners, although his term was not without controversy. Martín Chávez and other prominent citizens attended a large meeting held inside the Capitan schoolhouse to express their dissatisfaction with the board of commissioners and Sheriff John W. Owen on March 26, 1906. Those in attendance formed the Lincoln County Taxpayers' Association and submitted a report accusing commissioners Solomon C. Wiener, Paul L. Crause, and Yginio Salazar of conspiring with Sheriff John W. Owen in "illegal and corrupt practices in the administration of their duties." The association further claimed they had affidavits that proved Sheriff Owen and the commissioners had "violated their obligations to the people of this county." Martín Chávez was one of the representatives of thirteen precincts who signed their names to authorize the establishment of a finance committee to carry out an investigation. The association's leading point of contention was a contract with a businessman named William Booth for the construction of a road that would impede on the banks of the Río Bonito. The finance committee selected Judge Humphrey Bennett Hamilton as their legal advisor and instructed him to take whatever steps were necessary in preventing any further payments on the Booth contract and recovering any previously paid sums.[31]

The Lincoln County Taxpayers' Association obtained an order from the district court prohibiting County Clerk William E. Kimbrell from paying any further county funds to the William Booth contract before assembling for the second time on March 31, 1906. The association's finance committee appointed two separate committees to inspect the road and examine the county records, although their petition for an injunction was denied by Judge Edward A. Mann in Alamogordo on April 10. The following month Chairman Solomon C. Wiener tried to shift the blame onto Paul L. Crause and Yginio Salazar when insisting "the other two members were the ones behind all the evil." Whatever shady dealings for which Solomon C. Wiener, Paul L. Crause, Yginio Salazar, and Sheriff John W. Owen may have been liable, the calls for their removal from office never materialized. Yginio and his fellow commissioners finished out their terms, and John W. Owen won a second term as county sheriff on the Democratic ticket that November.³²

While Yginio Salazar focused on farming and raising his adopted daughter Margarita following his controversial stint as a county commissioner, Martín Chávez proudly watched his eldest son Modesto marry 16-year-old Trinidad Montoya in 1906. Martín and Juanita Chávez soon became grandparents when their daughter-in-law Trinidad gave birth to a son in Picacho on February 22, 1907. The infant was christened Martín Chávez in honor of his grandfather. Modesto and Trinidad made their home at Martín Sr.'s Sunset Ranch, where the patriarch of their growing family continued prospering. Martín and his employees arrived in Roswell, Chaves County, with eight wagons loaded with ninety-one sacks of the previous year's wool clippings on April 4, 1907. The mayordomo of Picacho shipped the eighteen thousand pounds of wool to the Aurora Scouring Mills in Illinois.³³

When Martín Chávez wasn't shipping large quantities of wool to Illinois, the astute businessman also operated a grocery store called Martin Chavez & Sons inside the same adobe building that served as the Picacho Post Office. His son Modesto worked as the bookkeeper. Martín was making enough money to hire two servants named José Antonio Romero and Antonio Gonzáles, both of whom lived with the Chávez family on their ranch. Like the late Juan Patrón decades earlier, Martín's mere presence in town had become a newsworthy item. "Martin Chaves, mayor of Picacho, was here on business today," the *Roswell Daily Record* announced on September 10, 1907.³⁴

Shortly after Martín's presence on the streets of Roswell was announced to the public, the former leader of the McSween partisans began making travel preparations when called upon by the new governor. President Theodore Roosevelt had appointed former Lincoln County sheriff, Spanish-American War veteran, and seasoned politician George Curry to the position on April 20, 1907. In September Governor Curry handpicked two sets of delegates to represent their territory at the upcoming National Civic Federation in Chicago and National Farmers' Congress in Oklahoma City the following month. Martín Chávez and the famous Pat Garrett were among the ten delegates selected to represent New Mexico at the National Farmers' Congress in the Oklahoma Territory.³⁵

Martín Chávez's disdain for the lawman who had killed his amigo Billy the Kid was probably of little concern to Pat Garrett when the six-day National Farmers' Congress commenced with a record-breaking 986 delegates from twenty-seven states and territories in Oklahoma City on October 17, 1907. The former sheriff of Lincoln and Doña Ana Counties had fallen on hard times. The 57-year-old Garrett was in considerable debt and frequently unable to pay his bills following years of failed business ventures and alcoholism. The famed lawman had also grown tired of people reminding him of his greatest claim to fame. "I sometimes wish that I had missed fire, and that the Kid had got his work in on me," the depressed Alabaman informed one contemporary.[36]

Four months after Pat Garrett returned from Oklahoma City, the slayer of Billy the Kid was shot and killed on the side of a road near Las Cruces on February 29, 1908. The 31-year-old Jesse Wayne Brazel was involved in a bitter land dispute with Garrett and probably responsible for the shooting, although he was later acquitted when standing trial. Patrick Floyd Jarvis Garrett's lengthy corpse was laid to rest alongside his daughter Ida's grave in Las Cruces on March 5, 1908. "He was entirely fearless, cool in emergencies, a dead shot and his work in enforcing the law in the lawless days of the rustlers in southwestern New Mexico will never be forgotten," the *Roswell Daily Record* declared. Martín Chávez and many amigos of the late William Bonney did not share the sentiments expressed by the *Roswell Daily Record* and other Anglo newspapers across the country.[37]

"He was lucky," Yginio Salazar later said of Pat Garrett. "That is, he was for a long time, and he gained a great reputation, but he finally got what was coming to him."[38]

***

The 57-year-old José Chávez y Chávez had served ten years in the territorial penitentiary when Governor George Curry received a sealed envelope from Lincoln County in December 1907. Inside was a letter written by his old friend Scipio Salazar and a petition calling for José Chávez y Chávez to receive an early release from prison on Christmas Day. "Have mercy on this poor old man and send him home rejoicing," Scipio Salazar pleaded. "Justice is satisfied in his case. No one is benefited by his further imprisonment and no harm is done if you pardon him. The fact is that all those who know him would be glad to see him out of prison spending his last years with his family and friends."[39]

José's wife Leonora Lucero de Chávez, their children Adecasio, Beatriz, Dionicio, and Bessie, and daughter-in-law Marines Chávez, had all signed their names on the petition mailed to Governor Curry calling for his release. So had Martín Chávez, Modesto Chávez, Florencio Cháves, Fernando Herrera, Francisco "Kiko" Trujillo, George Kimbrell, Probate Clerk William E. Kimbrell, County Assessor Porfirio Chávez, members of the Brady family, and hundreds of Hispano residents of Lincoln County. "The record of his good behavior while an inmate of the above said institution, his age, and the satisfaction which we have that the said Jose Chaves y Chaves will be a good and useful citizen in the future," the petition read. "Our most urgent request, with which, if your Excellency sees fit to comply, you will confer a great favor not only to our friend the prisoner but to all of us."[40]

Governor George Curry did not comply with the request for the early release of José Chávez y Chávez in December 1907 but changed his tune after the convicted murderer assisted the guards during a prison riot the following year. The fact that José had also been in charge of the prisoners working on the roads outside the penitentiary walls for the previous two and a half years without incident further convinced the governor that inmate no. 1089 was no longer a danger to society. Judge William J. Mills recommended clemency for the convict he sentenced to life imprisonment eleven years earlier, and Governor Curry granted conditional parole for José Chávez y Chávez on January 11, 1909:

EXECUTIVE OFFICE
SANTA FE.

WHEREAS, At the regular November A.D. 189[6] term of the district court sitting within and for the county of San Miguel, territory of New Mexico, Jose Chavez y Chavez was tried and convicted of the crime of murder; and

WHEREAS, Hon. Wm. J. Mills, the trial judge in the case, also the county officials of San Miguel county, and many responsible citizens of the territory of New Mexico, recommend that executive clemency be granted to said prisoner; and

WHEREAS, it has been shown that said Jose Chavez y Cjavez [sic] has at all times conducted himself in an exemplary manner since his incarceration in the penitentiary, has worked hard and faithfully at the tasks imposed upon him, and for the past two and one half years has had charge of the other prisoners engaged in work on the public roads of the territory; that he is now reaching an advanced age; and

WHEREAS, the undersigned has no doubt of the guilt of the prisoner at the time of conviction, still at the same time believing that the ends of justice in this case have been met, and that to recognize the meritorious life of a prisoner will encourage the other unfortunate inmates of the institution to emulate such conduct;

NOW THEREFORE, I, GEORGE CURRY, Governor of the Territory of New Mexico, by virtue of the authority in me vested, being fully advised in the premises, do hereby grant to the said Jose Chavez y Chavez a parole from further service of his sentence, upon the condition that during his liberty he shall at all times conduct himself in a law-abiding manner, and from time to time in writing duly inform the superintendent of the territorial penitentiary of his whereabouts and occupation, and any failure on the part of said Jose Chavez y Chavez to fulfil these conditions shall render this order null and void. The superintendent of the territorial penitentiary is hereby directed to release the said Jose Chavez y Chavez from further custody on February 1, 1909, subject to the conditions in this executive order.

> Done at the Executive Office this the 11th Day of January, A.D. 1909.
> WITNESS MY HAND AND THE GREAT SEAL OF THE TERRITORY OF NEW MEXICO.
> George Curry[41]

José Chávez y Chávez was released from the territorial penitentiary on February 1, 1909, after spending the previous 4,089 nights inside his cell. He presumably returned to Las Vegas, although his activities throughout the next decade remain a mystery. "Jose Chavez y Chavez reached town this afternoon from Cerillos," the *Las Vegas Optic* reported on September 16, 1909. The San Miguel County newspaper was likely referring to the Civil War veteran and former Bernalillo County politician named José Chávez y Chávez residing in Santa Fe County at the time. It was probably the same José Chávez y Chávez to whom the *El Paso Times* referred when reporting the capture of some escaped prisoners from the penitentiary two years later. "David Cuellar, who was serving a life [sentence] in the territorial penitentiary, and Anastacio Vigil, a short-timer who recently escaped from their guards between Las Vegas and Mora, were captured at the ranch of Sheriff Casaus on the Salado, Guadalupe County, by Jose Chavez y Chavez and were brought back to the penitentiary by Warden Cleofos Romero," the *El Paso Times* announced on July 12, 1911.[42]

If no news is good news, it appears the former Lincoln County Regulator named José Chávez y Chávez complied with the terms of his parole and lived a quiet, uneventful life somewhere in Nuevo México following his release from the penitentiary. His eldest son Adecasio and daughter-in-law María bequeathed the ex-convict with a granddaughter named Erenia in 1913.

Having once been the talk of the territory for his crimes, José Chávez y Chávez suddenly faded into obscurity. Public fascination with his old compadre Billy the Kid eventually brought him back into focus.[43]

***

Martín Chávez continued succeeding as a prominent businessman in Lincoln County as much as his family continued growing on his Sunset Ranch in Picacho. His son Modesto and daughter-in-law Trinidad had welcomed the birth of their second child, a boy named Roy Benjamin Chávez, on September 11, 1908. Martín's daughter Josefita Chávez then tied the knot with a 28-year-old salesman from Roswell named Francisco "Frank" Santana that November. Frank and Josefita had originally planned to make their home in Roswell, but they decided to stay on the family ranch when Martín offered his new son-in-law a position as a salesman in the nearby Martin Chavez & Sons store. Martín and his wife Juanita were undoubtedly thrilled when Josefita gave birth to a son named Henry Santana in 1909.[44]

While Martín and his family were thriving in Picacho, the residents of Lincoln were up in arms after losing a referendum to move the county seat from their town to Carrizozo on August 17, 1909. Established a decade earlier, the town of Carrizozo became the leading town in Lincoln County due to its station on the El Paso and Northeastern Railway line. As Carrizozo continued developing, Lincoln and White Oaks were considered old news, and became neglected, dusty monuments to the frontier days of Billy the Kid. Representatives of Lincoln filed an injunction to prevent the county commission from moving the county seat, and a four-year legal battle ensued until the New Mexico Supreme Court eventually ruled in Carrizozo's favor.[45]

As the citizens of Lincoln were fighting a losing battle to retain the county seat, the 57-year-old Martín Chávez had become such an esteemed figure that even his most innocuous activities were covered by the local newspapers. "Martin Chaves and Mrs. Modesto Chaves, his daughter-in-law, came up from Picacho last Sunday, for a visit with the family of W. O. Norman," the *Carrizozo Outlook* announced on February 18, 1910. William Olaf Norman was a 50-year-old proprietor of a dry goods store in Lincoln whom Martín had befriended in recent years. Martín's business dealings were also subject to newspaper coverage. A special correspondence informed the *Albuquerque Journal* that Martín had arrived in Roswell, Chaves County, to sell twenty thousand pounds of wool that May.[46]

In late October 1910, Martín and his beloved Juanita traveled southwest into Texas to spend several days enjoying the festivities provided by the El Paso Fair during the first week of November. The businessman probably tried to win some cigars by participating in the many contests held during the fair. Martín and Juanita undoubtedly enjoyed some hamburgers and lemonade, attended some of the musical comedy shows, and watched the eagerly anticipated motorcycle race held on November 5. While the fun never stopped at the El Paso Fair, Martín had to deal with a more serious matter shortly after returning to Picacho. Patricio Ramos and another of Martín's ranch hands were injured by a cave-in when digging a well on the Sunset Ranch. "At last report both men were getting well although one of them was said to have two or three ribs broken," the *Carrizozo Outlook* announced on November 11, 1910.[47]

The following summer Martín sold twenty-five thousand pounds of wool to Jaffa, Prager & Co. of Roswell in a deal announced by both the *Albuquerque Journal* and the *El Paso Times*. He then attended the Democratic Convention held in Lincoln on September 26, 1911. Don Martín was unanimously elected the temporary chairman of the central committee during proceedings. He was also one of the seven delegates appointed to represent the local Democrats during the upcoming territorial convention in Santa Fe. Many buildings in the territorial capital were draped with colorful pennants when Martín and his fellow delegates convened at the Democratic State Convention on October 3, 1911. An electric sign proclaiming "Welcome to the Capital City" could be observed on an arch at the southwestern corner of the plaza. "All Santa Fe is in gala attire in honor of her guests, the Democrats," the *New Mexican* proudly announced. The 58-year-old Martín Chávez was one of the twenty-six delegates appointed to the Democratic committee for permanent organization on October 10.[48]

Although the Democrats in Santa Fe prematurely described their assembly as a "State Convention," the population of New Mexico would not have to wait long for such a declaration to become a reality. Governor William J. Mills had been assured of statehood by President William Howard Taft on August 15, 1911. Former Lincoln County commissioner and Carrizozo resident William Calhoun McDonald won the election on the Democratic ticket to become the first governor-elect of the state of New Mexico that November. After decades of deliberation and proposals for statehood, New Mexico Territory was officially admitted to the Union as the forty-seventh state by President William Howard Taft at 1:30 on the afternoon of January 6, 1912. "The proclamation was signed in duplicate," the *Washington Times* announced in the District of Columbia. "The original will be kept in the files of the Department of State and the copy will be turned over to the New Mexican Historical Society for preservation." The 53-year-old William C. McDonald was inaugurated as the first governor of the state of New Mexico to great fanfare in the state capital of Santa Fe on January 15, 1912.[49]

Now a resident of the state of New Mexico, Martín Chávez continued thriving as a sheep rancher and merchant throughout the remainder of the decade. In October 1912 Martín and Corona sheepman Thomas Mickey Dubois were nominated as the representatives for Lincoln County on the executive committee for the New Mexico Wool Growers' Association. The following Autumn Martín traveled to Albuquerque, Bernalillo County, to take his seat on the petit jury during the District Court of the United States session with Judge William H. Pope presiding in October 1913.

"Martin Chavez was over 60 years of age but declined to claim immunity from service on that account," the *Las Vegas Optic* announced.⁵⁰

The First World War had commenced in Europe when Martín Chávez, Frank Gurney, and Chairman W. G. Downing represented Lincoln County as members of the state central committee at the Democratic State Convention in Albuquerque in August 1914. Martín's sons Modesto and Benjamin "Bennie" Chávez eventually registered with the draft board, although neither was called into service by the military. In October 1914 the 61-year-old Martín Chávez was selected to represent Lincoln County alongside Frank Coe, George Ulrick, Dr. James W. Laws, and Samuel M. Johnson as members of the board of control for the Eastern New Mexico Good Roads Association at a meeting held in Roswell, Chaves County. Considered an object of fascination for the citizens of New Mexico a decade earlier, the automobile had become a popular mode of transportation across the American Southwest. Benjamin "Bennie" Chávez was now making a living as an automobile mechanic in Picacho. "The object of the association is the promotion of road building," the *New Mexican* declared. "It will take a hand in securing the fullest co-operation of the state highway commission and a fair distribution of state road funds."⁵¹

As the world continued changing around Martín Chávez in Lincoln County, the socialist-revolutionary spirit of Los Gorras Blancas had resurfaced south of the Río Grande on a significantly larger scale with the Mexican Revolution, exemplified by the leadership of land-reformist Emiliano Zapata and guerrilla-bandit Francisco "Pancho" Villa. President Woodrow Wilson overreacted to the Mexican government's brief detainment of nine American sailors found in off-limit areas in Tampico by launching an invasion of Veracruz in April 1914. The conflict in Mexico spilled across the border again when Pancho Villa commanded a raid on Columbus in southwestern New Mexico on March 9, 1916. President Wilson ordered thousands of American troops into Mexico to pursue him. "The chase of Villa will resolve itself into a replica of the famed quest of the Golden Fleece by the Argonauts," the *New Mexican* declared in Santa Fe on May 20, 1916. "And Golden Fleece is an appropriate term for the peon chief in more ways than one."⁵²

Age did not slow the 63-year-old Martín Chávez's political ambitions in Lincoln County while Gen. John Pershing, American troops, and Apache scouts were pursuing Pancho Villa across the border in Mexico. Martín and other members of the Democratic State Central Committee had attended a large Democratic rally in Santa Fe on February 4, 1916. Three months later Martín was chosen by the local Democrats to represent Lincoln County alongside Governor William C. McDonald, his friend William Olaf Norman, Frank Gurney, H. Doyle Murray, and H. S. Campbell at the Democratic State Convention in Albuquerque on May 24. Martín Chávez, Governor William McDonald, and William O. Norman also attended the Lincoln County Democratic Convention in Carrizozo on August 18, during which they were selected as delegates for the upcoming State Democratic Convention in Santa Fe. The delegates were instructed to vote for Susan McSween-Barber's second husband George B. Barber in the race for district attorney of the local judicial district. Martín Chávez and Frank Gurney were subsequently reappointed to the Democratic State Central Committee at the convention held in the state capital on September 1, 1916.[53]

On the heels of his success as a member of the Democratic State Central Committee, Martín decided to take another crack at winning the office of probate judge of Lincoln County during the fall of 1916. The mayordomo of Picacho secured the nomination on the Democratic ticket for the third time in his life that autumn but fell short once again when the elections took place on November 7. Although George B. Barber won the race for district attorney ahead of Judge Humphrey B. Hamilton as the local Democrats had hoped, Republican candidate Elerdo Chávez received 851 votes ahead of Martín's 750 to win the office of probate judge.[54]

Martín Chávez never achieved the kind of political success the late Juan Patrón had enjoyed, but the leading citizen of Picacho had little else to complain about on the Río Hondo. He continued excelling as a businessman, and his sons and eldest daughter bestowed him with more grandchildren to entertain with stories. His eldest son Modesto provided for his wife Trinidad and their growing number of children in Picacho by working as an independent sheep rancher. His younger son Benjamin "Bennie" Chávez had recently tied the knot with the late George W. Peppin's daughter Emma Peppin. Their union produced a son named Benjamin Martín Chávez Jr. on October 18, 1916. Martín's eldest daughter Josefita and her husband Frank Santana had blessed their eldest son Henry with a younger brother named Felipe and two sisters named Annie and Esiquia. Whatever became of Martín's adopted son David Billescas unfortunately remains lost to history.[55]

The 64-year-old Martín Chávez, Corona resident Earl L. Moulton, Carrizozo banker Ernest M. Brickley, and the late William Brady's son Roberto "Robert" Brady were appointed to the Lincoln County Board of Education by District Judge Edward L. Medler in early 1917. "The county educational boards were recently created by the legislature and have practically all the financial matters of the county schools under their supervision," the *Carrizozo Outlook* declared. Martín attended a meeting called by Superintendent of Schools John E. Koonce inside the Carrizozo courthouse on May 16, 1917. The board was organized during proceedings, with Earl Moulton elected vice president and Ernest Brickley elected secretary.[56]

The Lincoln County Board of Education convened for the second time in Carrizozo on July 2, 1917. Vice President Earl Moulton was absent that day, but Martín Chávez, Ernest Brickley, and Roberto Brady all took their oaths. Several petitions for the establishment of new school districts in Lincoln County were tabled and referred to Superintendent John E. Koonce for consideration. Probate Judge Elerdo Chávez also appeared before the board to discuss "changing the boundaries of District 27 so that the children of his neighborhood could be included in District 20 and be allowed to attend the Hondo school." His proposal was referred to Martín Chávez and Roberto Brady for investigation. Martín and the rest of board unanimously ruled that schoolhouses should only be used for the educational purposes and the "habit of holding dances and entertainments of a like character" inside the buildings "be at once discontinued."[57]

Martín worked with the board to ensure that every school in Lincoln County was administrated efficiently. The wealthy businessman wanted the best education available in New Mexico for his own teenage daughter Marillita "María" Chávez. "Mr. and Mrs. Martin Chavez, son and daughter spent the night here [Carrizozo] Wednesday enroute from their home in Picacho to Santa Fe," the *Albuquerque Morning Journal* announced on September 9, 1917. "They go to place their daughter in the Sister's school."[58]

Don Martín Chávez became so well-regarded in New Mexico that even his farming activities on the Río Hondo were considered newsworthy. "Martin Chavez of Picacho reports that he has just harvested a wonderful crop of beans," the *Spanish-American* and other newspapers declared in October 1917. "He planted three and one-half acres of Hondo land to pink beans, and from this small acreage has threshed 4,000 pounds of a very fine quality." Martín's presence in Santa Fe during the Christmas and New Years celebrations that year was also reported by *El Nuevo Mexicano* in the state capital: "Martin Chavez, of Picacho, Lincoln County, member of the firm of Martin Chavez and Sons, rancher and merchant, influential person in the business and politics of his county, has been with us from December 22, until January 6 when he returned to his home. We had the pleasure of having him pay us a visit."[59]

The 65-year-old Martín Chávez was probably already thinking about relocating to Santa Fe County when attending a land sale in Carrizozo with his son Modesto on March 26, 1918. Already a member of the Democratic State Central Committee and the Lincoln County Board of Education, Martín also joined the Lincoln County Council of Defense. Former governor William C. McDonald and Roberto Brady were among the men elected to the local council in Carrizozo the previous August. "April sixth, next, is the first anniversary of our entry into the war for the freedom of the world," a proclamation from Governor Washington Ellsworth Lindsey declared in March 1918. "This is a time [of] sacrifice and labor. Let us save food, save clothing, buy Liberty Bonds and rededicate our lives, our fortunes and our sacred honor to the support of the Government in the prosecution of the war. This is a time for militant patriotism. Let us cease to speak of peace without victory, prod the citizen who sleeps while Liberty perishes, suppress the seditious, kill the traitor and entrain the spy for hell." The State Defense Councils pushed for the improvement of highways, and Martín attended a county council meeting held in the Carrizozo courthouse on July 24, 1918. The Defense Councils also served as representatives of the War Industries Board in efforts to cease any "unnecessary" construction taking place in New Mexico until the Allied Powers emerged victorious on November 11, 1918.[60]

Having fought alongside Billy the Kid, raised a family, and served the community of Lincoln County in a variety of ways, Martín Chávez packed his belongings and relocated to Santa Fe by the spring of 1919. While

Martín's eldest son Modesto remained in Picacho, his younger son Benjamin and son-in-law Frank Santana accompanied the esteemed businessman to the state capital with their respective families. Martín, his wife Juanita, and their teenage daughter Marillita "María" Chávez moved into their new house at 316 College Street on the south side of the city. Benjamin Chávez moved his wife Emma and their son Benjamin Jr. into their own nearby house on Santa Fe Avenue. Martín's son-in-law Frank Santana, his daughter Josefita, and their children Henry, Felipe, Annie, and Esiquia made their home a little farther north in a house on San Francisco Street.[61]

Martín Chávez opened a general merchandise store called Martin Chavez & Sons at 309 San Francisco Street shortly after moving to Santa Fe. He also established a large ranch on the outskirts of the Holy City. Frank Santana continued working alongside his father-in-law in the merchandise store while Benjamin Chávez provided for his family by working as a garage mechanic. Martín soon received a letter from his son Modesto assuring the old man of his prospects as a sheep farmer despite the heavy rain in Picacho during the spring of 1919. "Martin Chaves, of College Street, this city, has received encouraging reports from his son, Modesto Chaves, who is at Picacho, Lincoln County," the *Nuevo Mexicano* announced on May 15. "He writes that the prospects for lambing were never brighter and that this season is likely to be the best in the past ten years with indications that 95 percent of the lambs will be saved. From 555 ewes, Mr. Chaves says he has 554 lambs, these being from small herds. He has 1,000 lambs from larger herds."[62]

While Martín was undoubtedly proud of his son Modesto's success as a sheep farmer, the 66-year-old merchant decided his own time in the wool trade had come to an end. The businessman brokered a highly profitable deal with Jaffa, Prager & Co. in Roswell for the sale of all his sheep in the autumn of 1919. "This is one of the biggest sheep deals handled in this section for years," the *Roswell News* announced when the deal was finalized that October. "The deal involves approximately $50,000."

José Martín Chávez had come a long way from the orphaned teenager who established a modest farm for himself and his late grandmother Magdalena outside the small village of Picacho five decades earlier.[63]

Chapter 18

Game to the Last

Although his soul has taken flight,
his foot-steps echo still.
—James W. Whilt

José Chávez y Chávez was living on the arid outskirts of a village called Milagro, or Miracle in English, located thirty-five miles west of Santa Rosa in what was once again known as Guadalupe County in 1920. The former lawman and ex-convict described himself as a farmer when a census taker came knocking on his door in February of that year, having filed an application for 160 acres of land in keeping with the Homestead Act of 1862. It was said that José's hometown received its name after some early Hispano travelers "miraculously" discovered the Milagro Spring four miles west of the placita many decades earlier.[1]

The 70-year-old José Chávez y Chávez was now living with his second wife, Ruperta Selgado de Chávez. His first wife, Leonora Lucero de Chávez, had passed away during the previous decade. Tradition has it that the 59-year-old Ruperta Selgado de Chávez was formerly the wife of notorious outlaw Nicolas Aragón, although she may have been the widow of a local farmer named Diego Valverde. The married couple lived alone on their farm, where Ruperta often played the role of caretaker. A dairy farmer named Luis María

Cabeza de Baca later recalled seeing José at a political rally held in Pintada, Guadalupe County, in 1920. The elderly desperado was blind and seemed particularly frail to the 30-year-old Cabeza de Baca at the time.[2]

While Milagro was a quiet, innocuous place for an old badman like José Chávez y Chávez to call home, Guadalupe County became a potential hotspot for oil and gas drilling in 1920. Geologist N. H. Darton of the United States Geological Survey for the Department of Interior had spent the previous four years investigating various parts of New Mexico in search of reservoirs and domes containing oil and gas. "In Guadalupe County, for example, the apex of one of the most clearly marked domes is in the west-central part of township 11n-19e," the *Petroleum Journal* announced in Kansas. "On Pintada Creek, in the center of township 8n-19e, there is a smaller dome involving the same strata, and a slightly less pronounced dome is indicated in the same canyon a few miles above Pintada post office." Nelson A. Field, the commissioner of public lands for the state of New Mexico, announced that hundreds of acres of communal pastures in Guadalupe, San Miguel, and other counties were available for lease to the highest bidders "for the exploration, development and production of oil and gas" during the spring of 1920.[3]

As the search for oil and gas commenced across his homeland, José Chávez y Chávez continued living the uneventful life of a farmer with his wife Ruperta outside Milagro. He became particularly close friends with another farmer named Liberato C. Baca, who lived with his wife Teodorita and their children and grandchildren on their neighboring homestead. José also spent time around a schoolteacher named Juan Jorge Clancy, who was born in Puerto de Luna in 1879 and lived most of his life in Guadalupe County. "Chavez was a tall, heavyset man, of vivid, picturesque turns of humor," Clancy later recalled. "He was given to boasting as to his trigger ability, especially with a .44 Winchester."[4]

It was later said that José Chávez y Chávez entertained various curious onlookers with demonstrations of his marksmanship before losing his eyesight. A pistolero of frontier times was considered an object of fascination in the age of automobiles and airplanes. José also enjoyed telling tales of El Bilito and the Lincoln County War for anyone wishing to listen. "I remember that he was always connected with Billy the Kid in the sense that they were bully good amigos," recalled Juan J. Clancy. "He had a big and delectable fund of bad man stories with which he entranced and awed his listeners; he was wont to indulge in native pastoral doggerel, and I have a faint recollection that it was he for one who made up some sort of ballad like verse about his great amigo, el Bilito."[5]

Public fascination with the late Henry McCarty, alias William H. Bonney, persisted into the early twentieth century. The average Americano was far more interested in the demonic Billy the Kid persona created by the press and sensationalist writers rather than the affable vigilante whom the Hispanos of southeastern New Mexico had known and adored. An Illinois newspaper columnist named Arthur Chapman demonized the famous bandido in his wildly inaccurate article "Billy the Kid, a Man All Bad" in 1901. Former White Oaks resident Emerson A. Hough also portrayed El Bilito as an insidious psychopath in an article titled "Billy the Kid: The True Story of a Western Bad Man" in 1901. Hough published more of the same in his book *The Story of the Outlaw* in 1907.[6]

Former Pinkerton detective Charles A. Siringo had spent a little time around William Bonney on the Texas Panhandle and threw his hat into the mythmaking circle with the publication of his embellished book *The History of Billy the Kid* in the summer of 1920. "Billy the Kid is advertised as having killed 21 men, not including Indians," the *Albuquerque Morning Journal* declared. "Which makes Custer, Buffalo Bill and other redskin fighters look like pikers." In reality, Billy Bonney had killed less than half the number of men as suggested. Various old-timers dubiously claimed to have been friendly with the famous outlaw, and their fanciful stories were often printed as facts. "The life story of Billy-the-Kid; the Lincoln desperado, is now on sale at $1.00 the copy," the *Albuquerque Journal* announced on June 30, 1920. "But any E. P. & S. W. train conductor will tell you a more exciting version for a friendly cigar."[7]

It seemed almost everyone wanted a piece of William Bonney's legacy. When Republican jefe Eugenio Romero succumbed to a lengthy illness in Las Vegas on September 30, 1920, one of his obituaries contained a reference to three nameless outlaws having once been hired by Los Gorras Blancas to carry out his assassination, one of whom "was a member of the famous band of Billy the Kid."

A budding historian named Robert Norville Mullin had met Pat Garrett when he was a young boy in El Paso, Texas, and developed a fixation with Billy the Kid and the Lincoln County War. Mullin subsequently contacted José Chávez y Chávez's old comrade Yginio Salazar seeking information. The 61-year-old Salazar tried to answer Mullin's questions about the Lincoln County War and the five-day siege when writing a letter of reply on October 9, 1920:

Lincoln NM
October 9 1920

Mr. RN Mullin
Dear sir:

The first trouble that we had was in the year 1877.
    The principles was the death of J. Tonsel—the partner of McSween.
The names of the principles on both sides is it was John Chisum & the father of J. Tonsel, on the sides of McSween. On the other side of Murphy it was Catron, well I think this is about as near as I can ans your ques, I am sorry for delaying your letter the reason is that I a—
    This fellow Kinnie who help Murphy, he came from Las Cruces .n.m but he couldn't as many thing with his gang they have to call on the colonel Dudley from Ft. Stanton. he brought one company to fight with us, that was the 19 of July 1878 when they burn the house of McSween.
    The day we saw the troops comming we could get out but McSween received a letter Where Colonel Dudley told him not to worry about the troops that he was going over to some other places and the first thing they do is that they run away the other support we have in 3 houses.

Yours truly
Yginio Salazar.[8]

On the east coast, a play titled *Billy the Kid* had enjoyed seven seasons of production before playwright James Hoadley's sequel, *Billy the Kid in Mexico*, premiered in the state of New York that winter. A young actor named Berkley Haswell played the lead role in the "moving melodrama" that focused on a fictional love affair between the Kid and a sweetheart named Nelly.

Closer to home in New Mexico, the *Albuquerque Morning Journal* published a charming poem about the days of Billy the Kid titled "The Pecos Trail," courtesy of an old-timer called H. Dorsey, on December 2, 1920:

> It is over forty years ago
> Since I came up the Pecos Trail,
> Trailin' some cattle from Angelo,
> And it would make a man turn pale
> To hear of the stirrin' times we had
> In long about seventy-eight.
> Fer most men were rough and some were bad,
> And the bad wouldn't hesitate
> About shootin' up their enemies,
> Just fer to even up a score.
> And enemies were thick as bees,
> Durin' the Lincoln County War.
>
> There wasn't very much settlement—
> This town was jest a cow camp then,
> But there was a lot of devilment,
> And some shootin' among the men
> Who were divided in two factions.
> 'Twas many a killin' they did,
> And you could jest tell by their actions
> Those fer Chisholm or fer the Kid,
> For Chisholm's herds ran on the Pecos;
> Billy the Kid his cattle stold,
> So there was jest many a fracas
> In them thrillin' days of old.
>
> A brother came out here to see me,
> And it jest sort o' made me mad
> When the gang they wouldn't let him be;
> He was jest a sprite of a lad,
> And in the course of a week or so
> I found him dyin' by our shack,
> Fer that gang of cowards, don't you know,
> They jest shot him behind his back.
> I knew every feller in the bunch
> And trailed them fer many a day,
> So don't tell if I give you a hunch

> That none of them got away
> Well, Old Sherrif Garrett has passed on
> And John Chisolm has passed away,
> And Billy the Kid is dead and gone—
> Us Old Timers are scarce today.
> But as I was statin' before,
> It would jest make a man turn pale
> To hear 'bout the Lincoln County War,
> Fer there is jest many a tale
> That hasn't been told ner won't be told;
> But them old days is past and done.[9]

While José Chávez y Chávez and Yginio Salazar were happy to discuss "them old days" with anyone interested, the elderly farmers presumably scoffed when Catron County was established in western New Mexico in February 1921. The former Regulators probably felt justice was a long time coming for those who suffered at the hands of the Santa Fe Ring when the county's namesake, Thomas Benton Catron, died in the state capital on May 15, 1921. Catron served as one of New Mexico's first United States senators shortly following statehood, but his Santa Fe Ring had crumbled by the time he exhaled his final breath in the Holy City. "Political power was meat and drink to him," the *New Mexican* declared while singing the political giant's praises.[10]

Thomas B. Catron's controversial legacy would endure in Nuevo México, but it was public fascination with the late William Bonney that led the 73-year-old José Chávez y Chávez back to his old stomping grounds of Las Vegas on May 17, 1923. Having spent more than a decade out of the public eye, the aging farmer was undoubtedly thrilled to find himself the center of attention when entertaining the citizens of Las Vegas with tales of Billy the Kid and the Lincoln County War. Misleadingly described as "the sole survivor of that notorious gang, led by Billy the Kid," José's presence in the metropolis was publicized by the *Las Vegas Daily Optic*, the *Alamogordo Daily News*, and the *Santa Fe New Mexican*. "Although Chaves is now over seventy-five years old, he possesses the keen eye of the marksman and 'old timers' in this city that he could repeat his stunt of making tin cans dance to the tune of six shots from his favorite single action hammer revolver," one local reporter sensationally declared. "He related today the details of the battle between the cattle thieves and ranchers, the latter led by Pat Garrett, the sheriff of Lincoln County at the time. Billy the Kid, Chaves declared, accounted for twenty-one victims, the record of which he kept by notches on the stock of his revolver." There were merely glimmers of truth in such declarations, but that hardly mattered to the elderly pistolero. For just one day, José Chávez y Chávez felt important again.[11]

The 73-year-old José Chávez y Chávez returned to his farm in Milagro, Guadalupe County, after basking in the spotlight of Billy the Kid mythology in Las Vegas. His days were coming to an end. José may have described himself as "born to die" when facing the gallows, but he had outlived many of his unruly contemporaries. The Hispano farmer had survived the Lincoln County War, his many years of service as a lawman, the White Cap uprising in San Miguel County, a death sentence imposed by the courts for the crime of murder, and an eleven-year stretch in the penitentiary, but he could not outrun Father Time.

José Teodoro Chávez y Chávez received the last rites and died peacefully with his amigo Liberato C. Baca at his bedside in Milagro, Guadalupe County, on July 17, 1923. The funeral service was held in a local Roman Catholic chapel, and his battle-scarred corpse was laid to rest in the Milagro cemetery. José's widow Ruperta Selgado de Chávez would have been present for the service. His children Adecasio, Beatriz, Dionicio, and Bessie were presumably in attendance, along with Liberato Baca and other local friends and their families.[12]

Two years later a US marshal named Secundino "Sec" Romero informed a reporter in Santa Fe that "New Mexicans should remember one Jose Chaves y Chaves when they discuss Billy the Kid," for the badman was "not only the side kicker, right or left bower of Billy the Kid, and quite a worthy rifle shot, but a man of honor." While José would remain in the shadow of the legendary Billy the Kid, the Hispano ruffian had cemented his own stormy and occasionally embellished legacy in American frontier history. "He was an extraordinary individual," the *New Mexican* declared. "He was a remarkable shot—he could hit a ten-cent piece at a great distance. He was a man six feet tall, and had the steady nerves and keen eyesight of the great desperadoes of Wild Western days."[13]

José Chávez y Chávez would not be forgotten.

***

Martín Chávez had established himself as a prominent citizen of Santa Fe by the time José Chávez y Chávez passed away in the summer of 1923. His store, Martin Chavez & Sons, proved a successful venture on San Francisco Street. Martín and various other businessmen had sent gifts to the local Knights of Columbus to assist the Catholic fraternity with the construction of a new building in the Holy City in the autumn of 1919. Martín also generously donated $250 to a hotel drive before attending a banquet held in the Woman's Board of Trade building that December.[14]

While Martín's reputation as a generous pillar of the community was flowering in Santa Fe, the Hispano merchant was fortunate to survive a health scare the following year. Martín became so grievously ill inside his house on College Street that his son Benjamin was called home from business in Silver City, Grant County, in the summer of 1920. Modesto Chávez also arrived in the state capital to take a seat at his father's bedside. Whatever illness gave Martín such cause for concern, the patriarch of the Chávez family eventually recovered. "Martin Chavez who has been seriously ill in his home on College Street is now much improved," the *New Mexican* informed the public on August 19, 1920.[15]

Having recovered from his life-threatening illness, Martín invested in local real estate by purchasing various lots and properties in the state capital. The citizens of Santa Fe were advised to inquire in the Martin Chavez & Sons store on San Francisco Street about a three-bedroom brick house available for rent on Santa Fe Avenue in January 1922. Martin Chavez & Sons officially sold an apartment house located at 346 San Francisco Street to a local hombre named M. A. Ortiz in a deal brokered by real estate agent Edgar Knight five weeks later. Martín then made a personal donation of $5 to the Santa Fe Fire Department to assist in their quest to raise $500 worth of funds in April 1922.[16]

Martín Chávez was also a witness to New Mexico political history during the autumn of 1922. Less than two years after the female citizens of the United States of America won the right to vote in their homeland, Adelina Otero-Warren became the first woman in New Mexico to secure a nomination for Congress when soundly defeating Republican incumbent Nestor Montoya in Santa Fe. Although Mrs. Otero-Warren came up short when running against Democratic candidate John R. Morrow during the elections, the Hispana won an impressive number of votes and set an example for other women to pursue political success in New Mexico.[17]

The 70-year-old Martín Chávez reached the summit of his own political success the following spring when Governor James F. Hinkle personally nominated him to replace Félix García on the New Mexico State Tax Commission on March 9, 1923. The senate quickly confirmed Martín Chávez's appointment to the board. The Hispano businessman would work alongside Chairman Joseph Exum Saint, a Republican, and Carrizozo resident George Ulrick, a familiar fellow Democrat. While J. E. Saint was required to work full-time, his associate tax commissioners were limited to 150 days service each year—on a salary of ten dollars per day—for a six-year term. Chairman Saint was absent from the sixth state legislature due to illness when Martín and George Ulrick appointed former secretary of the Democratic State Central Committee and Roswell resident Byron O. Beall to succeed Van L. White as the secretary of the tax commission on March 23.[18]

Martín Chávez was among the prominent Democrats who met with former Secretary of the Treasury and Director General of Railroads William G. McAdoo in Governor James F. Hinkle's office on the morning of July 24, 1923. Several days later, Martín Chávez, Joseph E. Saint, George Ulrick, and Byron O. Beall were among the thirty-four delegates appointed by Governor Hinkle to represent New Mexico at the upcoming National Taxation Conference scheduled to commence in White Sulphur Springs, West Virginia, on September 24. Martín traveled east to attend the four-day conference that autumn before making the return journey to Santa Fe with Byron O. Beall and Don Hunsaker, the manager of the Mountain States Telephone & Telegraph Company. Secretary Beall and various other officials would push for the following autumn's National Taxation Conference to be held in Santa Fe, although the Holy City ultimately lost out to St. Louis, Missouri.[19]

The following spring Martín Chávez's name was mentioned as a potential candidate to run for mayor of Santa Fe during the Democratic State Convention in March 1924. Although Martín never ran for mayor, it would prove a busy year for the 71-year-old merchant in a variety of ways. The businessman was undoubtedly saddened when hearing news of his brother-in-law and longtime friend George Kimbrell's death in Picacho on March 25, 1924. "He was known all over the state and leaves a host of friends to mourn his passing," the *New Mexican* informed the public on April 23, 1924.

In early July 1924, Martín Chávez, George Ulrick, and Byron O. Beall set off on a two-thousand-mile round trip through twelve counties in southern and eastern New Mexico to "investigate dry farming land values." The two tax commissioners and their secretary were delayed because of heavy rain in both Chaves and Lea Counties during their excursion. Martín informed the *New Mexican* that he was pleased to see "fine crops and cheerful farmers" throughout his journey when returning to Santa Fe. The New Mexico State Tax Commission then began hearings on county budgets on August 4. Several weeks later Martín was one of the eighty delegates chosen by Governor James Hinkle to attend the seven-day National Taxation Conference scheduled to commence in St. Louis, Missouri, on September 13, 1924.[20]

Martín had returned from the National Taxation Conference in St. Louis when he probably scolded his 17-year-old grandson Martín Chávez Jr. for speeding in his automobile. Benjamin Chávez had joined the Santa Fe police force and was now working as the "speed cop" in the Holy City, spending his days patrolling the streets in a red car equipped with a speedometer. Benjamin issued five-dollar fines to fifteen different motorists for traveling twenty-five miles or more over the speed limit during the first week of October 1924. One of the lead-footed motorists whom Bennie pulled over and fined that week was his brother Modesto's eldest son Martín Jr.[21]

A speeding ticket was the least of Martín Sr.'s concerns when tragedy struck the Chávez family just over a week later. Martín was serving two customers in his renamed New York store on San Francisco Street when his son-in-law Frank Santana entered the nearby toilet and locked the door in the early afternoon of October 15, 1924. Frank was reportedly intoxicated at the time, despite Prohibition having come into effect across the United States of America four years earlier. Martín and his customers were stunned to hear a gunshot coming from the lavatory moments later. The proprietor broke through the toilet door with the help of his patrons and found his son-in-law's body lying on the floor. A .38-caliber revolver lay beside him. The 44-year-old Francisco "Frank" Santana had committed suicide by shooting himself through the heart.[22]

Informing his eldest daughter Josefita Chávez-Santana of her husband's shocking death would have been one of the most heart-wrenching moments of Martín Chávez's life on the afternoon of October 15, 1924. The suddenly widowed Josefita was devastated beyond words, having been left to raise her five children Henry, Felipe, Annie, Esiquia, and 11-month-old Frank Santana Jr. without their papá. A coroner's jury ruled that Francisco Santana died by his own hand later that evening. "No one appeared willing to make a definite statement as to a possible motive," the *New Mexican* announced. "Before going into the toilet, Santana gave no hint of his intention and no one in the store knew he had the gun."

Francisco Santana's funeral procession began at Martín and Juanita Chávez's house at 316 College Street at 6:45 on the morning of October 17, 1924. The service was held in the Cathedral Basilica of Saint Francis of Assisi (St. Francis Cathedral), before the deceased was buried in the Rosario Cemetery on North Guadalupe Street. A message of thanks to all those in attendance was published in the *New Mexican* the following day:

> We wish to extend our heartfelt
> thanks to all friends who were so
> kind to us at the time of our bereavement
> in the death of Frank Santana.
> MRS. FRANK SANTANA AND
> CHILDREN.
> MARTIN CHAVES AND FAMILY[23]

As his daughter Josefita Santana was adjusting to life without her husband, Martín returned to the Rosario Cemetery to serve as a pallbearer alongside Chief Justice Frank W. Parker and "Colonel" George W. Prichard during the funeral service of esteemed widow Josefita Sena de Luna on the morning of December 9, 1924. The late Mrs. Luna had been the first honor graduate of the Sisters of Loretto Academy and was renowned as a charitable pillar of the Roman Catholic community in Santa Fe. "The funeral service was notable for the number and beauty of the floral offerings," the *New Mexican* reported that evening. Martín Chávez would have been honored to serve as a pallbearer at the funeral of such a pious woman, having become a member of the St. Francis Cathedral and the church societies of Saint Joseph and Saint Francis in the Holy City.[24]

No amount of religious faith could have saved Martín Chávez's six-year term as a state tax commissioner from unravelling that winter when Socorro attorney William J. Eaton filed a lawsuit for $15,000 worth of delinquent taxes collected in the seventh judicial district of Socorro, Valencia, and Sierra Counties. Eaton also claimed that Chairman Joseph E. Saint, Martín Chávez, and George Ulrick were personally indebted to him for an additional $15,000. "Eaton alleges he was employed as special counsel to collect delinquent taxes in these counties on June 1, 1919, on a contingent fee and that he has copied the tax rolls of the three counties from 1903 to 1919, both inclusive made abstracts of all delinquent taxes and followed more than 2,000 suits to collect the delinquent taxes," the *New Mexican* announced on December 30, 1924. "The plaintiff charges the three members of the commission 'appropriated' the commissions due him and made themselves personally responsible to him." If Martín was guilty of appropriating funds as Eaton alleged, it was his only known transgression in an otherwise exemplary life of public service.[25]

The lawsuit filed by William J. Eaton and recent death of his son-in-law Frank Santana probably played some part in Martín's decision to sell his general merchandise store at 309 San Francisco Street to fellow Santa Fe merchant John Rousseau Martin in January 1925. "We thank each and every one of our customers for all their past business given us, and hope you will continue to buy from him," a public notice from Martin Chavez & Sons announced on January 19, 1925. The following month, the recently inaugurated Governor Arthur T. Hannett requested the resignations of his fellow Democrats Martín Chávez and George Ulrick from the New Mexieo State Tax Commission. "On what grounds the governor's action is based is not known," the *New Mexican* announced. Governor Hannett wanted to clean house and also requested the resignations of the entire State Penitentiary Commission.[26]

When Martín Chávez and George Ulrick refused to resign from the tax commission as requested, Governor Arthur Hannett exercised his constitutional right to relieve them of their positions on the grounds of incompetence on March 31, 1925. Hannett appointed Tucumcari resident Felipe Sánchez y Baca to replace Ulrick and Las Vegas resident John S. Clark to replace Chávez. The governor also appointed Byron O. Beall to replace Joseph E. Saint as chairman on the grounds that "Uncle" Joe's term had expired. "Tax Commission is Fired," a headline announced in the *New Mexican* the following day.[27]

Martín Chávez had retained Judge Edward R. Wright as his attorney while George Ulrick had acquired the legal services of Judge Charles J. Roberts when they appeared before Governor Hannett to "show cause as to why they should not have been and should not be removed for incompetency" on the morning of April 13, 1925. Martín stood accused of incompetency due to his "advanced age" and neglect of duty for holding "unnecessary sessions of the tax commission and drawing per diem and expenses." George Ulrick stood accused of "returning or causing to be returned for taxation 6,000 head of cattle owned by a company in which he is interested at $100,000 and mortgaging or causing to be mortgaged 8,000 head for $180,000." Martín and George denied the charges against them during proceedings. Governor Hannett insisted Chávez had verbally agreed to resign on March 17 only to later withdraw his resignation in writing. Hannett claimed that he "took that as confession of the charges."[28]

The situation turned ugly when Governor Hannett refused to see Martín Chávez, Edward R. Wright, George Ulrick, and Charles J. Roberts when they arrived outside his office to hear his ruling on the removal case at ten o'clock on the morning of April 21, 1925. Later that afternoon Hannett issued a second order removing Martín Chávez and George Ulrick as associate members of the State Tax Commission in adherence with his previous holding. The governor cited "specific grounds of incompetency" on the part of Martín Chávez, as "old age such that he has been weakened in both body and mind to such degree that he is unable to further discharge the duties of said office and because of said condition has neglected to perform the duties incumbent upon him." Whether the 72-year-old Martín Chávez was truly guilty of negligence or merely a victim of ageism remains indeterminable. Byron O. Beall resigned as chairman of the tax commission one week later and was quickly replaced by state school auditor Judson E. Owens.[29]

Martín Chávez and George Ulrick's attorneys took their respective cases before District Judge Milton J. Helmick in Santa Fe on July 23, 1925. Helmick subsequently ruled that Governor Hannett had exercised his legal right to remove Chávez and Ulrick from office. While Martín and Edward R. Wright accepted Judge Helmick's ruling that afternoon, Ulrick and Charles J. Roberts decided to file an appeal to the New Mexico Supreme Court. The "state tax war" finally concluded when the supreme court ruled in Governor Hannett's favor sixteen months later.[30]

Martín Chávez effectively retired from public service following his dismissal from the state tax commission. He enjoyed the fruits of his many labors with his wife Juanita, continued practicing his devout religious faith in the St. Francis Cathedral, and naturally spent time with his children and grandchildren. His daughter Marillita "Mary" Chávez had married an educated young man named Manuel R. Baca, a member of the Knights of Columbus who eventually worked on the New Mexico State Tax Commission himself. The young couple lived on Delgado Street in Santa Fe and their union had produced two daughters named Lucia and Josina.[31]

Don Martín remained very proud to have called the famous William Bonney his amigo, and undoubtedly thrilled his grandchildren with tales of the gentlemanly bandido. The journeyman was given the chance to reminisce about Billy and the old days when receiving a visit from a Chicago journalist and published author named Walter Noble Burns in the early 1920s. Burns had become entranced by the legend of Billy the Kid and was determined to write a book about the infamous outlaw. The author rapidly scribbled notes while Martín Chávez provided some of his recollections of William Bonney and the Lincoln County War. Martín recalled leading the McSween partisans into battle, unfairly dismissed Pat Garrett as a "coward," and reminisced about his friend El Bilito.[32]

Martín Chávez was not the only old-timer from whom Walter Noble Burns drew information and creative inspiration. The author also traveled to Fort Sumner to speak with Paulita Maxwell-Jaramillo; discussed Willie Bonney, John Chisum, Pat Garrett, and the old days with Sallie Chisum-Robert in Roswell; visited Susan McSween-Barber in White Oaks; and conducted an interview with John W. Poe before the former Lincoln County sheriff died of pneumonia in Battle Creek, Michigan, on July 17, 1923. Poe's manuscript, *The Death of Billy the Kid*, was published by Houghton Mifflin Co. in Boston, Massachusetts, a decade after his death.[33]

In his quest to gather firsthand recollections from those who had known the late William Bonney, Walter Noble Burns also traveled to Baca Canyon, Lincoln County, to meet with Yginio Salazar. Life was good for Yginio and his wife Isabel at the time. Their adopted daughter Margarita had recently married a plumber named Bernardo Salazar who worked at the Fort Stanton Hospital. Margarita and Bernardo had welcomed the birth of a daughter named Ida Mae Salazar—the first of many children their marriage produced—in around 1923. Margarita also gave birth to a son named Elias "Ed" S. Salazar on March 28, 1925.[34]

A talented writer, Walter Noble Burns later described the scenery enveloping Yginio and Isabel Salazar's adobe house in Baca Canyon in idyllic fashion: "Looking out across Bonito Valley a few miles west of Lincoln, a quaint adobe farmhouse stands to-day on a shelf of land at the foot of tall hills from whose slopes the winds bring the fragrance of piñon. Fields of wheat, oats, and alfalfa spread to the little river which here loiters in lazy loops and still pools. Cattle and sheep graze in the pastures. Orchards hang heavy with apples, pears, plums, and peaches. Within a few yards of the farmhouse door, a brimming asequia sings a song of peace."[35]

Don Yginio Salazar, whom Walter Noble Burns described as "a cheery, gravely courteous man" with "iron-gray hair and moustache" and a "tall, broad-shouldered frame that suggests the power that must have been his in his younger years," was more than happy to discuss Billy the Kid and the Lincoln County War. He spoke rapidly in Spanish when reminiscing with the author, sometimes rising to his feet and gesturing with his hands as if reliving the moments he described. "The old man has a histrionic flair," Burns later wrote. Yginio vividly recalled watching Billy smoke a cigarillo in the northeast kitchen of the burning McSween home and having feigned death while making his escape. Burns was impressed and devoted an entire chapter to Old Man Salazar's recollections titled "The Man Who Played Dead."[36]

Walter Noble Burns's *The Saga of Billy the Kid* was published by Doubleday Page & Co. in early 1926. The book proved a well received hit from coast to coast. More than any previous author who tackled the subject, Burns had cemented Billy the Kid's place in American folklore. Although the author deserved praise for having interviewed some of William Bonney's contemporaries and his undeniably enthralling narrative, *The Saga of Billy the Kid* was more a work of romantic fiction than reasoned history. The book featured countless embellishments and numerous instances of fictitious dialogue, and perpetuated the myth that William Bonney had killed twenty-one men.[37]

When Martín Chávez read his copy of *The Saga of Billy the Kid* in Santa Fe, he was no more impressed with Walter Noble Burns's version of events than when reading Pat Garrett and Charles Siringo's books about his famous amigo.[38]

***

The 66-year-old Yginio Salazar was going about his business when two automobiles pulled up outside his adobe house in Baca Canyon, Lincoln County, on the morning of July 9, 1926. The elderly farmer immediately recognized longtime Lincoln resident Miguel Luna stepping from one of the vehicles. Miguel had been playing marbles outside the old courthouse when Billy the Kid made his famous jailbreak decades earlier. He was now serving as a tour guide for his three neatly dressed companions. Yginio quickly realized these were no ordinary guests. It was the former governor Miguel Antonio Otero Jr. himself, accompanied by his friends Marshall Latham Bond and Marshall Bond Jr.[39]

Yginio politely welcomed each of his guests with a handshake before introducing them to his wife Isabel, their daughter Margarita, and some of the Salazar family children. The 66-year-old Miguel Antonio Otero Jr. was working on his own book about Billy the Kid in Santa Fe that summer. Gilley considered the young desperado whom he had befriended "a man more sinned against than sinning." He was also tired of the nonsensical rumors that Bonney was somehow still alive. Like Walter Noble Burns, the first Hispano governor of New Mexico Territory hit the road to visit a handful of William Bonney's contemporaries. Otero Jr., Marshall Bond, and Marshall Bond Jr. had already met with George B. Barber in Carrizozo and interviewed Susan McSween-Barber in White Oaks several days earlier. "The Kid was not half as bad as some of those who were after him and determined to kill him," George Barber informed Otero. "The native citizens, in particular, loved [Billy] because he was always kind and considerate to them and took much pleasure in helping them and providing for their wants," his wife Susan recalled.[40]

Now it was Old Man Salazar's turn to reminisce about his famous compadre with Miguel Antonio Otero Jr. in Baca Canyon. The humble farmer in his buttoned shirt and tattered trousers, and the former governor in an elegant suit and tie, quickly bonded over their mutual affection for the late William Bonney. "I wanted to talk with him because he was one of the few survivors of the McSween side," Otero later wrote. Yginio naturally talked about having feigned death during the climax of five-day-siege in Lincoln and Dr. Daniel Appel saving him from the wrath of a vengeful John Kinney the following morning. He also claimed the Murphy-Dolan faction had trumped up "false charges of some kind or another against me and were constantly getting out warrants for my arrest."

Yginio took several shots at Pat Garrett while chatting with his guests, insisting the famous lawman was "not the brave man many think he was." He also praised his amigo William Bonney's fearlessness and generosity toward the Hispano population. The former rustler dismissed the rumors that his compadre was still alive. "I lived at Fort Sumner for a while and know many people there who saw Billy's body after Pat Garrett killed him," Yginio declared. "There is absolutely no doubt in my mind about William H. Bonney, the Billy the Kid I knew and fought with, having been killed by Pat Garrett in Pete Maxwell's bedroom." Miguel A. Otero Jr. was grateful for Yginio Salazar's candor and had some photos snapped with the old farmer and members of his family before driving back to Lincoln. Yginio also posed for a photograph standing alongside Miguel Luna, with the Salazar family dog resting on the porch behind them.[41]

Miguel Antonio Otero Jr., Marshall Bond, and Marshall Bond Jr. also spent time with George and Frank Coe on the Río Ruidoso before driving north to old Fort Sumner. Miguel Antonio visited William Bonney's burial site with the arthritic Paulita Maxwell-Jaramillo during their stay. Although Pablita had denied being Bonney's querida when meeting with Walter Noble Burns, the mother of three let her guard down in the presence of the former governor. "[Billy] was a wonderful dancer and I might have married him—had he asked me," Paulita remarked. Gilley soon spoke with the Kid's impassioned surrogate mother Deluvina Maxwell, who still despised the men who had killed her "little boy." The former governor also conversed with the famous desperado's surviving amigos Jesús Silva, Vicente Otero, and Francisco Lovato.[42]

Miguel Antonio Otero Jr. and his companions decided to make one more stop at Don Martín Chávez's house on College Street when returning to Santa Fe. Like Yginio Salazar, the former tax commissioner was happy to discuss the old days with his three guests. Martín insisted that "most of the accounts of the Lincoln County War are far from true" when referencing the books published by Pat Garrett, Charles Siringo, and Walter Noble Burns, as well as an article published by a novelist named Harvey Fergusson that controversially suggested his amigo Billy the Kid had been forgotten. Martín also cited the lack of Hispano perspective regarding his demonized friend's legacy. "We have not put our impressions of [Billy] into print and our silence has been the cause of great injustice to the Kid," the Lincoln County War veteran informed Miguel Otero.

The 73-year-old Martín Chávez recalled leading the McSween partisans during the five-day siege in Lincoln with considerable detail when conversing with Miguel Otero Jr. He also spoke of the kindness his friend Billy Bonney had shown him. "He was not bloodthirsty," Martín said. "He was forced into killing in defense of his own life." Martín occasionally drifted into the realm of mythology when reciting tales of the Kid's exploits to which he had not been present, but humbly conceded that his knowledge of Billy's capture and death at the hands of Pat Garrett was hearsay.

"I felt grateful to Martín Chávez for his recollections of Billy the Kid and the Lincoln County War," Miguel Otero Jr. later wrote. "He fought side by side with the Kid in the days when Lincoln County was a by-word for lawlessness." The former governor devoted a chapter to Martín's recollections titled "An Old Friend of the Kid Speaks," although his manuscript,

The Real Billy the Kid: With New Light on the Lincoln County War, would not be published for another ten years.⁴³

***

In the summer of 1927, the 67-year-old Yginio Salazar received another visit from someone wanting to hear about the old days in Lincoln County. A 26-year-old Texan named James Evetts Haley wished to speak with as many interesting old-timers about their lives on the frontier as possible. The enthusiastic historian had already interviewed Deluvina Maxwell in Fort Sumner earlier that summer. He also recorded the recollections of Florencio Cháves in Lincoln on August 15, 1927. Haley sat down with Yginio Salazar in Baca Canyon and inscribed the Hispano farmer's words two days later. Old Man Salazar reached into the dusty corners of his memory when providing details about his arrival on the Río Bonito as a young boy, his adolescent years in Missouri Plaza, his near-death experience during the Lincoln County War, and his friend Billy Bonney's arrival at the Salazar home in Las Tablas shortly after putting James W. Bell and Bob Olinger in their graves.⁴⁴

Two months after Yginio Salazar spoke with J. Evetts Haley in Lincoln County, his old comrade Martín Chávez made a pretty peso in Santa Fe when selling a house located at the corner of Burro Alley and lower San Francisco Street to the Greer Loan Company for the sum of $18,000. "The property has a frontage of 82 feet on San Francisco Street and a depth of 135 feet," the *New Mexican* announced on October 10, 1927. "The deal was put through direct." The Greer Loan Company were planning to construct a four-thousand-seat auditorium on Burro Alley, with the basement serving as an "aristocratic club room." With an additional $18,000 in his bank account, Martín and his wife Juanita moved into a house at 518 College Street to enjoy their autumn years.⁴⁵

The following month Martín Chávez and Yginio Salazar undoubtedly heard the news that their amigo William Bonney's surrogate mother Deluvina Maxwell had died in an Albuquerque hospital on the morning of November 27, 1927. Deluvina would have been delighted that the *Albuquerque Journal* described her as "a warm friend of Billy the Kid" when announcing the elderly Navajo woman's passing the following day.⁴⁶

Two years later, Martín and Yginio would have heard about the death of their late friend's querida Paulita Maxwell-Jaramillo in Fort Sumner on December 17, 1929. "She was the daughter of Lucien B. Maxwell and Luz B. Maxwell, who were well known here in the days of Billy the Kid," the *Albuquerque Journal* announced. Pablita was buried in the same cemetery in which William Bonney had been laid to rest forty-eight-years earlier.[47]

While some of William Bonney's closest contemporaries were shaking off their mortal coil, any lingering doubts over the perennial fame and commercial appeal of the famous bandido were obliterated when King Vidor's motion picture *Billy the Kid* was released in theaters across the United States of America during the autumn of 1930. Governor Richard Charles Dillon enjoyed a private screening of the picture courtesy of Metro-Goldwyn-Mayer Studios in Santa Fe on September 24, 1930. The governor's personal endorsement of the film would appear on screen before the opening credits, although the Missourian later said that he wished the gentleman who portrayed Pat Garrett—the short, heavyset Wallace Beery—was "just a little taller." Families lined up around the block to see Johnny Mack Brown's portrayal of the famous Billy the Kid when the talkie based on Walter Noble Burns's book premiered at the Mission Theater in Albuquerque on November 1, 1930.[48]

Like Governor Richard C. Dillon, many people of New Mexico enjoyed King Vidor's artistic impression of events, some of which had been filmed in Gallup, McKinley County. The *Deming Headlight* described Vidor's *Billy the Kid* as an "Epic of 1,000 thrills" and "a great talking picture." Other citizens were appalled by the picture's sympathetic portrayal of a famous outlaw like William Bonney. "Such movies are outrageous travesties upon history and upon the character of men like Pat Garrett and John Poe," the *Roswell Record* declared. "It is an infamous libel and should be suppressed." John W. Poe's widow Sophie A. Poe was not impressed with the film, as she informed King Vidor himself. Susan McSween-Barber was disgruntled that she wasn't portrayed by a younger, more attractive actress than the 52-year-old Blanche Friderici.[49]

Yginio Salazar and Martín Chávez undoubtedly watched King Vidor's *Billy the Kid* with their families, although their reactions to the movie's portrayal of events remain lost to history. For all of the film's historical inaccuracies, the Kid's affectionate relationship with the Hispano population was demonstrated by an on-screen friendship with a fictional character named Santiago, played by Yaqui-Hispano actor Chris-Pin Martin. The late William Bonney was portrayed as a deadly pistolero who was willing to engage in violence against his enemies but who possessed an otherwise warm disposition and fierce loyalty toward his friends. In that sense the film's portrayal of El Bilito was not all that different from the affable bandido whom Yginio Salazar and Martín Chávez had known.

Johnny Mack Brown's taller, dark-haired version of Billy the Kid frequently smiled and joked, demonstrated his considerable dancing skills, and avenged the murder of his English employer Jack Tunston by waging war against a crooked sheriff of Lincoln called Col. William P. Donovan, an obvious amalgam of Lawrence Murphy, James J. Dolan, and William Brady. King Vidor's adaption of Walter Noble Burns's book provided filmgoers with a fantastical happy ending. Wallace Beery's Pat Garrett allowed Mack Brown's William Bonney to escape across the border to begin a new life with his deceased English employer's former fiancé Claire Randall, an entirely fictional character played by starlet Kay Johnson.

When watching King Vidor's *Billy the Kid* on the big screen, old Yginio Salazar undoubtedly smiled when Johnny Mack Brown's William Bonney casually lit a cigarillo on a piece of debris inside the burning McSween house, just like he remembered.[50]

***

The 77-year-old Martín Chávez was enjoying a peaceful retirement with his wife Juana in Santa Fe when tragedy struck their family again during the spring of 1930. Their daughter Josefita's eldest son Henry Santana was driving home from Springer with his friend Arthur Lucero when his Ford Coupe struck a cattle guard on a highway seven miles outside of Watrous at around two o'clock in the morning of April 10, 1930. The 21-year-old Henry Santana had allegedly fallen asleep at the wheel and was thrown one-hundred yards from his overturned vehicle when the accident occurred. A westbound Atlantic & Pacific bus driver discovered the car wreck a short time later and rushed the two severely wounded young men to Las Vegas. They arrived outside a hospital at around 3:15 that morning.

The 18-year-old Arthur Lucero was fortunate to come away from the automobile accident with merely a broken collarbone. Henry Santana had suffered a fractured skull and never regained consciousness. His distraught mother Josefita Chávez-Santana was by his side when the popular Santa Fe High School student was pronounced dead shortly before midday. Henry's corpse was delivered to the Nolan Funeral Home and transported back to Santa Fe by automobile that afternoon. "He was a grandson of Martin Chavez, prominent rancher of Lincoln County, well known in this community," the *Las Vegas Daily Optic* announced. Santa Fe Traffic Officer Benjamin Chávez conducted his own investigation of the crash that claimed the life of his nephew and insisted a blown-out tire had caused the fatal accident. Don Martín Chávez and his grandson Roy Chávez served as pallbearers during Henry Santana's funeral service inside the St. Francis Cathedral and burial in the Rosario Cemetery on April 12, 1930.[51]

While Martín Chávez survived the sorrow of burying his grandson Henry Santana that spring, the senior citizen may have sensed that his own time was coming to an end when he fell ill with pneumonia in November 1931. Although Martín became bedridden inside his home on College Street that month, he was still determined to attend the Roman Catholic mass scheduled to commence in the Cathedral Basilica of Saint Francis of Assisi at 10:30 on the night of Sunday, November 22. His wife Juanita and their concerned relatives believed he was too weak to make the journey and refused to escort the Lincoln County War veteran to the cathedral as requested. When none of his relatives were looking, Martín quietly sneaked out of his house like a teenage runaway. The cold night air did Martín's lungs no favors as the stubborn old-timer ambled down College Street and made the six-block journey over to the St. Francis Cathedral to attend mass. His relatives were shocked when discovering the patriarch of their family "ran away" and escorted him home later that night. It was the last time Don Martín was spotted outside his house by the citizens of Santa Fe.[52]

José Martín Chávez died of pneumonia inside his home at 2:30 on the afternoon of Tuesday, December 8, 1931. He was 78-years-old. As Martín's loving wife of fifty-six years Juanita Romero-Chávez began the grieving process with the couple's four children and many grandchildren, the *New Mexican* published a partially accurate account of her husband's exploits the following day:

> Martin Chaves, "compadre" of Billy the Kid and veteran of the Lincoln County War died peacefully at his home, 51[8] College Street, at 2:30 yesterday afternoon. Enfeebled by the weight of years, the man who had survived the bullets of the most famous war of the southwestern cattle country, succumbed to a severe cold. He carried scars received in battle alongside Billy the Kid to his death. . . .
>
> Don Martin belonged to the McSween section, the crowd of which Billy the Kid was the hero. Interviewed in recent years by authors of Billy the Kid books, Don Martin stoutly resented word pictures that made the Kid appear in the role of a "crook." He was loyal to his friends, he said, not a killer for the sake of killing.
>
> Don Martin's name appears in Walter Noble Burns' "Saga of Billy the Kid" in connection with the battle at McSween's house in Lincoln more than half a century ago. Billy and some of his followers were besieged in the McSween house by 50 or more of the Murphy-Dolan faction. Gathering what forces he could together, Chaves rode to his rescue. They were prevented from getting into the McSween house; the town was full of troops from Fort Stanton. Taking up stations in the Montano and Patron houses in the east end of the town, Don Martin, then a young rancher, and his followers carried on the battle from these points. Chaves and his followers were forced to retreat when Colonel Dudley, training gatling guns on the Montano and Patron houses, threatened to riddle them if he didn't withdraw.
>
> Two sons survive, Benny and [Modesto], the former being the traffic officer, two daughters, Mrs. Manuel Baca and Mrs. Frank Santana. Don Martin's widow also survives.
>
> Don Martin was born at Manzano, but "drifting down" to Picacho he became a rancher in Lincoln County in the days when history was being made with six-shooters.[53]

The *New Mexican* published an obituary for the late businessman the same day. "Although Mr. Chaves was a busy man, he found time and pleasure in taking active part in the political life of his state, always identified with activities of the Democratic party," the newspaper announced. "Mr. Chaves was a Christian man, actively engaged in the work of his church." Martín's passing was also announced by the *Albuquerque Journal* in Bernalillo County, the *Casper Star-Tribune* in Wyoming, and *The Daily Sentinel* in Grand Junction, Colorado.[54]

Martín Chávez's funeral service was held inside the St. Francis Cathedral at nine o'clock on the morning of Friday, December 11, 1931. His widow Juanita Romero-Chávez, their four children, grandchildren, and many friends were in attendance. A solemn high mass was performed by Rev. Leonard Holtkamp with the assistance of Father Jerome Hesse and Father Camillius Fangman. "There were many beautiful floral designs, each bearing a message of deep sympathy in the loss to the community of so valuable a citizen as Mr. Chaves was," the *New Mexican* announced that evening. Former governor James F. Hinkle, George Ulrick, and "Colonel" George Prichard served as honorary pallbearers, and helped transport one of Lincoln County's greatest Hispano success stories to his final resting place in the Chávez family plot in the Rosario Cemetery on North Guadalupe Street.[55]

***

When announcing the death of Martín Chávez in Santa Fe, the *New Mexican* declared that "only two survivors of the Lincoln County War remain." The two men in question were "George Coe, of Glencoe N. M., and Eugenio Salazar, of Lincoln, N. M." The newspaper had it wrong. The mild-mannered Yginio Salazar could still reminisce about escaping the burning McSween house with the 80-year-old Florencio Cháves on the Río Bonito. Florencio lived alone on the main street of Lincoln, having never remarried following the death of his wife Teodora Brady-Cháves two decades earlier.[56]

While Don Yginio Salazar could discuss the Wild West of his youth with a handful of old-timers like Florencio Cháves and George Coe, there was no question that times had changed by 1932. Long gone were the days of Billy the Kid. The frontier gunman, bandido, lawman, cavalryman, and hostile Indian were now merely caricatures on a movie screen, where actors like Tom Mix, Hoot Gibson, and a young man called John Wayne dressed in costumes and tried to portray the lifestyle Old Man Salazar had known. The newspaper headlines devoted to those living outside the law were now dominated by ruthless gangsters such as Al Capone. They used automobiles and machine guns rather than horses and six-shooters. While the Santa Fe Ring once held New Mexico firmly in their grasp, the insatiable J. Edgar Hoover had ushered in a new era of law enforcement and would attempt to exert control over the entire country. There was also trouble stirring over in Germany, where an Austrian named Adolf Hitler would soon take power.

It seemed there was little room left in the world for a decrepit frontiersman like Yginio Salazar as the elderly farmer continued living the simple life with his wife Isabel in Baca Canyon. Unlike Isabel Salazar, some Hispanas still wore their rebozos and used an *horno* to cook meals for their families. That made them an object of curiosity for gawking Anglo travelers, as if they were living remnants of a fading way of life. Every now and then, a journalist wearing a fashionable fedora hat showed up in Lincoln wanting to speak with the locals about the old days. George Coe gave a speech at a community picnic held near the old Mescalero Agency, during which various historic sites related to the Lincoln County War were marked, on June 12, 1932. The following month Yginio Salazar received a surprise visit from Hollywood stars Johnny Mack Brown and Douglas Fairbanks Sr. The two actors also spoke with Florencio Cháves in Lincoln before departing. The legend of Billy the Kid was becoming a magnet for tourists, and some people were pushing for a monument to be erected on William Bonney's gravesite in old Fort Sumner. There was money to be made from the desperado's fame.[57]

The 73-year-old Yginio Salazar also received a visit from a journalist named Wilber Smith before the year was out. "His rancho is just a little off the 'Outlaw Trail,'" Smith later wrote. "It is at Double Crossing on the Fort Stanton-Lincoln road, U. S. Highway 380." The journalist found Old Man Salazar an amiable host upon his arrival in Baca Canyon, later describing the elderly farmer as possessing "all the politeness and courtesy of his generation."

Yginio Salazar and Wilber Smith were soon discussing the old days. The Hispano farmer recalled arriving on the Río Bonito from Valencia County as a young boy. Naturally, Smith was more eager to hear about William Bonney and the Lincoln County War. It was a subject that Yginio had discussed on countless occasions over the years, but one that he never seemed to grow tired of talking about. "When he is not up on the range, tending to his rancho, he enjoys nothing better than a good chat about his old amigo, Billy the Kid,"

Smith later wrote. Yginio wiped his gray moustache and smiled before reminiscing in Spanish. His companion quickly noticed the same dramatic hand gestures that made an impression on Walter Noble Burns years earlier.

"*¡Por Dios!*" Old Man Salazar exclaimed. "Those were the days!"

Yginio discussed the McSween and Murphy-Dolan factions who went to war in Lincoln County when he was still a teenager. He remembered feeling as if everyone had to choose a side, as if neutrality was not an option at the time. He also mentioned the contrast between the Bible-thumping Alexander McSween and the pistol-packing Billy Bonney, the Scotsman's "strong man" who "depended upon his six-shooter."

"'Billy the Kid is supposed to have killed twenty-one men, a man for each year of his life," Smith asked. "Is that true?"

Yginio nodded in agreement, having succumbed to one of the many layers of mythology that had enveloped his famous amigo.

"*Muy posible*," Salazar replied. "But I cannot account for them all. There is one that I do not know about!"

"He was then an out-and-out killer," Smith suggested. "Something like the gangsters of Chicago?"

Yginio threw his hands up in exasperation at such a comparison.

"God forbid!" the elderly frontiersman exclaimed. "Those *ladrones* are rats! They have machine guns. Fast automobiles. Billy the Kid was not like that. He had a horse. A pair of six guns. He was *muy caballero*. He fought face to face with his enemies. He gave them a chance to draw."

Old Man Salazar recalled William Bonney's iron nerve, unfailing sense of humor, and infectious childlike laughter. He gleefully told Smith about the time his and Billy's wagon turned over in their haste to reach Fort Sumner one Christmas day, and about the clump of snow having been shot from off the top his head by his friend's revolvers.

"[Billy's] sense of humor never left him, no matter how tense and dangerous the situation," Yginio informed Wilber Smith. "He could've killed many more men than he did and he would have been justified in doing so. You know the Kid was notorious and there was always some hard boiled hombre, looking for a chance to down him, so that he would be known as the brave man who had killed the Kid."

Don Yginio Salazar recalled watching his friend Billy Bonney scare a "hard-boiled hombre" out of a cantina on one occasion. The man in question had pretended he was drunk when Bonney entered the establishment and insisted the Kid have a drink with him. The former deputy sheriff was in his element while describing the incident for an enthralled Wilber Smith:

> He wanted to catch Billy as he raised his glass to his mouth and away from his holsters. But the Kid must have sensed the danger. He lifted his glass. He threw the whiskey in the man's face. The man had already started for his gun. Billy laughed. "Let's play the trick over," he said. "You drink this time. Let's see whether I can get you!" The jaw of that hard-boiled hombre fell to the floor. He was one scared man. "I got to see a man about a paint pony," he stammered, terrified; and he dashed out of the saloon as if ten bobcats were after him. We all bent over and nearly split our sides with laughter at the way the bogus *valiente* ran.
>
> The Kid ran to the door and called after him. "Better luck next time, fellow! You are not the only one who has failed to get me. Even old Pat Garrett hasn't got me yet." Billy came back into the saloon. The smile was gone from his face. He talked as if he were thinking aloud. "Yeah, either I am going to get Pat or he is going to get me."

Having listened to Yginio Salazar's colorful recollections, Wilber Smith decided to broach a touchy subject for many of William Bonney's old friends.

"And Sheriff Pat Garrett did get him?" the journalist asked.

Yginio glanced at his guest but merely responded with stony silence.

"Oh, I see," Smith presumptuously remarked. "You are like many more people around here who think the Kid is still alive? You and George Coe are the only men now living who belonged to the Kid's faction. And Coe has declared many times that he did not believe the Kid was killed. Many think it was a frame up between those who wanted the reward and the Kid who was willing to clear out. Another thing. There was a big standing reward for the Kid, and Sheriff Pat Garrett did not collect it after he was supposed to have killed the Kid."

"*Muy posible*," Yginio politely answered, effectively ending their conversation.

Wilber Smith had demonstrated his ignorance regarding the death of William Bonney. Yginio's old comrade George Coe firmly believed their friend Billy the Kid had died at the end of Pat Garrett's revolver in Fort

Sumner, and the sheriff had indeed collected the $500 reward for killing New Mexico's most famous desperado. "Billy the Kid is like a character out of a Homeric epic," Smith would accurately inform his readers. "One does not know just where to separate mythology from fact." His article about Yginio Salazar and the fantastical rumors of William Bonney's survival, "The Amigo of Billy the Kid: The Man Who Fought Side by Side With Lincoln County's Outlaw Character Tells About the Days of Judge Colt's Rule," was published by *New Mexico Magazine* the following spring.[58]

Yginio Salazar and George Coe had lost another old comrade by the time Wilber Smith's article was published. The 82-year-old Florencio Cháves passed away in Lincoln on February 21, 1933. Yginio presumably attended the funeral service held in Lincoln the next day and followed Florencio's coffin to the community cemetery just east of town. It was a peaceful place for an elderly vaquero like himself to rest his bones when the time came. With Florencio's passing, Yginio was the last known McSween partisan to have escaped the Scotsman's burning house at the height of the Lincoln County War.[59]

On the Río Ruidoso, George Coe was frequently busy detailing his life story and recollections of the Lincoln County War with his ghostwriter Nan Hillary Harrison, a renowned poet and writer from Texas. The former Regulator and Mrs. Harrison decided to pay Yginio Salazar and his family a visit in Baca Canyon while working on their manuscript. Señora Isabel Salazar greeted Coe and Harrison at the door when they arrived and led them inside her "spotlessly clean little parlor." Isabel naturally proved "a most hospitable hostess" during their stay. Coe and Harrison noticed the walls inside the Salazar home were "lined with pictures; some of them fine old Spanish portraits."

Yginio Salazar cheerfully greeted his friend George Coe and his lady companion, although the farmer wished the "cattle rustlers would lay off his beat" at the time. The Great Depression had led to a minor resurgence in stock theft throughout the region. A new generation of outlaws like the affable John Dillinger, the psychopathic Lester "Baby Face" Nelson, the whiny Charles "Pretty Boy" Floyd, and the malicious Clyde Barrow and Bonnie Parker were consuming the newspaper headlines across the country at the time. J. Edgar Hoover and his Bureau of Investigation had their hands full pursuing bank robbers who used machine guns and automobiles.

Isabel Salazar quickly deciphered George Coe and Nan Harrison's broken Spanish while they chatted with her husband about the wild days and realized the purpose of their visit. Señora Salazar cordially invited her two guests to follow her into another room, where she retrieved a hidden key. She wanted to show them something. Coe and Harrison watched with curiosity as Isabel unlocked a cabinet drawer and removed a bundle wrapped inside a faded silk kerchief. The elderly Hispana smiled when handing Coe and Harrison a photograph of her husband in his younger years. She then produced a copy of the only known photograph of New Mexico's most famous desperado.

"Beely the Keed," Isabel whispered with a smile. "Beely the Keed."

George Coe knew as well as anyone how much his old friend William Bonney meant to the Salazar family and the local Hispano population. No matter what the Americanos said or wrote about the famous pistolero, he would always be their friend and hero Beely the Keed.

"Those few words spoke volumes," George Coe's memoir *Frontier Fighter* declared when published in 1934. "For 'Beely the Keed' is a fascinating legend for the natives, who could never be bought to betray him."[60]

***

The 75-year-old Yginio Salazar knew his time was finally coming when confined to his bed inside his home in Baca Canyon in early January 1935. His devoted wife Isabel Paniague de Salazar had passed away seven months earlier on May 15, 1934. The bedridden widower probably should have died in the McSween yard fifty-six years earlier. Fate dealt him a fortunate hand that night, but now it was almost time for him to meet Dios like so many of his comrades and friends before him. At least he would pass away surrounded by loved ones, unlike his amigo Billy the Kid, who had died alone and gasping for air in the darkness of Pedro Maxwell's bedroom.

Yginio Salazar died peacefully in his bed on January 9, 1935. His adopted daughter Margarita was present with her husband Bernardo and their children Ida Mae, Elias, Rogerio, Viola, and Flora. Yginio's older brother José Salazar still lived nearby and would have been in attendance with his wife Ginovera and their own children and young grandchildren. Baca Canyon eventually became known as Salazar Canyon owing to their family's longtime presence in the area.[61]

"One by one, the glamorous, gun-fighting men of the Old West fall like wheat before the sickle of time," the *Fort Stanton Caduceus* declared two months later. "Among the last were Ygenio Salazar, friend of law and outlaw. He passed away in bed at his home in Baca Canyon early in January." The *New Mexican* would publish most of Yginio Salazar's obituary—which naturally mentioned his miraculous escape from the burning McSween house—on March 22, 1935:

> He lay there three hours feigning death while the officers of the law held a wild celebration about the blazing house. Andy Boyle was for pumping another bullet into Salazar "just to make sure" but someone advised him, "don't waste a cartridge on a dead Mexican."
>
> SALAZAR BADLY WOUNDED
> Towards midnight the victors straggled away to bed and Salazar dragged his bleeding body across the wall and down along the Rio Bonita to the house of a relative. It was six months before he rode again.
> Salazar had many other brushes with outlaws and cattle thieves in those stirring times but the foregoing is his most famous exploit. Later, after Billy the Kid was captured and again escaped, killing two deputy sheriffs, he headed across the Capitan mountains. Salazar, then living at Las Tablas, furnished him food, blankets and a horse.
>
> MILD OLD GENTLEMAN
> In recent years Salazar looked nothing like the man who at 19 had ridden with the Kid. He was a mild mannered old Mexican gentleman with gray hair and [a] long white [moustache], thick bodied and broad shouldered . . .
> So passed one of The Kid's henchmen, game to the last. Unlike most of his companions in arms he died in bed with his boots off.[62]

Yginio Salazar was buried alongside his wife Isabel Paniague de Salazar in the community cemetery just east of Lincoln on January 10, 1935. The former vaquero, vigilante, rustler, deputy sheriff, and county commissioner remained a man of frontier values to the very end. Several hours before he died, the elderly farmer called his son-in-law Bernardo Salazar into his bedroom to offer some parting advice.

"Never run from cattle thieves," Yginio told him. "Stand and fight them."[63]

Epilogue

> *We are a multicultural country—always have been,*
> *and to our credit, always will be. It is something that*
> *we should be very proud of and embrace.*
> —Cheech Marin

The deceased Yginio Salazar and Martín Chávez's recollections of Billy the Kid and the Lincoln County War once again became available to the public when Miguel Antonio Otero Jr.'s *The Real Billy the Kid: With New Light on the Lincoln County War* was finally published in March 1936. Otero's book portrayed the famous outlaw as Yginio Salazar and Martín Chávez had remembered him—an amiable desperado who never shot a man without some justification, and a true friend of the Hispano population of southeastern Nuevo México. "Billy the Kid has a defender in former New Mexican official," the *Sacramento Bee* declared in California on March 28, 1936. "Frankly, it must be said former governor Otero is sympathetic toward the Kid and the faction with which he fought in the Lincoln fracas."[1]

Miguel Antonio Otero Jr. had relied far too heavily on the fantastical writings of Ash Upson when detailing much of Billy the Kid's legendary exploits, but the former governor opened a window to the Hispano perspective of William Bonney and the Lincoln County War for a future generation of researchers. Astonishingly, it took more than seventy years before another writer approached the subject in such a fashion. Author and historian Lynda A. Sánchez admirably started laying the groundwork for writing a book about Billy the Kid from the Hispano perspective in the 1980s, but ultimately shifted her focus elsewhere. It was not until former California politician Paul L. Tsompanas published his commendable effort *Juan Patrón: A Fallen Star in the Days of Billy the Kid* in 2012 that the Hispano side of things received the kind of literary focus it deserved. New Mexican historian Daniel B. Flores also published his findings about José Chávez y Chávez in a book titled *José Chávez y Chávez: The Outlaw Who Died of Old Age* in August 2014.[2]

The history of Billy the Kid and the Lincoln County War has endured, but for hombres like José Chávez y Chávez, Juan Patrón, Martín Chávez, and

Yginio Salazar, it was merely one storied chapter in a much broader history of resistance against bossism in Nuevo México. While Martín Chávez's grandson Martín N. Chávez and other Nuevomexicanos served their country during the Second World War, dozens of Hispano families on the Parajito Plateau in Los Alamos were forced to flee their homes within forty-eight hours to allow for the construction of the military lab in which the atomic bomb was created in 1942. Their houses were bulldozed and their livestock slaughtered or turned loose with little compensation. "These were Hispanic American homesteaders, which perhaps explains why this dark episode in American history is so ignored," remarked Los Alamos computer scientist Loyda Martínez shortly after the release of Christopher Nolan's film *Oppenheimer* in July 2023. The effects of the radiation caused by the US government's Trinity nuclear test in New Mexico during the summer of 1945 are still felt by the families of those who were living in the surrounding areas. "They'll never reflect on the fact that New Mexicans gave their lives," says cancer survivor Tina Cordova. "They did the dirtiest of jobs. They invaded our lives and our lands and then they left."[3]

Although the kind of widespread armed resistance carried out by Los Gorras Blancas never resurfaced in New Mexico, the Herrera brothers would have been pleased that Mexican Americans continued their struggle for self-preservation in a variety of ways. The racist term "greaser" of frontier times mutated into equally derogatory slurs such as "spic" and "wetback." A racial divide persisted, and some of the descendants of Spanish settlers formed organizations like the League of United Latin American Citizens to safeguard themselves from prejudice in the early twentieth century. From that seed eventually arose the Chicano Movement, or El Movimiento, personified by social activists like the famous César Chávez, Dolores Huerta, Rodolfo "Corky" Gonzáles, Rosalio Muñoz, Oscar Zeta Acosta, and Reies López Tijerina. Numerous subgroups like the militant Brown Berets, the Mexican American Youth Organization (MAYO), and the Raza Unida Party emerged during the movement's quest for worker's rights, racial equality, cultural identity, the alleviation of poverty, and communal autonomy throughout the decades following the Second World War. "I can remember my older cousins not being taught to speak Spanish so they wouldn't be discriminated against," recalls Margaret Chávez Slayton, the granddaughter of José Chávez y Chávez. "We were proud to be a Chávez and to bring honor to our family in all we did, and I still hold that standard today."[4]

The conflict over land grants also continued in northern New Mexico. Chicano activist Reies López Tijerina, originally a native of south Texas, formed the Alianza Federal de Mercedes (Federated Alliance of Community Grants) in northern New Mexico in 1963. Tijerina ambitiously sought the return of communal land grants to the Nuevomexicano population, as well as recognition of the United States government's violation of the Treaty of Guadalupe Hidalgo. The feisty activist famously led members of his Alianza Federal de Mercedes in a raid on the Tierra Amarilla courthouse in Rio Arriba County on June 5, 1967. Their intention was to carry out a citizen's arrest of their adversary Alfonso Sánchez, the district attorney. Sánchez was nowhere to be found, and two law officials were wounded in the resulting chaos. The Aliancistas took a journalist and a deputy hostage before fleeing into the mountains. The Tierra Amarilla Courthouse Raid received national press and a federal manhunt began. Reies López Tijerina, alias El Tigre, eventually surrendered to the authorities in Albuquerque. He was sentenced to two years in prison for the destruction of federal property and assault on a federal officer in 1970. Two years later a policy was instituted in which the northern Nuevomexicano population's cultural ties to grazing lands must be recognized by agencies. As recently as the autumn of 2017, a group of Nuevomexicano ranchers were left disappointed when their suit against the US Forest Service for limiting grazing on historic land grants was dismissed.[5]

While discord over the remaining land grants persists in northern New Mexico more than 170 years after the signing of the Treaty of Guadalupe Hidalgo, the neglected history of Los Gorras Blancas was celebrated with an exhibition of religious artifacts connected to the vigilante group in the City of Las Vegas Museum during the spring of 2022. "The land grants that still exist, is the legacy of Los Gorras Blancas," says Rock Ulibarri, the great-grandson of Juan José, Pablo, and Nicanor Herrera's older sister Juanita Paula Herrera-Ulibarri. "The struggle for preservation of land grants and our traditional way of life continues today, and knowing our history and lineage drives our passion to sustain it." The exhibition in Las Vegas was quickly shut down when Mayor Louie Trujillo ignorantly assumed the *gorras* worn by several men in attendance were symbolic of White supremacy. "The Hispano population of New Mexico has persevered through the years despite the challenges it has faced," says Roberto Martínez, the great-grandson of a proud White Cap. "It still survives to this day and will always survive as we pass on our traditions and stories to the next generations." Inroads have been made, and many Americans of various ethnic backgrounds celebrate National Hispanic Heritage Month from September 15 to October 15 on an annual basis.[6]

In contrast with the history of Los Gorras Blancas, the story of Billy the Kid and the Lincoln County War has remained the subject of countless books and dozens of films throughout the last century. José Chávez y Chávez became the most famous Nuevomexicano participant of the Lincoln County War with the release of *Young Guns* in 1988. The successful Western portrayed the pistolero as a Mexican Indian of Hispano and Navajo lineage who relies on his deadly skill with knives more than a rifle or six-shooter. Although the quiet, contemplative sage played by Lou Diamond Phillips bore little resemblance to the boastful, ruthless Chávez y Chávez of history, the film broadened the Hispano ruffian's fame significantly. Millions of people around the globe learned the name José Chávez y Chávez, something that would have undoubtedly pleased the notorious badman himself. The racial prejudice Nuevomexicanos often endured in frontier times was also demonstrated on screen. Lou Diamond Phillips reprised the role in *Young Guns II*, released in 1990. In the sequel Chávez y Chávez was inaccurately portrayed as dying in Fort Sumner from a gunshot wound inflicted by Pat Garrett's posse during the capture of Emilio Estevez's Billy the Kid at Stinking Spring.

Juan Patrón's name was mentioned by Terence Stamp's John Tunstall in the opening line of *Young Guns* in 1988, although the Hispano entrepreneur was never portrayed on screen throughout the remainder of the film. More recently, José Chávez y Chávez, Juan Patrón, and Yginio Salazar showed up as characters in Michael Hirst's dreadfully inaccurate television series *Billy the Kid*, which premiered on MGM+ in the spring of 2022. Martín Chávez has continually proven the most forgotten Hispano participant of the Lincoln County War. Despite leading the McSween partisans during the five-day siege in Lincoln, the mayordomo of Picacho has never been featured or mentioned in any of the films about his amigo Billy the Kid. More alarmingly, historians have mostly disregarded Martín's recollections of the conflict procured by Miguel Antonio Otero Jr. during the summer of 1926.[7]

José Chávez y Chávez, Juan Patrón, Martín Chávez, and Yginio Salazar each blazed their own individual paths in the years preceding the Lincoln County War. They continued doing the same in its aftermath. While there is no shame residing in the shadow of Billy the Kid along with everyone else in New Mexico's vast history, the colorful lives of José Chávez y Chávez, Juan Patrón, Martín Chávez, and Yginio Salazar are a small testament to their own people's imperishable legacy in frontier times and the early twentieth century.

Endnotes

Note for the Prologue

1. The various details of Johnny Mack Brown and Douglas Fairbanks Sr.'s travels through New Mexico and meeting with Yginio Salazar in Lincoln County in 1932 are featured in *Roswell Daily Record*, July 21, 1932; *Clovis (NM) News-Journal*, July 22, 1932; *Albuquerque Journal*, July 23, 1932; *Roswell Daily Record*, July 25, 1932; *Albuquerque Journal*, July 26, 1932; *Alamogordo Daily News*, July 28, 1932; and *Santa Fe New Mexican*, July 29, 1932.

Notes for Chapter 1

1. Daniel Flores, *José Chávez y Chávez: The Outlaw Who Died of Old Age* (pub. by author, 2014), 11. J. H. Hunter to Governor M. A. Otero, October 25, 1897, Omaha, NE, collection 1959-090: Governor Miguel A. Otero Papers (Otero Papers), Penal Papers, Commutations, box 14070, folder 267: Jose Chavez y Chavez October–November 1897, New Mexico State Records Center and Archives (NMSRCA), Santa Fe.
2. Flores, *José Chávez y Chávez*, 11. 1850 United States Federal Census. 1860 United States Federal Census. The correct date of José Teodoro Chávez y Chávez's birth in Cebolleta can be found in Bautismos: Acoma, Cebolleta, Cubero, La Laguna, San Mateo y San Rafael – del Diocese de Gallup, New Mexico, 1 Septiembre 1754—19 Diciembre 1885, extractions by David Gonzales, data entry by Edward J. Schoolcraft, NMSRCA. While José Chávez y Chávez's name was somewhat unique, there was a different José Chávez y Chávez residing in New Mexico throughout the same period. The other José Chávez y Chávez was born in New Mexico in around 1835 and served in the Grand Army of the Republic during the Civil War. This José Chávez y Chávez lived most of his life in Bernalillo County, where he became a minor political figure before eventually moving to Santa Fe. He died in the state capital on July 28, 1914. The other José Chávez y Chávez's obituary can be found on page 2 of the *Evening Herald* (Albuquerque), July 28, 1914.
3. Robert Julyan, *The Place Names of New Mexico*, rev. ed. (Albuquerque: University of New Mexico Press, 1998), 329–30.
4. Details about Hispano culture in New Mexico Territory can be found in various sources listed in the bibliography. Two indispensable studies are Arthur L. Campa, *Hispanic Culture in the Southwest* (Norman: University of Oklahoma Press, 1979), and Aurelio M. Espinosa, "New-Mexican Spanish Folk-Lore," *Journal of American Folklore* 23, no. 90 (October–December 1910): 395–418. Charles F. Lummis's *The Land of Poco Tiempo* (New York: Charles Scribner's Sons, 1897) also provides valuable insight. The collection of sources related to Hispano frontier culture listed in the bibliography will now be cited as Hispano New Mexico Sources. 1860 United States Federal Census.
5. *Santa Fe Weekly Gazette*, November 13, 1858. Julyan, *Place Names*, 329–30.
6. Lummis, *Land of Poco Tiempo*, 248. Hispano New Mexico Sources. All translations are by the author.
7. Paul L. Tsompanas, *Juan Patrón: A Fallen Star in the Days of Billy the Kid* (Richmond, VA: Belle Isle Books, 2013), 5.
8. *Richmond Weekly Palladium*, March 17, 1852.
9. Marta Weigle and Kyle Fiore, *Santa Fe and Taos: The Writer's Era, 1916–1941* (Santa Fe: Sunstone Press, 2008), 3.

10. Howard Bryan's *Santa Fe Tales & More* (Santa Fe: Clear Light, 2010) remains an enjoyable book about Santa Fe and its colorful history.
11. *Richmond Weekly Palladium*, March 17, 1852. For Jean Baptiste Lamy, see Paul Horgan, *Lamy of Santa Fe* (New York: Farrar, Straus, and Giroux, 1975). W. W. H. Davis, *El Gringo: New Mexico and Her People* (Lincoln: University of Nebraska Press, 1982), 232.
12. Tsompanas, *Juan Patrón*, 7–8.
13. *Santa Fe Weekly Post*, April 26, 1862. For the Civil War in New Mexico Territory, see Donald S. Frazier's *Blood & Treasure: Confederate Empire in the Southwest* (College Station: Texas A&M University Press, 1995); Alvin M. Josephy's *The Civil War in the American West* (New York: Alfred A. Knopf, 1991); Flint Whitlock's *Distant Bugles, Distant Drums: The Union Response to the Confederate Invasion of New Mexico* (Boulder: University Press of Colorado, 2006); Don Alberts's *The Battle of Glorieta: Union Victory in the West* (College Station: Texas A&M University Press, 1996); and Ray Colton's *The Civil War in the Western Territories: Arizona, Colorado, New Mexico and Utah* (Norman: University of Oklahoma Press, 1984).
14. Tsompanas, *Juan Patrón*, 8–9.
15. Davis, *El Gringo*, 217.
16. Julyan, *Place Names*, 220–21.
17. Margaret Leonard Windham and Evelyn Lujan Baca, comp., *New Mexico Baptisms: Nuestra Señora de la Inmaculada Concepción de Tomé*, vol. 2, *11 February 1847–12 June 1881*, extracted by Donald S. Dreeson and Lila Armijo Pfeufer (Albuquerque: New Mexico Genealogical Society: 2017), 71. New Mexico, US, Deaths, 1889–1945, Ancestry.com. 1850 United States Federal Census. 1860 United States Federal Census. 1870 United States Federal Census. Ernest S. Sánchez & Paul R. Sánchez, *"Nuestros Antepasados" (Our Ancestors): Los Nuevo Mexicanos del Condado de Lincoln (Lincoln County's History of Its New Mexican Settlers)* (Bloomington, IN: AuthorHouse, 2015), 173–75.
18. Billy Charles Patrick Cummings, *Frontier Parish: Recovered Catholic History of Lincoln County, 1860–1884*, book 4 (Lincoln, NM: Lincoln County Historical Society Publication, 1995), 34–36. Sánchez and Sánchez, *"Nuestros Antepasados" (Our Ancestors)*, 173–75.
19. For the Virgin of Guadalupe, see Carl Anderson and Eduardo Chávez, *Our Lady of Guadalupe: Mother of the Civilization of Love* (New York: Image, 2009).
20. For *Los Penitentes*, see Marta Weigle's *Brothers of Light, Brothers of Blood: The Penitentes of the Southwest* (Albuquerque: University of New Mexico Press, 1976). Louisa R. Stark, "The Origin of the Penitente 'Death Cart,'" *Journal of American Folklore* 84, no. 333 (July–September 1971): 304–10. Fray Angélico Chávez, *My Penitente Land: Reflections on Spanish New Mexico* (Albuquerque: University of New Mexico Press, 1974), 203.
21. Cummings, *Frontier Parish*, 34–36.
22. Marriage records show that the future Paula Salazar, the daughter of Diego Antonio Chávez and María Rosalia Varela-Chávez, married her first husband, José Ventura Sedillo, the son of José María Sedillo and Juana Sánchez-Sedillo, in Tome, New Mexico, on December 21, 1845. The 1850 United States Federal Census shows that Teofilo Salazar was living with his future wife Paula, her first husband José Ventura Sedillo, and the couple's eldest child Lugarda in Tome five years later. Margaret Leonard Windham, comp., *New Mexico Marriages: Churches of Immaculate Conception of Tomé and Our Lady of Belén*, extracted by Raymond P. Salas (Albuquerque: New Mexico Genealogical Society, 1994).

There has been much conjecture over Yginio Salazar's birthdate. His headstone in the old Lincoln cemetery reads that he was born on February 14, 1863. This is clearly incorrect, as Yginio is recorded living with his family three years earlier in the 1860 United States Federal Census. When Yginio Salazar filled out an insurance form with the Union Central Life Insurance Company of Cincinnati, Ohio, for himself and his wife Isabel Salazar in the early twentieth century, he recorded his own birthdate as September 18, 1859. Yginio also recorded Manzano as his place of birth. As it came from the man himself, it is this record on which I have relied regarding his birthdate. Yginio Salazar's insurance policy for both he and his wife: Identifier: S/2/18, Herman B. Weisner Papers (Weisner Papers), Río Grande Historical Collections, New Mexico State University Library, Archives and Special Collections (NMSU LASC), Albuquerque (hereafter cited as Salazar insurance policy). 1860 United States Federal Census. 1880 United States Federal Census. 1885 New Mexico Territorial Census. Hispano New Mexico Sources.

23. 1860 United States Federal Census. Campa, *Hispanic Culture*, 237. Lummis, *Land of Poco Tiempo*, 217–35. Hispano New Mexico Sources.
24. Wilbur Smith, "The Man Who Fought Side-by-Side with Lincoln County's Outlaw Character Tells All about the Days of 'Judge Colt's Rule,'" *New Mexico Magazine*, April 1933. Yginio Salazar interview with J. Evetts Haley, August 17, 1927, Haley Memorial Library, Midland, TX (hereafter cited as Salazar interview). 1860 United States Federal Census. Clark S. Knowlton, "Patron-Peon Pattern among the Spanish Americans of New Mexico," *Social Forces* 41, no. 1 (October 1962): 12–17.
25. For the Mexican-American War, see Peter Guardino's *The Dead March: A History of the Mexican-American War* (Cambridge: Harvard University Press, 2017); and Karl Jack Bauer's *The Mexican War: 1846–1848* (Lincoln: University of Nebraska Press, 1992). William S. McFeely, *Grant: A Biography* (New York: W. W. Norton, 1981), 30–38.
26. Erlinda Gonzáles-Berry and David R. Maciel, *The Contested Homeland: A Chicano History of New Mexico* (Albuquerque: University of New Mexico Press, 2000), 44–45. For the Treaty of Guadalupe and its ramifications, see Richard Griswold Del Castillo, *The Treaty of Guadalupe Hidalgo: A Legacy of Conflict* (Norman: University of Oklahoma Press, 1990),
27. Gonzáles-Berry and Maciel, *Contested Homeland*, is an indispensable source for the cultural, political, economic, and social conflict between Mexican Americans and Anglo Americans in New Mexico. For Mexican American resistance against Anglo expansion in the Southwest, see Robert J. Rosenbaum's *Mexicano Resistance in the Southwest* (Austin: University of Texas Press, 1981). Although blinded by a sense of racial superiority, Davis's *El Gringo* provides valuable firsthand insight into the cultural conflict between Mexican Americans and Anglo Americans in New Mexico Territory. For a solid study of the conflict over land in New Mexico and the Southwest, see María E. Montoya's *Translating Property: The Maxwell Land Grant and the Conflict over Land in the American West, 1840–1900* (Lawrence: University Press of Kansas, 2005). *Thibodaux (LA) Minerva*, November 26, 1853. Hispano New Mexico Sources. Campa, *Hispanic Culture*, 190. Lummis, *Land of Poco Tiempo*, 3.

Notes for Chapter 2

1. Salazar interview. Frederick Nolan, *The Lincoln County War: A Documentary History* (Norman: University of Oklahoma Press, 1992), 49.
2. Salazar interview.
3. Lynda A. Sánchez, *Apache Legends & Lore of Southern New Mexico* (Charleston, SC: History Press, 2014), 59. For Kit Carson and his campaigns, see Hampton Sides's *Blood*

and Thunder: An Epic of the American West (New York: Doubleday, 2006). Lynn Robison Bailey's *The Long Walk: A History of the Navaho Wars, 1846–1868* (Tucson: Westernlore Press, 1964); and Gerald Thompson's *The Army and the Navajo: The Bosque Redondo Reservation Experiment, 1863–68* (Tucson: University of Arizona Press, 1976) are also valuable sources. For the Bosque Redondo reservation, also see Lynn R. Bailey's *Bosque Redondo: An American Concentration Camp* (Pasadena, CA: Socio-Technical Books, 1970). For the Navajo see Pete Iverson, *Diné: A History of the Navajos* (Albuquerque: University of New Mexico Press, 2002).

4. See Andrés Reséndez's *The Other Slavery: The Uncovered Story of Indian Enslavement in America* (Boston: Houghton Mifflin Harcourt, 2016) for a concise history of Indian slavery. *Santa Fe Weekly Post*, May 23, 1868.
5. Salazar interview. James B. Mills, *Billy the Kid: El Bandido Simpático* (Denton: University of North Texas Press, 2022), 353. John R. Englekirk, "The Passion Play in New Mexico," *Western Folklore* 25, no. 1 (January 1966): 17–33.
6. Salazar interview.
7. Salazar interview. John P. Wilson's *Merchants, Guns, and Money: The Story of Lincoln County and Its Wars* (Santa Fe: Museum of New Mexico Press, 1987) remains an excellent source on the history of Lincoln County.
8. Wilson, *Merchants*, 23–24. *Santa Fe Weekly Post*, August 21, 1869.
9. For Saturnino Baca see Harold L. Edwards, "Capt. Saturnino Baca in the Shadow of the Lincoln County War," *Los Amigos* 2, no. 2 (April 1993), no. 3 (July 1993), no. 4 (October 1993). 1860 United States Federal Census. 1870 United States Federal Census. 1880 United States Federal Census.
10. Flores, *José Chávez y Chávez*, 11, 84. 1870 United States Federal Census. 1880 United States Federal Census. 1900 United States Federal Census. 1910 United States Federal Census. 1920 United States Federal Census. US World War I Draft Registration Cards, 1917–1918, Ancestry.com. Lincoln County Marriages, June 1869–December 1910, Church of Jurisdiction in Santa Rita Catholic Church, Carrizozo, Territory of New Mexico, microfilm FHL 016-756, NMSRCA.
11. *Santa Fe New Mexican*, September 13, 1870.
12. Tsompanas, *Juan Patrón*, 12. 1870 United States Federal Census. 1880 United States Federal Census. 1885 New Mexico Territorial Census. Juan Patrón's older sister Juana Patrón de Ramírez's obituary can be found on page 6 of the *Albuquerque Citizen*, January 31, 1902. She is also traceable through various census records and is listed as residing in Santa Fe in 1880 with her husband and daughter.
13. Wilson, *Merchants*, passim.
14. Amelia Bolton-Church interview by Louis Blachly on August 9 and 10, 1952, transcription by S. J. Morgan for the Lincoln County Historical Society, June 20, 2003, Chuck Usmar Collection, Albuquerque (hereafter cited as Bolton-Church interview by Blachly).
15. Tsompanas, *Juan Patrón*, 13–16.
16. 1870 United States Federal Census. 1880 United States Federal Census. 1885 New Mexico Territorial Census. US Civil War Pension Index: General Index to Pension Files, 1861–1934; Series T288, Roll 332; Record Group 15: Records of the Department of Veterans Affairs, 1773–2007; National Archives and Records Administration at Washington, DC (NARA). Bolton-Church interview by Blachly.
17. Interview in 1950 of Amelia Church of Roswell, NM, by Mary Peterson (typescript), Chuck Usmar Collection (Usmar Collection), Albuquerque.
18. For details about William Brady, see Donald R. Lavash's *Sheriff William Brady: Tragic Hero of the Lincoln County War* (Santa Fe: Sunstone Press, 1987), although the author's

highly contentious reasoning and cherry-picking of sources remain an example of how not to conduct historiography.
19. For Lawrence G. Murphy, see Mills, *Billy the Kid*, 92–96.
20. *The Borderer*, May 19, 1871.
21. For a good political history of New Mexico Territory, see Robert W. Larson's *New Mexico's Quest for Statehood, 1846–1912* (Albuquerque: University of New Mexico Press, 1968).
22. For the Santa Fe Ring, see Gale Cooper's *The Santa Fe Ring versus Billy the Kid* (Albuquerque: Gelcour Books, 2018); David L Caffey's *Chasing the Santa Fe Ring: Power and Privilege in Territorial New Mexico* (Albuquerque: University of New Mexico Press, 2014); Larson, *New Mexico's Quest*; and Howard Roberts Lamar's *The Far Southwest, 1846–1912: A Territorial History* (New Haven: Yale University Press, 1966). For Thomas B. Catron, see Victor Westphall's *Thomas Benton Catron and His Era* (Tucson: University of Arizona Press, 1973), although the book is frequently contradictory and highly romanticized.
23. *Santa Fe New Mexican*, May 1, 1871. *Weekly New Mexican* (Santa Fe), May 2, 1871. *Santa Fe New Mexican*, September 2, 1871.
24. *Santa Fe New Mexican*, December 4, 1871. Tsompanas, *Juan Patrón*, 18.
25. 1870 United States Federal Census. Wilson, *Merchants*, 20. Julyan, *Place Names*, 265–66.
26. Sánchez and Sánchez, *"Nuestros Antepasados"* (*Our Ancestors*), 174–75. James B. Mills, "Hombres Valientes in the Lincoln County War," *Wild West*, December 2020. 1860 United States Federal Census. 1870 United States Federal Census.
27. 1870 United States Federal Census. 1880 United States Federal Census. Mills, *Billy the Kid*, 144. A reference to Florencio Gonzáles having received an education in France can be found on page 1 of the *Lincoln County Leader* (White Oaks, NM), October 20, 1888.
28. *Las Vegas (NM) Gazette*, May 3, 1873. For the New Mexico sheep trade, see John O. Baxter's *Las carneradas: Sheep Trade in New Mexico, 1700–1860* (Albuquerque: University of New Mexico Press, 1987); and Alvar Ward Carlson, "New Mexico's Sheep Industry, 1850–1900: Its Role in the History of the Territory," *New Mexico Historical Review* 44, no. (1969): 25–49.
29. Ann Lacy and Anne Valley-Fox, *Stories From Hispano New Mexico: A New Mexico Federal Writers' Project Book* (Santa Fe: Sunstone Press, 2012), 64–69.
30. *Las Vegas Gazette*, May 3, 1873.
31. For John S. Chisum, see Bill O'Neal's *John Chisum: Frontier Cattle King* (Fort Worth: Eakin Press, 2018); Richard Weddle's "Chisum: Cattle King of the Pecos," *Wild West*, August 2014; Harwood P. Hinton's "John Chisum, 1877–84," *New Mexico Historical Review*, July 1956–January 1957; and Clifford R. Caldwell, *John Simpson Chisum: The Cattle King of the Pecos Revisited* (Santa Fe: Sunstone Press, 2010). Report of Inspector E. C. Watkins, Report No. 1981, June 27, 1878, Record Group 75, Records of the Bureau of Indian Affairs, Inspectors' Reports, 1873–80, NARA (hereafter cited as Watkins Report).
32. For details of the widespread livestock theft throughout the Southwest during this period, see Bob Alexander, *Desert Desperadoes: The Banditti of Southwestern New Mexico* (Silver City, NM: Gila Books, 2006). Rustling activities and their occasional repercussions were frequently reported in the *Santa Fe New Mexican* and other newspapers of the period in the American Southwest. David Johnson, *The Horrell Wars: Feuding in Texas and New Mexico* (Denton: University of North Texas Press, 2014), 52. *Santa Fe New Mexican*, August 21, 1872. *Santa Fe New Mexican*, February 18, 1873. *Santa Fe New Mexican*, March 8, 1873.
33. Rosenbaum, *Mexicano Resistance*, 95–98.

34. *Santa Fe New Mexican*, January 17, 1873. *Weekly New Mexican*, February 25, 1873.
35. *Weekly New Mexican*, February 25, 1873.
36. *Weekly New Mexican*, February 25, 1873.
37. *Weekly New Mexican*, February 25, 1873. Returns from US Military Posts, 1800–1916; Microfilm Serial: M617; Microfilm Roll: 1217; NARA.
38. *Weekly New Mexican*, February 25, 1873. *Daily New Mexican*, February 25, 1873.
39. Tsompanas, *Juan Patrón*, 23.
40. *Las Vegas Gazette*, May 10, 1873.
41. Tsompanas, *Juan Patrón*, 23. Nolan, *Documentary History*, 49.
42. 1870 United States Federal Census. Tsompanas, *Juan Patrón*, 23. *Santa Fe New Mexican*, September 29, 1873. *Santa Fe New Mexican*, December 20, 1873. Robert A. Casey interview with J. Evetts Haley, June 25, 1937, Haley Memorial Library (hereafter cited as Casey interview).

Notes for Chapter 3

1. Larson, *New Mexico's Quest*, 85–86. *Las Vegas Gazette*, January 11, 1873. For the Texas Revolution, see Stephen L. Hardin's *Texian Iliad: A Military History of the Texas Revolution, 1835–1836* (Austin: University of Texas Press, 1996); and Bryan Burrough et al., *Forget the Alamo: The Rise and Fall of an American Myth* (New York: Penguin Press, 2021).
2. Although Frederick Nolan's *Bad Blood: The Life and Times of the Horrell Brothers* (Stillwater, OK: Barbed Wire Press, 1994) remains a commendable study, it has since been surpassed by Johnson, *Horrell Wars*.
3. Johnson, *Horrell Wars*, 32–50.
4. Johnson, *Horrell Wars*, 19. *Santa Fe New Mexican*, December 20, 1873.
5. Lily Klasner, *My Girlhood Among Outlaws*, ed. Eve Ball (Tucson: University of Arizona Press, 1972), 100. W. D. Casey to J. Evetts Haley, March 30, 1932, Haley Memorial Library. Casey interview.
6. Mills, *Billy the Kid*, 94–96.
7. *Las Vegas Gazette*, July 5, 1873. *Las Vegas Gazette*, July 19, 1873.
8. Johnson, *Horrell Wars*, 59–61. Nolan, *Bad Blood*, 50.
9. Nolan, *Bad Blood*, 50–51. Johnson, *Horrell Wars*, 62–64. *Santa Fe New Mexican*, December 9, 1873. Casey interview. Amelia Bolton Church as told to Eve Ball, "Early Days in Lincoln," *True West*, August 1978. James D. Shinkle, *Reminiscences of Roswell Pioneers* (Roswell, NM: Hall-Poorbaugh Press, 1966), 96.
10. Nolan, *Bad Blood*, 50–51. Johnson, *Horrell Wars*, 62–64. *Santa Fe New Mexican*, December 9, 1873. Casey interview. Bolton Church, "Early Days." Shinkle, *Reminiscences*, 96.
11. Johnson, *Horrell Wars*, 63–65. *Santa Fe New Mexican*, December 9, 1873.
12. *Santa Fe New Mexican*, December 20, 1873. Major John S. Mason to Assistant Adjutant General, December 25, 1873, Letters Received, District of New Mexico, NARA. Frank Coe interview with J. Evetts Haley, March 20, 1927, Haley Memorial Library (hereafter cited as Frank Coe interview). *Santa Fe New Mexican*, December 9, 1873.
13. Mason to Assistant Adjutant General, December 25, 1873, Letters Received, District of New Mexico, NARA.
14. Casey to Haley, March 30, 1932. Mason to Assistant Adjutant General, December 25, 1873, Letters Received, District of New Mexico, NARA.
15. *Arizona Weekly Citizen* (Tucson), December 27, 1873. Nolan, *Bad Blood*, 56. Mason to Assistant Adjutant General, December 25, 1873, Letters Received, District of New Mexico, NARA.

Notes for Chapter 3

16. *Arizona Weekly Miner* (Prescott), December 27, 1873. Philip J. Rasch, *Gunsmoke in Lincoln County* (Laramie, WY: National Association for Outlaw and Lawman History, 1997), 27. Deposition of Juan Patron, Frank Warner Angel Report, "Report on the death of John H. Tunstall," Victor Westphall Collection, New Mexico State Record Center and Archives, Santa Fe (hereafter cited as Angel Report).
17. 1870 United States Federal Census. Mason to Assistant Adjutant General, December 25, 1873, Letters Received, District of New Mexico, NARA. Johnson, *Horrell Wars*, 73.
18. Tsompanas, *Juan Patrón*, 26–27. *Arizona Weekly Citizen*, January 17, 1874. Casey interview.
19. Tsompanas, *Juan Patrón*, 27. 1860 United States Federal Census. 1870 United States Federal Census. 1880 United States Federal Census.
20. *Arizona Weekly Citizen*, January 17, 1874. Bill Jones interview with J. Evetts Haley, January 13, 1927, Haley Memorial Library.
21. Johnson, *Horrell Wars*, 78. *Arizona Weekly Citizen*, January 17, 1874. *Santa Fe New Mexican*, January 2, 1874.
22. *Santa Fe New Mexican*, January 2, 1874. Casey interview.
23. Tsompanas, *Juan Patrón*, 28. *Pioche (NV) Record*, January 31, 1874. *Galveston Daily News*, February 13, 1874.
24. *Arizona Weekly Citizen*, January 17, 1874.
25. Cummings, *Frontier Parish*, 22. *Arizona Weekly Citizen*, January 17, 1874. *Newport (RI) Daily News*, December 31, 1873. *Wathena (KS) Reporter*, January 8, 1874. Author correspondence with Chuck Usmar, November 2020.
26. Tsompanas, *Juan Patrón*, 28.
27. Johnson, *Horrell Wars*, 80. Nolan, *Bad Blood*, 60–61.
28. Johnson, *Horrell Wars*, 80. Nolan, *Bad Blood*, 60–61. *Chicago Tribune*, January 15, 1874.
29. *Holmes County Republican* (Millersburg, OH), January 1, 1874. *Santa Fe New Mexican*, December 29, 1873.
30. Tsompanas, *Juan Patrón*, 28. Nolan, *Bad Blood*, 68–71.
31. *Santa Fe New Mexican*, January 2, 1874. *Santa Fe New Mexican*, January 10, 1874.
32. *Santa Fe New Mexican*, January 9, 1874.
33. Nolan, *Bad Blood*, 65. Klasner, *Girlhood*, 102–3. 1870 United States Federal Census.
34. Deposition of Juan Patron, Angel Report. *Santa Fe New Mexican*, January 20, 1874.
35. *Santa Fe New Mexican*, January 20, 1874. William Price to J. P. Willard, January 18, 1874, M1088, Roll 23, Letters Received, District of New Mexico, NARA.
36. Nolan, *Bad Blood*, 75–76. Johnson, *Horrell Wars*, 86.
37. Johnson, *Horrell Wars*, 86–87. *Santa Fe New Mexican*, January 27, 1874.
38. Klasner, *Girlhood*, 104–5. Nolan, *Bad Blood*, 80.
39. Nolan, *Bad Blood*, 80–81. Johnson, *Horrell Wars*, 87. Casey to Haley, March 30, 1932. Klasner, *Girlhood*, 104–5.
40. Klasner, *Girlhood*, 106. Casey to Haley, March 30, 1932. Casey interview. Nolan, *Bad Blood*, 80–83. Johnson, *Horrell Wars*, 87.
41. Klasner, *Girlhood*, 106. Sánchez & Sánchez, *"Nuestros Antepasados" (Our Ancestors)*, 175. John Nichols interview with J. Evetts Haley, May 15, 1927, Haley Memorial Library. Major William Price would report to J. P. Willard on January 25, 1874, that the man who killed Ben Turner "came to the Placita, boasted of the act and it was proposed to raise a purse of $100 for him. He is well known having murdered a Mexican a short time since." As Frederick Nolan noted in *Bad Blood*, 81, this may suggest the man who killed Ben Turner was an Anglo, not a Hispano like Martín Chávez. John Nichols, who was in the Jicarilla mines at the time, later suggested it was Juan Gonzáles who killed Turner. For what it is worth, there is no record of Martín Chávez ever denying responsibility for the shooting. ¿Quién sabe?

42. Nolan, *Bad Blood*, 82–83. 1870 United States Federal Census.
43. Nolan, *Bad Blood*, 84–85. *Santa Fe New Mexican*, January 27, 1874.
44. Nolan, *Bad Blood*, 85.
45. Tsompanas, *Juan Patrón*, 31–32. *Santa Fe New Mexican*, February 3, 1874.
46. Nolan, *Bad Blood*, 87. Johnson, *Horrell Wars*, 89–90.
47. Nolan, *Bad Blood*, 87. Johnson, *Horrell Wars*, 89–90. *Santa Fe New Mexican*, February 6, 1874. *Weekly New Mexican*, February 10, 1874.
48. Nolan, *Bad Blood*, 86. Crawford, Edith L, and Jose Apodaca, "Jose Apodaca," New Mexico, 1939, Manuscript/Mixed Material, retrieved from the Library of Congress. 1870 United States Federal Census. 1900 United States Federal Census.
49. Klasner, *Girlhood*, 105–6. Johnson, *Horrell Wars*, 90. Nolan, *Bad Blood*, 186–87.
50. Klasner, *Girlhood*, 106–7. *Santa Fe New Mexican*, March 17, 1874.
51. *Santa Fe New Mexican*, March 17, 1874.
52. Johnson, *Horrell Wars*, 91. Tsompanas, *Juan Patrón*, 32.
53. For the fate of the Horrell brothers, see Johnson, *Horrell Wars*.
54. Casey to Haley, March 30, 1932. Tsompanas, *Juan Patrón*, 32. Deposition of Juan Patron, Angel Report.

Notes for Chapter 4

1. Julyan, *Place Names*, 319–20. George W. Coe, *Frontier Fighter: The Autobiography of George W. Coe* (Chicago: Lakeside Press, 1984), 362.
2. Frederick Nolan, *The West of Billy the Kid* (Norman: University of Oklahoma Press, 1998), 134.
3. Florencio Cháves interview with J. Evetts Haley, August 15, 1927, Haley Memorial Library (hereafter cited as Cháves interview). Casey interview. 1880 United States Federal Census. 1885 New Mexico Territorial Census.
4. Mills, *Billy the Kid*, 95. *Santa Fe New Mexican*, August 15, 1874. *Weekly New Mexican*, November 10, 1874.
5. *Las Vegas Gazette*, January 9, 1875.
6. *Weekly New Mexican*, January 19, 1875. 1870 United States Federal Census.
7. *Santa Fe New Mexican*, March 22, 1875.
8. For Alexander and Susan McSween, see Frederick Nolan, "The Search for Alexander McSween," *New Mexico Historical Review* 62, no. 2 (July 1987): 287–301; and Kathleen P. Chamberlain, *In the Shadow of Billy the Kid: Susan McSween and the Lincoln County War* (Albuquerque: University of New Mexico Press, 2012). Account by Frances E. Totty from Mrs. Carlota Brent (nee Baca, daughter of Saturnino Baca), December 6, 1937, WPA Files, Folder 212, "Lincoln County War," Robert M. Utley Research Files (Utley Files), NMSRCA (hereafter cited as Totty account).
9. *Weekly New Mexican*, January 12, 1875. *Weekly New Mexican*, March 23, 1875. *Weekly New Mexican*, March 30, 1875. *Weekly New Mexican*, April 27, 1875. *Weekly New Mexican*, May 25, 1875.
10. *Weekly New Mexican*, May 25, 1875.
11. *Daily New Mexican*, May 8, 1875. *Las Vegas Gazette*, May 22, 1875. *Weekly New Mexican*, September 28, 1875. 1880 United States Federal Census. True Bill of Grand Jury, Lincoln County, April 23, 1875, criminal case file no. 149, *Territory v. Juan Patron*, NMSRCA. True Bill of Grand Jury, Lincoln County, April 23, 1875, *Territory v. A. H. Mills*, criminal case file no. 151, NMSRCA. True Bill of Grand Jury, Lincoln County, April 24, 1875, criminal case file no. 158, Utley Files.
12. Tsompanas, *Juan Patrón*, 34–35. *Mesilla (NM) News*, August 18, 1875.
13. *Santa Fe New Mexican*, June 9, 1875. *Santa Fe New Mexican*, June 9, 1875. *Santa Fe New Mexican*, July 6, 1875. Cooper, *Santa Fe Ring*, 182–83.

Notes for Chapter 4	487

14. Nolan, *Documentary History*, 69. Deposition of Juan Patrón, Angel Report.
15. *Santa Fe New Mexican*, August 9, 1875. *Weekly New Mexican*, September 7, 1875.
16. *Santa Fe New Mexican*, August 9, 1875. *Weekly New Mexican*, September 7, 1875. Nolan, *Documentary History*, 71. Klasner, *Girlhood*, 133–36. 1880 United States Federal Census.
17. *Weekly New Mexican*, September 14, 1875. *Weekly New Mexican*, September 28, 1875. Depositions of Juan Patron and Florencio Gonzáles, Angel Report.
18. Tsompanas, *Juan Patrón*, 56.
19. *Weekly New Mexican*, September 21, 1875. *Mesilla News*, September 22, 1875. *Weekly New Mexican*, September 28, 1875. *Evansville (IN) Journal*, September 20, 1875.
20. *Weekly New Mexican*, September 21, 1875. *Mesilla News*, September 22, 1875. *Weekly New Mexican*, September 28, 1875.
21. Lincoln County, District Court Journal, 1875–79, Fall term, 1875, 3-95, Utley Files.
22. *Weekly New Mexican*, March 7, 1876. *Weekly New Mexican*, March 21, 1876. 1870 United States Federal Census. True Bill of Grand Jury, Lincoln County, October 12, 1875, *Territory v. A. H. Mills*: Manslaughter, criminal case file no. 163, Utley Files.
23. Lincoln County, District Court Journal, 1875–79, Fall term, 1875, 3-95, Utley Files.
24. *Mesilla News*, December 18, 1875. *Weekly New Mexican*, December 21, 1875. 1870 United States Federal Census. Although the murder of Tomás Archuleta has been previously written of as occurring on November 19, 1875, a letter from a citizen of Lincoln published in the *Weekly New Mexican*, December 21, 1875, proves the murder took place around one o'clock in the morning of December 8, 1875.
25. Klasner, *Girlhood*, 134–35. Tsompanas, *Juan Patrón*, 37–38. A. A. McSween to "Dear Capt.," December 16, 1875, MS 141, box 204, C. L. Sonnichsen Special Collections Department (Sonnichsen Collections), University of Texas at El Paso. *Las Vegas Gazette*, December 25, 1875.
26. *Weekly New Mexican*, November 15, 1875. *Santa Fe New Mexican*, August 15, 1876.
27. Mills, "Hombres Valientes."
28. *Santa Fe New Mexican*, January 4, 1876. Sheriffs and Deputies, file - box 12, folder S- Folder 3, a) listing of Sheriffs and Deputies, Weisner Papers.
29. Mills, *Billy the Kid*, 85. *Las Vegas Gazette*, February 19, 1876.
30. *Weekly New Mexican*, March 7, 1876. *Weekly New Mexican*, March 21, 1876.
31. *Mesilla News*, December 26, 1874. *Weekly New Mexican*, March 21, 1876. *Mesilla Valley Independent*, October 13, 1877. Frank Coe on Blazer's Mill, typescript in Robert N. Mullin Research Files (Mullin Files), Haley Memorial Library.
32. *Santa Fe New Mexican*, April 11, 1876. Wilson, *Merchants*, 53. Tsompanas, *Juan Patrón*, 126.
33. *Weekly New Mexican*, May 30, 1876.
34. *Santa Fe New Mexican*, July 17, 1876. *Santa Fe New Mexican*, November 17, 1876. *Santa Fe New Mexican*, November 23, 1876.
35. *Santa Fe New Mexican*, July 17, 1876. *Santa Fe New Mexican*, November 17, 1876. *Santa Fe New Mexican*, November 23, 1876.
36. *Weekly New Mexican*, July 25, 1876.
37. George Coe interview with J. Evetts Haley, June 12, 1939, Haley Memorial Library (hereafter cited as George Coe interview). Philip J. Rasch, *Warriors of Lincoln County* (Laramie: National Association for Outlaw and Lawman History, 1998), 184. Nolan, *Documentary History*, 137–38.
38. Coe, *Frontier Fighter*, passim. Mills, *Billy the Kid*, 121. For the Colfax County War, see Corey Recko's *The Colfax County War: Violence and Corruption in Territorial New Mexico* (Denton: University of North Texas Press, 2024); David L Caffey's *When Cimarron Meant Wild: The Maxwell Land Grant Conflict in New Mexico and Colorado* (Norman: University of Oklahoma Press, 2023); and Louis Serna's *Clay Allison and the Colfax County War* (pub. by author, 2012).

39. *Santa Fe New Mexican*, August 15, 1876. 1880 United States Federal Census. Special Schedules of the Eleventh Census (1890) Enumerating Union Veterans and Widows of Union Veterans of the Civil War; Series M123; RG 15, Records of the Department of Veterans Affairs; NARA (hereafter cited as Special Schedules of the 1890 Census).
40. *Weekly New Mexican*, August 1, 1876. *Santa Fe New Mexican*, August 31, 1876. *Weekly New Mexican*, September 5, 1876. *Santa Fe New Mexican*, September 11, 1876. *Santa Fe New Mexican*, September 16, 1876. *Santa Fe New Mexican*, September 19, 1876. *Weekly New Mexican*, September 19, 1876.
41. Lincoln County, District Court Journal, 1875–79, October 1876 term, October 3–9, 1876, pp. 181–228, Utley Files. *Santa Fe New Mexican*, November 20, 1876. Mills, *Billy the Kid*, 90.
42. Tsompanas, *Juan Patrón*, 39. For the Fritz insurance funds case, see Herbert Marsh Jr., "Blood Money of the Lincoln County War," *Wild West History Association Journal*, June 2019.
43. Nolan, *West of*, 39–40. For John Henry Tunstall, see Frederick Nolan, *The Life & Death of John Henry Tunstall* (Albuquerque: University of New Mexico Press, 1964).
44. Nolan, *Tunstall*, 190–91.
45. Nolan, *Tunstall*, 190–91.
46. Ms 0249, box 11, folder 2, Elected County Officials Lincoln County, 1872–1974, Weisner Papers. Tsompanas, *Juan Patrón*, 44. *Santa Fe New Mexican*, January 22, 1877. *Las Vegas Gazette*, January 27, 1877.
47. *Santa Fe New Mexican*, November 17, 1876. *Santa Fe New Mexican*, November 23, 1876.
48. *Santa Fe New Mexican*, December 23, 1876. *Weekly New Mexican*, January 2, 1877.
49. *Weekly New Mexico*, January 2, 1877. Nolan, *Documentary History*, 103.
50. *Las Vegas Gazette*, December 30, 1876. Marsh, "Blood Money." Mills, *Billy the Kid*, 128–30.
51. Tsompanas, *Juan Patrón*, 44. *Santa Fe New Mexican*, January 22, 1877. *Las Vegas Gazette*, January 27, 1877.
52. *Santa Fe New Mexican*, January 23, 1877. *Las Vegas Gazette*, March 3, 1877. *Weekly New Mexican*, October 23, 1877. 1880 United States Federal Census.
53. Nolan, *Documentary History*, 98–100.
54. Nolan, *Tunstall*, 212–14.
55. Cháves interview, August 15, 1927. Deposition of Alexander McSween, Angel Report.
56. *Santa Fe New Mexican*, May 16, 1877. William Wier interview with J. Evetts Haley, Monument, NM, June 22, 1937, Vandale Collection 2H482, Barker Texas History Center, Dolph Briscoe Center, University of Texas at Austin (hereafter cited as Wier interview). Mills, *Billy the Kid*, 107.
57. Stephen Bogener, "Land, Speculation, and Manipulation on the Pecos," *Great Plains Quarterly* 28, no. 3 (Summer 2008): 216.
58. Salazar insurance policy. 1880 United States Federal Census.
59. Salazar interview. 1870 United States Federal Census. 1600s–Current, FindaGrave.com. Ancestry.com.
60. Wilson, *Merchants*, 60. Nolan, *Documentary History*, 120–23. *Mesilla News*, August 16, 1881.
61. Salazar interview. Wilson, *Merchants*, 60. Nolan, *Documentary History*, 120–23. *Mesilla News*, August 16, 1881.
62. Wilson, *Merchants*, 60. Nolan, *Documentary History*, 120–23. *Mesilla News*, August 16, 1881.
63. Wilson, *Merchants*, 60. Nolan, *Documentary History*, 120–23. *Mesilla News*, August 16, 1881. William R. "Jake" Owens interview with J. Evetts Haley, March 2, 1933, Haley Memorial Library (hereafter cited as Owens interview).

64. *Santa Fe New Mexican*, May 4, 1877. *Weekly New Mexican*, May 15, 1877. *Weekly New Mexican*, May 22, 1877.
65. Mills, *Billy the Kid*, 87. Deposition of Juan Patrón, Angel Report.
66. Deposition of Juan Patrón, Watkins Report. *Las Vegas Gazette*, October 13, 1877.
67. Chamberlain, *In the Shadow*, 89–93.
68. Mills, *Billy the Kid*, 113.
69. *Las Vegas Gazette*, March 31, 1877. *Las Vegas Gazette*, May 12, 1877. *Weekly New Mexican*, June 19, 1877. 1880 United States Federal Census.
70. Marsh, "Blood Money."
71. *Mesilla Valley Independent*, August 25, 1877. *Las Vegas Gazette*, August 4, 1877. Chamberlain, *In the Shadow*, 90–91.
72. Wilson, *Merchants*, 63–67. Chamberlain, *In the Shadow*, 91–92.
73. George Coe interview, June 12, 1939. *Mesilla Valley Independent*, September 8, 1877. *Las Vegas Gazette*, September 1, 1877. *Santa Fe New Mexican*, August 21, 1877.
74. *Mesilla Valley Independent*, October 13, 1877. Nolan, *Documentary History*, 170. Bolton-Church interview by Blachly.
75. Lincoln County, District Court Journal, 1875–79, October 1877 term, October 1–9, 1877, pp. 231–65, Utley Files. *Weekly New Mexican*, October 23, 1877.
76. *Mesilla Valley Independent*, September 29, 1877. Tsompanas, *Juan Patrón*, 126.

Notes for Chapter 5

1. For Henry McCarty, alias William H. Bonney, see Mills, *Billy the Kid*; Nolan, *West of*; and Robert M. Utley, *Billy the Kid: A Short and Violent Life* (Lincoln: University of Nebraska Press, 1989).
2. Smith, "Man Who Fought."
3. *The Sentinel* (Carlisle, PA), November 17, 1931. Marriage Certificate for William Antrim and Catherine McCarty, AC 017-P, William H. Bonney Collection (Bonney Collection), Fray Angélico Chávez Library, Palace of the Governors, Santa Fe. Waldo E. Koop, "Billy the Kid: Trail of a Kansas Legend," in Frederick Nolan, *The Billy the Kid Reader* (Norman: University of Oklahoma Press, 2012).
4. For an indispensable study of Henry McCarty's early years in New Mexico and Arizona, see Jerry Weddle's *Antrim Is My Stepfather's Name* (Phoenix: Arizona Historical Society, 1993). Also see Mills, *Billy the Kid*, 7–78.
5. For Jessie Evans see Grady E. McCright and James H. Powell, *Jessie Evans: Lincoln County Badman* (College Station: Creative Publishing, 1983). *Mesilla Valley Independent*, September 29, 1877. Nolan, *Tunstall*, 243–44.
6. Mills, *Billy the Kid*, 99–100. *El Paso Times*, September 16, 1923. Klasner, *Girlhood*, 169–170. Lily Casey Klasner, "The Kid," in Nolan, *Billy the Kid Reader*, 239–40.
7. Eugene Cunningham, *Triggernometry: A Gallery of Gunfighters* (Caldwell, ID: Caxton Printers, 1952), 131, 170.
8. Mills, *Billy the Kid*, 103–4. Tsompanas, *Juan Patrón*, 53–55.
9. Bolton-Church interview by Blachly. Tsompanas, *Juan Patrón*, 53–55. 1880 United States Federal Census.
10. Nolan, *Tunstall*, 250–52.
11. Tsompanas, *Juan Patrón*, 54–55. Depositions of Juan Patrón and Alexander McSween, Angel Report. Nolan, *Tunstall*, 252–54.
12. *Mesilla Valley Independent*, November 10, 1877. *Santa Fe New Mexican*, November 20, 1877. *Mesilla Valley Independent*, December 1, 1877. *Silver City (NM) Herald*, December 1, 1877. 1870 United States Federal Census. 1880 United States Federal Census.
13. *Mesilla Valley Independent*, December 15, 1877. Mills, *Billy the Kid*, 108–9.

14. *Mesilla Valley Independent*, December 15, 1877. Depositions of Juan Patrón and Alexander McSween, Angel Report. Mills, *Billy the Kid*, 109.
15. Alexander, *Desert Desperadoes*, 67–68, 81–82.
16. Casey interview. Bolton-Church interview by Blachly.
17. Casey interview. Klasner, "The Kid," in Nolan, *Billy the Kid Reader*, 241. Mills, *Billy the Kid*, 110. *El Paso Times*, September 16, 1923.
18. Miguel Antonio Otero Jr., *The Real Billy the Kid: With New Light on the Lincoln County War* (1936; repr., Houston: Arte Público Press, 1998), 98. E. L. Crawford & F. Gomez, (1938) Francisco Gomez, New Mexico, [Manuscript/Mixed Material] retrieved from the Library of Congress. Walter Noble Burns, *The Saga of Billy the Kid* (Garden City, NY: Doubleday, 1952), 16.
19. Robert F. Kadlec, *They "Knew" Billy the Kid: Interviews with Old-Time New Mexicans* (Santa Fe: Ancient City Press, 1987), 66–67. Totty account. Smith, "Man Who Fought."
20. Marsh, "Blood Money." Deposition of James J. Dolan, Angel Report.
21. Mills, *Billy the Kid*, 135–36.
22. *Las Vegas Gazette*, January 5, 1878. *Weekly New Mexican*, January 1, 1878. 1880 United States Federal Census. 1870 United States Federal Census.
23. Tsompanas, *Juan Patrón*, 56–58.
24. *Weekly New Mexican*, January 12, 1878. Tsompanas, *Juan Patrón*, 58–59.
25. *Las Vegas Gazette*, January 12, 1878. *Weekly New Mexican*, January 12, 1878. *Weekly New Mexican*, January 1, 1878. Tsompanas, *Juan Patrón*, 59.
26. *Mesilla Valley Independent*, January 12, 1878.
27. *Las Vegas Gazette*, January 12, 1878.
28. Tsompanas, *Juan Patrón*, 59–63. *Las Vegas Gazette*, January 19, 1878. *Mesilla Valley Independent*, January 19, 1878. *Las Vegas Gazette*, February 16, 1878.
29. Tsompanas, *Juan Patrón*, 64–70. Billy Charles Cummings, "Patrón, Axtell Fight Over Jesuits," *Los Amigos*, July 1995, Lincoln County Heritage Trust Newsletter.
30. Tsompanas, *Juan Patrón*, 64–70. Cummings, "Patrón, Axtell Fight Over Jesuits," *Los Amigos* (Lincoln County Heritage Trust Newsletter), July 1995.
31. *Mesilla Valley Independent*, January 19, 1878. *Mesilla Valley Independent*, January 26, 1878. *Las Vegas Gazette*, January 26, 1878. *Las Vegas Gazette*, February 2, 1878. Tsompanas, *Juan Patrón*, 64–70.
32. Cummings, "Patrón, Axtell." *Weekly New Mexican*, February 9, 1878.
33. *Weekly New Mexican*, February 23, 1878.
34. *Las Vegas Gazette*, February 16, 1878. Tsompanas, *Juan Patrón*, 64–72.
35. Depositions of Alexander McSween, Adolph P. Barrier, James J. Dolan, and Florencio Gonzáles, Angel Report. Mills, *Billy the Kid*, 136.
36. Photocopy of mortgage deed, January 19, 1878, box 12, folder 4, Maurice G. Fulton Collection (Fulton Collection), University of Arizona Library, Tucson. Joel Jacobson, *Such Men as Billy the Kid: The Lincoln County War Reconsidered* (Lincoln: University of Nebraska Press, 1994), 47.
37. Nolan, *Tunstall*, 255–60. *Mesilla Valley Independent*, January 26, 1878.
38. *Santa Fe New Mexican*, February 9, 1878. Nolan, *Documentary History*, 183–84. Deposition of Juan Patrón, Angel Report.
39. Marsh, "Blood Money." Mills, *Billy the Kid*, 140–41.
40. Depositions of Alexander McSween and Adolph P. Barrier, Angel Report.
41. Deposition of Robert Widenmann, Angel Report. Mills, *Billy the Kid*, 143–44.
42. Depositions of James Longwell, Alexander McSween, Adolph P. Barrier, and Robert Widenmann, Angel Report. Nolan, *Tunstall*, 259.
43. Nolan, *Documentary History*, 190–92. Jacobson, *Such Men*, 70–76.

44. Depositions of Robert Widenmann, William Bonney, Jacob B. Mathews, John Middleton, and Gottfried Gauss, Angel Report.
45. Depositions of Alexander McSween, Robert Widenmann, and James Longwell, Angel Report.
46. Mills, *Billy the Kid*, 153–54.
47. Nolan, *Documentary History*, 195.
48. Depositions of Robert Widenmann, William Bonney, and Gottfried Gauss, Angel Report.
49. The members of the posse can be compiled through various testimonies in the Angel Report.
50. Depositions of Gottfried Gauss and Jacob B. Mathews, Angel Report.
51. Depositions of Alexander McSween, William Bonney, John Middleton, Robert Widenmann, Albert Howe, John Patton, Florencio Gonzáles, and Samuel Perry, Angel Report.
52. Deposition of Robert Widenmann, Angel Report.
53. Frank Coe interview, March 20, 1927. Susan E. Barber interview with J. Evetts Haley, August 26, 1927, Haley Memorial Library (hereafter cited as Barber interview). Maurice G. Fulton, *History of the Lincoln County War* (Tucson: University of Arizona Press, 1968), 125–26. Deposition of Florencio Gonzáles, Angel Report.
54. For Taylor F. Ealy and the Ealy family, see Norman J. Bender, *Missionaries, Outlaws, and Indians: Taylor F. Ealy at Lincoln and Zuni, 1878–1881*; Ellen Marie Cain, "Testing Courage in New Mexico: Taylor Ealy and the Lincoln County War, 1878." *American Presbyterians* 72, no. 1 (Spring 1994): 11–22; Ruth R. Ealy, *Water in a Thirsty Land* (Las Cruces: Doc45 Publishing, 2021); and the Taylor F. Ealy Papers (Ealy Papers), University of Arizona Library, Tucson.
55. *El Paso Times*, September 16, 1923.
56. Cháves interview, August 25, 1927.
57. *Las Vegas Gazette*, March 23, 1878. Depositions of Atanacio Martínez and Millard Goodwin, Angel Report.
58. Deposition of Atanacio Martínez, Angel Report. Nolan, *West of*, 109. Nolan, *Tunstall*, 287. Nolan, "Dick Brewer: The Unlikely Gunfighter," *NOLA Quarterly* 15, no. 3 (July–September 1991): 19–27. Mills, *Billy the Kid*, 165.
59. Deposition of Florencio Gonzáles, Angel Report.
60. Depositions of George W. Peppin and James Longwell, Angel Report. Court Records, Lincoln County, District Court, civil case no. 141, *Fritz and Scholand v. McSween*, assumpsit; affidavit of Sheriff George W. Peppin, Lincoln, April 15, 1878, sworn before John S. Crouch, clerk of the court, Utley Files. Nolan, *Documentary History*, 212–17.
61. Wier interview. Typed copy of will of A. A. McSween from Book A Journal and Record of Probate Court, p. 100, box 12, folder 2, Fulton Collection. Mills, *Billy the Kid*, 169–70. David G. Thomas, *The Frank W. Angel Report on the Death of John Tunstall* (Las Cruces, NM: Doc45 Publishing, 2022), 31.
62. Totty account. Mills, *Billy the Kid*, 169–70.

Notes for Chapter 6

1. Pat F. Garrett and Frederick Nolan, *Pat F. Garrett's "The Authentic Life of Billy, the Kid,"* annotated ed. (Norman: University of Oklahoma Press, 2000), 59–61. For Ash Upson see John LeMay, *The Man Who Invented Billy the Kid: The Authentic Life of Ash Upson* (Roswell, NM: Bicep Books, 2020).
2. Mills, *Billy the Kid*, 171–74. Coe, *Frontier Fighter*, 132.
3. Garrett and Nolan, *Authentic Life*, 59–61. David S. Turk, *Blackwater Draw: Three Lives, Billy the Kid and the Murders That Started the Lincoln County War* (Santa Fe: Sunstone

Press, 2011), 94–101. Sallie Chisum Notebook, Chávez County Historical Society, Roswell, NM.
4. Garrett and Nolan, *Authentic Life*, 59–61. Cháves interview, August 15, 1927. Deposition of John Middleton, Angel Report. Frank Coe interview, August 14, 1927. *Albuquerque Review*, March 30, 1878.
5. *Las Vegas Gazette*, March 30, 1878. Mills, *Billy the Kid*, 176–77.
6. Deposition of Robert Widenmann, Angel Report. Bender, *Missionaries*, 24–28. Ash Upson to my Dear Niece [Muzzy] Roswell, March 5, 1878, box 11, folder 4, Fulton Collection.
7. Cháves interview, August 15, 1927.
8. Kadlec, *They Knew*, 32. T. F. Ealy to Dear Mary, Lincoln, March 4, 1878, Ealy Papers.
9. William A. Keleher, *Violence in Lincoln County, 1869–1881* (Albuquerque: University of New Mexico Press, 1957), 93.
10. Mills, *Billy the Kid*, 180.
11. Jacobson, *Such Men*, 127–30.
12. Mills, *Billy the Kid*, 181–82.
13. Edith Crawford, Billy the Kid, and Francisco Trujillo, "Billy the Kid," New Mexico, 1937, manuscript/mixed material, retrieved from the Library of Congress (hereafter cited as Crawford et al., "Billy the Kid"). 1880 United States Federal Census.
14. Crawford et al., "Billy the Kid." Mary R. Ealy to Maurice G. Fulton, Pittsburgh, PA, January 16, 1928, box 1, folder 8, Fulton Collection.
15. Crawford et al., "Billy the Kid."
16. Account of Gorgonio Wilson, age 66, Roswell, taken by Edith Crawford, rec'd in Santa Fe February 5, 1938, WPA Files, folder 212, History of Lincoln County War, Utley Files. Bolton-Church interview by Blachly. Bob Boze Bell, *The Illustrated Life a Times of Billy the Kid*, rev. and expanded 2nd ed. (Phoenix: Tri Star-Boze, 1996), 60–61. Nolan, *Documentary History*, 245–49. Taylor F. Ealy, "The Lincoln County War as I Saw It," n.d., c. 1927, Ealy Papers. Robert M. Utley, *High Noon in Lincoln: Violence on the Western Frontier* (Albuquerque: University of New Mexico Press, 1987), 61. Original Indictment, *Territory v. Wayt* for murder, April 22, 1878, Mullin Files. Mary R. Ealy to Fulton, Pittsburgh, PA, January 16, 1928, box 1, folder 8, Fulton Collection. *Santa Fe New Mexican*, April 13, 1878. Mills, *Billy the Kid*, 183–87.
17. Otero, *Real Billy*, 122. Deposition of Taylor F. Ealy, Watkins Report.
18. Mills, *Billy the Kid*, 189–90.
19. R. M. Barron, *Court of Inquiry: Lieutenant Colonel N. A. M. Dudley, Fort Stanton, New Mexico, May-June-July 1879*, 2 vols. (Edina, MN: Beaver's Pond Press, 1995). References to the inquiry will hereafter be cited as DCOI. Exhibit 77, vol. 1, no. 3, DCOI. Testimony of David M. Easton, June 7, 1879, RG 153, JAGO, records relating to the Dudley Inquiry (QQ 1284), Utley Files (hereafter cited as Easton testimony). Otero, *Real Billy*, 122.
20. *Mesilla Valley Independent*, April 27, 1878.
21. Frank Coe on Blazer's Mill, typescript, Mullin Files. Easton testimony. Frank Coe interview, March 20, 1927. Nolan, *West of*, 127–33. Utley, *Violent Life*, 71–74. Rasch, *Gunsmoke*, 110–16. Coe, *Frontier Fighter*, 93–104. Jacobson, *Such Men*, 140–45. W. C. Jameson, "Buckshot Roberts," *Wild West*, June 2006. *Mesilla Valley Independent*, April 13, 1878. *Santa Fe New Mexican*, April 13, 1878. Almer Blazer, "The Fight at Blazer's Mill, in New Mexico," *Frontier Times* 16, no. 11 (August 1939). A. N. Blazer to Fulton, Mescalero, NM, August 27, 1937, box 1, folder 7, Fulton Collection. Blazer to Fulton, April 24, 1931. Paul Blazer, "The Fight at Blazer's Mill: A Chapter in the Lincoln County War," *Arizona and the West* 6, no. 3 (Autumn 1964): 203–10.

Notes for Chapter 6

22. Lincoln County, District Court Journal, 1875–79, April 1878 term, April 8–24, 1878, pp. 264–91, Utley Files (hereafter cited as Lincoln County DC Journal, April 1878). Mills, *Billy the Kid*, 191–92.
23. Lincoln County DC Journal, April 1878.
24. Hispano New Mexico Sources. Bolton-Church interview by Blachly.
25. Lincoln County DC Journal, April 1878. *Mesilla Valley Independent*, May 4, 1878.
26. Lincoln County DC Journal, April 1878.
27. *Mesilla Valley Independent*, May 4, 1878.
28. *Mesilla Valley Independent*, May 4, 1878.
29. *Mesilla Valley Independent*, May 4, 1878.
30. *Mesilla Valley Independent*, May 4, 1878. *Mesilla Valley Independent*, May 11, 1878. Frank Coe interview, February 20, 1928. Mills, *Billy the Kid*, 204–5.
31. Owens interview, June 24, 1937. Mills, *Billy the Kid*, 321. *Mesilla Valley Independent*, May 11, 1878. *Weekly New Mexican*, May 11, 1878.
32. Mills, *Billy the Kid*, 206–8.
33. Mills, *Billy the Kid*, 206–9. Frank Coe interview, August 14, 1927.
34. Frank Coe interview, August 14, 1927. Coe, *Frontier Fighter*, 119–22. *Mesilla Valley Independent*, May 11, 1878. *Santa Fe New Mexican*, June 1, 1878.
35. Mills, *Billy the Kid*, 210–13. Crawford et al., "Billy the Kid."
36. Mills, *Billy the Kid*, 216–17. Crawford et al., "Billy the Kid." Cháves interview, August 15, 1927.
37. Crawford et al., "Billy the Kid." A. P. "Paco" Anaya, *I Buried Billy* (College Station: Creative Publishing, 1991), 28.
38. Crawford et al., "Billy the Kid."
39. Angel Report, passim. Also, David G. Thomas, *The Frank W. Angel Report on the Death of John Tunstall* (Las Cruces, NM: Doc45 Publishing, 2022), passim.
40. Mills, *Billy the Kid*, 215–16.
41. *Santa Fe New Mexican*, May 25, 1878.
42. Tsompanas, *Juan Patrón*, 91.
43. *Mesilla Valley Independent*, May 4, 1878. *Mesilla Valley Independent*, May 11, 1878.
44. Deposition of Juan B. Patrón, Angel Report.
45. *Mesilla Valley Independent*, May 11, 1878. Tsompanas, *Juan Patrón*, 92.
46. Mills, *Billy the Kid*, 218.
47. Depositions of Juan Patrón and Alexander McSween, Watkins Report.
48. Mills, *Billy the Kid*, 219–20. Cooper, *Santa Fe Ring*, 411–15. Frank Coe interview, August 14, 1927.
49. Testimony of Juan Patron, DCOI. Exhibit No. 29, DCOI. Exhibit No. 30, DCOI.
50. Tsompanas, *Juan Patrón*, 93.
51. Salazar interview. Smith, "Man Who Fought." *New Mexico Magazine*, April 1933. Yginio Salazar, copy of affidavit sworn before J. P. Wilson, Lincoln, July 20, 1878, Lincoln County War, National Archives, Utley Files (hereafter cited as Salazar affidavit, Utley Files).
52. Frank Coe interview, August 14, 1927.
53. Mills, *Billy the Kid*, 218–19.
54. Cháves interview, August 15, 1927.
55. *Weekly New Mexican*, July 6, 1878. Testimony of Jack Long, DCOI. Original warrant for arrest of Alexander McSween, written and signed by John B. Wilson, J. P., June 29, 1878, box 12, folder 2, Fulton Collection. Exhibit 77, vol. 1, no. 45, DCOI. Exhibit 78, vol. 2, no. 2, DCOI. George Coe interview, March 20, 1927. Coe, *Frontier Fighter*, 128. Utley, *High Noon*, 84–85.
56. Capt. Thomas Blair, 15th Inf., to Lt. Col. N. A. M. Dudley, Fort Stanton, July 12, 1878, box 11, folder 7, Fulton Collection.

57. Blair to Dudley, July 12, 1878. Chamberlain, *In the Shadow*, 121.
58. Blair to Dudley, July 12, 1878. Mills, *Billy the Kid*, 224.
59. Blair to Dudley, July 12, 1878.
60. Blair to Dudley, July 12, 1878. *Cimarron (NM) News and Press*, July 25, 1878.
61. Otero, *Real Billy*, 122.
62. Coe, *Frontier Fighter*, 148–49, Rasch, *Warriors*, 80–81.
63. Testimony of Saturnino Baca, DCOI.
64. Nolan, *Documentary History*, 311–12. Cooper, *Santa Fe Ring*, 424.
65. Testimony of Jack Long, DCOI.

Notes for Chapter 7

1. Coe, *Frontier Fighter*, 152–53.
2. Coe, *Frontier Fighter*, 152–53.
3. Coe, *Frontier Fighter*, 152–153. Mills, *Billy the Kid*, 235.
4. Coe, *Frontier Fighter*, 152–55. Testimony of Martín Chávez, Josefa Montaño, Teresa Philipowski, and Saturnino Baca, DCOI. The locations of various McSween partisans can be compiled through various testimony in the DCOI, although curiously unaccounted for are Fred Waite and Frank Coe.
5. Coe, *Frontier Fighter*, 153–56. T. F. Ealy to Rev. Dr. (Sheldon) Jackson, Anton Chico, August 13, 1878, in Pioneer Presbyterian Missions, 1878, vol. 8, 193–94, Mullin Files. Testimony of Andrew Boyle and David Easton, DCOI.
6. Testimony of Saturnino Baca, DCOI.
7. Mills, *Billy the Kid*, 234–35. Testimony of George W. Peppin, Jack Long, David Easton, Marion Turner, and James J. Dolan, DCOI.
8. Testimony of José María de Aguayo, DCOI. Otero, *Real Billy*, 122. Nolan, *Documentary History*, 312–13. Mills, *Billy the Kid*, 235.
9. Exhibit no. 47-A, DCOI. Exhibit 78, vol. 2, no. 4, DCOI. Testimony of Daniel Appel, Susan McSween, and Saturnino Baca, DCOI.
10. Exhibit no. 58, DCOI. Exhibit no. 52, DCOI. Testimony of Daniel Appel and Saturnino Baca, DCOI.
11. Like the McSween partisans, the identities of most of the Dolan partisans can be compiled from various testimony in the DCOI. Rasch, *Warriors*, 141. Owens interview, June 24, 1937. Testimony of José María de Aguayo, David Easton, Andrew Boyle, William Powell, Josiah Nash, Marion Turner, and Jack Long, DCOI.
12. Bender, *Missionaries*, 50–51.
13. Testimony of José María de Aguayo, Saturnino Baca, and David Easton, DCOI. Otero, *Real Billy*, 122.
14. Testimony of David Easton, DCOI. Exhibit no. 48, DCOI.
15. Exhibit 78, vol. 2, no. 16, DCOI. Jacobsen, *Such Men*, 176.
16. Exhibit 78, vol 2, no. 18, DCOI. Exhibit 78, vol. 2, no. 15, DCOI. Jacobsen, *Such Men*, 176–78. Testimony of George W. Peppin, DCOI.
17. Mary Ealy to Fulton, n.d., ca. 1928, box 1, folder 8, Fulton Collection. Mills, *Billy the Kid*, 241. Otero, *Real Billy*, 123. Testimony of José María de Aguayo and Saturnino Baca, DCOI.
18. Nolan, *Documentary History*, 316. Testimony of Saturnino Baca, DCOI.
19. Otero, *Real Billy*, 122–23. Utley, *High Noon*, 94. Testimony of Saturnino Baca, DCOI.
20. Exhibit 78, vol. 2, no. 18, DCOI. Testimony of George Purington and Daniel Appel, DCOI. Rasch, *Warriors*, 141.
21. Testimony of Juan Patrón, Nathan Dudley, and Daniel Appel, DCOI.

22. Bender, *Missionaries*, 50–52. 1880 United States Federal Census. Testimony of José María de Aguayo, DCOI.
23. Mills, *Billy the Kid*, 246. Testimony of Alex Rudder, Jack Long, Samuel G. Beard, and Andrew Boyle, DCOI.
24. Mills, *Billy the Kid*, 245–47. Otero, *Real Billy*, 123. Mary Ealy to Fulton, n.d., ca. 1928, box 1, folder 8, Fulton Collection.
25. Testimony of Juan Patrón, DCOI.
26. Testimony of Alex Rudder and Samuel G. Beard, DCOI. Exhibit 78, vol. 2, no. 19, DCOI.
27. Nolan, *Documentary History*, 322. Burns, *Saga*, 144. Joseph J. Smith to Mr. Capper, office of John H. Tunstall, Lincoln, July 19, 1878, box 11, folder 7, Fulton Collection.
28. Testimony of Martín Chávez, Daniel Appel, and William Bonney, DCOI.
29. Testimony of Martín Chávez, DCOI. Exhibit 78, vol. 2, no. 19, DCOI. Otero, *Real Billy*, 123.
30. Martín Chávez interview by Walter Noble Burns (typed transcript), Usmar Collection (hereafter cited as Chávez interview). Testimony of Martín Chávez, William Bonney, José Chávez y Chávez, Susan McSween, Isaac Ellis, and Daniel Appel, DCOI.
31. Chávez interview. Testimony of Martín Chávez, DCOI. Nolan, *Documentary History*, 324–25. Otero, *Real Billy*, 123. Mills, *Billy the Kid*, 251–52.
32. Chávez interview. Testimony of Teresa Philipowski and Francisco Romero y Valencia, DCOI. Mills, *Billy the Kid*, 252–53. Barber interview.
33. Testimony of John B. Wilson, Susan McSween, Marion Turner, and George W. Peppin, DCOI. Susan McSween interview with J. Evetts Haley, August 26, 1927, Haley Memorial Library (hereafter cited as McSween interview).
34. Testimony of Susan McSween, Nathan Dudley, George W. Peppin, DCOI. McSween interview.
35. Testimony of Susan McSween, William Bonney, and Jack Long, DCOI. Coe, *Frontier Fighter*, 169. Mills, *Billy the Kid*, 256.
36. Testimony of Andrew Boyle, DCOI. E. L. Crawford and M. L. Miranda, (1939) Mrs. Lorencita Miranda, New Mexico [manuscript/mixed material], retrieved from the Library of Congress. Barber interview. Mills, *Billy the Kid*, 257.
37. Mills, *Billy the Kid*, 253–57. Otero, *Real Billy*, 98. Barber interview.
38. Testimony of Taylor F. Ealy, Josefa Montaño, and Teresa Philipowski, DCOI. Bender, *Missionaries*, 52. Exhibit 78, vol. 2, no. 19, DCOI. Nolan, *Documentary History*, 329. Barber interview. Chamberlain, *In the Shadow*, 132–33.
39. Otero, *Real Billy*, 124. Chávez interview.
40. Mills, *Billy the Kid*, 259–60. Testimony of William Bonney, DCOI. Smith, "Man Who Fought." *New Mexico Magazine*, April 1933. Chávez interview.
41. Burns, *Saga*, 144–45. Owens interview, June 24, 1937.
42. Burns, *Saga*, 144–45.
43. Testimony of William Bonney, José Chávez y Chávez, Milo Pierce, Andrew Boyle, Josiah Nash, William Powell, and Jack Long, DCOI. Frank Coe interview, March 20, 1927. Mills, *Billy the Kid*, 260–61.
44. Burns, *Saga*, 145. Salazar affidavit, Utley Files.
45. Salazar interview. Burns, *Saga*, 145.
46. Mills, *Billy the Kid*, 261–62.
47. Mills, *Billy the Kid*, 262–63.
48. Burns, *Saga*, 145–48. Otero, *Real Billy*, 96–97.
49. Burns, *Saga*, 145–48. Otero, *Real Billy*, 96–97.
50. Burns, *Saga*, 145–48. Otero, *Real Billy*, 96–97.
51. Burns, *Saga*, 145–48. Otero, *Real Billy*, 96–97.
52. Burns, *Saga*, 145–48. Otero, *Real Billy*, 96–97. Notes of Dr. D. M. Appel, Fort Stanton, July 20, 1878, Utley Files (hereafter cited as Appel notes). Salazar affidavit, Utley Files.

53. Exhibit 78, vol. 2, no. 19, DCOI. Testimony of David Easton and Susan McSween, DCOI. Nolan, *Documentary History*, 333–34. Appel notes. Mills, *Billy the Kid*, 262–64.
54. Otero, *Real Billy*, 125. Chávez interview.
55. Kadlec, *They Knew*, 76–77.

Notes for Chapter 8

1. Otero, *Real Billy*, 125. Chávez interview.
2. Otero, *Real Billy*, 125. Mills, *Billy the Kid*, 266. George Coe interview, March 20, 1927.
3. Otero, *Real Billy*, 125. *Las Vegas Gazette*, July 27, 1878.
4. Burns, *Saga*, 148.
5. Mills, *Billy the Kid*, 268–69. Frank Coe interview, August 14, 1927. George Coe interview, March 20, 1927, and June 12, 1939. Records of the Adjutant General's Office, AGO LR 1871–80, File 1405, AGO 1878, M666, Reels 397 and 398, Lincoln County War, NARA. Copy, Godfroy to Post Adjt., Fort Stanton, August 3, 1878, Encl. to Dudley to AAG DNM, August 3, 1878, Utley Files. Capt. Thomas Blair to Post Adjt., Fort Stanton, August 9, 1878, Encl. to Dudley to AAG DNM, August 10, 1878, Utley Files. Godfroy to Dudley, South Fork, August 8, 1878, Encl. to Dudley to AAG DNM, August 10, 1878, Utley Files. Capt. Thomas Blair to Post Adjt., Fort Stanton, August 9, 1878, Encl. to Dudley to AAG DNM, August 10, 1878, Utley Files. Copy, SO 73, Fort Stanton, August 9, 1878, Encl. to Dudley to AAG DNM, August 10, 1878, Utley Files. Bell, *Illustrated Life and Times*, 79.
6. Nolan, *West of*, 170–71. Sallie Chisum Notebook, Chávez County Historical Society.
7. Frank Coe interview, August 14, 1927. Kadlec, *They Knew*, 66–67.
8. Burns, *Saga*, 188. 1880 United States Federal Census.
9. Burns, *Saga*, 189.
10. Frank Coe interview, August 14, 1927, and February 20, 1928. Coe, *Frontier Fighter*, 201–3.
11. *Las Vegas Gazette*, August 24, 1878. *Las Vegas Gazette*, August 31, 1878. *Las Vegas Gazette*, September 21, 1878. *Las Vegas Gazette*, September 28, 1878.
12. Mills, *Billy the Kid*, 287–88.
13. *Weekly New Mexican*, August 17, 1878. Records of the Adjutant General's Office, AGO LR 1871–80, File 1405, AGO 1878, M666, Reels 397 and 398, Lincoln County War, NARA. Dudley to AAG DNM, Fort Stanton, Sept. 7, 1878, Utley Research Files. Mills, *Billy the Kid*, 274.
14. Mills, *Billy the Kid*, 274-75. Totty account.
15. Exhibit 78, vol. 2, no. 42, DCOI. Records of the Adjutant General's Office, AGO LR 1871–80, File 1405, AGO 1878, M666, Reels 397 and 398, Lincoln County War, NARA. Dudley to AAG DNM, Fort Stanton, Sept. 7, 1878, Utley Files. Nolan, *West of*, 174. Mills, *Billy the Kid*, 276–85. Some interesting recollections of William Bonney's time in Tascosa can be found in Henry Hoyt's memoir *A Frontier Doctor* (Chicago: Lakeside Press, 1979); and Frederick Nolan's "Billy Hits Tascosa," *True West*, October 2002.
16. *Las Vegas Gazette*, September 21, 1878. *Las Vegas Gazette*, September 28, 1878. Chamberlain, *In the Shadow*, 146. Mills, *Billy the Kid*, 293.
17. Leon C. Metz, *John Selman: Gunfighter* (Norman: University of Oklahoma Press, 1992), passim.
18. Nolan, *West of*, 216–17. Chuck Parsons, "Reese Gobles: Predator," *NOLA Quarterly* 14, no. 2 (Summer 1990). Owens interview, March 2, 1933. Author correspondence with Chuck Parsons and David Johnson, June 2023.
19. Exhibit 78, vol. 2, no. 43, DCOI.

20. Exhibit 78, vol. 2, no. 43, DCOI.
21. Nolan, *West of*, 179. Exhibit 78, vol. 2, no. 44, DCOI. Fulton, *Lincoln County War*, 292.
22. Exhibit 78, vol. 2, no. 44, DCOI. Exhibit 78, vol. 2, no. 48, DCOI. *Mesilla Valley Independent*, October 5, 1878. William Bonney notes recorded by Lew Wallace, Lincoln, March 23, 1879, Wallace Papers. Wilson, *Merchants*, 105.
23. Exhibit 78, vol. 2, no. 44, DCOI. Exhibit 78, vol. 2, no. 47, DCOI. Exhibit 78, vol. 2, no. 48, DCOI. Frank Coe Interview, August 14, 1927.
24. Exhibit 78, vol. 2, no. 44, DCOI. Exhibit 78, vol. 2, no. 45, DCOI. Exhibit 78, vol. 2, no. 46, DCOI. Exhibit 78, vol. 2, no. 49, DCOI.
25. Exhibit 78, vol. 2, no. 48, DCOI.
26. Exhibit 78, vol. 2, no. 47, DCOI. Nolan, *West of*, 180.
27. Tsompanas, *Juan Patrón*, 102–4. Rasch, *Gunsmoke*, 196.
28. Mills, *Billy the Kid*, 290. Tsompanas, *Juan Patrón*, 104. Exhibit 78, vol. 2, no. 53, DCOI.
29. Tsompanas, *Juan Patrón*, 104.
30. Tsompanas, *Juan Patrón*, 102–3. Wilson, *Merchants*, 108–9. *Weekly New Mexican*, November 9, 1878. *Weekly New Mexican*, November 16, 1878.
31. Mills, *Billy the Kid*, 292. E. L. Crawford and Abran Miller, New Mexico [manuscript/mixed material], retrieved from the Library of Congress.
32. Mills, *Billy the Kid*, 293–95.
33. Cooper, *Santa Fe Ring*, 483–84.
34. Wallace Proclamation, Exhibit no. 3, DCOI. Cooper, *Santa Fe Ring*, 483–84.
35. Mills, *Billy the Kid*, 285–87, 294–97. Exhibit no. 25, DCOI. Exhibit 79, vol. 3, no. 40, DCOI.
36. *Santa Fe New Mexican*, December 14, 1878. Exhibit 79, vol. 3, no. 13, DCOI.
37. DCOI, 679–700. Nolan, *Documentary History*, 363–68.
38. Tsompanas, *Juan Patrón*, 109. Jas J. Dolan to Wallace, December 31, 1878, Wallace Papers. Mills, Billy the Kid, 299.
39. Mills, *Billy the Kid*, 300. *Mesilla Valley Independent*, January 11, 1879.
40. *Mesilla News*, January 18, 1879. Tsompanas, *Juan Patrón*, 107. Mills, *Billy the Kid*, 301. *Mesilla Valley Independent*, February 8, 1879.
41. *Weekly New Mexican*, February 8, 1879. Exhibit 79, vol. 3, no. 37, DCOI.
42. William H. Bonney to Wallace, March 13, 1879, Wallace Papers. Retrospection, by Edgar A. Walz, October 1931, Museum of New Mexico Library. S. R. Corbet, P. M., to John Middleton [in Kansas], Lincoln, February 3, 1880, box 11, folder 8, Fulton Collection.
43. Edgar A. Walz, "Retrospection," October 1931, Museum of New Mexico Library (hereafter cited as Walz, "Retrospection"). *Mesilla Valley Independent*, July 5, 1879. *Las Cruces Thirty-Four*, March 5, 1879. Exhibit 79, vol. 3, no. 42, DCOI. Exhibit 79, vol. 3, no. 43, DCOI. Bonney to Wallace, March 13, 1879, Wallace Papers.
44. Exhibit 79, vol. 3, no. 37, DCOI. Exhibit 79, vol. 3, no. 42, DCOI. Exhibit 79, vol. 3, no. 43, DCOI. *Las Cruces Thirty-Four*, March 5, 1879. Walz, "Retrospection." George Curry later wrote that José Chávez y Chávez and Martín Chávez were members of William Bonney's peace party in Lincoln on the night of Huston Chapman's murder. They may have been, although their presence cannot be definitively stated. George Curry, *An Autobiography* (Albuquerque: University of New Mexico Press, 1958), 36–37.
45. Walz, "Retrospection." *Mesilla Valley Independent*, July 5, 1879. *Las Cruces Thirty-Four*, March 5, 1879. Tsompanas, *Juan Patrón*, 72.
46. *Mesilla Valley Independent*, July 5, 1879. *Las Cruces Thirty-Four*, March 5, 1879. Walz, "Retrospection." Huston Chapman Autopsy Report, Usmar Collection. Copy, George Kimbrell to Lt. M. F. Goodwin, Lincoln, February 20, 1879, Wallace Papers. Nolan, *West of*, 187.

47. Exhibit 79, vol. 3, no. 37, DCOI. Exhibit 79, vol. 3, no. 38, DCOI. Exhibit 79, vol. 3, no. 41, DCOI. Exhibit 79, vol. 3, no. 42, DCOI.
48. Exhibit 79, vol 3, no. 40, DCOI. Exhibit no. 59, DCOI. Copy, Col. Nathan Dudley to AAG DNM, Fort Stanton, February 24, 1879, Utley Files.
49. Copy, George Kimbrell to Lt. M. F. Goodwin, Lincoln, February 20, 1879, Wallace Papers. Exhibit 79, vol 3, no. 40, DCOI. *Mesilla Valley Independent*, March 8, 1879.
50. Cooper, *Santa Fe Ring*, 503–5. Wilson, *Merchants*, 108–9.

Notes for Chapter 9

1. Utley, *High Noon*, 138–39. Nolan, *Documentary History*, 379–80. Tsompanas, *Juan Patrón*, 111.
2. Exhibit 79, vol. 3, no. 57, DCOI. Exhibit 79, vol. 3, no. 58, DCOI. Mills, *Billy the Kid*, 309.
3. Nolan, *Documentary History*, 382–83. Tsompanas, *Juan Patrón*, 111. Rasch, *Gunsmoke*, 211.
4. Exhibit no. 70, DCOI.
5. Exhibit no. 71, DCOI. Wilson, *Merchants*, 119.
6. William H. Bonney to Lew Wallace, March 13, 1879, Lew Wallace Papers. Wallace to Bonney, March 15, 1879, Lew Wallace Papers. The exchange of letters between Bonney and Wallace originally come from the Lew Wallace Papers, 1879–1881 (Wallace Papers), Indiana Historical Society, Indianapolis. They have also been faithfully reproduced in various books, including Gale Cooper, *The Lost Pardon of Billy the Kid* (Albuquerque: Gelcour Books, 2018). All of William Bonney's presently known correspondence can be found in Gale Cooper, *Billy the Kid's Writings, Words & Wit* (Albuquerque: Gelcour Books, 2011).
7. Tsompanas, *Juan Patrón*, 114–15.
8. Fulton, *Lincoln County War*, 340. Keleher, *Violence*, 218.
9. *Indianapolis World*, June 8, 1902. Otero, *Real Billy*, 98.
10. Tsompanas, *Juan Patrón*, 115. Lew Wallace to Juan Patrón, March 19, 1879, Wallace Papers.
11. William H. Bonney to John B. Wilson, March 20, 1879, Wallace Papers. Wallace to Wilson and Bonney, March 20, 1879, Wallace Papers. Bonney to Wallace, March 20, 1879, Wallace Papers.
12. Mills, *Billy the Kid*, 317. William Bonney ("Kid") Notes, Lew Wallace, March 23, 1879, Wallace Papers. Casey interview.
13. *Las Vegas Gazette*, December 28, 1880. Cooper, *Lost Pardon*, 583–86.
14. Keleher, *Violence*, 215–16. Tsompanas, *Juan Patrón*, 117–18.
15. Juan B. Patrón to Ben Ellis, April 12, 1879, Wallace Papers. Tsompanas, *Juan Patrón*, 118–19.
16. Mills, *Billy the Kid*, 323. Nolan, *Documentary History*, 383.
17. Lincoln County, District Court Journal, 1875–79, April 1879 term, April 14–May 1, 1879, pp. 296–387, Utley Files (hereafter cited as Lincoln County DC Journal, April 1879).
18. Lincoln County DC Journal, April 1879. Ira Leonard to Wallace, April 20, 1879, Wallace Papers.
19. Lincoln County DC Journal, April 1879.
20. Lincoln County DC Journal, April 1879. Cooper, *Lost Pardon*, 604–5. Utley, *High Noon*, 149.
21. DCOI, passim.
22. Testimony of Juan B. Patrón, Isaac Ellis, John B. Wilson, Susan McSween, and William Bonney, DCOI.

23. Testimony of José Chávez y Chávez, DCOI.
24. Testimony of Milo L. Pierce, DCOI.
25. Testimony of Martín Chávez, DCOI.
26. Testimony of Saturnino Baca, José Chávez y Baca, José María de Aguayo, James J. Dolan, Jack Long, and George Peppin, DCOI. DCOI, passim. Leonard to Wallace, June 6, 1879, Wallace Papers.
27. Mills, *Billy the Kid*, 335–36.
28. Tsompanas, *Juan Patrón*, 123–26. Garrett, *Authentic Life*, 113.
29. Tsompanas, *Juan Patrón*, 123–26. 1880 United States Federal Census. Afamilyofthewest.com, Family ID F3356.

Notes for Chapter 10

1. *Chicago Tribune*, July 23, 1879. A colorful overview of the history of Las Vegas, especially East Las Vegas, can be found in Howard Bryan, *Wildest of the Wild West* (Santa Fe: Clear Light, 1988). A more in-depth study of Las Vegas can be found in Lynn Irwin Perrigo's *Gateway to Glorieta: A History of Las Vegas, New Mexico* (Santa Fe: Sunstone Press, 2010).
2. *Mesilla Valley Independent*, June 14, 1879. *Inter-Ocean* (Chicago), July 2, 1879.
3. *Chicago Tribune*, July 23, 1879. *Inter-Ocean*, July 2, 1879. *Weekly Palladium* (Benton Harbor, MI), July 18, 1879.
4. *Chicago Tribune*, July 23, 1879. *Weekly Palladium*, July 18, 1879. *Mesilla Valley Independent*, July 5, 1879.
5. *Las Vegas Daily Gazette*, August 12, 1879. *Chicago Tribune*, July 23, 1879. *Inter-Ocean*, July 2, 1879. *Weekly Palladium*, July 18, 1879.
6. *Chicago Tribune*, July 23, 1879. Bryan, *Wildest of the Wild West*, passim. Mills, *Billy the Kid*, 367.
7. *Inter-Ocean*, July 2, 1879. David Correia, "'Retribution Will Be Their Reward': New Mexico's Las Gorras Blancas and the Fight for the Las Vegas Land Grant Commons," *Radical History Review*, no. 108 (Fall 2010): 49–57.
8. Tsompanas, *Juan Patrón*, 125–28. Julyan, *Place Names*, 278. *Las Vegas Gazette*, October 26, 1880. Daniel Flores's *Puerto de Luna* (pub. by author, 2010) remains a good source for Puerto de Luna and its history.
9. Francis C. Kajencki, "Alexander Grzelachowski: Pioneer Merchant of Puerto De Luna," *Journal of the Southwest* 26, no. 3 (Autumn 1984): 243–60. 1880 United States Federal Census.
10. William H. Bonney to Lew Wallace, December 12, 1880, Wallace Papers.
11. For Victorio see Kathleen P. Chamberlain, *Victorio: Apache Warrior and Chief* (Norman: University of Oklahoma Press, 2007). For the Victorio Campaign, see Robert N. Watt's *"I Will Not Surrender the Hair of a Horse's Tail": The Victorio Campaign, 1879* (Warwick, UK: Helion, 2017); and *"Horses Worn to Mere Shadows": The Victorio Campaign 1880* (Warwick, UK: Helion, 2019).
12. *Weekly New Mexican*, September 20, 1879. Nolan, *West of*, 215–16. W. R. Jake Owens, interview with J. Evetts Haley, June 24, 1937, Haley Memorial Library. Eve Ball, *Ma'am Jones of the Pecos* (Tucson: University of Arizona Press, 1969), 174–75. Gus Gildea to Maurice Fulton, Pearce, Arizona, January 16, 1929, box 2, folder 2, Fulton Collection.
13. *Amarillo Daily News*, November 13, 1936. Garrett, *Authentic Life*, 106–7, 113. Anaya, *I Buried Billy*, 82. Mills, *Billy the Kid*, 371–73.
14. Mills, *Billy the Kid*, 370–71. Utley, *Violent Life*, 121. Fulton, *Lincoln County War*, 370.
15. *Weekly New Mexican*, July 26, 1879. *Weekly New Mexican*, January 10, 1880.
16. Smith, "Man Who Fought Side-by-Side." *New Mexico Magazine*, April 1933.

17. Anaya, *I Buried Billy*, 77–81. 1880 United States Federal Census. Kadlec, *They Knew*, 39. A vivid description of the Fort Sumner cemetery, and the locations of Joe Grant, Charlie Bowdre, Tom Folliard, and William Bonney's gravesites, was provided by an impartial observer with the initials I. N. P. in the *Las Vegas (NM) Daily Optic*, January 16, 1882.
18. Garrett, *Authentic Life*, 113–14. Mills, *Billy the Kid*, 384. Frederick Nolan, "So, Who Was Dan Dedrick?" *True West*, June 2011. Vaden, Clay W., and Dr. Felipe Padilla, "Mexican Boy Captured by Apache Indians," New Mexico, 1936, manuscript/mixed material, retrieved from the Library of Congress.
19. *Weekly New Mexican*, January 31, 1880.
20. *Las Vegas Daily Gazette*, January 21, 1880. Flores, *José Chávez y Chávez*, 15–16.
21. *Las Vegas Daily Gazette*, January 28, 1880. *Weekly New Mexican*, January 31, 1880.
22. *Weekly New Mexican*, February 14, 1880. *Kansas City (MO) Times*, February 10, 1880.
23. *Weekly New Mexican*, February 21, 1880.
24. *Kansas City Times*, February 18, 1880.
25. The various details of the New Mexico excursion and its passengers' activities in Kansas and Kansas City, Missouri, are detailed in *Kansas City Times*, February 18, 1880. Juan Patrón's name is listed among the special guests on the train.
26. *Kansas City Times*, February 18, 1880. *Las Vegas Daily Gazette*, February 26, 1880.
27. *Las Vegas Daily Gazette*, March 3, 1880. *Santa Fe New Mexican*, March 3, 1880. *Las Vegas Daily Gazette*, March 4, 1880.
28. *Santa Fe New Mexican*, March 14, 1880.
29. *Santa Fe New Mexican*, March 14, 1880.
30. *Santa Fe New Mexican*, March 14, 1880.
31. *Las Vegas Gazette*, August 5, 1880. *Las Vegas Gazette*, November 16, 1880. *Santa Fe New Mexican*, November 13, 1875.
32. The best source on White Oaks, New Mexico, is Roberta Key Haldane's *Gold-Mining Boomtown: People of White Oaks, Lincoln County, New Mexico Territory* (Norman: University of Oklahoma Press, 2012). *Las Vegas Daily Gazette*, March 28, 1880.
33. *Santa Fe New Mexican*, July 14, 1880.
34. *Lincoln County News*, May 8, 1969. 1880 United States Federal Census.
35. 1880 United States Federal Census. 1885 New Mexico Territorial Census. 1900 United States Federal Census. Mills, "Hombres Valientes." Bryan, *Wildest of the Wild West*, 244.
36. *Las Vegas Gazette*, July 7, 1880. *Las Vegas Gazette*, October 1, 1880. *Las Vegas Gazette*, October 30, 1880.
37. E. L. Crawford and A. Chavez, "Ambrosio Chavez," New Mexico, (1938), [manuscript/mixed material] retrieved from the Library of Congress (hereafter cited as Crawford and Chavez, "Ambrosio Chavez"). 1880 United States Federal Census. 1885 New Mexico Territorial Census. 1900 United States Federal Census. Find a Grave, 1600s–Current, Ancestry.com.
38. Walter Noble Burns interview notes with Martín Chávez (typed transcript), Usmar Collection. John P. Meadows, *Pat Garrett and Billy the Kid as I Knew Them*, ed. John P. Wilson (Albuquerque: University of New Mexico Press, 2004), 28–33. Haldane, *Gold-Mining Boomtown*, 15–16. Secret Service Agent Azariah Faxon Wild's reports are found in Reports of Special Operative Azariah F. Wild (T915, Roll 308), RG 87, Records of US Secret Service Agents, 1875–1936, Records of the United States Secret Service, US Treasury Department, Secret Service Division, New Orleans District, NARA (hereafter cited as Wild Reports).
39. Otero, *Real Billy*, 125–26. Crawford and Chavez, "Ambrosio Chavez." Kadlec, *They Knew*, 42.
40. Crawford and Chavez, "Ambrosio Chavez." Otero, *Real Billy*, 129.

Notes for Chapter 11

41. Mills, *Billy the Kid*, 357–61. Otero, *Real Billy*, 98. Totty account.
42. *Albuquerque Journal*, September 24, 1931. Mills, *Billy the Kid*, 371–73.
43. Deluvina Maxwell interview with J. Evetts Haley, June 24, 1927, Haley Memorial Library (hereafter cited as Maxwell interview). Hoyt, *Frontier Doctor*, 261–63. Mills, *Billy the Kid*, 398–403.
44. Mills, *Billy the Kid*, 401–2.
45. For Pat Garrett see Leon C. Metz, *Pat Garrett: The Story of a Western Lawman* (Norman: University of Oklahoma Press, 1974); and Mark Lee Gardner, *To Hell On A Fast Horse: The Untold Story of Billy the Kid and Pat Garrett* (New York: William Morrow, 2010).
46. Afamilyofthewest.com. Tsompanas, *Juan Patrón*, 144. 1900 United States Federal Census. Find a Grave, 1600s–Current, Ancestry.com.
47. Tsompanas, *Juan Patrón*, 128–29. Mills, *Billy the Kid*, 348.
48. *Las Vegas Gazette*, October 6, 1880. *Las Vegas Gazette*, October 14, 1880. *Las Vegas Gazette*, October 15, 1880. *Santa Fe New Mexican*, October 18, 1880.
49. Chamberlain, *Victorio*, 204–7. *Las Vegas Gazette*, October 22, 1880.
50. Chamberlain, *Victorio*, 204–7. *Santa Fe New Mexican*, October 23, 1880.
51. Metz, *Pat Garrett*, 53–57.
52. Metz, *Pat Garrett*, 53–57. Mills, *Billy the Kid*, 373–75. Gardner, *Fast Horse*, 29–31. Burns, *Saga*, 17–18.
53. Mills, *Billy the Kid*, 373–76, 415–17. Gardner, *Fast Horse*, 94–96.
54. Wild Reports. Burns, *Saga*, 197. Otero, *Real Billy*, 98.
55. Lacy and Valley-Fox, *Stories From Hispano New Mexico*, 205.

Notes for Chapter 11

1. Wild Reports.
2. Wild Reports.
3. Wild Reports. Charles Bowdre to Capt. Lea, Fort Sumner, December 15, 1880, Bonney Collection. J. C. Lea to Lew Wallace, Roswell, December 24, 1880, Bonney Collection.
4. Metz, *Pat Garrett*, 53–57. Joan M. Jensen and Darlis A. Miller, *New Mexico Women: Intercultural Perspectives* (Albuquerque: University of New Mexico Press, 1986), 179. Burns, *Saga*, 197.
5. Wild Reports. Metz, *Pat Garrett*, 59. *San Francisco Examiner*, November 4, 1900.
6. Wild Reports. 1880 United States Federal Census. Haldane, *Gold-Mining Boomtown*, 44–48. James Townsend, "James W. Bell: Marylander, Texas Ranger, Fugitive," *Billy the Kid Coalition Press*, vol. 3 (2023).
7. Wild Reports. Jim East interview with J. Evetts Haley, September 27, 1927, Haley Memorial Library (hereafter cited as East interview). L. P. Bousman interview with J. Evetts Haley, October 23, 1934, Haley Memorial Library (hereafter cited as Bousman interview). Details about Frank Stewart and the Panhandle posse can be found in Kurt House and Roy B. Young, *Chasing Billy the Kid: Frank Stewart and the Untold Story of the Manhunt for William H. Bonney* (San Antonio: Three Rivers, 2022); and Nolan, "Billy Hits Tascosa."
8. Wild Reports. Garrett, *Authentic Life*, 114–15, 127–28.
9. Wild Reports. Mills, *Billy the Kid*, 422–23. Nolan, "Who Was Dan Dedrick?"
10. Wild Reports. William A. Keleher, *The Fabulous Frontier: Twelve New Mexico Items* (Albuquerque: University of New Mexico Press, 1962), 70–72. Garrett, *Authentic Life*, 121. Nolan, *West of*, 232–35. Haldane, *Gold-Mining Boomtown*, 56–57. Mills, *Billy the Kid*, 423–27. *Las Vegas Gazette*, December 24, 1880. *Las Vegas Daily Optic*, January 21, 1881. William Bonney to Lew Wallace, December 12, 1880, Wallace Papers.

11. Wild Reports. Garrett, *Authentic Life*, 128–32.
12. Garrett, *Authentic Life*, 131–33.
13. Garrett, *Authentic Life*, 132–33.
14. Garrett, *Authentic Life*, 134–37. Metz, *Pat Garrett*, 61–65. *Santa Fe New Mexican*, December 17, 1880.
15. *Las Vegas Gazette*, December 3, 1880.
16. Bonney to Wallace, December 12, 1880, Wallace Papers. Mills, *Billy the Kid*, 433–36. Nolan, *West of*, 238.
17. Mills, *Billy the Kid*, 433–36. Garrett, *Authentic Life*, 170.
18. Garrett, *Authentic Life*, 137–43. Gardner, *Fast Horse*, 117–18. Frank Clifford, *Deep Trails in the Old West: A Frontier Memoir*, ed. Frederick Nolan (Norman: University of Oklahoma Press, 2011), 81–86. House and Young, *Chasing Billy the Kid*, 191. East interview. Bousman interview. Jim East to Judge William H. Burgess, Douglas, Arizona, May 20, 1926, Mullin Files.
19. Garrett, *Authentic Life*, 142–44. East interview. Bousman interview.
20. Mills, *Billy the Kid*, 441–42. East interview.
21. Garrett, *Authentic Life*, 146–47. Metz, *Pat Garrett*, 72-73.
22. Garrett, *Authentic Life*, 146–48. Anaya, *I Buried Billy*, 98. Otero, *Real Billy*, 98. Metz, *Pat Garrett*, 74. East interview. Bousman interview. East to Judge Burgess, Douglas, Arizona, May 20, 1926, Mullin Files. James H. East to Charlie Siringo, Douglas, Arizona, May 1, 1920, typescript in Rasch Collection (O'Folliard File), Lincoln State Monument, Utley Files. *Las Vegas Gazette*, December 27, 1880.
23. Garrett, *Authentic Life*, 147–48. *Bisbee (AZ) Daily Review*, March 8, 1908. East interview. *Las Vegas Daily Optic*, January 16, 1882.
24. Garrett, *Authentic Life*, 151–52. Anaya, *I Buried Billy*, 101–7. House and Young, *Chasing Billy the Kid*, 219–23. East interview. Bousman interview.
25. Garrett, *Authentic Life*, 152–53. Anaya, *I Buried Billy*, 101–7. Otero, *Real Billy*, 98. East interview. Bousman interview.
26. Garrett, *Authentic Life*, 153–55. Anaya, *I Buried Billy*, 101–7. House and Young, *Chasing Billy the Kid*, 219–23. East interview. Bousman interview. *Las Vegas Gazette*, December 27, 1880.
27. Garrett, *Authentic Life*, 152–56. Anaya, *I Buried Billy*, 101–7. East interview. Bousman interview.
28. Garrett, *Authentic Life*, 155–56. Anaya, *I Buried Billy*, 101–7. East interview. Bousman interview.
29. James H. East to Charlie Siringo, Douglas Arizona, May 1, 1920, Utley Files. Burns, *Saga*, 186. Louis Leon Branch, *Los Bilitos: The Story of Billy the Kid and His Gang* (New York: Carlton Press, 1980), 214. Mills, *Billy the Kid*, 452. *Las Vegas Daily Optic*, January 16, 1882.
30. Maxwell interview. Keleher, *Violence*, 344–46. Keleher, *Fabulous Frontier*, 74–76. Rose P. White, "Full Many a Flower," *New Mexico Folklore Record*, no. 4 (1949–50): 15–16. Burns, *Saga*, 195.
31. James H. Earle, *The Capture of Billy the Kid* (College Station: Creative Publishing, 1988), 88. Burns, *Saga*, 195. East interview.
32. Mills, *Billy the Kid*, 454–58. *Las Vegas Gazette*, December 27, 1880.
33. *The Sun* (New York), December 27, 1880. *Las Vegas Daily Gazette*, January 20, 1881.
34. Mills, *Billy the Kid*, 462–66. *Las Vegas Gazette*, December 27, 1880.
35. Mills, *Billy the Kid*, 470–73. *Santa Fe New Mexican*, December 28, 1880.
36. Mills, *Billy the Kid*, 474. *Las Vegas Daily Gazette*, January 20, 1881. Bonney to Wallace, January 1, 1881, Wallace Papers. Bonney to Lew Wallace, March 2, 1881, Wallace Papers.

Notes for Chapter 11

Bonney to Wallace, March 4, 1881, Wallace Papers. Bonney to Wallace, March 27, 1881, Wallace Papers.
37. *Santa Fe New Mexican*, March 1, 1881. Otero, *Real Billy*, 132–34.
38. Details about William Bonney's trials can be found in Randy Russell's *Billy the Kid: The Story-The Trial* (Lincoln: Crystal Press, 1994); and David G. Thomas's *The Trial of Billy the Kid* (Las Cruces: Doc45 Publishing, 2021). *Mesilla News*, April 15, 1881. Nolan, *West of*, 264. Mills, *Billy the Kid*, 492–99.
39. Mills, *Billy the Kid*, 501–4. Otero, *Real Billy*, 127–28. *Lincoln County Leader*, March 1, 1890. Severo Gallegos interview with Eve Ball, April 5, 1949, Ruidoso, New Mexico, Eve Ball Papers, MSS 3096, box 11, folder 21, L. Tom Perry Special Collections, Harold B. Lee Library, Brigham Young University, Provo, Utah (hereafter cited as Gallegos interview).
40. Otero, *Real Billy*, 127–28. Chávez interview. Garrett, *Authentic Life*, 161. Mills, *Billy the Kid*, 504–5.
41. *San Francisco Examiner*, November 4, 1900. *Lubbock Avalanche-Journal*, September 21, 1930.
42. Casey interview.
43. Salazar interview. *Lincoln County Leader*, March 1, 1890.
44. Mills, *Billy the Kid*, 508–9. Gardner, *Fast Horse*, 143. *San Francisco Examiner*, November 4, 1900.
45. *Lincoln County Leader*, March 1, 1890. Gallegos interview. *Clovis News-Journal*, July 26, 1938. Mills, *Billy the Kid*, 511–7. Meadows, *As I Knew Them*, 47–50. Garrett, *Authentic Life*, 168.
46. Leslie Traylor, "Facts Regarding the Escape of Billy the Kid," *Frontier Times* 13, no. 10 (July 1936): 510. Salazar interview. *Lincoln County Leader*, March 1, 1890.
47. Salazar interview. John Meadows interview with J. Evetts Haley, June 13, 1936, Haley Memorial Library. Meadows, *As I Knew Them*, 50–52. Mills, *Billy the Kid*, 520.
48. Emerson Hough, *The Story of the Outlaw: A Study of the Western Desperado* (New York: Cooper Square Press, 2001), 305. Metz, *Pat Garrett*, 95–96. Garrett, *Authentic Life*, 171. Mrs. Sophie Poe to W. T. Moyers, attorney at law, letter undated, Mark Lee Gardner Collection (Gardner Collection), Colorado.
49. *Las Vegas Morning Gazette*, May 3, 1881. *Santa Fe New Mexican*, May 3, 1881. *Las Vegas Daily Optic*, May 4, 1881. *St. Louis Daily Globe-Democrat*, May 16, 1881. *Glasgow Evening Citizen*, June 22, 1881. *Manchester Courier and Lancashire General Advertiser*, June 23, 1881. *Belfast Morning News*, June 24, 1881. *Dublin Evening Telegraph*, June 23, 1881. Otero, *Real Billy*, 128.
50. Chávez interview.
51. *Las Vegas Daily Optic*, July 18, 1881. *London Times*, August 18, 1881. *Montreal Star*, July 19, 1881. *New York Times*, July 19, 1881. *Santa Fe New Mexican*, July 18, 1881. Mark J. Dworkin, *American Mythmaker: Walter Noble Burns and the Legends of Billy the Kid, Wyatt Earp, and Joaquin Murrieta* (Norman: University of Oklahoma Press, 2015), 32. Mills, *Billy the Kid*, 530–33. Chávez interview. Otero, *Real Billy*, 133.
52. Metz, *Pat Garrett*, 98. Earle, *Capture*, 58. John W. Poe, *The Killing of Billy the Kid* (1919; repr., Barto, PA: Creative Texts Publishers, 2015), 10, 21–22. Garrett, *Authentic Life*, 174–75. *Albuquerque Journal*, February 9, 1958. Chávez interview. *La Voz Del Pueblo* (Santa Fe), December 21, 1901.
53. Otero, *Real Billy*, 116–19. Anaya, *I Buried Billy*, 125–27. *Amarillo Daily News*, November 13, 1936. Poe, *Killing of*, 25.
54. Otero, *Real Billy*, 119. Poe, *Killing of*, 24. Kadlec, *They Knew*, 79. Cunningham, *Triggernometry*, 131, 170. Mark Lee Gardner, "A Belle of Old Fort Sumner," *True West*,

April 2018. Maxwell interview. *Amarillo Daily News*, November 13, 1936. *Las Vegas Daily Optic*, January 16, 1882.
55. Mills, *Billy the Kid*, 548, 552–54. *St. Louis Globe-Democrat*, August 3, 1881. Chávez interview.
56. *Eastern New Mexico News, The Clovis*, July 22, 2020. Otero, *Real Billy*, 121.

Notes for Chapter 12

1. Tsompanas, *Juan Patrón*, 144. Rayitos (Patrón) Hinojos to Lewis A. Ketring, Jr., August 2, 1962, Binder "Residents of Lincoln County, N-S," box 14, folder 1 (mixed materials), Lewis A. Ketring, Jr. collection of Lincoln County research, Ms 0519, NMSU LASC. *Las Vegas Gazette*, April 11, 1884.
2. *Las Vegas Gazette*, August 10, 1881. *Las Vegas Gazette*, August 17, 1881. Michelson, *Confining Winter*, 271-74.
3. *Santa Fe New Mexican*, February 24, 1882. *Santa Fe New Mexican*, February 7, 1882. *Santa Fe New Mexican*, February 1, 1881. Robert R. White, "The Murder of Colonel Charles Potter," *New Mexico Historical Review* 62 (July), 1987.
4. 1900 United States Census. Tsompanas, *Juan Patrón*, 144.
5. *Las Vegas Gazette*, October 4, 1882. *Las Vegas Gazette*, October 19, 1882. 1860 United States Federal Census. 1880 United States Federal Census.
6. *Las Vegas Gazette*, October 19, 1882. *Las Vegas Gazette*, October 4, 1882. *Las Vegas Gazette*, June 4, 1882. *Las Vegas Gazette*, June 3, 1882. *Las Vegas Gazette*, May 28, 1882.
7. *Las Vegas Gazette*, November 5, 1882. *Las Vegas Gazette*, November 7, 1882. *Las Vegas Gazette*, November 12, 1882. The vote returns for San Miguel County were published on page 4 of the *Las Vegas Gazette*, November 15, 1882.
8. 1860 United States Federal Census. 1880 United States Federal Census. Find a Grave, 1600s–Current, Ancestry.com. *Las Vegas Gazette, December 8, 1882*. Tsompanas, *Juan Patrón*, 144.
9. Juan Patron vs. George Mitchell, March 1884, case no. 1816, box 13541, folder 20, collection 1960-043: Records of the United States Territorial and New Mexico District Courts for San Miguel County, NMSRCA (hereafter cited as Patron vs. Mitchell).
10. *Santa Fe New Mexican*, July 14, 1883. *Las Vegas Gazette*, May 5, 1883. *Las Vegas Gazette*, March 21, 1884. 1880 United States Federal Census.
11. 1900 United States Federal Census.
12. *Las Vegas Gazette*, February 26, 1882.
13. *Las Cruces Sun-News*, July 22, 1882. *Las Vegas Gazette*, January 23, 1883. *New Mexican Review* (Santa Fe), June 9, 1883. *Lincoln County Leader*, November 11, 1882.
14. James B. Mills, "Slaughter in Seven Rivers," *True West*, June 2022. Author correspondence with Lynda A. Sánchez, August 2023. Garrett, *Authentic Life*, passim.
15. Metz, *Pat Garrett*, 135. Gardner, *Fast Horse*, 186–87.
16. 1880 United States Federal Census. Afamilyofthewest.com, Family ID F1105. Lacy and Valley-Fox, *Stories From Hispano New Mexico*, 215–17.
17. *Santa Rosa (CA) News*, June 7, 1940.
18. Lacy and Valley-Fox, *Stories From Hispano New Mexico*, 215–17. 1940 United States Federal Census.
19. *Las Vegas Gazette*, January 10, 1884. Mills, "Slaughter in Seven Rivers."
20. *Las Vegas Gazette*, January 10, 1884. *Weekly New Mexican Review* (Santa Fe), January 12, 1884. *Weekly New Mexican Review*, January 17, 1884. Mills, "Slaughter in Seven Rivers."
21. *Las Vegas Gazette*, January 10, 1884. *St. Louis Globe-Democrat*, January 15, 1884. Mills, "Slaughter in Seven Rivers."

Notes for Chapter 12 505

22. Mills, "Slaughter in Seven Rivers." *Las Vegas Gazette*, January 10, 1884. *Santa Fe New Mexican*, January 11, 1884. *Deseret News* (Salt Lake City, UT), January 19, 1884.
23. *White Oaks Golden Era*, February 7, 1884. *Las Vegas Gazette*, February 14, 1884.
24. *Lincoln County Leader*, February 23, 1884.
25. Rasch, *Warriors*, 129-131. Gardner, *Fast Horse*, 197. *Las Cruces Sun-News*, July 14, 1883. *White Oaks (NM) Golden Era*, February 7, 1884. *Lincoln County Leader*, February 16, 1884. *Las Vegas Gazette*, February 28, 1884. *Las Vegas Gazette*, February 15, 1884. *Lincoln County Leader*, February 23, 1884. 1880 United States Federal Census.
26. *Lincoln County Leader*, February 23, 1884.
27. *Las Vegas Gazette*, March 8, 1884. Gonzáles-Berry and Maciel, *Contested Homeland*, 62. Rosenbaum, *Mexicano Resistance*, 99–101.
28. *Las Vegas Gazette*, March 8, 1884.
29. *Las Vegas Gazette*, March 8, 1884. *Las Vegas Daily Optic*, March 7, 1884.
30. Tsompanas, *Juan Patrón*, 144.
31. *Las Vegas Gazette*, March 21, 1884. 1880 United States Federal Census. 1885 New Mexico Territorial Census. Tsompanas, *Juan Patrón*, 145.
32. Patron vs. Mitchell. *Las Vegas Gazette*, March 22, 1884.
33. *Las Vegas Gazette*, April 2, 1884. *Las Vegas Gazette*, April 11, 1884.
34. Rayitos (Patrón) Hinojos to Lewis A. Ketring Jr., August 2, 1962, Ms 0519, binder "Residents of Lincoln County, N-S," box 14, folder 1 (mixed materials), Lewis A. Ketring Jr. Collection of Lincoln County Research (Ketring Collection), NMSU LASC.
35. 1880 United States Federal Census. 1885 New Mexico Territorial Census. *Santa Fe New Mexican*, April 15, 1884. *Las Vegas Daily Optic*, April 14, 1884. Tsompanas, *Juan Patrón*, 145–46.
36. There is no valid reason to question either the recollections of Michael Maney in the *Las Vegas Daily Optic*, April 13, 1884, or the testimony sworn in affidavits by William Ruth and Thomas Jones in the case file regarding what occurred the night Juan Bautista Patrón was shot, unless one wishes to portray the Hispano businessman's death as some form of martyrdom. Juan Patrón was a remarkable man of his time and place, but he was no saint. His death, while certainly tragic, came as the result of his own notorious foolishness when under the influence of alcohol. Territory vs. Michael Erskin Maney, Murder of Juan B. Patron, 1885, case no. 6391, box 18193, folder 71, collection 1972-011: Records of the United States Territorial and New Mexico District Courts for Santa Fe County, Criminal, NMSRCA (hereafter cited as Territory vs. Maney). *Las Vegas Daily Optic*, April 13, 1884.
37. Territory vs. Maney. *Las Vegas Daily Optic*, April 13, 1884. 1885 New Mexico Territorial Census. *Las Vegas Gazette*, April 12, 1884. *Las Vegas Daily Optic*, April 14, 1884.
38. Territory vs. Maney. *Las Vegas Daily Optic*, April 13, 1884.
39. Territory vs. Maney. *Las Vegas Daily Optic*, April 13, 1884. Hinojos to Ketring, August 2, 1962, Ketring Collection.
40. Territory vs. Maney. *Las Vegas Daily Optic*, April 13, 1884. Tsompanas, *Juan Patrón*, 148–51.
41. Territory vs. Maney. *Las Vegas Daily Optic*, April 13, 1884. Tsompanas, *Juan Patrón*, 148–51.
42. Territory vs. Maney. *Las Vegas Daily Optic*, April 13, 1884. Tsompanas, *Juan Patrón*, 148–51. *Las Vegas Gazette*, April 12, 1884.
43. Territory vs. Maney. *Las Vegas Daily Optic*, April 13, 1884. Tsompanas, *Juan Patrón*, 148–51. *Las Vegas Daily Optic*, April 9, 1884.
44. Territory vs. Maney. *Las Vegas Daily Optic*, April 13, 1884. Tsompanas, *Juan Patrón*, 148–51. *Las Vegas Gazette*, April 12, 1884. *Las Vegas Daily Optic*, April 14, 1884.
45. Territory vs. Maney. *Las Vegas Daily Optic*, April 13, 1884. Tsompanas, *Juan Patrón*, 148–51. *Las Vegas Gazette*, April 12, 1884. 1860 United States Federal Census.

46. Tsompanas, *Juan Patrón*, 152. *St. Louis Globe-Democrat*, April 12, 1884. *Journal-Democrat* (Dodge City, KS), April 19, 1884. *Superior (WI) Times*, April 19, 1884. *Rock Island (IL) Argus*, April 14, 1884. *Baltimore Sun*, April 12, 1884. *Dayton (OH) Herald*, April 14, 1884. *The Republic* (Columbus, IN), April 14, 1884. *Independent-Record* (Helena, MT), April 12, 1884. *Urbana (OH) Daily Citizen*, April 14, 1884. *Daily Register* (Wheeling, WV), April 14, 1884. *Daily Memphis Avalanche*, April 12, 1884. *Lincoln (NE) Journal Star*, April 14, 1884. *Buffalo Morning Express*, April 12, 1884. *San Francisco Chronicle*, April 12, 1884. *Montreal Star*, April 12, 1884. *Pacific Bee* (Sacramento, CA), April 19, 1884. *Record-Union* (Sacramento, CA), April 12, 1884.
47. *Las Vegas Gazette*, April 11, 1884. *Santa Fe New Mexican*, April 12, 1884. *Albuquerque Evening Democrat*, April 14, 1884.
48. *New Mexican Review*, April 17, 1884. *Santa Fe New Mexican*, April 15, 1884.
49. J. M. J. to the Las Vegas *Stock Grower*, reproduced in the *White Oaks Golden Era*, April 24, 1884.
50. *Las Vegas Gazette*, April 12, 1884.
51. Tsompanas, *Juan Patrón*, 150–51. *Las Vegas Gazette*, April 12, 1884.
52. *Las Vegas Gazette*, April 11, 1884. *Santa Fe New Mexican*, April 12, 1884.
53. Hinojos to Ketring, August 2, 1962, Ketring Collection.

Notes for Chapter 13

1. *White Oaks Golden Era*, March 6, 1884. *Las Cruces Sun-News*, April 5, 1884. *Las Vegas Gazette*, April 3, 1884. *Albuquerque Journal*, April 2, 1884. 1870 United States Federal Census. 1880 United States Federal Census. 1885 New Mexico Territorial Census.
2. *Santa Fe New Mexican*, April 21, 1884. *Las Cruces Sun-News*, April 19, 1884. *White Oaks Golden Era*, March 6, 1884. *Santa Fe New Mexican*, April 8, 1884. *Las Cruces Sun-News*, April 5, 1884.
3. 1900 United States Federal Census. *Lincoln County Leader*, May 12, 1883. *Lincoln County Leader*, March 3, 1883. *Lincoln County Leader*, November 22, 1884. Wilson, *Merchants*, 143–45, 155.
4. The report of José Sambrano Tafoya's accident and death can be found on page 4 of the *Lincoln County Leader*, June 28, 1884. Details of Sambrano Tafoya's success as a missionary on the Mescalero reservation can be found on page 4 of the *Las Cruces Sun-News*, June 16, 1883. For Chief San Juan, see Morris Edward Opler and Catherin H. Opler, "Mescalero Apache History in the Southwest," *New Mexico Historical Review* 25, no. 1 (January 1950): 1–36. Author correspondence with Lynda A. Sánchez.
5. Warrant for Salazar, Salazar, Higinio – file – box: 12, folder: s-folder 6, f), Weisner Papers (hereafter cited as Warrant for Salazar). *White Oaks Golden Era*, August 21, 1884.
6. Warrant for Salazar. Find a Grave, 1600s–Current, Ancestry.com. 1870 United States Federal Census. 1900 United States Federal Census. US Civil War Pension, General Index to Pension Files, 1861–1934, T288, Roll 38; Records of the Department of Veterans Affairs, 1773–2007, Record Group 15; NARA.
7. Warrant for Salazar. Territory vs. Yginio Salazar, 1884–1888, serial 14609, page 78, collection 1976-034: Records of the United States Territorial and New Mexico District Courts for Lincoln County, NMSRCA (hereafter cited as Territory vs. Salazar). *White Oaks Golden Era*, October 9, 1884.
8. Details of the shooting of Ephraim Richards and Henry Lackey, and the testimony provided at the coroner's inquest held by Justice Aguayo, can be found on page 1 of the *White Oaks Golden Era*, August 21, 1884, and page 4 of the *Lincoln County Leader*, August 23, 1884. 1860 United States Federal Census. 1880 United States Federal Census. 1885 New Mexico Territorial Census.

9. "Melvin Emyor Richardson Sr.," Find a Grave, accessed February 12, 2025, https://www.findagrave.com/memorial/58334877/melvin-emyor-richardson. "Ephraim Wilson Richards," Find a Grave, accessed February 12, 2025, https://www.findagrave.com/memorial/6727399/ephraim-wilson-richards.
10. *Lincoln County Leader*, May 10, 1884. *Lincoln County Leader*, September 13, 1884. Kadlec, *They Knew*, 20.
11. *White Oaks Golden Era*, October 9, 1884. *White Oaks Golden Era*, January 15, 1885.
12. *Lincoln County Leader*, October 4, 1884. *Lincoln County Leader*, October 11, 1884. *Lincoln County Leader*, October 18, 1884.
13. 1870 United States Federal Census. *Las Vegas Gazette*, October 21, 1884. *White Oaks Golden Era*, October 30, 1884. *Las Vegas Gazette*, November 2, 1884.
14. Territory vs. Salazar. *Lincoln County Leader*, October 18, 1884. *Lincoln County Leader*, May 23, 1885.
15. *White Oaks Golden Era*, November 6, 1884. *Lincoln County Leader*, November 8, 1884. *White Oaks Golden Era*, January 5, 1885. Afamilyofthewest.com, Family ID F2935. Mills, *Billy the Kid*, 555.
16. Wilson, *Merchants*, 143–49.
17. *White Oaks Golden Era*, February 12, 1885. *Las Vegas Gazette*, January 27, 1885. *Las Vegas Gazette*, January 29, 1885. *Las Vegas Gazette*, January 31, 1885. *Las Vegas Gazette*, January 20, 1885. *New Mexican Review*, July 23, 1885. *New Mexican Review*, February 5, 1885. Mrs. Sophie Poe to W. T. Moyers, attorney at law, letter undated, Gardner Collection.
18. *White Oaks Golden Era*, July 2, 1885.
19. Tsompanas, *Juan Patrón*, 152–56. *Las Vegas Daily Optic*, May 11, 1885. *Santa Fe New Mexican*, May 12, 1885. *Santa Fe New Mexican*, May 14, 1885. New Mexico, US Deaths, 1889–1945, Ancestry.com 1910 United States Federal Census. 1920 United States Federal Census. 1930 United States Federal Census. Find a Grave Index, 1600s–Current, Ancestry.com.
20. 1885 New Mexico Territorial Census. *White Oaks Golden Era*, May 7, 1885. *Santa Fe New Mexican*, May 7, 1885. *Lincoln County Leader*, May 9, 1885. *Las Cruces Sun-News*, May 16, 1885. *St. Louis Globe-Democrat*, May 12, 1885. *Sacramento Bee*, May 14, 1885. *Hickman (KY) Courier*, May 15, 1885. *Indianapolis Journal*, May 7, 1885. *New York Times*, May 7, 1885. *Nebraska City News*, May 9, 1885. 1880 United States Federal Census. 1900 United States Federal Census. 1910 United States Federal Census. 1920 United States Federal Census. 1940 United States Federal Census. Find a Grave Index, 1600s–Current, Ancestry.com. Iowa, US Select Marriages Index, 1758–1996, Ancestry.com.
21. *Las Cruces Sun-News*, April 25, 1885. *Lincoln County Leader*, May 23, 1885. *White Oaks Golden Era*, May 21, 1885. *New Mexican Review*, May 28, 1885. *White Oaks Golden Era*, July 2, 1885. 1880 United States Federal Census. Find a Grave Index, 1600s–Current, Ancestry.com.
22. *New Mexican Review*, March 5, 1885. *Lincoln County Leader*, May 23, 1885. *Santa Fe New Mexican*, May 28, 1885. *New Mexican Review*, June 11, 1885. *Santa Fe New Mexican*, June 25, 1885. Judith Boyce DeMark, *Essays in Twentieth-Century New Mexico History* (Albuquerque: University of New Mexico Press, 1994), 120–21. Details of Catarino Romero's escape attempt and death at the end of Joseph Smith Lea's revolver can be found on page 1 of the *White Oaks Golden Era*, June 11, 1885.
23. *White Oaks Golden Era*, July 2, 1885. *Santa Fe New Mexican*, July 6, 1885. *Santa Fe New Mexican*, July 7, 1885. *New Mexican Review*, July 23, 1885.
24. *New Mexican Review*, February 5, 1885. *White Oaks Golden Era*, March 19, 1885. *Santa Fe New Mexican*, July 17, 1885. *New Mexican Review*, July 23, 1885.

25. *Santa Fe New Mexican*, July 17, 1885. *New Mexican Review*, July 23, 1885. *Lincoln County Leader*, July 25, 1885. *Lincoln County Leader*, October 1, 1885.
26. *White Oaks Golden Era*, October 15, 1885. *Lincoln County Leader*, January 24, 1885. *Lincoln County Leader*, July 11, 1885. *Lincoln County Leader*, October 10, 1885. *Lincoln County Leader*, December 19, 1885. *Lincoln County Leader*, January 16, 1886. *San Francisco Examiner*, October 10, 1905.
27. *White Oaks Golden Era*, June 18, 1885. *White Oaks Golden Era*, July 16, 1885. 1885 New Mexico Territorial Census.
28. *White Oaks Golden Era*, April 9, 1885. The depositions from Ash Upson and Charles H. Slaughter can both be found on page 3 of the *White Oaks Golden Era*, December 17, 1885. Bogener, "Land, Speculation, and Manipulation," 219. Stephen Dean Bogener, "Ditches Across the Desert: The Story of Irrigation Along New Mexico's Pecos River," (PhD diss., Texas Tech University, December 1997), 104–9.
29. *White Oaks Golden Era*, April 30, 1885. *Lincoln County Leader*, August 22, 1885. *White Oaks Golden Era*, October 29, 1885. *White Oaks Golden Era*, December 31, 1885. 1880 United States Federal Census. 1885 New Mexico Territorial Census. Special Schedules of the 1890 Census.
30. Territory vs. Maney. Flores, *José Chávez y Chávez*, 45, 87.
31. *Las Vegas Gazette*, July 1, 1885. 1885 New Mexico Territorial Census. Flores, *José Chávez y Chávez*, 45.
32. *St. Louis Post-Dispatch*, May 6, 1884. *Evening News* (Emporia, KS), May 7, 1884. Mark Lee Gardner, "The Strange and Mesmerizing Death of the Outlaw Jesse James," *True West*, February/March 2023.
33. Miguel Antonio Otero, *My Life on the Frontier, 1882–1897: Facsimile of Original 1939 Edition* (Santa Fe: Sunstone Press, 2007), 180. *Albuquerque Democrat*, March 27, 1885. Bryan, *Wildest of the Wild West*, 204–5. *Las Vegas Gazette*, March 26, 1885.
34. Bryan, *Wildest of the Wild West*, 205.
35. *White Oaks Golden Era*, January 14, 1886. *White Oaks Golden Era*, January 28, 1886. *Lincoln County Leader*, July 3, 1886. Sophie A. Poe, *Buckboard Days* (Caldwell, ID: Caxton Printers, 1936), 255. Totty account.
36. *Lincoln County Leader*, September 4, 1886. *Albuquerque Journal*, September 7, 1886.
37. Yginio Salazar, affidavit sworn before Jose Cordoba, Justice of the Peace, Lincoln County, New Mexico, July 25, 1888, Salazar, Higinio, file —, box 12, s-folder 6, Weisner Papers.
38. Details of the mass meeting in Lincoln can be found on page 2 of the *Santa Fe New Mexican*, January 18, 1887.
39. Afamilyofthewest.com: Family ID F2735. 1900 United States Federal Census. *Santa Fe New Mexican*, February 13, 1888. *Lincoln County Leader*, September 8, 1888. *Lincoln County Leader*, October 20, 1888. *Lincoln County Leader*, October 27, 1888. *Lincoln County Leader*, November 17, 1888. *Lincoln County Leader*, December 22, 1888. *Lincoln County Leader*, February 23, 1889. *Lincoln County Leader*, November 26, 1887. Find a Grave Index, 1600s–Current, Ancestry.com. Montana, US County Marriage Records, 1865–1993, Ancestry.com.
40. *Santa Fe New Mexican*, February 26, 1889. *Albuquerque Journal*, February 24, 1889. *Albuquerque Morning Democrat and Albuquerque Morning Journal*, February 24, 1889. "SFTA Hall of Fame: Felipe Chávez," *Wagon Tracks* 30, no. 1 (November 2015), 13. Bogener, "Land, Speculation, and Manipulation," 212–21. Gardner, *Fast Horse*, 190–91. Contrary to the popular belief that Chaves County was named after J. Francisco Cháves, newspaper reports from that period suggest the county was named after Felipe Cháves of Belen.

41. Otero, *Real Billy*, 123. 1900 United States Federal Census. A detailed obituary for Lucio Montoya's daughter Floripa Montoya-Flores can be found on page 3 of the *Alamogordo Daily News*, February 10, 1961. Find a Grave Index, 1600s–Current, Ancestry.com.
42. Martín Chávez and the other thirteen delegates elected to appear at the Democratic Convention in Roswell, Chaves County, are listed on page 1 of the *Santa Fe New Mexican*, August 19, 1890. *Santa Fe New Mexican*, July 3, 1890. *Las Vegas Daily Optic*, September 13, 1890. 1900 United States Federal Census. Find a Grave Index, 1600s–Current, Ancestry.com. Alexander L. Morrison's wife Jane Clark-Morrison's obituary can be found on page 4 of the *Las Vegas Daily Optic*, July 10, 1899.
43. *Carlsbad (NM) Current-Argus*, August 23, 1890.
44. *Steuben Republican* (Angola, IN), February 20, 1889. Gonzáles-Berry and Maciel, *Contested Homeland*, 60. *Las Vegas Daily Optic*, March 10, 1890. J. H. Hunter to Governor M. A. Otero, Omaha, Nebraska, October 25, 1897, Otero Papers.
45. Gonzáles-Berry and Maciel, *Contested Homeland*, 60–62. Correia, "Retribution Will Be Their Reward," 54.
46. Correia, "Retribution Will Be Their Reward," 54.
47. Gonzáles-Berry and Maciel, *Contested Homeland*, 63–64. 1850 United States Federal Census. 1860 United States Federal Census. 1870 United States Federal Census. 1880 United States Federal Census. 1885 New Mexico Territorial Census. 1900 United States Federal Census. American Civil War Research database. Ancestry.com. Geneanet Community Trees Index, Ancestry.com. Territory of Wyoming, 1869, Wyoming State Archives, Cheyenne, Wyoming. Territory vs. Juan Jose Herrera, Assault to Murder, 1886, case no. 2590, box 45149, folder 3, collection 1960-043: Records of the United States Territorial and New Mexico District Courts for San Miguel County, NMSRCA (hereafter cited as Territory vs. Herrera, case no. 2590). Robert W. Larson, "The White Caps of New Mexico: A Study of Ethnic Militancy in the Southwest," *Pacific Historical Review* 44, no. 2 (May 1975): 181–82. Tanner and Tanner, *New Mexico Territorial Penitentiary (1884–1912): Directory of Inmates* (Santa Fe: published by the authors, 2002), 22.
48. Correia, "Retribution Will Be Their Reward," 60–61. Gonzáles-Berry and Maciel, *Contested Homeland*, 63–64. Larson, "White Caps of New Mexico," 174–75, 181–82. For the People's Party of the United States, see Lawrence Goodwyn's *The Populist Moment: A Short History of Agrarian Revolt in America* (New York: Oxford University Press, 1978); and Robert C. McMath Jr.'s *American Populism: A Social History, 1877–1898* (New York: Hill & Wang, 1992). For the Knights of Labor, see Leon Fink's *Workingmen's Democracy: The Knights of Labor and American Politics* (Urbana: University of Illinois Press, 1983); and Carroll D. Wright, "An Historical Sketch of the Knights of Labor," *Quarterly Journal of Economics* 1, no. 2 (January 1887): 137–68.

Notes for Chapter 14

1. Rosenbaum, *Mexicano Resistance*, 99. Miguel Salazar to Governor L. Bradford Prince, July 23, 1890, roll 121, frame 570, Special Reports and Issues, The White Caps, Las Gorras Blancas, box 13931, folder 93, 1890–1893, collection 1959-088: Governor L. Bradford Prince Papers (Prince Papers), Territorial Archives of New Mexico, NMSRCA.
2. *Chicago Tribune*, March 13, 1889. *Las Vegas Daily Optic*, April 3, 1889. Gonzáles-Berry and Maciel, *Contested Homeland*, 64. Rosenbaum, *Mexicano Resistance*, 120–21. Larson, "White Caps of New Mexico," 176.
3. Prince to Secretary John W. Noble, August 11, 1890, Prince Papers. Miguel Salazar to Prince, July 23, 1890, Prince Papers. Territory vs. Jose Lucero, Juan Jose Herrera, Pablo Herrera, et al., 1889–1890, case no. 3316, page 365, box 45155, collection 1960-

043: Records of the United States Territorial and New Mexico District Courts for San Miguel County Criminal Cases, NMSRCA (hereafter cited as Territory vs. Lucero et al.). Correia, "Retribution Will Be Their Reward," 59.

4. The report of the ambush at the Quarrell and Rawlins ranch can be found on page 1 of the *Santa Fe New Mexican*, June 28, 1889. Governor Prince would also recall Tom Williams being wounded in Prince to Noble, August 11, 1890, Prince Papers.

5. José Y. Lujan to Prince, July 25, 1890, Prince Papers. Miguel Salazar to Prince, July 23, 1890, Prince Papers. Rosenbaum, *Mexicano Resistance*, 102–4, 167. *Santa Fe New Mexican*, August 6, 1889. *New Mexican Review*, May 3, 1888. The most concise study of the White Cap organization's motivation being class struggle rather than ethnic hostility is Correia, "Retribution Will Be Their Reward."

6. Manuel C. de Baca to Prince, October 10, 1892, Prince Papers. *Santa Fe New Mexican*, December 12, 1889. *Santa Fe New Mexican*, October 7, 1892. Flores, *José Chávez y Chávez*, 25. *Santa Fe New Mexican*, May 20, 1890.

7. Flores, *José Chávez y Chávez*, 17. 1880 United States Federal Census. 1885 New Mexico Territorial Census. 1900 United States Federal Census.

8. Correia, "Retribution Will Be Their Reward," 59. *Santa Fe New Mexican*, July 20, 1889.

9. Correia, "Retribution Will Be Their Reward," 59. 1870 United States Federal Census. 1880 United States Federal Census. 1885 New Mexico Territorial Census. Find a Grave Index, 1600s–Current, Ancestry.com. Rosenbaum, *Mexicano Resistance*, 167. *Santa Fe New Mexican*, May 15, 1888. Andrew B. Schlesinger, "Las Gorras Blancas, 1889–1891," *Journal of Mexican American History* 1, no. 2 (Spring 1971): 98. Weigle, *Brothers of Light*, 86.

10. *Las Vegas Daily Optic*, October 23, 1889.

11. Miguel Salazar to Prince, July 23, 1890, Prince Papers. Correia, "Retribution Will Be Their Reward," 60. Rosenbaum, *Mexicano Resistance*, 104–5. Find a Grave Index, 1600s–Current, Ancestry.com. 1880 United States Federal Census. 1885 New Mexico Territorial Census.

12. Prince to Noble, August 11, 1890, Prince Papers. *Santa Fe New Mexican*, November 4, 1889. *Las Vegas Daily Optic*, November 2, 1889. *Las Vegas Daily Optic*, June 26, 1890.

13. Miguel Salazar to Prince, July 23, 1890, Prince Papers. *Las Vegas Daily Optic*, November 9, 1889. *Las Vegas Daily Optic*, November 12, 1889. *Albuquerque Journal*, November 12, 1889. Details about Romualdo Fernandez, such as his being African American and having adopted a Mexican American name, can be found in the *Las Vegas Gazette*, March 12, 1882.

14. Miguel Salazar to Prince, July 23, 1890, Prince Papers. The identity of the railroad agent at Rowe whose name District Attorney Miguel Salazar had forgotten, Daniel B. Hampe, is revealed in *The Rustler* (Cerrillos, NM), January 10, 1890. Correa, *Retribution Will Be Their Reward*, 59. Schlesinger, "Las Gorras Blancas," 98. Rosenbaum, *Mexicano Resistance*, 167. *Las Cruces Sun-News*, November 9, 1889.

15. Miguel Salazar to Prince, July 23, 1890, Prince Papers. Records of the AGO, 1780s–1917; Record Group 94; Series Number M427; Roll 0038, NARA. Territory vs. Juan Jose Herrera, April 22, 1889, case no. 3316, Docket Book "C," 1888–1891, 14771, collection 1960-043: Records of the United States Territorial and New Mexico District Courts for San Miguel County Criminal Cases, NMSRCA (hereafter cited as Territory vs. Herrera, case no. 3316). Territory vs. Lucero et al. *Santa Fe New Mexican*, December 12, 1889. *Santa Fe New Mexican*, December 16, 1889. *Santa Fe New Mexican*, December 17, 1889. 1880 United States Federal Census. 1885 New Mexico Territorial Census. 1900 United States Federal Census.

16. Correia, "Retribution Will Be Their Reward," 58. San Miguel County Clerk M. A. Otero to Prince, August 9, 1890, Prince Papers.

17. Warrant No. 3316, Territory of New Mexico vs. Juan Jose Herrera, filed December 14, 1889, District Court, County of San Miguel, NMSRCA. Territory vs. Lucero et al.

Notes for Chapter 14

Warrant No. 3316, Territory of New Mexico vs. Pablo Herrera, filed December 14, 1889, District Court, County of San Miguel, NMSRCA. Territory vs. Lucero et al. Sheriff Lorenzo Lopez, telegram to Prince, December 11, 1889, Prince Papers. *Santa Fe New Mexican*, December 12, 1889. *Santa Fe New Mexican*, December 14, 1889. Schlesinger, "Las Gorras Blancas," 99.

18. Prince to Noble, August 11, 1890, Prince Papers. Appearance bond for Juan Jose Herrera, no. 3116, filed December 17, 1889, NMSRCA. Territory vs. Lucero et al. Appearance bond for Pablo Herrera, no. 3116, filed December 17, 1889, NMSRCA. Territory vs. Lucero et al. *Santa Fe New Mexican*, December 12, 1889. *Las Vegas Daily Optic*, December 17, 1889. *Santa Fe New Mexican*, December 16, 1889. Schlesinger, "Las Gorras Blancas," 99–100. Gonzáles-Berry and Maciel, *Contested Homeland*, 65.
19. Miguel Salazar to Prince, July 23, 1890, Prince Papers. Rosenbaum, *Mexicano Resistance*, 166.
20. Miguel Salazar to Prince, July 23, 1890, Prince Papers.
21. Schlesinger, "Las Gorras Blancas," 100. *Santa Fe New Mexican*, December 20, 1889. *Santa Fe New Mexican*, December 27, 1889. 1885 New Mexico Territorial Census. *Albuquerque Journal*, January 27, 1890. *Santa Fe New Mexican*, September 2, 1887.
22. Gonzáles-Berry and Maciel, *Contested Homeland*, 120. Larson, *New Mexico's Quest*, 148, 162–64. Larson, "White Caps of New Mexico," 177.
23. *Las Vegas Daily Optic*, March 7, 1890.
24. Otero, *Life on the Frontier, 1882–1897*, 249. *Las Vegas Daily Optic*, March 12, 1890.
25. Rosenbaum, *Mexicano Resistance*, 119. *La Voz Del Pueblo*, March 15, 1890.
26. Prince to Noble, August 11, 1890, Prince Papers. *Santa Fe New Mexican*, March 31, 1890. *Las Vegas Daily Optic*, March 18, 1890. Otero, *My Life, 1882–1897*, 248–49. Gonzáles-Berry and Maciel, *Contested Homeland*, 67.
27. *Las Vegas Daily Optic*, March 26, 1890.
28. Prince to Noble, August 11, 1890, Prince Papers. *Santa Fe New Mexican*, January 30, 1888. *Santa Fe New Mexican*, March 31, 1890. *Las Vegas Daily Optic*, April 1, 1890. *Las Vegas Daily Optic*, April 9, 1894. *Las Vegas Daily Optic*, March 31, 1890. 1880 United States Federal Census. 1885 New Mexico Territorial Census.
29. *Las Vegas Daily Optic*, April 5, 1890. *Las Vegas Daily Optic*, April 9, 1890. Schlesinger, "Las Gorras Blancas," 102.
30. Frank C. Ogden et al. to Terrance V. Powderly, August 8, 1890, Prince Papers. Miguel Salazar to Prince, July 23, 1890, Prince Papers.
31. *Las Vegas Gazette*, April 19, 1890. *Las Vegas Daily Optic*, May 5, 1890. *Santa Fe New Mexican*, April 25, 1890. 1885 New Mexico Territorial Census. 1900 United States Federal Census. 1910 United States Federal Census. Schlesinger, "Las Gorras Blancas," 109. Otero, *My Life, 1882–1897*, 249. Rosenbaum, *Mexicano Resistance*, 167.
32. *Las Vegas Daily Optic*, April 21, 1890. James O'Brien's detailed obituary can be found on page 1 of the *Caledonia (MN) Argus*, November 12, 1909. 1880 United States Federal Census. 1900 United States Federal Census. Minnesota, US Civil War Records, 1861–1865, Ancestry.com.
33. *Las Vegas Daily Optic*, May 5, 1890. *Las Vegas Daily Optic*, January 6, 1890. Prince to Noble, August 11, 1890, Prince Papers. Interestingly, Albert Alberti's previous home near the Las Vegas Hot Springs was also burned down in February 1889, as detailed on page 4 of the *Albuquerque Journal*, February 19, 1889. The perpetrators were never identified.
34. Miguel Salazar to Prince, July 23, 1890, Prince Papers. Territory vs. Lucero et al. Territory vs. Herrera, case no. 3316.
35. Prince to Noble, August 11, 1890, Prince Papers. Rosenbaum, *Mexicano Resistance*, 119. Schlesinger, "Las Gorras Blancas," 110. Territory vs. Herrera, case no. 3316.

36. *Santa Fe New Mexican*, May 20, 1890. *Santa Fe New Mexican*, April 22, 1895.
37. Tanner and Tanner, *New Mexico Territorial Penitentiary*, 87.
38. *Las Vegas Daily Optic*, June 5, 1890. J. B. Stouffer to Prince, September 7, 1890, Prince Papers. Prince to Noble, August 11, 1890, Prince Papers. Find a Grave Index, 1600s–Current, Ancestry.com. 1885 New Mexico Territorial Census. *Santa Fe New Mexican*, October 4, 1889.
39. *Las Vegas Daily Optic*, June 17, 1890. 1880 United States Federal Census. 1885 New Mexico Territorial Census. 1890 United States Federal Census. 1900 United States Federal Census. Prince to Noble, August 11, 1890, Prince Papers. Special Schedules of the 1890 Census. Find a Grave Index, 1600s–Current, Ancestry.com. US General Land Office Records, 1776–2015, Ancestry.com. *White Oaks Golden Era*, April 23, 1885.
40. *Las Vegas Daily Optic*, July 30, 1890. *White Oaks Golden Era*, April 23, 1885. *Las Vegas Daily Optic*, April 3, 1890. *Las Vegas Daily Optic*, April 17, 1890. 1870 United States Federal Census. 1880 United States Federal Census. 1885 New Mexico Territorial Census. 1890 United States Federal Census. 1900 United States Federal Census. Prince to Noble, August 11, 1890, Prince Papers. Schlesinger, "Las Gorras Blancas," 110. Geneanet Community Trees Index, Ancestry.com. Octavo Geoffrion's detailed obituary can be found in the *Las Vegas Daily Optic*, August 20, 1914.
41. Gonzáles-Berry and Maciel, *Contested Homeland*, 68–69. *La Voz Del Pueblo*, July 12, 1890. *Las Vegas Daily Optic*, July 5, 1890. Weigle, *Brothers of Light*, 86.
42. *Las Vegas Daily Optic*, July 5, 1890. *La Voz Del Pueblo*, July 12, 1890. 1880 United States Federal Census. 1900 United States Federal Census.
43. Mary Romero, "Class Struggle and Resistance Against the Transformation of Land Ownership and Usage in Northern New Mexico: The Case of Las Gorras Blancas," *Chicana/o-Latina/o Law Review* 26, no. 87 (2006): 98–99. Gonzáles-Berry and Maciel, *Contested Homeland*, 69. Schlesinger, "Las Gorras Blancas," 112. Mark Boardman, "The Assassination of Charles Bent," *True West*, February/March 2020.
44. Prince to Noble, August 11, 1890, Prince Papers. W. J. Mills to Prince, July 19, 1890, Prince Papers. Mills to Prince, July 22, 1890, Prince Papers. *Santa Fe New Mexican*, July 12, 1890. *Las Vegas Daily Optic*, July 19, 1890. *Deming (NM) Headlight*, July 16, 1890. 1885 New Mexico Territorial Census. Rosenbaum, *Mexicano Resistance*, 167–68.
45. Mills to Prince, July 19, 1890, Prince Papers. Mills to Prince, July 22, 1890, Prince Papers.
46. Mills to Prince, July 19, 1890, Prince Papers. Mills to Prince, July 22, 1890, Prince Papers. Prince to Noble, August 11, 1890, Prince Papers. Miguel Salazar to Prince, July 23, 1890, Prince Papers. *Las Vegas Daily Optic*, July 23, 1890. *Omaha Evening Bee*, July 16, 1890. *Current Wave* (Eminence, MO), July 24, 1890. *Atchison (KS) Daily Champion*, July 16, 1890. *Sioux City (IA) Journal*, July 16, 1890. *The Sentinel*, July 16, 1890. *Meriden (CT) Daily Republican*, July 16, 1890. *Morning Post* (Camden, NJ), July 16, 1890. *St. Paul Globe*, July 16, 1890. *Indianapolis Journal*, July 16, 1890. *Arkansas City (KS) Daily Traveller*, July 16, 1890. *The Times* (Streator, IL), July 17, 1890.
47. *Las Vegas Daily Optic*, July 30, 1890. *Las Vegas Daily Optic*, June 17, 1890. *Santa Fe New Mexican*, July 29, 1890. 1885 New Mexico Territorial Census. Prince to Noble, August 11, 1890, Prince Papers.
48. *Albuquerque Journal*, August 3, 1890. *Santa Fe New Mexican*, August 14, 1890. Schlesinger, "Las Gorras Blancas," 113.
49. *Las Vegas Daily Optic*, August 4, 1890. *Santa Fe New Mexican*, September 1, 1890. *Las Vegas Daily Optic*, November 3, 1890. 1880 United States Federal Census. US Register of Civil, Military, and Naval Service, 1863–1959, Ancestry.com.
50. Prince to Noble, August 11, 1890, Prince Papers. Schlesinger, "Las Gorras Blancas," 113–15.

51. Larson, "White Caps of New Mexico," 180. Schlesinger, "Las Gorras Blancas," 112–13. Ogden et al. to Powderly, August 8, 1890, Prince Papers. For Terence V. Powderly, see Vincent J. Falzone's *Terence V. Powderly: Middle Class Reformer* (Washington, DC: University Press of America, 1978); and Craig Phelan's *Grand Master Workman: Terence Powderly and the Knights of Labor* (Westport, CT: Greenwood Publishing).
52. *Las Vegas Daily Optic*, August 18, 1890. *Las Vegas Daily Optic*, September 25, 1890. Larson, "White Caps of New Mexico," 179–80. Schlesinger, "Las Gorras Blancas," 114.
53. Schlesinger, "Las Gorras Blancas," 115–17. *Las Vegas Daily Optic*, August 18, 1890.
54. *Las Vegas Daily Optic*, August 25, 1890. Territory vs. Nicanor Herrera, Carrying Arms, 1890, case no. 3429, box 45156, folder 3, collection 1960-043: Records of the United States Territorial and New Mexico District Courts for San Miguel County, NMSRCA.
55. Gonzáles-Berry and Maciel, *Contested Homeland*, 72–73. Schlesinger, "Las Gorras Blancas," 117–20.
56. *Las Vegas Daily Optic*, September 9, 1890.
57. Gonzáles-Berry and Maciel, *Contested Homeland*, 73–74. *La Voz Del Pueblo*, September 13, 1890. 1885 New Mexico Territorial Census. 1900 United States Federal Census.
58. *Santa Fe New Mexican*, September 8, 1890. *Santa Fe New Mexican*, September 9, 1890.
59. *Las Vegas Daily Optic*, September 25, 1890. *Santa Fe New Mexican*, September 26, 1890. *The Rustler*, September 26, 1890. *Carlsbad Current-Argus*, October 4, 1890. *Santa Fe New Mexican*, October 7, 1890. 1885 New Mexico Territorial Census. 1900 United States Federal Census.
60. *Las Vegas Daily Optic*, October 1, 1890. Gonzáles-Berry and Maciel, *Contested Homeland*, 73–74. 1880 United States Federal Census. 1885 New Mexico Territorial Census. 1900 United States Federal Census.
61. *Santa Fe New Mexican*, October 2, 1890. *Santa Fe New Mexican*, October 7, 1890. *Santa Fe New Mexican*, October 9, 1890. *Santa Fe New Mexican*, October 16, 1890. *Santa Fe New Mexican*, October 23, 1890. Larson, *New Mexico's Quest*, 164, 169–70.
62. *Las Vegas Daily Optic*, October 20, 1890. *Albuquerque Journal*, October 10, 1890. *Las Vegas Daily Optic*, October 15, 1890.
63. *Santa Fe New Mexican*, October 27, 1890. *Santa Fe New Mexican*, November 1, 1890. *Santa Fe New Mexican*, October 11, 1890. *Santa Fe New Mexican*, August 30, 1890. *Santa Fe New Mexican*, November 28, 1890. 1900 United States Federal Census.
64. *Albuquerque Journal*, March 1, 1890. *New Mexican Review*, May 26, 1887. *Santa Fe New Mexican*, November 3, 1890. 1870 United States Federal Census. 1880 United States Federal Census. 1885 New Mexico Territorial Census. 1900 United States Federal Census.
65. *Santa Fe New Mexican*, November 3, 1890.
66. *Las Vegas Daily Optic*, October 30, 1890. *Las Vegas Daily Optic*, November 1, 1890. *Las Vegas Daily Optic*, July 26, 1890.
67. *Las Vegas Daily Optic*, November 13, 1890. *Las Vegas Daily Optic*, October 1, 1890. *Las Vegas Daily Optic*, October 23, 1890. Rosenbaum, *Mexicano Resistance*, 169. 1880 United States Federal Census. 1885 New Mexico Territorial Census. 1900 United States Federal Census.
68. *Santa Fe New Mexican*, November 7, 1890. Gonzáles-Berry and Maciel, *Contested Homeland*, 74. *La Voz Del Pueblo*, November 22, 1890. *Las Vegas Daily Optic*, November 10, 1890.
69. Rosenbaum, *Mexicano Resistance*, 130. Otero, *My Life, 1882–1897*, 251.
70. *Las Vegas Daily Optic*, November 10, 1890. *La Voz Del Pueblo*, January 3, 1891. *Las Vegas Daily Optic*, January 3, 1891. *La Voz Del Pueblo*, January 17, 1891. *Las Vegas Daily Optic*, January 26, 1891. *Santa Fe New Mexican*, December 29, 1890.

71. *Santa Fe New Mexican*, December 29, 1890. *El Nuevo Mexicano* (Santa Fe), January 3, 1891. *Santa Fe New Mexican*, December 30, 1890. *Santa Fe New Mexican*, May 15, 1889.
72. *El Nuevo Mexicano*, January 3, 1891. *El Nuevo Mexicano*, January 17, 1891.
73. *El Nuevo Mexicano*, January 17, 1891. *Emporia (KS) Daily Republican*, January 26, 1891. *La Voz Del Pueblo*, January 17, 1891.
74. *El Nuevo Mexicano*, January 31, 1891. *Sierra County Advocate* (Kingston, NM), February 13, 1891.
75. *Santa Fe New Mexican*, February 6, 1891. *San Francisco Examiner*, December 15, 1899. *The Eagle* (Silver City, NM), April 15, 1896. Romero, "Class Struggle," 101–2. Tobias Duran, "Francisco Chavez, Thomas B. Catron, and Organized Political Violence in Santa Fe in the 1890s," *New Mexico Historical Review* 59, no. 3 (1984): 294. *Las Vegas Daily Optic*, February 23, 1891. One can read Charles Siringo's recollections of his time spent undercover with Los Gorras Blancas in his *A Cowboy Detective: A True Story of Twenty-Two Years with a World-Famous Detective Agency* (Arcadia Press, 2017), 48–50. Although, like much of Siringo's writings, it reads as somewhat embellished and self-aggrandizing.
76. *Santa Fe New Mexican*, February 26, 1891. Rosenbaum, *Mexicano Resistance*, 129. *Santa Fe New Mexican*, February 27, 1891. Schlesinger, "Las Gorras Blancas," 123.
77. Schlesinger, "Las Gorras Blancas," 123.
78. *Santa Fe New Mexican*, February 27, 1891. *La Voz Del Pueblo*, April 11, 1891.
79. Rosenbaum, *Mexicano Resistance*, 129.
80. *La Voz Del Pueblo*, April 11, 1891. *La Voz Del Pueblo*, March 7, 1891. *La Voz Del Pueblo*, March 28, 1891. *Las Vegas Daily Optic*, March 20, 1891. Duran, "Francisco Chavez," 294.

Notes for Chapter 15

1. *La Voz Del Pueblo*, April 11, 1891. Flores, *José Chávez y Chávez*, 46.
2. The two primary sources on Vicente Silva and the Society of Bandits of New Mexico are Manuel Cabeza de Baca, *Vicente Silva and His Forty Bandits: His Crimes and Retributions* (Santa Fe: Sunstone Press, 2022); and McGrath, *Vicente Silva and His Forty Thieves: The Vice Criminals of the 80's and 90's* (pub. by author, 1960). Titbits of information can also be found in Otero, *My Life, 1882–1897*. Although riddled with obviously fictional dialogue for dramatic effect, Cabeza de Baca's version of historical events in *Vicente Silva and His Forty Bandits* is reasonably reliable when compared to contemporary documents and reports.
3. 1860 United States Federal Census. 1870 United States Federal Census. 1880 United States Federal Census. 1885 New Mexico Territorial Census. Cabeza de Baca, *Vicente Silva*, 16–18. *Las Vegas Free Press*, June 25, 1892. Jesus Silva Death Certificate, photocopy, James B. Mills Collection, Australia (Mills Collection).
4. Cabeza de Baca, *Vicente Silva*, 16–17. Otero, *My Life, 1882–1897*, 168–69.
5. Otero, *My, 1882–1897*, 168. *Las Vegas Daily Optic*, September 23, 1890.
6. Cabeza de Baca, *Vicente Silva*, 18–19. Otero, *My Life, 1882–1897*, 169–70.
7. Otero, *My Life, 1882–1897*, 167–71. Cabeza de Baca, *Vicente Silva*, 20–21. 1870 United States Federal Census. 1880 United States Federal Census. 1885 New Mexico Territorial Census.
8. 1860 United States Federal Census. 1870 United States Federal Census. 1880 United States Federal Census. 1885 New Mexico Territorial Census. 1900 United States Federal Census. *Las Vegas Daily Optic*, May 12, 1891. *La Voz Del Pueblo*, May 16, 1891.
9. *La Voz Del Pueblo*, May 16, 1891. *Las Vegas Daily Optic*, May 12, 1891.

10. *La Voz Del Pueblo*, May 16, 1891. *Las Vegas Daily Optic*, May 11, 1891. *Las Vegas Daily Optic*, May 12, 1891. *Santa Fe New Mexican*, May 12, 1891. *Santa Fe New Mexican*, May 15, 1891. *El Nuevo Mexicano*, May 16, 1891. *Santa Fe New Mexican*, May 18, 1891. *Santa Fe Weekly Sun*, May 16, 1891. 1860 United States Federal Census. 1870 United States Federal Census. 1880 United States Federal Census. 1900 United States Federal Census. Tanner and Tanner, *New Mexico Territorial Penitentiary*, 20. Territory vs. Pablo and Nicanor Herrera, Assault with the intent to murder, 1891, case no. 3599, box 45158, folder 2, collection 1960-043: Records of the United States Territorial and New Mexico District Courts for San Miguel County, NMSRCA (hereafter cited as Territory vs. Pablo and Nicanor Herrera, case no. 3599). Territory vs. Pablo and Nicanor Herrera, murder, 1891, case no. 3600, box 45158, folder 2, collection 1960-043: Records of the United States Territorial and New Mexico District Courts for San Miguel County, NMSRCA (hereafter cited as Territory vs. Pablo and Nicanor Herrera, case no. 3600).
11. *Las Vegas Daily Optic*, May 13, 1891.
12. *Las Vegas Daily Optic*, May 11, 1891. *La Voz Del Pueblo*, July 25, 1891. 1885 New Mexico Territorial Census. Judge Henry Stiles Wooster's obituary can be found in the *Santa Fe New Mexican*, January 1, 1906.
13. *Santa Fe New Mexican*, May 12. 1891. *La Voz Del Pueblo*, May 16, 1891. *Las Vegas Daily Optic*, May 11, 1891. *Las Vegas Daily Optic*, May 12, 1891.
14. *La Voz Del Pueblo*, May 23, 1891. *Las Vegas Daily Optic*, June 8, 1891. *Santa Fe New Mexican*, May 18, 1891. *La Voz Del Pueblo*, June 13, 1891. *El Nuevo Mexicano*, May 23, 1891. 1885 New Mexico Territorial Census. Find a Grave Index, 1600s–Current, Ancestry.com. Sheriff José L. Lopez later filed expenses of $56.90 for the transportation of Pablo Herrera and W. B. Tipton to the Mora jail, as reported by *La Voz Del Pueblo*, November 26, 1891.
15. *Santa Fe New Mexican*, February 19, 1891. *Las Vegas Daily Optic*, June 8, 1891. *La Voz Del Pueblo*, August 8, 1891. Schlesinger, "Las Gorras Blancas," 124–25. *El Nuevo Mexicano*, June 13, 1891. *La Voz Del Pueblo*, May 16, 1891. *Las Vegas Daily Optic*, May 12, 1891.
16. *Santa Fe New Mexican*, April 23, 1889. *Santa Fe New Mexican*, August 10, 1891. *Santa Fe New Mexican*, August 11, 1891.
17. Rosenbaum, *Mexicano Resistance*, 129–30.
18. Territory vs. Juan Jose Herrera, assault with intent to murder, 1891, case no. 3598, box 45158, folder 2, collection 1960-043: Records of the United States Territorial and New Mexico District Courts for San Miguel County, NMSRCA. Territory vs. Juan Jose Herrera, attempt to murder, 1892, case no. 3621, box 45158, folder 4, collection 1960-043: Records of the United States Territorial and New Mexico District Courts for San Miguel County, NMSRCA. Territory vs. Pablo and Nicanor Herrera, case no. 3599. Territory vs. Pablo and Nicanor Herrera, case no. 3600. *Las Vegas Daily Optic*, May 31, 1892.
19. *Santa Fe New Mexican*, November 16, 1891.
20. *Las Vegas Daily Optic*, May 25, 1892. *Santa Fe New Mexican*, May 28, 1892. *Las Vegas Daily Optic*, May 31, 1892.
21. Duran, "Francisco Chavez," 297–300. *El Nuevo Mexicano*, December 17, 1892. *La Voz Del Pueblo*, June 4, 1892.
22. *Las Vegas Free Press*, August 3, 1892. *Las Vegas Daily Optic*, May 4, 1892. *La Voz Del Pueblo*, April 2, 1892.
23. *Santa Fe New Mexican*, October 17, 1892. *Las Vegas Free Press*, October 6, 1892. *Santa Fe New Mexican*, October 7, 1892.
24. *Las Vegas Free Press*, October 10, 1892. *Las Vegas Free Press*, October 7, 1892. *La Voz Del Pueblo*, October 15, 1892.

25. Rosenbaum, *Mexicano Resistance*, 132–33. *Las Vegas Free Press*, October 10, 1892. *Las Vegas Free Press*, October 7, 1892.
26. Manuel C. de Baca to Prince, October 10, 1892, Prince Papers. Tanner and Tanner, *New Mexico Territorial Penitentiary*, 40.
27. *Las Vegas Free Press*, October 10, 1892. *Las Vegas Free Press*, October 12, 1892. *La Voz Del Pueblo*, October 15, 1892.
28. Cabeza de Baca, *Vicente Silva*, 23–27. *Las Vegas Free Press*, October 29, 1892. *Las Vegas Free Press*, October 24, 1892.
29. *La Voz Del Pueblo*, October 29, 1892. *Las Vegas Free Press*, October 29, 1892. *Las Vegas Free Press*, October 24, 1892.
30. Rosenbaum, *Mexicano Resistance*, 178. *Santa Fe New Mexican*, November 12, 1892. *La Voz Del Pueblo*, November 12, 1892. *Las Vegas Free Press*, November 10, 1892. *Santa Fe New Mexican*, December 23, 1892.
31. *Santa Fe New Mexican*, November 21, 1892. *Santa Fe New Mexican*, November 18, 1892. *Albuquerque Journal*, November 20, 1892. *El Nuevo Mexicano*, December 17, 1892.
32. *Santa Fe New Mexican*, December 12, 1892. *El Nuevo Mexicano*, December 17, 1892.
33. *Santa Fe New Mexican*, January 21, 1893. Otero, *My Life, 1882–1897*, 167.
34. Rosenbaum, *Mexican Resistance*, 132–134. Gonzáles-Berry and Maciel, *Contested Homeland*, 76. Correia, "Retribution Will Be Their Reward," 65.
35. *Santa Fe New Mexican*, May 25, 1894. Cabeza de Baca, *Vicente Silva*, 21. Flores, *José Chávez y Chávez*, 46.
36. Territory vs. Jose Chavez y Chavez, murder, 1894, case no. 3765, box 45160, folder 1, collection 1960-043: Records of the United States Territorial and New Mexico District Courts for San Miguel County Criminal, NMSRCA (hereafter cited as Territory vs. Chavez y Chavez, case no. 3765). *Santa Fe New Mexican*, May 25, 1894. 1885 New Mexico Territorial Census. 1860 United States Federal Census. Cabeza de Baca, *Vicente Silva*, 53.
37. Julyan, *Place Names*, 208. Cabeza de Baca, *Vicente Silva*, 28. *Santa Fe New Mexican*, March 18, 1895.
38. Cabeza de Baca, *Vicente Silva*, 28–30. *La Voz Del Pueblo*, January 28, 1893. Otero, *My Life, 1882–1897*, 177–78.
39. *Santa Fe New Mexican*, May 12, 1894. *Santa Fe New Mexican*, April 13, 1894. *Santa Fe New Mexican*, May 25, 1894. 1880 United States Federal Census.
40. For the murder of Gabriel Sandoval, I have largely relied on the testimony of Guadalupe Caballero, Julian Trujillo, and José Valdéz provided during the trial of Julian Trujillo, found in Territory vs. Julian Trujillo, 1895, case no. 3755, box 45159, folder 5, collection 1960-043: Records of the United States Territorial and New Mexico District Courts for San Miguel County, Proposed Record and Bill of Exceptions, NMSRCA (hereafter cited as Territory vs. Trujillo). Naturally, Julian Trujillo tied to distance himself from the murder when providing his testimony by unconvincingly portraying himself as a reluctant participant. Documents related to the José Chávez y Chávez case can be found in Territory vs. Chavez y Chavez, case no. 3765. A relatively accurate report drawn from the case testimony provided during the Chávez y Chávez trial can be found in *Las Vegas Daily Optic*, October 27, 1897. Manuel Cabeza de Baca's depiction of the murder of Gabriel Sandoval in *Vicente Silva*, 35–41, is unfortunately riddled with obviously fictional dialogue. Incidentally, when Cabeza de Baca published his *Vicente Silva and His Forty Bandits*, the author changed the name of Silva's mistress to Flor de la Peña, clearly to protect the identity of the woman in question. Miguel Otero did the same when using the pseudonym Flor de la Peña in *Life on the Frontier, 1882–1897*. There is no contemporary record demonstrating the

existence of a woman with that name in Las Vegas, San Miguel County. It is obvious from the Territory vs. Trujillo case file, and other reports, that the real name of Vicente Silva's mistress was Rosario Lucera de Baca.

41. Flores, *José Chávez y Chávez*, 51–52.
42. Cabeza de Baca, *Vicente Silva*, 45–46. 1900 United States Federal Census. *Santa Fe New Mexican*, April 10, 1893.
43. *Santa Fe New Mexican*, May 5, 1893. *Santa Fe New Mexican*, May 9, 1893. Geneanet Community Trees Index, Ancestry.com. 1860 United States Federal Census. 1870 United States Federal Census. 1880 United States Federal Census. 1900 United States Federal Census.
44. Cabeza de Baca, *Vicente Silva*, 42–44, 47–50.
45. Territory vs. Jose Chavez y Chavez, assault and battery, 1893, case no. 3715, box 45159, folder 2, collection 1960-043: Records of the United States Territorial and New Mexico District Courts for San Miguel County Criminal, NMSRCA. *Santa Fe New Mexican*, May 11, 1893. Flores, *José Chávez y Chávez*, 52.
46. *Santa Fe New Mexican*, May 12, 1893.
47. *Santa Fe New Mexican*, May 5, 1893. *Santa Fe New Mexican*, May 12, 1893.
48. Cabeza de Baca, *Vicente Silva*, 50–52.
49. Cabeza de Baca, *Vicente Silva*, 47–51, 68.
50. *San Francisco Call*, July 3, 1898. *Santa Fe New Mexican*, March 18, 1895. Cabeza de Baca, *Vicente Silva*, 67.
51. The obituary for Emma Silva-Waers can be found in the *Kansas City Times*, December 7, 1957. 1880 United States Federal Census. 1900 United States Federal Census 1910 United States Federal Census. Missouri Death Certificates, 1910–1969, Missouri Office of the Secretary of State, Jefferson City. Missouri Marriage Records [microfilm], Missouri State Archives, Jefferson City. Find a Grave Index, 1600s–Current, Ancestry.com. *Las Vegas Daily Optic*, July 7, 1893. Details about the brief return of Emma Silva-Waers to New Mexico can be found in *La Voz Del Pueblo*, July 11, 1903; *Albuquerque Morning Journal*, July 9, 1903; and *Las Vegas Daily Optic*, July 7, 1903. Otero, *My Life, 1882–1897*, 178.
52. *Santa Fe New Mexican*, May 31, 1893. *Santa Fe New Mexican*, May 27, 1893. *La Voz Del Pueblo*, June 3, 1893. Cabeza de Baca, *Vicente Silva*, 73–74.
53. *Santa Fe New Mexican*, June 23, 1893. *Santa Fe New Mexican*, July 28, 1893.
54. *Santa Fe New Mexican*, August 3, 1893. *Santa Fe New Mexican*, December 5, 1893. 1860 United States Federal Census. 1870 United States Federal Census. 1880 United States Federal Census. 1900 United States Federal Census. Geneanet Community Trees Index, Ancestry.com.
55. *La Voz Del Pueblo*, December 16, 1893.
56. *Santa Fe New Mexican*, December 21, 1893. *Santa Fe New Mexican*, December 23, 1893.
57. *Santa Fe New Mexican*, April 12, 1894. *Santa Fe New Mexican*, May 18, 1894. *La Voz Del Pueblo*, May 19, 1894. *La Voz Del Pueblo*, April 7, 1894. Rafael Romero's obituary can be found in the *Spanish-American* (Roy, NM), July 27, 1918.
58. *Santa Fe New Mexican*, April 12, 1894. *Santa Fe New Mexican*, May 18, 1894. *La Voz Del Pueblo*, May 19, 1894. Testimony of Dr. M. M. Milligan, Territory vs. Trujillo. The coroner's report for Gabriel Sandoval and details about the discovery of his corpse can be found in the *Las Vegas Daily Optic*, April 13, 1894.
59. *Las Vegas Daily Optic*, April 11, 1894. *Santa Fe New Mexican*, April 13, 1894.
60. *Santa Fe New Mexican*, April 12, 1894. *Las Vegas Daily Optic*, April 13, 1894.
61. Flores, *José Chávez y Chávez*, 68–69.

62. A detailed account of the capture of Germán Maestas, including the snippets of dialogue, can be found in *El Independiente*(Las Vegas, NM), April 21, 1894. *Santa Fe New Mexican*, May 25, 1894. Cabeza de Baca, *Vicente Silva*, 75–78.
63. *Santa Fe New Mexican*, April 17, 1894. *Santa Fe New Mexican*, May 25, 1894. 1870 United States Federal Census. 1880 United States Federal Census. 1885 New Mexico Territorial Census. Cabeza de Baca *Vicente Silva*, 56.
64. Cabeza de Baca, *Vicente Silva*, 58. *Santa Fe New Mexican*, April 17, 1894. *Santa Fe New Mexican*, April 21, 1894. *Santa Fe New Mexican*, May 25, 1894.
65. Flores, *José Chávez y Chávez*, 53–74. *Santa Fe New Mexican*, April 21, 1894. When called to the stand during his trial in 1896, José Chávez y Chávez would testify that he remained in Las Vegas following the discovery of Gabriel Sandoval's corpse until fleeing the city on the night of April 24, 1894. He also claimed to have had no knowledge of the arrest of his fellow policemen Eugenio Alarid or Manuel Gonzáles y Baca at the time. A letter written in Las Vegas on April 20, 1894 (published by the *Santa Fe New Mexican* the following day), states that more than a dozen arrests had been made by that time. The letter further states that "twenty-one persons have been indicted" for the murder of Patricio Maes, and "three men have been indicted for the murder of Gabriel Sandoval." José Chávez y Chávez would have had to have been deaf and blind to be unaware of the arrest of Eugenio Alarid and various other individuals by that point in time. He was either misleading the jury or simply mistaken about the date of his departure when testifying at his trial. In all probability, Chávez y Chávez fled Las Vegas at least several days prior to April 24. The "public meeting" that was held "at the Opera House" on the night of April 20—as detailed by the letter published in the *Santa Fe New Mexican* the following day—was likely the "great deal of noise in the plaza" to which Chávez y Chávez was referring when describing the night of his departure in his testimony.
66. Flores, *José Chávez y Chávez*, 73–77.
67. Flores, *José Chávez y Chávez*, 81–82.
68. Flores, *José Chávez y Chávez*, 82–84.
69. *Santa Fe New Mexican*, May 3, 1894.
70. *Las Vegas Daily Optic*, May 3, 1894. *Santa Fe New Mexican*, April 27, 1894. *Santa Fe New Mexican*, May 4, 1894.
71. *Santa Fe New Mexican*, May 28, 1894. Cabeza de Baca, *Vicente Silva*, 58.
72. *Santa Fe New Mexican*, May 1, 1894. *New Mexican Review*, May 10, 1894. *Santa Fe New Mexican*, May 24, 1894. *Santa Fe New Mexican*, May 25, 1894. Cabeza de Baca, *Vicente Silva*, 59.
73. *Santa Fe New Mexican*, May 11, 1894.
74. *Santa Fe New Mexican*, May 12, 1894.
75. Details about the execution of Germán Maestas, including the snippets of dialogue, can be found in the *Santa Fe New Mexican*, May 25, 1894, and the *Santa Fe New Mexican*, May 26, 1894.
76. US World War I Draft Registration Cards, 1917–1918, Ancestry.com. 1880 United States Federal Census. 1885 New Mexico Territorial Census. 1900 United States Federal Census. New Mexico, US, Deaths, 1889–1945, Ancestry.com. *Santa Fe New Mexican*, May 25, 1894. *Santa Fe New Mexican*, May 26, 1894. *La Voz Del Pueblo*, May 26, 1894.
77. Flores, *José Chávez y Chávez*, 75.
78. *La Voz Del Pueblo*, July 28, 1894. *Santa Fe New Mexican*, July 26, 1894. *Santa Fe New Mexican*, July 28, 1894.
79. *Santa Fe New Mexican*, July 27, 1894. *La Voz Del Pueblo*, July 28, 1894. *Santa Fe New Mexican*, July 28, 1894.
80. *La Voz Del Pueblo*, July 28, 1894. *Las Vegas Daily Optic*, July 27, 1894. *Santa Fe New Mexican*, July 28, 1894. *Santa Fe New Mexican*, July 30, 1894.

81. *La Voz Del Pueblo*, August 4, 1894. *El Independiente*, August 4, 1894. *Santa Fe New Mexican*, August 6, 1894. *El Independiente*, August 25, 1894. Rosenbaum, *Mexicano Resistance*, 135.
82. Rosenbaum, *Mexicano Resistance*, 35–36. For Simón Bolívar, see Marie Arana, *Bolívar: American Liberator*.
83. Flores, *José Chávez y Chávez*, 84–87.
84. There are multiple reports of Pablo Herrera's death in contemporary newspapers. The most detailed report, which includes information about the coroner's inquest, can be found in *La Voz Del Pueblo*, December 29, 1894. It is that report which I have used as my primary source for the death of Pablo Herrera. The other contemporary reports, which frequently conflict with each other regarding details, can be found in *Santa Fe New Mexican*, December 24, 1894, *Evening Citizen* (Albuquerque), December 24, 1894, *Santa Fe New Mexican*, December 26, 1894, *New Mexican Review*, December 27, 1894, and *New Mexican Review*, January 3, 1895.

Notes for Chapter 16

1. *Santa Fe New Mexican*, March 18, 1895.
2. *Santa Fe New Mexican*, March 18, 1895. *Santa Fe New Mexican*, April 1, 1895. *Santa Fe New Mexican*, April 13, 1895. *Santa Fe New Mexican*, November 19, 1895. Cabeza de Baca, *Vicente Silva*, 79–85.
3. *Santa Fe New Mexican*, April 22, 1895. *La Voz Del Pueblo*, April 25, 1895.
4. *Sierra County Advocate*, June 7, 1895. 1870 United States Federal Census. 1880 United States Federal Census.
5. *Sierra County Advocate*, June 7, 1895.
6. *Sierra County Advocate*, June 7, 1895. *Santa Fe New Mexican*, June 1, 1895. *La Voz Del Pueblo*, June 1, 1895.
7. Duran, "Francisco Chavez," 300–307. Otero, *My Life, 1882–1897*, 264. *Santa Fe New Mexican*, January 26, 1894. *Santa Fe New Mexican*, January 23, 1894. *La Voz Del Pueblo*, June 1, 1895. *La Voz Del Pueblo*, June 8, 1895. *Santa Fe New Mexican*, June 7, 1895. *Santa Fe New Mexican*, June 15, 1895. *Santa Fe New Mexican*, June 17, 1895.
8. Duran, "Francisco Chavez," 300–307.
9. *Santa Fe New Mexico*, June 10, 1895. *Las Vegas Daily Optic*, November 18, 1897.
10. *Santa Fe New Mexican*, November 16, 1895. *Sierra County Advocate*, November 1, 1895. *Santa Fe New Mexican*, November 13, 1895. *Santa Fe New Mexican*, November 20, 1895. 1885 New Mexico Territorial Census. 1880 United States Federal Census. Flores, *José Chávez y Chávez*, 43. *Las Vegas Daily Optic*, September 3, 1896. 1910 United States Federal Census.
11. *Santa Fe New Mexican*, November 19, 1895.
12. For the murder and disappearance of Albert and Henry Fountain, see Corey Recko's *Murder on the White Sands: The Disappearance of Albert and Henry Fountain* (Denton: University of North Texas Press, 2007).
13. *Las Vegas Daily Optic*, March 7, 1896. *Santa Fe New Mexican*, March 9, 1896. *Albuquerque Journal*, March 10, 1896. *La Voz Del Pueblo*, July 25, 1896. *La Voz Del Pueblo*, July 4, 1896. *La Voz Del Pueblo*, April 25, 1896.
14. *Santa Fe New Mexican*, May 15, 1896. Tanner and Tanner, *New Mexico Territorial Penitentiary*, 102.
15. *Las Vegas Daily Optic*, April 16, 1896. *Las Vegas Daily Optic*, April 21, 1896. *Santa Fe New Mexican*, June 5, 1896. *Albuquerque Journal*, June 2, 1896. *Albuquerque Journal*, May 21, 1896. *Las Vegas Daily Optic*, May 27, 1896.

16. *Las Vegas Daily Optic*, May 28, 1896.
17. *Las Vegas Daily Optic*, May 28, 1896. Tanner and Tanner, *New Mexico Territorial Penitentiary*, 65. *Santa Fe New Mexican*, May 15, 1896. Flores, *José Chávez y Chávez*, 45.
18. Daniel Flores admirably reproduced the testimony of José Chávez y Chávez during his trial in *José Chávez y Chávez*, 43–89, although the trial occurred in late May–early June 1896, not June 1895.
19. *Las Vegas Daily Optic*, June 2, 1896. *Las Vegas Daily Optic*, June 13, 1896. *Santa Fe New Mexican*, June 15, 1896. *Las Vegas Daily Optic*, June 12, 1896.
20. *Las Vegas Daily Optic*, July 21, 1896. *Albuquerque Journal*, September 2, 1896. Flores, *José Chávez y Chávez*, 92.
21. Lincoln County Marriages, June 1869–December 1910, Church of Jurisdiction in Santa Rita Catholic Church, Carrizozo, Territory of New Mexico, microfilm FHL 016-756, NMSRCA. *Las Vegas Daily Optic*, September 7, 1896.
22. *Las Vegas Daily Optic*, November 25, 1896. *Las Vegas Daily Optic*, November 27, 1896. *Las Vegas Daily Optic*, December 1, 1896.
23. *Las Vegas Daily Optic*, December 1, 1896. *Las Vegas Daily Optic*, December 11, 1896. *Santa Fe New Mexican*, December 11, 1896.
24. *Las Vegas Daily Optic*, December 11, 1896.
25. *Las Vegas Daily Optic*, December 11, 1896. *Las Vegas Daily Optic*, December 14, 1896.
26. Duran, "Francisco Chavez," 305–306. *La Voz Del Pueblo*, June 1, 1895.
27. *El Independiente*, May 22, 1897. *Las Vegas Daily Optic*, November 15, 1898.
28. *Santa Fe New Mexican*, February 24, 1897. Otero, *My Life, 1882–1897*, 288–89.
29. Otero, *My Life, 1882–1897*, 289–94. *Santa Fe New Mexican*, June 14, 1897. Incidentally, a week after Miguel Antonio Otero Jr. swore his oath as governor in Santa Fe, the former district attorney for San Miguel County, Miguel Salazar, suddenly died from "stomach trouble" while visiting his father in Colorado on the morning June 22, 1897, as reported by the *Santa Fe New Mexican*, June 23, 1897.
30. *Santa Fe New Mexican*, August 25, 1897. *Santa Fe New Mexican*, August 26, 1897. *Sacramento Daily Record-Union*, October 3, 1897. *San Francisco Chronicle*, October 3, 1897. *Arizona Daily Star*, October 3, 1897. *El Paso Herald*, October 8, 1897. *Santa Fe New Mexican*, October 4, 1897. Flores, *José Chávez y Chávez*, 106.
31. *Las Vegas Daily Optic*, October 4, 1897. *Santa Fe New Mexican*, October 5, 1897. *Las Vegas Daily Optic*, October 12, 1897. *Santa Fe New Mexican*, October 11, 1897.
32. *Las Vegas Daily Optic*, October 4, 1897. *Las Vegas Daily Optic*, October 19, 1897. John D. W. Veeder to Governor M. A. Otero, Las Vegas, New Mexico, October 12, 1897, Otero Papers. Veeder & Veeder application for commutation of in the case of Jose Chavez y Chavez, 1897, Otero Papers.
33. *Santa Fe New Mexican*, November 9, 1896. *The Eagle* (Sierra County, NM), November 4, 1896. *Western Liberal* (Lordsburg, NM), November 13, 1896. *Western Liberal*, December 11, 1896. *Santa Fe New Mexican*, October 12, 1897. *Las Vegas Daily Optic*, October 19, 1897. *Las Vegas Daily Optic*, October 4, 1897.
34. Juan Ortega et al. to Otero, October 1897, Otero Papers. Demetrio Perea et al. to Otero, Lincoln County, New Mexico, Otero Papers.
35. Gideon D. Bantz to Otero, October 12, 1897, Silver City, New Mexico, Otero Papers. Needham C. Collier to Otero, October 13, 1897, Albuquerque, New Mexico, Otero Papers. Andrieus A. Jones to Otero, October 13, 1897, East Las Vegas, New Mexico, Otero Papers. Adin H. Whitmore to Otero, October 16, 1897, East Las Vegas, New Mexico, Otero Papers.
36. Frank Springer to Otero, October 16, 1897, Otero Papers. J. M. Cunningham to Otero, October 16, 1897, Otero Papers.
37. *Las Vegas Daily Optic*, November 19, 1897.

38. E. V. Long to Otero, October 20, 1897, East Las Vegas, New Mexico, Otero Papers. *Las Vegas Daily Optic*, October 19, 1897. *Santa Fe New Mexican*, October 25, 1897. Long to Otero, November 6, 1897, Las Vegas, New Mexico, Otero Papers.
39. Charles Springer to Otero, October 20, 1897, Raton, New Mexico, Otero Papers. Proclamation of Governor Otero regarding the sentence and scheduled execution of Jose Chavez y Chavez, Santa Fe, New Mexico, October 23, 1897, Otero Papers. *Santa Fe New Mexican*, October 23, 1897.
40. J. H. Hunter to Otero, October 25, 1897, Omaha, Nebraska, Otero Papers. 1900 United States Federal Census.
41. Reprieve for Jose Chaves y Chaves, signed by Miguel Antonio Otero, Governor of New Mexico Territory, Executive Office, Santa Fe, New Mexico, October 26, 1897, Otero Papers. *Santa Fe New Mexican*, October 25, 1897.
42. *Las Vegas Daily Optic*, October 27, 1897.
43. Harry Whigham to Otero, November 1, 1897, Raton, New Mexico, Otero Papers. Long to Otero, November 6, 1897, Las Vegas, New Mexico, Otero Papers. *Las Vegas Daily Optic*, November 12, 1897.
44. *Santa Fe New Mexican*, November 17, 1897. *Las Vegas Daily Optic*, November 18, 1897.
45. *Las Vegas Daily Optic*, November 18, 1897. *Las Vegas Daily Optic*, August 1, 1896. *Las Vegas Daily Optic*, November 15, 1897. *Albuquerque Journal*, November 20, 1897.
46. *Las Vegas Daily Optic*, November 18, 1897. *Santa Fe New Mexican*, November 19, 1897.
47. Long, Wm H. Pope to Otero, telegram, Plaza Hotel, Las Vegas, New Mexico, November 20, 1897, Otero Papers. John D. W. Veeder to Otero, telegram, Plaza Hotel, Las Vegas, New Mexico, 2:02 p.m., November 20, 1897, Otero Papers. Commutation for Jose Chaves y Chaves, signed by Miguel Antonio Otero, Governor of New Mexico Territory, Executive Office, Santa Fe, New Mexico, November 20, 1897, Otero Papers.
48. *Los Angeles Times*, November 22, 1897. *Larimer County Independent* (Fort Collins, CO), November 25, 1897. *San Francisco Call*, November 22, 1897. *Record-Union*, November 22, 1997. *Morning News* (Wilmington, DE), November 23, 1897. *St. Helena (CA) Star*, November 26, 1897. *Salt Lake Herald*, November 22, 1897. *Buffalo Inquirer*, November 22, 1897. *Las Cruces Sun-News*, November 26, 1897. *St. Louis Globe-Democrat*, December 12, 1897.
49. A. A. Jones's obituary can be found in the *Indianapolis Times*, December 21, 1927. 1900 United States Federal Census. 1910 United States Federal Census. Biographical Directory of the United States Congress, 1774–2005, Find a Grave Index, 1600s–Current, Ancestry.com. Miguel Antonio Otero, *My Nine Years as Governor of the Territory of New Mexico, 1897–1906: Facsimile of Original 1940 Edition* (Santa Fe: Sunstone Press, 2007), 106–7.
50. Special Schedules of the 1890 Census. 1870 United States Federal Census. 1880 United States Federal Census. *Santa Fe New Mexican*, November 23, 1897. *Santa Fe New Mexican*, February 27, 1897. *Las Vegas Daily Optic*, November 4, 1897. *Albuquerque Journal*, November 6, 1897.
51. Tanner and Tanner, *New Mexico Territorial Penitentiary*, 87.

Notes for Chapter 17

1. 1900 United States Federal Census. *White Oaks (NM) Eagle*, October 13, 1898. Ms 0249, box 11, folder 2, Elected County Officials Lincoln County, 1872–1974, Weisner Papers.
2. *White Oaks Eagle*, October 18, 1894. *White Oaks Eagle*, November 15, 1894. *White Oaks Eagle*, September 17, 1896. *Santa Fe New Mexican*, August 14, 1894. *Santa Fe New Mexican*,

June 13, 1896. *Santa Fe New Mexican*, September 21, 1894. *Santa Fe New Mexican*, November 13, 1896. *Santa Fe New Mexican*, May 9, 1896. *White Oaks Eagle*, August 23, 1894.
3. *White Oaks Eagle*, January 27, 1898. *New Mexican Review*, March 3, 1898. *White Oaks Eagle*, January 20, 1898. *White Oaks Eagle*, April 21, 1898.
4. Lincoln County Marriages, June 1869–December 1910, Church of Jurisdiction in Santa Rita Catholic Church, Carrizozo, Territory of New Mexico, microfilm FHL 016-756, NMSRCA (hereafter cited as Lincoln County Marriages, June 1869–December 1910). *White Oaks Eagle*, November 24, 1898.
5. For Miguel Antonio Otero Jr.'s time as governor of New Mexico Territory, see Otero, *My Nine Years as Governor*. For the Spanish-American War, see David F. Trask's *The War with Spain in 1898* (Lincoln: University of Nebraska Press, 1996). For Leonard Wood see Jack McCallum's *Leonard Wood: Rough Rider, Surgeon, Architect of American Imperialism* (New York: New York University Press, 2006).
6. *White Oaks Eagle*, May 25, 1899.
7. *El Paso Herald*, November 15, 1899. *White Oaks Eagle*, May 31, 1900.
8. *White Oaks Eagle*, December 14, 1899.
9. 1900 United States Federal Census. Lincoln County Marriages, June 1869–December 1910.
10. 1900 United States Federal Census. Yginio Salazar wrote his name as "Yginio Salazar (de Chavez)" when filling out an insurance form with the Union Central Life Insurance Company of Cincinnati, Ohio, for himself and his wife Isabel in the early twentieth century. Salazar insurance policy.
11. Wilson, *Merchants*, 156–60. Lummis, *Land of Poco Tiempo*, 13. *White Oaks Eagle*, January 25, 1900. *White Oaks Eagle*, June 28, 1900. Find a Grave Index, 1600s–Current, Ancestry.com
12. Margarita Salazar was recorded as the biological daughter of José and Ginovera Salazar in the baptismal records of the Santa Rita Catholic Church, Carrizozo, for 1901, which would explain why Margarita was initially recorded as Yginio and Isabel Salazar's "niece" in the 1910 United States Federal Census when residing with the couple. Baptismal Records for 1901, page no. 99, Santa Rita Catholic Church Records, Carrizozo, New Mexico (Xerox copy, courtesy of Massimo De Vito), Mills Collection. 1910 United States Federal Census. Find a Grave Index, 1600s–Current, Ancestry.com. Social Security Administration, Washington, DC, Social Security Death Index, Master File.
13. *White Oaks Eagle*, May 24, 1900.
14. *White Oaks Eagle*, May 31, 1900. *White Oaks Eagle*, July 26, 1900.
15. *White Oaks Eagle*, October 4, 1900. *White Oaks Eagle*, November 15, 1900. *Las Vegas Weekly Optic and Stock Grower*, January 19, 1901.
16. *Las Vegas Weekly Optic and Stock Grower*, January 19, 1901.
17. *White Oaks Eagle*, November 7, 1901. *Socorro (NM) Chieftain*, November 30, 1901. *White Oaks Eagle*, July 17, 1902. *White Oaks Eagle*, August 21, 1902. *White Oaks Eagle*, September 18, 1902. AFamilyofWest.com. 1910 United States Federal Census.
18. *White Oaks Eagle*, May 11, 1899. *Albuquerque Daily Citizen*, April 18, 1902.
19. *Albuquerque Daily Citizen*, April 18, 1902.
20. Tanner and Tanner, *New Mexico Territorial Penitentiary*, 103.
21. *Santa Fe New Mexican*, April 10, 1902. *Albuquerque Citizen*, April 10, 1902. *Albuquerque Citizen*, April 11, 1902. 1870 United States Federal Census.
22. *La Voz Del Pueblo*, October 11, 1902. *Albuquerque Citizen*, October 8, 1902.
23. James Bailey Blackshear, *Honor and Defiance: A History of the Las Vegas Land Grant in New Mexico* (Santa Fe: Sunstone Press, 2013), 156–59. Rosenbaum, *Mexicano Resistance*, 139. *Albuquerque Journal*, September 6, 1904. *Las Vegas Daily Optic*, November 3, 1903. *Deming Headlight*, December 3, 1903.

Notes for Chapter 17

24. Flores, *José Chávez y Chávez*, 11. California Death Index, 1940–1997, Ancestry.com. 1900 United States Federal Census. 1910 United States Federal Census. Dionicio Chávez Death Certificate, photocopy, courtesy of Margaret Chávez Slayton. Author correspondence with Margaret Chávez Slayton, October 2023. Lincoln County Marriages, June 1869–December 1910.
25. *White Oaks Eagle*, February 26, 1903. *Las Vegas Daily Optic*, March 7, 1903. *White Oaks Eagle*, April 23, 1903. *White Oaks Eagle*, January 1, 1903.
26. *White Oaks Eagle*, January 22, 1903. 1900 United States Federal Census. *Albuquerque Weekly Citizen*, August 29, 1903. *White Oaks Eagle*, August 6, 1903. *Santa Fe New Mexican*, August 13, 1903. *Roswell Daily Record*, November 11, 1903. *Roswell Daily Record*, November 10, 1903. *Roswell Daily Record*, October 31, 1903. *Las Vegas Daily Optic*, April 11, 1905.
27. *La Voz Del Pueblo*, December 26, 1903.
28. *Albuquerque Morning Journal*, January 24, 1904. *Santa Fe New Mexican*, June 7, 1904. *Albuquerque Journal*, September 23, 1904.
29. *Albuquerque Journal*, November 28, 1904. *Las Vegas Daily Optic*, November 28, 1904. *Santa Fe New Mexican*, November 28, 1904. *Las Vegas Daily Optic*, November 29, 1904. *Santa Fe New Mexican*, November 30, 1904. *Albuquerque Journal*, November 30, 1904. *Albuquerque Journal*, December 7, 1904. *Roswell Daily Record*, August 14, 1907. *Albuquerque Journal*, January 25, 1905. *Albuquerque Journal*, August 8, 1907. *Albuquerque Journal*, January 27, 1905. *Santa Fe New Mexican*, November 29, 1904. Find a Grave Index, 1600s–Current, Ancestry.com.
30. 1900 United States Federal Census. 1910 United States Federal Census. *White Oaks Eagle*, August 7, 1902. *Roswell Daily Record*, September 22, 1904. *El Farol* (Capitan, NM), April 10, 1906. *Santa Fe New Mexican*, February 17, 1906.
31. *El Farol*, April 10, 1906.
32. *El Farol*, April 10, 1906. *El Farol*, April 17, 1906. *El Farol*, May 15, 1906. *El Farol*, June 12, 1906. *El Farol*, November 20, 1906. *Santa Fe New Mexican*, April 5, 1906. *Albuquerque Journal*, April 2, 1906.
33. 1910 United States Federal Census. Trinidad Montoya-Chávez's obituary can be found in the *Santa Fe New Mexican*, February 12, 1957. Martín Chávez Jr.'s obituary can be found in the *Santa Fe New Mexican*, February 10, 1987. Find a Grave Index, 1600s–Current, Ancestry.com. *Roswell Daily Record*, April 5, 1907. *El Paso Herald*, April 9, 1907.
34. 1910 United States Federal Census. *Roswell Daily Record*, September 10, 1907.
35. *Albuquerque Citizen*, September 27, 1907. *Wichita (KS) Beacon*, October 1, 1907. *El Paso Herald*, September 28, 1907. *Roswell Daily Record*, September 30, 1907. *Binger (OK) Journal*, November 1, 1907.
36. *Gotebo (OK) Gazette*, November 1, 1907. *Binger Journal*, November 1, 1907. Mills, *Billy the Kid*, 559–60.
37. *Roswell Daily Record*, March 2, 1908. For the death of Pat Garrett, see David G. Thomas, *Killing Pat Garrett: The Wild West's Most Famous Lawman—Murder or Self-Defense?* (Las Cruces, NM: Doc45 Publishing, 2019).
38. Otero, *Real Billy*, 98.
39. Scipio Salazar to Governor George Curry, December 11, 1907, box 18032, folder 234, Penal Papers, Paroles, Jose Chavez y Chavez 1907–1910, collection 1959-092: Governor George Curry Papers (Curry Papers), NMSRCA.
40. Petition to Governor Curry, Curry Papers.
41. Governor Curry executive order for the conditional parole of Jose Chavez y Chavez, January 11, 1909, Curry Papers.
42. *Las Vegas Optic*, September 16, 1909. *El Paso Times*, July 12, 1911.

43. 1920 United States Federal Census.
44. *Roswell Daily Record*, November 17, 1908. 1910 United States Federal Census. Find a Grave Index, 1600s–Current, Ancestry.com.
45. Wilson, *Merchants*, 162–64.
46. *Carrizozo (NM) Outlook*, February 18, 1910. *Albuquerque Journal*, May 31, 1910. 1910 United States Federal Census. Find a Grave Index, 1600s–Current, Ancestry.com.
47. *Carrizozo Outlook*, November 11, 1910. *El Paso Herald*, November 3, 1910.
48. *El Paso Times*, June 9, 1911. *Albuquerque Journal*, June 9, 1911. *Carrizozo Outlook*, September 29, 1911. *Santa Fe New Mexican*, October 2, 1911. *Carlsbad Current-Argus*, October 13, 1911.
49. *Washington Times*, January 6, 1912. *Albuquerque Journal*, January 15, 1912.
50. *Albuquerque Journal*, October 13, 1912. *Evening Herald*, October 14, 1912. *Evening Herald*, October 21, 1913. *Las Vegas Optic*, October 22, 1913. 1910 United States Federal Census. Lincoln County, New Mexico, World War I Draft Registration Cards, 1917–1918, Ancestry.com.
51. *Carlsbad Current-Argus*, August 21, 1914. Lincoln County, New Mexico, World War I Draft Registration Cards, 1917–1918, Ancestry.com. *Santa Fe New Mexican*, October 23, 1914. 1910 United States Federal Census.
52. For Emiliano Zapata see John Womack Jr.'s *Zapata and the Mexican Revolution* (New York: Vintage Books, 1970). For Pancho Villa see Friedrich Katz, *The Life and Times of Pancho Villa* (Stanford, CA: Stanford University Press, 1998). For the Mexican Revolution see Frank McLynn's *Villa and Zapata: A Biography of the Mexican Revolution* (London: Pimlico, 2000); and John Reed's *Insurgent Mexico* (New York: D. Appleton, 1914). For the invasion of Veracruz, see Jack Sweetman's *The Landing at Veracruz: 1914* (Annapolis, MD: Naval Institute Press, 1968). *Santa Fe New Mexican*, May 20, 1920.
53. Lynda A. Sánchez, "The Last Hurrah," *True West*, May/June 2024. *El Nuevo Mexicano*, January 27, 1916. *El Nuevo Mexicano*, May 18, 1916. *Carrizozo Outlook*, August 25, 1916. *Albuquerque Journal*, September 2, 1916.
54. *Carrizozo Outlook*, November 10, 1916.
55. 1920 United States Federal Census. Benjamin Martin Chavez Death Certificate, 1994, roll 08, Indiana Archives and Records Administration, Indianapolis.
56. *Carrizozo Outlook*, May 18, 1917. 1910 United States Federal Census. 1920 United States Federal Census.
57. *Carrizozo Outlook*, July 6, 1917.
58. *Albuquerque Morning Journal*, September 9, 1917.
59. *Spanish-American*, October 13, 1917. *Estancia (NM) News-Herald*, October 11, 1917. *Taiban Valley (NM) News*, October 12, 1917. *El Nuevo Mexicano*, January 10, 1918.
60. *Carrizozo Outlook*, March 29, 1918. *Carrizozo Outlook*, April 5, 1918. *Carrizozo Outlook*, August 17, 1917. *Santa Fe New Mexican*, January 16, 1918. *Carrizozo Outlook*, July 26, 1918. *Carrizozo Outlook*, October 4, 1918.
61. 1920 United States Federal Census. *El Nuevo Mexicano*, May 15, 1919.
62. 1920 United States Federal Census. *El Nuevo Mexicano*, May 15, 1919.
63. *Albuquerque Journal*, October 6, 1919.

Notes for Chapter 18

1. 1920 United States Federal Census. Daniel Flores, *Billy the Kid: His Legacy in Guadalupe County* (pub. by author, 2017), 77–78. Julyan, *Place Names*, 228–29.
2. Flores, *Billy the Kid*, 77–78. Fabiola Cabeza de Baca, *We Fed Them Cactus* (Albuquerque: University of New Mexico Press, 1954), 97. 1920 United States Federal Census. 1910 United States Federal Census. 1930 United States Federal Census.

Notes for Chapter 18

3. *Petroleum Journal* (Topeka, KS), May 6, 1920. *Clovis (NM) News*, April 8, 1920. *New Mexico State Record*, May 7, 1920. *New Mexico State Record* (Santa Fe), April 2, 1920. 1920 United States Federal Census.
4. Flores, *José Chávez y Chávez*, 119. 1920 United States Federal Census. J. J. Clancy to M. G. Fulton, Anton Chico, NM, November 26, 1932, Ms 0519, Ketring Collection.
5. Clancy to Fulton, November 26, 1932, Ketring Collection.
6. Arthur Chapman, "Billy the Kid: A Man All 'Bad,'" *Outing Magazine* 46, no. 1 (April 1905). Emerson Hough, "Billy the Kid: The True Story of a Western 'Bad Man,'" *Everybody's Magazine*, September 1901. Hough, *Story of the Outlaw*, passim.
7. Charles A. Siringo, *The Story of Billy the Kid* (Badgley Publishing Company, 2012), passim. *Albuquerque Morning Journal*, July 9, 1920. *Albuquerque Journal*, June 30, 1920.
8. *Albuquerque Journal*, October 1, 1920. *Santa Fe New Mexican*, October 1, 1920. 1920 United States Federal Census. Robert N. Mullin, "The Boyhood of Billy the Kid," in Nolan, *Billy the Kid Reader*, 214. Yginio Salazar to R. N. Mullin, Lincoln, NM, October 9, 1920, Mullin Files.
9. *Star-Gazette* (Elmira, NY), December 30, 1920. *Star-Gazette*, December 31, 1920. *Albuquerque Morning Journal*, December 2, 1920. *Press and Sun-Bulletin* (Binghamton, NY), January 3, 1921. *Press and Sun-Bulletin*, January 4, 1921. *Star-Gazette*, January 3, 1921. *Star-Gazette*, January 4, 1921. *Star-Gazette*, January 5, 1921. *Star-Gazette*, January 6, 1921.
10. *Santa Fe New Mexican*, May 16, 1921.
11. *Alamogordo Daily News*, May 20, 1923. *Santa Fe New Mexican*, May 17, 1923.
12. Find a Grave Index, 1600s–Current, Ancestry.com. Flores, *José Chávez y Chávez*, 119.
13. *Santa Fe New Mexican*, June 9, 1925.
14. *Santa Fe New Mexican*, October 28, 1919. *El Nuevo Mexicano*, December 11, 1919.
15. *Santa Fe New Mexican*, August 19, 1920.
16. *Santa Fe New Mexican*, January 31, 1922. *Santa Fe New Mexican*, March 5, 1922. *Santa Fe New Mexican*, April 24, 1922.
17. Gonzáles-Berry and Maciel, *Contested Homeland*, 204–5. *Albuquerque Journal*, November 5, 1922. *Santa Fe New Mexican*, November 9, 1922.
18. *Santa Fe New Mexican*, March 10, 1923. *Santa Fe New Mexican*, March 23, 1923. 1920 United States Federal Census. Find a Grave Index, 1600s–Current, Ancestry.com. *Santa Fe New Mexican*, April 1, 1925.
19. *Santa Fe New Mexican*, July 24, 1923. *Santa Fe New Mexican*, July 31, 1923. *Independent-Herald* (Hinton, WV), September 20, 1923. *Santa Fe New Mexican*, October 8, 1923. *Hinton (WV) Daily News*, September 28, 1923. *St. Louis Globe-Democrat*, September 14, 1924.
20. *Santa Fe New Mexican*, March 26, 1924. *Santa Fe New Mexican*, April 3, 1924. *Santa Fe New Mexican*, July 28, 1924. *Santa Fe New Mexican*, August 25, 1924. *Alamogordo Daily News*, July 31, 1924. *Santa Fe New Mexico*, August 23, 1924. *Santa Fe New Mexican*, April 23, 1924. Find a Grave Index, 1600s–Current, Ancestry.com.
21. *Santa Fe New Mexican*, October 7, 1924.
22. *Santa Fe New Mexican*, October 15, 1924.
23. *Santa Fe New Mexican*, October 15, 1924. *Santa Fe New Mexican*, October 16, 1924. *Santa Fe New Mexican*, October 17. 1930 United States Federal Census. Find a Grave Index, 1600s–Current, Ancestry.com.
24. *Santa Fe New Mexican*, December 6, 1924. *Santa Fe New Mexican*, December 9, 1924. Find a Grave Index, 1600s–Current, Ancestry.com. 1910 United States Federal Census. 1920 United States Federal Census. *Santa Fe New Mexican*, December 9, 1931.
25. *Santa Fe New Mexican*, December 30, 1924.
26. *Santa Fe New Mexican*, January 19, 1925. *Santa Fe New Mexican*, November 18, 1927. 1920 United States Federal Census. US City Directories, 1822–1995, Ancestry.com. *Santa Fe New Mexican*, February 20, 1925. *Albuquerque Journal*, March 20, 1925.

27. *Santa Fe New Mexican*, April 1, 1925.
28. *Santa Fe New Mexican*, April 1, 1925. *Santa Fe New Mexican*, April 13, 1925. 1930 United States Federal Census.
29. *Santa Fe New Mexican*, April 21, 1925. *Santa Fe New Mexican*, April 22, 1925. *Santa Fe New Mexican*, April 28, 1925. *Santa Fe New Mexican*, May 1, 1925. 1930 United States Federal Census.
30. *Albuquerque Journal*, July 24, 1925. *Santa Fe New Mexican*, August 18, 1925. *Santa Fe New Mexican*, December 17, 1926. *Albuquerque Journal*, December 28, 1926.
31. 1930 United States Federal Census.
32. Walter Noble Burns interview notes with Martín Chávez (typed transcript), Usmar Collection.
33. Burns, *Saga*, passim. Walter Noble Burns interview with Martín Chávez, Chuck Usmar Collection. Draft chapter for *Saga of Billy the Kid*, MS 157, box 16, Leon C. Metz Papers, Sonnichsen Collections. Death Records, Michigan Department of Community Health, Division for Vital Records and Health Statistics, Lansing. Michigan Death Records, 1867–1952, Ancestry.com.
34. Find a Grave Index, 1600s–Current Ancestry.com. 1930 United States Federal Census. 1940 United States Federal Census. Ed Salazar's obituary can be found on page 5 of the *Daily Spectrum* (St. George, UT) June 2, 1998. Margarita Salazar's obituary can be found on page 8 of the *El Paso Times*, April 22, 1997.
35. Burns, *Saga*, 144.
36. Burns, *Saga*, 144–49.
37. Burns, *Saga*, passim. *St. Louis Post-Dispatch*, July 4, 1926. *Fort Worth Record-Telegram*, August 9, 1926. *St. Louis Post-Dispatch*, July 11, 1926.
38. Otero, *Real Billy*, 121.
39. Otero, *Real Billy*, 95–96.
40. *Santa Fe New Mexican*, June 24, 1926. *Santa Fe New Mexican*, July 14, 1926. Otero, *Real Billy*, 85–94, 134.
41. Otero, *Real Billy*, 96–99.
42. Otero, *Real Billy*, 114–20. *Santa Fe New Mexican*, July 14, 1926.
43. Otero, *Real Billy*, 121–29. Harvey Fergusson, "Billy the Kid," *American Mercury* 5, no. 18 (June 1925).
44. Maxwell interview. Cháves interview, August 15, 1927. Salazar interview.
45. *Santa Fe New Mexican*, October 10, 1927. 1930 United States Federal Census.
46. *Albuquerque Journal*, November 28, 1927.
47. *Albuquerque Journal*, December 22, 1929. Find a Grave Index, 1600s–Current, Ancestry.com.
48. *Albuquerque Journal*, November 2, 1930. *Albuquerque Journal*, September 25, 1930.
49. *Gallup Independent*, April 25, 1930. *Santa Fe New Mexican*, April 11, 1930. *Deming Headlight*, February 12, 1931. *Albuquerque Journal*, November 30, 1930. Richard W. Etulain, *Thunder in the West: The Life and Legends of Billy the Kid* (Norman: University of Oklahoma Press, 2020), 296.
50. King Vidor, dir., *Billy the Kid* (Turner Entertainment, 1930).
51. *Las Vegas Daily Optic*, April 10, 1930. *Santa Fe New Mexican*, April 10, 1930. *Santa Fe New Mexican*, April 12, 1930. *Santa Fe New Mexican*, April 15, 1930.
52. *Santa Fe New Mexican*, December 9, 1931.
53. *Santa Fe New Mexican*, December 9, 1931.
54. *Santa Fe New Mexican*, December 9, 1931. *Albuquerque Journal*, December 10, 1931. *Albuquerque Journal*, December 11, 1931. *Casper (WY) Star-Tribune*, December 10, 1931. *Daily Sentinel* (Grand Junction, CO), December 10, 1931.
55. *Santa Fe New Mexican*, December 11, 1931. US City Directories, 1822–1995, Ancestry.com.

56. *Santa Fe New Mexican*, December 9, 1931. 1930 United States Federal Census. Find a Grave Index, 1600s–Current, Ancestry.com.
57. *Roswell Daily Record*, June 9, 1932. *Roswell Daily Record*, July 21, 1932. *Clovis News-Journal*, July 22, 1932. *Albuquerque Journal*, July 23, 1932. *Roswell Daily Record*, July 25, 1932. *Albuquerque Journal*, July 26, 1932. *Alamogordo Daily News*, July 28, 1932. *Santa Fe New Mexican*, July 29, 1932. Smith "Man Who Fought Side-by-Side."
58. Smith, "Man Who Fought Side-by-Side."
59. Find a Grave Index, 1600s–Current, Ancestry.com.
60. Coe, *Frontier Fighter*, 184. For an enjoyable study of Depression Era outlaws, see Bryan Burrough's *Public Enemies: America's Greatest Crime Wave and the Birth of the FBI, 1933–34* (New York: Penguin Books, 2004).
61. Yginio Salazar's headstone in the old Lincoln Cemetery reads that his death occurred on January 7, 1936. However, his death is recorded as occurring on January 9, 1935, in Lincoln County Death Records for 1935, page 50, Santa Rita Catholic Church Records, Carrizozo, New Mexico (Xerox copy, courtesy of Massimo De Vito), Mills Collection. Although Isabel Salazar is pronounced as having passed away on May 15, 1935, on the same headstone in the old Lincoln Cemetery, Isabel's death is recorded as occurring one year earlier on May 15, 1934, in Lincoln County Death Records for 1934, page 46, Santa Rita Catholic Church Records, Carrizozo, New Mexico (Xerox copy, courtesy of Massimo De Vito), Mills Collection. Social Security Death Index, Master File, Social Security Administration, Washington, DC. 1930 United States Federal Census. 1940 United States Federal Census. Find a Grave Index, 1600s–Current, Ancestry.com.
62. *Santa Fe New Mexican*, March 22, 1935. A lengthy obituary for Yginio Salazar, published on page 4 of the *Santa Fe New Mexican*, March 22, 1935, makes a direct reference to a report of Yginio Salazar's death in early January 1935 by the *Fort Stanton Caduceus*. This is further proof that Yginio's death occurred in January 1935, not January 1936 as his headstone reads. Despite my efforts, a death certificate for Yginio Salazar has yet to be located in the archives.
63. Find a Grave Index, 1600s–Current, Ancestry.com. *Santa Fe New Mexican*, March 22, 1935.

Notes for the Epilogue

1. *Santa Fe New Mexican*, March 3, 1936. *Santa Fe New Mexican*, March 7, 1936. *Sacramento Bee*, March 28, 1936. *Santa Fe New Mexican*, March 3, 1936. *Santa Fe New Mexican*, March 7, 1936. *Sacramento Bee*, March 28, 1936.
2. Otero, *Real Billy*, passim. Author correspondence with Lynda A. Sanchez. Tsompanas, *Juan Patrón*, passim. Flores, *José Chávez y Chávez*, passim.
3. WWII Draft Registration Cards For New Mexico, 10/16/1940-03/31/1947, Records of the Selective Service System, 147; Box 23, National Personnel Records Center, St. Louis, Missouri. US World War II Draft Cards, Young Men, 1940–1947, Ancestry.com. Hospital Admission Card Files, ca. 1970; NAI: 570973; Records of the Office of the Surgeon General (Army), 1775–1994; Record Group 112; NARA. US World War II Hospital Admission Card Files, 1942–1954, Ancestry.com. US Department of Veterans Affairs BIRLS Death File, 1850–2010, Ancestry.com. "Here's the story not told in Nolan's Oppenheimer about those forced off their land in New Mexico," *CBC*, July 29, 2023, https://www.cbc.ca/news/world/oppenheimer-new-mexico-land-removed-1.6922402. Susan Montoya Bryan, "'Oppenheimer' Extols Atomic Bomb Triumph But Ignores Health Effects on Those Living Near Test Site," *LA Times*, July 19, 2023, https://www.latimes.com/science/story/2023-07-19/oppenheimer-extols-atomic-bomb-triumph-but-ignores-health-effects-on-those-living-nearby.

4. For the Chicano movement, see F. Arturo Rosales's *Chicano! The History of the Mexican American Civil Rights Movement* (Houston: Arte Público Press, 1997). For César Chávez see Matt Garcia, *From the Jaws of Victory: The Triumph and Tragedy of Cesar Chavez and the Farm Worker Movement* (Berkeley: University of California Press, 2012). For Rodolfo "Corky" Gonzales, see Christine Marín's *A Spokesman of the Mexican American Movement: Rodolfo "Corky" Gonzales and the Fight for Chicano Liberation, 1966–1972* (San Francisco: R. and E. Research Associates, 1977). Author correspondence with Margaret Chávez Slayton.
5. For Reies López Tijerina and the Tierra Amarilla Courthouse raid, see Reies López Tijerina's *They Called Me "King Tiger": My Struggle for the Land and Our Rights*, trans. and ed. José Ángel Gutiérrez (Houston: Arte Público Press, 2000); Lorena Oropeza's *The King of Adobe: Reies López Tijerina—Lost Prophet of the Chicano Movement* (Chapel Hill: University of North Carolina Press, 2019); Peter Nabokov's *Tijerina and the Courthouse Raid* (Albuquerque: University of New Mexico Press, 1969); and Richard Gardner's *¡Grito! Reies Tijerina and the New Mexico Land Grant War of 1967* (New York: Harper Colophon Books, 1970). Phillip B. Gonzáles, "Struggle for Survival: The Hispanic Land Grants of New Mexico, 1848–2001," *Agricultural History* 77, no. 2, Minority Land and Community Security (Spring 2003): 293–324. Susan Montoya Bryan, "New Mexico Grazing Rights Case: Court Rules Against Hispanic Ranchers," Patch.com, October 25, 2017, https://patch.com/new-mexico/across-nm/new-mexico-grazing-rights-case-court-rules-against-hispanic-ranchers.
6. Daniel J. Chacón, "Exhibit of Religious Items at Las Vegas Museum Sparks Controversy," *Santa Fe New Mexican*, March 26, 2022, https://www.santafenewmexican.com/news/local_news/exhibit-of-religious-items-at-las-vegas-museum-sparks-controversy/article_d657779e-abc7-11ec-a34f-3ff1937d7c7e.html. Author correspondence with Rock Ulibarri, November 2023. Author correspondence with Roberto Martínez, November 2023.
7. For Billy the Kid films, see Johnny D. Boggs, *Billy the Kid on Film, 1911–2012*. Insights can also be found in Jon Tuska's *Billy the Kid: His Life and Legend* (Albuquerque: University of New Mexico Press, 1994); Richard W. Etulain's *Billy the Kid: A Reader's Guide* (Norman: University of Oklahoma Press, 2020); and Etulain's *Thunder in the West*.

Bibliography

Archival Collections and Unpublished Materials

Arizona Department of Health Services, Phoenix.
Arizona Historical Society, Tucson.
Barker Texas History Center, Dolph Briscoe Center, University of Texas at Austin.
    Vandale Collection
C. L. Sonnichsen Special Collections Department. University of Texas at El Paso.
    Leon C. Metz Papers
Chávez County Historical Society, Roswell, New Mexico.
Chuck Usmar Collection, Albuquerque, New Mexico.
Fray Angélico Chávez Library, Palace of the Governors, Santa Fe.
    William H. Bonney Collection
Haley Memorial Library, Midland, Texas.
    Robert N. Mullin Bio Notes, Research Files, and Source Notebook
Historical Center for Southeast New Mexico, Roswell.
Indiana Archives and Records Administration, Indianapolis.
James B. Mills Collection, Australia.
John L. McCarty Papers. Amarillo Public Library, Texas.
L. Tom Perry Special Collections. Harold B. Lee Library, Brigham Young University, Provo, Utah.
Lew Wallace Papers. Indiana Historical Society, Indianapolis.
Lynda A. Sánchez Collection, Lincoln, New Mexico.
Mark Lee Gardner Collection, Colorado.
Michigan Department of Community Health. Division for Vital Records and Health Statistics, Lansing.
Missouri Office of the Secretary of State, Jefferson City.
Missouri State Archives, Jefferson City.
National Archives and Records Administration, Washington, DC.
National Personnel Records Center, St. Louis, Missouri.
New Mexico Department of Health Services, Santa Fe.
New Mexico State Records Center and Archives, Santa Fe.
    Governor George Curry Papers
    Governor L. Bradford Prince Papers
    Governor Miguel A. Otero Papers
    Lincoln County Marriages
    Museum of New Mexico Library
    New Mexico Marriages
    Records of the United States Territorial and New Mexico District Courts for Lincoln County, San Miguel County, Santa Fe County
    Robert M. Utley Research Files (Digitized)

Territorial Archives of New Mexico
Victor Westphall Collection
New Mexico State University Library, Archives and Special Collections, Albuquerque.
Herman B. Weisner Papers
Lewis A. Ketring Jr. Collection of Lincoln County Research
Philip J. Rasch Collection, Lincoln Historic Site.
Texas Department of State Health Services, Austin.
University of Arizona Library, Tucson.
Maurice G. Fulton Collection
Taylor F. Ealy Papers
Wyoming State Archives, Cheyenne.
All federal, territorial, state census records, and military records have been acquired from Ancestry.com, unless otherwise cited.

Newspapers

Alamogordo Daily News
Albuquerque Citizen
Albuquerque Daily Citizen
Albuquerque Democrat
Albuquerque Evening Democrat
Albuquerque Journal
Albuquerque Morning Democrat and Albuquerque Morning Journal
Albuquerque Review
Albuquerque Weekly Citizen
Amarillo Daily News
Arizona Daily Star
Arizona Weekly Citizen (Tucson)
Arizona Weekly Miner (Prescott)
Arkansas City (KS) Daily Traveller
Atchison (KS) Daily Champion
Baltimore Sun
Belfast Morning News
Binger (OK) Journal
Bisbee (AZ) Daily Review
The Borderer
Buffalo Inquirer
Buffalo Morning Express
Caledonia (MN) Argus
Carlsbad (NM) Current-Argus
Carrizozo (NM) Outlook
Casper (WY) Star-Tribune
Chicago Tribune
Cimarron (NM) News and Press

Bibliography

Clovis (NM) News
Clovis (NM) News-Journal
Current Wave (Eminence, MO)
Daily Illini (Urbana, IL)
Daily Memphis Avalanche
Daily Register (Wheeling, WV)
Daily Sentinel (Grand Junction, CO).
Daily Spectrum (St. George, UT)
Dayton (OH) Herald
Deming (NM) Headlight
Deseret News (Salt Lake City, UT)
Dublin Evening Telegraph
The Eagle (Sierra County, NM)
The Eagle (Silver City, NM)
Eastern New Mexico News, The Clovis
El Farol (Capitan, NM)
El Independiente (Las Vegas, NM)
El Nuevo Mexicano (Santa Fe)
El Paso Herald
El Paso Times
Emporia (KS) Daily Republican
Estancia (NM) News-Herald
Evansville (IN) Journal
Evening Citizen (Albuquerque)
Evening Herald (Albuquerque)
Evening News (Emporia, KS)
Fort Worth Record-Telegram
Gallup Independent
Galveston Daily News
Glasgow Evening Citizen
Gotebo (OK) Gazette
Hickman (KY) Courier
Hinton (WV) Daily News
Holmes County Republican (Millersburg, OH)
Independent-Herald (Hinton, WV)
Independent-Record (Helena, MT)
Indianapolis Journal
Indianapolis Times
Indianapolis World
Inter-Ocean (Chicago)
Journal-Democrat (Dodge City, KS)
Kansas City (MO) Times
La Voz Del Pueblo (Santa Fe)

Larimer County Independent (Fort Collins, CO)
Las Cruces Sun-News
Las Cruces Thirty-Four
Las Vegas (NM) Daily Optic
Las Vegas (NM) Free Press
Las Vegas (NM) Gazette
Las Vegas (NM) Morning Gazette
Las Vegas (NM) Weekly Optic and Stock Grower
Lincoln County Leader (White Oaks, NM)
Lincoln (NE) Journal Star
London Times
Los Angeles Evening Post-Record
Los Angeles Times
Lubbock Avalanche-Journal
Manchester Courier and Lancashire General Advertiser
Meriden (CT) Daily Republican
Mesilla (NM) News
Mesilla Valley Independent
Montreal Star
Morning News (Wilmington, DE)
Morning Post (Camden, NJ)
Nebraska City News
New Mexican Review (Santa Fe)
New Mexico Magazine
New Mexico State Record (Santa Fe)
New York Times
Newport (RI) Daily News
Omaha Evening Bee
Pacific Bee (Sacramento, CA)
Petroleum Journal (Topeka, KS)
Pioche (NV) Record
Press and Sun-Bulletin (Binghamton, NY)
Record-Union (Sacramento, CA)
The Republic (Columbus, IN)
Richmond Weekly Palladium
Rock Island (IL) Argus
Roswell Daily Record
The Rustler (Cerrillos, NM)
Sacramento Bee
Sacramento Daily Record-Union
Salt Lake Herald
San Francisco Call

San Francisco Call and Post
San Francisco Chronicle
San Francisco Examiner
Santa Fe Daily Democrat
Santa Fe New Mexican
Santa Fe Weekly Gazette
Santa Fe Weekly Post
Santa Rosa (CA) News
The Sentinel (Carlisle, PA)
Sierra County Advocate (Kingston, NM)
Silver City (NM) Herald
Sioux City (IA) Journal
Socorro (NM) Chieftain
Spanish-American (Roy, NM)
St. Helena (CA) Star
St. Louis Daily Globe-Democrat
St. Louis Globe-Democrat
St. Louis Post-Dispatch
St. Paul Globe
Star-Gazette (Elmira, NY)
Steuben Republican (Angola, IN)
The Sun (New York)
Superior (WI) Times
Taiban Valley (NM) News
Thibodaux (LA) Minerva
The Times (Streator, IL)
Urbana (OH) Daily Citizen
Washington Times (Washington, DC)
Wathena (KS) Reporter
Weekly New Mexican (Santa Fe)
Weekly New Mexican Review (Santa Fe)
Weekly Palladium (Benton Harbor, MI)
Western Liberal (Lordsburg, NM)
White Oaks (NM) Eagle
White Oaks (NM) Golden Era
Wichita (KS) Beacon

Books, Articles, and Essays

Abbott, E. C., and Helena Huntington Smith. *We Pointed Them North: Recollections of a Cowpuncher.* Norman: University of Oklahoma Press, 1976.

Adams, Clarence S., and Joan N Adams. *Riders of the Pecos & the Seven Rivers Outlaws.* Roswell, NM: Pioneer Printing, 1990.

Adams, Ramon F. *A Fitting Death for Billy the Kid.* Norman: University of Oklahoma Press, 1960.

Alberts, Don. *The Battle of Glorieta: Union Victory in the West.* College Station: Texas A&M University Press, 1996.

Alexander, Bob. *Desert Desperadoes: The Banditti of Southwestern New Mexico.* Silver City, NM: Gila Books, 2006.

Alexander, Bob. *Six-Guns and Silver-Jacks: A History of Silver City and Southwestern New Mexico.* Silver City, NM: Gila Books, 2005.

Anaya, A. P. "Paco." *I Buried Billy.* College Station: Creative Publishing, 1991.

Anderson, Carl, and Eduardo Chávez. *Our Lady of Guadalupe: Mother of the Civilization of Love.* New York: Image, 2009.

Anderson, George B. *History of New Mexico: Its Resources and People.* Los Angeles: Pacific States Publishing, 1907.

Arana, Marie. *Bolívar: American Liberator.* New York: Simon & Schuster, 2014.

Bailey, Lynn R. *Bosque Redondo: An American Concentration Camp.* Pasadena, CA: Socio-Technical Books, 1970.

Bailey, Lynn Robison. *The Long Walk: A History of the Navaho Wars, 1846–1868.* Tucson: Westernlore Press, 1964.

Ball, Eve. *Ma'am Jones of the Pecos.* Tucson: University of Arizona Press, 1969.

Ball, Larry D. *Desert Lawmen: The High Sheriffs of New Mexico and Arizona, 1846–1912.* Albuquerque: University of New Mexico Press, 1992.

Barron, R. M. (editing and typescript). *Court of Inquiry: Lieutenant Colonel N. A. M. Dudley, Fort Stanton, New Mexico, May-June-July 1879.* 2 vols. Edina, MN: Beaver's Pond Press, 1995.

Bartholomew, Ed. *Jesse Evans: A Texas Hide-Burner.* Houston: Frontier Press of Texas, 1955.

Bauer, Karl Jack. *The Mexican War: 1846–1848.* Lincoln: University of Nebraska Press, 1992.

Baxter, John O. *Las carneradas: Sheep Trade in New Mexico, 1700–1860.* Albuquerque: University of New Mexico Press, 1987.

Beck, Warren A. *New Mexico: A History of Four Centuries.* Norman: University of Oklahoma Press, 1962.

Bell, Bob Boze. *The Illustrated Life and Times of Billy the Kid: The Final Word.* Cave Creek, AZ: Two Roads West, 2021.

Bell, Bob Boze. *The Illustrated Life and Times of Billy the Kid.* Rev. and expanded 2nd ed. Phoenix: Tri Star-Boze, 1996.

Bender, Norman J. *Missionaries, Outlaws, and Indians: Taylor F. Ealy at Lincoln and Zuni, 1878–1881.* Albuquerque: University of New Mexico Press, 1984.

Blackshear, James Bailey. *Honor and Defiance: A History of the Las Vegas Land Grant in New Mexico.* Santa Fe: Sunstone Press, 2013.

Blazer, Almer. "The Fight at Blazer's Mill, in New Mexico." *Frontier Times* 16, no. 11 (August 1939).

Blazer, Paul. "The Fight at Blazer's Mill: A Chapter in the Lincoln County War." *Arizona and the West* 6, no. 3 (Autumn 1964): 203–10.

Boardman, Mark. "The Assassination of Charles Bent." *True West*, February/March 2020.

Bogener, Stephen. "Ditches Across the Desert: The Story of Irrigation Along New Mexico's Pecos River." PhD diss., Texas Tech University, December 1997.

Bogener, Stephen. "Land, Speculation, and Manipulation on the Pecos." *Great Plains Quarterly* 28, no. 3 (Summer 2008): 209–29.

Bibliography

Boggs, Johnny D. *Billy the Kid on Film, 1911–2012*. Jefferson, NC: McFarland & Company, 2013.

Bolton Church, Amelia, as told to Eve Ball. "Early Days in Lincoln." *True West*, August 1978.

Boomhower, Ray E. *The Sword and the Pen: A Life of Lew Wallace*. Indianapolis: Indiana Historical Society Press, 2005.

Branch, Louis Leon. *Los Bilitos: The Story of Billy the Kid and His Gang*. New York: Carlton Press, 1980.

Brown, Lorin W. *Hispano Folk Life of New Mexico*. Albuquerque: University of New Mexico Press, 1978.

Bryan, Howard. *Santa Fe Tales & More*. Santa Fe: Clear Light, 2010.

Bryan, Howard. *Wildest of the Wild West*. Santa Fe: Clear Light, 1988.

Buffington, Ann. "Woman of Lincoln County." *True West*, July 2000.

Burns, Walter Noble. *The Saga of Billy the Kid*. Garden City, NY: Doubleday, 1952.

Burrough, Bryan. *Public Enemies: America's Greatest Crime Wave and the Birth of the FBI, 1933–34*. New York: Penguin Books, 2004.

Burrough, Bryan, Chris Tomlinson, and Jason Stanford. *Forget the Alamo: The Rise and Fall of an American Myth*. New York: Penguin Press, 2021.

Cabeza de Baca, Fabiola. *We Fed Them Cactus*. Albuquerque: University of New Mexico Press, 1954.

Cabeza de Baca, Manuel. *Vicente Silva and His Forty Bandits: His Crimes and Retributions*. Santa Fe: Sunstone Press, 2022.

Caffey, David L. *Chasing the Santa Fe Ring: Power and Privilege in Territorial New Mexico*. Albuquerque: University of New Mexico Press, 2014.

Caffey, David L. *Frank Springer and New Mexico: From the Colfax County War to the Emergence of Modern Santa Fe*. College Station: Texas A&M University Press, 2006.

Caffey, David L. *When Cimarron Meant Wild: The Maxwell Land Grant Conflict in New Mexico and Colorado*. Norman: University of Oklahoma Press, 2023.

Cain, Ellen Marie. "Testing Courage in New Mexico: Taylor Ealy and the Lincoln County War, 1878." *American Presbyterians* 72, no. 1 (Spring 1994): 11–22.

Caldwell, Clifford R. *John Simpson Chisum: The Cattle King of the Pecos Revisited*. Santa Fe: Sunstone Press, 2010.

Campa, Arthur L. *Hispanic Culture in the Southwest*. Norman: University of Oklahoma Press, 1979.

Carlson, Alvar Ward. "New Mexico's Sheep Industry, 1850–1900: Its Role in the History of the Territory." *New Mexico Historical Review* 44, no. 1 (1969): 25–49.

Carlson, Alvar W. *The Spanish-American Homeland: Four Centuries in New Mexico's Río Arriba Country*. Baltimore: John Hopkins University Press, 1990.

Carrigan, William D., and Clive Webb. *Forgotten Dead: Mob Violence Against Mexicans in the United States, 1848–1928*. New York: Oxford University Press, 2017.

Chamberlain, Kathleen P. *In the Shadow of Billy the Kid: Susan McSween and the Lincoln County War*. Albuquerque: University of New Mexico Press, 2012.

Chamberlain, Kathleen P. *Victorio: Apache Warrior and Chief*. Norman: University of Oklahoma Press, 2007.

Chapman, Arthur. "Billy the Kid: A Man All 'Bad.'" *Outing Magazine* 46, no. 1 (April 1905).

Chávez, Fray Angélico. *My Penitente Land: Reflections on Spanish New Mexico*. Albuquerque: University of New Mexico Press, 1974.

Chávez, John R. *The Lost Land: The Chicano Image of the Southwest.* Albuquerque: University of New Mexico Press, 1984.

Clifford, Frank. *Deep Trails in the Old West: A Frontier Memoir.* Edited by Frederick Nolan. Norman: University of Oklahoma Press, 2011.

Cline, Don. *Antrim & Billy.* College Station: Creative Publishing, 1990.

Cline, Don. "Tom Pickett: Friend of Billy the Kid." *True West*, July 1997.

Coe, George W. *Frontier Fighter: The Autobiography of George W. Coe.* Chicago: Lakeside Press, 1984.

Colton, Ray. *The Civil War in the Western Territories: Arizona, Colorado, New Mexico and Utah.* Norman: University of Oklahoma Press, 1984.

Cooper, Gale. *Billy the Kid's Pretenders: Brushy Bill and John Miller.* Albuquerque: Gelcour Books, 2018.

Cooper, Gale. *Billy the Kid's Writings, Words, & Wit.* Albuquerque: Gelcour Books, 2011.

Cooper, Gale. *The Coroner's Jury Report of Billy the Kid.* Albuquerque: Gelcour Books, 2020.

Cooper, Gale. *The Lost Pardon of Billy the Kid.* Albuquerque: Gelcour Books, 2018.

Cooper, Gale. *The Santa Fe Ring Versus Billy the Kid.* Albuquerque: Gelcour Books, 2018.

Correia, David. *Properties of Violence: Law and Land Grant Struggle in Northern New Mexico.* Athens: University of Georgia Press, 2013.

Correia, David. "'Retribution Will Be Their Reward': New Mexico's Las Gorras Blancas and the Fight for the Las Vegas Land Grant Commons." *Radical History Review* no. 108 (Fall 2010): 49–72.

Cozzens, Gary. "A Parting Shot." *El Palacio*, Fall 2016.

Cramer, Dudley T. *The Pecos Ranchers in the Lincoln County War.* Oakland, CA: Branding Iron Press, 1996.

Cummings, Billy Charles Patrick. *Frontier Parish: Recovered Catholic History of Lincoln County, 1860–1884.* Book 4. Lincoln: Lincoln County Historical Society Publication, 1995.

Cummings, Billy Charles. "Patrón, Axtell Fight Over Jesuits." *Los Amigos* (Lincoln County Heritage Trust Newsletter), July 1995.

Cunningham, Eugene. *Triggernometry: A Gallery of Gunfighters.* Caldwell, ID: Caxton Printers, 1952.

Curry, George. *An Autobiography.* Albuquerque: University of New Mexico Press, 1958.

Davis, Jerry A. "Matilda Allison on the Anglo-Hispanic Frontier: Presbyterian Schooling in New Mexico, 1880–1910." *American Presbyterians* 74, no. 3 (Fall 1996).

Davis, W. W. H. *El Gringo: New Mexico and Her People.* Lincoln: University of Nebraska Press, 1982.

Davis, William C. *American Frontier: Pioneers, Settlers & Cowboys.* Reprint, New York: Smithmark, 1995.

Deutsch, Sarah. *No Separate Refuge: Culture, Class, and Gender on an Anglo-Hispanic Frontier in the American Southwest, 1880–1940.* New York: Oxford University Press, 1989.

DeMark, Judith Boyce. *Essays in Twentieth Century New Mexico History.* Albuquerque: University of New Mexico Press, 1994.

DeMattos, Jack. "The Search for Billy the Kid's Roots." *Real West*, no. 21 (November 1978).

DeMattos, Jack. "The Search for Billy the Kid's Roots Is Over." *Real West*, no. 23 (January 1980).

Dolan, Samuel K. *The Line Riders: The Border Patrol, Prohibition, and the Liquor War on the Rio Grande.* Essex, CT: TwoDot, 2022.

Dormandy, Thomas. *The White Death: A History of Tuberculosis*. New York: New York University Press, 2000.

Duran, Tobias. "Francisco Chavez, Thomas B. Catron, and Organized Political Violence in Santa Fe in the 1890s." *New Mexico Historical Review* 59, no. 3 (1984): 291–310.

Dworkin, Mark J. *American Mythmaker: Walter Noble Burns and the Legends of Billy the Kid, Wyatt Earp, and Joaquin Murrieta*. Norman: University of Oklahoma Press, 2015.

Ealy, Ruth R. *Water in a Thirsty Land*. Las Cruces: Doc45 Publishing, 2021.

Earle, James H. *The Capture of Billy the Kid*. College Station: Creative Publishing, 1988.

Edwards, David G. *Billy the Kid: As He Was Reported in Newspapers from the 1870s and 1880s*. Published by the author, 2018.

Edwards, Harold L. "Capt. Saturnino Baca in the Shadow of the Lincoln County War." *Los Amigos* 2, no. 2 (April 1993), no. 3 (July 1993), no. 4 (October 1993).

Edwards, Harold L. "The Short and Violent Life of Juan Patrón." *True West*, March 1991.

Englekirk, John R. "The Passion Play in New Mexico." *Western Folklore* 25, no. 1 (January 1966): 17–33.

Espinosa, Aurelio M. "New-Mexican Spanish Folk-Lore." *Journal of American Folklore* 23, no. 90 (October–December 1910): 395–418.

Etulain, Richard W. *Billy the Kid: A Reader's Guide*. Norman: University of Oklahoma Press, 2020.

Etulain, Richard W. *Thunder in the West: The Life and Legends of Billy the Kid*. Norman: University of Oklahoma Press, 2020.

Falzone, Vincent J. *Terence V. Powderly: Middle Class Reformer*. Washington, DC: University Press of America, 1978.

Fergusson, Harvey. "Billy the Kid." *American Mercury* 5, no. 18 (June 1925).

Fink, Leon. *Workingmen's Democracy: The Knights of Labor and American Politics*. Urbana: University of Illinois Press, 1983.

Flores, Daniel. *Billy the Kid: His Legacy in Guadalupe County*. Published by the author, 2017.

Flores, Daniel. *José Chávez y Chávez: The Outlaw Who Died of Old Age*. Published by the author, 2014.

Flores, Daniel. *Puerto de Luna*. Published by the author, 2010.

Frazier, Donald S. *Blood & Treasure: Confederate Empire in the Southwest*. College Station: Texas A&M University Press, 1995.

Freiberger, Harriet. *Lucien Maxwell: Villain or Visionary?* Santa Fe: Sunstone Press, 2007.

Fulton, Maurice G. *History of the Lincoln County War*. Tucson: University of Arizona Press, 1968.

Galeano, Eduardo. *Open Veins of Latin America: Five Centuries of the Pillage of a Continent*. New York: Monthly Review Press, 1997.

García, Elbert A. *Billy the Kid's Kid: The Hispanic Connection*. Santa Rosa, NM: Los Products Press, 1999.

García, Mario T., and Ellen McCracken. *Rewriting the Chicano Movement: New Histories of Mexican American Activism in the Civil Rights Era*. Tucson: University of Arizona Press, 2021.

Garcia, Matt. *From the Jaws of Victory: The Triumph and Tragedy of Cesar Chavez and the Farm Worker Movement*. Berkeley: University of California Press, 2012.

Gardner, Mark Lee. "A Belle of Old Fort Sumner." *True West*, April 2018.

Gardner, Mark Lee. "Billy the Tintype." *True West*, July 2019.

Gardner, Mark Lee. "Pat Garrett: The Life and Death of a Great Sheriff." *Wild West*, August 2011.

Gardner, Mark Lee. "The Strange and Mesmerizing Death of the Outlaw Jesse James." *True West*, February/March 2023.

Gardner, Mark Lee. *To Hell on a Fast Horse: The Untold Story of Billy the Kid and Pat Garrett*. New York: William Morrow, 2010.

Gardner, Richard. *¡Grito! Reies Tijerina and the New Mexico Land Grant War of 1967*. New York: Harper Colophon Books, 1970.

Garrett, David. *Blood on the Saddle: The Life of Doc Scurlock*. Published by the author, 2020.

Garrett, Pat F., and Frederick Nolan. *Pat F. Garrett's "The Authentic Life of Billy, the Kid."* Annotated ed. Norman: University of Oklahoma Press, 2000.

Gibson, A. M. *The Life and Death of Colonel Albert Jennings Fountain*. Norman: University of Oklahoma Press, 1965.

Gómez, Laura E. *Manifest Destinies: The Making of the Mexican American Race*. 2nd ed. New York: New York University Press, 2008.

González, Deena J. *Refusing the Favor: The Spanish-Mexican Women of Santa Fe, 1820–1880*. New York: Oxford University Press, 2001.

Gonzáles, Phillip B. "Struggle for Survival: The Hispanic Land Grants of New Mexico, 1848–2001." Minority Land and Community Security, *Agricultural History* 77, no. 2, (Spring 2003): 293–324.

Gonzales, Samuel Leo. *The Days of Old*. Published by the author, 1993.

Gonzáles-Berry, Erlinda, and David R. Maciel. *The Contested Homeland: A Chicano History of New Mexico*. Albuquerque: University of New Mexico Press, 2000.

Goodwyn, Lawrence. *The Populist Moment: A Short History of Agrarian Revolt in America*. New York: Oxford University Press, 1978.

Greenberg, Amy S. *Manifest Destiny and American Territorial Expansion: A Brief History with Documents*. Boston and New York: Bedford/St. Martin's, 2012.

Griego, Alfonso. *Good-Bye My Land of Enchantment: A True Story of Some of the First Spanish-Speaking Natives and Early Settlers of San Miguel County, Territory of New Mexico*. Published by the author, 1981.

Griego, Alfonso. *Voices of the Territory of New Mexico: An Oral History of People of Spanish Descent and Early Settlers Born During the Territorial Days*. Published by the author, 1985.

Griswold Del Castillo, Richard. *The Treaty of Guadalupe Hidalgo: A Legacy of Conflict*. Norman: University of Oklahoma Press, 1990.

Guardino, Peter. *The Dead March: A History of the Mexican-American War*. Cambridge: Harvard University Press, 2017.

Gutiérrez, Ramón A. *When Jesus Came, the Corn Mothers Went Away: Marriage, Sexuality, and Power in New Mexico, 1500–1846*. Stanford: Stanford University Press, 1991.

Haldane, Roberta Key. *Gold-Mining Boomtown: People of White Oaks, Lincoln County, New Mexico Territory*. Norman: University of Oklahoma Press, 2012.

Haley, J. Evetts. *Charles Goodnight: Cowman and Plainsman*. Norman: University of Oklahoma Press, 1981.

Haley, J. Evetts. *The XIT Ranch of Texas and the Early Days of the Llano Estacado*. Norman: University of Oklahoma Press, 2013.

Hall, Thomas D. *Social Change in the Southwest, 1350–1880*. Lawrence: University Press of Kansas, 1989.

Hardin, Stephen L. *Texian Iliad: A Military History of the Texas Revolution, 1835–1836*. Austin: University of Texas Press, 1996.

Henn, Nora True. *Lincoln County and Its Wars*. Roswell, NM: Southwest Printers, 2017.
Hertzog, Peter. *Little Known Facts About Billy the Kid*. Santa Fe: Press of the Territorian, 1964.
Hinton, Harwood P. "John Chisum, 1877–84." *New Mexico Historical Review* 31–32 (July 1956–January 1957).
Horgan, Paul. "In Search of the Archbishop." *Catholic Historical Review* 46, no. 4 (January 1961).
Horgan, Paul. *Lamy of Santa Fe*. New York: Farrar, Straus, and Giroux, 1975.
Horn, Calvin. *New Mexico's Troubled Years: The Story of the Early Territorial Governors*. Albuquerque: Horn & Wallace Publishers, 1963.
Hough, Emerson. "Billy the Kid: The True Story of a Western 'Bad Man.'" *Everybody's Magazine*, September 1901.
Hough, Emerson. *The Story of the Outlaw: A Study of the Western Desperado*. New York: Cooper Square Press, 2001.
House, Kurt, and Roy B. Young. *Chasing Billy the Kid: Frank Stewart and the Untold Story of the Manhunt for William H. Bonney*. San Antonio: Three Rivers, 2022.
Hoyt, Henry F. *A Frontier Doctor*. Chicago: Lakeside Press, 1979.
Hunt, Frazier. *The Tragic Days of Billy the Kid*. Santa Fe: Sunstone Press, 2009.
Hunter, J. Marvin. *The Trail Drivers of Texas*. Austin: University of Texas Press, 1985.
Hutton, Paul Andrew. *The Apache Wars: The Hunt for Geronimo, the Apache Kid, and the Captive Boy Who Started the Longest War in American History*. New York: Broadway Books, 2016.
Hyde, Albert E. "Billy the Kid and the Old Regime in the Southwest," reprint of "The Old Regime in the Southwest: The Reign of the Revolver in New Mexico." *Century Magazine*, no. 63 (March 1902).
Iacampo, Mark. "Recollections of the Kid." *Wild West*, Autumn 2022.
Iverson, Pete. *Diné: A History of the Navajos*. Albuquerque: University of New Mexico Press, 2002.
Jacobsen, Joel. *Such Men as Billy the Kid: The Lincoln County War Reconsidered*. Lincoln: University of Nebraska Press, 1994.
Jameson, W. C. "Buckshot Roberts." *Wild West*, June 2006.
Jensen, Joan M., and Darlis A. Miller. *New Mexico Women: Intercultural Perspectives*. Albuquerque: University of New Mexico Press, 1986.
Jernado, Don. *The True Life of Billy the Kid*. New York: F. Tousey, 1881.
Johnson, David. *The Horrell Wars: Feuding in Texas and New Mexico*. Denton: University of North Texas Press, 2014.
Josephson, Matthew. *The Robber Barons: The Great American Capitalists, 1861–1901*. New York: Harcourt, Brace and Co., 1934.
Josephy, Alvin M. *The Civil War in the American West*. New York: Alfred A. Knopf, 1991.
Julyan, Robert. *The Place Names of New Mexico*. Rev. ed. Albuquerque: University of New Mexico Press, 1998.
Kadlec, Robert F. *They "Knew" Billy the Kid: Interviews with Old-Time New Mexicans*. Santa Fe: Ancient City Press, 1987.
Kajencki, Francis C. "Alexander Grzelachowski: Pioneer Merchant of Puerto De Luna, New Mexico." *Journal of the Southwest* 26, no. 3 (Autumn 1984): 243–60.
Katz, Friedrich. *The Life and Times of Pancho Villa*. Stanford: Stanford University Press, 1998.
Kaye, E. Donald. *Nathan Augustus Monroe Dudley, 1825–1910: Rogue, Hero, or Both?* Denver: Outskirts Press, 2006.

Keleher, William A. *The Fabulous Frontier: Twelve New Mexico Items.* Albuquerque: University of New Mexico Press, 1962.

Keleher, William A. *The Maxwell Land Grant: A New Mexico Item.* Santa Fe: Rydal Press, 1942.

Keleher, William A. *Turmoil in New Mexico, 1846–1868.* Albuquerque: University of New Mexico Press, 1952.

Keleher, William A. *Violence in Lincoln County, 1869–1881.* Albuquerque: University of New Mexico Press, 1957.

Klasner, Lily Casey. "The Kid." In Nolan, *Billy the Kid Reader.*

Klasner, Lily. *My Girlhood Among Outlaws.* Edited by Eve Ball. Tucson: University of Arizona Press, 1972.

Knowlton, Christopher. *Cattle Kingdom: The Hidden History of the Cowboy West.* Boston: Houghton Mifflin Harcourt, 2017.

Knowlton, Clark S. "Patron-Peon Pattern Among the Spanish Americans of New Mexico." *Social Forces* 41, no. 1 (October 1962): 12–17.

Koop, Waldo E. "Billy the Kid: Trail of a Kansas Legend." In Nolan, *Billy the Kid Reader.*

Lacy, Ann, and Anne Valley-Fox. *Stories from Hispano New Mexico: A New Mexico Federal Writers' Project Book.* Santa Fe: Sunstone Press, 2012.

Lamar, Howard Roberts. *The Far Southwest, 1846–1912: A Territorial History.* New Haven: Yale University Press, 1966.

Larson, Robert W. *New Mexico Populism: A Study of Radical Protest in a Western Territory.* Boulder: Colorado Associated University Press, 1974.

Larson, Robert W. *New Mexico's Quest for Statehood, 1846–1912.* Albuquerque: University of New Mexico Press, 1968.

Larson, Robert W. "The White Caps of New Mexico: A Study of Ethnic Militancy in the Southwest." *Pacific Historical Review* 44, no. 2 (May 1975): 171–85.

Lavash, Donald R. *A Journey Through New Mexico History.* Portales, NM: Bishop Publishing, 1971.

Lavash, Donald R. *Sheriff William Brady: Tragic Hero of the Lincoln County War.* Santa Fe: Sunstone Press, 1987.

Lavash, Donald R. *Wilson & The Kid.* College Station: Creative Publishing, 1990.

Leckie, William H. *The Buffalo Soldiers: A Narrative History of the Negro Cavalry in the West.* Norman: University of Oklahoma Press, 1967.

Leighton, Harry. *The Story of Richard M. Brewer, 1850–1878: Frontier Fighter, Farmer, Cowboy.* Mesilla, NM: Billy the Kid Outlaw Gang, 2016.

LeMay, John. *The Man Who Invented Billy the Kid: The Authentic Life of Ash Upson.* Roswell, NM: Bicep Books, 2020.

Lummis, Charles F. *The Land of Poco Tiempo.* New York: Charles Scribner's Sons, 1897.

Marín, Christine. *A Spokesman of the Mexican American Movement: Rodolfo "Corky" Gonzales and the Fight for Chicano Liberation, 1966–1972.* San Francisco: R. and E. Research Associates, 1977.

Marsh, Herbert, Jr. "Blood Money of the Lincoln County War." *Wild West History Association Journal,* June 2019.

Martinez, Monica Muñoz. *The Injustice Never Leaves You: Anti-Mexican Violence in Texas.* Cambridge, MA: Harvard University Press, 2018.

McCallum, Jack. *Leonard Wood: Rough Rider, Surgeon, Architect of American Imperialism.* New York: New York University Press, 2006.

McCarty, John L. *Maverick Town: The Story of Old Tascosa*. Norman: University of Oklahoma Press, 1946.

McChristian, Douglas C. *Regular Army O! Soldiering on the Western Frontier, 1865–1891*. Norman: University of Oklahoma Press, 2017.

McCright, Grady E., and James H. Powell. *Jessie Evans: Lincoln County Badman*. College Station: Creative Publishing, 1983.

McFeely, William S. *Grant: A Biography*. New York: W. W. Norton, 1981.

McGrath, Tom. *Vicente Silva and His Forty Thieves: The Vice Criminals of the 80's and 90's*. Published by the author, 1960.

McLynn, Frank. *Villa and Zapata: A Biography of the Mexican Revolution*. London: Pimlico, 2000.

McMath, Robert C., Jr. *American Populism: A Social History, 1877–1898*. New York: Hill & Wang, 1992.

Meadows, John P. *Pat Garrett and Billy the Kid as I Knew Them*. Edited by John P. Wilson. Albuquerque: University of New Mexico Press, 2004.

Meier, Matt S., and Feliciano Rivera. *The Chicanos: A History of Mexican Americans*. New York: Hill and Wang, 1972.

Metz, Leon C. *The Encyclopedia of Lawmen, Outlaws, and Gunfighters*. New York: Checkmark Books, 2003.

Metz, Leon C. *John Selman: Gunfighter*. Norman: University of Oklahoma Press, 1992.

Metz, Leon C. *Pat Garrett: The Story of a Western Lawman*. Norman: University of Oklahoma Press, 1974.

Michelsohn, Lynn. *Billy the Kid in Santa Fe: Young Billy*. Roswell, NM. Cleanan Press, 2014.

Michelsohn, Lynn. *Billy the Kid's Jail*. Santa Fe: Cleanan Press, 2011.

Michelsohn, Lynn. *A Confining Winter: Billy the Kid in Santa Fe*. Santa Fe: Cleanan Press, Inc, 2019.

Miller, James M. *The Early Days & Pecos Valley Life of James M. Miller: Reminiscences of Billy the Kid and John Chisum*. Published by the author, 2018.

Mills, James B. *Billy the Kid: El Bandido Simpático*. Denton: University of North Texas Press, 2022.

Mills, James B. "Billy the Kid and the Apaches." *True West*, July/August 2021.

Mills, James B. "Hombres Valientes in the Lincoln County War." *Wild West*, December 2020.

Mills, James B. "Slaughter in Seven Rivers." *True West*, June 2022.

Mills, James B. "They Called Him Bilito." *Wild West*, December 2020.

Mills, James B., and Bob Boze Bell. "True West Exclusive! Long Lost Jailhouse Interview with Billy the Kid and Illustration Uncovered." *True West*, April 2020.

Montgomery, Charles. "Becoming 'Spanish-American': Race and Rhetoric in New Mexico Politics, 1880–1928." *Journal of American Ethnic History* 20, no. 4 (Summer 2001).

Montoya, María E. *Translating Property: The Maxwell Land Grant and the Conflict over Land in the American West, 1840–1900*. Lawrence: University Press of Kansas, 2005.

Morsberger, Robert E., and Katharine M. Morsberger. *Lew Wallace: Militant Romantic*. San Francisco: San Francisco Book Co., 1980.

Mullin, Robert N. *The Boyhood of Billy the Kid*. Southwestern Studies 5, no. 1, monograph no. 17. El Paso: Texas Western Press 1967.

Mullin, Robert N. "The Boyhood of Billy the Kid." In Nolan, *Billy the Kid Reader*.

Mullin, Robert N. "Here Lies John Kinney." *Journal of Arizona History* 14, no. 3 (Autumn 1973).

Mullin, Robert N., and Charles E. Welch Jr. "Billy the Kid: The Making of a Hero." *Western Folklore* 32, no. 2 (April 1973).

Munk, Joseph A. *Arizona Sketches*. New York: Grafton Press, 1905.

Murphy, Lawrence R. *Lucien Bonaparte Maxwell: The Napoleon of the Southwest*. Norman: University of Oklahoma Press, 1983.

Murphy, Lawrence R. *Philmont: A History of New Mexico's Cimarron Country*. Albuquerque: University of New Mexico Press, 2014.

Myers, Lee. *Fort Stanton, New Mexico: The Military Years, 1855–1896*. Lincoln, NM: Lincoln County Historical Society.

Nabokov, Peter. *Tijerina and the Courthouse Raid*. Albuquerque: University of New Mexico Press, 1969.

Noble, David Grant. *Pueblos, Villages, Forts & Trails: A Guide to New Mexico's Past*. Albuquerque: University of New Mexico Press, 1994.

Nolan, Frederick. *Bad Blood: The Life and Times of the Horrell Brothers*. Stillwater, OK: Barbed Wire Press, 1994.

Nolan, Frederick. "Billy Hits Tascosa." *True West*, October 2002.

Nolan, Frederick, ed. *The Billy the Kid Reader*. Norman: University of Oklahoma Press, 2012.

Nolan, Frederick. "Boss Rustler: The Life and Crimes of John Kinney." *True West*, September 1996, October 1996.

Nolan, Frederick. "Dick Brewer: The Unlikely Gunfighter." *NOLA Quarterly* 15, no. 3 (July–September 1991): 19–27.

Nolan, Frederick. "Dirty Dave: The Life and Times of Billy the Kid's Worst Friend." *The Kid*, December 1989.

Nolan, Frederick. "Here He Lies." *Western Outlaw Lawman Association Journal* (Spring 2003).

Nolan, Frederick. "Hunting Billy the Kid." *Wild West*, June 2003.

Nolan, Frederick. *The Life & Death of John Henry Tunstall*. Albuquerque: University of New Mexico Press, 1964.

Nolan, Frederick. *The Lincoln County War: A Documentary History*. Norman: University of Oklahoma Press, 1992.

Nolan, Frederick. "The Private Life of Billy the Kid." *True West*, July 2000.

Nolan, Frederick. "The Search for Alexander McSween." *New Mexico Historical Review* 62, no. 2 (July 1987): 287–301.

Nolan, Frederick. "So, Who Was Dan Dedrick?" *True West*, June 2011.

Nolan, Frederick. *The West of Billy the Kid*. Norman: University of Oklahoma Press, 1998.

Nostrand, Richard L. *The Hispano Homeland*. Norman: University of Oklahoma Press, 1992.

O'Keefe, Michael. *The Literature of Billy the Kid and the Lincoln County War: 1952–2022*. Published by the author, 2023.

O'Neal, Bill. "Henry Brown: Hired Gun of the Lincoln County War." *True West*, February 1984.

O'Neal, Bill. *Henry Brown: The Outlaw Marshal*. College Station: Early Press, 1980.

O'Neal, Bill. *John Chisum: Frontier Cattle King*. Fort Worth: Eakin Press, 2018.

Opler, Morris Edward, and Catherin H. Opler. "Mescalero Apache History in the Southwest." *New Mexico Historical Review* 25, no. 1 (January 1950): 1–36.

Oropeza, Lorena. *The King of Adobe: Reies López Tijerina—Lost Prophet of the Chicano Movement*. Chapel Hill: University of North Carolina Press, 2019.

Otero, Miguel Antonio. *My Life on the Frontier, 1864–1882*. New York: Press of the Pioneers, 1935.

Otero, Miguel Antonio. *My Life on the Frontier, 1882–1897: Facsimile of Original 1939 Edition*. Santa Fe: Sunstone Press, 2007.

Otero, Miguel Antonio. *My Nine Years as Governor of the Territory of New Mexico, 1897–1906: Facsimile of Original 1940 Edition*. Santa Fe: Sunstone Press, 2007.

Otero, Miguel Antonio, Jr. *The Real Billy the Kid: With New Light on the Lincoln County War*. 1936. Reprint, Houston: Arte Público Press, 1998.

Parsons, Chuck. "Reese Gobles: Predator." *NOLA Quarterly* 14, no. 2 (Summer 1990).

Pearson, Jim Berry. *The Maxwell Land Grant*. Norman: University of Oklahoma Press, 1961.

Perrigo, Lynn Irwin. *Gateway to Glorieta: A History of Las Vegas, New Mexico*. Santa Fe: Sunstone Press, 2010.

Phelan, Craig. *Grand Master Workman: Terence Powderly and the Knights of Labor*. Westport, CT: Greenwood Publishing, 2000.

Poe, John W. *The Killing of Billy the Kid*. 1919. Reprint, Barto, PA: Creative Texts Publishers, 2015.

Poe, Sophie A. *Buckboard Days*. Caldwell, ID: Caxton Printers, 1936.

Rasch, Philip J. *Gunsmoke in Lincoln County*. Laramie, WY: National Association for Outlaw and Lawman History, 1997.

Rasch, Philip J. *Trailing Billy the Kid*. Laramie, WY: National Association for Outlaw and Lawman History, 1995.

Rasch, Philip J. *Warriors of Lincoln County*. Laramie, WY: National Association for Outlaw and Lawman History, 1998.

Recko, Corey. *The Colfax County War: Violence and Corruption in Territorial New Mexico*. Denton: University of North Texas Press, 2024.

Recko, Corey. *Murder on the White Sands: The Disappearance of Albert and Henry Fountain*. Denton: University of North Texas Press, 2007.

Reed, John. *Insurgent Mexico*. New York: D. Appleton, 1914.

Reséndez, Andrés. *Changing National Identities at the Frontier: Texas and New Mexico, 1800–1850*. Cambridge: Cambridge University Press, 2004.

Reséndez, Andrés. *The Other Slavery: The Uncovered Story of Indian Enslavement in America*. Boston: Houghton Mifflin Harcourt, 2016.

Roberts, Calvin A., and Susan A. Roberts. *New Mexico*. Rev. ed. Albuquerque: University of New Mexico Press, 2006.

Romero, Mary. "Class Struggle and Resistance Against the Transformation of Land Ownership and Usage in Northern New Mexico: The Case of Las Gorras Blancas." *Chicana/o-Latina/o Law Review* 26, no. 87 (2006): 87–109.

Romo, David. *Ringside Seat to a Revolution: An Underground Cultural History of El Paso and Juárez, 1893–1923*. El Paso: Cinco Puntos Press, 2005.

Rosales, F. Arturo. *Chicano! The History of the Mexican American Civil Rights Movement*. Houston: Arte Público Press, 1997.

Rosenbaum, Robert J. *Mexicano Resistance in the Southwest*. Austin: University of Texas Press, 1981.

Russell, Randy. *Billy the Kid: The Story, The Trial*. Lincoln: Crystal Press, 1994.

Sánchez, Ernest S., and Paul. R Sánchez. *"Nuestros Antepasados" (Our Ancestors): Los Nuevo Mexicanos del Condado de Lincoln (Lincoln County's History of Its New Mexican Settlers)*. Bloomington, IN: AuthorHouse, 2015.

Sánchez, George I. *Forgotten People: A Study of New Mexicans*. Albuquerque: Calvin Horn Publisher, 1967.

Sánchez, Lynda A. *Apache Legends & Lore of Southern New Mexico*. Charleston, SC: History Press, 2014.

Sánchez, Lynda A. "El Jovencito." *True West*, July 2011.
Sánchez, Lynda A. "The Last Hurrah." *True West*, May/June 2024.
Sánchez, Lynda A. "They Loved Billy the Kid." *True West*, January 1984.
Schlesinger, Andrew B. "Las Gorras Blancas, 1889–1891." *Journal of Mexican American History* 1, no. 2 (Spring 1970): 87–143.
Serna, Louis. *Clay Allison and the Colfax County War*. Published by the author, 2012.
"SFTA Hall of Fame: Felipe Chávez." *Wagon Tracks* 30, no. 1 (November 2015): 13.
Shinkle, James D. *Fort Sumner and the Bosque Redondo Indian Reservation*. Roswell, NM: Hall-Poorbaugh Press, 1965.
Shinkle, James D. *Reminiscences of Roswell Pioneers*. Roswell, NM: Hall-Poorbaugh Press, 1966.
Sides, Hampton. *Blood and Thunder: An Epic of the American West*. New York: Doubleday, 2006.
Simmons, Marc. *Spanish Pathways: Readings in the History of Hispanic New Mexico*. Albuquerque: University of New Mexico Press, 2001.
Siringo, Charles A. *A Cowboy Detective: A True Story of Twenty-Two Years with a World-Famous Detective Agency*. Arcadia Press, 2017.
Siringo, Charles A. *The Story of Billy the Kid*. Badgley Publishing Company, 2012.
Siringo, Charles A. *A Texas Cowboy, or Fifteen Years on the Hurricane Deck of a Spanish Pony*. New York: Penguin Books, 2000.
Slatten, Josh. "Jose Chavez y Chavez: The Good Side of a Not So Bad Man." *Wild West History Association Journal* 15, no. 4 (December 2022).
Slatten, Josh. "White Oaks, Dark Roots." *Wild West*, Autumn 2022.
Smith, Wilbur. "The Man Who Fought Side-By-Side with Lincoln County's Outlaw Character Tells All about the Days of 'Judge Colt's Rule.'" *New Mexico Magazine*, April 1933.
Sonnichsen, C. L. *The Mescalero Apaches*. Norman: University of Oklahoma Press, 1973.
Stahl, Robert J. "We Saw Billy the Kid Dead." *Wild West History Association Journal*, December 2019.
Stanley, F. *Dave Rudabaugh: Border Ruffian*. Denver: World Press, 1961.
Stark, Louisa R. "The Origin of the Penitente 'Death Cart.'" *Journal of American Folklore* 84, no. 333 (July–September 1971): 304–10.
Steele, Thomas J. *Archbishop Lamy: In His Own Words*. Albuquerque: LPD Press, 2000.
Steele, Thomas J., S. J. Paul Rhetts, and Barbe Awalt. *Seeds of Struggle/Harvest of Faith: The Papers of the Archdiocese of Santa Fe Catholic Cuatro Centennial Conference—The History of the Catholic Church in New Mexico*. Albuquerque: LPD Press, 1998.
Sweeney, Edwin R. *Mangas Coloradas: Chief of the Chiricahua Apaches*. Norman: University of Oklahoma Press, 1998.
Sweetman, Jack. *The Landing at Veracruz: 1914*. Annapolis, MD: Naval Institute Press, 1968.
Tanner, Karen Holliday, and John D. Tanner Jr. *New Mexico Territorial Penitentiary (1884–1912): Directory of Inmates*. Santa Fe: Published by the authors, 2002.
Tatum, Stephen. *Inventing Billy the Kid: Visions of the Outlaw in America, 1881–1981*. Albuquerque: University of New Mexico Press, 1982.
Thomas, David G. *Billy the Kid's Grave: A History of the Wild West's Most Famous Death Marker*. Las Cruces, NM: Doc45 Publishing, 2017.
Thomas, David G. *Dirty Dave Rudabaugh: Billy the Kid's Most Feared Companion*. Las Cruces, NM: Doc 45 Publishing, 2023.

Thomas, David G. *The Frank W. Angel Report on the Death of John Tunstall*. Las Cruces, NM: Doc45 Publishing, 2022.

Thomas, David G. "He Shot the Sheriff." *Wild West*, February 2021.

Thomas, David G. *Killing Pat Garrett: The Wild West's Most Famous Lawman—Murder or Self-Defense?* Las Cruces, NM: Doc45 Publishing, 2019.

Thomas, David G. *The Trial of Billy the Kid*. Las Cruces: Doc45 Publishing, 2021.

Thompson, Gerald. *The Army and the Navajo: The Bosque Redondo Reservation Experiment, 1863–68*. Tucson: University of Arizona Press, 1976.

Tijerina, Reies López. *They Called Me "King Tiger": My Struggle for the Land and Our Rights*. Translated and edited by José Ángel Gutiérrez. Houston: Arte Público Press, 2000.

Tower, Mike. "Big Jim French and the Lincoln County War." *Wild West*, December 2004.

Tower, Mike. *The Outlaw Statesman: The Life and Times of Fred Tecumseh Waite*. Bloomington, IN: AuthorHouse, 2007.

Townsend, James. "James W. Bell: Marylander, Texas Ranger, Fugitive." *Billy the Kid Coalition Press*, vol. 3 (2023).

Townsend, James. "Justified Homicide." *True West*, July-August 2021.

Trask, David F. *The War with Spain in 1898*. Lincoln: University of Nebraska Press, 1996.

Traylor, Leslie. "Facts Regarding the Escape of Billy the Kid." *Frontier Times* 13, no. 10 (July 1936): 506–13.

Tsompanas, Paul L. *Juan Patrón: A Fallen Star in the Days of Billy the Kid*. Richmond, VA: Belle Isle Books, 2013.

Turk, David S. *Blackwater Draw: Three Lives, Billy the Kid and the Murders That Started the Lincoln County War*. Santa Fe: Sunstone Press, 2011.

Turk, David S., and Rick Parker. "The Search for Jessie Evans." *Wild West*, August 2009.

Tuska, Jon. *Billy the Kid: His Life and Legend*. Albuquerque: University of New Mexico Press, 1994.

Usmar, Chuck. "Billy the Irish." *True West*. May 2015.

Usmar, Chuck, III. "Was Billy's Mother a Five Points Prostitute?" *True West*, July/August 2021.

Utley, Robert M. *Billy the Kid: A Short and Violent Life*. Lincoln: University of Nebraska Press, 1989.

Utley, Robert M. *High Noon in Lincoln: Violence on the Western Frontier*. Albuquerque: University of New Mexico Press, 1987.

Vidor, King, dir. *Billy the Kid*. Turner Entertainment, 1930

Vigil, Ernesto. *The Crusade for Justice: Chicano Militancy and the Government's War on Dissent*. Madison: University of Wisconsin Press, 1999.

Wahll, Andrew J. *Maxwell's Ranche, Territory of New Mexico*. Berwyn Heights, MD: Heritage Books, 2013.

Wallace, Lew. *An Autobiography*. 2 vols. New York: Harper & Bros., 1906.

Wallis, Michael. *Billy the Kid: The Endless Ride*. New York and London: W. W. Norton, 2007.

Ward, Nathan. *Son of the Old West: The Odyssey of Charlie Siringo: Cowboy, Detective, Writer of the Wild Frontier*. New York: Atlantic Monthly Press, 2023.

Watt, Robert N. *"Horses Worn to Mere Shadows": The Victorio Campaign, 1880*. Warwick, UK: Helion, 2019.

Watt, Robert N. *"I Will Not Surrender the Hair of a Horse's Tail": The Victorio Campaign, 1879*. Warwick, UK: Helion, 2017.

Weddle, Jerry. *Antrim Is My Stepfather's Name*. Phoenix: Arizona Historical Society, 1993.

Weddle, Jerry. "Apprenticeship of an Outlaw: Billy the Kid in Arizona." *Journal of Arizona History* 31, no. 3 (Autumn 1990).

Weddle, Richard. "Chisum: Cattle King of the Pecos." *Wild West*, August 2014.

Weddle, Richard. "Shooting Billy the Kid." *Wild West*, August 2012.

Weigle, Marta. *Brothers of Light, Brothers of Blood: The Penitentes of the Southwest*. Albuquerque: University of New Mexico Press, 1976.

Weigle, Marta, and Kyle Fiore. *Santa Fe and Taos: The Writer's Era, 1916–1941*. Santa Fe: Sunstone Press, 2008.

Weiss, Elaine. *The Women's Hour: The Great Fight to Win the Vote*. New York: Penguin Books, 2019.

Westphall, Victor. *Mercedes Reales: Hispanic Land Grants of the Upper Río Grande Region*. Albuquerque: University of New Mexico, 1983.

Westphall, Victor. *Thomas Benton Catron and His Era*. Tucson: University of Arizona Press, 1973.

White, Robert R. "The Murder of Colonel Charles Potter." *New Mexico Historical Review* 62, no. 3 (1987).

White, Rose P. "Full Many a Flower." *New Mexico Folklore Record*, no. 4 (1949–50): 15–16.

Whitlock, Flint. *Distant Bugles, Distant Drums: The Union Response to the Confederate Invasion of New Mexico*. Boulder: University Press of Colorado, 2006.

Wilson, John P. *Merchants, Guns, and Money: The Story of Lincoln County and Its Wars*. Santa Fe: Museum of New Mexico Press, 1987.

Windham, Margaret Leonard, comp. *New Mexico Marriages: Churches of Immaculate Conception of Tomé and Our Lady of Belén*. Extracted by Raymond P. Salas. Albuquerque: New Mexico Genealogical Society, 1994.

Windham, Margaret Leonard, and Evelyn Lujan Baca, comp. *New Mexico Baptisms: Nuestra Señora de la Inmaculada Concepción de Tomé*. Vol. 2, *11 February 1847–12 June 1881*. Extracted by Donald S. Dreeson and Lila Armijo Pfeufer. Albuquerque: New Mexico Genealogical Society: 2017.

Womack Jr., John. *Zapata and the Mexican Revolution*. New York: Vintage Books, 1970.

Wright, Carroll D. "An Historical Sketch of the Knights of Labor." *Quarterly Journal of Economics* 1, no. 2 (January 1887): 137–68.

Young, Roy B. "Billy, the Kid Who Never Grew Up." *Wild West History Association Journal*, June 2020.

Acknowledgments

I owe thanks to numerous people for varying degrees of assistance while I put this book together, but none more so than the spectacular Dena Hunt—the best archivist in the state of New Mexico—at the New Mexico State Records Center and Archives in Santa Fe. No task was too much for Dena as she happily sought out and scanned any and all materials that I requested. We also developed a wonderful friendship. To say that I owe Dena a fancy dinner for her help would be an understatement.

As usual, I owe much thanks for my wonderful circle of friends in the American West history field for their affection and support: Bob Boze Bell, Lynda A. Sánchez, Chuck Usmar, Roy B. Young, Chuck Parsons, Mark Boardman, Stuart Rosebrook, Erik "Eazy-E" Wright, John LeMay, Richard W. Etulain, Mark Lee Gardner, James Townsend, Corey Recko, Herbert Marsh Jr., Samuel K. Dolan, and Matthew Bernstein.

Appreciation also goes to numerous other friends and colleagues for their assistance, inspiration, or moral support: Rock Ulibarri, Roberto Martínez, Margaret Chávez Slayton, Ed Romero, Massimo De Vito, Art T. Burton, John Boessenecker, Janice Dunnahoo, the late Drew Gomber, David Lauterborn, Greg Lalire, Jack DeMattos, Michael Wallis, Robert Ray, Daniel B. Flores, Mark Warren, Gordon Fikes, Bob Reece, Michael O'Keefe, Susan Stevenson, Gary Jones, Benjamin Doss, Fredrick Balduini, Will Courtney, Mike Mayberry, Brandon Dickson, Cindy A. Medina, Melanie Hubner, Josh Slatten, Christopher Anderson, Rick Beyer, David Woodbury, Robert Fiorent, Nathalie Bleser, Domenica Bongiovanni, Kathy Radina, Thomas Bell, Keegan Cool, Dana Condel, Carolyn Danza Ossorio, John Fusco, and Emilio Estevez.

I owe thanks to my editor Ron Chrisman at University of North Texas Press, our wonderful copyeditor Amy Maddox, the amazing Cathy Smith at the Haley Memorial Library, the wonderful Heather McClure at the Fray Angélico Chávez Library, Gail Packard of the State Archives of New Mexico, the delightful Teddie Moreno, Cindy Abel Morris, and Christopher Geherin at the University of New Mexico, Dennis Daily, Jennifer Olguin, and Elizabeth Villa at the New Mexico State University Library, Abbie H. Weiser and Claudia Rivers at the University of Texas at El Paso Library, Kim Montoya-Hopkins at the Rosario Cemetery in Santa Fe, Matthew Hill at the Brigham Young University, Findlay Martin, and the late Charles R. Cross. I also extend a personal thanks to Scott Arthur, Stuart Lewis, Blair Forrest, and Steven "Sid" Best.

Last, but certainly not least, I owe a colossal thank you to my remarkable mother, Diane Mills, and the two furry little fellows to whom this book is lovingly dedicated: my dog, Dennis, and my cat, Bernard.

James B. Mills
jamesmills83@yahoo.com

Index

A

Abeyta, Agapito, 356
acequias (irrigation ditches), 10, 272, 305
Acosta, Oscar Zeta, 476
Aguayo, Aristotle, 231–33
Alamogordo, New Mexico, 5, 432
Alarad, Trinidad, 227
Alarid, Eugenio, 353, 362, 365, 368–70, 380, 382–83, 400, 408, 427
Alarid, Laureano "Chino," 396, 405
Alberti, Albert, 326–27
Alborado, Santiago, 268
Albuquerque, New Mexico, 4, 300, 306, 356, 358, 377, 381–82, 430, 439–41, 449, 463–64
Alcock, James A., 299
Alianza Federal de Mercedes (Federated Alliance of Community Grants), 477
Allen, James, 47, 229–30, 297
Allen, Lyman Sprague, 296
Allison, Clay, 79
Álvares, Nicodemos, 78
Anaya, Apolicarpio "Paco," 222
Anaya, Josefa, 257
Anaya, Pablo, 182, 221, 223, 230, 280–81
Ancheta, José Arturo, 346
Anderson, William E., 286, 296
Angel, Clemente, 354
Angel, Frank Warner, 139, 141, 182
Anthony, George T., 225–28
Anton Chico, New Mexico, 181–82, 220–21, 237, 239, 246–48, 267, 270, 314, 318, 331
Antrim, William, 96
Apaches, 28–29, 33, 47–48, 62, 65, 67, 179, 225, 411
Apodaca, Desiderio, 230
Apodaca, Severanio, 62
Appel, Daniel, 155, 159–60, 164, 174–75, 189, 461

Applegate, Bill, 63–64
Aragón, Nicolas, 290, 292–94, 297–98, 445
Aragón, Pablo, 339, 342, 344–45
Aragón, Ruperta, 292, 298, 445
Aragón, Simón, 386
Archibeque-Herrera, María Paula, 307
Archibique, Sostenes, 78
Archuleta, Tomás, 74
Archulete, Lucio, 84, 99–100
Arizona, 20, 39, 95–96, 180, 271, 380, 383, 388–89, 394–95
Armijo, Perfecto, 266
Atencio, Dario, 317, 327
automobiles, 3–4, 430, 440, 446, 454, 460, 466, 468, 470, 472
Axtell, Samuel Beach, 70, 77, 81, 106–9, 123–24, 134–35, 139, 148, 182, 275, 282

B

Baca, Albino, 342, 371
Baca, Carlota, 68, 102, 119, 176, 183, 235, 262, 302
Baca, Celso, 267
Baca, Juana, 53, 149, 155, 256
Baca, Liberato C., 446, 451
Baca, Manuel R., 458
Baca, Pedro, 353, 380, 382
Baca, Saturnino, 29, 36–37, 70–71, 74, 76–78, 81, 83–84, 134, 136, 144, 146–49, 154–55, 158–59, 187, 189
Baca, Serafin, 364, 381, 399, 401, 413
Baca y Sedillo, José, 104, 108
Bacheldor, Edward Norman, 342
Bado de Juan Pais, New Mexico, 381
Bail, John D., 255
Baker, Frank, 98, 100–101, 113, 115–17, 122–23, 126
Ballard, A. J., 191

549

Bantz, Gideon D., 408, 415
Barber, George B., 242, 302, 441, 461
Barcelo, Gertrude, 12
Barela, Manuel, 217–18
Barnes, Sydney M., 226, 293
Baros, Gregorio, 280
Barragon, Ramón, 178
Barrett, A. H., 273
Barrier, Adolph P., 110–12, 119, 125
Barrow, Clyde, 472
Bates, Sebrian, 157–58, 166, 174
Beale, Yank, 272
Beall, Byron O., 453–54, 457
Beall, George T., Jr., 296
Beck, Herman, 295–96
Beckwith, Hugh Mercer, 87
Beckwith, Refugia, 87
Beckwith, Robert, 63, 87–88, 115, 138, 143, 148, 155, 165–66, 171–73, 175, 200
Beery, Wallace, 464–65
Belen, New Mexico, 304, 397
Bell, James W., 243, 245, 256–60, 463
Bennett, James M., 287
Bennett, Thomas, 288–89, 291, 296
Bent, Charles, 331
Bergman, Edward Henry, 416–17, 426
Bernalillo County, New Mexico, 352, 377, 436, 439, 468
Bernard, Joseph, 333
Bernard, Louisa Desmarais, 330, 333
Bernstein, Morris J., 179
Biederman, Charles R., 300
Billescas, Casimiro, 306
Billescas, David, 269, 291, 305, 419, 421, 442
Billescas-Chávez, Marines "María," 429
Blackwood, William, 425
Blair, Thomas, 147–48, 159, 168
Blake, Francis A., 309, 336
Blakely, Joe, 381–82, 399
Blanchard, Charles, 182, 331
Blanchard, William F., 287, 422
Blazer, Henry, 130
Blazer, Joseph H., 76–77, 132

Blazer's Mill, New Mexico, 130–31, 142, 204
Bojorquez, Roberto, 80
Bolden, Joe, 47
Bolívar, Simón, 388
Bolton, Amelia, 32, 62, 98, 101, 127
Bolton, Ellen, 153
Bolton, John, 50, 58
Bond, Marshall Latham, 460
Bond, Marshall, Jr., 460–61
Bonney, William H. "Billy," 4–6, 95–97, 101–2, 112–18, 126–28, 135–38, 167–71, 177–81, 190–96, 200–204, 206, 221–25, 233–37, 239–63, 270–71, 447–51, 458–62, 464–65, 467–72, 474–75
  Antrim, Henry "Kid," 95, 192, 201, 203
  Billy the Kid, 1–2, 4–6, 101–2, 127–28, 167–71, 175–78, 180–81, 192–93, 195, 200–204, 206, 221–22, 224, 233–37, 239–63, 434, 447–51, 458–65, 467–75, 478
  El Bilito, 97, 235, 241–63, 271, 446–47, 458, 465
  McCarty, Henry, 1, 95, 97, 253, 255, 262
Booth, Stephen E., 335
Booth, William, 432
Borrego, Inocencio, 413
Bosque Redondo, New Mexico, 26–27, 180, 259
Bousman, Lou, 248, 251–52
Bowdre, Charles Meriwether, 92–93, 124, 127, 130, 133, 137–38, 142, 145, 204–5, 221–22, 235–36, 246, 250–52
Bowdre, Manuela, 252
Bowen, Bill, 47–48
Bowen, Tom, 47–48
Boyle, Andrew "Andy," 100, 155, 161, 167–68, 171–73, 200, 474
Brady, María Bonifacia Chávez-Montoya, 33
Brady, Robert "Roberto," 289, 442–43

Brady, William J., 33, 36–37, 42–44, 55, 58, 82–87, 92–93, 98–100, 110–15, 118–19, 123–29, 131–32, 149, 206, 232, 442–43
Brady, William, Jr., 149
Brady-Cháves, Teodora, 468
Branch, Alejandro, 105
Brazel, Jesse Wayne, 434
Brazil, Manuel, 246, 250, 252
Breedon, Marshall A., 297
Breedon, William, 35, 80, 108, 226, 293, 297–98
Brent, James R., 286, 290, 292, 296–97, 300, 302–4
Brewer, Richard M. "Dick," 83, 85, 97–98, 101, 113–20, 122, 124, 126, 129–31, 135
Brickley, Ernest M., 442
Brinkerhoff, Henry R., 207
Bristol, Warren, 58, 73, 80, 103, 110–12, 131–32, 141, 205, 222, 226, 255
Britton, Frank, 47
Brothers, James A., 39, 304
Brown, Henry, 114, 120, 123, 127, 130, 132, 153–54, 178, 183, 190, 200, 206
Brown Berets, 476
Brunswick, Marcus, 254, 344
Brunton, William B., 339
Bryant, "Rustling Bob," 184, 188
Bullene, T. B., 228
Bureau of Investigation, 472
Burns, Walter Noble, 5, 458–60, 462, 464–65, 467, 470
Burns, William, 67, 346, 459–60, 465
Bursum, Holm Olaf, 394–95, 426
Burt, Billy, 259
Bushnell, Samuel, 58
Butler, Benjamin F., 332

C

Caballero, Guadalupe "El Lechuza," 353, 367–69, 371, 373, 379, 383, 399, 401–2

Cabeza de Baca, Luis María, 446
Cabeza de Baca, Manuel, 336, 361, 366, 371, 375, 379, 383, 388, 393, 398–99, 412
Cabra Arenoso, New Mexico, 224
Caffrey, William, 302
Cahill, Frank, 96
Cajul, Antonio, 355
California, 20, 47–48, 81, 266, 282, 296, 333, 416, 475
California Gold Rush, 20
Camp Grant, Arizona, 96
Campbell, Bill, 83, 193–95, 199, 201–4, 206–7, 441
Campbell, H. S., 441
Canada, 81, 244, 258, 282, 331
canciones (songs), 18
Candelario, Andres, 53–54
Candelario, Casimiro, 53–54
Candelario, José, 53–55, 57, 331
Capitan Mountains, 25, 86–87, 92, 177–78, 259
Capone, Al, 468
Carlson, J. C., 430
Carlyle, James, 245–47
Carr, Eugene A., 406
Carrizozo, New Mexico, 29, 53, 85, 199, 420, 422–23, 429, 437–39, 441–43, 453, 461
Carroll, Henry, 186, 196, 200–201
Carson, Kit, 11, 26
Carvallo, Carlos Narziso, 71–72
Casaus, Porfirio, 390
Casey, Lily, 48, 57, 59–60, 63
Casey, Robert, 48, 54, 57, 66, 70–71, 73–74, 204
Casey, William, 48, 59, 64, 71, 73–74
Catron, Thomas Benton
Catron County, New Mexico, 341, 450
Cebolleta (modern-day Seboyeta), New Mexico, 7–9, 29
Chambers, Lon, 248, 250
Chaplin, Charlie, 3
Chapman, Arthur, 447

Chapman, Huston L., 183, 189–90, 192, 194–96, 201, 223
Cháves, Amado, 220, 226
Cháves, Dionicio, 299
Cháves, Felipe, 304
Cháves, Florencio, 97, 102, 117, 123–24, 161, 163, 169, 171, 463, 468–69, 472
Cháves, J. Francisco, 36, 108, 226, 228, 274, 303, 321, 344–45, 431
Cháves, Manuel Antonio, 220
Chaves County, New Mexico, 4, 304–6, 433, 438, 440
Chávez, Adecasio, 29, 215, 232, 270, 314, 402, 429, 435, 451
Chávez, Ambrosio, 233–34, 421
Chávez, Ana María, 8
Chávez, Anacleto, 265–66
Chávez, Beatriz, 270, 429, 435, 451
Chávez, Benjamin, 419, 437, 440–42, 444, 454, 466
Chávez, Benjamin Martín, Jr., 442, 444
Chávez, Bessie, 429, 435, 451
Chávez, César, 199, 476
Chávez, Dionicio, 429, 435, 451
Chávez, Elerdo, 441–42
Chávez, Erenia, 437
Chávez, Feliciano, 384, 394, 397
Chávez, Francisco "Frank," 349, 359, 396, 405, 437
Chávez, Isadora, 7–10
Chávez, José María, 153, 170, 215
Chávez, José "Modesto" Francisco, 291
Chávez, Josefa "Josefita," 303–5, 437, 442, 444, 455, 465–66
Chávez, Juan, 1, 7–8, 10, 15, 19, 23, 147, 202–3, 381, 427, 429, 475, 478
Chávez, Juan José, 7–8, 10, 147, 364, 427
Chávez, Juana, 8, 149, 178, 215, 261, 291, 303, 305, 465
Chávez, Juliana V., 396
Chávez, Magdalena, 15, 36
Chávez, María de los Angeles, 422
Chávez, María Lauriana, 15
Chávez, Marillita "María," 426, 442, 444

Chávez, Martín, 14–17, 36–40, 150–54, 156–59, 161–63, 165–67, 175–78, 185–87, 233–35, 260–61, 269–70, 285–87, 289–91, 303–6, 419–21, 429–35, 437–44, 452–58, 462–66, 475–76
Chávez, Martín, Jr., 442, 454
Chávez, Pasqual, 225
Chávez, Porfirio, 427, 435
Chávez, Roy Benjamin, 437
Chávez y Baca, José, 144–47, 155, 215
Chávez y Chávez, José, 7–10, 29–30, 137–39, 153–54, 169–71, 179–81, 231–32, 270–71, 300–302, 313–14, 360, 364–66, 368–72, 379–85, 394–417, 426–30, 434–37, 445–46, 450–52, 478
Chávez y Sánchez, Clato, 185–86
Chávez y Sánchez, Desiderio, 185
Chávez y Sánchez, José, 185–86
Cherry, Wesley, 47
Chicago, Illinois, 5, 219, 433, 458, 470
Chicano Movement, 476
Chihuahua, Mexico, 238
Chisum, John Simpson, 39, 87–88, 103, 138, 222, 291
Chisum, Pitzer, 39, 87
Chisum, Sallie, 122, 179, 458
Christie, Follett G., 89, 112
Church, Josh, 302
Civil War, 13, 15, 19, 29, 32–33, 35, 88, 90, 178, 308–9, 326, 329, 332
Clancy, Juan Jorge, 446–47
Clark, Jasper L. "Jap," 429
Clark, John, 119, 457
Clay, Thomas F., 374, 386, 389
Clay County, Missouri, 374
Clendenin, David Ramsay, 61, 64, 68
Cleveland, Grover, 303, 372
Clifton, Arizona, 96
Cochrane, Tom, 115
Coe, Frank, 77–79, 97, 102, 116, 119, 130, 135–37, 144, 178–81, 185, 189
Coe, George, 79, 129–31, 136–37, 140, 142, 144–45, 151–54, 167, 170, 178–79, 181, 468–69, 471–73

Index

Coghlan, Pat, 236
Cole, Emily Catherine, 374
Cole, Jesse Richard, 373–74
Colfax County, New Mexico, 79, 90, 298, 372
  Colfax County War, 79, 90
Collier, Joseph B., 419–20
Collier, Needham C., 408, 415
Collier, Thomas Willis, Jr., 406
Collins, Frank, 200, 288
Collins, John, 184, 197, 200
Colorado, 20, 39, 96, 181, 228–29, 308–9, 341, 430, 468
Columbus, New Mexico, 440, 452, 458
Conklin, Anthony M., 217
Conklin, Charles, 254
Cook, Joe, 244
Cooper, Tom, 236, 241–44
Copeland, John, 40–43, 84, 131, 134, 136–37, 139, 145, 191–92, 196
Corbet, Sam, 129, 137, 187, 196, 256, 289–90
Córdova, José, 259, 303, 390
Córdova, Nicolás T., 390
Cordova, Tina, 476
Corn, Jasper, 290, 292, 298
Crause, Paul L., 431–32
Crawford, Charlie, 100, 155–56, 158–61
Crompton, Zacharias, 49–50, 64
Cronin, Michael, 79, 143, 286, 290, 303
Crouch, John S., 103, 108–9, 131
Cullins, Tom, 153, 170–71, 176
Cummings, W. R., 273
Cummins, Josh, 288
Cunningham, J. M., 409
Cunningham, William P., 383–84
Curry, George, 419, 433–36

D

Daniels, Henry, 407
Daniels, James M., 47
Darton, N. H., 446
Davidson, George V., 230, 281, 283
Davis, George, 98, 115, 133, 145, 147, 187, 200, 246–47

Davis, William Watts Hart, 14
Dawson, Byron, 195
Dawson, J. B., 398–99
de Aguayo, José María, 156, 158, 161, 215, 232, 288
de Baca, Amado, 230
de Baca, Ezequiel, 365
de Baca, Tomás, 267
de Guevara, Maximiano, 98–99, 190–91
Dedrick, Mose, 225, 236
Dedrick, Samuel, 236
Delano, Columbus, 56
Delgado, Juan, 227, 275
Denman, M. J., 299
Denson, Shadrack T., 46
Denver, Colorado, 329, 346, 349, 377, 430
Desmarais, Frédéric-Alexis, 329
Desmarais, Miguel F., 358
DeVours, James, 242
dichos (rhymes), 10
Dickey, George, 288–89, 291, 296
Dillinger, John, 472
Dillon, Jerry, 88, 92
Dillon, Richard Charles, 464
Dixon, Joe, 158, 163–64, 166
Dolan, James J., 48, 60–62, 85–93, 102–3, 110–12, 114–19, 122–23, 132–37, 139–50, 152–63, 165–76, 178–80, 182–83, 185–86, 188–89, 191–95, 199–207, 215–16, 222–23, 420
Domingues, José, 77
Domínquez, Ponciano, 113
Doña Ana County, New Mexico, 34, 88–89, 93, 97, 99–100, 103, 105–11, 131, 133, 140–41, 206–7, 255, 285
Dorsey, H., 449
Dow, Elisha, 77
Dow, Eugene, 71
Dowlin, Paul, 58, 76, 88–89, 93, 105
Dowlin, William, 58, 67, 82
Downey, John, 273
Downing, W. G., 440
Dubois, Thomas Mickey, 439

Dudley, Nathan, 129, 134–35, 137, 141–43, 147–49, 155, 157, 159–60, 162–69, 183–87, 189–92, 195–96, 200, 207–10, 213–15
Duford, William, 292
dummy, 153–54, 167, 172
Dunn, Richard, 267
Duran, Leonardo, 355
Durán, Rosita "Rosa," 379

E

Ealy, Mary, 117, 124, 126, 161
Ealy, Taylor F., 117–18, 123–24, 128–29, 131, 136, 153, 156, 160–61
Earp, Wyatt, 219
East, Jim, 248–49, 251–53
Easton, David, 238
Eaton, William J., 456
Eddy, Charles Bishop, 299, 304–5
Eddy, Henry, 47
Eddy County, New Mexico, 304
Edwards, Robert "Buck," 244
Eguillon, Peter, 357
El Burro, New Mexico, 309, 316
El Cuervo, New Mexico, 320, 360
el Día de San Juan (St. John's Day), 27, 32, 143, 268, 275
El Partido del Pueblo Unido (The United People's Party), 336–40, 342–44, 347–48, 352, 357, 361–62, 365, 387
El Paso, Texas, 438, 448
El Salitre, New Mexico, 309, 313, 316
Elkins, Stephen Benton, 35, 80, 406
Elliot, Richard, 293
Elliott, H. W., 100
Ellis, Ben, 134, 160–61, 174, 196, 202, 205
Ellis, Isaac, 90, 118, 134, 137, 164, 183, 187, 206, 208, 226
Ellis, Leslie, 424
Ellis, Will, 137
Emory, Tom, 248
Esquibel, Félix, 428
Esquibel, José Santos, 282, 300, 379

Esquibel, Perfecto, 104, 107, 416
Esquibel, Refugio, 366
Estabrook, Marcos, 77
Estevez, Emilio, 478
Evans, Jessie, 97–101, 111, 113, 115–16, 119, 125, 129, 133, 140–42, 187, 192–94, 199–204, 206–7
Evarts, William, 189

F

Fairbanks, Douglas, Sr., 3, 6, 469
Fall, Albert Bacon, 346–47, 397
Fangman, Camillius, 468
Farmer, Henry, 10, 68, 82
Fechét, Edmund Gustave, 55
Fennessey, Thomas, 273
Fergusson, Harvey, 462
Fernandez, Romualdo, 316
Fewell, Lucien N., 341–42
Field, Nelson A., 446
Finley, James, 243
First World War, 440
Fisher, Daniel, 77
Flores, Daniel B., 1, 272, 475
Floyd, Charles "Pretty Boy," 472
Flynn, William H., 294, 296
Folliard, Tom, 170–71, 190, 192, 195, 200, 203, 205–6, 209, 215, 221–22, 233–35, 244, 246, 250, 252
Ford, Charley, 301
Ford, Robert, 301–2
Fort, Lewis C., 329, 358, 379–80, 383, 386–87
Fort Stanton, New Mexico, 25–29, 33–34, 39–43, 51–52, 58–59, 61, 71–73, 76–78, 125, 128–29, 136–37, 143, 149, 155, 157, 159–63, 183–86, 190–93, 199–205, 207
Fort Sumner, New Mexico, 178–80, 183, 215–16, 221–25, 236, 239–40, 243–44, 246–47, 249, 252, 260–63, 458, 461, 463–64, 469–70
Fort Union, New Mexico, 12
Fort Wingate, New Mexico, 9, 26

Index

Fountain, Albert Jennings, 80, 255, 296, 397
Fountain, Henry, 397–98
Fox, Lafayette, 407
Frank, William, 48, 59, 115, 117, 122–23, 126, 253–54, 370–72, 381, 456, 461
Freeman, Frank, 83, 92
French, James, 190–91
French, Jim, 120, 127–29, 153, 166–67, 170–71, 176, 178, 183, 190, 200
Friderici, Blanche, 464
Frietz, Daniel, 100
Fritz, Carolina, 223
Fritz, Charles, 67, 81, 84, 91, 93, 111, 186
Fritz, Emil, 33, 48, 67, 81, 303, 420
Frost, Max, 341–42

G

Gadsden Purchase, 20–21
Galindre, José L., 354, 390
Galisteo, New Mexico, 81, 227, 313, 345
Gallegos, Cresenciano, 276–77, 279–80
Gallegos, Isidoro, 428
Gallegos, José Delores, 390
Gallegos, José M., 67
Gallegos, Juan, 50, 101, 145–46, 249–50, 268, 276, 279–80, 337, 374, 390, 396
Gallegos, Juan J., 249
Gallegos, Lucas, 42, 50, 84, 93, 98, 100–101, 207
Gallegos, Nestor, 337, 386–87
Gallegos, Pantaleon, 115–16, 145–46, 154
Gallegos, Román, 265, 276–77
Gallegos, Santos, 318
Gallegos, Severo, 256, 259
Gallegos, Tomás, 268, 276
Gallup, New Mexico, 464
García, Apolinario, 54
García, Dionicio, 237, 308
García, Félix, 339, 342, 344–45, 453
García, Higinio, 249–52
García, José de Jesús, 104
García, Pedro, 356
García, Sostero, 84, 207
García y Trujillo, José, 271
Garfield, James A., 255
Garrett, Patrick "Pat" Floyd Jarvis, 238–44, 246–58, 260–62, 270–73, 286, 291–92, 305, 433–34, 448, 451, 458, 460–62, 464, 471
Gasparri, Donato, 107
Gates, Susan, 117
Gauss, Gottfried, 114–15, 223, 256, 258–59
Gavarro, Ignacio, 84
Geoffrion, Octave, 329
Georgetown, Texas, 47
Gibson, Hoot, 468
Giddings, George, 281–82
Giddings, Marsh, 35, 55–57, 61, 69
Giddings, William Baxton, 268, 281
Gildea, Augustus "Gus," 184, 222
Gill, William, 61, 397
Ginn, George, 90
Gobles, Reese, 184
Godfroy, Fred, 112, 130, 142, 179
Gómez, Francisco, 102, 189, 422
Gómez, Ignacia, 289
Gonzáles, Antonio, 82, 326, 370, 388, 396, 399, 405, 433
Gonzáles, Florencio, 37, 39, 71, 76, 79–80, 82, 84, 100, 103, 118, 134, 286, 290
Gonzáles, Jacinto, 44, 49–50
Gonzáles, José, 53, 78–79, 134, 286, 290, 370, 379, 381, 399–401, 405, 408
Gonzáles, Juan, 42, 50–52, 57–58, 62, 71, 78–80, 82–83, 100, 118, 134, 379
Gonzáles, Patricio, 66, 353, 355, 381, 383, 388, 396, 405
Gonzáles, Pilar, 53
Gonzáles, Rodolfo "Corky," 476
Gonzáles y Baca, Manuel, 353, 367, 370, 373, 377–81, 399–402
Gonzáles y Blea, Martín, 370, 373, 379
Gonzáles y Borrego, Antonio, 396, 405
Gonzáles y Borrego, Francisco, 359, 396, 405

González, Ignacio, 56, 129, 137, 153, 170–71, 177–78
Goodley, Joel, 320
Goodley, Stan, 320
Goodley, William, 320
Goodnight, Charlie, 39, 236
Goodwin, Millard, 118, 179, 196, 199, 203
Gordon, M. G., 323
Gould, Wallace, 308
Grand Junction, Colorado, 468
Grant, Joe, 224, 250, 252
Grant, Ulysses S., 20, 35
Grant County, New Mexico, 79, 89, 93, 96, 99–100, 103, 346, 407, 452
Gray, Bill, 47
Gray, Elias, 202
Great Britain, 261
Great Depression, 472
Greathouse, Jim, 244–46
Green, Elias, 386–87
Green, Tom, 115–16
Green, William "Billy," 288, 354–55, 364, 381–82, 385–87, 389–90
Greene, Charles W., 305
Gregg, James E., 297
Gregg, John, 61
Greiner, John, 11–12, 21
Griego, Candalario, 80
Griego, Nicolas, 281
Griffith, Bill, 272–73
Grizzell, James, 47
Gross, Jacob, 267
Grzelachowski, Alexander, 221, 244, 247, 249, 253, 278, 281
Guadalupe County, New Mexico, 348, 363, 365, 381, 388, 421, 437, 445–46, 451
Gurney, Frank, 440–41
Gurulé, Antonia, 63
Gutiérres, Cisto, 272–73
Gutiérres, Faustino, 266
Gutiérres, Rafael, 82
Gutiérrez, Apolinaria, 239
Gutiérrez, Juana Saturnina, 237
Gutiérrez, Manuel, 44, 51, 56, 147

Gutiérrez, Rafael, 53, 155, 216, 236
Gutiérrez, Regino, 270–71
Gylam, Jacob Lewis, 42, 49–51, 69

H

Hadley, Ozra Amander, 329, 339
Haley, J. Evetts, 5, 463
Hall, Lee, 248, 251, 300, 379
Hamilton, Humphrey Bennett, 396, 432
Hampe, Daniel B., 316
Hannett, Arthur T., 456–58
Hardy, R. F., 340, 342–43
Harrison, Benjamin, 326
Harrison, Nan Hillary, 472
Harrold, Mahlon, 57, 339
Hart, Edward, 59–60, 63
Haskins, Joe, 50, 62–63
Haswell, Berkley, 448
Hatch, Edward, 77, 190, 192, 199–200, 226–27
Hawkins, Mike G., 80
Haydon, William Gill, 397
Hayes, Rutherford B., 80, 123, 125, 134, 182, 187, 275
Head, R. G., 339
Heckle, George G., 330
Helmick, Milton J., 458
Henry, Edward, 119, 330, 416, 426
Herlow, Paul, 81, 230, 297
Hernández, Jesús, 390
Herrera, Delores, 420
Herrera, Fernando, 127, 159, 161, 165, 177–78, 202, 435
Herrera, Juan José, 307–9, 312, 315, 317, 319, 323–25, 330, 334–37, 342–43, 348–49, 354–57, 360–65, 375, 388, 427–28
Herrera, Manuel, 307, 336, 353, 361, 379, 388
Herrera, Nestor, 336, 339, 342, 344–45, 353, 380, 382, 401
Herrera, Nicanor, 307–9, 312, 317, 327, 330, 336–37, 339, 349, 354–57, 361, 372
Herrera, Pablo, 307–9, 312, 317–18, 327, 330, 334, 339, 342–49,

Index 557

353–56, 358–59, 361–65, 372, 375, 389–91
Herrera-Ulibarri, Juanita Paula, 354, 477
Hesse, Jerome, 468
Hewitt, J. Y., 419
Higgins, John "Pink," 64
Highsaw, James M., 87
Hill, Tom, 15, 98, 113, 115–16, 124
Hindman, George, 113, 115–17, 127–28, 133
Hinkle, James F., 419, 453–54, 468
Hirst, Michael, 478
Hitler, Adolf, 469
Hittson, John N., 40
Hobart, Edward F., 312
Hobbs, Bud, 429
Hocradle, Jerry, 59
Holliday, John "Doc," 219
Holt, Wallace, 302
Holtkamp, Leonard, 468
Hommel, Mary Ann, 330
Hoover, J. Edgar, 469, 472
Horrell, Benjamin, 46
Horrell, Elizabeth, 46
Horrell, James Martin "Mart," 46–47
Horrell, Merritt, 46–47, 51, 63–64
Horrell, Samuel, 46–48, 51, 63–64
Horrell, Thomas "Tom," 46–48, 64
Horrell brothers, 46–64, 76, 78, 282
Horrell ranch, 51–52, 59–61
Horrell War, 55, 64, 282
Hough, Emerson A., 447
Houston, John K., 103–4, 106, 108–9
Huber, George, 295
Hudgens, William H., 184–85, 236, 244–45
Huerta, Dolores, 476
Huff, Daniel, 156–58
Humphreys, Henry H., 207–15
Hunsaker, Don, 453
Hunter, Alf, 421
Hunter, James H., 306, 410–11
Hunter, Robert D., 91
Hurley, Johnny, 113, 115–16, 135, 155, 165–66, 171, 242–43, 246, 289, 292, 297–98

I

Ilfeld, Charles, 428
Iowa, 269, 296
Irvin, Jim, 184, 200

J

Jacobson, Isaac, 371
James, Frank, 135, 200, 206, 373, 440
James, Jesse, 219, 301, 373
Jaramillo, Hiraldo, 88
Jaramillo, Telesfor, 180–81
Jesuits, 107–10, 193, 356
Jilson, Arthur, 381
Johnson, Kay, 465
Johnson, Samuel M., 440
Johnson, William, 87–88, 135, 161
Jones, Andrieus A., 408
Jones, Heiskell, 48, 59
Jones, John, 165, 172, 197, 200, 222, 404
Jones, Thomas, 280
Joseph, Anthony, 323
Joseph, Antonio, 237, 284, 323, 340, 342, 363, 388
Joy, John C., 296–97

K

Kansas City, Missouri, 4, 227–28, 374
Kayse, Thomas, 306
Keenan, Thomas, 63
Keller, William H., 267
Kelley, Alexander, 78
Kelly, Edward "Choctaw," 255
Kimbrell, George, 37, 63, 187, 190–93, 195–96, 199, 202–3, 206–7, 233, 236, 238–39, 242–43, 289–90, 421, 424–25
Kimbrell, William E., 432, 435
King, C. W., 63
King, Thomas, 63, 83
Kinney, John, 101, 141–42, 144–46, 149, 152, 154–56, 162, 166, 171, 173, 175
Kiser, Frank, 273

Kistler, Russel A., 321–24, 334–36, 340, 343, 412–13
Kitt, George, 115, 130
Kline, August, 186, 269, 289, 303, 420, 424
Knight, Edgar, 452
Knights of Columbus, 452, 458
Knights of Labor, 309, 314, 318, 322, 324–25, 330–31, 335, 348–49, 356, 359, 365
Kohn, Samuel, 38
Koogler, J. H., 247
Koonce, John E., 442
Kruling, Charlie, 115–16, 135–36
Ku Klux Klan, 312
Kuch, Fred, 245–46

L

La Mesilla, New Mexico, 34, 88–89, 93, 97, 99–100, 103, 105–11, 131, 133, 140–41, 206–7, 255, 285
La Sociedad de Bandidos de Nuevo México (The Society of Bandits of New Mexico), 352–53, 362, 364–67, 370–74, 377–80, 382–83, 394, 397–99, 426
la Virgen de Guadalupe (the Virgin Mary), 9, 15, 388, 423
Labadie, Lorenzo, 220, 229–30, 237, 265, 274–76, 281–82, 340, 342
Labadie, Rallitos, 220, 275–76, 279
Labadie, Román, 276–77
Labadie, Tranquilino, 14, 104–5, 216, 220, 237, 274
Lackey, Henry, 288–89, 291, 296
Lampasas, Texas, 46–48, 64
Lamy, Anthony, 74
Lamy, Jean Baptiste, 12–14, 31, 74, 107, 132, 304, 357
Lamy, New Mexico, 12, 31, 228, 274, 341–42, 379
Lane, Alexander G., 292, 298
Largo, Jesús, 78–79
Larn, John, 184
Larue, Joseph A., 238, 241, 286

Las Cruces, New Mexico, 47, 101, 103, 109, 114, 135, 285–86, 289, 293, 434, 448
Las Tablas, New Mexico, 86, 178, 200, 202, 235, 239, 257, 287, 289, 291, 463
Las Vegas, New Mexico, 192–94, 217–21, 228–30, 253–55, 265–70, 274–76, 281–83, 300–301, 315–19, 321–24, 326–31, 333–40, 357–58, 360–61, 366–67, 370–84, 386–87, 393–96, 407–11, 426–30
Las Vegas Land Grant, 307, 313, 315, 317, 319, 333, 338, 357, 365, 375–77, 428
Lassaigne, Pedro, 43, 52, 55
Laub, John Lawrence, 334
Laughlin, Napoleon Bonaparte, 398
Lawrence, Kansas, 228
Laws, James W., 440
Le Duc, Frank, 323
Lea, Joseph, 236, 238, 242–44, 246, 286, 297, 300
Lea, Joseph Smith, 297, 300
Leach, Fred, Jr., 219
League of United Latin American Citizens, 476
Leckie, Joseph, 328, 394, 398
Lee, Oliver M., 397
Leiva, Mariano, 247, 266
Leon, Charles T., 346
Leonard, Ira, 196, 206–7, 215, 239, 241–42, 255
Leonard Wood County, New Mexico, 421, 430
Leverson, Montague, 125, 129, 139
Lewis, Charles, 3
Liddel, Dick, 301
Lincoln, New Mexico, 1, 3, 29, 36, 57, 124, 187, 189, 192, 213, 260
Lincoln County, New Mexico, 28–30, 33–37, 42–44, 46–49, 55–59, 63–65, 67–77, 79–83, 88–90, 109–10, 121–24, 139–41, 187–92, 199–201, 241–43, 286–87, 298–99, 302–4, 422–26, 439–44

Index 559

Lincoln County War, 1–2, 143–44, 176, 178, 192–93, 201, 222–23, 424–25, 448–51, 458–59, 462–63, 466–69, 472, 475, 478
Lindsey, William Ellsworth, 443
Lloyd, Dick, 122
Lloyd, S. N., 83
Lloyd, S. W., 76
Long, Elisha Van Buren, 315–18, 397, 399–401, 409, 411, 414, 428
Long, Jack, 112–13, 119, 127, 144–45, 150, 153–56, 158, 161, 167, 189, 191
Longwell, James, 97, 112–13, 119
López, Adolfo, 429
López, Felipe, 389–90
López, José L., 340, 343, 355–56, 358, 360, 364, 383, 387
López, Lorenzo, 220, 313–15, 317, 320, 327, 330–31, 337–38, 340, 363, 365, 367, 378–79, 386–89
Lorenzo, Vicenzo, 301
Los Alamos, New Mexico, 107, 268, 363, 367, 370–73, 377, 379, 381, 383, 393, 476
Los Gorras Blancas (The White Caps), 311–49, 351, 356–58, 365, 389, 394, 398, 427, 440, 447, 476–78
Los Pastores, 27
Los Penitentes, 16–17, 282, 313, 315
Los Portales, New Mexico, 236, 246
Louisiana Purchase, 21
Lovato, Francisco, 262, 462
Lucero, Antonio, 317, 327, 388, 399
Lucero, Arthur, 465–66
Lucero, Cecilio, 374–75
Lucero, José, 29, 215, 232, 289, 317, 327, 366, 369, 375, 399, 435
Lucero, Juan, 42, 146, 317, 327, 375
Lucero, Lorenzo, 185, 388
Lucero, Pablo, 317, 327, 353, 366
Lucero, Rosario, 367–69, 373, 379, 399
Lucero de Baca, Rosario, 367–69, 373, 379, 399, 401
Lucero de Chávez, María Leonora, 29, 66, 215, 232, 270, 300, 428–29, 435, 445

Lucero y Romero, Manuel, 42
Luhan, José Y., 313
Lujan, Rafael, 317, 327
Luma, Francisco, 86, 178, 187, 289
Lummis, Charles, 423
Luna, Miguel, 78, 247, 348, 460–61
Lynch, James Wilson, 315, 329
Lyon, William B., 186, 195

M

Mack Brown, Johnny, 3, 5–6, 464–65, 469
Mackel, Peter, 273
Mackie, Johnny, 96
MacNab, Frank, 117, 120, 123, 127–28, 130, 135–38, 206, 223
Madrid, José Leon, 341
Maes, Felipe, 362–63
Maes, Patricio, 353, 362–63, 371, 375, 380–83, 386, 397
Maes, Zenon, 353, 380, 382
Maestas, Germán, 353, 364–66, 379–80, 382–85, 397
Maestas, Lauteres, 385
Maestas, Macedonio, 385
Maldonado, Manuel, 380
Maney, Barbara Mae (Caldwell), 293
Maney, Henry, 293
Maney, Michael Erskine, 277, 281–82, 293
Mann, Edward A., 432
Manzanares, Francisco "Frank" Antonio, 267, 323, 331
Manzano, New Mexico, 14–15, 17, 36–37, 40, 75, 233, 467
Manzano Mountains, 14–15, 377
Mares, Higinia, 352
Mares, Hilario, 380
Mares, José, 360
Marshall, Charlie, 115
Martin, Chris-Pin, 465
Martin, John Rousseau, 456
Martin Chavez & Sons, 433, 437, 443–44, 452, 456
Martínez, Atanacio, 118, 126, 133, 138, 145, 153, 165, 177–79, 300, 303

Martínez, Benigno, 374
Martínez, Eduardo, 267, 275, 331
Martínez, Félix, 332, 335, 337, 339, 342, 357–59, 363, 365, 388, 390, 398
Martínez, Francisco, 126, 230, 359
Martínez, José, 126, 153, 177, 331, 339–40, 342, 357, 365, 379, 386, 388
Martínez, Juan, 44, 49–52, 267, 275, 337, 339, 342, 357, 365, 374, 379
Martínez, Juanita, 239
Martínez, Loyda, 476
Martínez, Roberto, 477
Martínez, Tomás, 267, 275, 394, 397
Martíni, Chaffre, 101
Martz, Martin, 114–15
Mason, Barney, 239, 244, 246–49, 251, 292
Mason, John, 51–52, 55–56
Mateos, Diego Corrientes, 370
Mathews, Jacob B. "Billy," 92, 100, 113–15, 127–28, 133, 153–54, 158, 161, 191, 193, 199–201, 206
Maxwell, Deluvina, 252–53, 262, 462–63
Maxwell, Lucien B., 252, 464
Maxwell, Luz B., 180–81, 252, 464
Maxwell, Paulita, 180, 239, 243, 248, 252, 259, 261, 458, 462, 464
Maxwell, Pete, 249, 261, 461
Maxwell City, New Mexico, 372
Maxwell Land Grant Company, 79, 398
Mayberry, Amanda, 294, 296
Mayberry, Edward F., 294
Mayberry, John William, 294
Mayberry, Nellie Maude, 294, 296
Mayberry, William F., 294, 296
McAdoo, William G., 453
McAllister, H. D., 341
McBee, James, 273
McBride, M. F., 288
McCallum, Frank, 59
McCarthy, James, 296–97
McCarty, Catherine, 95
McCloskey, William J., 114, 122–23
McCullum, Frank, 195, 289

McDaniels, Jimmy, 129, 153–54
McDonald, William Calhoun, 439, 441, 443
McFarland, James, 346, 349
McGee, Charles F., 296
McKibbin, Chambers, 42–43, 51
McKinley, William, 405–6
McKinley County, New Mexico, 464
McKinney, Thomas "Kip," 262
McSween, Alexander, 68, 73–75, 81, 83–85, 89–91, 100–103, 110–14, 116–20, 125–29, 132–37, 140–46, 148, 150–53, 155–56, 158–60, 162–64, 166–76, 189–92, 207–10, 448
McSween, Susan, 89–90, 125, 146–47, 153, 155, 164, 166, 168, 182–83, 189–92, 195–96, 207–8, 459, 461, 464
McSween home, 91–92, 112–14, 116–17, 128–29, 153–54, 156–57, 160–61, 164–69, 171, 175–76, 207, 209, 211, 213
  burning, 4, 6, 169, 172, 208, 213, 459
Medler, Edward L., 442
Médran, Florentino, 370, 372–73, 393
Melendes-Montoya, Josefa, 285
Melville, Andrew, 47
Meras, Nico, 50
Meridian, Texas, 64
Mes, Felipe, 175, 191
Mescalero Apache Agency, 112, 142, 300, 469
Mescalero Apaches, 7, 26–27, 29, 47, 62, 67–68, 76–77, 225, 286, 410–11
Mescalero reservation, New Mexico, 34, 39, 89, 97, 129, 178, 221, 225, 269, 286
Mexican American Youth Organization, 476
Mexican Revolution, 440
Mexican-American War, 14, 20, 45, 220
Michaelis, R., 421
Middleton, John, 115–17, 119–20, 123, 127–28, 130–32, 137, 142, 178, 183, 190, 200, 206

Milagro, New Mexico, 445–46, 451
Milhiser, Philip, 317
Miller, Abran, 188
Miller, Charles, 59
Miller, William H. H., 304
Mills, Alexander Hamilton "Ham," 39, 44, 51–52, 57, 59–62, 64, 68–69, 71, 73–74, 80–81, 89, 93, 332
Mills, María, 127
Mills, Theodore B., 330, 336–38, 340, 342, 344, 346–47, 362
Mills, William J., 332, 403, 428, 435, 439
Minner, John A. C., 352
Miranda, Lorencita, 124, 167
Miranda, María Inez, 305
Missouri Plaza, New Mexico, 26–28, 59, 66, 463
Mitchell, George W., 268, 276
Mix, Tom, 468
Moise, Columbus, 276
Montaño, José, 53, 58, 68–69, 71, 73, 79, 134, 153, 158, 191, 286, 289–90, 303
Montaño, Josefita "Josefa," 53, 153–54, 168
Montaño, Manuel, 317, 327
Montaño store, 32, 37, 102, 143, 153–54, 156–59, 161–66, 169, 174, 199, 241
Montoya, Augustine, 237
Montoya, Domingo, 285
Montoya, Felipe, 390
Montoya, Floripa, 305
Montoya, José, 145, 202, 235, 330, 336, 340, 343, 345, 380, 383, 390
Montoya, José Tiburcio, 380, 383
Montoya, Lisandro, 380
Montoya, Lucio, 145, 154, 156, 158–59, 305
Montoya, Nestor, 322, 330, 335–39, 342, 344–45, 348, 380, 452
Montoya, Rafael, 58
Montoya, Ramón, 115, 202, 399
Moore, Charles Hayes, 277
Moore, Domingo, 390

Mora County, New Mexico, 78, 308, 316, 323, 329, 335, 339, 348, 356, 358, 367
Morales, Jesús, 218
Morehead, James A., 229
Morris, Harvey, 153, 170–73, 175, 209, 212
Morrison, Alexander L., 306, 406
Morrison, Arthur, 237
Morrow, John R., 453
Morrow, Ratliff, 243
Morton, William S. "Buck," 86
Moulton, Earl L., 442
Muller, H. L., 80, 300
Mullin, Robert Norville, 448
Muñoz, Rosalio, 476
Murphey, Edward G., 389
Murphy, Israel, 200
Murphy, Lawrence G., 33–34, 36–37, 41, 48–49, 52, 55, 57–58, 62, 64, 66, 68–71, 77, 83
Murray, H. Doyle, 441

N

Nana, 221
Nash, Josiah, 111, 135, 172
National Hispanic Heritage Month, 477
Navajo, 8–9, 11–12, 26, 29, 180, 252–53, 262, 382, 463, 478
Neal, John S., 273
Neill, Hymàn G., 219
Nelson, John, 184, 294, 296, 472
Nelson, Lester "Baby Face," 472
Nelson, Martin, 294–96
Nelson, Peter, 294
Nesmith, George, 67
New, J. N., 273
New Hampshire, 294
Newcomb, John, 70, 83, 100, 117–18, 206, 255
Nixon, Milton V., 274
Noble, John Willcock, 323
Nolan, Christopher, 466, 476
Norman, William Olaf, 438, 441
Nowlin, Daniel C., 304

Nuestra Plataforma (Our Platform), 319–21, 336
Nuñez, Camilo, 202

O

Oakley, Robert, 329
O'Brien, James, 326–28, 333, 358, 364, 371
Ogden, Frank C., 335
Oklahoma City, Oklahoma, 433–34
Olinger, Bob, 115, 135, 155, 222, 242–44, 246, 256–58, 463
Olinger, John Wallace, 115, 135
Omaha, Nebraska, 306, 410
Ortega, Juan, 403, 408
Ortega, Theodore, 48
Ortiz, Emimia, 427
Ortiz, Juan, 317, 327
Ortiz, Louis M., 308
Ortiz, M. A., 452
Ortiz, Ramón, 20
Osborne, Nathan W., 207
Otero, José, 174–75, 406, 408, 410–12
Otero, Miguel Antonio, Jr., 1, 5, 174, 255, 321, 326, 352–53, 405–17, 421, 460–62, 475, 478
Otero, Page Blackwood, 383, 431
Otero, Vicente, 80, 462
Otero-Warren, Adelina, 452
Owen, John W., 429, 432–33
Owens, Judson E., 458
Owens, William, 88, 135, 184, 277–78, 280
Owens, William R. "Jake," 88, 135, 184, 200, 277–78

P

Pacheco, Anselmo, 98
Pacheco, Francisco, 132, 178
Pacheco, Nicolecita, 174
Padilla, Adecasio Juan, 314
Padilla, Catalina, 53–54
Padilla, Felipe, 225
Padilla, Francisco, 317

Padilla, Isidro, 53–55, 57
Padilla, José Delores, 54–55, 313–14, 317
Padilla, Marcellina, 313–14
Padilla, Pablo, 317
Padilla, Viviana, 53–54
Paniague, Luis, 422
Paniague de Salazar, Isabel, 422, 473–74
Parada, Juan José, 145, 147
Parker, Bonnie, 472
Parker, Frank W., 455
Patrón, Encarnación, 30, 52–53
Patrón, Felipa Martínez, 10, 30
Patrón, Isidro, 10–11, 14, 30, 52–55
Patrón, Juan Bautista, 1, 11, 13–14, 19, 23, 30–33, 35–37, 41–44, 48–52, 54–59, 61–62, 64, 67–75, 77, 79–82, 84–86, 88–90, 92–93, 99–101, 103–4, 106–11, 114, 116–21, 124, 127, 131–34, 136, 139–42, 147, 160–62, 182–83, 187–94, 196–97, 199–207, 215–16, 219–21, 225–30, 237–38, 265–68, 270, 274–80, 282–85, 293, 429, 475, 478
Patrón, Juana, 53, 216, 266
Patrón, María Delores Felipa, 275
Patrón, Rayitos, 236, 265, 276, 279, 284
Patrón, Sivoriano, 11
Patrón, Juan Secundino Ramón Jesús, Jr., 266
Paxton, George, 288
Paxton, Louis, 87–88
Peacock, George C., 277, 282
Pearl, William S., 273
Pennypacker, Galusha, 207
people's movement, the, 338, 340–41, 348, 356, 359, 376, 388, 427
Peppin, George W., 90, 92, 119, 127–28, 135, 141–45, 154–57, 159–60, 163–67, 174–75, 189–92, 206–8, 289–90, 420, 441
Perea, Demetrio, 408
Perea, Escolastico, 266
Perea, Pedro, 406
Perea-Silva, Dolores, 352
Perez, Demetrio, 368

Index 563

Perry, Sam, 115–16, 135, 153–54, 162
Pershing, John, 441
Pettyjohn, John Barney, 343
Pfingston, Fred, 431
Philipowski, Teresa, 153
Phillipowski, Lyon, 67
Phillips, Lou Diamond, 478
Picacho, New Mexico, 25–26, 37–38, 59–60, 75–76, 150–52, 176, 185–87, 233–34, 257, 269–70, 303–6, 421–22, 424–26, 429, 433, 437–38, 440–44
Pickett, Tom, 236, 242, 244, 246, 250–51, 253, 272–73
Pickford, Mary, 4
Pierce, Frederick Harrison, 428
Pierce, Milo, 135, 148, 155, 173, 213, 222
Pile, William A., 35
Pino, José de la Cruz, 274
Pino y Pino, Pablo, 68–69, 397
Pintada, New Mexico, 446
Poe, John W., 258, 260–62, 270, 273–74, 286–88, 290–93, 296–97, 302, 459, 464
Poe, Sophie, 260, 292, 464
Polanco, Librado, 383
Pope, William H., 197, 414, 439
Potter, Charles, 266, 297
Powderly, Terence Vincent, 335
Powell, Thomas "Buck," 87, 135
Prescott, C. H., 228
Price, Hugh H., 406
Price, William, 58–59, 61, 406
Prichard, George W., 267, 276, 326, 360, 363, 455, 468
Prince, LeBaron Bradford, 225–27, 230, 314, 317–18, 320–21, 326–27, 330–35, 346, 348–49, 361, 406
Pringle, George, 288
Puerto de Luna, New Mexico, 181–82, 220–21, 223–24, 229, 237, 247, 249, 253, 265, 267–68, 275–77, 279, 281–84
Purington, George, 87, 118, 128, 159–60, 163–64, 203–4

Q

Quarrell, W. D., 311–13, 317
Quemado, New Mexico, 394
Quintana, Juan, 363

R

Rael, Candelario, 331
Rael, Nicacio, 382
Rael, Procopio, 353, 364, 371, 375, 378, 382
Rainbolt, Amanda Drucilla, 63
Rainbolt, James Polk, 63
Ramírez, Juan, 30, 216, 266
Ramírez, Melquiades, 237
Ramos, Patricio, 132, 438
Randlett, James, 48, 52–53, 57
Raton, New Mexico, 410, 412
Raton Pass, 228
Rawlins, William, 311–12
Ray, Charles "Pony Diehl," 286
Raynolds, Jefferson, 376–77, 406, 428
Raza Unida Party, 476
Reagan, Frank, 48, 59
Redman, James, 193
Redon, Auguste "Antonio," 237, 284
Reese, Jim, 143, 161, 182, 184, 200, 207
Regulators, 120, 122–31, 133, 135–38, 142–54, 157, 160, 164–65, 167–68, 175–76, 178–83, 188, 190–92, 200, 203–4
Richards, Ephraim Wilson, 288–89, 291, 296
Richardson, Melvin "Mel" Emyor, 288–89
Ricos, 19, 313
Riggins, Frank, 28
Riley, John H., 37, 40–43, 72–73, 78, 80, 86–88, 91–93, 97, 110–14, 116, 119, 133, 135, 137, 141
Rio Arriba County, New Mexico, 104, 308, 359, 416, 477
Risque, John P., 71
Ritch, William G., 225–27, 229, 248, 254, 262
Rivera, Demetrio, 405

Roberts, Andrew L., 113, 115, 124, 130–31, 133, 142, 204, 255
Roberts, Charles J., 457–58
Roberts, William M., 273
Robinson, Berry, 157, 159, 166
Robinson, George, 128–29, 133, 166
Rociada, New Mexico, 427
Rock Creek, New Mexico, 328, 394
Rodríguez, Jesús, 145, 202
Rodríguez, Marcial, 67
Rodríguez, María, 67, 202
Rogers, John, 404
Roival, José, 249
Romero, Adolfo, 232
Romero, Benigno, 218
Romero, Catarino, 84, 93, 98–99, 296–97, 389–90, 399
Romero, Cleofes, 427
Romero, Desiderio, 132, 181, 229, 237, 247, 253
Romero, Eugenio, 274–75, 321, 328, 330–31, 343, 363, 388, 428, 447
Romero, Francisco, 83–84, 132, 174, 187
Romero, Hilario, 292–93, 300–301, 380, 395, 416
Romero, J. Placido, 315
Romero, José Antonio, 433
Romero, Manuel B., 429
Romero, María, 15, 75, 153, 170, 178, 233
Romero, Pedro, 379–80, 382, 397
Romero, Rafael, 228, 378–79, 393
Romero, Ricardo, 380–81
Romero, Sabino, 390
Romero, Secundino "Sec," 451
Romero, Trinidad, 233
Romero, Vicente, 15, 37, 75, 132, 152–53, 161–62, 165, 169–70, 172–73, 175–76, 178
Romero family, 15, 37, 176, 389
Romero y Lueras, Francisco, 82–84
Romero y Luma, Francisco, 187
Romero y Valencia, Francisco, 132, 174
Romero-Chávez, Juanita, 75, 234, 269, 419, 425, 467–68
Romero-Kimbrell, Paulita, 37
Romeroville, New Mexico, 315, 320, 332

Roosevelt, Theodore, 433
Rose, George, 153–54, 162
Ross, Edmund G., 303, 307–8
Rossell, Eugene, 404
Roswell, New Mexico, 59, 61, 63, 121–23, 138, 161, 205, 244, 303–4, 306, 421–22, 429, 433–34, 437–38, 440
Rowe, New Mexico, 316, 323, 334
Rudabaugh, Dave, 236, 242, 244–47, 250–55
Rudder, Alex, 202
Rudulph, Charles, 249, 340, 343, 363, 365, 388
Ruffley, John, 300
Ruth, William, 277, 280
Rynerson, William L., 35, 74, 103, 109, 113–14, 131–33, 140–42, 205–6, 222, 255

S

Saint, Joseph Exum, 16–17, 53, 65, 422, 453, 455–57, 466
Sais, Carpio, 300, 366, 380, 404, 413
Salas, Ascención, 422
Salas, Juan D., 431
Salas, Octaviano, 175
Salas, Teodoso, 313, 317, 327
Salazar, Bernardo, 431, 459, 473–74
Salazar, Elias "Ed" S., 459, 473
Salazar, Enrique H., 337, 363, 365, 371, 388
Salazar, Eugenio, 432, 468
Salazar, Francisco, 17, 212, 290
Salazar, Ginovera Lucero, 289
Salazar, Guadalupe "Lupita," 423
Salazar, Ida Mae, 459, 473
Salazar, Isabel, 422, 424, 459–60, 469, 472–74
Salazar, José, 1, 17, 19, 23, 26, 151, 153–54, 156–57, 161, 163, 167, 169, 175, 192, 202–3, 226, 259, 289, 303, 306, 312, 327, 408, 423–24, 429, 434, 448, 450, 473, 478

Salazar, Lugarda, 17
Salazar, Magencia, 17
Salazar, Margarita, 424, 433, 459–60, 473
Salazar, Martena, 153
Salazar, Miguel, 5, 192, 223, 259, 312, 315–17, 320, 323, 325–27, 332–33, 460–61
Salazar, Paula, 17–18, 27, 289, 423
Salazar, Pilar, 422
Salazar, Rómulo, 17, 289, 423
Salazar, Scipio, 153–54, 259, 290, 300, 429, 434
Salazar, Teofilo, 17, 19, 27, 86, 289, 423
Salazar, Victoriana, 289, 423
Salazar, Yginio, 1, 3–6, 17–19, 23, 25–29, 86–88, 95, 102, 115, 135, 143–44, 151, 153–54, 156–57, 161, 163, 166–75, 178–79, 192–96, 200, 202–3, 212, 215, 221–26, 235, 240, 250–51, 257, 259, 261, 263, 287, 289–91, 293–94, 296–98, 300, 302–3, 306, 408, 422–24, 429, 431–34, 448, 450, 459–65, 468–76, 478
Salazar family, 19, 26, 28, 87, 259, 422–24, 460–61, 473
Salpointe, Jean-Baptiste, 334, 357
San Gerónimo, New Mexico, 309, 311–12
San Juan County, New Mexico, 238, 430
San Miguel County, New Mexico, 178–79, 181–82, 220, 229–30, 246–47, 266–68, 270–71, 306–9, 311, 313–16, 321–22, 324, 331–34, 336, 338–48, 361–63, 377–79, 386–88, 401–3, 427–28
San Patricio, New Mexico, 101, 208
Sánchez, Alfonso, 477
Sánchez, Estólano, 202
Sánchez, Gregorio, 185–86
Sánchez, Isabella, 257
Sánchez, Lynda A., 475
Sánchez, Martín, 84, 185–86, 202, 204, 206, 408, 421
Sánchez, Mauricio, 33, 58
Sánchez, Raimonda, 421

Sánchez, Sequio, 66, 93, 126, 138–39, 145, 202, 257, 408
Sánchez y Baca, Felipe, 457
Sandoval, Donaciano, 386–88
Sandoval, Doroteo, 354–56
Sandoval, Florencio, 354–56, 358, 364
Sandoval, Gabriel, 352, 367–71, 378–83, 395, 397–403, 405, 408, 412–13
Sandoval, Plácido, 363
Sandoval, Remigio, 353, 373, 383
Sandoval de Silva, Telésfora, 353–54, 362, 367–73, 378, 380, 382–84, 393–94, 400–401
Sanger, Ira Everett, 419–20
Santa Fe, New Mexico, 10–15, 27–31, 55–58, 67–68, 78–81, 103–5, 109–11, 187–89, 225–31, 253–54, 306, 347–49, 357–58, 396–98, 405–7, 412–16, 439–44, 450–56, 458, 462–66
Santa Fe County, New Mexico, 27, 30, 78–79, 230, 293, 298, 328, 341, 345, 349, 353, 383–84, 394
Santa Fe Railway Company, 182, 218, 220, 226–27, 229, 268, 321, 329, 333
Santa Fe Ring, 2, 35, 43, 67, 70, 74, 79–80, 86, 103, 108–13, 123, 126, 142, 150, 196, 205, 207, 222, 226, 236, 238, 254, 274–75, 282, 307, 331, 340, 359, 450, 469
Santa Fe Trail, 12, 227
Santa Rosa, New Mexico, 216, 220, 225, 237, 265–66, 268, 270, 275–77, 281, 445
Santana, Francisco "Frank," 437, 455
Santana, Henry, 437, 442, 444, 455, 465–66
Saunders, Ab, 78, 135–36
Schaefer, George, 96
Scholand, Emilie, 81
Schurz, Carl, 204
Scott, G. O., 329
Scott, Jerry, 46–49, 53
Scroggins, John, 129, 137–38, 142, 183

Scurlock, Josiah "Doc," 78, 80, 204
Second World War, 476
Sedillo, Antonio A., 82
Sedillo, José, 17, 104, 108, 202, 419
Sedillo, José Ventura, 17
Segovia, Manuel "The Indian," 113, 115, 133, 135–36, 138–39
Segura, Alejandro, 224
Segura, José, 78, 343
Segura, Nepomuceno, 343
Selgado de Chávez, Ruperta, 445, 451
Selman, John, 184–86, 188, 200, 207
Selman, Tom, 184, 188, 200, 205
Semana Santa (Holy Week), 16, 132, 285
Sena, Andres, 267–68, 275
Sena, José D., 227, 230, 298
Sena de Luna, Josefita, 455
Serno, José, 175
Seven Rivers, New Mexico, 26, 87–88, 97–101, 135, 188, 203, 222, 272–73, 299
Seven Rivers Warriors, 87–88, 101, 135–37, 148, 184
Shank, John, 340, 343
Shedd, Warren H., 97, 111
Sheldon, Lionel A., 255, 272–73, 290, 293
Shelley, George M., 228
Shield, David P., 90–91, 128–29
Shield, Elizabeth, 90, 153, 167–68
Short, Mark, 46
Short, Wash, 46
Sibley, Henry, 13
Silva, Antonio, 352–53, 370
Silva, Emma, 352, 367, 372–74
Silva, Felipe, 146–47, 390
Silva, Jesús, 222, 250–52, 262, 352, 394, 462
Silva, Juan, 147, 337, 354, 365, 390
Silva, Manuel, 337, 367, 370, 373, 375, 378, 380, 383, 393, 398
Silva, Teodocis, 352
Silva, Vicente, 349, 352–54, 362, 365–73, 378, 380, 383–85, 393–94, 398–400, 411, 413
Silva Gang, 395, 399, 404, 410, 416

Silver City, New Mexico, 71, 96, 100, 407, 452
Siringo, Charles A., 346, 349, 447, 460, 462
Sisneros, Dionicio, 353, 370, 373, 379–80, 383, 427
Slaughter, Charles H., 299
slavery, 12, 26–27
Slayton, Margaret Chávez, 476
Smith, Dick, 87
Smith, George W., 125, 128
Smith, Joseph J., 153, 161, 163, 170–71
Smith, Sam, 120, 153–54, 170
Smith, Thomas, 379, 382–83, 387, 389–90, 396, 398–99, 402–3, 407
Smith, Wilber, 469–72
Snouffer, John Boon, 328
Snow, Charles, 184
Socorro County, New Mexico, 29, 104, 222, 382, 389, 394–95, 426
Solano, Antonio, 340, 342–43
Soto, Eduardo, 71
Speakes, Bob, 184
Spiegelberg, Levi, 83, 91
Spies, Charles, 428
Springer, Charles, 410
Springer, Frank, 226, 326, 409
Springer, New Mexico, 298, 410, 465
St. Francis Cathedral, 455–56, 458, 466, 468
St. John, John, 229
St. John's Day, 27, 32, 143, 268, 275. *See also* el Día de San Juan
St. Louis, Missouri, 103, 179, 229, 377, 453–54
Stamp, Terence, 478
Stanley, Stephen "Steve," 60–63, 68, 71, 76, 93, 112–13, 142
Steck, James F., 268, 276
Steck, Joe, 245–46
Stedman, Clarence A., 226
Steele, William J., 301
Stephens, Steve, 129, 142, 153
Stewart, Frank, 244, 247–54, 258
Stinking Spring, New Mexico, 250, 478
Stone, Edmund Thomas, 273, 289

Index

Storms, Joseph, 83
Sullivan, Dan, 308

T

Tafolla, Francisco, 224
Tafoya, Jesús María, 340, 343
Tafoya, José Sambrano, 15, 17, 32, 75, 269, 286–87, 304
Tafoya, Tomás, 267, 275
Taft, William Howard, 439
Taos County, New Mexico, 27, 326, 330
Tascosa, Texas, 183, 382
Taylor, DeWitt Clinton, 295
Taylor, Dorothy Caldwell, 4
Tecolote, New Mexico, 329, 363, 371
Tecolote Creek, 311–12, 330
Terrazas, Joaquin, 238
Terrell, Frank, 273
Terrell, Samuel S., 273
Tessiere, Julian, 328, 394
Texas, 19–20, 26–27, 39–40, 45–48, 63–64, 183–85, 188, 190, 202, 204–5, 234–36, 243–44, 249, 292–94, 447–48
Texas Revolution, 19
Thomas, Benjamin Morris, 344
Thompson, Albert W., 241, 428
Thornton, Edward, 119
Thornton, William, 254, 372, 375, 379, 387, 394, 399
Thornton, William Taylor, 372
Tiedemann, H. G., 42
Tijerina, Reies López, 476–77
Tillotson, Thomas C., 420
Tipton, William Bryant, 356
Tolby, Franklin J., 79
Tome, New Mexico, 15, 17, 37
Torrance County, New Mexico, 431
Torres, Nicholas, 187, 274
Tracy, L. P., 278
Treaty of Guadalupe Hidalgo, 20–21, 187, 307, 338, 477
Trementina, New Mexico, 330, 333
Trujillo, Apolonio, 317, 327
Trujillo, Francisco "Kiko," 126, 137–39, 290, 435

Trujillo, Jesús, 328, 394
Trujillo, José Gregorio, 137, 147, 187
Trujillo, Juan, 101, 206, 317, 327
Trujillo, Julian, 328, 353, 362, 365–70, 378–80, 382–83, 394, 399–402, 408
Trujillo, Julianna, 427
Trujillo, Louie, 477
Trujillo, Luciano, 425
Trujillo, Porfirio, 313, 318, 320, 323, 328, 358, 361, 377, 394, 398, 427
Trujillo, Seledon, 263
Trujillo, Severiano, 51
Trujillo, Severino, 316
Trujillo, Vicente, 368–69, 378, 398, 427
Tsompanas, Paul L., 1, 475
Tucker, Thomas H., 394
Tucson, Arizona, 383
Tularosa, New Mexico, 28, 41, 43, 49, 52, 55, 97, 124, 144, 179, 182
Tularosa Ditch War, 43
Tunstall, John Henry, 81–82, 85–86, 89–91, 97–102, 110–20, 122–23, 126–29, 135–37, 141–42, 167–68, 170–71, 175, 191–92, 209–11, 223
Turner, Ben, 47–48, 59–60, 76
Turner, Marion, 135, 144, 148, 155, 166, 200, 206
Tuscola, Illinois, 312

U

Ulibarri, Gumecindo, 354
Ulibarri, Meliton, 354
Ulibarri, Pablo, 354, 378–79, 386, 390, 477
Ulibarrí, Ramón, 343
Ulibarri, Rock, 477
Ulibarri, Róuiulo, 390
Ulrick, George L., 287, 290, 419, 440, 453–54, 456–58, 468
Underwood, Nathan, 87, 111
Union County, New Mexico, 428
Upson, Marshal Ashmun "Ash," 121–23, 162, 186, 270, 273, 299, 475

V

Valdéz, Antonio José, 370, 397–99
Valdéz, Antonio Lino, 254
Valdéz, José, 249–52, 337, 340, 343, 358, 370, 397–99
Valdéz, Manuel, 78, 370, 398–99
Valencia, Patricio, 396, 405
Valencia County, New Mexico, 8, 14–15, 17, 19, 37, 82, 315, 377, 397, 469
Valentine, Tomás, 274, 423
Valenzuela, Gregorio, 73–74, 80
Valizan, Dario, 54–55
Valles, Domingo, 431
Valverde, Diego, 445
Varela, Gregorio, 313, 390
Varela, Marcos, 380
Vaughn, James Lewis, 286
Veeder, Elmer Ellsworth, 397
Veeder, John D. W., 357, 361, 363, 409, 411, 414
Veeder, John De Witt, 397
Veracruz, Mexico, 440
Verelles, Jesús, 250–52
Vialpando, Jesús, 353, 394, 397
Vickey, Charles, 73
Victorio, 221–22, 225, 238, 248
Vidor, King, 4, 464–65
Vigil, Hermerejildo, 340, 343–44
Vigil, Joaquin, 405
Vigil, José Trinidad, 233
Villa, Francisco "Pancho," 440
Villezea, Jesús, 386–87

W

Waddingham, Wilson, 332
Waers, Jesse William, 374
Waite, Fred, 102, 112–14, 118–20, 127–28, 132–33, 142, 183, 190, 200
Waldo, Henry L., 207, 215, 225–26
Walker, John, 53
Wallace, George H., 406
Wallace, Lew, 184, 187, 189, 192, 196–97, 199–204, 207, 221, 225–27, 242, 254, 260, 262
Walz, Edgar, 149, 193, 195–96, 241–42
Warner, David C., 49
Warnock, Joe, 62
Washington, District of Columbia, 439
Washington, George, 113, 128–29, 133, 137, 145, 157, 174, 202, 273
Watkins, Erwin Curtis, 142
Watrous, New Mexico, 329, 335, 339, 465
Wayne, John, 468
Weaver, James B., 361
Webb, John Joshua, 246–47, 254
Welding, Simeon E., 273
West, William H., 241, 244–45
Wheeler, Roswell G., 179, 200, 333
Whigham, Harry, 412
Whitaker, V. R., 184
Whitcraft, Allen, 47
White, Van L., 453
White Oaks, New Mexico, 231, 233, 236, 241, 243–46, 248, 258, 260, 287, 289, 304, 306, 422–23, 431–32, 459
White Sands, New Mexico, 397
White Sulphur Springs, West Virginia, 453
Whitmore, Adin H., 292, 408
Wichita, Kansas, 96
Widenmann, Rob, 90, 112–16, 118–19, 123–25, 128–29, 133, 137, 139, 141–42, 183
Wiener, Solomon C., 431–32
Wier, William, 119
Wiggins, Joseph "José," 394
Wilburn, Aaron, 63
Wilburn, Frank, 63
Wilcox, Thomas, 249–52
Wild, Azariah, 241–44
Wilkons, J. C., 202
Williams, Bob, 248
Williams, George, 421–22
Williams, Pony, 272
Williams, Thomas, 46–47
Williams, Tom, 46, 248, 272, 312–13
Wilson, Andrew, 132, 289
Wilson, Billy, 225, 236, 241–47, 250–51, 253–55, 272–73

Wilson, George, 117, 119, 175, 187, 196, 231, 249, 288
Wilson, John B., 111, 114, 117–19, 128, 131, 164, 166, 175, 187, 195–96, 201–3, 206, 208, 213
Wilson, Sidney, 205
Wilson, Stephen S., 296
Wilson, William, 70–71, 73–75, 117, 119, 195, 202, 241, 244–45, 251, 253
Wilson, Woodrow, 440
Woltz, Charles M., 87–88
Wood, David, 125
Wooster, Henry Stiles, 355, 371–72, 404
Wortley, Sam, 70, 73, 77, 83, 152, 154, 156–57, 159, 161, 163–64, 258
Wright, Edward R., 457–58
Wright, W. C., 329
Wylie, Robert, 87–88
Wynkoop, Edward W., 318
Wyoming, 20, 308, 468

Y

Yerby, Tom, 246
Young Guns, 478
Young Guns II, 478

Z

Zamora, Francisco, 153, 170, 172–73, 175–76, 178, 212
Zapata, Emiliano, 440